The Elementary School Teacher

THE

ELEMENTARY SCHOOL TEACHER

VOLUME VIII

SEPTEMBER, 1907—JUNE, 1908

CHICAGO
The University of Chicago Press
1908

Published
September, October, November, December, 1907
January, February, March, April, May, June, 1908

Composed and Printed By
The University of Chicago Press
Chicago, Illinois, U. S. A.

INDEX TO VOLUME VIII

INDEX TO ARTICLES

INDEX TO AUTHORS

INDEX TO BOOK REVIEWS

VOLUME VIII NUMBER I

THE ELEMENTARY SCHOOL TEACHER

SEPTEMBER, 1907

THE DEVELOPMENT OF TECHNICAL EDUCATION

JAMES P. HANEY
Director of Manual Training in the New York City Public Schools

Industrial training has too long been neglected in our general scheme of education; it has come to be a real and crying need. Our schools have, on the one side, seen our apprenticeship system decline and die, while they have witnessed, on the other a vast development of the country's mechanical resources. It is necessary that we revise some of our current notions regarding educational practice. We are still confused by the idea that as we live under a democratic government every child should receive the same kind of schooling. Our older educational ideals were clerical. Education was made up of a study of the Humanities; culture was its aim. At one time one mind could grasp a knowledge of many fields of human activity; now these fields have so multiplied that one mind finds it difficult to grasp all the details of a single aspect of man's work. Our interests as a civilized people are becoming more complex each year, and each man becomes perforce a specialist.

It is fortunate that man has a variety of interests, and those who deal with pupils in the schools know that these interests early express themselves. Some by nature turn to clerical pursuits, some to commercial vocations, and some to the arts and crafts. One sees men who are born doctors, others who are born lawyers, and others who are born craftsmen. Education of old took little heed of the latter; even now it does little to encourage the artisan to become a thoroughly skilled worker. We have offered the same schooling to all, and have shut our eyes to the fact that many found such schooling not adapted to their interests and capacities. These are the pupils who are virtually forced out of the school because they cannot square with the clerical ideals. We mourn their early leaving, but never stop to question as to whether they might not have been retained in school had they been offered work so plainly useful that it would have been to their interests to stay to take, saving thereby the tedious ill-paid and ill-taught training, which is all the apprentice can now secure. Nowhere in the educational field is there a condition more plainly demanding attention. Man must early specialize in his education, as he must early specialize in work. Schoolmen, as a body, resist acknowledging the necessity of such early specialization, but economic pressure is forcing the matter to solution.

Some think that manual training in the elementary school will help to solve the problem. Undoubtedly it will help, but it only leads the boy a few steps on the path he must travel. Manual training in the elementary school is an essential. It is necessary that the boy grow on his physical and motor side as well as on his mental side. It helps to give him the right point of view toward the constructive world which surrounds him. It teaches him the power which lies in his own fingers.

The boy who finishes the elementary-school course is only at the beginning of his training. More schooling is necessary for such a one, if he is to specialize effectively at a later stage. It must be offered to save for such a pupil those years now called by the *Douglas Report* "the wasted years of the boy's life," when he has not skill enough to earn a living wage, and is given so little opportunity to learn that the time from the fourteenth to the seventeenth year is of no educative value. These years are of no profit to the child or the state—they are of no profit, but incalculable loss to both.

We are, perhaps, not yet prepared for trade-schools, but more opportunity must be offered in secondary schools for those boys who are anxious to specialize along mechanical lines. We have many technical schools of college rank to supply us with engineers, but what we need are secondary schools in which those men may be trained who come between the engineers and the artisans. Such schools should educate their students as future foremen and superintendents in factories. They should be day schools, giving not only the literary elements of a secondary-school education, but also additional instruction in mechanics, physics, chemistry, and mathematics in their application to various industries. They should give instruction in design, in freehand and mechanical drawing. The latter should receive particular attention. Shop-practice should also be given that the pupils may learn those principles of instruction which are at the foundation of most trades.

Such schools would serve a double purpose. They would act not only as does the manual training high school, as such school is now frequently seen (that is, a school giving a general high-school training with some manual work), but would also serve specifically to lead their pupils into the trades. They would not be trade-schools, but would aim to give training essential to the skilled artisan. They would also fit their students to go on to higher technical schools if they so desired.

The arguments in favor of a development of industrial education are weighty. Chief among them stands the economic necessity of such training being given to an industrial people like ourselves. Increasing pressure from many foreign points with insistence to this necessity. Germany is dotted with technical schools and busy with the development of plans for the training of skilled artisans. France and Italy are not idle, and statesmen in England are studying the problem with feverish anxiety. Those who will look may also see in the Orient a great nation rousing itself from its sleep. Before long it must be plain to the dullest that the occidental worker will have to labor in world-competition with an almond-eyed artisan of deft fingers and no mean intelligence. Industrial and technical education is but one way of spelling economic prosperity. It is the way in which great nations are to fight a war which is already on. National disarmament may come, but every machinist who stops making cannons will be set to making gears, cams, and dynamos, and that nation whose artisans are the cleverest, and whose designers are the most artistic, stands to win. We live in the age of the machine, but there must always be a man behind it.

Our country has in its raw material a wealth that is astounding, but to realize upon such material it must be manufactured. We now send abroad raw stuffs which we buy back at a vastly increased value because of the skill of the worker which has gone into the making of the raw material into the manufactured product. The money so lost is given away by us to the superior state-trained artisans of France and Germany. They are an industrious people by natural advantages and by inclination. We must develop an industrial scheme of education adequate to the needs of our present-day life.

From every shop in our country there comes a single-voiced demand—a demand for skill. Our schools give science, and science is good; but skill they must also give, if they are to fulfil the first requirement of all schooling, that education fit for environment. Our environment is one which demands both science and skill. As a constructive people we must be given constructive knowledge. The conditions in our workshops do not serve to produce more skill but rather to produce less skill. Specialization in the workshop tends to narrow the worker. Specialization in the school, with its broader training, will serve to give the skill now demanded.

Related to this question of handwork in the school is one of vital importance to every artisan. Our education, it has been said, of old held up clerical ideals. It cultivated respect for the skilled thinker, but ignored the skilled worker. Manual work put in school sees its own dignity enhanced. Hand labor has not been dignified in education. The skilled laborer has not been pointed to with the pride that has distinguished the skilled physician or lawyer. (The future will see a change in this.)

There is nothing of more significance for all labor, whether organized or unorganized, than the general development of manual training in the elementary- and high-school systems. The introduction of such handwork in schools attacks at its root a true economic error—the lack of school respect for such work. Nothing ever done for labor has such importance for the individual laborer in his social standing as the change in educational standards that is being effected before our very eyes. As a constructive people we have come to have respect for those whose life is devoted to the constructive arts. There is to be a raising of the whole standard of respect for those who work with their hands.

THE PUBLIC SCHOOL SYSTEM OF THE STATE OF OKLAHOMA: ITS ORGANIZATION

L. W. BAXTER
Ex-State Superintendent

The destiny of the commonwealth depends upon the training of its youth. The public-school system is the source of the major portion of this training. It obtains, then, that the school system of the great state of Oklahoma, "the new star on the flag," should be systematically organized and adequately maintained.

Section 13 of the Enabling Act provides that "the laws in force in the territory of Oklahoma, as far as applicable, shall extend over and apply to said state until changed by the legislature thereof." And section 21 of the same act reads:

> and the officers of the state government formed in pursuance of said constitution as provided by said constitutional convention, shall proceed to exercise all the functions of such state officers; and *all laws in force* in the territory of Oklahoma at the time of admission of said state into the Union shall be in force throughout said state, except as modified by this act or by the constitution of the state, and the laws of the United States not locally inapplicable shall have the same force and effect within said state as elsewhere within the United States.

I take it for granted, therefore, that after the adoption of the constitution, the election of state and county officers, the present Oklahoma school laws will be the laws of that portion now known as Indian Territory as well as that portion now known as Oklahoma Territory, until such time as the legislature of the new state shall change the same. In passing, let me plead with all the teachers and patrons of the new state of Oklahoma to wipe out this imaginary line between the two territories. Let us forget it entirely. Already it has caused, and is causing, unnecessary trouble. We will be one, with common interests, for weal or woe. Let us be undivided, harmonious, fraternal, in all our rich young life.

Among other officers the laws will doubtless provide for the election of a county superintendent in each county. By the present Oklahoma laws it is made the duty of the county superintendent of public instruction

to divide the county into a convenient number of school districts, and to change such districts when the interests of the people may require it, by making them conform to existing topographical and physical conditions; and to appoint the time and place for the said first district meeting, which shall then proceed as by law required. Such superintendent shall number school districts when they are formed, and he shall keep in a book for that purpose a description of the boundaries of each school district and part of district in his county, with a plat of same, date of organization, date and full record of all changes of boundaries, and a list of district officers in his county, the date of election or appointment, and the time the term of each is to expire.

The special district meeting shall elect officers, and transact such business as is prescribed by law for regular school district meetings.

The school district, under the Oklahoma system, is usually three miles square, thus containing nine square miles of area.

The school district is deemed duly organized when the officers are elected, and have qualified, and signed an acceptance of office. The school district is a body corporate, and possesses the usual powers of a corporation for public purposes.

The first district meeting may appoint a chairman, elect officers, designate a site for the district schoolhouse, vote an annual tax sufficient for the various school purposes, direct the sale of any school property, determine the length of time the school shall be taught, *when* such school shall be taught, and whether the money shall be used for summer or winter term of school.

The said school board shall purchase, or lease, a site as designated by the voters; hire, purchase, or build a schoolhouse as directed; look after the care and keeping of the same; provide the necessary supplies and furniture; make necessary rules and regulations; hire a qualified teacher, and provide for the opening of school.

Thus the school is started. The machinery is simple. It

makes little difference whether one school district is to be formed in one county, or whether one hundred districts are to be formed in each of as many counties. The machinery is the same. It is true that it will require a little more work on the part of the superintendents. It is also true that many tantalizing and nerve excruciating petty difficulties, barriers to be surmounted, will arise; these are to be expected, endured, settled, and the work should proceed.

The Oklahoma schools are already organized and in running order. I do not regard it as a difficult task to organize the schools of Indian Territory. If the state officers take charge June 1, I can see no good reason why Indian Territory ought not to have the majority of its schools running the school year of 1907 and 1908. The schools in the cities are already fairly well organized and are doing good work. Our intelligent citizenship will soon establish the rural or district schools.

If the Oklahoma system is followed, school district should be made as large as possible. The greatest detriment to our school system is the small district. It is a relic of the past, and should be so recognized by our people. School district boundaries should be on half-section lines, so that schoolhouses may be properly located at the crossroads, and not in the middle of a section of land.

In the newly organized district, district boards should be conservative in expending the public money the first year or two, and not mortgage the future for a period of twenty years, and make it impossible to have good schools.

In the election of county superintendents great care should be exercised to elect only highly qualified, self-sacrificing, professional men. The schools should be organized by schoolmen who know from training and experience the school needs. The school district officers selected should be intelligent, conservative, men of affairs, who are able to see beyond personal greed.

If the constitutional convention, now sitting, makes not other provisions, thus will our schools be organized. However, I feel that this convention should take some decisive action and provide for the introduction of the township system of schools in Indian

Territory, instead of the present Oklahoma district system. If the constitutional convention does not act, it will be too late for the first legislature to move, as the Oklahoma district system will be fastened on to Indian Territory.

The township system is so much superior, less expensive, affords the graded school more highly trained teachers, longer school terms, a better body of directors, more satisfactory schoolhouses, better school equipment, and larger and richer libraries. I hope that the teachers throughout the new state of greater Oklahoma will take a bold stand for the township school system, and will use all of their influence with the members of the convention to establish this system in Indian Territory, and to make a provision whereby the Oklahoma school district may gradually be consolidated, and all pupils transported to and from school.

The common school is the foundation of the school system, "the university of the masses." After this is provided for, adequate provision should be made so that every boy and girl may attend a good high school within a reasonable distance of his home. The township system will provide the necessary secondary instruction. One, two, three, or four years of high-school work may be done in the township school. However, if the pupil cannot get this work in his district school, a high school should be established in every county, maintained at state and county expense, where the boy or girl may receive this training.

Oklahoma's high-school system is the weak link in her educational chain. A good system of high schools in the new state will strengthen our educational system more than anything else. The present constitutional convention would build for itself an everlasting monument, if it were to establish a county high school in every county in the new state.

Having established the rural school and the high school, it is then time to establish the state institutions of higher learning. Ordinarily, in the history of America, the custom has been to found the higher institution first and the common school last. This is wrong. We now have plenty, if not a superfluity, of higher educational institutions. Too much work done by them should be done in the lower schools. They should be confined to their appointed fields, and should not attempt to take the place of other needed schools.

Usually these state institutions are conceived and fostered in the mind of the real-estate boomer, for personal ends, rather than to satisfy the real needs of the people. Let us divorce ourselves from the usual historical custom, and build our schools to satisfy the actual needs of the pupils. Let us found our rural school, then the high school, then the institution of higher learning. It is understood, of course, that the articulation between these schools will be perfect; more properly, they are simply divisions of one great public-school system made for the purpose of intelligent discussion.

Many additional problems in the matter of organization will present themselves. Among others may be mentioned the installation of a satisfactory system of taxation, the passing of an effective compulsory educational law, a plan for the certification of teachers, the adoption of modern textbooks, the inauguration of a separate school system, the outlining of an adequate system of supervision, and the arrangement of the course of study. Already the so-called "Nationalized Illinois Course of Study" has been adopted in the two territories, and will certainly be continued in the new state. It is probably the most perfect course of study yet outlined, and has proved eminently satisfactory.

The present system of supervision in Oklahoma, consisting of a state board of education, a state superintendent, city superintendents, and county superintendents, has stood the test of years, and in my estimation should be continued by the legislative department of the government. The state board of education is a very valuable part of this system of education. It outlines the general educational policy, and its duties and powers should be increased rather than decreased. The state superintendent is practically the executive officer of the state board of education. He should be in the field, visiting the schools, and not compelled to remain in the office to do clerical work. This may also be said of the county superintendents. My experience in the past has convinced me that our superintendents are very worthy, honorable, competent, painstaking, and ambitious officers—ambitious for the schools. Their faithfulness and self-sacrifice are to be most highly commended.

In conclusion, I cannot refrain from expressing a word of thanks to the teachers of Oklahoma for their uniform, hearty, and worthy support in all matters of administration in the past six years. My term of office expired with the past year, as a result of my voluntary resignation; and go with the most pleasant memories and the highest word of commendation and appreciation for the great body of teachers who have done and are doing so much for the future commonwealth of Oklahoma. May their labors in the future be as effective in the development of a citizenship and a commonwealth as they have been in the past! May the blessing of heaven rest upon each and every one of them. May the rose and daisy ever bloom in their pathway.

Thomas Jefferson said of his Scotch professor, William Small: "He was the man who fixed the destinies of my life." You, my friends, the school teachers of Oklahoma, are to fix the destinies of our 225,000 growing youth of Oklahoma, the future citizens of our beloved commonwealth and of our greatly revered nation. They will be the dominant factors tomorrow. May they all be "men, high-minded men; men who their duties know, and knowing dare perform;" and thus by their workmanship prove the labors of the master-minds who fixed their destinies—the school-teachers of Oklahoma.

NORMAL SCHOOLS OF THE NEW STATE

N. S. COWART
Superintendent of City Schools, Wilburton, I. T.

That there is a crying need for normal schools in our new state of Oklahoma may be seen on every hand. In many places it has been impossible to get normal-trained teachers for the schools in Indian Territory; some places have been filled by girls who had only finished the sixth grade, for the reason that better teachers could not be secured. In all the states there is a scarcity of well-prepared teachers, and even in Massachusetts, the cradle of the normal school in the United States, only 48 per cent. of the teachers are normal graduates.

If we are to have an ideal commonwealth; if we are to have the best possible schools; if we expect to build a citizenship that will maintain and further develop our public institutions, we must not be satisfied with teachers that are in any way inferior to those of any state, or any country of the world.

Experience is a great factor in successful work in the schoolroom, and teachers having special preparation stay longer in the work, and therefore accomplish more. Those not well fitted become discouraged, disgusted with their own efforts, and quit the work often just at the time when they should be coming into their useful period. These persons are largely responsible for low salaries and the failure of teachers' unions.

The first normal school in the United States was started in Massachuetts in 1839. The idea grew rapidly and spread from state to state. At present Massachusetts' number has reached ten, while New York and Pennsylvania each has fifteen normal schools. These three states have nearly one-fourth of all the normal schools, and more than one-third of the normal students, in the United States. While these states are leading in this important work, many others are following them closely; and, notwithstanding the fact that the colleges and universities have tried to show cause why the normal school should not exist, the idea is constantly growing, and we might with safety say that a state's educational standing may be measured by its institutions for the training of teachers.

Oklahoma now has three such institutions, and from reports they are all doing good work. We need more.

We should have one strong central normal school equipped to do all that any school of the kind can do, and several rightly located ones that would be at least sufficiently complete to prepare teachers for the common schools. In all, we should have, in my opinion, not fewer than four, and not more than six, of these schools. Later, as our population and schools increase more can be established, if necessary.

It would be better if the teachers in these schools could first have a college or university course, and then a normal course. This would prevent the oft-occuring trouble of having teachers in the faculty who are not thoroughly in sympathy with normal school work. The academic work of the normal school should be as well taught as that of the university, and then so recognized by the state; for a normal-school student must have not only a reciting knowledge of a subject, but also a teaching knowledge; and this should mean a thoroughness not attempted by many of our university students.

A normal school should have a model, a practice, and a experimental department. The first two are nearly always in evidence, but the experimental department is doubtless too much neglected. Dr. Roark says that each professor of teaching, and his body of carefully selected, fit students, should try to push the frontier of pedagogy a little farther out, and that there can be no good reason given why they should not have the franking privilege, that they may send out the results of their experiments even to the most remote country districts, just as many states send out reports of agricultural experiments.

There is a school in Indiana and one in Oregon that maintain practice departments for rural schools; and why such an important thing should be overlooked by most of our normal schools I am unable to see. In West Virginia and Arizona the students visit the rural schools accompanied by the teacher of pedagogy. So far as I am able to learn, there are only six schools in the United States that maintain practice departments for the high-school work. In our new state it would probably be better to have this work only in our central school.

Theory and practice should go hand in hand, and the teacher of methods should be the one to apply them in the model department. Only about one-tenth of our schools have this arrangement.

If the normal school has a right to exist, it deserves more recognition than is given it. If it be required of the state to furnish such schools, it should be required of the teachers that they attend these schools. I believe our new state should take a step in advance of what has been done elsewhere, and require all teachers not now in the service, after a certain fixed period of time, to present a normal diploma as a certificate to teach.

Our central school should have a course for county and city superintendents and institute workers, and the people should demand this preparation. And I can see no reason why we should not also have normal extension work and a library course. In my judgment, the state will be amply able to support these schools.

The Indian Territory will want at least two of the schools, and the teachers will do their best to see that they are located where they will serve the greatest number of people, and not placed by the overanxious town-boomers.

We would recommend that a committee be appointed by this association to take such steps as may be necessary to protect all the educational interests of the new state.

THE MAKING OF A PLAY[1]

MARTHA FLEMING

The history in the sixth grade was early Greek—the myth-making period. Many old Greek and Latin stories and some tree-myths were read, among the latter the modern story "Old Pipes and the Dryad," by Frank R. Stockton. As soon as the children had read this story they proposed to play it. Last year some of them had written and acted a play founded on Irving's *Rip Van Winkle,* and no doubt Old Pipes and his mother and the echo-dwarfs suggested Rip, Gretchen, and the dwarfs of the Catskills.

With the play in mind we reread the story carefully to see whether it was the right kind of material for a play. Each child took a copy of the story, which he carried home and studied for himself. The children decided that they could make a play out of it. Next we retold the story in as few words as possible, rejecting everything not suitable for our purpose, and holding the whole together by the natural order of incidents. The divisions of the story we wrote on the board and considered as a unit.

Preliminary notes.—Old Pipes, helped up the hill by the children, discovers that his pipes are no longer heard by the cattle. He resolves to return the wages just paid to ihm. Release of the dryad. Old Pipes made twenty years younger. The cave of the echo-dwarfs. The angry echo-dwarf vows vengeance. He steals the pipes and attempts to shut the dryad up again in her tree. The dryad shuts the echo-dwarf in the tree, restores the pipes to Old Pipes, and roams the forest for the remainder of the summer. The mother of Old Pipes is made twenty years younger. The discovery of the dryad's tree by the children. The dryad kisses Old Pipes and his mother again, lets the dwarf out, and goes back to the warmth and comfort of her tree.

Then we discussed the presentation of these different parts. We were without stage, curtains, scenery, or properties of any

[1] This play has been reprinted from the issue of May, 1902, in response to the many calls that have been made for it.—EDITOR.

kind, and even without a platform. Everything had to be planned and made by the children. We were obliged to go over the details very carefully, and we rejected many things as impossible under the circumstances. The children drew on the blackboard the scenes as they would like to have them, and sketched the characters in costume, each giving his opinion freely and illustrating his ideas with the chalk. They made drawings of the mountains, the rocky path, and the dryad tree. Many of the elaborate plans for the scenery we were unable to carry out.

As we worked out the scenery and action, the dialogue developed. Each child contributed. One proposed a speech, the others considered and criticized. The final result in each case was written on the blackboard. In the Francis W. Parker School the whole text was written in this way. In the School of Education, after the first two scenes were written, each child completed the work for himself. Then we compared results and selected from the whole what we considered best. Some of the most dramatic actions and speeches came out at the very last rehearsal.

The whole now took shape on the stage. After the first full rehearsal the children felt that something was wrong, and they were discouraged. The next morning, before school, while they were talking it over, one remarked: "There is too much talk and too little acting in this for a play. It drags out too long." They then decided that they would act, and talk only when speech was absolutely necessary. The dialogue was cut wherever it was possible to substitute action that would tell the story.

Still there was great disappointment in the result. The children began to feel that they had made a mistake, and some of them were quite ready to give up the play. One said: "There is not trouble enough in this story for a play. Things just go on. Enough does not happen." "Well," said another, "let us make more trouble. We don't need to have it just as it is in the story." They had made the discovery that the struggle between the good and the evil forces was not great enough, that the story itself was not sufficiently dramatic. This led to many interesting discussions and warm debates. A variety of plans was suggested, but finally it was agreed that the echo-dwarf was the mischief-maker, that the struggle was between him and the dryad, and that he might be allowed to plan a greater revenge and to carry his plans farther than in the story without interfering with the final outcome. He must steal the pipes, try to destroy them, then hide them, and proceed in his attempt to get the dryad back into her tree again; the dryad must discover the plot just in time, and, after shutting the dwarf up in the tree, find the pipes and put all things right again. The children of the Francis W. Parker School allowed the dwarf to keep the pipes hidden over one night, thus causing Old Pipes and the villagers sore trouble. Except for the difference at this point, the two versions follow nearly the same lines. The dialogue varies, the language in many cases being entirely different, although dealing with the same situations.

One of our greatest difficulties was to end our play. The ending of the story the children would not consider at all. That no one should ever know what became of the dryad outraged all their sense of right. At first they proposed to end by leaving the dryad free. Later they decided this would not be an end at all. They objected to shutting her up again, but at last decided that, since the tree was her home, and she *wanted* to go back into it, and could shut *herself* in and could come out again in the summer, the real end was to let her do it. As she goes to her tree she kisses Old Pipes and his mother, who are enjoying their evening meal outside the cottage, leaving them each thirty years younger than they were at the beginning of the play.

We never talked about any other meaning to this story than what lay on the surface. The children talked of the characters as real persons and of the incidents as real happenings. However, as we neared the time for presenting our work at a morning exercise, and they realized more and more the joy of the dryad in her own happiness and her delight in giving happiness to others, they called her the spirit of spring, of youth, of life, and of joy.

The rocky path and the cave of the echo-dwarfs we made of boxes, baskets, and benches covered with dark-gray cambric. The dryad tree was made in the manual-training room. It was a flat-surface frame, with the door opening outward. The frame was covered with heavy paper and calcimined to resemble the bark of an oak tree. Holes were bored in the wood and real twigs thrust in. The cottage of Old Pipes was a framework covered with cloth and calcimined a dull yellow. The latticed window, painted red, opened like a shutter.

The costumes were all simple, designed by the children, and constructed for the most part out of materials and costumes on hand. Old Pipes wore a hunter's dress; the dryad, a soft Greek robe; the dwarfs, gray suits in one piece, with pointed cap and shoes; the mother of Old Pipes, the dress of an old German woman; and the children, the dress of German peasant children, for somehow they had the impression that this was a German story.

Dramatis personae: Old Pipes; Echo-Dwarf and other dwarfs; dryad; mother; children—boys and girls.

SCENE I.

(*A rocky path. A large oak tree at left. Cottage to right. Rustic seat and small table outside.*)

Enter Old Pipes with children, two boys and a girl. Boys holding Old Pipes' arms, and helping him along. Girl pushing him from behind. He sinks exhausted on the seat. The children sit on the ground about him; each pulls a piece of bread from his pocket and eats.

Old Pipes. I am very tired tonight. I don't know that I could have climbed up this steep path to my home if you had not helped me. (*Gives each of the children a copper coin.*) I am sorry I tired you so much.

Boy. Oh, that would not have tired us, if we had not been so high up on the mountains for the cattle today.

Old Pipes (*in great surprise*). Had to go high up on the mountains for the cattle? What do you mean? (*Girl goes behind Pipes, puts her hand on her mouth, and makes all sorts of signs to the boy to stop. He does not notice her.*)

Boy. Why, you see, sir, that, as the cattle can't hear your pipes now, the chief villager has hired us to drive them down from the mountain every night.

Old Pipes (*in great distress*). How long have you done this? (*Girl tries to stop the boy as before.*)

Boy. Almost a year now. I think ever since the people felt that the cattle could not hear your pipes, and we have not heard the echoes for a long time. But we are rested now, and must go home. Good night, sir. (*The children go, the girl scolding the boys all the way out.*)

Girl. It was a secret. The old man did not know that the cattle can't hear him, and you have made him so unhappy.

Old Pipes (after sitting awhile silent and in deep trouble). Mother! mother! *(Goes to the latticed window, where she sits spinning, and shouts again.)* Mother! mother! *(Old woman comes hobbling out; she is very deaf, and Pipes speaks very loud as both move toward the seat.)*

Old Pipes. Mother, did you hear what those children said?

Mother (speaking in Pipe's ear). Children! I did not know that there were children here.

Old Pipes. Why, they say that the cattle can't hear my pipes any more, and that the villagers are paying me for nothing.

Mother (shouting). They can't hear you! Why, whats the matter with the cattle?

Old Pipes. Nothing's the matter with the cattle. It is with me and my pipes. But one thing is certain; if I do not earn the wages, I shall not take them. *(Takes money from a bag that hangs at his side and counts it out.)*

Mother (very angry). You piped the best you could, and what are we to do without the money?

Old Pipes. I don't know, but I shall go straight down to the village and give back the money they paid me today. *(Starts off. Mother goes into the house, grumbling.)*

Mother. Foolish! foolish! What are we to do without the money?

Old Pipes (dropping wearily under a tree). I cannot go tonight, I am too tired; but tomorrow—*(Leans heavily against the tree; a tapping is heard; listens; it is heard again; listens; a voice is heard.)*

Voice. Let me out, let me out.

Old Pipes (springing to his feet). This must be a dryad tree, and she wants to get out. I'll let her out if I can. It is summer time, and the moon rises tonight before the sun goes down; I must find the key, and if I do I shall surely turn it. *(He comes all around the tree trying to turn every little bit of bark that he finds sticking out; one turns quite around.)* Here it is! *(A large part of the side of the tree is pushed open, and a beautiful dryad steps quickly out. She stands motionless, looking out over the mountains and all before her.)*

Dryad. Lovely! lovely! How good of you to let me out! I am so happy, so thankful! *(Kisses him on both cheeks.)* Oh, it's glorious! glorious! I am so happy! What can I do for you, my kind friend?

Old Pipes (who has been gradually straightening up since receiving the dryad's kiss, is standing with eyes and mouth wide open, hardly able to speak for surprise). Well! well! I am glad that I let you out, but I must tell you that I turned the key because I wanted to see a dryad. I knew that your people lived in the trees, and that you were happy to come out in the summer time, and now I am glad that I let you out, because you are so happy; but if you want to do something for me, you can take this money down to the chief villager for me. It is the money paid me for calling the cattle home from the mountains. It is more than a year now since I have been able to make them hear my pipe, and I can't receive pay for what I cannot do.

Dryad (*taking the money*). To the village! I will go any place for you. Often, in my tree, I have heard the sweet notes of your pipes. (*Moves away, looking at the beautiful things about her.*)

Old Pipes (*following her to the entrance, watching her as far as he can see*). Now I have seen a dryad! (*Begins to move toward the house, and notices how light and free he feels. Throws his arms about, and goes quickly to the house.*) Why! I feel quite rested. I can walk quite easily. My! I feel so strong, and I am very hungry. I shall go home and eat my supper, and tomorrow go to the forest and cut some fuel for mother. (*Exit.*)

SCENE II.

(Same as scene I. Time the next evening.)

Enter Old Pipes, carrying a large armful of wood. He crosses the stage, and begins to pile it up against the side of the cottage.

Old Pipes. There, mother, I have done a fine day's work. If I keep on this way, we shall have plenty of fuel for next winter. Now it is time to call the cattle home. I must get my pipes. (*Goes into the cottage, and comes out, followed by his mother.*)

Mother. What are you going to do now? If you will not take the money, why will you pipe?

Old Pipes. I am going to play for my own pleasure. (*Plays a strong, full note. A faint echo is heard.*) Ha! ha! What has happened to my pipes? (*Plays again.*) They must have been stopped up of late, but they are as clear and good as ever! (*Plays again. Echo is heard as before. Pipes looks up toward the mountains.*) See, mother! see! the cattle are coming down as they used to do. (*Rising as the truth flashes upon him.*) O, I see it all now, mother! I had forgotten that a kiss from a dryad makes one ten years younger. She kissed me twice. I *am* really younger. Look! mother, look! (*Begins a joyous dance across the stage to show his mother how young he is.*) Come, come, mother, come! She must kiss you too! (*Tries to pull her with him.*) Well, then, I'll find her and bring her to you. (*Dances off the stage in search of the dryad.*)

Mother (*looking after him in astonishment*). He's bewitched! O Pipes! Pipes! when will you be old enough to have ordinary common-sense? (*Turns toward the cottage.*) He's bewitched!

SCENE III.

(Cave of the echo-dwarfs. Rocks lying all about.)

Dwarfs of all sizes running about, playing. One echoes back the sound of laughter that comes from the distance; another, the sound of a blacksmith's hammer; another, the call of a voice. One big, fat, lazy-looking dwarf is lying on a rock, sound asleep. The notes of Old Pipes' pipes sound in the distance. They all stop to listen and, when it is repeated, run to wake the big dwarf. He rolls to his feet, and begins to echo back the notes of the pipes. He is very angry at being disturbed, and, as soon as the piping stops, moves about shaking his head and fists and grinding his teeth.

Echo-Dwarf. I thought those pipes had stopped forever. I have been deceived. I'll go and find out how long this is to last. I will find the piper himself. (*Starts to run off. Meets the dryad.*) Ho! ho! what are you doing here? How did you get out of your tree?

Dryad. Doing! I am being happy that's what I'm doing. I was let out by the good old man who plays the pipes to call the cattle home, and I've kissed him and made him young enough to play as well as ever.

Echo-Dwarf (*pale with anger, moves toward her in threatening way*). And you are the cause of this great evil that has come upon me? You are the wicked creature who has again started this old man upon his career of pipe-playing? What have I ever done to you that you should condemn me for years and years to echo back the notes of those wretched pipes?

Dryad (*laughing merrily*). What a funny little fellow you are! Anyone would think that you had been condemned to toil from morning till night. Fie upon you, Echo-Dwarf! You are lazy and selfish; and that is what is the matter with you. Instead of grumbling, you should rejoice at the good fortune of the old man who has regained so much of his strength and vigor. Go home, do your work, and learn to be generous, and then you may be happy. Good-by! (*Moves off in the direction of the forest.*)

Echo-Dwarf (*growing more angry and more savage, dances about, shakes his fist, and shouts at the dryad*). Insolent creature! I'll make you suffer for this! You shall find out what it is to heap injury and insult upon one like me. I have earned my rest by long years of toil. (*Follows her, then turns back.*) I'll find the piper, steal his pipes, and hide them!

SCENE IV. (SAME AS SCENE I.)

Enter Echo-Dwarf from behind the cottage. He looks all about. Old Pipes comes out, looking about; dwarf grinds his teeth, and motions that he would like to kill Old Pipes, but runs after him and stops him.

Echo-Dwarf. What are you looking for, old man?

Old Pipes. I am looking for a dryad whom I let out of her tree. She kissed me twice, and made me young enough to call the cattle home again, and I want her now on account of my old mother. I want to ask her to make my mother younger, as she did me. When I was old myself I did not notice how feeble mother was. Now it shocks and grieves me.

Echo-Dwarf (*his eyes glistening*). That's a noble idea! But you know a dryad can make no person younger but the one who lets her out of her tree. But, then, that is easy. You must find the dryad, tell her what you want, and ask her to step inside her tree; you shut her in and run for your mother. She will open it, let the dryad out, and you will have your wish.

Old Pipes. Good! good! I will go at once, but I must first get my pipes, lest I should be late in returning.

Echo-Dwarf (*rubbing his hands in glee*). She is quite foolish enough to do it. Then, when he goes for his mother, I'll take a stone and break off the key, so nobody can ever turn it again. She shall see! she shall see! (*Enter Old Pipes.*) Take me with you; you can carry me on your shoulder; and I'll help you. (*Old Pipes picks him up. The dwarf snatches the pipes, and begins to bend and bite at them. They move on. Soon the dwarf catches sight of the dryad in the distance. Before she enters, Old Pipes discovers his loss, and is hunting for the dwarf when the dryad enters.*) Oh, there she is! Put me down. Don't tell her I suggested the plan. (*Old Pipes puts him down; he runs off with the pipes and hides, but watches and listens. Enter dryad.*)

Old Pipes. I have been looking everywhere for you. Mother looks so old and feeble. Will you go into your tree for a few minutes? and I'll run and bring her to open it. Then kiss her as you did me just after you came out.

Dryad (*looking sadly at Pipes*). I should dislike it dreadfully, but if you wish it—(*Moves toward the tree, enters.*) I have thought of making you happier, and I have waited about your cottage many days for your mother; but she does not come out, and a dryad cannot enter a house. If you can get her to come out, I can make her younger any time without going into the tree. (*The echo-dwarf grows so anxious that he moves into sight. The dryad sees him.*) Did you think of this plan of shutting me up yourself?

Old Pipes (*hesitating*). No, no; a little dwarf, whom I met, proposed it to me.

Dryad. Oh, I see through it all. It is the scheme of that miserable echo-dwarf, your enemy and mine. Where is he? (*Dwarf hides. Pipes looks about.*) There he is. (*Pipes sees him. The dwarf tries to escape, but the dryad catches him, and drags him to the tree.*) We will put him in here. (*Old Pipes helps to thrust him in.*) Now we will shut him up, and I shall be safe from his mischief for the rest of the time that I am free. (*Shuts the door. There is a clicking sound of bark and root as the tree closes.*) There, no more need to be afraid of him.

Old Pipes. Oh, my pipes! The rascal has stolen them! (*Both search all about, and at last discover them under a rock. Old Pipes busies himself repairing them. Dryad helps. Pipes blows on them, making no noise.*)

Dryad. Now, will you not ask your mother to come out and meet me?

Old Pipes. Oh, it's no use. We must find some other way. She does not believe in dryads. She has forbidden me even to speak the name to her again. She says that I have been bewitched by a sorceress. (*Exeunt together.*)

Enter children, girl and small boy racing after the larger boy. He drops, breathless, under the oak tree.

Large boy. Ha! ha! you did not catch me, after all! (*A knocking is heard. All listen. Again the knocking is heard, also a voice, pleading.*)

Voice. Let me out! Let me out! (*All start up.*)

Large boy. Oh, this is a dryad tree, like the one Old Pipes found. Let's let her out. (*Hunts for the key.*)

Girl (*pulling him away from the tree*). No, no; what are you thinking about? I am the oldest here, and I am only thirteen. Do you want us all to be turned into crawling babies again?

Large boy. I want to see her! I want to see her!

Small boy (*tugging at large one*). No, no; every kiss from a dryad makes one ten years younger, and I am only nine. Where would I be? (*Both pull at large boy.*)

Girl. Are you crazy? Run! run! run! (*All run as fast as their legs can carry them.*)

Enter mother.

Mother. Alas! alas! the time has come when I am too old to work. I have grown utterly useless. Someone else will have to cook and sew for my son. I wonder where he is. (*Looks for him, but sinks exhausted into the chair, and soon falls asleep. The dryad enters, steps up lightly, and kisses the mother on both cheeks.*)

Dryad. Now Old pipes has his wish, and he will be happy. (*Disappears.*)

Mother (*waking, yawns, stretches herself*). My, how a little sleep does refresh one! It is astonishing how well I feel! (*Moves about quite easily, and, finding that she can walk without her cane, drops it, and turns quickly toward the cottage.*) I must hurry; my son will be here in a few minutes, and his supper must be ready. I do feel so well. (*Exit.*)

Enter Old Pipes with his pipes.

Old Pipes. This is the last time that I shall call the cattle down this year; the nights are growing colder, the mountains are bare, and the winter will soon be here. (*Sits and begins to play. Echo is heard from the tree.*)

Enter mother. She brings forward the little table, and sets the supper on; then seats herself beside Old Pipes, and, with a smile, watches the cattle coming down. Both begin to eat.

Enter dryad.

Dryad (*shivering*). The night winds chill me. How happy they look there together; but I do not believe it will hurt them to be a little younger. (*Steps up lightly and kisses each of them once. The mother kisses her son. Dryad shivers again.*) I must get back into my comfortable home in the oak. (*Goes to the tree, turns the key and calls to the dwarf.*) Come out. Winter is coming. I want the shelter of the tree myself. The cattle have come down for the last time this year, the pipes will sound no more, and you can go to your rocks and have a holiday until next spring. (*Echo-Dwarf skips out, and runs away among the rocks.*) Now he can break the key, it does not matter. Another will grow out in the spring, and I know that, when the warm days are here next year, the piper will come and let me out. (*Shivers again, wraps her robe about her, enters the tree, and pulls the door after her.*)

PRAIRIE VIEW FARM SCHOOL

CAROLINE M. HILL

The farm vacation-school experiment, plans for which were published in this magazine in February and March, 1905, was carried on again in the summer of 1906 in the hope that it would become a pathfinder in education. That it could not be a financial success and a primrose path of delight had been pretty well demonstrated by the first summer's experience, but those who had started the enterprise were not willing to give it up until they had tried it again under slightly different conditions. In the course of the two summers certain problems developed which may be of interest to educators.

Democratic education was the first principle in the minds of the two who planned this kind of school. But they were immediately confronted with the financial necessity which compelled them to accept only the children of those who were able to pay enough to make the enterprise self-supporting. Other plans were given a brief trial, but special terms to a few only made it necessary that others should pay enough more to restore the balance.

The next problem was one arising out of the previous education and training of the children who came. The colonial family was something like this one in size, but the children had been added one at a time and both parents and children had become inured to the necessities of the case. These children had been accustomed to be the idols of homes where children were few, and they believed that any real work was to be done by someone else. They had dipped into manual work at school, but only for its educational value. Of the educational value of work as work they had no idea, for it is contrary to the modern theory. It was a notable fact, however, that the most successful parents who sent their children to the farm had this idea for their children. The temporary parents of this summer group had unbounded faith in children and little experience with them, but when this second difficulty developed they could not break their second principle, which was that the work of the household, except the cooking and cleaning, should be done by members of the family.

In several ways life on the farm was a return to primitive conditions, and, on the whole, the children endured it better than the grown people, for children can do without any such artificialities as cleanliness and learning from books. They held firmly to the essentials of food, its production and preparation, and play. Their science teachers had been very successful in interesting them in their work during the school year, but in the summer could only get them to go on excursions if they were promised a swim afterward. The Professor-of-Things-in-General could get them to work with him on the farm and keep them at it if he paid them wages by the hour, but this led to so much contention and thought about the money that it finally had to be abandoned. This shows what the third and fourth difficulties that presented themselves naturally would be—the absence of school associations and of teachers fitted to carry on an entirely new kind of school.

Children are accustomed to drift in the summer and do not take kindly to anything that is like what they do in school in the winter. If they are to make use of their time in the summer it must be by means of a regular life and by doing certain things, different, of course, from what they do in the winter, whether they feel inclined to do them or not. Children go to school during the year and do their work regularly because they have behind them the force of parental and school authority and centuries of tradition. Most parents do not wish their children to exert themselves in the summer and many of them allow the children to stop doing a thing at the very point when the will begins to be educated—when they begin to be tired. Some mothers, like Mrs. Cheyne in *Captains Courageous*, wish to protect their children from the very training that would make them men and women.

Any new kind of school which is to secure a following must have teachers who have enough enthusiasm for their subjects to carry along even the unwilling. The French teacher secured for part of the summer of 1906 was able to do this, and one little boy (who, however, was not among the unwilling) did so much beginning French in September that he was given a year's credit for it on the first of October. The writer believes that this is only an instance of the saving of time that might be effected by combining school work and manual work in the right way during the entire year. Some parents felt that their children learned more in their first three months in the country than in any year in school. It should be possible by means of a reasonable amount of physical exercise, to do the brain work of a day at school in a fraction of the time usually given to it.

Such are the main difficulties encountered in two summers' experience. In what respects has the experiment proved a success?

1. No school can be a success if the children do not like to attend it. It may safely be said that in so far as this was not in any ordinary sense a school, the children liked it. At the end of the first summer a number of them expressed a desire to stay and go to school all winter, even if they did have to wear good clothes and study arithmetic and grammar.

2. The farm life proved to be most excellent as a training in general social efficiency, and this is the watchword of modern education. The situations which arose demanded more of inventiveness, adaptibility, and courage than any which are likely to come in the child's city experience, and the very fact that he was aiding in the production of the necessities of life gives his education a broader outlook than it had when his manual training was confined to woodwork and pottery. This life was an expansion of the manual training idea.

3. We may be very weary of hearing about the farmer's sons who have become the great men of the city, but has anyone written up the farmer's daughters who have become the competent women of the city? The farm experiences proved just as enjoyable for the girls as for the boys and the writer believes it to be even more valuable for them. Domestic science and library training may be obtained in the city but outdoor life and control over the forces of nature cannot be obtained there. Girls learn on the farm the differences between essentials and non-essentials, learn

to deal with larger problems, to overcome timidity, to use their larger muscles and brain-areas, and to meet emergencies. In the home life boys and girls live together and educate each other, on the farm they do the same. Some mothers who have only boys are afraid to send them where there are girls, but mothers who have both know the good influence they have upon each other. As a matter of home management the writer found the task much easier with both for they check each other's adolescent tendencies. To put it plainly the boys were less brutal and the girls less silly when both were represented. They had not yet reached the sentimental age, so few complications arose out of having them together.

4. Another opportunity which the farm school presents is for the moral and religious training of the child. A large family can give better moral training than a small one because it forms habits which enable children to live in harmony with other persons. To belong to a large family in isolation is to command resources, not merely to be free from intrusions. Religious feeling has developed among races that live close to nature. Under proper guidance a natural religion might be developed in the child. To most city children religion means nothing, it is a form to be gone through because parents wish it, or something to be scoffed at because parents do that. If it is right that the child in his school life should live over the industrial life of the race, why shall he not enter into its spiritual inheritance in the same way?

The writer believes in the plan as much as ever, and sees even more need for such an opportunity for the city child than it was possible to see before the experiment was tried. The physical energy which runs to waste and worse than waste in the summer time should be utilized in productive labor to the eternal welfare of the child. The old saying that it is but three generations from shirt-sleeves to shirt-sleeves might not be so true if the second generation had a shirt-sleeve period. It is the usual thing to see splendidly competent parents with callow, impudent, and lazy children, because the stage of involuntary training which made the parents has been omitted in the case of the child. On the other hand, it has become almost proverbial that the best men in business are those who have had to work their way through college or university.

The same arguments that pointed to such a summer experiment point now to the establishment of such a place on a permanent basis. An endowed school could afford to be democratic, could develop the manual training idea, which is now in its infancy, would be obliged to have the equipment necessary to give it a school atmosphere, and teachers who would be paid enough to make it worth while to give their time to it. The hardships attendant upon starting any new enterprise in the country are sufficient to discourage anyone who has no endowment back of him. The ideal head of such an institution would be someone who has had experience with both vacation schools and manual training schools, and who is willing to give his entire time to the development of the plan. The school has not been carried on during the past summer, but the persons who are interested in it hope that at some time it may be taken up by the right persons, under the right conditions.

BOOK-BINDING AS A SCHOOL CRAFT

GERTRUDE STILES
School of Education

There has been, within the past two or three years, a very keen interest in the subject of book-binding as hand-work in schools. Wood, pottery, metal, and the textiles, including all forms of weaving, having passed their probationary stage, seem now established as an important and necessary factor in the course of study. The crafts themselves have decided their own limitation and boundaries. The instructors in charge of the hand-work have not been slow to recognize these imposed boundaries; to see the possibilities lying within the confines. Therefore, the proper relation of the crafts to what might be called the regular school work has been the more readily established. Instructors in the crafts have been recruited from the ranks of the professional teacher, or have studied well the teaching questions and have a knowledge of the child, what he wants to do, what he can do, what is best for him to do, and what line of work will best promote his development.

So the three—the child's ability, the crafts' limitation, and the teacher's knowledge—have placed the hand-work in right relation to the more fully established studies.

The hand-work is universally recognized. Book-binding as one of the forms of hand-work has yet to fulfil its present alluring claims and promises.

Too well do we know the great wave of enthusiasm which sweeps us on in the study of any new subject. We neglect details and resist every suggested obstacle—possibilities are almost limitless. After this first burst, however, we are thrown back on the dry sands of limitation—it is not what we had thought—it is useless, barren, why have wasted the time? To do the best within these limitations—to discard, to select, and to arrange—is the problem.

I view the subject from the standpoint of a craftsman, having had but limited experience and small insight, I fear, into the realm of its educational possibilities. And what I say will be said tentatively (for we cannot as yet arrive at many conclusions) and with a suggestion or two of what it seems to me might be done, and, finally, of a few of the exhibited results which have so far been obtained.

The present chaotic state of book-binding in schools comes, I think, from a lack of interest on the part of the craftsmen. No one as yet has set himself to a study of its educational features, to a study of its simplification to elemental form, or even to any systematic outline of book-construction. Those who have undertaken its teaching have not, for various and obvious reasons, been able to master sufficient of the craft to reduce it to its simplest elements, or even to see fully the great possibilities *within* its limitations.

As an art, practiced by but few, it is most arduous, requiring skill beyond the average, practice of years (Cobden Sanderson says it takes ten years to make a book-binder), an exquisite judgment involving both artistic and literary taste, a combination of manual dexterity, of poetic and artistic feeling, of enthusiasm which shall carry one through many a Slough of Despond. It seems so far beyond the child's comprehension: why bring it from this high estate, where it has lived for centuries, loved and honored by the world's potentates, to place it in our common schools? How the patron saint of book-binding—Grolier, maybe—must groan in spirit at the atrocities committed in his name!

Is it so surprising, then, that a craftsman guards so jealously his craft? But the traditions of a craft need not be destroyed—by a judicious selection of certain forms which may be useful to us—any more than the beauty of any opera is destroyed by the rendering of a detached portion. And these portions prove stepping-stones to a bigger understanding of the whole.

Book-binding has been carried on with success in normal and high schools. Equipment and supplies, necessary working space, and students have all been ready at hand, proving again the keen interest in the work. In the elemenary schools, however, it has been confined to the making of portfolios and the small word-books of the earlier grades. These, both, are important steps in book-construction, and, with proper attention at their making, could be made the first movement toward a correct sequence of the various problems which book-binding involves. The portfolio is an exact duplicate of a case-binding minus the book. The word-books, tied with thread through the fold of the section, are of the simplest form of pamphlet binding, and often involve, if made of large sheets of folded paper, an immediate example of folio or quarto, as the paper may happen to be; if made of single sheets, punched with holes and tied, the book is an embryo photograph album. They are identical in construction, but somewhere the connection is lost; this little thread of instruction is either tied right there in a hard knot and forgotten, or it is allowed to drag through a few intermediate stages, trailing along, blown here and there, a bit of waste, unnoticed, unattached, until, if it *does* reach the book-binding classes, it is so worn and frayed, so shabby and tangled, as to be absolutely useless.

Book-binding seems forced to spell itself with a capital B; to stand apart, fenced about, just a little mysterious and unnatural, and all the time it is wishing to be spelt with a little b; to be allowed to take its upward shoot naturally, to grow a little each year, and to be right.

One seventh-grade boy retained a thread of what he had gained in the earlier years, when, in making a book for kodak pictures, he proclaimed it, rather contemptuously, a "kindergarten stunt." But as he worked, the problem lost its infantile character, and the boy after having done it all himself seemed rather proud of the result.

Book-binding touches closely the general cause of study at many points—as hand-work, art-work, and as a literary and historic study. As hand-work, the immediate needs of the children or the school offer a wide range in subject-matter, and as sufficient training is gained these needs can be supplied. Such work must be simple—not involving too much time—for should it be a book in constant use, it must be put into its cover quickly.

The question of utility is a large one in supplying these demands. Often, a small book in constant use is put in a case-binding without resewing, as sewing would place the book out of service for too long a time. The beginning French lessons were put into a simple tied cover, allowing more sheets to be added as the French lessons progressed. This is almost the only way we have of binding single sheets. Commercial houses do them differently, to be sure.

In the constructive work, there is a wide field in various forms of folios, with or without pockets. The child can make what he most needs in this line, working it out in size, shape, and style to suit himself. There are various related problems, such as the making of pocket-books, card-cases, stamp-books, writing folios—the list is endless—coming often under the head of "leather work," which should be included here, brought into line and recognized as a phase of book-construction.

As to books themselves, unless a blank book, the binder is more restricted. It is not purely creative, but a thing already existing about which he must build, using the book itself as an integral part of that construction. Tradition too binds him, for books can only be made in certain correct ways; yet, even in this, he can be given the initiative in choosing one of the few ways in which to do it. These ways must be taught and their various adaptabilities brought out as clearly as possible. In the earlier grades the boards should be cut for the children, but the practice in pasting and cutting and calculating of paper for covers can be gained. Later, when the child begins to cut boards for himself a distinct falling off in the appearance of the finished result will be unavoidable. A good-sized photographic cutter will be necessary. The use of the plough and press I think a little complicated for even the eighth grade, yet we have used it there. The children are invariably delighted with its use, and a few seem to understand it fairly well, but the many adjustments necessary, such as perfect pressure, cut against, level running of the knife, even screwing up of the pins, to say nothing of the sharpness of the knife, are so many that a child is apt to forget one or more in his eagerness. This eagerness is difficult at best to manage—

they see one point and *dive*. In this connection of helping the child to plan, and to consider the many points necessary a working formula could be made. The child could write out carefully, with the teacher's help, the processes involved in the making of his particular book—all the frequent pressings noted, all details recorded, in the order in which they should be followed, the color and kind of leather and paper he is to use, and keep this as a reference.

Pamphlet bindings are of various forms of making, and are a good problem for the first sewing—many of them with two kettle stitches, some larger books with three. Those going into covers of paper later, the same sewing can be combined with an advance in the manner of the attachment of the boards, using a different arrangement of leather or cloth, with the paper. Sewing on tapes comes next, and can be carried out in case-binding or in one or more forms of library binding. If in a library binding, we always back the book and attach the boards by either lacing the tapes through, or by using a split board. We have not tried with the children, and it would seem too advanced a form, the regular flexible sewing-on cords. Nor have we used the condemned sunken cord. The tapes seem to answer all purposes.

The children like the work and at the close of the hour over half the class will remain for "just a little more." Sometimes, to be sure, a child will complain of the care required, and one girl, after receiving criticism, said: "Have I got to do that over again? I just hate this. I wouldn't have come into the class, only I wanted the things we make." A frivolous remark, and from a girl not commended for serious work in any department, yet it proclaims a sentiment, a desire for some of the "things," and a wish to preserve work done in other lines.

Second, as art-work: In this, it extends its boundaries; for what *cannot* be lavished on the book! It first will join with the printing in producing a good "inside." This "inside," the real book, may have illustrations, fancy borders, head and tail pieces, initials, illuminations, what not? Passing, then, forward to the binding stage, it can have suitable and elaborate end-papers, designed and hand colored, they may be stenciled or done with wood blocks; the covers can also be stenciled or specially designed, decorative lettering becomes a feature in the titling. Covers could be made of cloth and embroidered in some simple outline stitch, or these, in turn, stenciled or blocked. So far, we have attempted no decoration, beyond a line or two following the outline of the tapes through the leather, across the back, based upon structural lines alone—the most legitimate form of decoration. We have tried to gain good color effects in our choice of leathers and papers. The various Japanese papers have been of great service.

We have made a decorative feature of the sewing by using bright-colored thread over leather or tape, and not covering this, but covering only the boards, allowing this to appear. The art and manual training can give each the hand of helpfulness in working out some delightful examples in this art.

Third, in correlation with history and literature. The study of the history of book-binding, of the glorious record of its faithful followers during the monastic period; its vital connection with the history of printing; the effect printing had upon its career; its connection with the goldsmith's art; the jewels used for its further enriching; the story of the Book of Kells; the great names of famous book-lovers of the past; the story of the first public libraries; the history of papyrus and parchment; study even the derivation of our words "volume" and "codex;" the whole history of the primer and the New England primer in particular, of which that charming reproduction was made a few years ago; the hornbook which they have duplicated in wood and isinglass; all this opens a field of unusual interest and beauty. Nothing more exquisite has been written than *Friar Jerome's Beautiful Book*. Read a bit of Eugene Field's *Love Affairs of a Bibliomaniac,* quaint and humorous. A few chapters in Brander Matthews' *Book-bindings, Old and New,* will stir the interest afresh. One chapter in it speaks only of cloth-covered, commercially bound books. What an interest can be aroused to a consideration of the art, the labor and thought expended on this most intimate object of our everyday use! In the smallest town interesting books are to be found. Why could these not be brought together by a class and investigated? Old books are intensely interesting in their making, and inquiring glances down their backs, to their sides, their heads and joints—all homely technical terms—will delight and reward a class who know something of how books are made. Surely all this is more or less cultural—an attempt to secure that intelligent interest in the pursuits and the products of others. Surely this cannot fail to bring about that more serious regard for books—the lack of which is sometimes bewailed; that love for books—without which no man is truly great.

GLAZE-WORK [1]

SABELLA RANDOLPH
College of Education, University of Chicago

Just how long the process of glazing has been in use is not known. Since pottery claims its greatest antiquity in Egypt, it is quite probable that the same may be claimed for the process of finishing the ware. The Egyptian explorer, Dr. Petrie, found evidences of its dating back before the time of Abraham, a period of nearly four thousand years.

The Egyptian glazed ware was of a sandy, porous body covered with an alkaline glaze. The ancient potters of India and Persia employed *engobe,* a coating of a white, flinty material, over a colored body upon which underglaze colors were painted, the whole being covered with a transparent alkaline glaze. Most of the ancient glazed ware—the Indian, Damascene, Rhodian, and Persian—is *engobe,* each having its beautiful and characteristic effect. All have transparent, bright glazes, supposed to have been made principally of soda and lime with quartz or silica. Different effects and brighter colors were obtained with the alkaline glazes from those produced by the lead glazes so much used today. On the other hand, the lead glazes are more easily handled and surer of results. Cheaper methods began to be sought for eventually, engobe was abandoned, and the processes which produced unique and most fascinating wares became a lost art. Fortunately tin, which was introduced into glazes later on, contributed a certain pleasing and singular quality to the glaze. It was the opaque quality, the highest form of which is found in the Delft ware of the sixteenth century. The decorations are painted over the glaze before the glaze is fired.

The inspiration of these old pieces brought down to us is such that the artist potter longs to find a process whereby he

[1] This article is based upon work done in the New York School of Ceramics under Professor Charles F. Binns.

POTTERY DONE IN MATT AND TRANSPARENT GLAZES

By Members of a College Class

may reproduce their effects. The empirical method was the method of the ancients. This resulted in receipts which are really of little or no value now since their ingredients have become unknown, some of them having belonged only to certain localities where they were used.

Ceramists have been endeavoring to get away from this method and to secure a method by which desired results may be prescribed on paper. Although absolute certainty as to results is impossible, because of physical properties that sometimes influence the mutual action of one material upon another, making a difference in the fineness of results, the relative contents of materials may be prescribed. This is done by the use of equivalents.

The use of equivalents assumes the construction of a molecule of glaze containing acids and bases, and we make our division of glazes according to the acids and bases contained: first, silicates; second, boro-silicates containing boric acid.

With this classification, all glazes being silicates, they are named according to their bases, or to the predominating base, if more than one base is contained.

There are three parts to the constitution of a glaze:

Base	Intermediate	Acid
RO	R_2O_3	SiO_2

The rule in glazes is to take the sum of the bases, or fluxing elements whose formula is of the type RO, such as lime (CaO), potash (K_2O), soda (Na_2O), lead (PbO), zinc (ZnO), etc., as unity; to gather the elements whose type-formula is R_2O_3 into an intermediary group—for example, alumina (Al_2O_3), iron (Fe_2O_3); and the third group of the acids, silica and boracic.

$$\text{Formula for the body of a glaze} \left\{ \begin{matrix} .50\ PbO \\ .35\ CaO \\ .15\ K_2O \end{matrix} \right\} \begin{matrix} Al_2O_3 \\ .35 \end{matrix} \Big\} \begin{matrix} SiO_2 \\ 1.484 \end{matrix}$$

Sum of bases 1.00

There are various considerations as to what bases shall be put into a glaze—the body, fire, and composition. Barium is harder to fire than calcium. In order to lower the fusibility of the glaze .1BaO may be substituted for .1CaO. The increase of PbO or the introduction of certain oxides of the heavy metals reduces the melting-point of the glaze. Zinc oxide will sometimes improve certain colors of a glaze, if used sparingly, otherwise it would impair the brilliancy of the glaze. It does not produce color, but it is very important in that it directs color. But, whatever the bases, their sum must always be unity.

The transfer of a formula into a common weight mixture is called translating. This is of greatest importance.

The above formula translated into a glaze mixture.

White Lead	129.00
Whiting	35.00
Spar	83.55
Calcined Kaolin	44.40
Flint	11.04
Batch weight in 302.99 parts or grams	302.99

From 1 to 3 per cent. of the metal oxides must be added to the batch weight to give color to the glaze; only 1 per cent. is used for the stronger oxides such as cobalt or copper.

A glaze must be compounded of insoluble ingredients. It is first ground in water, or blunged, so as to produce evenness. If a piece has to be handled much, 1 or 2 per cent. of soluble material—used purely for its physical properties for cementing—is added to bind the glaze. Many difficulties would arise if there were no way of making soluble material insoluble.

Fritting, also called *fretting,* takes its name from *fritt* which originally meant a conglomeration by fire; cintered by fire. It is a preliminary operation by means of which soluble substances are rendered insoluble, and infusible substances are rendered fusible. According to whether or not glazes contain a fritt they are named *raw* or *fritt glazes.*

In raw glazes we are limited to insoluble materials. They are composed of the following: kaolin, flint, feldspar, whiting, white lead, sometimes red lead, zinc oxide, and barium carbonate. They range from the red lead to the porcelain glaze with a high percentage of silica and alumina. The more or less opaque or rather translucent quality characteristic of matt glazes is due to the content of a high percentage of alumina, the greater part of which is held in supension, giving the glaze its peculiar matt quality. An increase of alumina in a glaze noticeably diminishes fusibility.

A very great variety of effects is possible with simple raw glazes, and for all public-school work the lower-temperature glazes are most practicable.

It is not too much to hold that in no other craft is the creative element so strong as in that of clay-working—the joy that comes with seeing the clay take form in one's hands is unlimited. Then, when one has done all that is possible for him to do with it, there is still the enchantment of the fire. The desire to abandon it never comes, if you have once entered the field of ceramics.

THE RATIONALE OF SPELLING

B. C. GREGORY
Superintendent of Schools, Chelsea, Mass.

The purpose of this discussion is by no means to solve offhand the spelling problem. It is merely an effort to throw a little light upon it through the medium of child-study. It has seemed to me that of all blind teaching we teachers do, the teaching of spelling is the blindest. It is empirical in most cases; reason (much less psychology) enters very little into our methods. We differ as to oral and written spelling, we differ as to the propriety of dictating words in sentences or in columns, and we differ as regards the use of spelling-books and the degree of difficulty of words used; but why we differ, or what is the psychological basis of this or that method, few of us can say. And so we go on, and the product is bad, and we are criticized severely by the public because our graduates can't spell. The present discussion arises from the fact stated: a sincere effort to apply the principles of psychology to facts drawn from the schoolroom. It is an effort, semi-scientific, at least, to get at causes. The inferences have seemed sufficiently important to warrant me in radical changes in methods in my own schools, and I offer them, not as finalities, but with the hope that they may turn your thought along somewhat new lines.

One March I sent to two classes in one of the Trenton, N. J. schools two extracts to be dictated by the teachers and written by the pupils. The classes selected were of the fifth and seventh grades. In that city, as in many others, the first grade usually represents two years: therefore, the pupils in the grades tested may be said to be in the 6th and 8th years in school; i. e., of an average of eleven years in one class, and thirteen in the other.

The extracts selected were the following:

Fifth grade.—Once upon a time a man and his son were going to market, and they were leading their donkey behind them. They had not gone far when they met a farmer and he said: "You are foolish to walk to town and that lazy donkey walking behind you." "What is a donkey good for if not to ride upon?" "Well, I never thought of that," said the man "and I am willing to please you;" so he put the boy on the donkey and started again on his journey. Soon they passed some men on the roadside. "See that lazy boy," said one of the men, "he rides the donkey and makes his poor old father walk behind." When the man heard this, he called to the boy and said: "Stop a minute, let us see if we cannot please these men." Then he told the boy to get off, and mounted the donkey himself.

Seventh grade.—One day, a ragged beggar was creeping along from house to house. He carried an old wallet in his hand, and was asking at every door for a few cents to buy something to eat. As he was grumbling at his lot, he kept wondering why it was that folks who had lots of money were never satisfied, but were always wanting more. "Here!" said he, "is the master of this house. He was always a good business man, and made himself rich a long time ago. Had he been wise, he would have stopped then. He would have turned his business over to some one else, and then he would have spent the rest of his life in ease. But, what did he do instead? He took to building ships and sent them to sea to trade with foreign lands. He thought he would get mountains of gold, but there were great storms on the water, his ships were wrecked, and his riches were swallowed up by the waves. Now, his hopes all lie at the bottom of the sea, and his great wealth has vanished like the dreams of the night."

The words misspelled were marked by the teachers of the classes and returned to me. Availing myself of the assistance of a bevy of high-school girls, I subjected the papers to the following treatment. At the bottom of each paper were written the words misspelled in each paper: in each case the word correctly spelled was first given, and the incorrect spelling followed. These records were afterward cut into slips and arranged alphabetically. An alphabetical table was then made out, giving under each word its various misspellings. To illustrate: *foreign* was spelled in six different ways, but there were nine cases of misspelling; *forign* four times, and once in each of the following ways: *foreigh, forhen, foren, forigen, forin.*

There were in all 324 cases of misspelling, seventy-seven words misspelled and 202 forms of misspelling. The lowest number of forms of misspelling was one, the highest eighteen, the latter in the case of the word *journey.* There were in all eighty papers examined. No attention was paid to the difference in grade. After this preliminary work of the investigation had been completed, and the matter was in systematic form, I called a conference of about thirty intelligent teachers and submitted the results of this investigation. The matter was discussed as thoroughly as the time permitted, and some light was thrown upon the meaning of the data. I make this statement to show that I conducted the inquiry with some little care.

Before considering the facts developed and the inferences drawn, a preliminary observation may be in order. It may be objected that the number of pupils tested is small. Usually in child-study investigations, a vast number of cases are treated. In answer, I merely desire to say that some of the lessons which I have drawn from this investigation are overwhelmingly indicated in the field covered, and I do not think that a wider field would reverse these conclusions. Regarding certain other conclusions found in this paper, I admit the paucity of data. In my own mind these latter conclusions are clearly indicated, although, of course, not proven. The investigation must, of course, be regarded as experimental or preliminary. A much wider field must be examined before all the inferences of this paper can be considered as established. I might add, on the other hand, however, that in widening the field we meet complications; introduce other considerations whose influence should not be lost in the mass, but should be estimated separately. For instance, the school investigated was located in one of the best portions of the city, and was composed of children of American parentage. Suppose I had mixed with the results I have obtained, those drawn from sections where the foreign population is in the ascendant. I think my results would have been confusing. The foreign children should be examined by themselves. They offer evidence of two kinds: first, evidence corroborating inferences drawn from other quarters—this evidence is just as valuable, considered separately, as if it had been drawn from a mass of mixed data; second, foreign localities teach a lesson peculiarly their own, and this we cannot afford to lose by mixing the data. Besides, in the investigation of spelling, do we not first need to know the difficulties which the native-born population finds; and secondly, those which the foreign encounters? The former are essential errors often perhaps inherent in the language. The special difficulties of the foreigner are inherent in the foreigner.

The disclosures of the investigation may be approached in a rather interesting way, by taking a few words and observing various forms of misspelling. I begin with the word *journey.* On this word the pupils have expended the wealth of their ingenuity. I could not have invented so many spellings. I give the entire list: *jorney, journy, jerney, gerney, jornay, jirney, jarnay, gourney, journei, jurony, jorney, yourney, jouery, jer, ji, jou.* Let us consider this list in some detail. It gives as will be seen later, a conspectus of nearly the whole field.

There are eighteen of these spellings, and the first thirteen are founded on aural percept; that is to say, the ear has determined the wrong spelling. Of these forms some are repeated by more than one pupil, thus: *jorney* is given five times; the thirteen forms, in fact, represent twenty-two mistakes. There were twenty-seven mistakes altogether in the spelling of *journey.* Therefore, almost 82 per cent. (22 out of 27) of the mistakes were ear-mistakes. I mean that in such mistakes the boy had a percept of the sound *journey* and he translated that sound into writing in his own way, and there are thirteen different ways. These pupils had seen the word *journey* many times, but they had also heard it many times; and it was the aural percept that dominated. Like as not, they had written the word *journey* in spelling-lessons, and had been corrected and made to spell it right. All futile—the sound of the word determined the spelling in accordance with the boy's views of orthographical combinations. I should like to give out the same exercises to the same pupils again. The same pupils would probably spell *journey* wrong again, and in accordance with the phonetic laws, but would they the second time adopt the same wrong spelling?

I may as well say here that the whole investigation clearly indicates this law: viz., that the sound is the dominating element in children's spelling. I might give many illustrations; one must suffice: *foolish* is spelled *foullosh, fulish, foulies, folish, follish, foulish, fourshil, furlash.*

Now, what does this teach? In my opinion this, at least, that the spelling cannot be taught by writing alone. When a boy writes *jerney,* that visual percept satisfies his view of the facts of the case. Of course, he does not see it to be wrong. But, when the word is corrected at the end of the lesson, does not that fix the proper spelling? Not always. The wrong form has been associated with the sound, and the association has not been broken. Why? In my opinion, because of the interval which elapses between the writing and the correction. First, the correction should be made instantly—with a shock, as it were—and this can be done only in oral spelling. Secondly, the association must be broken not once, but many times, if it is to be completely demolished. Now, oral spelling has greatly the advantage of written spelling in this respect: you can spell a word one hundred times orally while you are writing it ten times. Rapid oral spelling bears the same relation to written spelling that rapid mental arithmetic does to written arithmetic. In my judgment, the oral spelling should always both precede and follow the written spelling

In my case this means a complete overturning of my previous notions. For many years, I had argued in this way: spelling is used only in writing; therefore the visual picture of the word alone is of consequence; therefore, spelling should be taught exclusively by writing and in sentences. During the last few years, to be sure, I had been weakening on this theory; but rather because I could not see that my theory was turning out good spellers than because I saw flaws in the theory. But the overwhelming evidence presented by this investigation reduces the matter, in my mind, to a certainty. The psychology of the written method is incontestable, but hard oral drill is evidently suggested by the predominance of ear-mindedness, indicated in the present investigation.

Let me, in discussing this question of ear-mindedness, call attention to some subordinate considerations under the same general heading. They seem to me to be of great importance and throw a bright light on the relation of oral to written spelling.

First, it is to be remarked that not only do pupils know the sound of *journey,* but some of them know it wrong also: e. g., note *jorney.* The pupil who wrote this probably pronounces it with a long o. Take the word *swallowed.* I give the forms offered by the pupils: *swalloed, swolloed, swolid, swolled, swalled, sallowed, swolid.* Note that the boy who wrote *swalloed* has the correct sound, and yet he wrote it wrong; but the boy who wrote *swolid,* did not even have the correct sound; and he must write it wrong. The latter fact is true of the writers of *swolled* (four boys), and *swalled.* To proceed with a spelling-lesson when everybody has the correct pronunciation of the words does not always result in accurate spelling, as has been already suggested; but, to proceed, as many teachers do, without being sure of the pronunciation, is surely foolish. Take *wondrously,* spelled three times *wonderously* and once *wondersly.* Do not these represent wrong aural percepts to start with?

Again, still considering ear-mindedness, the investigation indicates the interesting fact that certain pupils attach certain phonetic power to certain letters or combinations of letters. Thus, returning to *journey,* in *gerney,* and *gourney,* this is the explanation of *g,* and in *jeirnie* of *ie* and probably of *ei;* in the spelling *creaping,* note *ea,* and in *creping,* e; etc. Now this trouble is inherent in our language and presents formidable difficulties. We have few rules, and they don't help us much. For instance, take the rule: *g* is soft before *e.* Well then, what's the matter with *gerney?* We certainly spell *germane* g-e-r-m-a-n-e. I call attention to this proposition: These wrong views on phonetics are probably individual with each pupil; they are idiosyncrasies. This is very important, if true. A little investigation, even notes taken from time to time, will reveal the tendencies of individual children in this matter and enable the teacher to anticipate what the child will do, and prevent his writing the wrong letter, not only in *journey,* but also whenever soft *g* is suggested. Thus: "We have *journey* in today's lesson. With what letter does it commence?" "With a *j,*" say the majority. "With a *g,*" say a few. "Now let us look," says the teacher. But note that this method of procedure is oral. It has to do with an aural percept and contemplates the immediate aural correction of incorrect aural percepts. I insist on immediateness of correction. To wait an hour will not do. And I insist on the first approach being made through the ear, for it is the ear-mind, if you will allow me the expression, that is in error.

Again, one of the interesting and amusing facts concerning this matter of ear-mindedness is the contempt which children have for unnecessary letters. I confess that I sympathize with them. Mark Twain once expressed his admiration of a young lady who, in a word-game, spelt *caf* for *calf*. He argued a certain directness, going straight to the point, in the young lady's make-up. And there is as much wisdom as wit in the story. It is our spelling that is irrational, and it is the bad speller that is rational. My investigation, of course, offers many illustrations of the tendency I am discussing. Thus, note *journy:* what's the use of the *e? Jurny:* what's the use of the *o?* Cf. *foks* for *folks, stoped* for *stopped, reck* for *wreck,* etc. In the word *swallowed* there were ten misspellings, and in only one of these did the last *w* occur.

What are we going to do about this? Phonetic methods of reading claim to have solved this problem. There are the phonetic alphabets and the double-printed books. I have not the time to discuss them, but I confess I do not see their value. So far as this investigation may suggest a remedy or method of teaching, I have the same inference to make as in the phase of the discussion just passed: viz., we should anticipate the cases in which letters are omitted, and by concentrating attention on those points, prevent the occurrence of the omission. Perhaps the tendency to the omission of a certain letter is an idiosyncrasy of the child. Have we ever thought of that?

In leaving this question of ear-mindedness, may I not suggest an explanation for the well-known fact that children spell unusual words well and familiar words incorrectly? The unusual words have never been used in such a way as to form an aural percept. The percept is visual, and therefore correctly written. But the child has learned to speak the familiar words before he saw them printed, and when he saw the correct form, it did not displace the incorrect form already in the mind.

An interesting psychological inquiry is this, and I earnestly urge it: Does there lie in some back corner of each child's mind a visual percept, which is the constant translation of the aural percept of the word the child knows—*jerney,* for instance? And when he transfers this percept to paper can he write anything else? Adults are often in doubt as to the spelling of a word but with regard to familiar words at least, the child is in no doubt; he writes *caf* with an insouciance that is simply delightful. If these visual images do subconsciously exist, notice how they persist year after year in spite of all our teaching. If they do exist, why not acknowledge their existence, expect them, and combat them first and last through the approach by which the image entered the mind, viz., the ear? To blame or reproach a child for such errors is like blaming him for being left-handed. I shall return to this consideration, but at present note that here again there is a suggestion of an idiosyncrasy.

I dismiss for the present the question of ear-mindedness and come to a class of errors that clearly arise, at least in part, from visual aberrations. My word *journey* does not help me here, and this, of itself, is an interesting fact. Let us take the word *foreign.* I give the spellings: *forign* (four times), *foreigh, forhen, foren, forigien, forgen.* Now, several of these spellings are entirely or practically phonetic; notice *foren.* But on the other hand, notice the letter *g* occurring in every spelling but two, i. e., in 78 per cent. of the cases. In the last spelling, *forgen,* it is hard to believe that there was any aural percept at all. The *g* shows that the eye has been active in every case but two; just as the last *w* was left out in *swalloed,* where the ear was concerned, the *g* is studiously put in where the eye is concerned. The pupil doesn't know how to spell *foreign,* but he knows there is a *g* in it somewhere. Take the word *minute.* I have twenty misspellings, taking seventeen forms. Now the phonetic errors given are these: *minnet, minuete, minnote, menat, minet, minete.* But, on the other hand, consider these, remembering that from the child's point of view, the letter *u* is the unreasonable part of the word: *minutt, mintue, munt, minut, minunt, minuate.* In some of these spellings the phonetic principle has still something to do, but the eccentric dancing around of that letter *u* is a purely visual matter.

For a moment consider the two words *minute* and *foreign* together. Certain peculiarities are observable when they are contrasted. *Minute* is a common word, and therefore there was a previous image corresponding to the sound. But the printed or written word was *outré* as far as the *u* was concerned, and hence arose errors which are not phonetic. *Foreign* is not a word for the child's vocabulary; it is purely visual, and hence the phonetic element enters very little into the misspelling. Notice also that there were only nine misspellings of *foreign,* while there were twenty of *minute.* Of course, *foreign* had no original settler to expel, and *minute* had, and in twenty cases the original settler held his ground.

I think this argument indicates that we need not fear the unusual words nor the danger of wrong percepts obtained visually. The fight must be made on familiar words, where aural percepts are concerned, for as I have already said, it is a fight to gain territory already occupied by residents as obstinate as Boers. With reference to the class of words typified by the word *foreign,* it is merely a question of learning; but the learning of the words typified by *journey,* means the unlearning of an alien language.

But teachers generally make their spelling-lessons out of the unusual words and every day violate the principle for which I am now contending. Spelling-books almost unanimously offer words unusual to the child. I almost think that if we taught well the child's own vocabulary, we could leave the new words to take care of themselves. When the child wants to use a new word, he can be taught to look up the spelling, as we adults do. We waste our ammunition in teaching spelling as we do.

I now desire to touch a galaxy of errors which cannot be classified under either of the headings, ear-mindedness or eye-mindedness. At first sight they seem to be matters of invention. Some of them are rather interesting. Note that peculiarity among children of putting in letters that have no force in the sound of the word. *Minent* and *minth,* for *minute; jernary* for *journey;*

medt for *met, pasend* and *pasted* for *passed; crepting* for *creeping; leanding* for *leading; satisfided* for *satisfied.* What do these mean? I have gone over several of these errors thoughtfully. I cannot say that I can offer anything profound, but two or three practical propositions seem to arise from the consideration.

1. The trouble may be that the child is of foreign birth or parentage. For instance, final *th* means *t* to a German. If you know the pupil to be foreign, you may have the key.

2. In not a few cases, where the pupil was uncertain about a word, while he was thinking he found himself compelled to hurry on because the teacher was dictating a new sentence. Some prominent sound or letter in the word, as *r* in *journey,* and *n* in *leading,* dominated and went down on the paper because the faculties were not acting normally. Take *elese* for *else.* Sometimes a sound or letter belonging to another word in the sentence was dominant, and introduced itself into the word being written.

3. I find the process of association very active in writing. In the instances given, note *crepting, leanding,* and *minth.* Think of the actual words *crept, lend,* and *month.* I do not say that these words were in the child's mind, but I have a little proof to show that they might have been. The investigation offers a number of instances in which other good English words were actually used for those dictated, the new words making no sense whatever, and yet leaving me entirely sure that the new word had taken the place of the old one. Take a few illustrations. *Wrecked* was spelled *wreathed* and *wretched.* This is not a case of misspelling. It is an actual intrusion of a new word in the place of the word dictated. Now, when *minth* was written for *minute,* might not *month* have intruded itself in the same way? To give other illustrations: *were* was spelled *where* and *was,* and *make* was used for *made.* In many other cases, at least, we cannot be sure that the child did not know how to spell the word, as when he spelled *farther* for *father.* I think in this case, that he knew how to spell *father,* but the word *farther* got into his mind. Children run off on tangents very easily, and many so-called errors in spelling are tangential errors.

4. Certain letters tend to intrude themselves with certain

children. *T* is a very intrusive letter. Why do people say *oncet?* I have on my list *pasted* for *passed, wonderstly* for *wondrously,* and *leiting* for *leading.* I knew a little girl who invariably put in an *n* after *say,* as "what was he sayning?" and "I was playning." I think these may be called idiosyncrasies, and should be treated as such. Similar considerations apply to the substitution of letters, as when *mourted* was written for *mounted.*

I pause here to direct attention as forcibly as I may to this fact applying to the present section of this discussion. It is its practical outcome. Such errors as we are now considering are not errors in spelling at all; that is to say, they don't indicate that the child doesn't know. They arise from haste or the domination of an associated idea. The teacher should not correct such errors, but should permit the child to discover them himself by reading over his paper several times, until he finds them; much less should the pupil lose marks for them. It is unjust to say the boy does not know how to spell when he has written *mourted.* Give him a chance to correct his own paper and see if this is not so.

But how few teachers seem to know this! There is only one fact in their minds when they correct a spelling-paper, and that is that the word was spelled wrong. Let me enforce the lesson I am now trying to teach by the consideration of a few more errors, kindred to those just considered, to which the practical statements I have just made apply with equal force.

There is a tendency, for instance, on the part of children to leave out letters. I have many illustrations in my table of errors. We are so familiar with this in our own writing that we should not be surprised. In our case it is not because we don't know, nor is it necessarily so in the child's case. It is the result of other causes, some of which have been referred to, which affect the manual act of writing. Here again the child should be permitted to find his own error, and should not be treated as if he did not know his lesson. The same argument and suggestion should be made again in cases in which a child has inverted letters, as *jurony* for *journey.*

So also must we regard the substitution of the singular for

the plural; as *ship* for *ships,* or the opposite; the putting-in of another part of the verb, as *sending;* the use of one word for another, as *then* for *them, the* for *they, though* for *thought.* They are not errors in spelling—or they may not be; at least the pupil ought to have the same privilege that we enjoy in our correspondence, that of reading it over to himself one or more times.

Permit me, for a moment only, to call attention to a class of very peculiar, but interesting, errors which deserves similar treatment. I refer to those cases in which the word isn't spelled at all. Take these spellings for *journey: jer, ji, jou.* Now, maybe the child did not have time for consideration, was nervous. The state of mind may be similar to that already described, in which I have tried to show why a boy put in an extra letter. Here again the child should be permitted to correct his own errors by reading over his own paper. It is not permitted to infer from this kind of error that the child doesn't know.

It is time for me to sum up. The charge is made against some child-study investigations that they traverse a great area to discover what we knew before. Maybe that is the case in the present investigation. Whether it be or not, I am certain of this, that the inferences to which I have been inviting attention represent principles which are every day violated by thousands of teachers. I desire in concluding this paper, therefore, to group my inferences and show how they collide with established custom.

1. I call attention to the broad inference from this investigation, that the criticism of spelling should be analytical. Errors in spelling differ in kind, and they differ as to their origin, and they demand varying treatment. But, in practice, there is no analysis in the treatment of spelling. The teacher recognizes the fact that seven words out of the fifty are wrong, and she recognizes no other fact. But the seven errors may each require special treatment. It has been shown that some are not errors in spelling at all. They are errors of nervousness, mental tricks, or merely errors of writing, as when a boy spelled *yourney* for *journey.* Furthermore, the pupil should be permitted to discover

his own errors in many cases. Such errors as he can discover should not be marked for him. Again, the error may be in the percept of the sound of the word, or it may be the sound and a certain spelling are so closely associated that hard knocks are necessary to break the connection; or the child may be in error as to the phonetic force of certain letters and combinations of letters; or he may have idiosyncrasies regarding spelling which require individual treatment; or, finally, the eye may be at fault.

Of course, all this means fewer dictation exercises and more detailed and analytical consideration of such exercises. The present plan of many exercises and a superficial correction evidently does little good. I think it may be shown that it even strengthens certain wrong tendencies.

2. The importance of a larger amount of oral work in spelling ought to be apparent; for, by far the larger portion of the errors arises from false percepts derived through sound. I have already called attention to the probability of there exisiting subconsciously in the child's mind a visual percept, which is the translation of the child's aural percept of a word. Note carefully that this relation between the false percept and the sound is probably individual and is intimate beyond belief. It takes a convulsion to separate them. The sound *journey* and the spelling *jernie* have been friends for a good while. This relation is a sort of Siamese-twin relation. You must utterly destroy it before you can establish a new one. This means a running fight with the false percept, not one fight but many; and this means much oral work, covering a limited area. It also means the correction of the error the instant it shows itself. It will not do to wait. Here again ample oral drill is demanded. The dictation exercise is important, but only at a test of the success of oral drill. Of course, I am here referring only to sound errors.

3. We are not to forget that the ultimate purpose in the teaching of spelling is that the pupil shall write correctly; not in columns, but in paragraphs. The oral drill and the column work must be considered not as ends in themselves, but in view of practical writing. Teachers are perfectly familiar with the fact that pupils will write the column lesson much better than

the dictation lesson. But success in the latter is the only true success and must, of course, be made the standard of attainment. The word drill and the column drill must be manipulated for the most part to prepare for the paragraph work, or to correct the errors found therein.

4. Note the great preponderance indicated in this investigation of what I have called sound errors, and note also that these errors have to do almost exclusively with familiar words; i. e., with the child's own vocabulary. This means that if we can extirpate such errors, we have largely cleared up the child's bad spelling. Why not do this? Why go on endeavoring to teach a new vocabulary and leave this mass of inaccuracy behind us? I submit that such a course of procedure is in the highest degree illogical. Yet it is the course followed by most teachers. I have already touched on this subject, but lay special emphasis on it at this point with a view of making a practical suggestion or two. Any observant teacher can within a year make a list of words which are actually used by her pupils, and, to a greater or less extent, used incorrectly. This is her most valuable spelling-book. I don't mean that no other spelling-books may be used, but their use must be subordinate and *not to teach spelling,* but to increase the vocabulary.

But regarding the increase of the child's vocabulary, a word of caution is necessary. Few of us realize how very small is the possible daily or weekly increase in the child's knowledge in any line. This is especially true with regard to language. No child can add to his vocabulary one-tenth the number of new words many teachers put in a spelling-lesson. Two, three, or at the most five are a large daily increment. We ourselves discover this in the learning of a new language; German, for instance. If this be true, the necessity for any large use of the spelling-book disappears and the drill falls back on the child's own vocabulary. When teachers grasp these two correlated essentials —first, drill on the child's own vocabulary; second, very small daily increment to that vocabulary—accuracy in spelling will result. In other words, when we stop trying to do so much we shall succeed in doing more.

I add a suggestion which is a logical corollary to what I have already offered. The increase in the child's vocabulary must be for use in that vocabulary and subject to subsequent drill. Therefore, the words must be easy. This principle is violated by most courses of study and therefore by most teachers. The child who reads in a third reader uses a vocabulary of the grade of a first or second reader. The fourth-reader pupil's own vocabulary is scarcely above that of the second reader. Here is the indication for the spelling-lesson so far as the new words are concerned. The words given out in our spelling-lessons are far too difficult.

5. I claim that children should correct most of their own errors. Not only so, but they should also find many of them without any help from the teacher. The blue pencil is used far too much. It is necessary, however, to note that the pupils probably will not be able to find the sound errors at first. *Jernie* will not arrest the child's attention. It looks perfectly natural. *Foring* for *foreign* will arrest his attention, for he is not sure about *foreign*, and he will consult the dictionary. But he is sure about *jernie* and passes on. When *jernie* does arrest his attention, then the association is broken.

Let the child do all he can for himself before you interfere. Then apply your skill on the residual errors and apply your skill skilfully.

6. Finally, I call attention to the moral phase of the problem. The right of children to help themselves, just discussed, is indeed a moral consideration, but there is another and a very serious one. Remember my claim that many errors are not spelling errors. They don't mean that that child can't spell the word. Now, when we mark ten words wrong, and six errors are of this character, we are unjust as well as unwise, for there are also errors which are those of pure carelessness, or which indicate wilful lack of study. In one set of cases the child has not tried, and in the other he has tried. By the usual process we make no distinctions. We hold the child up for unpleasant criticism and make unjust comparisons. Perhaps the child indicates no sense of injustice, but when we try the rôle of justice we see how quickly he responds. "Some of you have hurried and

wrote words you didn't mean to write. Now, look over your papers and I know you can correct many errors. I don't want to take advantage of you." Right gladly the normally-constituted child hands in his improved paper. Now, you may say: "You have only two errors," and that is more stimulating than to say: "You had eight errors." Try this plan for a few weeks and then go back to the old way and see if the child is not conscious of injustice. The only reason he wasn't conscious before was, that he did not know that there was any other way. It pays to be just, even in spelling.

But this moral question has one other phase. I am very fond of Froebel's claim that there is no true education where the child is not made conscious of power. And Froebel distinctly means power. The child is to be made conscious of power; he is not to be made conscious of failure. What does the teacher generally do? She emphasizes failure. It is a mistake. Emphasize success, emphasize power. By recognizing the child's ability to correct many of his own errors, we emphasize power. By holding up a long list of errors we discourage him; or, putting it more forcibly, we evolve consciousness of defeat. Give the child a chance and then say: "Well done, you had only one error today and I can see how you made that, and I know you won't make it again after you understand it," etc. There is always a response to this kind of treatment. We should not be so fond of the blue pencil, but, when we mark, mark the words written correctly, and then the blue will be on the paper and not in the child.

In conclusion, let me note that the inferences in this paper are of three kinds. First, those which seem to be reasonably grounded, and point clearly to certain methods of teaching. Second, those which carry with them a strong probability, strong enough to furnish a basis of experimental action; third, inferences merely indicated, but indicated with sufficient clearness to warrant further investigation. As I have already stated, I am only too well aware of the limitations of my investigation. I trust I may be able to continue it. I hope at least that somebody else will.

SONG OF THE OAK

Music and words by Fifth Grade, Autumn, 1904

EDITORIAL NOTES

Turn, turn my wheel, all things must change
To something new, to something strange.

The Mutability of Human Events

Mutability, at once the opener of new doors of opportunity, the bringer of new hopes, and the source of tragedies, plays its joyous and its tragic rôles in the world of schools and teachers. The deepest tragedy is worked in the soul of the one who cannot adjust himself to life under changed conditions. The peasant immigrant, who sees his children buoyantly stepping forth in the new customs of the New World, while he himself is set aside as too old-fashioned and clumsy to keep up with the procession, finds himself in isolation from the society into which he has drifted, and, sadder still, left behind by his Americanized children.

Tragedies Arising from a Changed Order

The teacher, who has been unable to find order and substance in a changed curriculum feels that the school in which he is placed is on the rapid way to disorganization, and that the old values of education are lost, while no new ones have risen up to take their place. The tragedy of the bewildered and disheartened schoolmaster whose guiding light is being clouded by the smoke of burning text-books is a very real one.

The tragedy comes to the one with a habit-fixed routine of thought. Years are nothing and fears seem vain to the one who has retained intellectual elasticity, and to him there is probably nothing fundamentally new in education. The eternal verities remain but change plays over the surface, producing new forms in which the everlasting truths clothe themselves. Changes in methods, materials, systems come and go, but the great forces of life are still the great forces to be reckoned with by all for whom the school is a profession or a benefit. Work, hope, fear, love, play, art, fellowship, and family, these are the great motives and relationships that operate to produce what we call education.

Much of that which seems permanent aside from the satisfaction and training of these great human needs is a thing here today and cast aside tomorrow. The school has had poured into it during all the ages the accumulations of knowledge and custom often to remain there long after society had outlived the same. Then it has taken many a great wrench and a tremendous warfare to oust these obsolete practices from their firm intrenchment. It is the really great teacher who has had the courage to reject, and who has had the power to discriminate between the transitory and the abiding, the non-essential and the essential.

The Old That is Ever New

We hail with shouts of acclamation that man who rises up out of the sensationalism, and confusion of modern life to proclaim, not the novel discovery, but the same old articles in a creed of fellowship, forbearance, honesty, charity, and justice. So comes a pastor Wagner, an Emerson, and so came Jesus, preaching in the streets. Among these preachers of the simple virtues came Froebel, teaching of the meanings of family and community life, of the poetry of play, of the value of early habits of industry, of the function of art in life, and the supreme importance of an early bias toward human sympathy and respect, and of the interpretation of the great arousal of religious and social interest at adolescence.

The Kindergarten Once an Innovation

The kindergarten, founded by Froebel was decried because it was a change, an innovation upon the *a-b-c* of primary education. And, at the same time, it was hailed in other quarters with approbation for its evident suitability to the real needs of little children. It is now being judged by less simple standards than in those early days, when the great test of desirability was whether the fathers and mothers of the rising generation had needed anything of the kind when they were children. The test now being put is rational and valid, namely, "Is a child better equipped who has had a year or more of kindergarten training?"

The case, moreover involves not merely the value of the kindergarten idea, but a judgment of the kindergarten "as she is taught." Someone has complained that the great difficulty with the kindergarten is that there are no two alike. This objection would soon vanish if some of the leaders among the kindergartners had their way. For then there would be but one mode of procedure for all; and that the right one. It should be a cause of hymns of thanksgiving that there is still not entire uniformity in the practice of kindergartening. Were such uniformity to prevail, the kindergarten would be ready for a decent interment; as it is, there is hope.

The Kindergarten Both a Philosophy and a System

Froebel never taught uniformity, but he gave so detailed an expression of his idea of the materials and methods adapted to the use of little children, that his followers have tended to solidify these into a fixed system. This has been done in direct opposition to his plea for spontaneity, creativeness, individuality, and freedom. These tools, the "gifts and occupations" of the kindergarten, are made use of by different teachers in three typical modes, according as temperament or training dispose the worker.

Different Types of Procedure

We have first the orthodox, who cling not only to Froebelian law, but to the letter. These fear novelty and dread change, and sometimes fail to see the changes demanded by a different generation and civilization. For these mutability will work tragedies as the old order is succeeded by a new. In the second class are the drifters, who are largely imitative and interested in novelty for novelty's sake, and are inclined to work along the line of least resistance without any very great development of the critical faculty. It is this type of teacher who is likely to bring the kindergarten into disrepute with school men and women. But these very critics forget the many, many teachers in other grades of work who fall similarly short, yet who are not taken as the evidence for denouncing elementary teaching as a whole.

Something may be said in favor of any institution which keeps children happily busy in a social group. Mild praise this is, and scarcely a justification.

In the third class are found those who have sought to revise the practice of the kindergarten, and to bring it into harmony with current psychology, and to adapt it to the kind of social environment in which children find themselves. In doing this no serious conflict has been found between the most important educational theories of Froebel, and modern thought. The emphasis has been changed however. Many points have been modified, and some discarded. The handwork has undergone radical changes.

We find ourselves now in this position; the public school is looking for results; where can it find a product that justifies the expense and trouble necessary to maintain the kindergarten as a first step in education.

Results Wanted

In some kindergartens the work is too intellectually logical. Long sequences of building and designing exercises are dictated to the children to the exclusion of playful making. The products of this work are to the children neither work, for they have no utility or meaning, nor play, for they have not been born of impulse and have brought no joy in the making. Boredom and listlessness mark the children's attitude. This is surely not the kindergarten of the Froebel who was wont to say, "Come children, let us sing and spring," as the signal for going to their games.

The shibboleth of the one who leans too far in this direction is found in the words, "obedience, order, attention, concentration." The kindergarten of this type should recommend itself to the advocate of that type of educational theory which places importance on a scheme of study involving a good deal of the disagreeable, because of the moral value of going through with it. But it must fail to satisfy the man who is looking for naturalness and joy as two qualities necessary to any plan for infant education.

The Discipline of the Disagreeable

We are thrown back upon a familiar question, "Do any children, save those in neglected homes, need the kindergarten?" The answer is found in a recognition of the fundamental human needs. Do children of that age hunger for companionship? Do they love to make and construct, to impersonate, sing, dance, play, hear stories? Do they love to feel their power growing over materials as they

The Answer Rests with the Children

fashion the crude blocks, and paper, clay, and sand to embody their ideas. If so, they need a most attentive and resourceful mother, a most unusual person if she be able to keep these impulses satisfied *and trained* in addition to her other duties as mother and home-maker.

As a "mother's helper," and a link between the nursery and the more formal school the kindergarten has its place.

B. P.

Mr. Carl J. Kroh, who has been head of the Department of Physical Training in the School of Education severs his connection with the University of Chicago this autumn to fill the office of president of the Normal College of the North American Gymnastic Union. Mr. Kroh was for many years the head of the physical training in the Cook County Normal School under Colonel Francis W. Parker, and is acknowledged to be one of the greatest teachers of educational gymnastics in the United States. The college is to be congratulated upon securing a master in his profession.

The college is an institution that has been graduating teachers of physical training for nearly 40 years. It has been located in Indianapolis and in Milwaukee during various periods of its history. It is now permanently located in Indianapolis, in a spacious and well-equipped building, and with a faculty composed of specialists in the three departments of the theory and practice of physical training, of anatomy, physiology and hygiene, and of letters and science. Mr. Kroh is dean of the Department of the Theory and Practice of Physical Training and professor of educational gymnastics.

The college is organized under the state law of Indiana as an institution empowered to confer academic and professional degrees and diplomas. It is under the control of the North American Gymnastic Union.

One interesting fact to be noted in this connection is the opening of the public schools of Indianapolis to the college for the purpose of giving its students practice teaching under supervision.

One of the epoch-marking events of the year has been the great play congress held in Chicago in the month of June. It was the first annual meeting of the Playground Association of America. This somewhat tardy notice of so great a series of meetings can but call the attention of our readers to two articles to appear in the October issue of this Journal by Mr. Perkins and Mr. Zueblin, on the question of playground control, and further to urge all teachers to possess themselves of the papers given during the three days of the congress. The August number of *Charities and the Commons* contains them all, and can be had by purchasing it at news-stands or by sending ten cents to the publication office, 616 The Rookery, Chicago, Ill.

BOOKS RECEIVED

A. S. BARNES & CO., NEW YORK

Composition in the Elementary School. By JOSEPH S. TAYLOR. Cloth. Pp. 197.

GINN & CO., CHICAGO

The Sunshine Primer. By MARION I. NOYES AND KATE LOUISE GUILD. Cloth. Illustrated. Pp. 128.

Earth and Sky: Number II. By J. H. STICKNEY. Cloth. Pp. 128.

The Richmond Second Reader. By CELIA RICHMOND AND HARRIET ESTELLE RICHMOND. Cloth. Illustrated. Pp. 134.

The Burt-Markham Primer. By MARY E. BURT AND EDWIN MARKHAM. Cloth. Illustrated. Pp. 119.

D. APPLETON AND CO., NEW YORK

The Culture Readers. Book I—Primer. By ELLEN E. KENYON-WARNER. Cloth. Illustrated. Pp. 124.

The Culture Readers. Book II. By ELLEN E. KENYON-WARNER AND JENNY B. MERRILL. Cloth. Illustrated. Pp. 124. Two copies.

The Cave Boy of the Age of Stone. By MARGARET A. MCINTYRE. Cloth. Illustrated. Pp. 131.

D. C. HEATH & CO., BOSTON, MASS.

The Beginner's Reader. By FLORENCE BASS. Board Covers, cloth back. Illustrated. Pp. 110.

Nature Stories for Young Readers: Animal Life. By FLORENCE BASS. Board Covers, cloth back. Illustrated. Pp. 172.

HENRY HOLT & CO., NEW YORK

A German Primer. By LEWIS ADDISON RHOADES AND LYDIA SCHNEIDER. Cloth. Illustrated. Pp. 109.

LITTLE, BROWN & CO., BOSTON.

The Man Without a Country. By EDWARD EVERETT HALE. Cloth. Illustrated. Pp. 60.

THE SUNDAY SCHOOL TIMES CO., PHILADELPHIA

The Making of a Teacher. By MARTIN G. BRUMBAUGH. Cloth. Pp. 351.

VOLUME VIII NUMBER 2

THE ELEMENTARY SCHOOL TEACHER

OCTOBER, 1907

GEOGRAPHY IN THE LIFE OF THE PUPIL

JAMES FRANKLIN CHAMBERLAIN
State Normal School, Los Angeles, Cal.

That our schools do not prepare those who attend them for the opportunities, the responsibilities, the problems of adult life is a statement frequently heard. If this charge be true, then our schools are failing to perform their essential function, for the great aim of education is to prepare for life in the highest sense. Its purpose is so to surround each child by the best influences and conditions, so to direct its physical, mental, and moral growth, that it shall, as a present and future member of society, live the highest life of which it is capable.

No one will question the statement that pupils should study those phases of human knowledge and human activity which will, in later years, enable them to be of the greatest service to themselves and to humanity. In fact, it may be said that the public school has no right to teach anything else. That these subjects should be so presented as to enter into the life interests of the learners is evident. Neither of these conditions is fully realized in practice, and hence the schools are not doing their full duty in training pupils for their life work.

Geography, as one of the fundamental subjects in the elementary school, should receive, as it has been receiving during recent years, the most careful consideration. Both subject-matter and methods of presentation are being examined in order to secure more valuable results. Until quite recently a knowledge of geography was not regarded as an essential part of one's education. Indeed, it seems that it is not generally so regarded today, for our high-school and college graduates know much more of Latin, French, and German than of geography. For the former, the average citizen has comparatively little use, while a knowledge of the latter is constantly demanded in conversation, reading, travel, and business.

The study of geography can and should make our pupils closer observers, clearer thinkers, better reasoners. It should furnish them with information which will be helpful in almost any occupation. It should make them broad and sympathetic in their views. It should remove superstition. It should make traveling, reading, and conversation more pleasurable and more profitable.

In spite of this, and in spite of the fact that geography treats of those things in which both children and adults are deeply interested, and with which they are vitally concerned, the subject is said to be poorly taught. It is said that as a rule it is dry and uninteresting to pupils. It is not long since Dr. Hall characterized it as the "sick man of the curriculum." That there is *some* force in these criticisms every teacher realizes. I wish to point out a few fundamental weaknesses in our work, and to suggest a few improvements.

The failure of geography to enter fully into the lives of the pupils in the elementary school is not a matter of failing to provide for instruction in the subject, but rather to unwise selection and presentation of subject-matter. Although geography has made a remarkable advance during the last two decades it is still too largely a memory subject. Mere exercise of the memory is not necessarily interesting or educative. Unless geography is training our pupils to put together the links in the chain of cause and consequence it is being poorly taught. More important than this is the fact that it is not developing the habit of reasoning without which our pupils will, as adults, be drifted by the currents of popular opinion, now this way, and now that.

The great problem in geography is how to make the subject enter into the conscious experience of the child, for only as it is to him a living reality, as it interests him, appeals to him, and influences his life in ways which are to him apparent, will he enter consciously and purposefully into its study. The subject must do more than offer information through the medium of the printed page; it should encourage the pupil to *experience* geography, and to contribute these experiences. Such opportunity as geography offers for the exercise of the constructive faculty should be used to the fullest extent. This can be carried out in the making of maps, charts, sketches, graphs, and models of various kinds. Where these conditions are not realized the results must always be meager, superficial, unsatisfactory.

The textbook still holds, and must always hold, an important place in the study of geography. The weaknesses of the book are therefore likely to be reflected in the work of pupil and teacher. Our geographies are too incomplete. The material is too fragmentary, too statistical. This is a necessary condition where the plan of treating all or a large part of the world in one book is followed. If each book dealt with the work of a single grade the topics taken up could be more fully and more interestingly presented. This would also make possible a larger number of maps and illustrations. In order to make good this deficiency in the text, supplementary readers should be very freely used. These bring out the human side of geography which always appeals to children. It is a mistake to use these books simply as readers. The topics should be studied and fully discussed by the pupils, and maps employed whenever they would be of service.

Under present conditions the questions in the text constitute an important factor in the work of the pupil. His preparation for the recitation is in large measure based upon these questions, and therefore very much depends upon their character. As a matter of fact the majority of the questions ignore the causal notion. Their study is dry and deadening to the pupil. In our very best texts about one-half of the questions tend to create thought.

Questions pertaining to position, dimensions, area, population are legitimate, and many such should be asked, but they should not dominate the work. The function of questioning is to develop thought, not simply to secure answers. We can increase the interest and the value of the work by supplying questions of the right sort.

The following, which are simply suggestive, indicate how this might be applied to the British Isles:

Using your map, find the latitude of the British Isles. Compare this with the latitude of your state, and with that of Labrador. Using the scale, find the length and the average width of Great Britain. Compare with the dimensions of your state. What is the nature of the coast line? Is such a coast line an advantage or a disadvantage? Make a list of the sea-ports. Make a list of those on the Atlantic coast of the United States. Has the English Channel helped or hindered the development of the British Isles? Give reason for your answer. What part of the British Isles is best watered? Explain. If the mountains extended east and west how would they influence rainfall? Examine an isothermal chart of the British Isles and compare the temperatures with those in New England. Account for the difference. Is there snow in London during the winter? Do people sleigh-ride? Do they skate? Compare with winter conditions in Boston.

What part of England is best adapted to agriculture? Comparing the population with the area, do you think that England's agriculural products supply her demand? If not, where might she purchase wheat, flour, cotton, sugar, fruits, etc.

Locate the coal and iron-producing sections. Locate the manufacturing areas. How are the two related? What is the meaning of the expression, "Carrying coals to Newcastle?" What advantages has Great Britain for shipping her manufactured products? What articles have you seen that were made in the British Isles? Why do people come to America from the British Isles? Why do people go from the United States to that country?

These questions are by no means exhaustive. Similar lists pertaining to other areas can be worked up and placed upon the board to be used by the pupils during the periods devoted to the study of geography.

Special investigation, as well as the experience of the teacher, has shown that the geographical interests of children center in peoples, products, and industries. Hence work involving these topics should be made the basis of introductory geography, and should receive attention throughout the grades.

Our texts give very scanty attention to the industrial and social phases of geography as constituting the basis of the subject. One of the best devotes 107 pages to home geography and of this number the first 79 pages treat of rivers, plains, mountains, the ocean, the air, etc. The remaining 28 pages, or about 25 per cent. of the whole, deal with the human side. Another recent text devotes 45 pages to home geography, 17 of which, or about 40 per cent., treat of the industrial and the social. In other texts introductory geography is almost entirely physical and astronomical.

The child has a more active interest in a snow-white cotton field, in the picking and the ginning of the crop, in its transportation to the mills, and its transformation into wearing apparel, than he has in the conditions of soil, temperature, and moisture, which make the crop possible. Not only this, he sees a closer connection between the industrial and social conditions and himself, than he does between the physical and his individual life.

The story of the necessities of life runs back and forth on bands of steel or over ocean wave, connecting the most distant lands and peoples with the community, with the pupil himself. This is home geography in the largest sense, for the home cannot be understood unless its relation to remote areas is seen. The people of a community and of the world are held together by the chains of mutual industrial, and social interdependence slowly forged through centuries of development in the habits and demands of daily life.

This study of the industrial and social does not ignore the facts of surface, climate, and location. These are of necessity taken up and given more meaning than they would otherwise have.

Among the lessons taught by this phase of geography is the great truth that physical labor is absolutely necessary and honorable. If the pupil sits beside a cheery coal fire while the snow is drifting out of doors, it is because deep beneath the earth's surface men with hands and faces blackened by contact with coal, with bodies weary from labor, toil day after day although constantly exposed to the most terrible dangers. This general truth of the necessity for co-operation and the dignity of labor is presented in different forms as each industry is studied.

While geography deals with the realities of life—human

beings, streams, forests, mountains, mines—these are for the most part studied through the use of symbols. Here we have another reason for the difficulty experienced in placing geography among the life-interests of the child. The great value of the excursion is now generally recognized, although it is still much more largely a matter of theory than of practice. Nothing else can give such life and value to geography. With the great inspiring picture spread out before us; the wonderful works of nature, and the marvelous works of man, we ask the pupil to step in doors, and *read about these things.*

That practical difficulties confront us when we attempt to do field work is well known, yet, if all teachers, school authorities, and parents realized fully the importance of this method of study, these obstacles would, in large measure, be removed. The taking of an occasional half day or entire day for excursions should not be regarded as an interference with the regular work of the school. The time is not far distant when out-of-door work will occupy a prominent place in elementary instruction. The excursion should by no means be limited to the observation and study of geographic forms and processes, but should include mills, factories, quarries, museums, and many other centers of human activity. The trips need not be and should not be expensive. If carefully planned and skilfully handled the danger attending them is not worth considering.

Pictures constitute a very valuable aid in the teaching of geography. Here again practice falls short of theory. Merely exhibiting the pictures is not enough, although there is value in this. The teacher should ask questions concerning them so as to encourage close observation.

The modern stereoscopic views are an inspiration to pupils. While using them one can easily imagine that he is observing the actual objects which they represent. The stereopticon should find a much more general use in the elementary school. By means of the slides we may take our pupils on in-door excursions to all parts of the world.

Much material in the form of raw and finished products can be brought into the schoolroom. In studying other states and countries, pupils should be encouraged to bring to the school articles which came from those regions. The list of materials easily obtained is a long one.

Through the efforts of pupils and teacher a school museum of some considerable value, can be worked up. The materials, in connection with pictures and descriptions written by the children, could be so arranged as to present a graphic history of some of the most important industries. When desired they could be so placed as to show their geographical distribution.

Travel is a most potent factor in vitalizing the work in geography. The knowledge and the inspiration obtained by every member of this association who has traveled across the continent to attend this convention can be used to great advantage for years to come. Pupils are always deeply interested in what the teacher has actually seen.

In many schools there are pupils who have enjoyed the benefits of some travel. This contact with geography at first hand should be drawn upon to the fullest extent. As early in the year as possible the teacher should learn just what regions have been seen by pupils. This information can be tabulated and the topics assigned pupils at the proper times. In all cases where trips are being described the routes followed should be carefully traced upon a map before the class.

The exchange of letters by schools in different parts of the country while by no means new, should be much more generally practiced. If one letter a month were written by each grade throughout the year, pupils would be in possession of a very valuable picture of changing landscape, planting, and harvesting of crops, weather conditions, migration of birds, blossoming of wild flowers. In addition there would be descriptions of the surface, natural resources, industries, and the daily lives of the people. If a different section were selected by each grade in the school, and the practice kept up from year to year, it would add immensely to the pupils' knowledge of geography. Pictures accompanying such letters would be a very valuable feature. Several pupils should have a hand in the writing of each geography-letter, thus multiplying the benefit received.

To summarize: Geography while intimately connected with daily life, is not as vital a part of school life as it should be or can be made. Our texts, while steadily improving, are still too meager and statistical in character. A striking weakness is shown by the map questions which do not serve sufficiently to develop thought. The books should be more limited in scope, thus making it possible to treat given areas more interestingly and fully. The map questions should be supplemented by others tending to create more interest and greater mental activity.

Introductory geography should be based upon the industrial and social phases of the subject, as investigation has shown that the geographical interests of children are strong along this line. Such study connects geography directly and vitally with the actual daily life of each pupil, not only as applied to the home, but as applied to the world as well. More use should be made of pictures, stereoscopic views, and slides, as well as of such materials, raw and manufactured, as can be supplied by pupils and teacher. Every school should start a museum which will increase in size and usefulness with each succeeding year.

Such knowledge of areas beyond the immediate vicinity as has been acquired by teacher or pupils through actual observation should be used to the fullest extent. The exchange of letters by schools in different parts of the country can be made a source of the greatest interest and profit.

In these ways geography can be made to enter more fully into the school life of the pupil, and to enlist his conscious and purposeful participation in its study. It will then be fulfilling its deeper function, the training for the larger experiences which follow those of school days.

SHOULD THE MUNICIPAL PLAYGROUNDS BE CONTROLLED BY THE BOARD OF EDUCATION?

DWIGHT HEALD PERKINS

A playground is an outdoor space where boys and girls may play without restriction; where "keep-off-the-grass" signs do not appear; where space for running and jumping and apparatus for play are provided, and where squealing is not prohibited. It differs from a park in that the emphasis is put upon play and not upon the beauties of nature. While growing green must be provided along the borders or in secluded spots, it must always be so arranged as not to interfere with the activities of children nor even be affected by their heedlessness.

Whether playgrounds be controlled by park boards or boards of education is to some degree a minor matter; it is all the municipality. Both are supported by funds raised by taxation imposed upon the citizens, who reap the benefits.

The discussion is, therefore, not one of principle, but one of expediency. It relates to the details of carrying out a scheme the general principles of which I believe we are all agreed upon.

It is admitted that playgrounds must be supervised; that rotation, equal opportunity, and proper use of facilities cannot be left to the children alone; they must be conscious of the presence of some authority. This supervision need not be oppressive, negative, or restrictive. It should be quite the opposite; it should be suggestive and should divert the mind from mischief-making into a line of activity which would cause the mischief-maker to forget his intended pranks. It must always be regarded by children as a privilege to enter a playground, and that privilege must be obtained and retained by proper behavior.

I wish to answer some objections often brought against the control of playgrounds by boards of education. It is often asserted that boards lack funds. This I regard as a temporary objection and not one based upon permanent principles. I see no reason for separating the funds of education from other municipal governing or taxing bodies. If the board cannot raise money—and I believe that it can as soon as the public is convinced of the necessity—it would certainly be possible for the municipal government to turn over to the board such amount of money as would be spent by it for playground purposes. With the increased funds from that source the board would be equipped with financial power, and would be in a position to work energetically on this problem.

It is also urged that teachers are already overworked, and that this would place on them an additional burden. I grant that they are overworked, but I think that you will also grant, if we may coin the phrase, that they are "underplayed" (as well as underpaid). I believe that the association of teachers with their pupils while at play would be just as much real recreation for the teachers as it is for the children. I believe that it would be money well spent if sufficient teachers were employed to give them time to direct the children in their play.

The objection, that it would put the playgrounds under the adverse influences of political machinery may be answered. My answer is that this objection insofar as it is true is a reflection only upon those people who stay away from the primaries and the polls and do not take an active part in politics. We may as well admit that we can do nothing to change this situation until we become politicians. We may as well admit that this country is governed, taxes are raised and expended, and public officers are nominated and elected by the people by means of political methods.

I of course assume that civil-service methods of appointment prevail—at least to the extent that they do in Chicago in 1907. I would not advocate playground management under either an educational board or a municipal government unless employees were selected and retained upon merit. If the opposite were the case it would be better to abolish playgrounds altogether.

It is useless to talk of avoiding the politician. If he does not do as he should, we must either take his place or abide the results uncomplainingly. I have had the pleasure of associating with politicians of both parties; men about whom we read uncomplimentary things in the press. I have seen them work energetically and unselfishly for the establishment of playgrounds. In my seven years' experience as a member of the special park commission of Chicago I have never received any interference from any politician. So far as my personal experience goes they have always assisted in a patriotic manner in the establishment and maintenance of small parks and playgrounds, and I am sure that their establishment could never have been brought about without such assistance. Aldermen are unpopular in their wards now unless they secure playgrounds for their constituents, and the political value of this movement is appreciated more by them than by outsiders. You should take advantage of that fact.

Playgrounds are not parks. They are for recreation, while parks are for rest. The parks attract a tired person, while playgrounds are for those having undirected and superfluous energy. In the parks one is brought into contact with flowers, shrubs, and trees. Their problem is bringing the country to the people if the people cannot be taken to the country, and it differs widely from that of the playgrounds.

Playgrounds are essentially educational; in fact they are the basis of the development of children. Being educational, they naturally should come under the board of education rather than under park supervision. The objection that is raised in regard to park people being more expert in that line is not an objection that is applicable to playgrounds nor one which should govern in this discussion.

It is said that the hours of school are limited from 9 A. M. to 3:30 P. M., and that the grounds are only open from 8 A. M. to 5 P. M. This is a mere matter of administration. I see no reason why the grounds should not be open from 6 A. M. to 11 P. M. This does not mean that attendants would have to stay that entire period; it merely means organization. Who would think of limiting our transportation facilities from 8 A. M. to 5 P. M.? They are practically in operation twenty-four hours a day, but their employees work but eight or nine hours each day. There is always a transfer of shifts.

Children are always doing something when they are awake, and there is no reason why their entire time should not be used in a pleasant, natural, and instructive manner. There is also no reason why this cannot be done in a schoolhouse as a neighborhood center without interfering with the ordinary life or functions of the home. Many of those functions, so far as recreation is concerned, are impossible in the home, and even if they could exist there it would be better to transfer them to the neighborhood center.

I submit the following affirmative reasons in support of the position which I have taken, and I further state that any person may be convinced of the correctness of the affirmative side of this question by reading an article entitled "The Playground as a Part of the Public School," written by Mr. Joseph Lee, of Boston. This and other articles of his contain sufficient argument, I believe, to maintain the position here taken. Several of the points which I have mentioned have been suggested by Mr. Lee's papers.

I know of nothing, unless it be the water and sewerage system, which so completely covers the entire area of the city as the public-school system does. The schools are within walking distance of everybody. As soon as an open prairie is converted into a thickly or even a sparsely inhabited district and the residents are too remote from the school to reach it by walking there is a demand for a new school building, and that demand is complied with just as soon as conditions permit. The schools are not only everywhere, but they represent in value the sum of $40,000,000.00. They belong to the people, and a calculation of the interest lost by the non-use of this investment for one-half or even one-third of the time would convince any business man, I believe, of the wisdom and necessity for making use of this plant twenty-four hours in the day, if that is a possible thing.

It is necessary to the work of the educator. This is true notwithstanding the fact that playgrounds are for all children old enough to walk prior to school age and all children so long as they are able to walk after their school life is over. The less separation between people under and over school age and those in school the better. The special park commission of Chicago has indorsed this contention by locating its playgrounds adjacent to schools wherever possible.

The combining of schools with playgrounds makes possible contact between teachers and pupils through play as well as study relations; each helps the other if the play is not advertised as "educational." The relation of play and physical culture to mental and character development should not be broken. There is a great opportunity for co-operation here. The unified organization and management and the avoidance of duplication should appeal to educators, park people, the business man, and taxpayers. No clashing of authority need arise under unified management. This should occur only in the case of dual management. The same would apply to the interference in programmes.

The schools run about nine months in the year. Under this management they should run twelve months in the year. The educational work at the University of Chicago runs twelve months in the year. This does not mean that teachers and students have no vacation, for they do, but there is an opportunity at all times for persons to study there. There should also be an opportunity at all times for pupils to improve by either study or play in the public-school buildings and grounds.

The apparatus could be made to conform to the educational necessities if the board of education had control over the funds with which to provide such apparatus. The providing and maintenance of pet animals and birds could be arranged for so that children might study their habits and enjoy their companionship. This is distinctly an educational feature which would require out-of-door space.

It is not necessary to speak of the educational and character-developing power of flowers. It is said that children wilfully destroy flowers. In answer to this I will say that when the flowers are constantly replaced, and the excitement of a chase or of escaping punishment is taken away, the child gradually loses his motive for destruction and grows into the desire to protect the plants.

In addition to the saving already mentioned is the saving in building construction. There is no reason why the basement of schools should not be used for toilet-rooms, shelters, etc., instead of duplicating them in the playgrounds. A great deal of money could be saved in this way, and as for the destruction of the school property by such use, it can be so built that it would be just as durable as the buildings erected in small parks for use by the public.

Playground space is needed for light and air for buildings.

It is not wasted, considering the interests of the pupils alone. We must have sunlight in every elementary classroom during some part of the day.

The board of education now, through its physician in the child-study department and through visiting nurses, concerns itself directly and actively in regard to the physical condition of the school children. Through its physical-culture director it develops children's bodies in order that they may become better students. Why should not the physical-culture director, who daily makes use of an indoor gymnasium, for the same reasons make use of an outdoor gymnasium? Why should not the work of the physician be supplemented by such work in the gymnasium as would remedy such defects as may be discovered by the physician.

The teacher's work, in my opinion, is the noblest of all professions. Teachers are, by their training and work, better fitted for the care of children and for the control of their symmetrical development than any other class of persons. It is, therefore, only natural that they would be the best persons who could be obtained to direct and co-operate in the physical exercises indulged in by the children. As a result of such co-operation a camaraderie can be established which will take the place of discipline.

In conclusion, after stating the above reasons for the affirmative side of this question, I wish to fall back for corroboration upon Professor Charles Zueblin of the University of Chicago. On pages 276 and 277 of his book entitled *American Municipal Progress* the following paragraph appears, which I quote in full, and which I submit as an authorative indorsement of the position which I have taken:

> Children's playgrounds are as necessary as schools to the welfare of the modern community. The idea that the public interest in the child ceases at the close of the school session has to be abandoned in the contemporary city. Along with the restricted opportunity for play in the city streets there has come a conception of the value of rational recreation which has its application in both city and country. Regularly equipped playgrounds with apparatus and the direction of skilled teachers or attendants, to encourage both individual and organized play, will soon doubtless be a part of the public-school system throughout the land.

REPORT FOR COMMITTEE OF NINETEEN OF THE INTERNATIONAL KINDERGARTEN UNION

LUCY WHEELOCK
Chairman

History repeats itself. This old saying was never more fully exemplified than in the present kindergarten situation. The various protesting movements in the church resulted in the division into sects and the formation of many creeds expressing all shades of belief. Today the liberal of even twenty years ago is a conservative, and there is a larger spirit of Christian unity than the world has ever known.

A Congress of Religions is possible, and an Educational Religious Association, which gives a platform to members of any denomination with a true and sincere message. There is a fraternity between orthodox and liberal, and "the brotherhood of man" is no mere phrase.

In the same way the kindergartners are approaching a larger spirit of unity through a process of reconciliation of differences. We are illustrating the Froebelian law of mediation in our recognition of the harmony possible, even where widest differences of opinion exist and are tolerated.

It is necessary for the encouragement and strengthening of the younger workers, who are disquieted "by wars and rumors of wars," to declare that the differences between us are the inevitable results of growth and freedom of thought; that they must express themselves in matters of technique and in our preferences for one school of philosophy and psychology or another; but they are not separating, and do not generally affect the aims and underlying principles controlling kindergarten practice.

Some of the apparent differences are mere variations of phraseology; some of them are indisputably different interpretations of theory and different illustrations of the same principles.

There has been a frank and friendly statement of our divergences and much discussion of the same. May there not now be a reconciling view, which shall help to bind us together in a united body, standing for one aim and one unified effort for the preservation in its integrity of the kindergarten as the finest type of early educational procedure?

The reactionary movement has been no doubt necessary and helpful as a protest against any chance of arrested development through a crystallization of practice and the ever-present danger of a perfection of system. It has had its effect in making us all give heed to our ways and reasons for the faith that is in us.

In order to come to a better understanding of the situation, each member of the Committee of Nineteen has been asked to prepare a statement of what seemed to her the points of issue between the two schools of kindergartners. To this request twelve members have responded. At first reading it seemed impossible to collate these statements and make any report from them. They are so varied in treatment and in the points of view that no composite can be made. I have not attempted to bring together the papers, nor to quote from them, but rather to present a report of the total impression conveyed, supplemented by my recollection of the fuller expansion of the topics in our previous discussions.

I have endeavored not to give a personal coloring to the matter except in a few instances where I have yielded to the temptation to declare my own belief and have so stated.

From the many points made by the writers of the statements I have selected those most frequently mentioned. A few declare differences between kindergartners to be essential and others superficial. Those who deem differences fundamental consider interpretation rather than the truth itself. The difference is one of emphasis or degree or of attitude, not of fundamental doctrine.

The topics most frequently mentioned as causing variation of practice are as follows: (1) Adherence to Froebel and Froebelian philosophy; (2) Theory of play, relation of play to work; (3) Place of instinct in early education; (4) The sense image versus the idea; (5) The doctrine of interest as applied to the programme; (6) Symbolism and the *Mother-Play*.

FROEBEL AND FROEBELIAN LITERATURE

There is undoubtedly a difference in the attitude of the kindergartners toward Froebel and Froebelian literature and the use of the established Froebel material in the kindergarten. No one for a moment holds that Froebel or any other man has said or ever will say a final word on education. A few believe that we have not yet understood Froebel and the fulness of his gospel, nor given sufficient study to his *Mother-Play* and other books. Others would give larger place to the study of other educational writers of the past and present and especial value to the contributions of modern genetic psychology and child-study. The latter group believes that in recent psychological studies we may find a more present help than in the philosophy of Froebel's time. All would agree in giving Froebel the first place as a pioneer in child-study and as a man rarely gifted with sympathy and insight.

In the use of the special Froebel material in the kindergarten and training-school there is evidently wide latitude. All kindergartners admit some outside material, although many would limit it to what is definitely in line with the established system. Some insist upon the importance of preserving the integrity of the gifts, of presenting them in logical sequence, of keeping unbroken the chain of connection from solid to point. No one discards the gifts altogether, but in many instances selections are made of building and other material for illustrative and group work. Some advocate reconstruction of the kindergarten hand-work from the standpoint of hygiene and of art. The original classification of the various forms made under the heads, Life, Knowledge, and Beauty, is considered of importance by many of the committee. Some members would not admit that arrangements of symmetry alone express children's aesthetic ideas and feelings. They depreciate the imposition of abstractions of knowledge in the mathematical and analytic lessons sometimes given with the gifts.

THEORIES OF PLAY AND WORK

There are, as among other observers of child-life, varying theories of play, and of the relation of play to work. Those who believe the child to be filled with reverberations from the past and impelled to physical movements and play activities practiced by a remote ancestry, select folk-plays and those imitating the movements of animals and gymnastic games which exercise the larger muscles. Those who prefer to consider the child as "father to the man," anticipating in play the practice of later life, will choose the plays illustrating human life and relationships—those which present in dramatic form great institutional ideals, which prefigure the child's place in a social whole.

From one view point the boy's impulse to climb a tree is due to the fact of his arboreal ancestry. To the other, it is his desire to transcend limitations, to find a new world, "to look abroad on foreign lands."

Is there after all any contradiction in these two views; is not the child both a rehearsal and the prophecy, a link between the past and the future? Do we not find Janus everywhere with faces looking both ways?

There is also a difference among kindergartners in the degree of freedom or organization of play. The advocacy of free play which was in reality free disorder has passed, and all agree with Plato, Froebel, and other observers of children as to the need of harmony, rhythm, law, and guidance in play. One of the special functions of the kindergarten is the educational guidance of the play activities of children toward desired ends.

The relation of play to work is another mooted question. One school would protect the child at the kindergarten stage from premature initiation into activities which take on an industrial form. The other school holds that play is the child's serious business; that it becomes more rational and interesting when a goal is set, which may be recognized and reached through the energizing impulses of play. It believes that the natural preparation for work is through a gradual transformation of the play instinct into productive activity.

THE RECOGNITION OF INSTINCTS IN EDUCATION

A matter closely related to the foregoing is the place of instinct in the early education. We divide here in reference to the recognition to be granted certain instincts during the kindergarten period. How far shall we yield to the taste for the crude and the barbaric in music, in art, and in story? How shall the child's instinct to represent be guided? How shall he use color? Can he appreciate the refinements of a landscape? Does he really feel the effects he seems to produce in making color sketches of sunsets, clouds, and mountains? Is his art sense best trained by formal arrangements of squares, triangles, and other geometric forms? Shall the stories told be so revised as to eliminate all reference to evil, cruelty, and wrong? Are they sometimes robbed of vigor in the process of refining? What is the place of imitation in art, in construction, in conduct? What is its relation to originality? Which instincts shall be strengthened and guided to full fruition, which shall be suppressed and cast off as soon as possible? These are some of the topics which have been touched upon in the discussions of the committee.

Another matter mentioned in several papers is the *sense image* versus the *idea.* Does the kindergarten child work from a clear and definite mental picture, which he tries to realize in outward form, or does he work from a general notion? Is it a concrete or an abstract table he represents? Does he work from the particular to the general, or vice versa, or is it a double process? Can he comprehend the generalized type forms, and do they aid him in his process of world discovery; or must he grasp many individual objects and build up his idea of the type through successive sense impressions? Is dictation to suggest the *image* or the *ideal* of the object to be made? These questions have been considered at our committee sessions, and there is a variation of belief and practice. Certain of our members believe that children work more intelligently when a clear mental picture precedes the act of making. Others emphasize the value of the creative process as a means of self-discovery. This question, as affecting methods of gift work, is most practical, and demands careful consideration. The teachers of psychology and kindergarten methods in the training-schools should give especial attention to this matter that the young kindergartner may have some guidance before her own experience entitles her to draw conclusions.

THEORY OF INTEREST

The theory of interest is another subject of practical import, as our programmes are the outgrowth of our special views thereon. The issue is not *interest* versus *will,* for we should all agree that the nature of mind hath joined these together, and only a very blundering teacher can put them asunder. To *will* and to *do* are two steps in any working process, and interest supplies the causal energy. The real question at stake is, Which interests are most beneficial in child development, and which should be appealed to in our choice of subject-matter? Children are interested in what is going on about them at home and in the community, in special days and occasions. The immediate environment is rich in its attractive suggestions. In the recurrence of the seasons, the varied aspects of old Mother Earth, the teeming life of the streets and the shop, and in the home and family circle we have subject matter of real and permanent value for reproduction in dramatic and constructive forms. Is this the whole environment of the child, or is there an intellectual as well as an accidental and immediate environment? Are there spiritual mansions as well as local habitations? One school of kindergartners assert that the mind is self-environing, that through imagination it may lay hold upon a larger world than that which the eyes behold. They would transcend the limits of the actual and often sordid environment. Those holding this faith would not give much time to the illustration of phases of experience, which are temporary and limited; but to those larger aspects which connect present and future by bonds of true and enduring worth. They demand continuity and logical sequence in the programme; stories modeled after certain universal types, plays which reveal the great institutional life of man in dramatic form, and present ideals of conduct which appeal to the imagination.

On the other hand, those who believe in the social training of children through their present recognition of social situations calling for an immediate response, believe that the natural subject-matter of a programme is found in the every-day experiences of children, which are largely bound up with the domestic and home occupations, and the fundamental industrial work of the community. These differences of belief plainly appear in the choice of giftwork and handwork. We have

The constructive	versus	The creative school
Use or Utility	versus	Beauty
The emphasis on constructive work in wood and paper, and sometimes in domestic processes	versus	Emphasis on distinction, classification and unification of elementary qualities.
Emphasis on the product	versus	Emphasis on the creative process
Emphasis on the craftsman or artisan	versus	Emphasis on the artist
Emphasis upon doing the *real* thing	versus	Emphasis upon *make-believe* play

There seems to be unanimity of opinion as to the desirability of some connected plan of work, which shall prevent a teacher from laying undue stress upon the temporary and accidental. There is a general assent to the position that no plan of work, however excellent, can be rigidly applied everywhere, and under all conditions. Whether the programme be made by a collective body or evolved by an individual to meet her own needs, the critical question is what are the true interests of childhood, which should grow into permanent tastes and tendencies? The choice of subject-matter is determined by our answers to this question.

SYMBOLISM

Here we find ourselves confronted with the matter of symbolism, which has not yet been taken up as a topic of discussion by the committee, although referred to in a few of the papers. As far as I can discover, differences here are more verbal than actual. We all hold that the child's realm by right of eminent domain is the realm of fancy. We believe in the fairy tale, the Mother Goose rhyme, and the dramatic play, which lead beyond the boundaries of the actual to

> Where the roads on every hand
> Lead onward into Fairyland.

"The child like the poet puts eyes and a tongue into all he sees." Things speak to him with a voice and a message, which he hears, although he cannot tell what they say. We all agree that any wise man may pluck a leaf and read a sermon on it. We know that there is an inner eye which is the bliss of solitude, that there are treasures which moth and rust cannot corrupt.

We do not need to agree in our opinions as to the symbolism of the gifts. That is a matter which concerns only the adult student, and has never colored our practice. We may believe in unity, and fail to see its embodiment in the ball. We may believe in evolution, and be unable to see it illustrated in the gift series; but the ball will be prized as a good plaything for children nevertheless, and the gifts furnish admirable building material.

We also must continue to differ in our estimate of the symbolic value of the *Mother-Play.* We differ in our use of it in our kindergarten programme, and in our choice of its plays; but we are of one mind as to the great service the book renders in classifying and arranging in practical form the most typical and important experiences of a normal child-life, and in illuminating the deep meaning "which oft lies hid in childish play." As we take individual instances of Froebel's symbolism divested of the artificiality often thrown around them by too much explanation, I think we should mostly agree as to their validity. That much of sentimentality and many mystifying interpretations have been connected with the use of this book we deplore; but is not this true of any great book, which attempts to set forth in poetic form the great relationships of a life? One may not agree with Froebel in his explanation of the fascination of a timepiece for a child. He frankly states that he does not force his conviction upon anyone, and adds that such a conviction harms no one, and, if generally shared, might result in great good to the rising generation. One is reminded of the answer of Turner to the woman, who complained that she could not see the colors he painted in the sky. "Don't you wish you could, Madam," was his pitying rejoinder. We are also reminded of the lines of an English poet of some eminence never accused of excessive sentiment, who apparently cherished Froebel's feeling of the significance of a clock.

> We take no note of time, save from its flight;
> To give it then a tongue were wise in man.

A clock means something to all of us. It is more than a mere combination of wood, metal, and glass, impressing a certain sound upon the auditory nerve. To the most careless in moments of pause it may say, "Forever, never; never, forever." In such moments it bids us value time as we value life, "for time is the stuff life is made of."

Our acceptance of symbolism is a matter of degree, and of individual capacity for seeing. We are not all of "the city," which Benson so eloquently describes in his *From a College Window,* but we may all at times dream of its lofty spires and walls of gold and pearl and amethyst. I believe, and this is my individual creed, that the highest service Froebel has rendered to those who study his educational theories is that of interpreter of the realities that surround us, and live within us; for "we live by admiration, faith, and love."

This very inadequate summary of the topics, which have forced themselves upon our consideration from the present kindergarten situation, is offered not for the purpose of more sharply defining differences; but as an effort to find the reconciling view, which shall enable us to strengthen our work and our influence as a body of educators through that union and co-operation necessary to the advance of any movement. Discussions are profitable; but dissension is not so. It is always right to dissent and to divide on matters of principle; but never on matters of opinion or individual interpretation. We may be of one faith although not of one practice; we may be members of one body, and recognize that each member has a different office. Is it not well now that we emphasize those things which we hold in common, and which are, after all, the essentials? May we not rally for the preservation of the kindergarten as a distinctive type of educational practice under the common standard of the master, who has given us our educational name and significance, and whose final charge to his friends was to strive for unity of life? May I be permitted also to remind you of the Great Teacher, who committed his gospel to a band of men ordained to carry it to the world, with this last prayer: "Neither pray I for these alone, but for them also which shall believe on me through their word, that they may all be one, that the world may believe that thou hast sent me."

HISTORY OF CHICAGO

PEARL BACKUS CARLEY
Third Grade, Francis W. Parker School

The children of the third grade have studied the history of the growth of Chicago from the time it was a mere trading-post and fort, environed by swamps, through its pioneer stage; and through their own struggles with some of the problems of these early settlers, they have come to a genuine, though childish realization of some of the most obvious of the present needs of the city.

The work will appear in *The Elementary School Teacher* in two sections; the first being "Chicago of Long Ago," and the second, "Some of the Past and Present Problems of Chicago—Transportation, Water Supply, and Drainage."

To present the work adequately it would be necessary to give much of the correlated work in geography, industrial science, mathematics, handwork, and art. It would be essential to give the reading-slips that have been specially adapted from reliable sources and printed for the use of the children. However, one child's work in the subject makes a book of about 150 pages. We are therefore forced, in reducing this material to the limit of two articles, to select from among the papers written by the children only those most essential in telling a brief story of Chicago's growth through the past century.

The motive of making a book of the history of Chicago which is to be both complete and beautiful appeals very strongly to the children of the third grade. Its tendency is to bring about the maximum of good careful work, and to reduce the amount of drill necessary to secure accurate formal work to the minimum. The second great incentive to careful work in expression has been the pictures with which the books are illustrated. Each child has nearly 50 pictures (obtained by teacher and reduced to proper size) from histories, books in the public library, pictures in buildings, and from historical landmarks, such as tablets and statues.

The index given below will give some idea of the contents of each child's book:

PART I

How Chicago Looked a Hundred Years Ago
- Swamps in Chicago
- Some of the Birds Found in Swamps
  - Red-winged Blackbird
  - Yellow-headed Blackbird
  - The King-fisher
  - The Snipe
  - The Turnstone
  - The Little Green Heron
  - The Great Blue Heron
  - Sora Rail
  - Wild Geese
  - Wood Duck
  - Woodcock

Stories of Indians
- Indians' Dress
- Indian Homes
  - Wigwam
  - Summer Home
  - Winter Home

Indian Village

How the Indians Travel

How They Cook Their Food

How They Light Their Fires

How They Gather Wild Rice

How They Hunt and Fish
- Elk Hunting
- Buffalo Hunting
- Hunting Buffalo with Decoys
- Antelope Hunting
- Hunting Deer with Decoys
- Hunting Bears
- Hunting on Snowshoes
- Story of Beavers
- Trapping Animals
- Fishing
- Fishing with Bow and Arrow
- Fishing with Soap Root

Picture-writing

Building Canoes

Indians in Lincoln Park

Building Fort Dearborn
Plan of Fort Dearborn
Mr. Kinzie Comes to Chicago
The Kinzie Mansion
Fur-trading
How Chicago Looked in 1812
Tecumseh
Revolutionary War
War of 1812
First Indian Trouble
Massacre of Fort Dearborn
Black Partridge
Captain William Wayne Wells
Fort Dearborn Statue

PART II

After the War of 1812
Fort Dearborn Rebuilt
Government Bought Land for Canal
Coming of Settlers
How They Traveled
  Traveling in Flat Boats
  Traveling in Prairie Schooners
  Traveling in Sledges
  Traveling in Ox Carts
  Traveling on Pack Horses
  Mr. and Mrs. Kinzie's Traveling Experiences
How Chicago Looked in 1831
Making Dip Candles
Making Candles with Molds
Making Gas
How Gas Is Collected
How Gas Is Made on a Large Scale
Old-fashioned Flint and Steel
Old-fashioned Fire Place
River Water
Sweep Wells
Selling Water from a Cart
Water System—Log Pipes—Pier 150 Feet Long
  First City Water Works
  Second City Water Works
    The Tunnel
    The Crib
  The Drainage Canal
  Plan for North Shore Sewers

How the River Used to Bend
Chicago Harbor
Lifting Chicago Out of the Mud
Intersecting Sewers
The Train of Cars
The F. W. P. Fast Freight

CHICAGO OF LONG AGO

PART I

HOW CHICAGO LOOKED A HUNDRED YEARS AGO

Long ago there were Indians all around Chicago. The only house was a log cabin on the north side of the river. There were swamps all around. In the swamps there were snipe, heron, wild geese and wild ducks. There were many wigwams on the south side of the river. In the log cabin there lived a Cuban, whose name was Mr. Au Sable. Mr. Au Sable came to Chicago to try to be an Indian chief, but the Indians would not have him, so he sold the cabin to Mr. LeMai. He came to trade with the Indians. Then he sold it to Mr. John Kinzie, who stayed here as long as he lived. In the tall grass there were prairie chickens, and further out on the prairies there were buffaloes. In the woods were bear, foxes, and wolves. There were deer in the woods too. There were no street lamps to be seen, no houses nor cars. The squirrels frisked in the trees. There were beautiful flowers in swamps and along the banks of the river. ELEANOR HOLBROOK

SWAMPS

If you had been in Chicago years ago you would have seen many swamps on the South Side. A man lived here in 1830 and wrote to his friend telling him how the hunting was, and this is a portion of the letter: "Vast quantities of water fowl were feeding on the wild rice, seeds, and insects in the swamps. . . . . Swan, geese, and brant, passing to and fro in clouds, keep up an incessant cackling. . . . . There were ducks of every kind, from the mallard and canvasback down to the tiny water-witch and blue-winged teel—while hundreds of gulls hovered gracefully over the swamp."

LUDWELL LINCOLN

We have not all visited the swamps but some of us have seen swamps. We had a number of pictures and slides of swamps. This is the way the swamp looked to us. The tall reeds, rushes, cat-tails, wild rice, and water lilies grew in them. You will find dragon-flies and fish and frogs there too. The yellow-headed blackbird and red-winged blackbird are swamp birds. They feed on the wild rice. ELIZABETH BECK

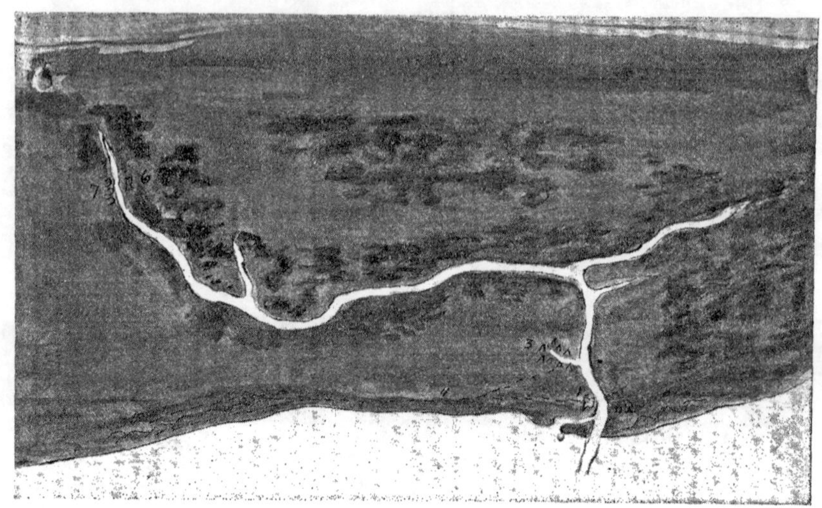

1. Fort Dearborn.—2. Kinzie House.—3. Indian Encampment.—4. Indian Trail.—5. Sand Hills—Battle Ground, 1812.—6. Lee's Cabin.—7. Hay Stacks.

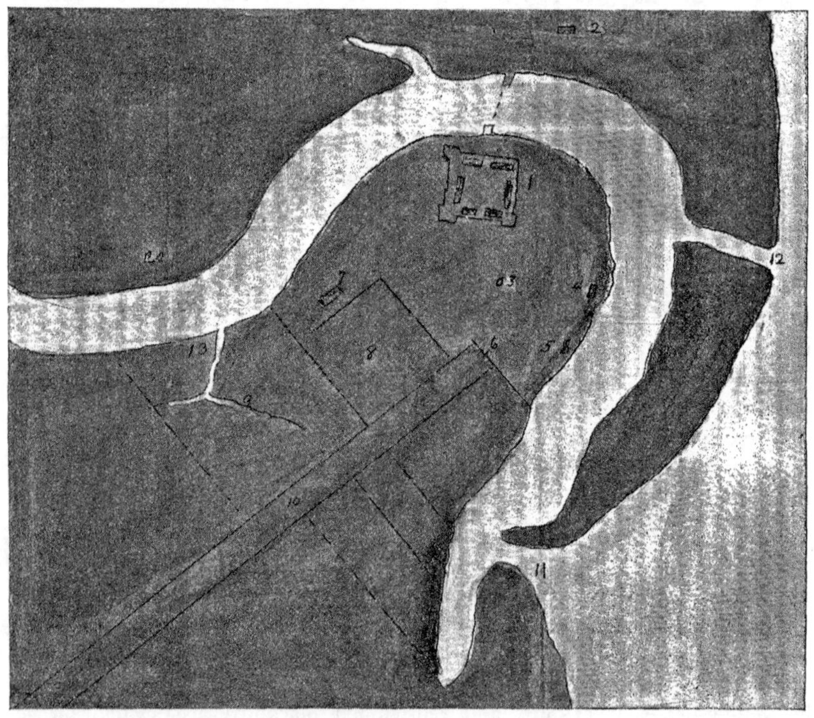

1. Fort.—2. Kinzie House.—3. Well.—4. Wash House.—5. Shop.—6. Gate.—7. Barn.—8. Garden.—9. Cultivated Field.—10. Road—11. Old mouth of river.—12. Channel cut in 1828.—13. Creek—where State Street is now.

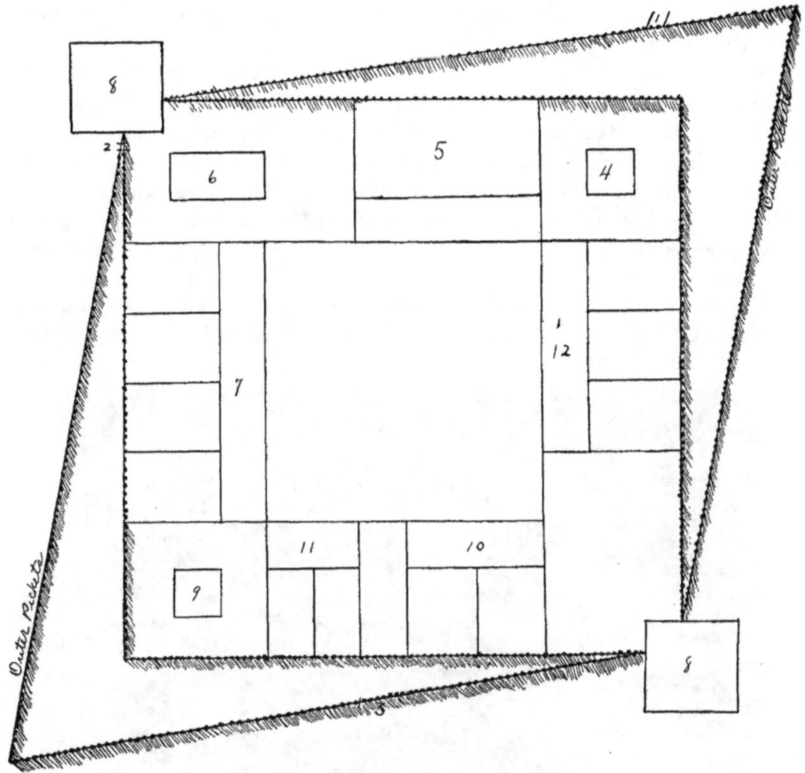

PLAN OF FORT DEARBORN

1. Tunnel and Underground Well.—2. Wicket Gate.—3. Main Gate.—4. Store House.—5. Contractor's Store.—6. Magazine.—7. Officers' Barracks.—8. Block Houses. 9. Stone House.—10. Soldiers' Barracks.—11. First Floor—Guard House. Second Floor—Hospital Store.—12. Commisary Officers' Barracks.

You would find the turnstone on the shore, turning stones over to get the insects under them. His bill is turned up a little bit, so he can turn the stones over.

MATILDA DELANO

The little green heron goes far out into the swamp to get his food. The great blue heron gets his food in the same way, only he wades out a little farther.

They walk out very slowly, and when they see a fish or frog come up above the surface they stick their long bill after it. We saw the great blue heron in Lincoln Park.

GENEVA HARRISON

The snipe has very large toes. They act like snowshoes, so that he can walk in marshy places without sinking. He likes to go into marshy places and put his bill in the mud and get worms. The snipe's bill is moveable at the end, and he has his eyes near the back of his head so when he is digging he can see a hunter come. The snipe is a good game bird, but he is very hard to catch.

The woodcock is very much like the snipe in habits. He likes to stay in marshy places too, and eat earthworms. The woodcock is disappearing very fast, because the laws do not protect him. He goes south in winter. Down in Texas they have a law that no game birds can be shipped out of the State. The time they are killed is mostly in the spring when they are nesting. They kill the old birds and the little ones are not strong enough to take care of themselves. HELEN BRECKER

Wild rice grew on the banks of the Chicago River. The Indian squaws would go out and gather it long ago. They would paddle along in their

CHICAGO A HUNDRED YEARS AGO

canoes. When they came to a big patch they would bend the rice stalks over their canoes and beat them. They had a big mat in the bottom. They would empty the rice into a big basket. They gathered until their baskets were filled. They used the rice for food. ENID WINGERT

HUNTING

The life and comfort of the Indian depended upon his skill and success in hunting. They needed the skins for clothing, for the wigwams, and the meat for food. The Indians had to learn the habits of the animals in order to catch them. FOWLER McCORMICK

BUFFALO HUNTING

When the Indians go to hunt Buffalo the whole village goes—the squaws, papooses, and all the children. They like to watch the hunt, and they are afraid to stay home. They climb a tree or hide behind the bushes. When they see the herd they give the signal. FRIEDA MAYNARD

Blackboard Drawing by Third-Grade Children

The Indians sometimes hunt the buffalo with decoys. When the Indians hunt with decoys they cover themselves with wolf skins. A herd of buffalo

WILD RICE

BUFFALO DANCE

is not afraid of one or two wolves. Then the Indians creep up near enough and use their bows and arrows. ARNOLD HORWEEN

ANTELOPE HUNTING

The Indians have to study the different habits of the animals. This is one of the ways the Indians hunt antelope. They put a stick with a piece

Hunting Buffalo with Decoys

of something that is red on it. They lower and raise it. They did this because they found that the antelope were very inquisitive and would come very near. The Indian would be hiding in the tall grass and would shoot with his bow and arrow.

Matilda Delano

DEER HUNTING

The Indians sometimes hunted deer at night in canoes. They would put a piece of birch bark in front of the canoe and sit behind the bark. They would hold a torch in front and it would blind the deer. Then they would paddle nearer and the deer was not able to get away because the light confused it.

HILDEGARDE PABST

HUNTING BEARS

The Indians held a bear dance before hunting bears.

The Indians worry the bears and tire them out before attacking them, because they are so ferocious. Sometimes bears are caught in traps.

RUTH COOPER

SNOWSHOE HUNTING

In snowshoe regions a snowshoe hunt was preceded by a dance giving thanks to the Great Spirit for the snow which would aid them in bringing

HUNTING BUFFALO ON SNOWSHOES

home their game. Snowshoes serve well in hunting moose and buffalo, as they could be easily surrounded or overtaken in the deep snow.

VINCENT FISCHER

FISHING WITH BOW AND ARROW

Usually the Indians spear the fish, but sometimes they shoot the sunfish with bow and arrow. There is a little string tied to the bow and arrow, so when the arrow goes into the water the fish will not take it away.

PAUL TABER

FISHING

They take a long pole, with barbs in the end of the pole, and put attractive bait on the barbs. They twirl the pole. That attracts the fish. It catches them on the barbs.

ARNOLD HORWEEN

The soap root was used at a low stage of water, late in summer. Indians dug the root and pounded it. This was rubbed by handfuls on rocks in streams. This roiled the water and made it somewhat foamy. Fish were affected by it. They became stupid and came to the surface. The Indians used scoop baskets to catch them. HELEN BRECKER

PICTURE-WRITING

I am going to tell you how the Indians write. They don't write. They make pictures instead of writing as we do. They write on skins—sometimes on deer skins, sometimes on buffalo skins, and sometimes on birch bark. When they want to remember anything they paint it, and that is the way they do. ENID WINGERT

FISHING WITH BOW AND ARROW

THE INDIANS IN LINCOLN PARK

The Indians came to Lincoln Park on Chicago's birthday, October, 1905. A hundred years ago the Indians' grandparents lived here. This is a picture of an Indian wigwam that was in Lincoln Park. ANNA WIEBOLDT

FORT DEARBORN

Fort Dearborn was built for the people and to protect the traders. The fort was built on the highest part of the river where it turned south. The government saw that they needed a fort, so they sent Captain Whistler to Chicago to build it. Captain Whistler came in a schooner and the soldiers came on foot. Captain Whistler got along very well until he came to the mouth of the river. It became so shallow there that they could see the sand at the bottom. He could not get his boat through, so he had to unload. Some Indians were standing on the shore and saw the schooner. One

INDIAN WIGWAM IN LINCOLN PARK

Indian said "Great bird." Another Indian chief said, "Canoe with wings." Captain Whistler's soldiers came to Chicago safely. It was very hard to build a fort.

ELIZABETH BECK

THE KINZIE HOME

Mr. Kinzie sent to Canada for some lumber. He enlarged his house by building rooms at the side. He made a garden around it. Then he planted Lombardy poplars in front of it. When Mr. Kinzie's house was finished it

FORT DEARBORN

was so snug and cozy that the other settlers called it the Kinzie mansion. The Indians were very friendly. They never knocked at the door. They would walk in and say "How, how." That meant hello. Then they would

THE KINZIE HOUSE

sit down and tell the children stories. Mr. Kinzie played the fiddle and the Indians liked to watch the children dance. MARGUERITE DOEPFNER

FUR-TRADING

When Fort Dearborn was built Mr. Kenzie built a trading post. At the trading post many Indians came to trade and many canoes dotted the river. The cabin in which the trading was carried on stood on the north side of the river and was built behind the cabin of Mr. Kinzie. The Indians in exchange for the furs got guns, kettles, hatchets, blankets, and sometimes ammunition. Some Indians came down the Mississippi River, up the Illinois, through the Des Plaines, across the Chicago portage to the Chicago river. Mr. Kinzie

INDIAN FUR-TRADING

had the Indians get furs for him because they could capture the animals more easily. They brought otter, mink, beaver, bear, martin, wolf, fox, wild-

MODEL OF FORT DEARBORN MADE BY THIRD-GRADE CHILDREN

cat and deer. The squaws sometimes brought little birch-bark boxes and canoes filled with maple sugar, because they wanted to get ribbons, beads, and looking-glasses.

HILDEGARDE PABST

THE REVOLUTIONARY WAR

The Revolutionary War was a war we had with England to free ourselves from them. The war of 1812 was another war we had with England. That was at the same time we had trouble with the Indians in Chicago.

In 1812 the Indians felt very brave, and they looked in at the fort and said, "The white squaws will not be so glad in a little while." The reason that the Indians felt so brave was because the English were against the people in Chicago.

HELEN STAUFFER

[*To be continued*]

READING FOR LITTLE CHILDREN

ELSIE AMY WYGANT
Second Grade, University Elementary School

The first half of the year the industrial history in this grade attempts to make vivid and to put meaning into the modern process of food-getting. To make it vivid the children go to the sources of supply and distribution about Chicago, a farm, the wholesale district on South Water Street, a bakery, a milk depot, a grain elevator, an express depot, and shipping docks. To give background and meaning to it, stories are told of a more primitive means of doing similar things.

The life of simple people is pictured by stories of Indians, the people of Borneo and New Guinea, of Hawaii, and others. With the environment thus given, the children suggest and experiment with possible ways and means of food-getting. After their experimentation and invention the means people actually employed is either told in stories or explanations of exhibits at the Field Museum, or is read from reading-slips prepared for this purpose.

While the "Story of Ab," the boy of the Stone Age in England, is told most fully as a type of a primitive people, yet the stories of other peoples are also told in order that the general idea may be broader, less individualistic.

The following series of reading will be used in this way:

I. Workers of Today.
II. The Indian Way.
III. "Indian Rice Harvest" by Jennie Hall (printed in *Francis W. Parker School Leaflets,* Series No. 2).
IV. Indian Harvest of Grass-seed.
V. Storing Food.

VI.	An Indian Tepee.	By Elsie A. Wygant, to be printed in successive numbers of the *Elementary School Teacher.*
VII.	A Sioux Brave.	
VIII.	The Daughter of a Sioux.	
IX.	The Indian Dresser of Skins.	
X.	The Field Museum.	
XI.	The Story of Sitkala-Sä.	

XII. Stories Adapted from Stanley Waterloo's "Story of Ab":

1. A Little Brown Baby.
2. Meeting a Hyena.
3. Inside the Cave.
4. A Meal in the Cave.
5. The Forest at Night.
6. Old Mok.
7. Evenings in the Cave.
8. The Great Stone Kettle.
9. The Feast About the Stone Kettle.

(Of the above XII, Nos. 1, 3, 4, and 5 appeared in the *Elementary School Teacher,* January, 1907, Vol. VII, No. 5, and the rest will appear in successive numbers of this Journal.)

XIII.	Flour.	By Jennie Hall, printed in the *Francis W. Parker School Leaflets,* Series No. 2.
XIV.	An Old Flour Mill.	
XV.	Mills.	
XVI.	Hominy.	
XVII.	How We Made a Mortar.	
XVIII.	Corn Husking, I and II.	
XIX.	Corn Meal in the South.	

XX. "Alice's Supper." Music by Eleanor Smith in "Songs for Little Children;" words reprinted in *Elementary School Teacher,* January, 1907, Vol. VII, No. 5.

WORKERS OF TO-DAY

We had a luncheon at school.

We had bread and butter, eggs and cocoa, berries and cream.

We cooked it all ourselves.

Yet it took at least fifty other people to get that luncheon.

The farmer, the miller, the dairy maid, the train hands, the teamsters, the wholesale merchants, the grocer, and the delivery boy all helped to get our luncheon.

At least fifty more people worked to make our clothes.

The farmer, the spinner, the dyer, the weaver, the tanner, the tailor, the train hands, the wholesale merchant, the retail merchant, and the delivery boy all helped to make our clothes.

At least one hundred more worked to build our house.

The men in the lumber camp, the stone-cutter in the quarry, the brick-makers, the glass-blowers, the paint-mixers, the mortar-makers, the iron-moulders, the architect, the digger, the mason, the plumber, the glazier, the plasterer, the painter, the roofer, and the gardener all helped to build our house.

> Richman, poorman, beggarman, thief,
> Doctor, lawyer, merchant, chief!

All except the beggar and the thief work for each other and for us.

THE INDIAN WAY

Long ago it was not so.

One family got its own food and clothes and home.

An Indian family even now get their own food, make their own clothes and build their own home.

The father goes out to hunt.

He kills an elk or deer or buffalo or beaver or mountain sheep; may be only a squirrel or rabbit.

The mother carries the animal home on a sled or on her back.

She makes the skin into clothes or into a cover for the tepee.

She cuts some of the meat to eat at once.

Some she hangs to dry in the sun or over a smoking fire.

She digs roots from the ground.

Arrow root, the root of the wild hyacinth, sassafras, and many others are good to eat.

The children gather nuts and berries; they search for bird's eggs and wild honey.

Some Indians gather water-lily seeds to grind into flour.

Some grind sun-flower seeds and make cakes of this flour.

Some make flour of acorns.

Some cut off the tender, green ends of cat-tails which makes a good soup.

Many gather the wild rice which grows in the swamp places.

Whatever they have, the father and mother and children must get for themselves.

INDIAN HARVEST OF GRASS-SEED

Many kinds of grass seed are good to eat.

Sand-grass grows in dry, sandy places.

It grows about Chicago.

It grows in California, too.

In California the Indian women gather the seed.

In the early fall when the seeds are ripe an Indian squaw goes out to gather them.

She carries a funnel-shaped basket in one hand.

In the other hand, she carries something that looks like a tennis racket.

She beats the grass heads over the basket with this racket.

The seeds fall into the basket.

When it is full she puts it on her back.

She holds it there with a band of buckskin which goes around her forehead.

She leans far forward as she walks.

The baskets are large and when they are full they are heavy.

When she gets home she puts the seeds into a shallow basket.

She drops hot coals in also and shakes the basket.

This roasts the seeds; then they are good to eat.

STORING FOODS

Indians must gather their seeds, acorns, berries, and nuts in the fall.

When the snow comes they can get no more.

They do not eat all the meat which they get on a hunt at one time.

Their food must be kept perhaps all winter.

Many foods must be kept dry or they spoil.

Some must be kept cold and damp to be good.

Dogs, rats, mice, squirrels, beetles, and ants all like these things to eat too.

Some men learned to store food where animals could not get it.

They learned to hide some things in dry rocky caves.

They learned to bury some in the cold damp ground.

Some people who live on an island far in the west put their food into gourds.

They set a tall pole in the dirt floor of their houses.

They put a cross-bar on this pole and here they hung the gourds full of food.

It was out of the reach of dogs and mice.

Some people in the south set a pole in the ground out of doors.

They make a great clay vase on top.

They put a thatch roof over the vase.

Here they keep corn and seeds.

One tribe of Indians used to build their storehouse together.

They made a circular wall of stone and earth.

They made a roof of branches, grass, leaves, and clay.

They set this house in a stream in a shady place.

Here they stored the corn, fruit, meat, and fish that belonged to all the tribe.

Some Indians move often from place to place.

These Indians store their food in clay jars and fine woven baskets which are easy to carry.

Many hundred years ago women learned that cats ate mice.

They knew that mice ate their grain.

So they went into the woods and got the young of the wild cats.

They were pets for the children.

As they grew up they were tame.

They kept the mice away from the grain.

And so it happens that we have cats about our homes today.

EDITORIAL NOTES

"In the Beginning"

The night was exceedingly beautiful, and the out-door sights and sounds lent their aid to the tender influences of the wonderfully inspiring music, skilfully rendered by the Thomas Orchestra at the last of the open-air concerts in Ravinia Park. Gentle memories were awakened of other wonderful evenings in the past, when, by some strange freak of memory, a picture flashed before our eyes of a scene in the dingy office of the superintendent of public schools in a city not a thousand miles from Chicago, one morning, not a dozen years ago. A committee of Benevolently Inclined Mothers waited upon the venerable educator to discuss plans for putting music into the public schools. The worthy man listened patiently, then, after due deliberation said that he had received *his* education in these same schools, and that what was good enough for him then was good enough for the children now. The committee retired and waited.

In Course of Time

In due time the worthy man died, unaided by chloroform. The Benevolently Inclined Mothers again called at the office, and when plans had been explained, and due assurance given that this would bring no added burden to the city finances, as the Mothers and Assisting Fathers would bear all expenses, the arrangements were completed. An enthusiastic, tactful, and, above all, capable teacher soon won a place for herself and music in the public schools.

Two years later when Children's Day exercises were given in that city in one of the large churches the children's singing was fine, but when, at the close, all in the large church were asked to rise and sing America, and all the children in the body of the church joined in song, heartily and sweetly, and all knew the words of every verse without book or leader, a thing unheard of in years gone by, one of the Assisting Fathers remarked to one of the Benevolently Inclined Mothers, "That is what your 'Music in the Public Schools' has done."

In another smaller city more than a thousand miles from Chicago we were present at the closing exercises of the grammar grades of the one school in the place, and saw the rendition of "Nearer My God to Thee," given as it had been for several years, following the directions in the "Model Exercise," printed in the *State Teachers' Manual,* something like this: "'Nearer My God to Thee,' [pupils stand reverently upon both feet and slowly roll the eyes upward as they sing,] 'E'en though it be a cross that raiseth me;' [raise the right hand slowly and point to an imaginary cross, then fold the hands upon the breast,]" and so on. Draw your own conclusions as to the aesthetic and ethic effect upon the minds of the singers.

The Body—Where is the Spirit?

The course of study prescribed for the public schools of that entire state outside of the few largest cities, lays much emphasis upon "the 45 combinations," upon "rules and definitions," which in arithmetic "must always be learned accurately and perfectly before any problems are solved," upon many other things which are Greek to the teacher who has not lived in Greece, and she is obliged "to promise to follow exactly in all details this course of study," and unless she can affirm "that she has so followed in all details this course of study," she forfeits her salary and her right to continue teaching in the schools of the state. Think of that, ye men and women who are allowed to teach every conceivable thing, in every conceivable manner, even though it may happen to lead to utter confusion, just as you believe something is about to be evolved.

Pharisee, Sinner, or Saint

Are we in danger of saying, "I thank Thee, Lord that I am not as other men"? How may the truth be reached, the truth of beauty, of sincerity, of high ideals? It is our earnest wish, our most cherished hope, that we may neither be blinded by egotistic satisfaction with self and with present conditions, nor, in our aspiration after better things, be led far from the truth by our false ideals, or by our lack of training, of keen perceptions, of clear brain looking to the desired end along vistas of sound common-sense.

VOLUME VIII NUMBER 3

THE ELEMENTARY SCHOOL TEACHER

NOVEMBER, 1907

SOCIAL WORK IN THE HAMLINE SCHOOL

LOUISE MONTGOMERY

Recent years have made us familiar with various forms of school extension designed to enlarge the function of the public school and make it serve the needs of an entire community. The rapid development of our great industries, the massing of population in large cities, and our practically unrestricted immigration are among the forces producing such radical changes in our social life that the public school must face new problems unknown to the village and to the educational theories of an earlier day. We are learning that the study of school problems should not be separated from the study of the social and industrial conditions of any given period, for ultimately the public school must respond to the needs of the community as created by such conditions. The wonderful changes in the course of study, the introduction into our public-school system of manual training and household arts, nature-study, school gardens, gymnasiums, and playgrounds, in brief, all the studies and the equipment but recently known as "the fads of our new education," have been a response to the cry that the school must be related to the whole of life, that it cannot afford to be isolated or stationary, unmindful of social and industrial progress.

We have enlarged our conception of what the school must do for the child, and we have not been able to do this without finding ourselves in the midst of perplexing questions arising from the relation of the school to the rest of the community.

The idea that the school should be at the service of the adult members of a neighborhood who for various reasons find themselves ill equipped for life and its work has its recognition in the evening school, and in the courses of free popular lectures now common in the larger cities. The next step in school extension is the social center. In an article on this subject in *The Elementary School Teacher*,[1] Dr. Dewey shows why we have reached this point in the development of our educational system, and are destined to go forward with the demand that "the school shall be related more widely, shall receive from more quarters, and shall give in more directions." But it is the practical side of this question that calls for present consideration.

> I do not feel [he writes] that the philosophical aspect of the matter is the urgent or important one. The pressing thing, the significant thing, is really to make the school a social center. That is a matter of practice, not of theory. Just what to do in order to make the schoolhouse a center of full and adequate social service, to bring it completely into the current of social life—such are the matters, I am sure, which really deserve the attention of the public.

It was this feeling of the present need of action that led the Educational Department of the Chicago Woman's Club to engage a social worker to give her entire time to the Hamline Public School and its immediate neighborhood. This school is on Forty-eighth and Bishop streets, in that part of Chicago popularly known as the Stockyards District. Germans, Bohemians, and Poles are well represented, relieved and enlivened by a few Irish families, and a limited number who insist upon being called "Americans" by the right of being one generation removed from "the old country." As the simplest beginning, Thursday afternoon was announced as the time when mothers would be welcome at the school to visit their children and gain some knowledge of the daily work, or to consult with the principal and teachers. Invitations, printed on the school press by the boys of the eighth grade, were sent through the children into the homes, with the hope of reaching enough mothers to form a permanent organization that should aid in discovering the best methods of making

[1] Vol. III, No. 2, p. 73.

the school a social center. The first efforts were an unlooked-for disappointment. Not only the first, but the second, third, and repeated invitations failed to bring a response from more than a dozen women. Then an interesting discovery was made. The printed slips had been left in desks and books or torn in bits and scattered on the street. Few had found their way into the homes. Children were suspicious and discussed this innovation among themselves. Why should their mothers come to the schoolhouse? Possibly it boded ill for them. At least, it was in their hands to prevent it, and they did. Of course explanations followed, but distrust was not confined to the children alone. Parents too often looked upon the call to attend a purely social gathering as an indication of wrong-doing on the part of their children. One Polish woman voiced a prevailing sentiment when she gave as proof of the good behavior of her children the fact that she herself in ten years had not once set foot inside the school building nor seen one of their teachers.

Possibly nothing could better illustrate one of the needs of a foreign neighborhood than just such results of a simple effort to bring the home and the school into a closer relation. It is unfortunate that in the past parents have considered their duties ended when they sent a child to school and kept him there, by force if necessary. The parent has been strangely silent, surrendering his child to the school system with a curious, unquestioning faith. It is difficult to understand this attitude, except in the light of the old idea of education as a purely intellectual process which must be intrusted to specialists and therefore beyond the comprehension of the average parent. The newer ideal, which seeks to relate the school life of the child to all that concerns him outside of it, is responsible for the parent-teacher associations that have been coming to life in all parts of the country. We have had women's clubs, child-study clubs, mothers' clubs, and congresses of mothers, but nothing comparable to the recent organizations of parents and teachers, meeting in the school building in which their common interests center. Such associations will present varying degrees of efficiency. Obviously the school located in a foreign neighborhood, facing differences in race, language, and customs, will find the process of unification so slow and difficult that little can be accomplished in the earlier years beyond simple social meetings. Each school district must face its own needs, and from the people themselves must come the growing consciousness of the larger function of the school.

Through the first unsuccessful beginnings with a small group of women this consciousness of larger opportunities both for themselves and for their children is coming to the neighborhood of the Hamline School. It was from them that the suggestion came to open the building one evening in each month. Among hard-working people where all the household duties and the care of a large family fall to one pair of unassisted hands, the number who can find the leisure to attend an afternoon club will always be limited. The opening of the building for evening lectures, entertainments, and social gatherings met a wider need. Two entertainments each year have been furnished by the children. School plays given by the children's dramatic club and choruses of national songs have proved most popular. Travel-talks upon different countries and cities, Washington, San Francisco, Scotland, Ireland, and Japan, illustrated by stereopticon pictures, have been offered by friends interested in the success of the work, and volunteers have not been wanting to help in making the social evenings a success. Men, women, and children of all ages have made up the number of those who are growing accustomed to the open school on one Friday evening in each month and who frankly express their pleasure in the new order.

Among the children the need of furnishing opportunities for the right kind of companionship and social life demanded attention. Here the field is still so large that it is appalling. The average home is not large enough to admit of children's parties, or even the spontaneous play of neighbors. The street in front, or the few feet of ground called the back yard and shared by the ten or fifteen children of a small tenement—these are the spaces in which children play and form the habits of a lifetime. Within easy reach of all, the five-cent theater and penny arcade create an abnormal desire for excitment, and through the vivid use of picture and song too often suggest the glamor of the life that throws aside the fundamental standards of morality. Here children unconsciously construct their standards of right and wrong and build their air-castles. The development of a high sort of social intercourse is essential to the creation of ethical ideals, and for this reason children's clubs hold an important place. There is enthusiasm in numbers, and it is natural to accept the ideals of an organization. Volunteer leaders were found to direct small clubs. Cooking, sewing, music, stories, books, pictures, and school dramas have been the basis of interest with different groups. The possibilities in this direction are limited by the difficulty in securing efficient leaders who can give the time such clubs demand if their success is assured.

With the coming of spring the desire for outdoor life and contact with growing things led to new plans. On May 1, 1906, a generous neighbor gave the use of two lots on Bishop Street for school gardens. The children of the upper grades cleaned the lots, made bonfires of its rubbish, spaded the ground, and laid it out in small plots ready for planting, incidentally adding to their knowledge of practical arithmetic through the need of finding the number of square feet in the entire space, and the size of the plot that could be allotted to each one of sixty-five children. Poor soil and a constant atmosphere of soot and smoke are not favorable to vegetation, and only the hardiest plants can be induced to thrive in that part of the city; but in spite of discouragements the little garden was counted a success, chiefly through the interest it aroused in the neighborhood and the stimulus it gave to the children to try to make the small spaces in their own yards more attractive. In a community where unassisted nature has apparently given up in despair and left the ground to the mercy of multiplying industries, the importance of even such small efforts can hardly be overestimated. Unfortunately the ground could not be secured the second year and the gardens were discontinued.

The school excursion furnished another means of increasing the interest in outdoor life. The value of the excursion is now recognized even in the city districts favorably located and in part free from the discomforts of a crowded population, but for the poorer quarters of the city it is not too much to say that trips to the country and to the city parks are a real necessity. Each year has brought its pathetic revelation in the number of children who have never seen a live robin, who scream in ecstasy at finding a frog, who marvel at the flock of sheep in Washington Park, to whom the first sight of Lake Michigan brings a moment of surprised awe. During the first year, excursions were confined to the first-grade children, owing to the lack of funds for streetcar fare, but the second year brought contributions large enough to include the entire school. Each room, accompanied by the teacher and a volunteer assistant, was given one excursion either to Jackson or Washington Park. Many of the rooms visited the Field Museum to see whether they could find among the stuffed birds any that looked like the colored pictures exhibited at the school each spring. Then they went to the Wooded Island to discover real birds. One boy of twelve years found and named correctly ten different varieties he had never seen before, identifying them solely from his observation of the pictures and the stuffed birds. Although other children often did much less, not one failed to make some discovery he could call his own, and the eager joy of this one child seemed full compensation for the cost and effort incident to the excursion.

In addition to these outdoor excursions, five upper-class rooms were given a winter trip to the Art Institute. Mrs. Schuhmann met each teacher with her pupils at the Field Memorial Room and gave them simple explanations of a selected group of pictures. Each trip furnished material for classroom work or compositions, and the results showed how much the children need and appreciate these glimpses of a larger world to which they have had no access.

The constant daily contact with these groups of children led to some observation of their physical and mental development, with the result that all who were noticeably below the grade in which they belonged were made the subject of a special study that is not yet completed.

The failure of any child to rank with the majority of his own age may be due to many causes, and it is unfortunate to reach conclusions on insufficient data, but this failure is at least an evidence that conditions exist which will bear investigation. Each child came under the examination conducted by the school medical inspector during the months of the general scarlet fever and diphtheria epidemic. The results showed marked physical defects in 200 out of the 208 examined. The suspicion that malnutrition and underfeeding might be the most common underlying causes led to an effort to learn something of the home surroundings of each child. A majority of the children slept in ill-ventilated rooms with windows invariably closed at night except in the hottest summer weather. The hours of sleep were irregular and insufficient for growing children. Out of the 208 only two were found who were not addicted to the use of strong tea and coffee two or three times daily. One of the most serious results of this habit is that the tea and coffee seem to take the place of sufficient food. Bread and coffee suffice for breakfast; bread and tea for supper. Practically there is but one adequate meal in the day. As one little girl innocently expressed it, when asked which one of these stimulants served as the drink for the third meal, "Oh, we always *eat* once a day." This condition arises partly from false notions of economy, largely from the easily formed habit of requiring a stimulant, and too often because the overworked mother finds it the quickest way to satisfy the demands of a large family. Many other factors not yet fully ascertained are a part of this slow process of physical deterioration, but these failures to observe the laws of simple hygienic living are given prominence because they may be made the basis of active educational work.

The interest in the physical welfare of school children is not new, but it is a growing interest, and discoveries similar to the above are unfortunately too common. The recent discussions on the subject of school medical inspection, the proposal to furnish lunches and even eyeglasses free of charge, show the recognition of a need that has not been met. Although so many causes combine in an industrial and crowded neighborhood to produce physical deterioration that no single remedy can be safely proposed, the solution of this problem will never be reached through charitable measures. A part, at least, of the underfeeding is due to ignorance rather than to poverty, and the school must be made the center of a persistent enlightenment not only on this but on all subjects pertaining to the physical life of the child. The disclosures incident to this partial study of 208 children furnished abundant material for discussion in the Mothers' Club and in many homes where a school visitor is always welcome, though both parents may refuse any active part in a club. To expect any sudden change in the habits of a lifetime as the outgrowth of such discussions is impractical, but it is indeed rare to find parents who will not listen to suggestions. However ignorant they may be, they long for the best for their children, and they work and sacrifice with a silent heroism that should bring their reward; but too often both work and sacrifice are in vain because they do not know. They need help and sympathy and understanding, and the school should be the center of a social work that will bring them what they need.

How far this development of different forms of school extension will continue is open to discussion. Nineteen years ago the charter of New York City was amended to give the Board of Education control of school property for "public education, recreation, and *other* public uses"—a free statement which has had a liberalizing effect on the whole system of education, not only there but in all parts of the country. The idea of the school as a social and educational center is growing steadily, but in practice the financial question has checked that growth in every city with the possible exception of New York. Upon whom shall the burden of this extension fall? This same question arose with the demand for kindergartens, evening, and vacation schools, but the gradual incorporation of all three into the public-school system of education is an expression of the conviction that the school must leave its traditional limits. Because the schools have been in the main closed to the growing needs of modern life, social settlements and other agencies for community improvement have been called upon to do a work which properly belongs to the school. For it is the public school in America that is the most purely democratic institution known to the people, and it stands in the minds of all as the center of progress regardless of differences in race, creed, custom, politics, or social position. After all, in this, as in every other question, public opinion is the final court of appeal. Schools cannot respond to a need until there is some notion in the community of what the need is. On the other hand it is the work of the schools to create new desires, to help in formulating new wants. Not only must the school accommodate itself to the growth of this form of social democracy; it must aid in that growth.

THE AMERICAN IDEAL OF THE KINDERGARTEN[1]

MOTIVE FOR WORK

MARGARET E. SCHALLENBERGER, PH.D.
Principal Training Department, Normal School, San José, Cal.

Perhaps no educational department is so widely known and so pronouncedly misunderstood as to its motive as the kindergarten. Not only may this be said of its patrons, fond and often ignorant mothers at all levels of the social strata; but it is true to an enormous and, at first glance, surprising extent of educators themselves. This gross general misconception is due probably to the fact that for a long time the kindergarten was set apart from the general scheme of education. There were the primary, grammar, and high schools, and, as a climax to the series, if one went on, the university. The kindergarten was a side issue—a little play or toy school—in the narrowest sense of the word play—sometimes functioning, sometimes not, always an extra, never an essential, always a special type, or variation, never a universally recognized and accepted form of education. This being the case, the kindergarten as a factor in child-development has not been seriously considered. Therefore its motive has not been seriously studied by educators at large. Here and there, to be sure, we find most careful investigators, many of whom are able writers, so that we in America now possess, aside from the contributions furnished by other countries, a kindergarten literature of our own of no mean quality; but comparatively few people have been inclined to read these publications, and a still smaller number have felt the necessity for doing so. Kindergartners themselves are partially responsible for this apathy. Their sunny child gardens were filled for long years, notwithstanding the protests of many able leaders, with ignorant, poorly paid women, who, dazzled by the bright colors and bewildered by the vast mass of novel material thrust upon them, flitted hither and thither among the little people and their

[1] Paper read at the meeting of the N. E. A., July, 1907.

"culture stuff" like giddy butterflies, and displayed little more reason while flitting than these care-free flower-lovers.

But all this is ancient history; the kindergarten has found its place in the educational scheme, and though there are striking exceptions, kindergartners today, as a rule, understand, at least as well as other teachers understand theirs, the problems set them. Nevertheless, for the reasons just stated, they by no means have as yet succeeded in making "the people" understand.

The great problem of the kindergartner is not different in the main from that of other educators. Can any clearer statement be made of it than the following by Professor Edward L. Thorndike in his *Educational Psychology?*

> The work of education is:
>
> 1. To supply the needs of the brain's healthy growth and to remove physiological impediments to it.
>
> 2. To provide stimuli to desirable mental variations and to withhold stimuli from the undesirable.
>
> 3. To make the outcome of desirable activities pleasurable and to inhibit their opposites by discomfort.
>
> The three chief practical problems of education would thus be those of hygiene, of opportunity, and of incentive and deterrents.

The conscientious teacher often asks herself, "How can I best deal with the child at this period of his life in order that it may yield its fullest and richest value?" It follows logically that an impoverished life at one period means a weakened life at the next, and conversely. The argument, often advanced, that a child entering the primary school directly from the home does brilliant work and advances rapidly through the primary and grammar grades is no criticism at all upon the kindergarten. Who can say how wonderful might have been his proficiency or how rapid his development had he been subject to kindergarten stimuli? The other thesis, that the kindergarten child does not always take to primary-school methods with ease and docility is likewise challengeable. The ease with which he does take to them may be due largely to his kindergarten life; or, we might ask, are the primary-school methods always those that well-developed six-year-olds find interesting and profitable?

The kindergarten, as well as the other departments of education, has been and is in progressive evolution. The intelligent kindergartner no longer follows blindly the theories of Froebel or Pestalozzi, any more than does the intelligent primary teacher depend altogether for guidance, as she did very generally not many years ago, upon the average accumulated experience of her predecessors. The kindergartner no longer points with pride, as she sometimes used to, to the results obtained in various forms of handwork, e. g., pricking patterns upon cardboard, any more than the thoughtful teacher in the grades congratulates herself upon the ability of her pupils to state certain facts in history, arithmetic, or grammar.

The emphasis today in education is an emphasis upon interest in what is worth knowing and zeal in its pursuit, rather than upon the accomplishment of a finished amount of work, mental or physical, or even than upon the ability to perform the work. We care less for what a man knows than for what he is desirous of knowing, less for what he can do than for his attitude toward work. The life of the educated man is a life of voluntary action in a right direction. It is the function of the school to provide, so far as possible, the proper stimuli and deterrents to make not only possible, but strongly probable, such life.

Psychology, sociology, ethics, as well as the long-established sciences, are gradually furnishing us with certain data upon which we formulate educational principles. The kindergartner in common with other educators eagerly seeks for these data. She knows that the mind of the little child is analogous to that of the adult; the two are similar but not alike. She learns as much as possible about the make-up and functioning of her own mind. She tries to apply this knowledge to the study of the child-mind. She studies the laws of society and tries to understand what is meant by a good citizen. She learns to discriminate finely between forms of right and wrong action, and turns to various sciences to see what they have to teach her of precision, accuracy, patience, conditions of experiment, truth. And then she turns again to her kindergarten to know as much as is possible of the physical and mental condition of each child under her direction, to study inherited traits and home environment, and with this knowledge to set about a work of definite and deliberate change to be wrought in each bit of humanity.

This is the self-constituted task of the professional-spirited kindergartner.

How does her work differ from that of other teachers? The work of the kindergartner is of a more positive nature. The child comes to her with less experience of the world of any kind. The influence of environment, good or bad, has not had time to change in any marked degree his original self. Action in any particular direction has not been continued long enough to become habit. Curiosity has not yet been killed or even very much curbed, neither has its field of operation been very wide or fertile. Imitation has not gone sufficiently far to become second-nature. Rivalry, emulation, courage, timidity, self-reliance, aggressiveness, selfishness, generosity, vanity, co-operation—no one of these tendencies has been given opportunities striking enough or often enough repeated to be classed as characteristic. In a word, the kindergarten child is more a bundle of material than of acquired tendencies. The kindergartner's problem is less complex than that of the child's later teachers. She has less to do with the breaking of habits, because, speaking broadly, we may say that no strong habits have been formed. She has much to do, however, with the formation of habits, and in providing opportunity for their proper development and exercise, she has a problem sufficiently important and difficult.

It is in the study of natural tendencies of individual children and their expression, in other words, in the study of children's motives and their direction into avenues of desirable work that her chief function lies. No teacher has so little exercise for repression, for the simple reason that there are fewer tendencies to suggest the method of repression; no teacher, perhaps, has so great a responsibility, for the simple reason that there are so many chances for wrong expression, bad habit-formation, undesirable work.

Any form of expression engaged in with zeal is work. Certain forms of what is commonly turned to play may very properly, according to this definition, be classed as work. This the writer understands; but the walls between play and work are so low and weak as constantly to need propping upon one side or the other, and the enormous gaps between the two fields are so apparent that it seems absurd to try to draw any hard and fast line between the two. The kindergarten, e. g., far from being a mere play school, might far more properly be called a garden in which children work, and the work done in a kindergarten, in which selection of stimuli has been careful and direction of child-motive is wise, certainly compare favorably in value to that done during any period of equal time during the child's school life.

The selection of work-inspiring stimuli rests of course with the kindergartner. The motive for work is to be found in the child himself. Artificial incentives for work in the kindergarten are neither necessary nor advisable, and their employment with all teachers is too often due to lack of knowledge of how to use motives already in the child-mind.

Roughly, then, the method of procedure is blocked out; it is the same for all kindergartners. What truths, if any, have been discovered? How is the kindergarten child differentiated from children of a larger growth and from adults? The most noticeable trait, apparent even to the casual observer, is physical activity. The kindergarten child is predominantly active, as compared with others. He likes movement for its own sake, and truly the granting of opportunity of movement for its own sake would be a boon to many a child. But the wise kindergartner utilizes this natural motive for motion and makes of it a motive for work involving motion. She realizes that this movement ought to be self-directed to a great extent, that it must call for the exercise of the power of choice, that it must lead to production of some kind, that in its progress it must not interfere with the rights of others, that it must take the form of co-operation, that it must be of such a nature and continue for such a time as to further, never to hinder, healthy, normal, physical development. Games, then, are not played for mere amusement; songs are not sung for entertainment. Handwork is not provided merely to keep the child busy, nor, on the other hand, for the finished production which may follow. Pictures are not drawn to serve as specimens of childish art. The work in the mind of the kindergartner to be wrought is real work, work that carries with it power and dignity, work that is thoroughly enjoyed, and the motive for it she finds in the child, in irrepressible movement.

But this tendency to irrepressible movement is not confined to his physical nature. His mind, as is ours, is in a constant state of flux. The mind of the young child, however, is in a special or unique state, that of passive attention. If he be a normal human being of four or five years he must attend to the sights, sounds, and other stimuli offered by the outside world. He is more of an animal than he will be later. The animal who refuses thus to attend fails to survive. The child who is unable thus to attend is abnormal, unfit. Yet these brief periods are at the same time periods of interest, and if the proper stimuli be provided, are periods of great and valuable mental growth. The motive for work in this case is simply an overpowering tendency to be constantly in a peculiar state of mental activity. The work is the change that goes on in the child's mental complex during these rapidly passing periods, under the influence of carefully directed stimuli. The motive for work then is again irrepressible movement, but in this case mental movement.

Much that this new and strange world brings to the child he is not ready to receive. It bears no content, carries with it no meaning, but there are certain tendencies either natural or easily and early acquired that almost never fail to appeal to him. Among these is the inclination to collect things, a form of activity both mental and physical. Given the proper stimuli, i. e., the one that appeals to the child as an individual, and this tendency to collect may result in work of huge proportions. If the tendency, as frequently happens, be merely the collection of any objects whatsoever, simply the gathering of material, then it is the kindergartner's privilege and duty to provide material of educative value or to lead the child to find it for himself. The child thus directed becomes a changed being, simply through the utilization of his motive for work, which was a crude, uncultivated restlessness forcing him to act in a certain ill-defined but positive way.

Lacking almost entirely the knowledge and content of words it is no wonder that the child's ideas are largely composed of symbols of a different kind. They seek for expression of their ideas, however, quite as eagerly as the children of a larger growth, but more emphatically than they in the form of dramatization. It is only through their bodies that they can make themselves clearly understood. It is only through the bodily actions of others that they are fully able to understand them. The same sort of irrepressible energy that impels them almost constantly merely to move, impels them frequently to move in living pictures. Life is a medley of disconnected incidents. The desire to set forth the incidents experienced is self-forceful. Surely it is not necessary to point out how eagerly the kindergartner seizes upon this tendency to accomplish work. The child in the kindergarten who has been permitted to work with ideas in this way knows far better how to work with them in a more abstract form when he is ready to step forth into the larger world of word ideas. Who shall say which form of work is the more valuable in bringing about desirable change? In fact, the change wrought in a child's mental and ethical nature by work done in a wisely selected drama can hardly be estimated, and its value can hardly be overestimated. Again we find the motive for work emanating from the child himself. Not only is the kindergarten child interested in his own action and that of his fellows, but all that moves holds him a willing captive. He unconsciously stretches forth his hands to the flying bird, imitates the motion of the running horse, or follows to its hiding-place the shy rabbit. All living, moving things wield a power over him. It is not that he wishes to attend; he must attend. And so the kindergarten is filled with live animals;, the living conditions of which are as nearly as possible like those of their free brothers, or, better still, the children and animals live together in a veritable out-of-door kindergarten—permissible in many parts of our country—and are taken frequently from their own little garden out into the larger one of the adjoining bit of world. Who can ever hope to trace the changes in brain-cell patterns that must result? The motive supplied by the child himself, intense active interest in living, moving animals, the kindergartner obtains, in addition to actual knowledge of animal life, increased sympathy, respect, pity, tenderness, love for, and actual care of, animals involving various forms of mental and physical work. The motive for work was once more child-born.

Sometimes two tendencies—two motives of action or work of opposite types—are made to co-operate admirably. There is in all animals—and the human being is no exception—the instinct for self-preservation expressing itself often in young children in a kind of aggressive self-defense exercised without necessary provocation. We say the child likes to fight. There is also prominent in most children the parental or protective trait, as shown in love and care of babies, dolls, animals, Teddy bears, etc. The desire to fight also can certainly be traced to this origin. The kindergartner simply directs the tendency into its proper channel. The kindergarten child who involuntarily flushes and clinches his small fists, when he sees an animal cruelly hurt or a weak child cruelly teased, is on the highroad to citizenship. The world needs fighters of this sort, and the motive for this form of the world's work does not have to be artificially supplied.

It is the tendency to imitate that leads a child to wish to do what he finds others doing. This is, obviously, one of the most fruitful sources of education. The amount of hard work accomplished through imitation among children is enormous. The kindergartner skilfully turns the motive for work of mere imitation into desire for co-operative work where imitation is more or less called into play.

But why multiply instances? The purpose of this paper has been accomplished if the following points have been made clear:

1. The kindergarten has a recognized place in the scheme of education.

2. It is in a state of progressive evolution.

3. Its general problem is not radically different from that of other educators.

4. It deals with children at a time when they are in a peculiar state of mental condition.

5. Its function, like that of other departments of education, is to supply desirable forms of work.

6. The motives for this work are to be found in certain powerful tendencies in the child himself.

DEMOCRACY IN EDUCATION

JESSE D. BURKS, PH.D.
Principal Teachers Training School, Albany, N. Y.

One of the most notable contributions made by the nineteenth to the twentieth century is the illuminating thought of John Fisk that the human species has reached its supreme position in the evolutionary scale very largely through the gradual lengthening of the period of infancy. Nicholas Murray Butler has seized upon this thought as the starting-point for a sound theory of education, and has pointed out with great clearness the logical identity of the period of infancy and the period of systematic education. From this point of view, the whole or the greater part of the period of infancy should properly be devoted to activities calculated to develop social intelligence, social sympathy, and social power, to the end that each individual, as completely as possible, may adjust himself to his own world.

In certain directions, this theory has resulted in a remarkable prolongation of the period of formal education. A person, for example, who pursues the entire course of training in elementary, secondary, and collegiate schools and, subsequently, a professional course in medicine, law, theology, or pedagogy, spends twenty years or more in his course of study and reaches the age of twenty-five years or over before he is ready to begin his professional career. Such a striking extension of the period of education, however, concerns directly only a small fraction of our population as will readily be recalled when we consider the facts in a single typical community.

In the city of Albany, the capital of the wealthiest and most populous state of the Union, there are approximately 1,600 pupils in each of the first four years of school. In the fifth year there are 1,300 pupils; in the sixth year 1,100; in the seventh year 700; and in the eighth year 500. Hardly one-third of the children enrolled in the fourth school year, it will be seen, reach the final year of the elementary school. In the high school of this city, the rate of decrease in number of pupils is even more rapid, the number in the four successive classes being 400, 300, 200, and 150. These figures represent a condition that is general throughout this country. The ratio of decrease in numbers from grade to grade no doubt varies considerably, but the essential fact is almost uniformly the same. The great mass of our boys and girls are not remaining even to the end of the elementary schools, and large numbers of them are leaving as early as the fifth or sixth school year.

In our educational organization and policy, we have evidently failed to grasp the full significance of a prolonged period of infancy as a factor in the development of the individual and of the race. It is possible that by artificial restriction we are shortening the normal period of plasticity, and are thus impairing the capacity of the rising generation to make the needed adjustments to a rapidly changing and exacting environment. There never was a time when there was more urgent need for every member of society to exercise intelligence and energy in adjusting himself to the economic, political, and ethical conditions of life. There can be no more serious educational problem than an inquiry into the methods by which a more complete adjustment may be assured the great majority of our boys and girls.

The present consideration of this problem will be limited to three of its many aspects: first, what are the chief reasons why so large a proportion of pupils now leave school before the end of the elementary course; second, in what ways may more adequate provision be made for the varied needs of children in the last years of the elementary-school period; and third, what effect would such provision probably have in prolonging the school life of pupils and in accomplishing more nearly the true purposes of our educational system?

Among the reasons assigned for the rapid dropping-out of pupils are age, lack of mental capacity, and dissatisfaction with the restraints of school life, on the part of pupils; lack of intelligence and interest, on the part of parents; deficiency of insight, sympathy, and tact, on the part of teachers; the economic necessity for children to assist in the earning of a family livelihood; and the ill adaptation of the courses of study to the special needs of the children. Very likely all of these influences are operative in greater or less degree. The relative weights of these several influences in determining the dropping-out of pupils is a matter to be settled by a consideration of the facts rather than by a mere expression of opinion. The facts, however, are difficult to ascertain, for the motives that influence individual boys and girls to leave school are by no means always clearly defined, even in their own minds. A child who is unhappy or backward in his school work is easily persuaded that the lack of adjustment is due to the prejudice or incapacity of his teachers or that the welfare of his family requires that he find employment and provide for his own support. It not uncommonly happens that a child whose abilities in certain directions are of high order finds it difficult or impossible to make satisfactory progress in one or more of the school subjects. It is easy for teachers, parents, and the pupil himself to attribute such failure to the stupidity of the pupil rather than to the fact the school makes no adequate provision for the special combination of abilities that this child possesses.

There is undoubtedly a widespread feeling among parents and children that the last years of the elementary school do not pay; that the opportunities of these years are of no direct value to children destined for industrial and domestic pursuits. At the close of the fifth or sixth year of school, pupils have attained moderate proficiency in reading, writing, and simple calculation, and have some knowledge of geography, and the history of their own country. The last years of the elementary course are devoted largely to an amplified study of these same subjects. To a child who can see no immediate application of these studies in solving the urgent problems of his own life, what serious loss can there be in leaving school as soon as the law permits, or sooner if the law can be evaded? Are not these two or three years of greater economic value when given to industrial pursuits than when wasted in the tiresome repetition of the traditional school "studies"?

It is easy enough for the schoolmaster to enter a general

denial of the charges implied in this very practical estimate of the relative value of training in the schools and of training in the world's work. He may characterize the estimate as basely utilitarian or he may point to the fact that those pupils who do complete the elementary course are found to have earning power superior to those who do not. The answer to this reply is that, whatever may be the facts, there is nevertheless the widespread opinion that the training offered in the last years of the elementary school has little practical value, and this opinion is one of the strongest influences in shortening the school life of pupils.

The recent report of the Massachusetts Commission on Industrial Training, though not conclusive on this point, furnishes strong indications that this attitude toward the practical value of school training has a much more direct effect upon the dropping-out of pupils from school than has economic pressure or the blindness of parents to the higher interests of their children. About half of the parents of children who had withdrawn from school before the age of sixteen stated definitely that, if there had been courses for industrial training offered in the public schools, they would have kept their children in school instead of allowing them to enter the low-grade and unskilled industries which alone are open to them. More than 75 per cent. of the parents of these children, according to the report, were financially able to keep their children in school if it had seemed desirable to do so.

It is evident, then, that the low estimate placed upon the value of the last years of elementary-school training is a powerful factor in determining the length of the school life of children. Let us now ask whether this estimate has proper foundation, or is based upon essential error.

Here again the report of the Massachusetts commission presents evidence of great value. It is shown that the years from fourteen to sixteen, whether spent in the school or at work, are wasted years so far as concerns the permanent earning capacity of the great mass of boys and girls who enter industrial and domestic as distinguished from commercial and professional pursuits. Those children who enter unskilled industries at the age of fourteen are put at work that requires extremely little intelligence and therefore possesses practically no educational value. Owing to this arrest of development, these children soon pass beyond the point where the opportunity is open or the impulse is active for them to enter skilled pursuits. They become more and more fixed in their low-grade pursuits. The wages of two to four dollars per week received at the outset are scarcely enough to meet the actual cost of living of a boy or girl, much less to enable him to begin the habit of systematic saving. Within a few years these children reach the maximum of their earning capacity at about nine dollars per week. This is at so low a level that they are condemned to lives of uncertainty and of poverty, if not of degradation.

Those children who remain in school until they are sixteen years old eventually reach a higher wage-earning level, it is true; but the uniform testimony of employers is that they are almost wholly lacking in the "industrial intelligence," and that accordingly they enter upon industrial occupations in no condition even to begin to learn the special processes involved in their respective vocations. The advantage, measured by wage-earning capacity, which these children eventually prove to possess over those children who leave school at the age of fourteen, is very likely due, in part at least, to the tendency of individuals of superior intelligence and ambition to remain in school until the completion of the elementary course. This tendency is strengthened by the traditional high value which public sentiment assigns to a complete "common-school education." Children who remain in school until the age of sixteen, therefore, form a select group having not only a relatively high degree of general maturity, but probably a distinct advantage in the way of native capacity and zeal. On account of the maturing of special capacities and tastes during the years between fourteen and sixteen, it is moreover probable that children at the more advanced age more often choose the kind of occupation in which they are naturally best qualified to succeed. The industrial superiority referred to may accordingly by no means so largely be due to the added two years of school training as is generally supposed.

Though there is no reason to doubt the value of the last few years of the elementary-school training as a means of increasing industrial efficiency, it might still appear to be the part of economic wisdom to accept the prevailing conditions of elementary education, with possibly a raising of the compulsory age limit and a more effective enforcement of compulsory-attendance laws. Such a conclusion, however, is not justified. The rational development of our educational system does not culminate in a condition under which attendance must be enforced by external authority; but rather in a condition which in itself possesses a compelling power sufficient to hold the great majority of our boys and girls through a period long enough for them to attain the genuine purposes of education. Such compelling power can be secured only through a reasonable adaptation of the training offered by the school to the concrete needs of the pupils.

The real secret of the loss of pupils in the upper elementary grades is to be found in our astounding failure to provide for some of the strongest psychological and social needs of many pupils as they approach these years. We take boys and girls at a time when their impulses are strong for active participation in the vital interests of life, and we confine them within narrow schoolroom cells, with books and pencils as their chief or sole means of participation; we take them when their desire for social co-operation is a dominant motive, and we require each to work for himself and by himself upon tasks which, so far as he can see, have little to do with the great world outside of the school walls; we take them at a period when their capacity and their instinct for individual initiative is strong, and we expect them to work under the constant direction and control of a teacher—their problems artificially assigned, their coming and going, their starting-points and stopping-places determined for them; we take them when their individual differences in capacity, interest, and prospective careers are properly matters of growing and vital concern, and we require them to pursue a uniform course of study having little direct relation to these specific powers, motives, and prospects.

Our attitude toward our boys and girls is not unlike that which has characterized our dealings with the American Indians. We placed the Indians upon reservations and took from them their native resources and occupations; we hedged them about with all manner of artificial restrictions, and placed overseers in charge of them to prevent outbreaks; we then found to our chagrin and to our occasional discomfiture that they were not altogether contented with the favors that we had forced upon them, and that they did not always make the rapid progress that we had planned for them. The analogy in our educational policy is not difficult to see. Let us look to it that the idleness, the irresponsibility, the passive indifference, and the physical and moral degeneration that we have forced upon our Indian wards is not repeated in the lives of our own children.

Much of the ill adaptation of our educational organization to the actual needs of our society is due to a false notion of democracy as applied to education. We very properly maintain that a true social and political democracy must rest upon equality of educational opportunity for all. We then proceed to interpret *equal* opportunity to mean the *same* opportunity and the mischief is done. We are failing in our educational policy to appreciate the fact that genuine opportunity consists not in what is offered to all alike but in what actually serves the concrete purposes of any individual concerned. What is a real opportunity to one person may fail utterly to meet the requirements of another.

Curiously enough this pseudo-democratic idea did not characterize our educational organization in the early period of our history. For the first two centuries of our colonial life, the distinct purpose of the schools was to train a comparatively few men for the responsibilities of leadership in church and state. For the rank and file, education was provided in the main through actual participation in the common activities of daily life—in political functions, in vocations, and in religion. With the expansion of our national life that has accompanied our growth in territory, in population, and in wealth, and with the increased complexity of our social, industrial, and political organization, demands have arisen for trained leaders in medicine, law, and engineering. In the higher stages of our educational system, we have made provision for the training of such leaders. Thus far, however, we have failed to provide for that great majority of our population that can never by any chance attain to the rank of leader. The school has taken over the entire responsibility for education which it formerly shared with the home, the farm, the apprenticeship, and a social order in which the individual was normally brought into direct contact with a great number of industrial processes. The school has assumed the entire responsibility, but it has not yet discovered how to supply the important factors in education that in other days were provided through activities outside the school.

Thus we boast of a system of universal education, but fall far short of educating all of our children. Our secondary schools are dominated by the idea of preparation for college. Our elementary schools are dominated by the idea of a single type of scholarship which directly concerns a small minority of our children. If instead of our abstract and misleading notion of equal educational opportunity for all, we should substitute the more concrete and sane idea of furnishing educational opportunities adapted to the needs of various groups of children, we might develop a system of education that should be actually and not merely nominally democratic.

If education is to enable each person to live the happiest and most useful life of which he is capable, it must meet all of the main requirements of such a life, not otherwise properly provided for. These may roughly be classified as the requirements of leisure and the requirements of vocational pursuits. The work of the elementary school is almost wholly designed to train children for the pursuits of leisure. The literature, history, geography, nature-study, music, and drawing are obviously adapted to the purposes of recreation and of general social intercourse, rather than to the more specific purposes of vocational pursuits. Even arithmetic and manual training, which are commonly considered as of high "practical value," have mainly indirect application to the peculiar problems of most vocations. Even assuming that the school as now constituted furnishes adequate training for professional and commercial pursuits, the fact still remains that, for industrial and domestic pursuits, there is absolutely no systematic training in most of our schools. It is impossible, on any grounds consistent with true democracy, to justify a system of education that is adapted to the needs of a small minority only; that so far fails to meet the needs of the whole body of our boys and girls that more than two-thirds of them refuse to accept, as a free gift, even the training offered in the elementary period of eight years.

Individual differences in native capacities and in prospective careers of pupils, it has been seen, appear with increasing force as the children are passing through the last few years of the elementary course. The disregard of these differences, in the organization of the school work, has been pointed out as one of the chief reasons for the rapid loss of pupils during these years. *There must be a reorganization of education, in accordance with the actual psychological development of children and with the requirements of genuine democracy, based upon a systematic recognition of special aptitudes.*

Such a recognition supplies the rational ground for the distinctions between elementary and secondary education. The distinction at present is purely formal and fortuitous and is evidently made at too late a period. Whatever may be the arbitrary and external organization of education, the actual secondary stage in the development of boys and girls will inevitably begin when the differences in their tastes, capacities, and ambitions become more conspicuous and important than the likenesses. The difference between elementary and secondary development is thus a matter of life; not a mere matter of convenient arrangement. Differences in abilities and in interests will always demand some differences in form of activity, and if these are not definitely provided in the school they will be found elsewhere, as they are at present during the last years of the elementary course. In view of the persistence with which we cling to our traditional organization of education, it might be supposed that a uniform eight years' elementary course was guaranteed by Magna Charta or that it was proclaimed in the Declaration of Independence as one of the inalienable rights of man. As a matter of fact, in failing to make the transition from the elementary to the secondary stage in our school system correspond with its appearance in the development of our children, we are guilty either of indefensible stupidity or of deliberate malfeasance.

The provision of alternative courses for vocational training, before the end of the present eight-year elementary course, implies, it is true, that each child will be called upon to choose the course that he will pursue. Here we shall encounter a storm of protest against the introduction of the "elective system" at this early stage of children's careers. The arguments against "early specialization" are of course thoroughly familiar. They were first brought forward with great vehemence in the discussions that accompanied the growth of the elective system in our colleges. They next appeared in the debate concerning the introduction of elective courses into our high schools. This debate is still in progress and the familiar arguments are constantly hurled by the reactionaries against the advocates of wider opportunity and greater freedom for pupils in high schools. These arguments will in turn be directed against every effort to extend the elective system backward to the logical beginning of the secondary stage of education. The outcome of the struggle between rigid prescription and free election must eventually be the same in all three of these fields for the conflict is really one and not three. The question is whether human beings who differ widely in native gifts and acquired tendencies shall be forced to pursue a single conventional course of training, or have the privilege of choosing a course that will equip them not only for the worthy use of their leisure but for the intelligent pursuit of their vocations. Life itself is from the beginning an elective process—each person selecting from the complex whole of experience those elements that accord with his native and acquired interests and rejecting those elements that serve no useful purpose in his life. Mental growth, if we are to accept the teaching of modern psychology, consists in the development of a multitude of specific forms of connection rather than of a few general faculties such as memory, judgment, and reasoning power. We cannot, therefore, justify a study or a course of study on the basis of the discredited theory that a few general mental faculties require the traditional school subjects for their proper discipline. As an individual mind can be expected to develop only a very small number of the innumerable connections possible at any stage of its growth, the problem of education becomes in large measure the problem of providing situations favorable to the selection by each child of the connections best suited to his needs. In the earlier stages of children's development these needs are fairly uniform and may be met by a relatively uniform course of study. This is the proper period for elementary education. With the appearance of distinct differences in individual requirements, as we have seen, a uniform school course is inadequate to the needs of all types of children. At this point the period of secondary education rationally begins, with its system of alternative courses adapted to the specific needs of various groups of children.

The elective system, then, is an unavoidable fact without regard to what the school organization may be at a given time and place. Under present conditions there are but two alternatives open to a pupil in our elementary schools. One is to continue in the single course offered by the schools; the other is to enter vocational work before the completion of the school course. The question is not, therefore, whether we shall extend the privilege of election to pupils in the elementary schools, but whether, by introducing courses for industrial and domestic training within the school, we shall widen the field within which election may be made.

A rational system of secondary education must provide not only for the training of special capacities but for making children conscious of the special capacities that they individually possess. One of the most serious weaknesses of the present organization of education is that the range of experience provided for in the schools is so narrow that many of the latent powers of children are not stimulated to activity. In some cases the special capacities of children appear early and in unmistakable form. In such cases it is relatively easy to supply the appropriate educational influences. More often, however, the specific characteristics of children require particularly favorable conditions to bring them to the surface. In order that a child may be placed in position to make proper choice of a school course and, ultimately, of a vocation it is often essential, therefore, that means be taken to ascertain what are the native capacities upon which his success in every undertaking must very largely depend. These capacities cannot always be determined with reference merely to the desires of parents and of pupils or to such general advice as teachers and principals of schools are commonly qualified to give. Teachers must be equipped to recognize, to search for, and to interpret the evidences of special aptitude. This will necessitate a fuller recognition of the influence of heredity upon mental and moral traits and a more vital and practical view of genetic psychology than is yet widely prevalent.

As to whether the school life of pupils can be prolonged by adequate provision for vocational training, our argument has been in the main indirect and deductive. In the absence of concrete data, however, such an argument is all that can be presented. It seems reasonable to assume that children will remain in school as long as they and their parents regard it as distinctly to their advantage to do so, and economic conditions do not prevent. The conclusion clearly indicated, accordingly, is that adequate provision for vocational training, beginning at about the sixth year of school, would tend to prolong the school life and increase the vocational efficiency of the great mass of children; especially of those who enter industrial and domestic pursuits.

The whole argument for vocational training is of course open to the familiar charge that it is basely utilitarian. As to the charge that vocational training is utilitarian, why should not the answer be one of "confession and avoidance"? Such training *is* utilitarian; but why *basely* so? Most men devote more than half of their waking hours to their vocations. Are their lives necessarily on that account basely utilitarian? Our war for independence had its origin in a question of taxation. Was it for that reason a basely utilitarian struggle for selfish ends? Almost every great national policy involves some matter of industry or commerce. Is our national life therefore unworthy of our loyal affection? The intellectual and moral progress of the race has always been in large measure dependent upon material and commercial prosperity. Are the achievements of the human spirit on that account insignificant or base? As a people we profess a belief in the dignity of work. Shall we hesitate to exemplify our belief by making it possible for every man to find his work and in his work to find a worthy means of enlarging and completing his life?

PLAYGROUNDS AND THE BOARD OF EDUCATION

CHARLES ZUEBLIN
University of Chicago

Municipal playgrounds should not be controlled by the board of education for three reasons: First, children's interests are not now covered by the activities of the board of education; second, playgrounds are not merely for children and are not used only for play; third, the administration of the increasingly complicated municipal functions involves a complete reorganization of municipal government.

First, The argument has been made that the administration of playgrounds should be given to the board of education because it has the supervision of the chief affairs of children. In that case the board of education might also be intrusted with the administration of parks, public baths, and beaches, libraries, museums, the juvenile court, legislation against child labor, medical inspection, hospitals, asylums, summer outings, and transportation. All of these activities affect children as much as adults, and in some cases, exclusively. As we have become more familiar with these newer functions, we have begun the attempt of co-ordination, and in some instances amalgamation has been proposed.

It is certainly desirable that each school house should have an adjoining playground, and that it should be equipped with shower baths, if not a swimming-tank. It is important that the teachers make use of the public museums and art galleries, for their own benefit and that of the children. There should be a branch of the public library in every school house. The problems of compulsory education and truancy are intimately identified with the service of the juvenile court. Experience in factory legislation restricting the employment of children in Chicago and elsewhere has proved the wisdom of intrusting some of the functions to the school authorities, such, for example, as licensing school boys to sell papers, and regulating the granting of certificates to children of school age. The school has proved a satisfactory place for medical inspection and vaccination, leading in New York City to the proposal to have eyeglasses furnished by the board of education. But a larger problem remains in the correlation of such activities of the board of education with the administration of hospitals and asylums. Even transportation service has been utilized by boards of education in providing scientific and recreative excursions and in conveying children to centralized schools. Professor Jackman proposed that city schools be all located in the suburbs, thus employing the dead cars which carry people in opposite directions during the rush hours. Nevertheless it does not seem desirable to burden the board of education with the entire administration of all these municipal and state functions.

Second, The development of the playground into the elaborately equipped recreative center of today has carried it beyond the conception of a space for the amusement or education of children, and has made expert administration and voluntary social co-operation imperative. The Chicago small parks contain provision for the athletic, recreative, and intellectual diversion of people of all ages at all hours of the day, every day in the year. It is true that the schoolhouse should be and that it is being similarly used. That indicates, however, the necessity for coordinating the various social activities of the city rather than merely enlarging the scope of the board of education. It is desirable that the public be allowed the free use of the library, baths, gymnasium, auditorium, and playground of the schoolhouse. But even that will not serve the manifold functions of one of our Chicago play centers.

The conception of public life is enlarging. The obligation of the city to its citizens is broader than before. The solution of the problem is to be found in enlightening the citizen regarding his obligations to the city, and in reorganizing completely the municipal administration. It has been pointed out that many expedients may be used for emergencies which will not satisfy the requirements of the future. Playgrounds under voluntary management or under independent municipal control have yielded to superior methods based on experience. The same thing will happen with playgrounds intrusted to the board of education. A new conception of public life is forcing itself upon patriotic citizens and intelligent municipal administrators.

Third, Municipal functions have already multiplied and in the future these are destined to be so much further increased that a reorganization of municipal government is inevitable. The plan followed by the British cities universally, adopted by three Texas cities, and just indorsed by Des Moines under an act providing for the administration of all the cities of Iowa, promises to solve the problem of playground administration along with the other questions from which it can hardly be separated. The old American distinction between administration and legislation is abandoned and all the administrative functions are intrusted to committees of the council. Only in this way is it likely that these new municipal services will be correlated. If one committee of the council controls the schools, another the libraries and museums, others parks, playgrounds and public baths, the various members of the council being placed on the different committees in which they have special interest, or on which they are peculiarly useful, we shall secure interrelation with expert service. If it be suggested that we cannot intrust these large vital functions to our present councilmen, it may be retorted that they were not elected for such services. In fact, they are generally chosen now by an unintelligent electorate to serve private rather than public interests, while the membership of school and park boards is parceled out among political favorites or inoffensive partisans.

Perhaps the rapid and extensive expansion of the playground idea may help to open the eyes of patriotic citizens to the larger municipal problem. Neither the board of education nor the park commission is likely to serve the public interests adequately, while the mayor and council are chiefly engaged in granting special privileges to otherwise honest citizens, who are thereby bribed to disbelieve in the city government. Eliminate the granting of franchises from the functions of the city; concentrate the authority in the hands of a council chosen in recognition of an enlarged public life, and the correlation of the various municipal functions, including schools and playgrounds, will inevitably ensue.

READING FOR LITTLE CHILDREN—PART II.

ELSIE AMY WYGANT
Secondary Grade, University Elementary School

IN AN INDIAN TEPEE

Far out west in Montana stands a tepee on a river bank.

It stands on the edge of a forest.

Great mountains rise behind it and in front at a distance are other mountains.

They look purple in the distance and their tops are always covered with snow.

The tepee is made of long poles that stick out of the skin cover at the top.

The covering is made of brown cow-hide.

Another cow-hide fastened on with wooden pegs makes the door.

A fire burns in the center of the tepee.

Here a woman is kneeling.

She broils meat on long sticks over the fire.

Other sticks lie by her side.

A wooden bowl is filled with red raspberries.

The bowl is made of maple wood; it is polished and the rim is set with pieces of shell.

A horn spoon lies by the bowl with a rattlesnake carved on its handle.

The tepee smells smoky, for all the smoke does not go out of the hole at the top.

TEPEE OF SIOUX INDIAN

A SIOUX BRAVE

Sioux Indians live in this tepee.

The man is a great warrior.

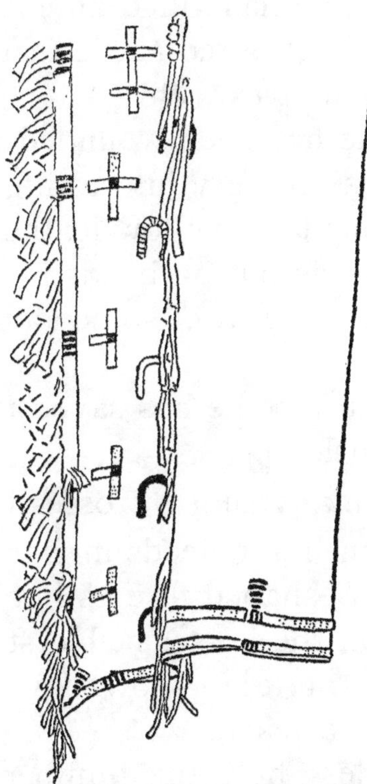

Leggin of Sioux Brave

His good wife has painted his deeds on his skin robe.

She has woven them in beads on his leggins.

He has a long pipe with a red stone bowl and a wooden handle.

The red stone cuts easily.

He has carved his deed on his pipe bowl.

His tribe have given him a queer head-dress to show that he is brave.

It is a circle made of cedar root.

The circle is bound and crossed with strips of leather; an eagle feather, painted red, hangs from the center.

This means he has killed an enemy in battle.

He owns a single red eagle feather too.

Sometimes he wears this.

It means he has been wounded in battle.

His leggins are very interesting.

They are made of yellow leather.

His squaw has put on beads in many patterns.

Along the side are some double crosses like this: ‡

These mean that he has saved the life of another warrior in battle.

There are many single crosses like this: + + +

These mean brave deeds in war.

There are *U*-shaped figures like this: *U*

These mean the horses he has stolen for his tribe.

Some red triangles show how many ponies he gave away at a feast.

Some circles show the number of buffaloes he has killed.

A snake means that he is a great medicine man.

THE DAUGHTER OF A SIOUX

A young Indian girl is coming through the forest.

She plays on a bone flute as she dances along.

It makes a high sweet sound like a bird call.

The beads in her long black hair shine in the sunshine.

Her pink shell ear-rings shake and glisten as she moves.

She has a dress of soft brown skin tied over her shoulder.

It hangs to her knees and is painted in many colors.

Her leggins are of buckskin with a wide border of heads.

Her buckskin moccasins are beaded too.

A beautiful bag hangs on her arm.

It is the white and yellow skin of a little fawn.

It is tied with beads and bird feathers, and bound with a blue bead band at the top.

As she comes near to the tepee she calls aloud.

Her mother comes to the door of the tepee.

Her father, who sits at the door, raises his long pipe and nods a greeting.

She holds her bag high over her head.

It is late summer.

She has been out on the hillside hunting for berries.

They see that she has had good luck.

Her bag is full.

THE INDIAN DRESSER OF SKINS

Near the tepee some stretchers stood in the sun one day.

A great brown hide was stretched on them near the ground.

At the door of the tepee a woman was kneeling.

A skin was pegged down on the ground before her.

She scraped something toward her over the skin.

Again and again she leaned forward with her arms outstretched.

Then she pulled this thing toward her over the skin.

It was a skin-scraper like the one in the picture.

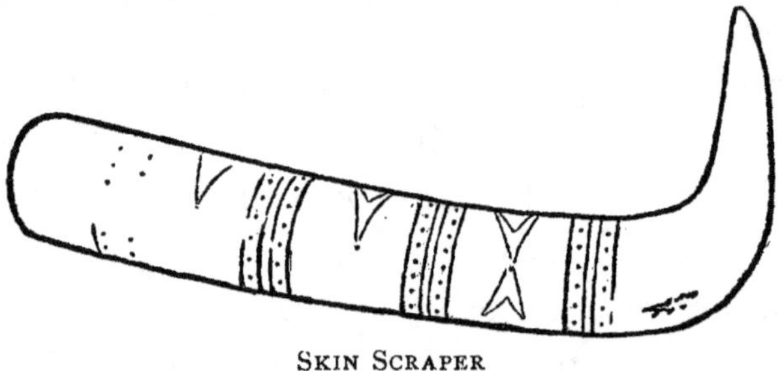

SKIN SCRAPER

But when she used it, it had an iron piece bound on the end.

This made it scrape better.

She had scraped the skin and dried it three times.

Then she had washed it and dried it again.

She had rubbed it and chewed it to make it soft.

Now she was scraping and cross-scraping it to make it more soft.

She wanted it to be as soft as a blanket.

While she was at work some men rode up to the tepee.

They watched the woman at work and saw her scraper made of elk horn.

They asked her what the signs on it meant.

She said the dots were the hides she had tanned.

The crosses were the tepees she had made.

THE FIELD MUSEUM

The Indian woman who owned the skin-scraper wanted beads and dye.

The men gave her these for the skin-scraper.

You can see it today in the Field Museum.

It is in a case marked: "Yankton, Sioux, Montana."

This means the woman belonged to the Yankton tribe of the great Sioux family of Indians, and she lived in Montana.

The leggins of the Sioux medicine man are there too.

So are his eagle feather and his pipe.

The robe of the Indian girl, her ear-rings, and her flute are there.

In fact all the things in the tepee are there.

And so is the tepee itself.

A POSITIVE FUNCTION FOR SCHOOL MUSEUMS

FRANK A. MANNY
New York City

As one visits the various school museums in Munich, Paris, Zürich, Berne, and other cities he is thankful that the functions that have called these into existence have been recognized. In the first-named city one can see a remarkable collection of school materials. The purpose is commercial as well as educational, and so the organization is such as to keep the museum up to date. In Paris one is impressed by the possibilities of accumulation. I wondered where in America would be found such a quantity of school exercises by American pupils as far back as 1878, to say nothing of those from all parts of Europe and even Japan. When we get around to the making of careful comparative studies of what has actually been done during the course of years in school subjects we shall wish that more such material had been saved. The results from the single set of old papers, preserved in Springfield, Mass., and so widely written up two years ago, have shown of how much service such studies can be in combating criticisms based for the most part on sentiment and old associations.

With the increased interest in pedagogical training, quite apart from whatever can be done by the libraries of the various universities, we need a center to which all can turn for material—a museum which has a positive function. By this I mean not mere accumulation and classification of materials, however valuable that may be, but a positive organization with reference to serving the needs of those who influence and, to some extent, determine our educational policy. For instance the *Fortbildung-schulen* of Germany have perhaps as much suggestion for American schools as any present-time movement in European schools. Few can take the time to visit the work in Germany, and the one who does so realizes how much need there is that those immediately concerned with the problem see what is being done. A careful expenditure of no large sum would bring together a collection of reports, work done, criticisms, etc., which would be of great value if shown in our leading cities. This would bring out the merits of the various schemes, as that of Dr. Kerschensteiner at Munich, Dr. Kuypers at Cologne, the industrial schools of M. Rombant in Brussels, etc.

This is one instance; there are scores of others all of which have significance for our present needs. Naturally such work as this could best be done by our national bureau, but to keep it up and to give an opportunity for it to exercise a positive function would mean the systematic expenditure of large sums of money. The returns, however, would amply justify this expenditure.

EDITORIAL NOTES

During the early autumn there came into the editor's office a heart-breaking communication from a mother whose children are being educated in the public schools, written in the conviction that it was the public duty of parents who believe in democracy to send their children to the people's schools. While supporting this belief to the uttermost, a quotation is given not merely to show what sacrifices are sometimes demanded in living up to this faith in democracy, but as a plea for work in these schools that will integrate and not disintegrate ideas; work that will put purpose in the place of mere passive following of directions, and interest in the place of dullness or irritation.

While the case to be cited may be an extreme one, the educational sins are typical ones; and like lies exist in all shades from black to rather light gray.

Wasteful cramming.—A class of children in the upper seventh grade the first day of school were given several long and deeply involved problems. These were written upon the board. The children were to copy them and solve them before the next day's recitation. They were difficult for even a mature brain—these children were 11, 12, and 13 years of age. One little girl worked for an hour over one problem—finally left it weeping. Her mother could not work it. The class evidently could not work it, and were given a sharp reprimand and told that it *must* be done by the next recitation. The second night the father explained and solved the little girl's lesson to their mutual satisfaction. The third morning the mother visited the school and told the teacher what difficulty the girl had. Her teacher replied, "Oh, I am not surprised at all that the class could not do that work. I copied those problems out of a book without even reading them through, and later it took me two days to find out how to do them myself. Last night it came to me and is really quite simple. But don't for the world let Mildred know I couldn't do them."

The same teacher assigned for two weeks' work—that is for eight recitations in geography—all the vast amount of information to be found in an advanced textbook on England, Ireland, Scotland, and Wales, utterly unrelated to any past information in history or literature, a lot of raw mental food crammed into a weary brain, causing mental nausea. This was the subject which, properly treated and correlated, would have been delightful past words to describe. Our girl's twin cousin spent this summer traveling in Great Britain. But we had no time to recall her letters and make these places real to Mildred; we must cram for the test questions at the end of the month.

During these weeks her spelling has been as follows. Judge how well it fits into a well regulated mental diet. To me it seems that spelling should be an aid in expressing Mildred's ideas of the above geography, arithmetic, etc., but look at this: 36 words ending in *-ish;* 36 words used in architecture; 120 derivatives from 24 utterly disassociated words; 28 marks used in printing; 104 unaltered Latin words.

The history work consisted in reading sixteen pages of disassociated facts cut up into short accounts utterly lacking in literary interest regarding the period of fifty years preceding the Revolution.

Add to this some work in physiology, singing, writing, drawing, reading from some classic, and an hour each day practicing upon the piano—is it a wonder that she grows skilful in only one thing, and this is her salvation, namely, in shirking—learning just enough to pass muster and make a passable recitation? No real inherent interest lies in any of this work. She gains little or nothing and at what tremendous cost—from 9:00 A.M. to 4:00 P.M. in uncomfortable seats, breathing close air, gaining wrong habits of study, hurried, slovenly habits of accepting and swallowing any and every fact without exercise of either the divine forces of imagination or reason, the constant pressure resulting in an eager, unrestful, harried, impatient, irritable moral nature. Physically, mentally, morally she is limited, stunted, and prevented from a free natural development.

The Root of The Trouble

The wail of protest recorded above was read to a class of young students who were just beginning their preparation for teaching. The majority of the class had but recently been graduated from various high schools. Without hesitation, and without leading, they pointed out the weak spots, and the more flagrant errors made by the teacher. Many perceived at once that the most serious source of trouble was found in the teacher's utter lack of a simple interest in the subjects taught; and in her complete indifference to the children, their point of view, capacity, and needs. Others pointed out the unwisdom of a curriculum that would require so large an amount of unrelated material.

Yet while these students could detect these defects by the mere use of common-sense, they were at the same time suffering, as most of us are, from these very mistakes in their earlier school life. The mother quoted complains of slovenly habits of thought and work. Possibly "slovenly" is too harsh a word to apply to the trait that the writer finds a most common and most baffling one in young candidates for the teaching profession. But that ineffectiveness is an *induced* characteristic seems almost certain. It is strongest in the younger members fresh from high school. If a period of home life, of college, or even of office work has intervened, the case is usually changed, partly because of mere years and consequent maturity, partly because the person has been engaged in some real work, practical, or intellectual.

The Passive Attitude

There is a certain type of young woman who enters the normal school, or college, with a sweet willingness to do any thing that she is told to do; she sits with passive face and quiet hands, volunteers no suggestions, and asks few questions, save those of the following character: "What do you want me to do?" "How do you want me to do it?" "How far do you wish us to read for tomorrow?" She has little curiosity, few intellectual interests, and no good habits of study.

In many of these still young people that youthful interest in all that lives and moves seems to have suffered a change. Perhaps that is natural; but the youthful quality of spontaneous interest has not been followed by persistent study, or reflective judgment. We know they all had a lively curiosity and a tendency to experiment as children; why have these not been developed into interests and a scientific attitude? These are some of the questions forced upon us.

Motive and purpose in a general sense they must have or they would not have enrolled themselves as prospective teachers. But alas, the tremendous handicap that the school has placed upon them! Passivity, that is the negative descriptive word. What could have been done to preserve freshness of interest, enthusiasm, and initiative?

Working for the Waste-Basket

One of the greatest dampers on individual effort is the extinguisher of the waste-basket. Not that it is clapped on the pupil as a material dunce-cap, but it serves to put out his light none the less. How should we grown-ups feel toward writing if we knew that every careful exercise, every bit of narrative, every letter, every record of experiments, were to be immediately consigned to the dust-heap, to be read by no recipient, to be, in short, communicated to no one and of use to nobody? How long, under such conditions, should we continue to "think with our pens," and to do our best?

And yet when it comes to the case of the little learner we think he should be quite satisfied to remember that he is learning to write and to read, and that some day he may use this power to write *to* someone, or read to those who want to hear. We want to give them ease and skill; we therefore divest their reading of meaning and make their writing a set of exercises unrelated to any use or thought appreciable by them. We make it the end and aim to secure repetition of the old vocabulary and to add to it, in the hope that it may soon be of use. Therefore, they write for the waste-basket.

The Place of Drill

The children do arrive at a point, certainly, when they are ready to practice in order to achieve ease and smoothness in any function, but this point comes when we have learned the meaning and purpose of the mode of expression we are using. When this time comes drill is stripped of much of its drudgery. One of our most common mistakes with children is to demand the drill before they really feel any need of it; thus continually we put the cart before the horse.

Is it not possible to have the children write *from the beginning* because they have something to say, and to read because something good to read is waiting to be read? May they not count and measure, add, substract, divide, because they *need* these processes, or need the results the processes will bring? The waste-basket may be the final destination of this written work, but not the immediate one. The whole difference in the two cases is summed up in the word "purpose."

The People Who Furnish the Padding

We have purposeless, vague, limp people in the world, partly because they were born so, but in ninety-nine cases out of one hundred it is because the school has trained all purpose and force out of them. Their ideas have been disintegrated. Just so soon as school activities offer as much opportunity for experiment and observation and original effort as play does, we may begin to hope for a subsequent generation of workers who will put brains into their work.

In a little sketch entitled *Mugby Junction,* Dickens gives us an admirable parallel to our apportionment of mental food to the youthful mind. The lady proprietess of a railway restaurant goes to France to study French methods of restaurant-keeping. Her own, and those demanded by the traditions of England, have been to supply tough sandwiches, leathery pies, flat ginger beer; in general, "to keep the public down" and "to smooth their cuffs and smile while the public foams." Returning, she calls together her assistants and describes the horrors she has seen: "juicy meat-pies, fresh bread, sweet milk, abundant portions," and to sum up the whole situation of offense to her profession *"eatable things to eat, and drinkable things to drink!"*

Are we afraid that we may not be able to "keep the public down" if we supply readable things to read, and writable things to write?

B. P.

BOOKS RECEIVED

CENTURY CO., NEW YORK

Southern Stories. Retold from *St. Nicholas.* Cloth, 12mo. Illustrated. Pp. 190.

Sea Stories. Retold from *St. Nicholas.* Cloth, 12mo. Illustrated. Pp. 200.

Western Frontier Stories. Retold from *St. Nicholas.* Cloth, 12mo. Illustrated. Pp. 198.

Stories of the Great Lakes. Retold from *St. Nicholas.* Cloth, 12mo. Illustrated. Pp. 185.

Island Stories. Retold from *St. Nicholas.* Cloth, 12mo. Illustrated. Pp. 190.

Stories of Strange Sights. Retold from *St. Nicholas.* Cloth, 12mo. Illustrated. Pp. 195.

THOMAS Y. CROWELL & CO., NEW YORK

Days Before History. By H. R. Hall. Sunshine Library. 8vo, cloth. Illustrated. Pp. 144. $0.50.

When America Was New. By Tudor Jenks. Cloth, 12mo. Illustrated Pp. 320. $1.25.

AMERICAN BOOK CO., CHICAGO

Brief History of the United States. By John Bach McMaster. Half leather, 8vo. Illustrated. Pp. 464. $1.00.

Outline for Review of Greek History. By Newton and Treat. Cloth, 16mo, pp. 51. $0.25.

Outline for Review of Roman History. By Newton and Treat. Cloth, 16mo, pp. 62. $0.25.

Half-Hours with Mammals. By C. F. Holder. Cloth, 12mo. Illustrated. Pp. 253. $0.60.

Composition Rhetoric. By Thos. C. Blaisdell. Cloth, 12mo. Illustrated. Pp. 405. $1.00.

Maxwell's School Grammar. By William H. Maxwell. Cloth, 12mo, pp. 317. $0.60.

A. S. BARNES & CO., NEW YORK

Memory Gems for School and Home. Arranged by W. H. Williams. Pp. 130. $0.50.

Day by Day in the Primary School. By Alice Bridgham. Pp. 142. $1.25.

HENRY ALTEMUS CO., PHILADELPHIA

The Bible as Good Reading. By Albert J. Beveridge. Pp. 94. Cloth $0.50. Ooze calf $1.00.

Good Stories from the Ladies' Home Journal. Pp. 128. Illuminated boards $0.50. Ooze calf $1.00.

GINN AND COMPANY, CHICAGO

The Child's Word-Garden. By J. S. Lansing. Illustrated. Pp. 96.

Lisbeth Longfrock. Translated from the Norwegian of Hans Aanrud by Laura E. Poulsson. Cloth, 16mo. Illustrated. Pp. 149. $0.40.

CHARLES E. MERRILL & CO., NEW YORK

The Ancient Mariner. By Samuel Taylor Coleridge. Introduction by Julian W. Abernethy. Pp. 155.

VOLUME VIII NUMBER 4

THE ELEMENTARY SCHOOL TEACHER

DECEMBER, 1907

EDUCATIONAL PROBLEMS OF ADOLESCENCE

KATHARINE M. STILWELL
Instructor Grade VIII, University Elementary School

Not all children develop alike, in truth no two develop in the same way; yet a knowledge of the nascent periods of development and of the aggregate interests of any age may prevent serious mistake in education.

The inherent difficulty of the subject lies in the fact that all study of the child must be objective. It must be made from an adult standpoint and is necessarily full of errors. We get at the mind through the body, which is the reservoir of habit. The mind is not static, but is continually changing and presents different and distinct features at each stage of growth. It grows only by social contact; cannot develop alone, but is a function of social life. It acts only through social stimuli, and develops only in response to social needs.

The educative period of human life has been divided by psychologists into four stages. These groups are not set off from one another sharply by marked lines, by sudden and abrupt changes of characteristics, but they blend into and overlap one another. They are not sorts of phenomena which occur at certain stated periods in the child's life, consisting of physical and mental upheavals.

Dr. Dewey says, "They are simply to be considered as the apexes of waves of greater amplitude. It is not so much that the old has fallen off, but that the new has come in, and coming in, it assimilates into itself a great many of the other features."

In other words each period is characterized by a new standpoint in which the old activities have not disappeared, but remain to show themselves under different conditions, while the new activities give character to the period.

Thus, then, in discussing the adolescent, one must bear in mind the characteristics of the preceding stages of growth, how these came to be, what they do, in short, what is their relation to the general scheme of development.

"Character in infancy is instinct, in childhood it is slowly made over into habits, while at adolescence it can be cultivated through ideals."

Adolescence differs from the preceding stages in that the changes are more marked and sudden. To the average observer it is almost a Minerva birth. From childhood the boy springs full grown to manhood, the girl to womanhood. It is literally a new birth, a time when physical, mental, and moral changes take new departures.

The most marked physical characteristic is of course the rapid growth. At this time the normal annual per centage of increase in height, weight, and strength is from 15 per cent. upward.

Although in varying ratios, the bones—the arms, the legs, the thighs—all grow both in length and in breadth.

The brain, which has almost reached its maximum size at the eighth year, continues to increase slightly, while the skull shares in the general development of the bones.

Muscular growth, especially in the larger fundamental muscles, is also rapid. Lungs and chest are augmented in size, while the heart increases its volume from an average of 160 to 225 cubic centimeters, and during this period, quite reverses its relation to the circulatory system.

Previous to adolescence the heart is small while the blood vessels are large, but in the adult, the opposite condition prevails.

One noticeable feature of this rapid physical growth is its lack of harmony. Asymmetries of form and function in the right and left half of the body are common. The shoulders or head tips slightly, or the spine curves, or there is a disposition to lop or stoop in standing and sitting.

The muscular growth is out of proportion to bone growth, sometimes resulting, when the linear growth of the bone is less than that of the muscles, in flexibility of the joints; when it is greater, if the unequal tension is extreme, in contractures or warping of the bones. The characteristic clumsiness of the adolescent is largely due to this disproportion between bone and muscle growth, together with the rapid development of the larger muscles and the retarded growth of the smaller and finer muscles which make all the delicate adjustments.

Adolescence is an apparently healthy stage, when judged by the low death rate. Yet it is, in truth, a period susceptible to disease. Childish disorders are still in evidence, and adult diseases have already made their appearance. Anemia, hysteria, epilepsy, heart trouble, nervousness, headache, eye disorders, some forms of chorea, spinal curvature, and digestive trouble; are all more or less familiar.

In addition to the diseases peculiar to the age, city life, with its impure air, its liability to contagion, and its distracting hindrances to that repose which is so essential to youth—city life is directly responsible for much ill-health.

Many of the digestive troubles are due to unwise habits of eating, which again have their origin in the vagaries of appetite, which is "not an infallible guide to physiological needs." Stanley Hall claims that this is the nascent period for establishing a well-balanced dietary, and wisely suggests the value of judicious oversight eked out on occasion by a little wholesome authority. It is probably true that the greater number of breakdowns in later student life is due to errors in diet. Much of this ill health, which is neither illness nor health, but on the border land between the two conditions, is owing to physical unbalance.

If any of the vital organs fail to grow in proportion to the growth of the body, they are subject to strain, become unable to do the work required of them, and tend to collapse. Any strain or tension now is dangerous. Curvatures are likely to result from an ill-fitting desk, or from any occupation that requires an unnatural position, or produces strain or excessive confinement.

There is an especial risk in commenting upon the increased height of a child as in his efforts to reduce or hide it, he may assume a crouching position which will affect the shape of the bones or depress the chest, which in turn may affect the lungs. More than one case of this has come under my observation.

Doubtless, the most important physical changes are involved in the development of the sex function. These changes are of vast importance, physically and mentally, furnishing, as they do, some explanation of the mental and moral characteristics of the period; but they do not naturally cause the pathological conditions emphasized by Dr. Hall. Normal functions under normal conditions do not bring about abnormal results.

As the most striking physical feature at this time is the rapid growth, so the most prominent mental characteristic is emotional instability, which at the beginning quite overshadows the intellectual changes. New emotions come into being, old emotions are intensified; desires, vague yearnings are felt. There is a great influx of nervous energy, a desire to do things, a consciousness of self, which leads to that overassertion of individuality that shows itself in boastfulness; this is sometimes the expression of conscious weakness assuming a strong position. Altruism and self-interest struggle for the mastery. It is a period of introspection and reverie, of self-consciousness and self-criticism, sometimes extending to morbidness. Imagination runs riot, the youth sees visions and dreams dreams. His power of imitation is strong, a new interest in speech develops, the use of slang culminates, while the dramatic instinct is at its height. It is withal a *social* period; intense and devoted friendships are formed, interest in adults and a desire to be treated as adult shows itself. The old occupations and amusements no longer suffice, new activities and new interests are demanded. The future for the first time becomes all-important, the present is overshadowed. There is a widening of the child's horizon, he begins to recognize his relation to society, and is interested in social life as it reveals to him his own place and its meaning. This enlargement of the sphere of his interests makes it also a period of personal readjustment to the new point of view, and the effort on the part of the individual to reconstruct himself, as it were, the effort to meet the new situation, is the primary cause of the emotional disturbances which have gained for this age the title of the "storm-and-stress period."

The intellectual changes are no less important than the physical and the emotional. The higher thought processes show themselves. Reasoning grows more formal and elaborate. The child becomes more reflective. He is interested in principles and makes large generalizations. He discovers and formulates relationships. Details have now new meaning—they are instances or examples of some general law.

But with this coming into function of new desires and new interests comes also normally the evolution of the higher powers of control and inhibition, and if the physical and mental characteristics of the previous periods of growth have been developed under proper conditions, the educational problems of adolescence resolve themselves into one problem, i. e., that of adjustment to the social organism. If, however, the preceding periods of growth have not been properly utilized, they give rise to important adolescent problems.

We are slowly coming to see that there is an order of development, physical and mental, and that education must observe that order. The details have not yet been worked out, but enough has been done to point the way. The theory of nascent periods of development maintains that if any power is not exercised properly at its appropriate time, it will be arrested in its development. Mr. O'Shea has pointed out that a nerve center loses its plasticity when the wave of ripening moves past it to other centers; and this results, not only in the arrest of this particular function, but it influences other functions by interfering with the readiness of association between centers that can become connected only through the undeveloped one.

In all the organs, periods of growth seem to alternate with

periods of functional activity. A period of unconscious ripening precedes functional activity. Frequently, moreover, the period of functional activity is succeeded by a further period of unconscious growth or incubation, followed by another and higher manifestation of functional activity, and so on, growth and activity sustaining a sort of rhythm with increasing richness and development.

The period of functional activity is the critical period both for the function itself and all the functions associated with it. This period may be sustained by proper nutrition and a basis be laid for future strength. Or, by a lack of nutrition it may be retarded, the effect of which would be seen in arrested development.

If a child is compelled to repeat any form of activity, when in the normal course of development the attention should be upon a higher activity, the higher powers do not mature. The tendency is to remain on the lower plane. Every teacher knows with what distaste adolescents respond to drill and repetition in studies that they commonly regard as belonging to childhood while they are amenable to forms of discipline that they consider a part of the life of their contemporaries and elders. Shop work with emphasis on technique, gymnastics, military drill, *do* seem to make more or less appeal to them. The adolescent is not concerned primarily in getting *control* of a tool, but in *using* that tool to work out his ideas, thus enlarging his experience. Drill prolonged beyond the nascent period, or overemphasis upon thoroughness, or excessive devotion to detail, will result not in mental growth, but in the arrest of growth.

There is also that other danger which perhaps is more apparent than arrested development. I refer to forcing or overstimulation—so often the result of parental vanity—resulting in the precocious child, whose powers, like the hothouse plant, forced to early maturity, soon decay.

In childhood, the second division of the periods of mental development, the emphasis is upon the motor side. At this time the child is interested in the process rather than in the product. Dr. Donaldson believes that the development of the higher areas of the brain depends upon the development of the motor areas. Since the motor areas function first, they should be exercised first educationally. If this is not done, the higher areas, which are in a measure dependent upon them, can never be completely developed. Psychologically, this means that muscular experiences are essential to the gaining of clear definite effective ideas of the world.

Childhood is the period for play, which at this time is not only a factor in the child's present growth, but it is an element of future efficiency. Play is the vicarious living of the child. He goes through typical race experiences, experiments; discovers, and forms habits. Doubtless, to the fact that many children are deprived of these muscular experiences is to be attributed the vague, formless images which many adolescents hold. But the important thing is that the child must carry on an activity in order to comprehend it. In early life all activities must be lived out; but the central elements of these activities remain with the individual in generalized form, and as he grows older, these only are needed for readjustment. It thus follows that in maturity the mental activity finds it easier to gain the ascendency.

It is evident, if the lines of development that I have indicated are in the right direction, the duty of training the adolescent is for the home as well as the school. The work of each is distinct from the other, and yet in perfect harmony one with the other. Today we are asking ourselves the question, What can the *school* do in this direction?

We Americans are proud of our public school. We deem it the panacea for all individual and social ills, and the condition of higher development. How is it meeting the needs of this period of life? If I were asked to name the most vital function of the school, I should unhesitatingly say, "To give its pupils worthy ideals of life." Theoretically, the old ideals of mere study and brain work are passing. Theoretically, "the old order changeth, yielding place to new." The public school is not primarily to better the material condition of any child. Its justification lies in gain to the state in terms of citizenship, and just so far as individual advancement means increased responsibility for one's fellows, loyalty to the community through efficient service, constructive appreciation of property rights, both public and private property, and a recognition of group interests, to that degree, and that only, the interest of the state and the success of the individual are one and the same.

The purpose of the curriculum is not alone to advance the pupil in knowledge. Any adequate curriculum must take into account the *whole* child, physical, intellectual, spiritual. It must take account of his present stage of growth, must know the relation of his present to his *past,* must *utilize* his past experiences, and above all recognize his present working capital—his mental equipment—and make no attempt to go back of or beyond that. This curriculum must have its foundations in the culture already achieved by the race. It must look forward to the child's future, to the society in which he is to live.

The material that enters into this curriculum should be selected in accordance with the normal development of the student, and with the direct purpose of aiding in that development. It should be material that arouses his interest, that demands his highest effort, and answers his present needs.

We believe that the mental state is to some extent dependent upon the physical condition. The school can do much physically for its pupils, both directly and indirectly. First, the amount of mental work in early adolescence, especially for boys, should be replaced by a great deal of physical work. In this same connection, let me recommend increasing the time devoted to sleep. I've noticed that many young people often object to early rising. This is probably due to the fact that they require more sleep than they are accustomed to take. If your child must sit up late at night to prepare his lessons for the next day, something is wrong. Either he has unduly postponed beginning his preparation or the work required is excessive, or he is advanced beyond his ability. Studying late at night is not a virtue. There should be no undue strain in intellectual work. Study should be a pleasure, and there should be time for recreation.

Much less time should be spent in the schoolroom and much more spent in the open air, in walking or running or skating or swimming; in playing ball or tennis or golf; in games and amusements appropriate to the season. For indoors, there are dancing, fencing, basket ball, and other games and plays which combine recreation with the needed muscular development. Walking is an especially valuable exercise. The adolescent should not be sent to school in an automobile. High-school girls suffer from a lack of physical exercise at this the golden age of development. This is the period for exercising the larger fundamental muscles that move the trunk, large joints, back, shoulders, hips, neck, elbows, and knees. Formerly when industries were carried on in the home the occupations were such as developed these basal muscles. But with the advent of the shop and factory, the occupations which our young people carry on require only the use of the finer muscles. When this work is fine, exact, and overprecise, we have again the danger of nervous strain and tension. For this reason sewing and much fine needlework are not well suited to girls in the upper grammar grades. Other forms of textile work are better adapted to this age.

Direct physical training should be part of the daily programme. In this exercise special attention should be paid to carriage and bearing. The work should consist of free gymnastics with exercises on the apparatus. Stress should be upon the larger muscles. The result of this work should appear in dexterity, alertness, in grace and ease of movement, as well as in increased strength and power of endurance. The exercises given to girls should not be the exercises given to boys. By this I do not mean that they should be *easier,* but that they should be different—planned in each case to meet the needs of the differently developing bodies. Plays and games, recreative gymnastics adapted to the stage of growth should form part of this course. Withal the exercises should be co-ordinated and progressive, leading on the one hand to physical and mental control, on the other to that natural democratic spirit which comes when young people meet on a common plane. For all who need it, this course should include corrective exercises to offset the defects of the school and home life; or the misfits between environment and nature. The changed relation between the parts of the body lessens for the time their co-ordination and unity. This renders it a plastic period, a time when previous abnormal growths may be overcome, both by nature and by physical training.

The problem as Dr. Hall states it is how far "to stimulate each part in its period of greatest or least development; whether to stimulate the powers that excel, to their highest possibilities, or to emphasize drill on the weaker part."

The mental traits of the adolescent indicate quite clearly what should be the essential characteristics of the studies chosen. They must be reflective and comparative, to accord with the newly born capacities. The increased nervous and mental energy must be occupied by studies of increasing difficulty. The interest in speech and language must be met by the study of foreign languages and formal grammar. The emotional life must find its outlet through oratory and the dramatic art. The tendency to introspection and analysis must be satisfied by the disclosing of the inner connections and deeper reasons of the subjects taught. The newly aroused social interests must be fostered by the introduction of social work. The desire to do things must be satisfied by the opportunity for creative work.

The right of constructive work to a place in the lower grades of elementary school is now practically conceded, although the work to be *added* to an already full curriculum. From the standpoint of mental growth, it has an equal right in the high school. While the adult is able to some extent to readjust the central elements of his previous activities, motor experiences in young children are fundamental. The adolescent is in transition from childhood to adult life, and his mental activities are still more or less (mostly more) dependent upon his muscular experiences. And so I repeat, from the standpoint of individual efficiency or control, the industrial arts are essential to the high-school student. Mind is a function of social life. "It is only through the development of the whole race that any one man can develop." These arts are in their very nature social. They have grown out of man's efforts to meet the needs of life. Their development, to quote Miss Clara Mitchell, has resulted "in our present state of society with its sum of *knowledge* and stored up *power;*

knowledge organized into science, mathematics, history, civil law, philosophy; *power* expressing itself as skill in the arts of living—agriculture, manufacturing, commerce, social government, language, literature, and the fine arts."

Economic and social principles have guided the race in the evolution of knowledge. Should not the individual, the unit of the race, apply the same principles? Should we not introduce our young people to the typical lines of *human experience*, not only in industry and trade, but also in intellectual and social activities?

Many things indicate general dissatisfaction with the existing intellectual methods in our high schools. Chief among these is the fact that so many of the brighter students, especially boys, leave school before the end of their course. The complaint, when stated, is that these studies as carried on have no connection with life, that they throw no light on the vital situation which the youth finds facing him.

It is a significant fact that so many are enrolling themselves in technological schools. This movement toward industrial education is not in the direction of commercialism. It is to be interpreted as a demand on the part of students for vital contact with life processes—a direct first-hand knowledge of the factors which control society.

Whatever our individual prejudices on the question of the race problem, we must all acknowledge the insight and genius directing the educational experiment at Tuskegee. There we see an inferior race being raised to a distinctly higher level of civilization—to better citizenship—through industrial education.

In the George Junior Republic, and as near home as Allendale, we see a lawless class of youths through industrial and social organization brought to nothing less than a marvelous degree of moral action. Our technical high schools have proved that boys who have taken the manual-training high-school course enter college better equipped in the academic studies, and at an earlier age than those who have taken only the classical course.

In response to the demand for individual activity, we have introduced handwork into many of our schools. As yet the general public questions their value and denies their right in the school curriculum. Last fall a prominent lawyer, whose son has been in our school six years, told me that he did not believe in handwork. He thought it all right for young children, had not seriously objected to it before his son entered the eighth grade, but now he wanted him to do *serious* work—meaning by that mathematics, Latin, and English. He expected his son to be a lawyer, and manual training would be of no advantage in that profession. Perhaps, rather doubtfully, it was all right for every boy to know *some* trade, yet none of the boys in the School of Education would ever follow a trade, and he really didn't see why this work had a place in the school.

The gentleman expressed a common point of view regarding social occupations. He perhaps expressed your own sentiments. They are good for young children, for the colored race, the laboring, and the lawless classes. But for your own children you want something more. And in one sense you are right. A smattering of knowledge, a minimum of skill in woodwork, metal-work, pottery, weaving, cooking, gardening, sewing, modeling, drawing, painting, bookbinding, or printing is not educative in the highest sense. Knowledge and skill in the fundamental processes of any or all of them, training for trade, does not necessarily educate. Only when these activities come into the school as vital parts of the curriculum, only when their social value is felt by all the workers, are they a means of education. When the work is broad enough and in sufficient variety to interest every pupil, when it is great enough to use all his powers, when it is connected with nature on the one hand and society on the other, it will be to the children the educational instrument it has been to the race.

It is the social and historic phases which make the difference between work as a trade and educative work, between the artisan and the artist. The one is material, the other spiritual, leading upward to a higher plane of living.

When the youth in the schoolroom is engaged in the activities that he sees going on in the larger world about him, he encounters difficulties which he cannot surmount except by the help of science. So the facts and principles of physics and chemistry and botany come in to aid in his daily living. He meets problems whose solution leads him to the past. History then throws light on his present, and becomes a living study. The interest in the work leads naturally to a study of the raw materials, to a study of the finished products, to comparison of the various methods, past and present, used in securing these products. It leads to an understanding of the facts and forces of the industrial world, organized industry, and commerce. It interests the students in the lives of other workers in these various kinds of work and their relation to the social whole. It forms the background for all industrial and social history. The pupil comes to all subjects a questioner with problems that have grown out of his own experience. Learning is no longer a matter of *memorizing*. Knowledge becomes the realization of a subject through a living experience; and so constructive work opens up all knowledge, affords training for all the mental faculties, socializes the individual.

We have introduced the social occupations into the school, but we have not yet socialized the school, so that these activities fall into their normal place. And herein lies the weakness of the present situation. A socialized school is one that organizes society to help the individual, one whose chief aim is to develop in the individual the power for and the inclination toward social usefulness.

The socialized school uses gymnasiums, studios, workshops, and laboratories as means of developing a socialized being. It is necessary that the individual should have experience in every one of the fundamental activities which have built up society before he can have an intelligent appreciation of the society. But the work of socialization in the individual is but half done when this fundamental experience has been gained. A further and equally important function of the school, and we have not always done this, is so to organize these various shops, studios, and gymnasiums, that the community life, thus brought about, may in itself call out the highest effort of each individual and return to him the larger culture which rightfully should be his.

The socialized school must organize itself in such a way that the school life is one with the community life, so that the youths are co-operators in the work of the world.

SOCIALIZING THE MATERIALS AND METHODS OF EDUCATION[1]

JOHN A. KEITH

I. Social efficiency of the actual and ideal types, as the dominant aim of education, and, therefore, as the dominant aim of all school work, is acceptable to all persons who are concerned in the process of education, viz.:

1. The philosophers, idealists, materialists, pragmatists, etc.
2. The statesmen—who seek social welfare—in office or out.
3. The public—who pays the bills, and furnishes the pupils.
4. The politicians—who echo the public.
5. The schoolmasters—who actually do the work, for it is a concrete and progressively realizable ideal that vitalizes every aspect of school work.

II. The deepest law of human nature is: *One becomes by being.*

1. Skill grows out of successive and repeated co-ordinations.
2. Qualities of mind are the outcome of processes.
3. The possibilities or potentialities bound up in a child at birth become realized or actualized *only by the activities of that child.*

III. These activities of the individual are of two types:

1. Those activities due to stress from within—unfolding or developing activities.
2. Those activities due to stimuli from without—infolding or integrating activities.

[1] Syllabus of address given at the Schoolmasters Club, Peoria, October 12, 1907.

Our conception of *cause* should be so modified as to include the mutual interconnectedness of things—sound—pencil—desk—air.

IV. The principle in III (above) yields the corollary that the activity of the mind, whether in the form of development or in the form of integration, is educative.

V. The fundamental problem of education and of the school is so to condition children that through their developing and integrating activities they may progressively become more socially efficient.

VI. The old idea of school work was to select certain *fundamentals* of effective living and present these to the child with the hope that he might some day come to appreciate their value through his use of them.

VII. The present idea of school work (or, at least, the one to be defended this morning) is to select certain significant aspects of the life about the child and present them in such a way that he progressively grows into a deeper appreciation of them—and thus comes to the *fundamentals*—to the *grounds of his own living.*

VIII. To state the idea differently, a child cannot really *study* anything except in so far as he can, through his own mental activities that are connected with it, secure *significance,* and significance is meaning, is felt mental relationship.

IX. The life of the child is inevitably matrixed in social relationship (even the nature about which he cares most is that which is connected with social uses and social estimates), and the greatest growth of the child into social efficiency is clearly in building up a wider and deeper significance (to him) of those relationships that radiate from his present social life into the life around him. (The line of least resistance is also the line of greatest educative effort.)

X. The so-called "subjects" of the curriculum are social products—are aspects of a past and existing social life, and have their values for education because of the increased social efficiency which their mastery confers on one.

XI. It follows (from the two propositions just preceding) that the "subjects" of the curriculum should receive an organization which is social and psychological rather than logical. This means that the child should approach the subject from that aspect of it which connects himself with others, and should proceed in it in accordance with his own ability to gain increased significance. (Wherever there is a priority of relationship which is necessary to mastery, the social and psychological organization is also logical.)

XII. The logical organization should be a secondary movement by the child, as it has been in the race, rather than a primary one.

XIII. Only in this way can school education be *genuinely practical* at every stage of its process.

XIV. The primary method of learning, in the race as in the child, is involuntary experience which includes spontaneous, impulsive, and instinctive movements, and suggestion.

XV. The derived form of learning, in the child as in the race, is planned (or purposed) activity, including imitation, invention, and discovery.

XVI. Imitation is the basal form of social transmission.

XVII. Invention and discovery are the basal forms of social progress.

XVIII. Since society is progressive, social efficiency demands that the child become inventive and discoverative.

XIX. The great thing in elementary and secondary education is to bring the child up to the present level of society, by making use of his tendencies to develop and by integration, in such a way that he is efficient and progressive.

XX. What is meant by socializing the materials and methods of education may be illustrated by a consideration of nature-study:

1. Criteria for the selection of materials:
   a) Select materials which reveal the controls which men have developed in their efforts to satisfy their felt needs.
   b) Select laws or uniformities which men have discovered and to which they conform in order that they may the more advantageously satisfy their felt wants.
   c) Select materials which have gained a social significance because of the curiosity and aesthetic activities of men.
2. Criteria for organization of materials:
   a) Begin with that aspect of the material which already has greatest significance to the child.
   b) Proceed in the order of the questions that arise in the child's mind.
   c) Provide for elaboration (working over) so that the temporary mental organization brought about by the child's perception of relationship (catching on, understanding, apperception) may become relatively permanent mental structure.
3. Criteria of method:
   a) Awaken in the child a sense of the value, to self or to the race, of the material to be studied.
   b) Arouse the inventive and discoverative attitudes toward the selected material.
   c) Provide abundant situations which require the communication or expression of the relations learned.
   d) Cultivate through construction (all forms of actual as opposed to symbolic doing) the social values of, the social estimate of, and the social attitude toward, the materials dealt with.

HISTORY OF CHICAGO. II

PEARL BACKUS CARLEY
Third Grade, Francis W. Parker School

CHICAGO OF LONG AGO

THE FIRST INDIAN TROUBLE

One day some Indians went into the Lee cabin frowning. Usually the Indians say "How." These Indians looked very cross and did not say a

MODEL OF FORT DEARBORN AT CHICAGO HISTORICAL BUILDING

word, but kept on frowning. The people in the Lee house were frightened. Two of them ran to the fort as fast as they could. They stopped at every house they passed and told the people to run to the fort. When they got to the fort they talked the matter over and decided what they had better do. And there was no more trouble.

THE MASSACRE OF FORT DEARBORN

In 1812 word came to Captain Heald to vacate Fort Dearborn and leave for Fort Wayne, as the English had already captured Detroit. Captain didn't think it safe enough to go alone for fear of an attack. Next day he held a council with the Indians and asked them to take him safely to Fort Wayne. He promised them all the ammunition in the agency house, and even more. That night everyone was so discouraged that Captain Heald himself saw what he had done. The following day when the Indians came to get the ammunition Captain Heald said he did not have time to give it to them. They decided to destroy everything and wanted time to do it. The

Indians knew at once that he meant to keep them out of it. At night they got as near as possible to the fort; they could smell the liquor in the river, and could hear the soldiers throwing the ammunition into the well. The next morning all started out along the lake shore. It was all right until they came to some sand dunes. Then the Indians went behind the sand hills. Some of the men noticed it. They told the others to get ready to fight. The chief of those Indians was Black Partridge. He once had received a peace medal from the government. The morning they left he went to the fort, put the medal on the table and said, "I tried my best to keep peace, but my warriors want to fight." An Indian had told Mr. Kinzie to get into a boat with his family. Mr. Kinzie put his wife and children in the boat. He said, "I am going to stay with the others. If something happens I want to help." In a little while the Indians started to fight. Many were killed. Mr. Wells said to the Indians, as they were going to kill the women and children, "Shame on you to fight against them. If you do that I shall go to the fort and attack your squaws and papooses." He went away. Some Indians followed and killed him. As one Indian was attacking Mrs. Helm, Black Partridge came and took her to the lake and held her in the water up to her neck. He pretended he was drowning her. That is the way he saved Mrs. Helm. The Indians afterward burned the fort, but Mr. Kinzie's home was not hurt. The prisoners were taken to Detroit and ransomed.

HILDEGARDE PABST

PROBLEMS OF TRANSPORTATION, WATER SUPPLY, AND DRAINAGE
PART II

AFTER THE WAR OF 1812

After the war of 1812 the soldiers spread the news all over the country of Illinois' good farming-land. They told about the good location Chicago had, about its good soil, vast prairies, and good timber land. Chicago had good waterways. You could travel from the Gulf of Mexico up the Mississippi River, up the Illinois River, up the Desplaines River, across the Chicago Portage, and through the Chicago River into Chicago When the people in the East heard about the good land for raising corn, wheat, and oats, people began to come to Illinois. In 1816 Captain Bradley was sent to rebuild Fort Dearborn. This time the fort was much larger than it was before. The logs that were used the second time were hewn. The government, meanwhile, had a treaty with the Indians for canal land. They were going to make a canal across the Chicago Portage. The people in the East thought what good waterways Chicago would have, and began to come.

GILBERT S.

FLAT BOATS

Some of the people built flat boats and keel boats and came down the Ohio River. When they came to a place they liked they stopped. Sometimes they would take their boat to pieces and build their cabin out of it. If they wanted to go up the Mississippi River they took a rope and put it around a tree ahead of them, and then they pulled up to that tree, and then they put

Flat Boat

Settling in Illinois

the rope around the next tree, and pulled up to that, and so on up the Mississippi River. They had to do this because they were going against the current. They would do this until they found a place where they wanted to stop. Sometimes they would go into the woods and cut down trees and build their houses.

James F.

TRAVELING IN PRAIRIE SCHOONERS

When people traveled in prairie schooners they sometimes went through woods. The men had to get out and chop down trees and make their own

TRAVELLING IN PRAIRIE SCHOONERS

roads. Sometimes they had to wade through streams. They stopped wherever they liked the location, where there was good farming-land, and usually near a stream.

SARAH G.

TRAVELING FROM BUFFALO

A tired party in two prairie schooners were going slowly along the lake shore on their way to Chicago. They had covered about 500 miles, having come from Buffalo. Three young men walked by the side of the wagons. Their clothes were spattered with mud and they looked as if they had more than once put their shoulders to the wheels. The roads were very bad, it seemed as if they had been out of one mud hole and into another all day. The horses looked as if they were pretty well tired out. The lighter of the two wagons was drawn by one horse. The heavier wagon was drawn by two horses. They had just left a tavern and had forty-two miles to go before they could reach another. They were going to travel along the lake shore near the sand. They unhitched the two horses from the heavy wagon, and had them pull the lighter wagon over to the shore, down where the sand was packed. It was easier to pull there. It was three o'clock in the afternoon before the large wagon overtook the small wagon. The old horse could go no farther, all urging could not make him move another step. Then they decided to turn the old horse loose.

A storm was coming up, the sky looked threatening, and they decided to have supper and camp for the night. They had hardly sat down when the threatening storm broke over their heads. They gathered all the food they could in the short time they had, and jumped into the prairie schooners. The three young men got into the smaller wagon. They thought they had the best of it, because that wagon carried the mattresses and blankets. But toward morning, the cover blew off, and they were drenched with rain before they got it back.

In the other schooner the people sat opposite each other and all were holding on to the cover to keep it from blowing away. The next morning they prepared breakfast; it was not easy to get because all the wood was saturated with water. They left the heavy wagon upon the beach, with all in it that they could spare, and pressed on with the smaller wagon.

They had written to a friend at Chicago to meet them with some oxen, and they were hoping that soon they would have the oxen to help them.

Travelling in a Sledge.

That day the friend did meet them with his oxen. It was easier to go along then. The two horses were almost dead, but they were not so tired but that they could help the oxen. They all reached the tavern.

The next morning the three young men went back with the oxen and horses for the schooner that they had left behind. At night they were in among the sand dunes and had to sleep in two inches of snow for a change. They had some pine twigs at their heads and a roaring fire at their feet. They rolled up in blankets and slept finely. They found the wagon the next night, just as they left it. They ate slap-jacks and honey for supper, and had a good time of it.

Tyler P.

TRAVELING IN A SLEDGE

Long ago in winter people used to ride in sledges instead of sleighs. Oxen pulled the sledges.

Margaret P.

TRAVELING IN AN OX CART

Mr. Beaubien came from Detroit in an ox cart. He had an Indian to guide him. He got knocked around because it was so humpy and the cart didn't have any springs.

JAMES F.

OX CART

PACK HORSES

TRAVELING ON PACKHORSES

A family was traveling from the East on packhorses to Chicago. Mr. King was walking in front with his dogs, and carrying a rifle. His wife was riding horseback. Behind her on a horse were some pots and dishes and things that were needed for cooking. They did not take any meat with them. They only took salt and cornmeal, because Mr. King expected to get meat by shooting deer or wild turkey in the woods. There was a small path that they were following, which was called an Indian trail. Another horse was tied to the back of Mrs. King's saddle. One packhorse carried a rake, a piece of iron for a plow, and small farm tools. These things did not have handles, except the hatchet, which was used on their way to cut firewood. One horse carried two baskets, a basket on each side. The baskets were filled with bedclothes, and in a hole in the middle of them the children sat. Other packhorses carried household goods. The hired man walked behind, to see that nothing was lost, and he also kept the cattle together.

GILBERT S.

MR. AND MRS. KINZIE'S TRAVELING EXPERIENCES

Mr. and Mrs. Kinzie started from Detroit to Ft. Winnebago. Mr. Kinzie was to have charge of the Agency House there. They took a steamer

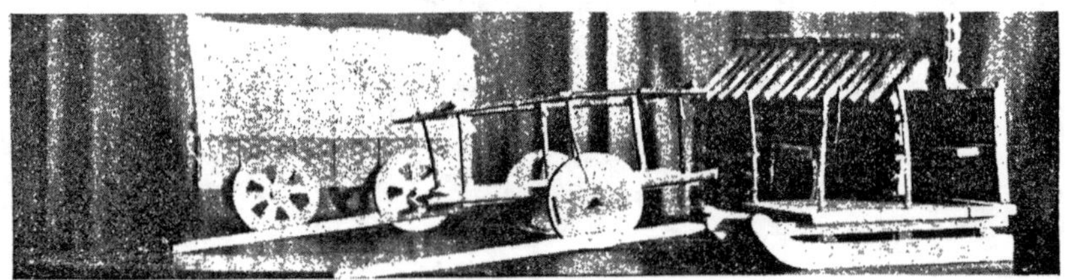

MODELS MADE BY THIRD-GRADE CHILDREN

and were much pleased that they were not going to travel in a schooner, as some of their friends had done, and were three months going from Detroit to Chicago. Even now a sailing-vessel can sometimes cover that distance in four days. I think our boats must be built in a very much better way nowadays.

HAROLD W.

They had a pleasant trip for the first twenty-four hours, but a storm came up and the rain was so severe that it made its way through the seams of the deck, and everything in the ladies' cabin was saturated. They went to the gentlemen's cabin, but it then began to rain there, and they had to get into the berths. Their dinners were served to them on their pillows. The gentlemen chose the dryest spots and sat around under umbrellas. They finally reached Mackinaw, and afterward went on to Green Bay.

FRANK P.

There a boat came for them from the fort. These Mackinaw row boats, as they were called, were thirty feet long. The center was a framework of posts covered with canvas, which could be let down at the sides and ends. A mattress was placed in the cabin and could be used at night if too unpleasant for camping.

HELEN S.

Mr. Kinzie took with them three Canadian boatmen, besides the crew of soldiers. These boatmen helped take charge of the boat, put up tents, lighted the camp fires, and prepared the meals. They usually dressed in tanned deer skin and wore red sashes and caps. JOSEPHINE P.

On their way they came to many rapids. If the rapids were very swift, the boat and baggage had to be carried to shore and on to smooth water.

MARION C.

Sometimes in rather shallow water the boat would get fastened between two stones. Then the men would all have to jump overboard and push and pull until the boat was released. Then they would get in and go on rowing in their wet clothes. LUCY S.

If the rowing and work was very hard they rested often. The French Canadians always smoked while resting. It was the custom for them to stop every six miles to rest and smoke, so in measuring distances it was so many "pipes" instead of so many miles. JAMES B.

When the rowing was easy they often sang funny little French songs, and the oars kept time to the music. Sometimes they sang:

Row, brothers, row, the stream runs fast,
The rapids are near, and the daylight's past.

KATHERINE T.

At night when they camped the boatmen pitched their tents, collected wood for the camp fires (they had no matches in those days but used flint and steel), and prepared the supper. The Frenchmen knew how to make delicious coffee. They broiled ham, using forked sticks, and made toast, bringing it fresh from the coals. They used tin plates and tin cups. Mrs. Kinzie enjoyed these suppers very much. Being out of doors all day and so thoroughly enjoying the scenery and the trip gave her a good appetite.

OWEN W...

They reached Ft. Winnebago after having traveled eight or nine days, and now that distance can be covered in four or five hours.

ROBERT M.

After Mrs. Kinzie had been at the fort many months she decided to visit their relatives in Chicago. They started one March morning. All were horesback, a packhorse carried the provisions and blankets, and each traveler carried his own hunting-knife. A tincup was fastened to each saddle, as no mess-basket could be taken. A canoe was put in an ox cart, which was to take them over a stream and a marsh beyond, which at that time of the year was covered with water. DOROTHY W.

The stream was crossed in safety, then they came to the marsh. Mrs. Kinzie's trunk and saddle were placed in the canoe. She got in and sat on the trunk. Just as Mr. Kinzie was going to push off and jump in, the two hounds, not liking to go through the cold water, gave a spring and landed on Mrs. Kinzie, upsetting boat, trunk, Mrs. Kinzie, and all. Mr. Kinzie then thought it best to carry her cver like a papoose. She did not stop to change her clothes, but rode on to a suitable camping-place.

MILDRED Z.

The tent was pitched and furs were spread down, and Mrs. Kinzie got into dry clothes. Her riding-habit was taken to the fire to dry, but it froze stiff, looking as if the lady had mysteriously disappeared from it.

DORIS H.

OLD FASHIONED FLINT AND STEEL

The weather grew colder, and before the horses could swim across the streams the ice had to be broken with an ax. One of the guides would mount a horse and reach out in front of him and break the ice so that all of the horses could swim over.

FREDERICK G.

One night it snowed and the wind was so strong. and the snow so heavy that the tent poles broke, and down they all came on Mrs. Kinzie. She had never traveled in the West before and was not properly clothed. She started with a straw hat and kid gloves. The wind was so cold that she used her husband's silk handkerchief for a veil.

FRIEDA M.

Sometimes they were able to stop at a cabin over night. One time they lost the trail and provisions became very scarce, but they found an Indian who guided them the rest of the way. They were all very happy when they finally reached Chicago. CHARLES W.

STORIES OF VILLAGE LIFE

In the early days of Chicago the people did not have the conveniences that the people have today. They did not have the daily mail, but they did

OLD FIRE PLACE

COUNTRY STORE

have a mail carrier who came from different towns. He had to camp out on the way, and kill birds and game for his meals. New York papers were two months old when they reached Chicago, but people were glad to get them. The matches were used as curiosities, and they used flint and steel to light their fires. JOSEPHINE P.

OLD-FASHIONED FIRE-PLACE

They used this fire-place in olden days for heating the house and for cooking. They baked their bread in a baking-pot, and hot wood ashes were put on top and under it.

DEDRICK P.

A COUNTRY STORE

Usually at a country store they sell a little of everything, dry goods, groceries, and sometimes mail would come there too. People would come to

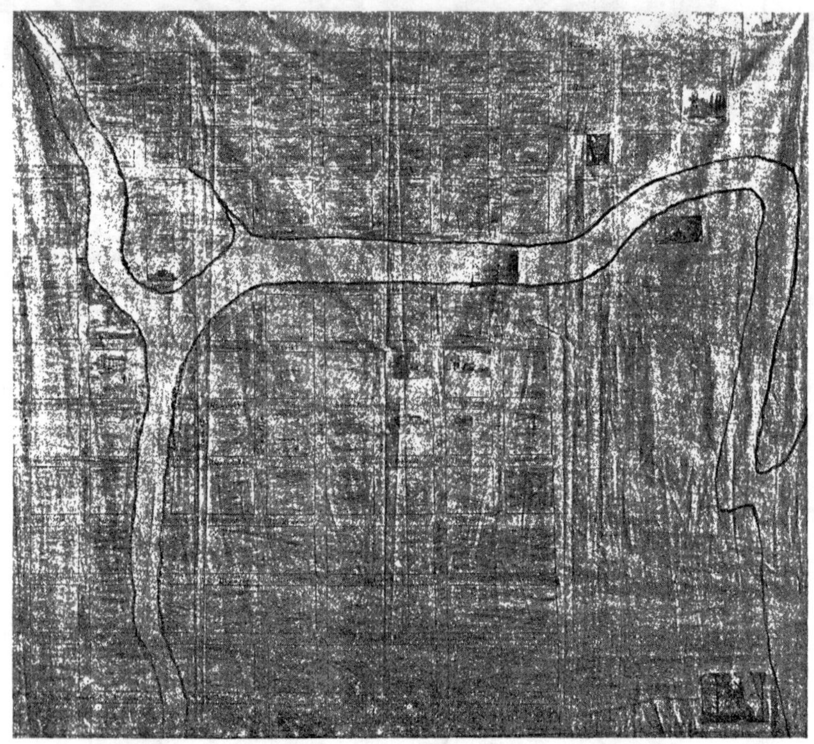

MAP OF EARLY CHICAGO

the store to get the mail, and sit around the stove and talk. Some of them would not get any mail, then the others would read theirs out loud.

MARGARET P.

STREET PROBLEMS

THE FIRST MAP OF CHICAGO

A long time ago the streets were crooked and muddy. The streets wound about from house to house. The people picked out the driest spots on which to build their log cabins. In 1830 the government sent surveyors to survey the canal land. They made the first map of Chicago, and the streets on the map were nice and straight.

SAMUEL B.

CHICAGO STREETS

Chicago was built on swamps. The streets were very wet and muddy. Sometimes wagons full of goods for the Chicago stores would get caught in the mud. The people said, "We must have better streets." One man said, "Have the streets slope to the river, and plank them." They did this. But when it rained muddy water settled beneath the planks, and when a team of oxen would step on one of the planks dirty water was splashed all over. Then a flood came and washed away the planks. This plan did not work. Then they said, "No more digging down for us."

HELEN B.

LIFTING CHICAGO OUT OF THE MUD

Chicago was unhealthful. The streets were bad. The people tried to fix them. Mr. Chesbrough's plan was this. He said, "We must raise the streets."

STREETS OF EARLY CHICAGO

The people laughed at him, but after a while they thought it would be best to follow his plan, so they did. Just at that time they were widening the river, and the dirt that was taken off from widening the river was used to make the streets higher. Some of the houses were raised up to the new street level, and some were not raised. So they had to have steps leading up and down.

MARGARET P.

OLD PLANK ROADS

At the time Chicago's streets were so muddy very few farmers came to bring in goods. So people said, "We must make better country roads too." They leveled the dry places. Most of these roads had been trails made by the Indians in traveling. These trails after leveling were planked. The man who had given the planks and who was to keep the road in good condition would put up a toll-gate. Wagons would be stopped by a pole across the road. The gate-keeper would ask for money. That money was used to keep the roads in order.

HILDEGARD P.

ILLINOIS AND MICHIGAN CANAL

People of Chicago said if Chicago had a canal their trade would be better. So the government bought the Chicago Portage from the Indians. The government sent surveyors to divide the ground into lots. These lots they sold to people who wanted to buy land. With the money the government started to build the canal. But alas, there was not enough money, and the banks failed all over the country. They left the canal, and weeds grew in it. Several years after the banks failed some rich men said to the government, "We will pay for the canal, and all the boats will have to pay toll until we get back as much money as we have spent. Then you can have the canal." The government said they could do that, so they hired some workmen and the work began again and in a few years the work was done.

FOWLER McC.

WATER SUPPLY

RIVER WATER

Years ago the river was so clear that you could see yourself in it. The water was blue and sparkling, and good to drink. People built little piers out into the river. They took wooden pails and went out on the piers and dipped the water up. But people grew careless after a while and threw garbage into the river. Then they could not drink the water. They felt they must get clean water to drink, and to cook things with.

LUCRETIA C.

SWEEP WELLS

People tried many ways to get water. The sweep wells were one way. But after a time that failed. The people grew very careless and threw their garbage and dishwater and other impurities on the ground. These impurities sank into the ground and spoiled the wells. Chicago looked very funny in those days. The sweep wells were a great deal higher than the houses.

MATILDA D.

WATER CART

A man said, "I know how to get pure water for Chicago. Why, there is plenty of pure water in Lake Michigan." People said, "Then get us pure water." So he got a hogshead and put it on a wagon. He went to the lake every morning, filled his barrel and drove around town. Ladies came out and said, "Fill my barrel." But too many people came to Chicago and the water wagon could not suppy them all.

SARAH G.

WATER SYSTEM—LOG PIPES

A company thought they could make money pumping water to the different houses. They built a pier 150 feet out into the lake. They laid pipes on the top of the pier. They turned the end pipe down into the water. The pipes were made of logs with holes bored in them lengthwise. They had an engine on shore to pump the water into a tank. Then it was pumped through the wooden pipes underground to the houses. This plan did not work well because the water was taken from too near the shore. Little fish came

Old Water Works

through the faucets, and little sticks that were floating in the water. The people had to pay for this water, and some were too poor to buy it. So some drank from their old sweep wells, some took from the river, and some still bought from the man with the water cart.

Arnold H.

FIRST CITY WATERWORKS, OR GETTING CLEAR WATER THROUGH A TRENCH

After the pier plan for getting water failed the people thought that if the city paid for good waterworks the water would be better and cheaper. Then the city hired some engineers. They worked for three years. They built a trench on the bottom of the lake. They turned the end of the pipe up, instead of down. When they finished it they built a crib over the bent-up end. They had a waterworks with a pump. Then they built a big brick tower. Then the engineer started the pump. It was a happy day for the people, because they thought they were at last going to have good water.

Fowler McC.

SECOND CITY WATERWORKS

After Mr. Chesbrough had built the tunnel and crib the people thought they would have pure water. But the sewers emptied into the river and the river emptied into the lake. The new cribs were built farther out into the lake but still the water was not pure. The people said, "We must dig a drainage canal so the river will flow backwards and take the sewage down the canal. Then the lake and river will be pure and clean." The drainage canal was a great success for Chicago. It did its work and the water was much better than before. But still the water is not pure, because the sewers

PLAN OF CRIB AND TUNNEL LEADING TO PUMPING STATION UNDER LAKE MICHIGAN

empty into the lake up north and the current of the water sends the sewage down. There are people who examine the water from the different pumping stations, and the newspapers tell when the water is impure, and suggest boiling or filtering.

GILBERT S.

BEACHES

Almost all the beaches along the north shore of Lake Michigan are on the north side of the piers. They are on the north side because the current comes from the north. It is farther out in the lake and brings great masses of sand in and the waves take it to shore. The people wrote to the government that the old mouth of the river was too shallow for boats to come through.

HILDEGARD P.

CHICAGO HARBOR

The river used to empty into the lake at Madison street, but the current of the lake brought sand into the mouth of the river. There was a long sandpit there. After a while the government sent men to cut a channel through. But that was not successful. The sand drifted in, and men were constantly dredging it out. Then the government built a government pier running east and west. But still sand drifted in. Then they built it longer. The government built another pier, running northwest and southeast.

MARGARET P.

OUR RIVER TRIP

We got on a little launch called Chicago and went out to see the harbor. We saw the lighthouses and life-saving station, and the oldest slip. The boat turned and we went up the south branch of the Chicago River. We saw many grain elevators and lumber yards. We visited one of them. We saw the old Illinois-Michigan Canal, and the Drainage Canal.

HELEN B.

We saw some canal boats that were used on the Illinois and Michigan Canal. They were used long ago for carrying freight, and sometimes for

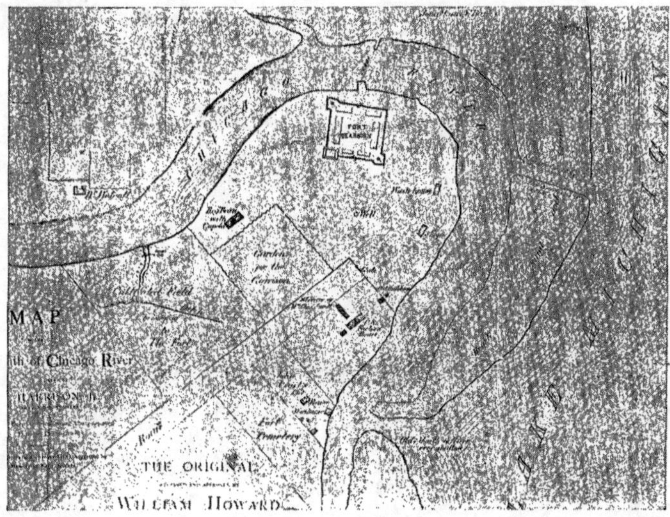

CHICAGO HARBOR

traveling. Then they were drawn by horses which walked along the bank. We saw one boat loaded with coal. Now the canal boats are drawn by tugs. Long ago the farmers brought all their grain to the city in wagons, but the roads were so muddy that the wagons got stuck. The canal was built so that things could be carried to market by water. In this way Chicago got much more grain and that helped Chicago to become a great city.

HILDEGARD P.

When our launch passed the place where the north branch joins the south we could see a distinct black line across the river. The north branch is all oily and bad. The south branch is lake green. Years ago all the river was like the north branch is now. The river used to flow into the lake, and made the drinking water impure, so Chicago built the Drainage Canal. The canal is six feet deeper at the west end than at the east, and is about twenty feet deeper than the lake. There is a plan to clear out the north branch. All the sewers on the north shore empty into the lake and the current brings it down here. The plan is to dig a big canal that will empty into the north branch and make a current, so as to clear it out.

We saw a few flat boats loaded with dirt coming from the north branch They are making the river wider.

FOWLER McC.

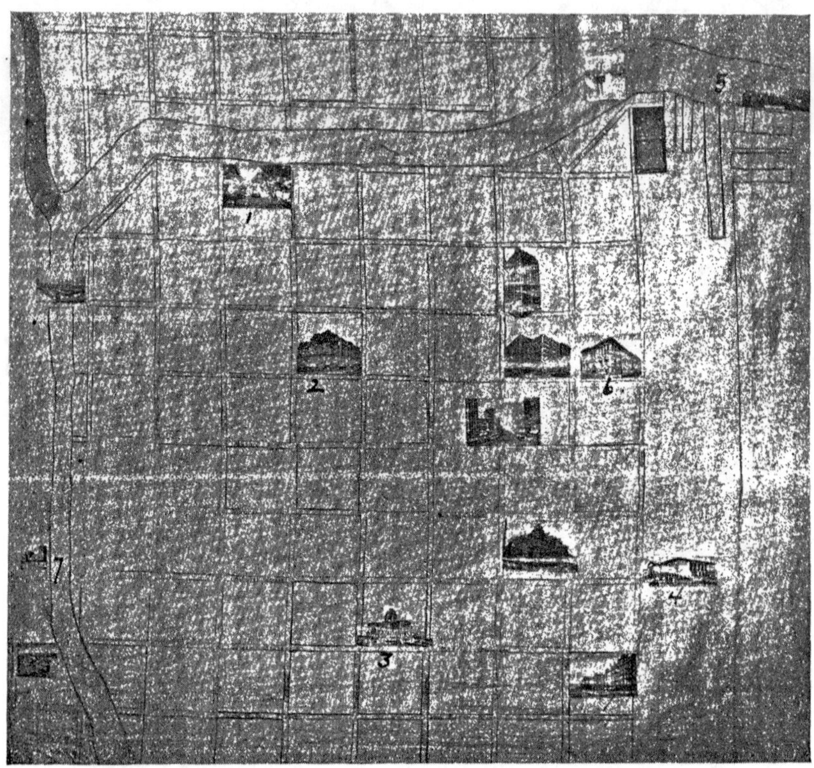

MAP OF CHICAGO AT PRESENT (PICTURES CUT OUT AND PASTED ON BY CHILDREN) 1 South Water Street; 2 Court House; 3 Post Office; 4 Art Institute; 5 Warehouses on River; 6 Public Library; 7 Union Depot.

In selecting the foregoing material from the work of the children, the purpose is to show rather fully what has been done along a few selected lines, transportation, water supply, and the various street problems. As the study of Chicago has seemed to be well adapted to stimulate the interest and activity of the third-grade children, it has been a subject of study in that class for several years. Each entering class has the benefit of what has been done by the preceding class, and also the incentive to leave something well worked out for classes to come.

The eighth grade has for several years also worked upon certain phases of civic development in Chicago, and thus—by

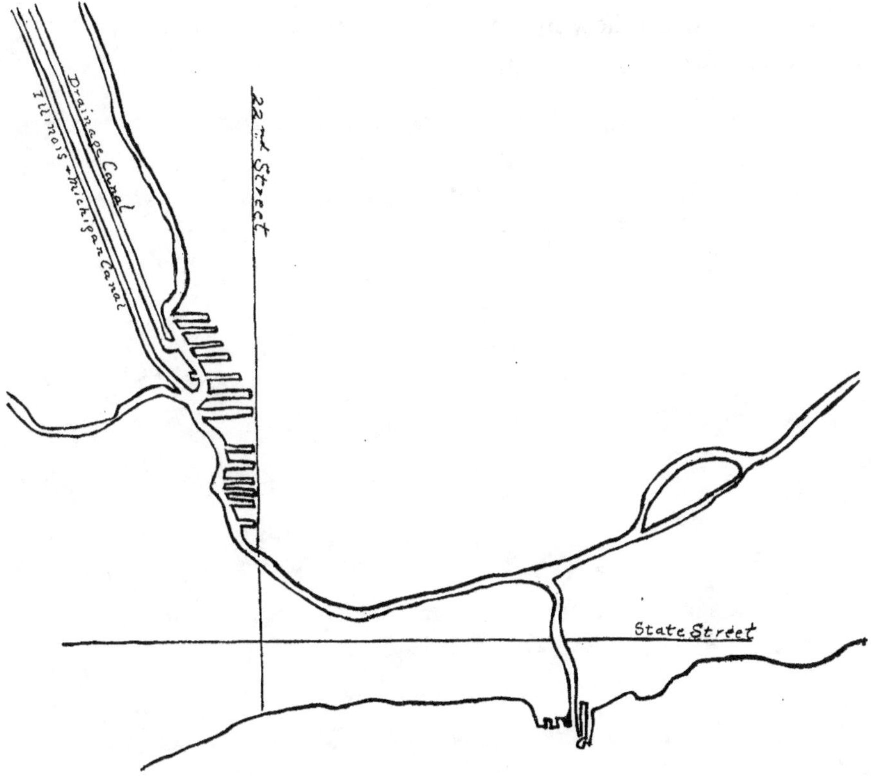

means of morning exercises—have kept the interest which has been awakened alive and growing in the children's minds throughout the entire school course.

It has been impossible in this article to show the full scope of the work. The use of the stereopticon, for taking imaginary trips to the swamps, on the lakes, to the Drainage Canal, and the actual trips to industrial centers, and the use of supplementary reading-slips can only be suggested. The work in construction, such as the making of flat boats, prairie schooners, sledges, ox carts, and trains, has been omitted; also the experimental work, although the experiments in connection with the purification of water, and those in connection with illumination—such as candle-making, generating gas, collecting gas, piping to the houses—are most valuable and educative experiences. A description of the work in construction, as given by the children in a morning exercise, will follow in the succeeding number of *The Elementary School Teacher.*

READING FOR LITTLE CHILDREN.—PART III

ELSIE AMY WYGANT
Second grade, University Elementary School

The six reading-lessons in this and the January number complete the series outlined in the October issue. Five are stories taken from Stanley Waterloo's "Story of Ab," published by Doubleday, McClure & Co., New York. These are not continuous, being Nos. 2, 6, 7, 8, and 9 of a series of these adaptations. The remainder, Nos. 1, 3, 4, and 5, were published in this journal, January, 1907.

It is with every apology that these are offered, and only in appreciation of the fine literary quality and dramatic element in the original were they ever attempted. These very elements are the qualities to be desired in even the beginnings of reading for little children, because they give a motive sufficient for, and a value equivalent to, the immense effort which a child puts into his first reading. Therefore with no desire for originality, and only a hope of retaining something of Mr. Waterloo's spirit and so much of his forceful phrasing as the demand for simplicity would allow, these sketches were constructed.

To use them isolated from the original text would be deplorable. The plan is to read Mr. Waterloo's story to the children sufficiently so that they get into the spirit of the thing. Then instead of reading, or before reading, one of these incidents or situations, such as "Meeting a Hyena," "Old Mok," etc., the children are given one of these adapted sketches to read.

The desire to know more of a story which they have gotten into furnishes motive for reading, the rapid action and short sentences adapt them to children's ability, but they are valuable only because suggestive of the larger, richer background which the original story holds.

The "Story of Zitkala-Sä" is taken in much the same way

from her own article published some years ago in the *Atlantic Monthly,* entitled, "The Story of My Indian Girlhood." In reading the article I was anxious that children should get that sense of first-hand knowledge given as simply and picturesquely as Zitkala-Sä herself gives it, and to that end the following is retold, using wherever possible the language and phrasing of the original.

THE STORY OF ZITKALA-SÄ

A tepee of weather-stained canvas stood at the foot of some hills.

A path led gently downward to a broad river.

Here morning, noon, and evening my mother came to draw water.

Always when my mother started I stopped my play to run along with her.

I was a wild little girl of seven.

I wore a slip of brown buckskin.

I was light footed, with a pair of soft moccasins on my feet.

During the summer my mother built her fire in the shadow of our tepee.

In the early morning our breakfast was spread on the grass west of the tepee.

My mother would sit by the fire and toast the dry meat.

It smelled good as it toasted.

I sat upon my feet near her eating my dried meat with bread and drinking strong coffee.

We were alone at breakfast.

At noon anyone who happened to be passing, stopped and ate with us.

But I loved best the evening meal.

That was the time the old stories were told.

When the sun hung low my mother sent me to invite the old men and women to eat supper with us.

I ran all the way to their tepees.

When I reached the door I said, "My mother says you are to come to our tepee this evening."

"Yes, yes, gladly I shall come," each replied.

I ran back skipping and jumping.

I told my mother, "Yes, yes, gladly they will come."

When they came I sat close to my mother.

We sat around the open fire.

When we finished eating, each in turn told a story.

I put my head on my mother's lap, and lay flat on my back and listened.

I watched the stars as they peeped out, one by one.

The old people said funny things and we all laughed.

Then we heard the wolves howl.

I was frightened, and got into my mother's lap.

She put more sticks on the open fire.

Then the bright flames leaped up higher.

I saw the faces of the old folks as they sat around in a great circle.

An old woman was telling a long story.

I fell asleep before the story was finished.[1]

[1] The stories which this daughter of the Dakotas heard are retold by herself in *Old Indian Legends*, retold by Zitkala-Sä, published by Ginn & Co.

MEETING A HYENA

It was a long, long time ago that a little brown baby lay asleep in a forest.

He lay on a bed of leaves under a beech tree.

When he awoke he began to cry.

His mother ran to him and tossed him in her arms.

He crowed and laughed and kicked his feet.

Suddenly she heard a sound.

She listened.

Then with her baby, she leaped and climbed into the beech tree above her.

She reached its high branches just in time.

Below her rushed a horrible wild beast.

It snarled and smelled the ground as it ran.

It was a dirty brown color, striped with a lighter brown.

It had a black nose like the snout of a hog.

Great fangs stuck out of its jaws.

I was a hyena hunting for food.

It was well that the mother and baby were safe in the tree.

There in the tree the mother laughed as the wild beast leaped toward them.

She knew that they were safe but her baby, little Ab, was hungry.

So she sent a strange call through the forest.

A call came in answer.

Again and again she called.

Nearer and nearer came the answer.

Soon the father came in sight.

He was not walking on the ground but swinging from branch to branch along the tree tops.

He knew by the call that there was danger below.

When he reached the beech tree he swung down beside the other two.

In his belt was a great stone axe.

He saw the hyena leaping below.

He too laughed at the wild beast.

He too knew that they were safe in the tree, but it was time to go home.

So he broke a great limb from the tree.

With this club he struck the beast as it leaped upward.

Then he swung down from the tree and killed the hyena with his stone axe.

Now they were safe.

Father and mother and baby went off through the forest to their home in the cave.

OLD MOK

As Ab grew older a little brother and sister came to live in the cave too.

The brother's name was Bark and the little sister was called Beechleaf.

One day when Ab was about ten years old, someone else came to live in the cave.

This was a man who was bent and old.

His hair was grizzled and his beard was short and stiff.

Below his skin robe, one of his legs was twisted and it was shorter than the other.

Mok was a cripple. He could not travel about nor hunt.

But his arms were strong and his fingers were skilful.

He had been a great hunter when he was young.

In fact he had been crippled in a hunt by a fierce cave tiger.

Now he could not hunt, but he could tell wonderful stories of beasts and birds and swimming things.

And best of all he could make stone weapons.

He could make better weapons than any man in the valley.

Therefore each man wanted him to come to live in his cave.

So old Mok had lived first with one and then with another.

But now he had come to spend the rest of his life with his old friend One-Ear.

Ab liked him at once, and Mok grew to love Ab more than anyone else in the world.

WEAVING IN THE ELEMENTARY SCHOOL

KATHARINE FRENCH STEIGER
Supervisor of Domestic Art in the Schools of Rochester, N. Y.

It has been truly said there is nothing new under the sun. As teachers and educators we plan year by year new courses of study and gather data from every source, but the most we have done has been to make an application of the principles which Froebel taught to the world before we were born. Broadly considered, standards in education at the present time are practically the same.

We agree that the development of the individual parallels that of the race; that the child is a distinct entity and not in any sense a diminutive adult; we translate subject-matter into terms of value, and in attributing to studies their relative worths, we regard the present as well as the future of the individual, or rather, we consider the present and hence the future of the individual. Method too is a determining element in the value of a study, for the worth of any instruction depends largely upon its manner of presentation. We note the dual nature of the educational problem; sociologically, the relation of the individual to society, and psychologically, the relation of the individual to himself. Notwithstanding all these signboards along the pedagogical way to avert a marked deviation from the true course, every traveler in a sense makes his own pathway, showing footprints distinct and individual. Each year, each section of country, and each pupil present problems which demand of the teacher careful consideration and tactful planning. The unquestioning acceptance of past standards do not lend themselves to open-mindedness and individual initiative. No one has entirely reared the superstructure of education needed today, so even the humble worker in a limited field can make observations which may furnish a contribution to the general good.

It is in this spirit that I enter a plea for handwork in the elementary school which will be vital and far reaching as an ethical influence. Generally speaking, one need no longer question the value of manual work or its claim to a stimulation of the mental faculties. Of course, I mean manual exercises which are not misfits, but logically based upon principles which make them of the highest possible value.

The one exercise however which seems to have been assigned a lower place than it merits in the scale of relative values is weaving. Of all the occupations for little fingers, with the exception of clay-modeling, there is none it seems to me which appeals to the child's interest and develops sustained application more fully than simple textile weaving. We recognize its value as a social occupation, we know that racial development has been along this line, that it is the earliest industrial art practiced by primitive peoples, and that pottery and textile remains are the books which reveal to us the life-history of a dim past. We know also that well-chosen exercises in weaving afford an opportunity for the child's initiative, choice of material, taste in color, originality in pattern; in other words, that they offer an opportunity for real development to the maker, through self-expression, after having acquired a small degree of skill of hand. Further, that textile materials and processes properly handled bring the user into contact with the industrial and geographical sources from which they come, giving much information in regard to the origin and meaning of the things made and the materials used. So the exercises given in the schoolroom by an alert teacher mean more than the making of a series of articles. An important part of the training lies in thus bringing before the child concretely much of the number-work, history, geography, and literature, which it interprets and makes applicable to the life of today.

It is interesting to note that teachers in various parts of our country, working independently of each other, have come to practically the same conclusion, namely, that clay-modeling and textile weaving furnish the basis for a systematic course in industrial work that shall be a means for helping the children to interpret the steps of human progress and that shall at the same time provide means of gaining an intellectual and practical control as progressive problems are met and solved. When one seeks some tangible evidence of this foundation, however, the results are not always encouraging. As I have already said weaving seems to have fallen low in the scale of educational values, much of the work being trivial in character and lacking in gradation and variation. Some of the reasons for this are obvious. The large number of pupils which the grade teacher has under her supervision, the difficulty of obtaining suitable materials for the work, the demand made upon the public-school treasury for this purpose, the slowness of the process, the articles made usually requiring time, patience, and a degree of skill not possessed by the average child; all have contributed to this result.

Some of the difficulty lies in our trying to imitate too closely the best efforts of primitive peoples. Rugs of overfine material and belts of rather intricate pattern are attempted in the second grade as well as in the fourth or the fifth grade. Preceding such work should come simpler exercises of course, pliable, inexpensive material leading up to the finer product. Under right laws should we not have a carefully planned gradation from coarse to finer work, the objects made leading up through the primitive to those suitable for school and home use? In the lower grades the textile arts are and should be largely social occupations. The things made should have a definite use and fill an immediate need. But is this a reason why overfine and rigid material should be used? Can we not get something better than paper, reed, splint, and raffia for developing little fingers and little lives? Is the weaving-needle with a spring to clasp flimsy paper strips a better tool than the fingers themselves in the kindergarten and the first grades?

One condition of socialized work is that it shall benefit not only the community but the worker himself. As a social organizer it is primarily the function of the teacher so to plan community work that it will be of the greatest value to the individual child. *What* to do, *how* to do it, and *what kind* of material to use have become the practical problem of today. For little people we must utilize materials soft and pliable, and the first tools should be the fingers. The beginning and the ending of woven pieces, even the simplest, present difficulties to the average child. So it seems to me as a forerunner the more plastic material, clay, should be used freely in the kindergarten and first grade. The weaving of these grades should be crude, coarse, and free in character. The clothing processes of the cave men, of the Lake-dwellers of Switzerland, of the North American Indian, of the Eskimo, of Hiawatha and Robinson Crusoe, the furnishing of a playhouse and the dressing of dolls, all contribute subject-matter for crude primary work.

If the little people are in localities where they can gather neighborhood grasses, twigs, and husks, and utilize them in their own way, the lessons will be appreciably richer. Familiarity with the sheep, the cocoon, the cotton plant, and flax, with the kind of weaving shown in birds' nests and in the lace tree, with the fine threads spun by spiders and caterpillars will lay a foundation for later work in the higher grades. There the processes of spinning, carding, and weaving, properly understood, lead to an intelligent understanding of the work of the modern machine and some introduction to the great social problems of today—child labor, the sweatshop system, home economics, industrial betterment, and social ethics.

In the schools of Rochester last year an attempt was made to introduce a systematized course of weaving based on educational principles. As these processes stand in close relation to the textile arts, the history of all mankind being implicated with the evolution of flax, wool, and cotton fibers into cloth, the weaving was made a part of the domestic art department. For convenience, however, it is taught to the primary-grade teachers by the special teachers of the manual-training department. The course begins with simple exercises for the kindergarten and the first grade, largely co-operative and closely related to the classwork. In the two lower grades the looms are furnished; they are also shifted from class to class, thus reducing expenditure somewhat. In the third and the fourth grades the pupils construct their own looms and also a crude spindle and whorl. Original patterns and color arrangement are also attempted. The warping is a steady gradation from simple to more difficult, while the spacing is based on the number-work of the respective grades

—one inch, one-half inch, one-quarter inch, etc. There is also oral-language work in connection with all courses. Practice is not confined to a few skilful hand-workers. Each pupil is given an opportunity to make some article of inexpensive material, while those who show skill are allowed to repeat the exercise using better material. By this method expense has been minimized. Waste and labor have also been reduced appreciably by putting into the hands of the grade teacher definite directions for the care, cutting, and distribution of materials. The city of Rochester has a population of two hundred and eighty thousand. Last year the expense of weaving-materials for all the schools amounted to less than five hundred dollars.

No attempt has been made to cover in one year the entire course of study, only one or two exercises, meeting present needs, being attempted in any class. If the child has responded to the purpose of his work, gaining in sympathy, self-control, and responsibility, the making of one object means more than a whole series wrought without this human insight. Social occupations along textile lines in the primary grades have led to special work of an excellent character in some of the grammar grades. Articles really worth while have been made for the home with a minimum expenditure of time and money. So the results are by no means discouraging though the crowded curriculum last year gave opportunity for nothing more than a mere beginning. Even in its incompleteness, the course has been adopted by the Mechanics' Institute of Rochester as a part of the training given students in preparation for public-school service.

The work done in the schools last year is as follows:

First grade.—Book bag (based on the Lake-dweller's fishing-net—an exercise in tying, knotting, and interlacing; looms furnished).

Second grade.—Doll's hammock; doll's muff and tippet (exercises in looping, braiding, and weaving; looms furnished).

Third grade.—Doll's hood or toboggan (measurements of dolls' heads taken and suitable looms constructed); small bath rug.

Fourth grade.—Bath slipper (loom made by child and constructed according to individual foot measurement); doll's Tam O'Shanter (based on measurement of doll's head).

Large co-operative pieces along the same lines were made in some classes, and were by no means a tedious occupation.

The complete outline of the course planned, a copy of which is placed in the hands of every grade teacher, is as follows:

KINDERGARTEN

Materials.—Swamp grasses, flat reed, husks, rags, Holland, braid, felt, etc.

Applications.—Rugs, matting, mats, porch curtain, etc. (For this class warp and weft should be free, not continuous.)

Language-work.—Talks on the sheep and wool; on the use of the loom and weaving.

FIRST GRADE

Materials.—Kindergarten materials, roving, coarse yarn, etc.

Applications—Repeat kindergarten exercises, fishing-nets, book bag, braided rag mat woven in circular form. (In this grade, use a continuous warp and a free weft.)

Language-work.—Talks on wool (simple story of raw material found in Poullson's *Child's World,* p. 413); talks on wool-washing and dyeing in simple form. Explain the meaning of warp and weft.

SECOND GRADE

Materials.—Roving, woolen and cotton yarns, twine, rags.

Applications—Repeat kindergarten exercises, fishing-nets, and history, weave dollhouse furnishings, mattings, nets, rags, curtains, bed spreads, table covers, table mats, also doll's muff and tippet. (In this grade use a continuous warp and weft.)

Language-work.—Talks on cotton and hemp; stories of raw material in Poullson's *Child's World,* p. 421. Explain the meaning of warp, woof, and selvedge.

THIRD GRADE

Materials.—Same as for previous grades.

Applications.—Mat made of rags, braided and sewed, Indian belt, marble bag, school bag, bean bag, coarse cushion cover, table cover, doll's clothes, hood or toboggan based on head measurements. (Construct a spindle and whorl, also a simple loom.)

Design.—Plan a school bag with colored borders.

Language-work.—Talks on flax (*Child's World*, p. 426); talks on carding and spinning.

FOURTH GRADE

Materials.—Any available materials.

Applications.—Purse for small change, handkerchief bag, protectors for large bags, baby socks, bed shoes, tea cozy, child's Tam O'Shanter or hood, rug, porch cushion, etc., set of table mats, cord or raffia. (Construct loom; use heddle or shed stick.)

Design.—Make a colored design of some article to be woven.

Language-work.—Talks on silk (worm, cocoon, raw materal, and manufactured articles. Keep these talks simple).

GRADES V, VI, VII, VIII; OPTIONAL WORK

Exercises.—Original work, study of tapestries, Indian rugs, etc.

Applications.—Textile furnishings for the home.

Suggestions.—Hammocks, rugs, covers for chairs, table, couch or pillow draperies, sets of table mats, woven borders for decorative purposes. Visit woolen mills if possible. (Navajo loom-principles of construction.)

In conculsion let me say that an old story has been retold, but I hope it will come with a new meaning to my fellow-workers. St. Paul's admonition: "Prove all things, hold fast to that which is good," applies here. The educative process is not yet complete. Someone has compared it to a circle not entirely closed. We are giving the child a large opportunity through subject-matter and method to derive ideas from his environment. If we give him an equal opportunity to use these new impulses in uplifting his environment, the circle will be nearer completion. It is no light task to train for a sane citizenship. This is the ultimate aim of all forms of art and handwork that have found a place in the school curriculum.

THE TROLLS' CHRISTMAS

GUDRUN THORNE-THOMSEN
The University of Chicago Elementary School

Scene I

(*A cozy room. Christmas Eve. The Christmas tree stands lighted in the middle of the room.*

Six children, the father and mother are singing and dancing around the tree when curtain rises.

Song—"This Tree Was Grown on Christmas Day.")

1st Child—Hush! I think I hear St. Nicholas at the door!

(*Children run to the door.*)

All—No, not yet.

2d Child—It was only the wind.

3d Child—I do wish he would hurry up and come.

4th Child—Let us tell stories while we wait.

5th Child—I'll tell you a story. Come, let us sit under the Christmas tree.

(*Children group themselves under the tree. 5th Child recites, " 'Twas the night before Christmas, when all through the house," etc., until the line, "I was sure 'twas St. Nick." A loud knock at the door; all the children get up, run to the door calling:*)

All—There he is, there he is; open the door.

(*Enter St. Nicholas nodding and smiling.*)

6th Child—Oh, I'm so glad you have come!

1st Child—We've been waiting so long.

2d Child—Are you cold?

3d Child—You must be tired.

4th Child—Come to the fire.

5th Child (*brushing off the snow from St. Nicholas' coat*)—Oh, you dear, kind St. Nicholas, what have you brought to us?

St. Nicholas (*looking from one to the other*)—Well, have you all been good children?

All—Oh, yes!

St. Nicholas—Then you shall all have *something*, but I have only half as many presents for you this year as I had last.

Children—Why?

St. Nicholas—I came through the North country, there I peeped into many homes and I found children who had little to wear, little to eat, and no Christmas presents at all. I gave half of your gifts to them. Did I do right?

Children (except 1st and 2d Child, Axel and Lottie by name) —Of course you did right.

St. Nicholas—(looking at Axel and Lottie)—Didn't I do right?

Axel—Last year I had twenty presents, and this year I'll have only ten.

Lottie—And last year I had thirty presents, this year I'll have only fifteen. The trolls will have a better Christmas than we.

Axel—Yes, I'm sure the trolls will have a much better Christmas than we.

St. Nicholas (looking sadly from one to the other)—Very well, if you want to see the trolls' Christmas, come with me. *(Grasping each by the arm, hurries out with them. They resist and call:)* Oh, no, no; let me go, let me go.

(Children, father, and mother run after them.)

Father and Mother—Axel! Lottie!

Curtain.

Scene II

(The foreground of the stage represents a forest, snow on the ground and on the pine trees. Back of the trees, and not seen when the curtain rises, is the trolls' cave. Darkness. Enter St. Nicholas with Axel and Lottie.)

St. Nicholas—Here you are. I have other and pleasanter business to attend to.

(Exit St. Nicholas.)

Axel (peering around the trees)—Lottie, where are we?

Lottie—St. Nicholas has left us; we are all alone. (*Wolves are heard howling.*) What's that awful sound?

Axel—O, sister I think it is the wolves howling.

Lottie—Axel, I'm afraid, oh, so afraid, and it is so dark, and I'm so cold.

Axel—Let us see if we can't find a house. Come sister you must be brave.

Lottie—I am so tired, Axel, I can't go far.

Axel (*who has been hunting for shelter among the trees*)—There, look there. I think I see a cave among the rocks. It will save us from the wolves at least. Come, Lottie, come!

(*The forest is removed. Children are seen entering the cave. They scream.*)

Lottie and Axel—The trolls!

Scene III

(*The trolls' cave. Darkness. King and queen of the trolls on thrones. A number of trolls sitting in a circle in front. Axel and Lottie crouching in a corner. Servant passes refreshments.*)

Troll Queen—I like snakes best. Ah, king, this spider was delicious!

1st and 2d Troll (*fighting*)—This snake is mine. No, mine, mine. I'll have it!

3d Troll (*blowing*)—This icicle is hot!

4th Troll—Stop stroking the cat, it makes it so light it hurts my eyes.

King (*rises*)—This is our great holiday. It is getting colder and colder, darker and darker. Soon there will be nothing but ice and snow in the world, and no light at all. Then we, the trolls, shall rule the whole world.

Trolls (*clapping hands*)—Hurrah, hurrah, we, the trolls, shall rule the whole world.

King—Send for the messenger.

(*Enter Messenger.*)

King—What did you see?

Messenger—I saw a faint glow in the east.

King—Go back and watch again.

(*Exit Messenger.*)

King—Let us dance.

(*Trolls caper about in a circle to Grieg's music, "In the Trolls' Hall."*)

King—Send for the messenger.

(*Enter Messenger.*)

King—What do you see now?

Messenger—No light at all, perfect darkness, perfect darkness.

All—Good, good, perfect darkness.

King—Now let us have a merry song.

Trolls (*singing*)—

Oh, who is so merry, so merry hi, ho,
As the gay little troll, hi, ho, hi, ho,
He dances and springs
To the tune that he sings
With a hey, and a hi, and a ho!

(*All turn summersaults. Messenger comes running, face covered by hands.*)

Messenger—Oh, Oh!

Trolls—What is the matter? What is it? Speak, speak!

Messenger—A light in the east! A bright, shining light I saw. It has blinded my eyes, I cannot see.

King—What can that be? Who can tell us what that means? (*Silence.*)

1st Troll—There, see, there are some children from the world; ask them.

King (*beckons to Axel and Lottie. They step before him*)—I can turn you into wolves, or frogs, or snakes if I please, but if you can tell me what that light in the east is, I'll let you go.

Axel—It is the star of Bethlehem.

King—What does that mean?

Lottie—It means that a babe was born this night, and he is the light of the world.

King—What is this baby's name?

Axel and Lottie—Jesus Christ.

(*Light enters the cave. Trolls' moan and fall to the ground turned to stone.*)

Axel—Look Lottie, look, the trolls! The light has turned them to stone.

Lottie (*feeling them*)—And they are icy cold.

Axel—Lottie, what shall we do?

Lottie (*looking and pointing to the light*)—The star, the star shall lead us home!

(*Children walk hand in hand looking at the light.*)

Curtain.

NOTE—The children of the Third Grade of the University Elementary School assisted in the making of this play. They had been studying the beginnings of trade and commerce as seen through the voyages of the early Norsemen, the climate, the character of the country, and the industries and customs of the people today. They had been told something of the Christmas festivities and of the customs that mark the season. They had also been told many of the old folk-tales from which they had gathered the Norse conception of the troll.

The troll takes the place of the Jotuns of more ancient myth. The Jotuns were the spirits of evil; they were known through cold, darkness, and winter death, while the heroes of Asgard were the powers of light, warmth, life, and goodness. When Christianity became the religion of the people the trolls gradually assumed something of the rôle formerly played by the more powerful Jotuns. The trolls are small, mean, mischievous spirits. They are little men, dwelling near to men in the forest or in the hills. The Jotuns were terrible and great, and dwelt afar off in the icy mountain heights. As in the old myth, the smile of Balder could overcome the evil Jotuns, so in later tales the sun or light is the force which can annihilate the troll power; or, as the tales symbolize it, "turn the trolls to stone."

From the most ancient days the people celebrated the coming of Balder, the turning of the sun again to the earth, and the beginning of returning warmth and life. The Christian religion did not utterly reject, but assimilated some of the old customs and reanimated a few of the old symbols in its Christmas festival which falls at the same time of the year as the older festival.

Among the stories told the children were "The Land East of the Sun and West of the Moon," and "The Trolls in the Hedal Forest," as told in

Popular Tales from the Norse, by Dasent. The play is freely adapted from a modern story by Zacharias Topelius.

The music used for the scene in the troll-king's palace is Grieg's "Troll-Dance." The music of the Brownie song is found in Reinecke's *Fifty Children's Songs,* and the Christmas song is "The Christmas Tree," by Myles Foster, and is found in the *Primer,* "Modern Music Series," Silver, Burdett and Co., publishers.—Editor.

CHRISTMAS SONG

CHARLES KINGSLEY | L. A. COONLEY–WARD

From *Songs in Season*, A. Flanagan, publisher. By permission.

EDITORIAL NOTES

NOTES FROM THE MEETING OF THE NORTHERN ILLINOIS TEACHERS' ASSOCIATION [1]

If the general trend of thought displayed at the recent meeting of the Northern Illinois Teachers' Association is any index of progress in teaching in the section of country there represented, we have reason for great encouragement. The topic was, "Nature-Study and Geography." Both the prepared addresses and the discussions showed a strong movement in the direction of real experience as the basis of all work from primary grades through the high school. Not only this, the speakers who took part in the discussions, almost without exception, urged the organization of geography and nature-study from the human standpoint, and about a large and rich organizing center. The "choppiness" of the old teaching of geography came up for the strongest kind of denunciation. The necessity was emphasized of so enlisting the pupil's interest that problems would arise out of his own desire for meaning and relation.

In the discussion of Mr. Otis Caldwell's paper on "Criteria for the Selection of Material in Geography and Nature-Study," Mr. Charles A. McMurry called attention to the unity from the first to about the fourth school year in subject-matter of nature-study and geography and then said that in discussions too often the general principles of teaching a subject would be laid down and the detail of selection would be left untouched. He said that we must go on from criteria of selection to selection of materials in a course of study; must not be afraid to risk our principles, but proceed to the detail of topics, and the treatment of topics throughout a progressive course. He said that the problem for all teachers was now a practical one, namely, "What is the outcome of theory?" He gave as his solution the conviction that for each school year the work in nature-study and geography should cluster about a few large topics, saying,

[1] Meetings held at the University of Chicago, November 1 and 2, 1907.

The best topics in any study are those that the study in itself is not big enough to hold; children can be most sincerely interested in a big comprehensive subject.

He suggested the topics, "The Farm," "Forest," and "Garden," as offering a combination of manual work and scientific and practical study. The coal industry was given as an example of a study that could be made far reaching in its ramifications, if studied as an organic thing; the transportation, machinery for blasting, hoisting, and weighing, the geography of coal-producing areas, the origin of coal, and the force of the coal industry in determining the whole question of manufacture in this country; the conditions under which the miners live, economic relations. All these gave to the topic great richness. The following quotations give the trend of Dr. McMurry's further discussion:

Any topic worth studying at all is worth studying in three or four different subjects. . . . . If education concentrates, we must pick out our topics not so much with relation to the logic of particular subjects, as with the view of illuminating these large relationships; and any teacher who is not big enough to deal with such a topic in its varied relationships is not big enough to deal solely with any one subject.

The great world is *one,* not two or twenty; this conception is not the only determining one in the selection necessary for forming a course of study, but it is a great one.

The increasing complexity of modern life is responsible for a complexity of studies in their interrelations; the course of study must throw light on these different and complicated social forces; history must show the development of man's institutions; natural science throw light on the application of the great inventions that have revolutionized industry, and art must bear an ever closer relation to modern industrial life.

The content studies all converge at one point, namely, in modern life, and topics must be selected from that point of view.

A growing and developing idea is what children need; every great topic is capable of upward development.

CRITERIA FOR ALL DETERMINATION IN THE COURSE OF STUDY

1. Large topics, reaching out in all directions, into other studies.

2. Topics found in types. Types are concrete problems, realities, but may contain in their development far-reaching generalizations. Illustration: In the study of one great commercial city we have the type of all.

The discussion of the grammar grade and high-school section in the afternoon centered about the paper: "An Outline for a

Course of Study in Nature-Study and Geography for the Period of Adolescence," by Miss Zonia Baber. Both the paper itself and the discussion which followed it showed the same prevailing tendencies as were evidenced in the earlier session. In the absence of Miss Baber, Mr. Wallace Atwood gave a brief analysis of the main points in her paper:

1. Adolescence is a period of enlargement of interests, of adjustment to a larger world. Study should be extensive rather than intensive; should cover a wide range.

2. Problems should arise from the industrial or practical side of school work, and schools should be so organized that these problems would appear naturally.

3. The work in these subjects, as in all others, should tend toward greater social efficiency in the pupils.

4. Reasons for the decrease in numbers electing science work in the high schools.

5. Necessity for fieldwork.

Mr. Atwood said in conclusion that the paper was written on a broad philosophic basis, from the general motive of the establishment of controlling principles.

Mr. John Tear opened the discussion with an expression of harmony with the general point of view of Miss Baber's outline. He confined his attention to points one and two of Mr. Atwood's analysis. He agreed entirely with the idea of approaching problems from the human standpoint and said:

The school should be an organization for activity and should organize interests. The child should have as vital an interest in the processes engaged in at school as the man has in his business. In such a school only, can social efficiency be developed.

I should not quite agree with the statement that work should be extensive rather than intensive; I think it can be both extensive and intensive to great advantage. The medium of the "type-study" gives this possibility. The type-study is so far reaching in so many lines that it gives the quality of extensiveness, while being intensive; in method it is extensive in being interpretative of similar conditions or places. Take, for example, a study of the wheat industry in the fifth grade; the interest becomes immediate and vital while the implications geographically, industrially, and scientifically are very broad.

In answer to the question, Why is science decreasing in popularity as a chosen subject in high school? I would say that considering geography "as she is taught," very few grammar-grade children would elect it if it were made optional; since no election is allowed there, all take it. Nor should the high school be allowed to elect.

The notion that science is a body of truth, fixed, absolute, and eternal; and the maintenance of a corresponding attitude on the part of the teacher is responsible for a great measure of the lack of interest in geography and science in high schools. If geography is taken up from the industrial side in the fifth grade and is carried out on the same fundamental lines in later grades, the children will begin to be ready by the seventh grade, or certainly by the eighth, for geography *per se.* In the ninth grade geography might be treated somewhat from the logical development of the subject, in the form of physiography, or physical geography. The more abstract sciences would follow.

In the eighth grade the child begins to become conscious of need for some systematic study. He will not get much out of systematic study until he comes to it with a great deal of knowledge, a great number of facts that have come to him vitally and that are crying out for reorganization. For example, the study of physics should come when he has had much experience in an informal way with the phenomena falling under that head and begins to feel the need of their relation to a larger whole.

Another aspect of the centralization of subjects was brought out in the discussion of the paper by Miss Marian Weller on "The Principles of Presentation of Geographic Material," namely the importance of presenting material in such form to children that they would grasp the causal relations existing between phenomena.

Miss Weller's thesis was as follows:

In the "old" geography, place and location formed the content of the subject-matter, and facts appeared wholly isolated and unrelated. This "new" geography of ours presents a striking contrast, in looking at the subject from a distinctly human view-point; in recognizing man as the unifying element.

Those principles, therefore, which, according to our modern ideas, should underlie and control the presentation of geographic material in the elementary school, may be stated in a general way, as follows:

1. The human element should be most prominent. Man in his social and industrial environment is the central figure, and therefore geography should be presented from the human point of view.

2. Causal connections and relationships should be looked for at each step, and there should be a constant relating of man to his environment through his own needs, so making geography in its broadest sense a "study of the earth in its relation to life."

3. A first-hand knowledge of geographic facts and conditions at home

is essential in order to have a basis for the understanding of those conditions which are far reaching in their effect upon peoples.

4. Concreteness of material and illustrations should be aimed at.

In the discussion of this paper Dr. Herman Lukens said that he would add to the fourth point the idea of concreteness not merely for the purpose of having a graphic presentation but because concrete material embodies causal relation. He believed the course of study should be organized to this purpose—to bring out causal relation. Dr. Lukens thought the usual study of geography was too fragmentary, that mere skeletons of life were taken up for study, not real, live, active conditions, he said:

> Material must be made over, and organized, to be sure that the causal relations are brought out, like the dramatist, the teacher, must choose elements artistically; the presentation must be of real life, but done as a work of art.

Dr. Lukens cited the type-studies of Dr. Charles A. McMurry as an example of concrete topics involving the presentation of material about some great situation until it becomes clear in its causal relations. He gave as an example the study of Niagara Falls and the great lakes extending over several weeks, covering the geology, history, manufactures, utilization of water power, great cities and reasons for their growth; afterward touching lightly on one or two other lakes and lake systems for comparison. He said that these causal relations must not be stated but must be thought out by the children, and to give them geographies that do state relations explicitly is to defeat one's purpose, which should be to have the work of discovery and organization done by the children. In speaking of contact with realities he said:

> No arm-chair philosopher could have discovered the causal relation between the earthworms and the soil; the discovery was the result of observations made *on the ground.*

B. P.

BOOKS RECEIVED

MAYNARD, MERRILL AND CO., NEW YORK

Graded Literature Readers—Sixth Book. By Harry Pratt Judson, LL.D., and Ida C. Bender. Cloth. Illustrated. Pp. 256. Two copies.

Graded Literature Readers—Seventh Book. By Harry Pratt Judson, LL.D., and Ida C. Bender. Cloth. Illustrated. Pp. 256.

Graded Literature Readers—Eighth Book. By Harry Pratt Judson, LL.D., and Ida C. Bender. Cloth. Illustrated. Pp. 256.

HENRY ALTEMUS COMPANY, PHILADELPHIA

Mother Goose's Puzzle Pictures. By Howard E. Altemus. Cloth. Illustrated. Pp. 77. Two copies.

W. H. WHEELER AND COMPANY, CHICAGO

Wheeler's Graded Readers—A Primer. By Gail Calmerton and William H. Wheeler. Cloth. Illustrated. Pp. 128.

AMERICAN BOOK COMPANY, NEW YORK

The Jingle Primer. By Clara L. Brown and Carolyn S. Bailey. Cloth. Illustrated. Pp. 128.

Carpenter's Industrial Reader—Foods. By Frank G. Carpenter. Cloth. Illustrated. Pp. 362.

Natural Introductory Geography. By Jacques W. Redway and Russell Hinman. Cloth. Illustrated. Maps. Pp. 146. $0.60.

Natural School Geography. By Jacques W. Redway and Russell Hinman. Cloth. Illustrated. Maps. Pp. 186. $1.25.

An American Book of Golden Deeds. By James Baldwin. Cloth. Illustrated. Pp. 304.

W. M. WELCH COMPANY, CHICAGO

First Lessons in Handicraft. By Maud Summers. Cloth. Illustrated. Pp. 100.

THE MACMILLAN COMPANY, NEW YORK

The Story of the Iliad. By Rev. Alfred J. Church, M.A. Cloth. Pp. 221.

Bacon's Essays. Edited by George Herbert Clarke, M.A. Cloth. Pp. 318.

The Story of the Odyssey. By Rev. Alfred J. Church, M.A. Cloth. Pp. 232.

The Iliad of Homer. Done in English Prose by Andrew Lang, M.A., Walter Leaf, Litt.D., and Ernest Myers, M.A. Cloth. Pp. 326.

Heroes and Hero-Worship. By Thomas Carlyle. Edited by Annie Russell Marble, A.M. Cloth. Pp. 417.

New Arithmetic—Book I. By John W. Hopkins and P. H. Underwood. Cloth. Pp. 258. Two copies.

THE PILGRIM PRESS, BOSTON

The Boy Problem. By WILLIAM BYRON FORBUSH. Pp. 220. $1.00.

LAIRD AND LEE, CHICAGO

The Wooster Juvenile Speaker. Compiled by LIZZIE E. WOOSTER. Cloth. Pp. 112. Special Frontispiece.

Edison's Handy Encyclopedia. Compiled and Revised by ALFRED B. CHAMBERS, Ph.D. Cloth. Illustrated. Pp. 512.

Webster's New Standard Dictionary. Elementary School Edition. Compiled by E. T. ROE, LL.B. Cloth. Illustrated. Pp. 384.

Conklin's Handy Manual. Compiled and Revised by JAMES A. BEATON, M.A. Cloth. 50 full-page maps. Pp. 532.

Modern Penmanship. By C. L. RICKETTS and G. F. HERHOLD. Cloth. Illustrated. Pp. 100.

ATKINSON, MENTZER AND GROVER, CHICAGO

The Art-Literaure Readers. Book III. By FRANCES ELIZABETH CHUTTER. Cloth. Illustrated. Pp. 220.

LITTLE, BROWN & CO., BOSTON

Daniel Webster for Young Americans. By CHARLES F. RICHARDSON. Cloth. Illustrated. Pp. 216.

Boy Blue and His Friends. By ETTA AUSTIN BLAISDELL and MARY FRANCES BLAISDELL. Cloth. Illustrated. Pp. 165.

ORANGE JUDD COMPANY, NEW YORK

Rural School Agriculture. By CHARLES W. DAVIS, B.S., M.S.A. Cloth. Illustrated. Pp. 300. $1.00.

GOVERNMENT PRINTING OFFICE, WASHINGTON

Annual Report of the Smithsonian Institution. 1906. By the BOARD OF REGENTS. Pp. 120.

THE CENTURY CO., NEW YORK

Father and Baby Plays. By EMILE POULSSON. Cloth. Illustrated. Pp. 98. Two copies.

HOUGHTON, MIFFLIN AND COMPANY, BOSTON

(THE RIVERSIDE PRESS, CAMBRIDGE)

Stories to Tell to Children. By SARA CONE BRYANT. Cloth. Pp. 243.

EDUCATIONAL PUBLISHING CO., BOSTON

Drawing with Colored Crayons. By D. R. AUGSBURG. Cloth. Illustrated. Pp. 64.

The Little Red Hen. By MARA L. PRATT-CHADWICK. Cloth. Illustrated. Pp. 102.

VOLUME VIII NUMBER 5

THE ELEMENTARY SCHOOL TEACHER

JANUARY, 1908

FIELD-WORK AND NATURE-STUDY
PART I
THE PEDAGOGICAL ASPECT

IRA B. MEYERS
School of Education

Field-work as used in this paper may be broadly interpreted as referring to any type of school-directed activity of such a character as to bring the children into direct contact with their out-of-door nature environment, from the standpoint of their own interests in nature. From this point of view the incorporation of the interests and experiences derived through this contact is most desirable and essential in elementary education.

It seems due time that steps should be taken, especially in our city schools, for bringing about more effective means and demands, through our school work, for taking children from the schoolrooms into gardens, truck-patches, parks, fields, and woodlands for the purpose of extending and intensifying their sense-contact experience with natural objects and phenomena and of fostering the "old naturalist" love of nature which seems so essential to child life.

No one subject, recognized as belonging to the elementary-school curriculum, has been so widely discussed, has received so much thoughtful consideration, during the past five years, as that of nature-study. It has been reviewed in all of its phases; its old aspect and its new; its aims and purposes; what it is and what it is not; and how it should be taught. Much of good has come out of all of this and the nature-study movement is stronger today, filled with more promise for effectiveness, than ever before. But this plea for the study of nature in our elementary schools is not new. Through the entire period of the past century the plea for the incorporation of more of the study of nature into our elementary-school curriculum never ceased. The conviction that this seemingly instinctive, deep-seated interest of children in nature should be a very potent factor in elementary-school work, has never been absent.

Yet during the century there never was a time when the study of nature gained sufficient foothold in the schools to insure its survival when it came into contention with the languages, number, history, literature, geography, etc. Doubt and confusion still exists in the minds of both teachers and parents as to the real purpose of nature-study or its relative educational value.

In the face of all that has been said and done, we need to seek the reason for this doubt and confusion. I believe that the answer is not to be found in the subject-matter of nature-study, but in our general conception of the aims and purposes of elementary education as a whole and the method of procedure by which these purposes are to be realized. Up to date we have no agreed-upon, conscious educational standards by which to test the educational-value-claim of nature-study nor of any other elementary-school subject of thought content. Our educational theories are to a certain extent formulated in the light of scientific progress, but our educational practices are directed by old traditions.

Our elementary-school system was organized to administer a course of study through the medium of textbooks and peculiarly adapted to schoolroom and class-group work. Studies which have been added from time to time have had to adapt themselves to this schoolroom and class-group idea with such modifications as laboratories and workshops. During its period of organization the public was dominated by the conception that education consisted in acquiring a certain fund of knowledge, or degrees of skill, in certain systems of subjects which man had arranged for study. And the school struggle was, and is yet, to get pupils to learn these formal systems. School work has fallen time and again into a dull routine and the warning that "the facts of science have been so abundantly acquired, so thoroughly systematized, and rendered so easily available through textbooks, manuals, and models that we frequently resort to the teaching of these schemes of knowledge instead of the knowledge itself" has had to be sounded at frequent intervals. Books, supplemented by the teacher, have been the reservoirs of knowledge. In the meantime the effort required to interest pupils in these studies, the meager results for the time and energy expended, the constant failure of subjects to stimulate any steady interest, and to impart to the pupil the delight and power they promised, have stimulated investigations into the act of teaching and learning and the principles involved.

As a result of these investigations there has been a gradual facing about in educational theory with a much slower adjustment in school organization and teaching methods. We have not yet been able to effect a coalescence of the two ideas, "education the act of learning subject," in the light of classical tradition; and "education for power and development" in the light of scientific progress. We find ourselves constantly attempting, urged forward by our old conceptions and established customs, to reach our present scientific conceptions through old traditional practices.

The facts relating to the purpose of elementary schools and the results which are desired are quite generally agreed upon. It is almost universally accepted that these schools are established for the purpose of educating children and that education has, as a part of its function, to do with aiding children in acquiring a certain skill in the use of number, spelling, reading, writing, drawing, etc., and a certain fund of information relating to the more fundamental facts in history, literature, sciences, etc. It is also to a certain extent accepted that education should have to do with individual development, generating power, and initiative, with growth into social efficiency.

Reduced to its simplest terms we have involved in elementary school work two prime factors: (1) Various subjects of study, the pursuit of which involves the acquirement of certain types and degrees of skill and information, and (2) the pupil. The process of educating is conceded to be through some interrelation of pupil with subject or subject with pupil. Our view-point as teachers, as to the desired nature of this interaction, is the crucial thing in educating. "What gets to the child is dependent upon what is in the mind of the teacher and how it is in his or her mind." In this, as has been pointed out, there exist two dominant ideals. Either these subjects which make up the course of study are selected as types of knowledge to be learned by the pupil, the amount learned or the skill acquired being the measure of educational progress; or they represent types of subjects, means, for the development of desired qualities in physique, mentality, skill, working efficiency, the qualities and power gained in these directions being the measure of educational progress. This distinction as to our attitudes in teaching may not at all times appear clear-cut or essential, but the path of elementary-school progress is strewn with the wrecks of methods and the mutilated forms of noble purposes which were foundered on the conception that teaching is wholly concerned with inducing children to learn the subject; and these methods have ranged from Grad Grinds through all types of (un)pedagogical novelties warranted to induce, lead, stimulate, or trick the pupil to learn the desired subject. Accompanying the growth of our knowledge of the laws which underlie human development has come a growing belief and confidence that the subjects, making up the elementary-school curriculum, may be so taught that the act of learning will prove the vital and essential factor in education; a conviction that children's interests may, and should, furnish the basis for educational method and progress. But to realize this we must find out their attitudes and view-points, and direct them rather than ignore them and set them to work from our own view-points. Paralleling this conception has come a fuller appreciation of the law of self-activity as an essential and fundamental condition for growth. This does not imply merely the self-effort of a pupil in acquiring certain facts pertaining to some subject which is taught, but it implies at its very foundation that this effort or action shall be a response to some deep-seated feeling or need, interest, desire, or conscious duty on the part of the pupil, and that the effort put forth shall be a direct response to this impulse from within the pupil. In making these assertions I am not unmindful of exceptional occasions when the present desires and interests of the child must give way to the needs and duties of the occasion, but these happenings in no way nullify the deeper fact that, for both the child and the adult, the best of education comes through direct response to individual interests and needs as determined by the individual himself.

No one seriously questions that, with an adult, power and control are obtained through the realization of personal ends and problems, through personal selection of means and materials which are relevant, and through personal adaptation and application of what is thus selected, together with whatever of experimentation and of testing is involved in this effort. Practically every one of these three conditions of increase in power for the adult is denied for the child. For him problems and aims are determined by another mind. For him material that is relevant or irrelevant is selected in advance by another mind. And upon the whole there is such an attempt to teach him a ready-made method for applying his materials to the solution of his problems, or the reaching of his ends, that the factors of selection and experimentation are reduced to a minimum. With the adult we unquestioningly assume that an attitude of personal inquiry, based upon the possession of a problem which interests and absorbs, is a necessary precondition of mental growth. Alertness is our ideal in the one case; docility in the other. With the one we assume that power of attention develops in dealing with problems which make a personal appeal, and through personal responsibility for determining what is relevant. With the other we provide next to no opportunity for the genesis and evolution of problems out of immediate experience, and allow next to no free mental play for selecting, assorting, and adapting the experiences and ideas that make for their solution.[1]

The desirability of acquiring a comprehensive fund of useful information, a high degree of skill, may pass unquestioned. But whether, in our efforts to induce children to acquire these, we do not too frequently suppress qualities without which there can be no great efficiency in either knowledge or skill is open to question.

The assumption is that no method can be adjudged right or wrong, no subject good or poor, no aim sufficient or insufficient,

[1] Dewey, *Psychology and Social Progress.*

except as they, in combination, influence the child and give scope in opportunity for approximating these conditions essential for growth. If field-work, as a method of school work, offers opportunity for the fulfilment of these requirements of conditions for growth—since no one can question the value of the subject-matter itself—then the problem which we have failed to meet is that of adjustment. Nature-study is in essence an out-of-door study, and it will succeed only to the degree in which we can afford children the out-of-door advantages which the study demands. If nature-study is to succeed we must be sure that it is really a study of nature. The inability of schools to establish a method of procedure which extends and incorporates into its work the out-of-door interests of children in nature has been the basal cause of the frequent failures in nature-study and its slow progress in securing a strong foothold in the curriculum. We have failed, or rather refused, to recognize seriously in school work the factor most vital in the interrelation of children with nature, namely that impulse from within the child which we term "love of nature." We seem to grope in the dark when we try to teach anything less crude than conscious knowledge. We have practically failed to direct or develop in any broad way those inner feelings or emotions which stimulate individual effort and vitalize the facts in learning. Nor yet have we been keen to detect the environmental conditions which generate and develop the feelings in a wholesome way. Wherever, in teaching, we have tried to recognize the importance of these feelings and to direct them, as in the teaching of ethics, morality, and religion, we have drifted to meaningless formalism or to sentimentality, until at the present time we are so thoroughly adrift in the matter that we avoid it altogether. So in nature-study, armed with our fragments of nature, books, and stories, we try to accomplish through formal teaching that which can only be accomplished by free and direct contact with out-of-door nature. But after this contact, if we are wise enough to utilize the best which results from this contact, we may accomplish with ease that which we failed to accomplish with effort before. Feeling, in nature, cannot be detached from facts and information without degenerating into sentimentality which on the whole is worse for the individual than formalism.

Trying to respect and take into account children's feeling for nature does not imply a lack of need or demand for information; it rather implies an increase in subject to meet the demand of that increase in mental capacity which always accompanies genuine interest. No teacher who has ever spent an hour in a rich out-of-door environment with a healthy class of pupils has been nearly so vividly impressed with his fund of information, in relation to their interests and questions, as he has been with his poverty of it. In order to utilize these interests, to enlist them in the service of human development and in the acquirement of knowledge and skill, we must give up our efforts to devise courses and methods which will communicate a fund of human knowledge to the children in the shortest possible time and must find out how to generate and direct interests which will give freedom to self-activity in the direction of that knowledge and skill which we deem essential to civilization.

We need to appreciate in all fulness what John Burroughs means when he says that in his contact with nature he has always "found feeling in advance of intellectualization." What Hall means when he says, "The spirit of botany is where plants and flowers grow; of geology in the field and not in the laboratory or cabinet; and of astronomy in the silence of the open night. . . . . Nature is sentiment before it is formulae, idea, or utility." To understand the need of the freedom of outdoors in all of its completeness is to catch the tone of Emerson's feelings when he said:

> All is needed by each one;
> Nothing is fair or good alone.
> I thought the sparrow's note from heaven,
> Singing at dawn on the alder bough;
> I brought him home, in his nest, at even;
> He sings the song but it cheers not now,
> For I did not bring home the river and sky;—
> He sang to my ear,—they sang to my eye.

This interest and sympathy between the child and nature is not in any sense conscious sentiment, as is frequently true in the adult, and any attempt to treat it as such must prove fatal. It exhibits itself in an insatiable curiosity and inquisitiveness which, if not suppressed by our own indifference and lack of means, will not be satisfied until the individual has experienced or until he knows. I risk the assertion that there is no sympathetic teacher or parent who does not feel that if she had the wisdom and knowledge to keep alive, to direct and feed this spirit of inquisitiveness, it would lead the child to an acquaintance with nature, a command and control of the elements of the sciences with a sureness and directness possible in no other way. To furnish a method of procedure which will foster this love of nature, which will secure an acquaintance and command of nature knowledge in a wholesome way, which will give a broad experience and a fund of information out of which, in proper season, the various natural sciences may be organized without quenching the fires of interest is the purpose of field-work. If we pursue the matter in a wholesome, genuine way we may rest assured that the pupil will reach in a surer and better way the end which we had hoped to gain through our more formal work. Our experience makes us perfectly aware that our indoor study has not succeeded in any adequate degree in aiding children to "read and enjoy the wonder-book of nature." We need not neglect any of the other purposes of nature-study, in trying to keep alive this interest; nor can we hope to succeed if we do not foster it, or if we conceive the idea that it can be kept alive by anything but free contact with out-of-door nature.

PEDAGOGICAL SCRAP-IRON, OR THE RUMINATIONS OF A NORMAL-SCHOOL VISITOR

JEAN SHERWOOD RANKIN
Minneapolis, Minn.

8:15 A. M. RECEPTION ROOM. My purpose in visiting this normal school is chiefly to note modern methods in teaching language. However, I hope I shall see something of the psychology and pedagogy also. How perfectly systematized all details of the day's work seem to be. Absolute discipline evident, yet its machinery wholly out of sight. And how delightful to have an usher thus assigned to help one put in every moment to the best advantage! What shall I visit first?

8:30. CLASSROOM A. *A recitation upon the "subjunctive mode in English."*—This lesson seems to be conducted in a clear-cut, definite way. The students quite glibly give specific forms called for under the name *subjunctive*. They do not, however, as they should if they have mastered the subject, present for consideration abundant citations showing use of the subjunctive in literature. To such use it is now, of course, practically confined, being almost obsolete in popular everyday discourse. I wonder whether these advanced pupils are aware that they are studying a phase of English dead except to the scholar, and that modern grammarians often discard the subjunctive mode entirely. Would they even recognize the "mode" if it should occur in their general reading?

8:45. Not a hint yet to indicate any intelligence upon the part of these embryo teachers as to the practical usefulness or otherwise of the subject they are reciting about. Doubtless they will go out into district schools to waste the time of country pupils with similar unapplied lessons upon this obsolescent phase of English. Ah, the usher comes for me, though I would fain see this ceremony in dead English through its final rites.

8:50. *A psychology class.*—And so these pupils are taught that "concentration of attention upon an act *will result in the act,* even though one make up his mind, that is, even though he will, not to do the deed." Examples given are, the man who jumps "unwillingly" from a cliff, and in certain cases the hypnotized person. This is "developed" from a bright girl whose modern English is guiltless both of subjunctives and of certain other requirements of the grammar books. But what a pity to leave this as final impression, unrelieved by the more comprehensive truths (1) that no person will ever commit a crime who firmly and constantly believes that he will not, and (2) that no persons are hypnotized except when either voluntarily, passively, or expectantly giving up their own self-control. Here lay ready at hand the practical applied lesson of self-control, self-direction, and persistency of moral attitude, which should have made this recitation rich in ethical culture. I am sorry that the bell for chapel rang so soon. Even if the moral application be presented tomorrow—as seems, however, doubtful from the trend of today's treatment—the postponed application cannot then be driven home with full force. Correct *de facto,* the lesson is incorrect *de jure,* except as reinforced by the larger psychological truth that man can and must *control his attention.* May Providence grant that no morbid weakling in this class ever use this recitation hour as scapegoat for future misdeeds!

9:30. *An eighth- and ninth-grade grammar class, analyzing and parsing Gray's "Elegy in a Country Churchyard."*—Either I have had trouble in hearing these pupils, or else I have been in a brown study, for since I sat here they have analyzed the following:

> Far from the madding crowd's ignoble strife,
> Their sober wishes never learn'd to stray;
> Along the cool sequestered vale of life
> They kept the noiseless tenor of their way.
>
> Yet e'en these bones from insult to protect
> Some frail memorial still erected nigh,
> With uncouth rhymes and shapeless sculpture deck'd,
> Implores the passing tribute of a sigh.

Their name, their years, spelt by the unletter'd Muse,
  The place of fame and elegy supply:
And many a holy text around she strews,
  That teach the rustic moralist to die.

I wish I had noted whether they disposed of "far" correctly. I recall what nonsense those two first lines used to make in my own mind because I construed "far" with "stray." I must at least be sure how they explain ungrammatical "teach." For here is a nugget of grammatical gold, an actual "disagreement" of verb and subject for the sake of rhythm! Will they seize the gold, I wonder, or will they go on picking up only worthless scrap-iron—because their eyes have been trained to recognize only the latter? Ah! it seems that neither this long-experimented-upon class nor their "critic teachers" have even perceived the ungrammatical expression. Not that I should care personally to have them do so. Love of the beautiful forbid! But this school claims to be teaching these pupils grammar; and if they do know even a little grammar they should surely demand concord between subject and verb, and not parse "agreement" where none exists. Even thus is many a child misled!

Clearly this is a case in absolute proof that study of grammar does not give grammatical perception. Now they go on again, parsing, inflecting, and construing each word, picking up busily the grammatical scrap-iron, and all oblivious of the mine of literary treasure over which they heedlessly tread. Very suavely I ask in a whisper of the "critic teacher," or "model teacher," or whatsoever her title may be, "How did the pupils construe 'to protect'?" "What did they make it modify?" " 'To protect,' " she informs me gravely, "has merely the adverbial relation, and does not modify anything." My surprise is so ill-concealed that she hastens to assure me, "The text we use indorses such use of the infinitive," and she points out the category which she has thus interpreted. I again cautiously press the inquiry, "But what does 'to protect' modify?" Quickly perceiving the true logical relation, she now answers me correctly. But is this a normal-school class in ninth-grade grammar?

Rather shamefacedly, because of my momentary inattention,

I ask, "Will you permit your pupils to read those two last lines as if they were prose instead of verse, changing any incorrect form?" But this, it seems, is a new and impossible task. Answers show conclusively that the thought in these stanzas is not comprehended, and that Lewis Carroll's "Jabberwocky" would probably have been better material for use. Finally, however, one little girl offers the needful "teaches," to our general relief. I do not venture to ask what is meant by "the unletter'd Muse," for I suspect—but there comes that most attentive usher. Never was there school where visitor's wishes received more courteous and watchful respect. However, I am glad to go; but I do wonder how much longer Gray's beautiful "Elegy" will be prostituted to these unseemly ends. Ah, yes, "Jabberwocky" would be delightful material for analysis and parsing. Thus it goes:

'Twas brillig, and the slithy toves
  Did gyre and gimble in the wabe;
All mimsy were the borogoves,
  And the mome raths outgrabe.

"Beware the Jabberwock, my son!
  The jaws that bite, the claws that catch!
Beware the Jujub bird, and shun
  The frumious Bandersnatch!"

He took his vorpal sword in hand:
  Long time the manxome foe he sought—
So rested he by the Tumtum tree,
  And stood awhile in thought.

And as in uffish thought he stood,
  The Jabberwock, with eyes of flame,
Came whiffling through the tulgey wood,
  And burbled as it came!

One, two! One, two! And through and through
  The vorpal blade went snicker-snack!
He left it dead, and with its head
  He went galumphing back.

"And hast thou slain the Jabberwock?
  Come to my arms, my beamish boy!
O frabjous day! Callooh! Callay!"
  He chortled in his joy.

'Twas brillig, and the slithy toves
Did gyre and gimble in the wabe;
All mimsy were the borogoves,
And the mome raths outgrabe.

This nonsense lyric is ideal material for the offices of the zealous diagrammer. In my mind's eye I behold it beautifully displayed upon the school blackboard in symmetrical sausage-links. Someone, I recall, became quite enthusiastic over the word "chortled." Since we need a single word to express the idea of talking nonsense, I believe "chortled" would fill a useful place. To my notion, these children have been "chortling."

10:00. *A sixth-grade class in language.*—These appear like bright pupils, and the teacher's every word and look denote poise and power. I shall settle down for a half-hour of solid comfort. I note a small dictionary on each desk, but no other text-book. The teacher is reading aloud—can I believe my ears?—Lowell's "Vision of Sir Launfal"! Apparently this is a class in ear-mindedness. But surely this is no suitable text for such purpose. For even if they had the text before their eyes, sixth-year children could not instantly comprehend the bare thought, to say nothing of appreciating this poem in its delicate imagery and its numerous contrasted pictures.

The teacher reads:

The drawbridge dropped with a surly clang,
And through the dark arch a charger sprang.

"What is a charger?" Recourse is instantly had by all to the dictionaries, and an acceptable definition is presently deduced. But if the next line had been read, either by pupils or by teacher,

Bearing Sir Launfal, the maiden knight,

time need not thus have been wasted by a score of children in looking up the word "charger." This is an extreme example of inexcusably bad method directly in opposition to the teachings of that wise man, Dr. Alexander Graham Bell. Several more lines are read by the teacher rapidly and well, with two or three pauses for the direction, "*Now make the picture;*" and so this absurd mixture of supposititious visualization and ear-training goes on, because, forsooth, it is supposed to be "pedagogic" and "psychologic." Ah, welcome is the usher! I could almost shed tears over this exercise. A brilliant teacher, an able class, a noble poem—but the combination a mere misfit. Oh, pedagogy, what crimes are committed in thy name!

10:30. *A fourth-year class in language.*—Another capable and charming teacher. The general subject is the King Arthur myths, and attention today centers upon the adventures of the fair-handed Geraint which result in his being knighted by Lancelot. A quick review is given yesterday's lesson for the purpose—of all things unsuitable!—of emphasizing the paragraphs it contained with the topic of each. Here is college composition work babyfied with a vengeance. Paragraphing for infants, I perceive, is one of our newest fads, and this although the subject is purely one of logic and of chief import to the maker of literature, not to the reader thereof. For the vast majority of pupils in the public-school grades who will never reach the high school this is about as complete a waste of time as could well be devised; and for the advanced student of logical mind, who has begun writing in earnest, the subject is one which will well-nigh take care of itself, since it is largely mechanical. Thus are these babes and sucklings made to begin at the wrong end of literature, the critical end. No surer way could be taken to prevent their becoming creative. Was there ever another school system, I wonder, so coarsely spongy as our own, soaking up thus as it does every device exploited by anybody and everybody in the name of education, and this, whether it be meat for man, or milk for babes, or wine for tippling youth?

At all events, this teacher reads these dear old myths delightfully and they are suited in grade to those who listen. However, the quaint diction somewhat lessens their value as material for training in ear-mindedness. Moreover, ear-mindedness comes more by nature than by acquirement, and most of these pupils are now chiefly eye-minded. These, at least, should be allowed to have the text in their hands; and, for that matter, so should all who prefer. Isn't it odd that our school system should take its pupils wholly ear-minded at entrance, neglect to avail itself of that ear-mindedness for several years when it would be of most use in acquiring a wide vocabulary, and then, after having inculcated a pretty general eye-mindedness, should in fourth, fifth, and sixth grades waste precious hours in attempting to undo what it has labored so hard to accomplish? Truly, wonders will never cease—wonders of folly, at least!

The only redeeming feature in this "recitation" is the admirable reading of the teacher. Every word falls like a bell-note, sweet, clear, and appropriate. The pupils seem to follow Frost's easy version with little need of explanation. They evidently enjoy the recital and are interested in the story. Ah, now she is through with the reading for today. She begins to discuss—the story? Alas, no; the paragraphs they shall make in their written work from the portion of the story which has just been read aloud. Heavens! I am humiliated to the depths of shame for my own country's school system. So this specious display of epic literature was for no good end in itself after all, but merely a thing whereon to hang written memory tests and drills in the logic of paragraphing; and this memory test is made to depend also upon the ear-mindedness of each child! Thus is the pure joy in beautiful literature for its own sake buried in the hearts of these poor children under an Egyptian pyramid of anxious care. This is cruelty to human animals. I cannot endure listening longer, and I shall not await the arrival of my usher.

10:50. Another grammar class, and the same teacher as in class number one. I shall have only ten minutes here as it is almost time for the intermission. Ah, what does that girl say?

. . . . And over the breast
Of the glimmering lake he spread
A coat of mail, that it need not fear
The downward point of many a spear
That he hung on its margin, far and near,
Where a rock would rear its head.

"*Need* is a form in which the *s* of the third person singular is omitted. It is in the indicative mode," and so forth. Well, well, well! and was it in this room an hour ago that this teacher taught English subjunctives? I have seldom seen so striking a proof that the study of mere grammar does not develop the grammatical sense. Here is a subjunctive beyond doubt, if we ever have one, yet it is not even recognized as such by the class nor by the teacher, although the latter is indeed author of the textbook in his own hand. How long, I wonder, will grammar be called a "practical" study? For my part, I am thoroughly delighted over the blunder. It merely proves what all great scholars claim, that grammar is largely a waste of time with pupils below high-school grade. This teacher is certainly a more than average grammarian, but he evidently has not the grammatical nose, which scents out as if by instinct the delicate flavor of the subjunctive. And what of it? Neither have all except one or two persons out of every thousand; and, hence, what need to teach subjunctives at all, except in high-school or college classes? Well, it is really delightful to have one's pet theories thus emphatically confirmed!

11:40. *A class in literature.*—Here I am again in the same room as at first. And so Lowell's "Commemoration Ode" is the literary nutriment adjudged suitable for these students, who seem so mature that I wondered just what "first year" means, as applied to them.

12:10. I have listened in considerable uneasiness while these pupils—mostly girls, of course, for all sensible boys save one have fled the precincts long ago—while these girls have recited *at* the greater part of this heavy poem. We have suffered together, they in striving to render orally the difficult constructions and involved thought, which they apparently do not quite comprehend nor certainly at all enjoy, and I in beholding their evident physical discomfort and nervous strain. Laboring to recall the words, they can hardly enjoy their own rendition. Their emphasis and pronunciation have frequently been faulty. Surely, every teacher of literature should first of all be an accomplished reader, who through the beautiful rendering of noble passages leads her pupils to the same attainment. Another dreary misfit! And how almost pessimistic it makes one feel! Well, I share the pupils' distaste. For this is a heavy poem of occasion, very uneven as to the beauty of its various portions, and best suited to the mature intellect. As a whole, it is ill chosen for adolescents. Is this in fact a class doing high-school work, or is it a "normal" class proper? If it be the latter, these pupils should rather be memorizing and comparing childish stories and merry jingles, and preparing their own collections of the same for future use when some of them will be miles from a good library. They should be cultivating their latent power of selection, through attempting to estimate the practical schoolroom value of numerous bits of choice verse culled from the fair field of poesy from Spenser down to Kipling. Could these sober-looking students enjoy Edward Lear and William Brighty Rands, I wonder, after the long focusing of their mental vision upon a commemoration ode? Truly it seems not likely, and they are losers in the training which would best have fitted them for their future work. How I wish I might ask each one to recite some short fairy tale such as she would choose in a primary grade to foster the ear-mindedness so potent in learning to understand and to speak even one's own language; or to give an anecdote suited to teach indirectly lessons of self-control or of presence of mind; or to render several bits of good magazine verse or of jolly folklore, which should tend to develop vocabulary; or to explain to me her individual test as to what one shall or shall not regard as literature; or to explain how she would seek to stimulate in her pupils a love for the beautiful in their own daily speech. But all this practical sort of thing would be unknown ground, I fear, to students who are drilled chiefly upon obsolescent English subjunctives, and who are taught that *shall* as used in the passage "Whatsoever a man soweth, that shall he also reap" expresses *determination* on the part of the speaker. However, were I but dictator, my "Thus shalt thou do" should indeed express an unchangeable determination that a new and rational sort of language teaching must come into being in American schools.

For far better might children be turned out to pasture than exposed unprotected to the graduated tortures which I have this day beheld. Normal? No! *abnormal* from beginning to end. And this so-called "normal" system can never be aught but abnormal, so long as it creates a false condition and then meets that condition with theoretical remedies. This exploiting of "model" departments sequestered far from the madding grade's noble strife is in itself a fallacious presumption. For these classes of English-speaking pupils, who have been brought largely from homes of culture, in no wise correspond to the polyglot groups of children forming public-school grades. Hence, even if the work I have seen today had been suited to its end, it would nevertheless still be unsuited to the unsifted collections of "graded" human units in our every public-school building.

Why not abolish these specious "model" departments which serve in effect to instil in hundreds of thousands of pupil-teachers a false conception as to fact and, hence, false ideals and false aims? Indeed, the ablest teacher I have met while visiting three normal schools has assured me that the normal school is not run for the children's good, but for that of the pupil-teachers! "But it would not do to say that publicly," he hastened to add in apology, upon my look of incredulous disapprobation. But why not, at the very least, let these pupil-teachers go out as assistants into congested school buildings, where they will face actual conditions and living problems? And why not let them help make *model schools* of these as far as possible in a quasi-application of the judicious "Batavia" system? The overcrowding of primary grades is the single greatest evil in the schools of America today; but a large body of normal-school assistants giving class or individual instruction even for an hour or two daily in these primary grades would insure a marvelous improvement all along the school line. Should this be done, no longer would there be as now a doubtful excuse for the existence of the American normal school.

This school, I remind myself, is no second-rate institution. On the contrary, it is doubtless one of the best in America. I shall not venture, I believe, to visit others less high in public esteem, lest I again behold these and similar follies, such as I fain would have become forgotten even by my subconscious self. Truly our great American school system is topheavy with a hydrocephalus which only heroic surgery can possibly relieve.

And what if the patient die under the knife? Well, better death than chronic disease, a bedridden patient, and final atrophy.

"Normal" lines and methods, being interpreted, seems to mean the magnification of means rather than ends, through over-elaboration of specific details supposedly in accord with the dictates of pedagogics and of psychology. A *little* psychology has indeed proved a dangerous thing for thousands of American teachers. I have visited today chiefly classes in English because I hold that a generous command over one's vernacular is the main gift which education can confer upon man; but all inspiration and original genius must evaporate from dead-English classes such as I have seen.

However, not this normal school alone, which is one of the best of its kind, but our entire educational system, whether within or without normal-school walls, should be cited to appear at the bar of American public common-sense, and there, pleading guilty to much ignorant evil-doing, it should give pledge for thorough reformation. Well, peace to these ashes! and may the phoenix of a New Education yet arise therefrom!

COOKING IN THE ELEMENTARY SCHOOL

JESSIE P. RICH
The University of Chicago Elementary School

There are few exceptions in the answers of little children to the question, "Do you enjoy your cooking?" Certain it is this activity affords to a majority of children a pleasurable experience, hence they admit they have an interest in it or "like it." To analyze this interest we find it need not arise alone (especially with children above Grade II) from a feeling of anticipation and accomplishment, but, under favorable conditions, it comes in some measure from mental growth, or is an intellectual interest.

This opportunity for the development of an intellectual interest is often neglected by teachers of cooking in the Elementary School. We flatter ourselves into believing that to arouse the social instincts and promote skill is the aim and end of the work. Surely this is something, but the growth and further acceptance of this branch as a school subject must come from this broader view; a view which includes not only the children and special teacher but the class teacher as well, and can only be carried out where such co-operation is possible. The object of this paper is to give an illustration of work from this point of view.

The work of Grade III centers about trade and trade conditions. The children discuss the beginnings of exploration and travel and develop a feeling for the growth and expansion of industrial and social life. It is from this thought that the following piece of work found its place.

The children were bartering and exchanging things of one section of the country for products of another: food-stuffs native to a moderate climate, for food-stuffs of a warm climate, as Illinois and California. Grapes were offered from California many times in trade, when one small child objected and said, "I can't take any more grapes, I just can't. I have so many now I can't sell them all." The salesman immediately saw the difficulty and offered raisins. "Yes. They'll keep and if I don't sell them all now it don't matter." Raisins were then discussed with the children. "What are they?" "Where do they come from?" "How do they grow?" "What kind of grapes make a good raisin?" Thus the children were eager to learn more, and it was planned to make raisins, and find answers to many of these questions.

Several varieties of grapes were obtained suitable and unsuitable for raisin making, and suggestions were given for their drying. The Concord, Cornican, and Tokay grapes were carefully weighed and placed in various places to dry. Some were hung in the sunshine out-of-doors, some were placed on the radiator, and others were put in a sunny window. Observations were made from time to time. All the grapes were noted to shrink and shrivel with a decrease of size and weight. Those on the radiator dried most quickly but did not produce as fine a product as the sun-dried fruit. The grapes in the window lost weight according to the following record:

October 18, 4 oz of fruit.
October 21, 3½ oz. of fruit.
October 25, 2 oz. of fruit.
October 31, 1½ oz. of fruit.
November 4, 1 oz. of fruit.

The grapes on November 4 were compared with store raisins and determined as "finished." From a comparison of the varieties the Concord were declared unfit for raisin making; the Tokay fair; and the Cornican good. (Could the White Muscat raisin grape of California be procured, still better results could be obtained.)

The children then wished to make an individual bunch of raisins. Parts were read or told them concerning "Raisin Curing" in *California Fruits*, and the chapter on "Grapes" in Carpenter's *How the World Is Fed*. This gave a clear picture of the real operation. Each child then weighed one-quarter of a pound of Cornican grapes, placed them on an individual rack made for that purpose, and set them in the sunshine. On each box was marked the date of starting and the weight. Each week additions were made to the record as new weighings were made.

In the reading it was found that the Spaniards make raisins by dipping grapes in a boiling solution of lye (one pound of lye being used to three gallons of water). This the class imitated by hanging the grapes on a long stick and dipping them quickly into the boiling solution and then into clear cold water. They found that the grapes shrank and that the flesh was cured more rapidly by this process; but the product was not comparable with the sun-dried fruit.

Thus far the exercise interpreted to the child a simple "product-making" process, an illustration of value, but by no means the highest value; nor did the work stop at this point. The children themselves were stimulated, during the manufacture to further questioning. To answer these questions lessons in science and mathematics were necessary.

Previous to this work the class had made grape juice, and as the raisins dried the children remarked, "All the grape juice is drying up, the raisins won't be any good." "But raisins are good, I think," said John; "maybe the good in the juice don't get out." So the class set about to find what "got away" or evaporated. Grape juice was again tasted and examined. Cloths were then moistened in it and dried by the children. "What had dried out?" "What remained?" Grapes were also boiled and the vapor caught on cold glass. Grape juice was distilled, and the distillate and residue tasted. One child suggested a grape be dried under a glass case and see if juice or water came out as the drying went on. The experiments were convincing that water alone evaporated and all the goodness of the grape remained. "It is the same as drying your hands in the sunshine," said one small boy, "the hands do not get away, just the water on them."

Then another question. "Why were the grapes so long in drying?" To meet this, four grapes were placed in a row, three of equal size and one very small one. The first grape had the skin entirely removed, the second half peeled, and the last two were intact. Observations made from day to day indicated that the skin had a great deal to do with the rate of drying, as had also the size of the fruit. This gave a new notion concerning the covering of the fruit—a point which will later be amplified in the lessons on "Parts of the Fruit."

Quantitative work on evaporation then followed to enforce and clear the ideas: (*a*) that surface exposure influences evaporation; (*b*) atmospheric conditions influence evaporation. Equal quantities of water were placed in deep, shallow, covered and uncovered vessels, and placed under the same conditions to observe the rate of evaporation. Equal quantities of water were placed in dishes of same size and shape and placed under different conditions of exposure. The comparative rate of evaporation was carefully observed and conclusions were reached for determining favorable and unfavorable conditions for evaporation. Application followed in discussing good days for drying clothes, and when to use and when not to use the cover on the cooking-pot.

No less important was the mathematics for carrying on this interest. The scales must be understood, the tables of ounces and pounds, pints, quarts, and gallons learned, the multiplication table of 3's and 4's drilled upon, and simple problems in addition and subtraction practiced. The records kept from time to time (as record of drying before given) gave basis for concrete problems as: Find the loss of water for the first four days; Find entire loss; Find the proportion of raisins to grapes; Find the necessary amount of grapes to make one pound of raisins; What is the cost of one pound of raisins if one pound of grapes cost 8c; Compare with cost at store; What is the amount of raisins produced from one of the large California trays of twenty-four pounds of grapes? Also each child had his individual problems from the record of his special tray.

The making of the tray was also a neat problem. Each had a one-quarter pound bunch of grapes for drying. Three or four of these bunches were measured and it was found a box 3×5 on the bottom was suitable. It was then for the children to determine the size of the paper to cut for the entire box with a depth of one inch and the size as before mentioned.

Without the co-operation of the class teacher, such work is impracticable, even if possible. The greater part of the mathematics and science of the grade must be carried on by the class teacher, and she needs this concrete work as a basis for such lessons. Also a large part of the cooking period must be laboratory work, but of such a nature that it need not stop here. It is high time for schools, where cooking is taught, to recognize this broader value and allow its worth to be estimated in terms broader than "a favorable cup of tea" or "a suitable sandwich."

THE TEACHERS' VIEW OF THE METHODS USED TO INSPIRE PROFESSIONAL INTEREST[1]

ANNA BROCHHAUSEN
Supervising Principal, Indianapolis, Ind.

In the spring of 1907, the Department of Education of Indiana University undertook an investigation to determine, if possible, the superintendents' and teachers' views of the methods employed to stimulate professional interest. The following questions were sent to teachers in different cities of New York, New Jersey, Missouri, Indiana, Minnesota, and Ohio:

1. What has aided and inspired you most as a teacher?
2. What assistance from superintendents (or supervisors) has been most helpful? Visits? Teachers' meetings? What kind of teachers' meetings have helped you most? Personal interviews?
3. Can you suggest anything more helpful to teachers than the means now employed?

To assure free expression, the teachers were requested to send their answers directly to Bloomington. About one hundred fifty answers were received. Whether the teachers really have expressed themselves frankly will probably be disputed. Nor can I decide the question. Our ideals are apt to speak when we record ourselves in black and white, but these ideals express our true selves.

This article will report a study of the teachers' answers under the following heads:

1. The teachers' attitude toward their work.
2. Their view of supervision.
3. Visiting other schools.
4. Teachers' meetings.
5. General suggestions.

[1] From the Pedagogical Seminary of Indiana University, J. A. Bergstrom, director.

1. Judging from the answers received, there is among teachers a prevailing spirit of earnestness and serious appreciation of the great responsibility resting upon them. They show a religious attitude toward their work, together with an intense desire for self-improvement. More than half the answers say that the greatest inspiration comes to the teacher from the children. They speak as if they were commissioned to promote the betterment of humanity. One calls herself a "Crusader against ignorance." All feel it a privilege to be of help, and ask in almost an injured tone, "Could any other inspiration be needed to make us realize that we have chosen the highest profession—the molding of the lives of the young?" Frequently an answer is stated thus: "If I could know that the boys and girls leave me a little better prepared for citizenship, for the duties of manhood and womanhood, I would feel that my efforts have not been in vain. Let each teacher have a deep and abiding love for each soul intrusted to her care and the knowledge of duty well done will bring joy and courage to continue." Numerous replies are as follows:

"That which has aided and inspired me most as a teacher has been the happiness derived from my contact with the children."

"The response, sympathy, and friendship given by the pupils."

"The encouragement received from pupils when they have grown several years older and they express their gratitude for the help received from me, while in my schoolroom, has aided and inspired me most."

These answers prove that most teachers are keenly sensitive to their duty and responsibility, and humbly appreciate their power to do good. Part of this inspiration which they receive from the children is possibly due to the feeling of success in their work. Indeed, several acknowledge this fact:

"The greatest inspiration to me is to see results from my work with the children."

"The encouragement that comes when one's own teaching shows successful results."

"This may seem egotistical: that inspiration is found in the successful termination of one's own efforts, but nevertheless I believe it is true."

Psychologically, it is undoubtedly true; but these teachers at the same time mention their love for children, and in their replies show devotion to their work.

Accompanying this religious attitude is a strong desire for higher scholarship. They feel the need of better preparation. One woman replies to Question 3, "A more rigid requirement for a license. Before a young person enters the teaching profession, he ought to be quite familiar with what is being done and what has been done by the most proficient men and women of the profession. He ought, also, to be a very close student of human nature. Such a student as only a somewhat extended study of psychology and pedagogy can produce." Another writes: "Require higher qualifications." Many long for the opportunity to travel and attend schools, and suggest that scholarships, like those given in Indianapolis, be awarded talented teachers.

In most cities there are classes, reading-circles, literary clubs, formed among the teachers. A letter received from a woman who once taught, speaks forcibly against these intellectual stimuli. She says: "The pleasure of study comes not from outside pressure." This truth is self-evident, but the history of these organizations proves that they originated among the teachers themselves. Upon inquiry, Superintendent Small of Providence, R. I., learned that two-thirds of the high-school and grade teachers had been studying either at the Rhode Island School of Design, or Brown University. "The general feeling of these men is that study is necessary for their own life and growth. As one puts it, he 'wants the tonic that comes from outside study.'"

Superintendent Small goes on to say, "It is surprising to what an extent *mood* has carried these teachers in their studies. Some have pursued systematic work for ten, fifteen, or twenty years, and they are still working." To the question, "Should teachers be *required* to present evidence of increased scholarship?" he answers, "No. The mood for increased scholarship is inherent in the good teacher."

This strain which teachers feel, I believe, is not due so much to the work which they do, as to the nervousness caused by examinations. Some teachers are evidently taking university extension courses at the same time that they attend institutes and reading-circles. They must take the examination for their university credit as well as the state examination. In general, a teacher who is ambitious enough to wish to do university work will see to it that he is well informed in the subjects he is expected to teach. He will gain a great deal more from classwork than from a superficial preparation for examination. As one teacher states: "A large majority of the teachers here are availing themselves of the educational courses extended by the college in our vicinity; and while following this line of work, are suddenly confronted by the reactionary movement on the side of state officials toward a return to the former periodic examinations for 'teachers' license.' If a teacher who is a student keeps in close touch with the pupils by being herself a learner, why should she not be accorded recognition for her college credits while climbing the hill, as well as after she has reached the top? Yes, more credit! Could not the colleges and universities act in conjunction with the state board of education in the grading of a teacher's standing? If such an arrangement could be worked out and put into operation, it would relieve many of us from the feeling of being goaded on all sides." This seems a reasonable request and deserves consideration.

A more ideal spirit than the combination of these two, the devotion spoken of above and this striving "mood" as a basis for the profession, can scarcely be imagined, and this is certainly a striking feature of the answers received.

2. Teachers have expressed themselves quite freely about supervision. From their answers, I conclude that practically none think that it can be dispensed with. It may be that they think otherwise, but only one speaks of the danger of over-supervision, and volunteers the remedy of having a supervisor for a month or six weeks about twice a year. Radically opposed to this teacher's view are those who state that each building should have its own supervisor, and those who say, "They (the supervisors) ought to come oftener and stay longer."

There is a general agreement in the fact that successful supervision depends upon the personality of the supervisor, or the superintendent. One goes so far as to say, "The influence of their visits depends nine-tenths on their personality." Another remarks, "Superintendents and principals should be persons of strong personality; of such faith in the work that we constantly feel a desire to do better." One claims that the greatest need today is inspiration from earnest leaders.

The characteristics of supervisors which receive favorable mention are enthusiasm and sympathy, as the following quotations show:

"Coming in touch with one who put her whole heart into her work has been a source of great inspiration to me. She was so enthusiastic that one could not be in her presence long without catching her spirit."

"One help I have always had when discouraged—my principal. She does not know what despondency means, nor can I when she talks to me, for in every storm her eyes can see the haven."

That supervisor is fortunate, indeed, of whom the following has been said, "My principal has a very pleasing way of offering her criticism. I do not realize at the time that my methods are being criticized. I try her suggestions because they are given as such, and find that her way is better. If she had done otherwise I should have been discouraged."

These quotations suffice to show the appreciated qualities of supervisors. Probably the greatest mistake of supervisors is lack of giving enough encouragement. It is sad that a teacher quotes from Dr. Hillis' *Quest of Happiness,* "This is an age of harsh judgments, cruel criticisms, and brutal blamings." Another puts it more mildly by saying, "The superintendent can be of great assistance by talking with the teacher about her work and giving her a word of praise when she deserves it." Still another says, "The fact that he always spoke a word of encouragement in regard to some point of success, at the same time that he pointed out mistakes, inspired me to accomplish better work. This I believe is *very* important in helping teachers."

"A little commendation from a supervising officer does much in the way of help. The average inexperienced teacher has not much confidence in her ability and she needs it before she can succeed to any great degree. I remember very well a time in my early years of teaching when I received a little commendation from a conservative person, in whose judgment I had great confidence. It was like a tonic. I think it helped me to grow in my profession more than all the criticism that was ever given me. Criticism is bad enough when it is coupled with a little commendation, but it is positively deadening without it. Under commendation, and not criticism, one finds his power."

Perhaps these quotations are convincing enough to show how much the teachers feel the absence of encouragement from conferences with supervising officers. They feel most keenly haughty, overbearing conduct on the part of supervisors. Note this reply, "In personal interviews more help is obtained by the sympathetic appreciation of a supervising officer than by supervisory airs and a general attitude of criticism." One emphatically states that "children at once detect a critical attitude." Another says, "Visits are helpful when the supervisor is sympathetic and enters into the work, and when he talks over the work after the lesson. The supervisor who is an inspector only, may help the system, but he is of little help to the individual teacher." Another asks, "Could not the supervisor give more attention to environment and work *with* the teachers rather than *over* them. In case of weakness could he not help them even as they strive with children to know the cause of failure, and to remove the obstacle?"

I believe that this is exactly what supervisors strive to do—to study the special power and need of the individual teacher; to be of help in developing every talent, and in overcoming difficulties. If they fail it is not due to lack of effort. These same things about which the teachers have complained have given superintendents and supervisors much occasion for thought. This fact would be acknowledged if all teachers could have heard Miss Harris, supervisor of schools in Rochester, N. Y., when she spoke to the superintendents at Louisville. In her paper she answered every criticism of the above quotations. She says, "The supervisor is not to sit in judgment, or to act as a disciplinarian; but he must be a sympathetic counselor who will guide the young teacher into right ways of teaching, and the older teachers, who do not understand the meaning of the course of study, to a wiser and clearer interpretation of the same.

"The function of the supervisor is not that of a police officer, nor of a detective to spy out weak teachers, nor even that of a critic; but primarily that of a helper and guide.

"The supervisor needs to carry into every classroom: one measure of ability to put himself in the teacher's place . . . . two measures of the saving sense of humor; three measures of appreciation for the effort put forth; four of timely suggestion; and five of stimulating words of encouragement and commendation."

As heartily as I believe in the excellent spirit of most teachers, I believe that the above quotations from Miss Harris's paper express the spirit of most supervisors and superintendents.

The teachers in their replies generally acknowledge that their greatest help from supervisors comes to them through personal interviews:

"By far the greatest assistance that comes to me is from my principal, and that chiefly through personal interviews. His sympathy, appreciation, and ever-ready helpfulness are of untold value."

"The greatest aid to me as a teacher has been the help given me by my principal. She has always criticized my work in the form of suggestion."

"Personal interviews in which definite lines of improvement were suggested, so that a certain result could be worked for, were most helpful."

One teacher offers as a suggestion, "More personal interviews with supervisors after their visits, when points good and bad would be made."

That these interviews ought to be frank seems an unnecessary statement, yet some teachers feel that they are not so. One remarks that "personal interviews are rarely honest;" and another states that, "A superintendent or supervisor who can get a teacher to talk to him of her problems, as she would to a fellow-teacher; and who instead of talking all around and outside the subject, or acting as if he would rather not be bothered, can and will give advice that 'will work,' is one most helpful to the individual teacher."

One feature of a supervisor's visits needs consideration, viz., that of interrupting the recitation. Though some consider it helpful, others strongly disapprove. One says, "The superintendent has helped me by visiting my school and taking part in a helpful way;" another that, "Visits in which supervisors and superintendents take part in recitations, followed by personal interviews when there has been perfect frankness on the part of both, are most helpful." Opposed to these views is the following: "I think supervising officers of all kinds, whether principals, supervisors, or superintendents, should be prohibited from going into any room where a recitation is going on, and addressing the teacher or class until the lesson is ended, or until the teacher gives some intimation that such a thing would be welcome. I think the average superintendent is thoughtful in regard to this point, but many principals are not. They do not recognize what someone has indicated as the 'sacredness of the recitation.' "

No doubt, interruptions, which can be interpreted by the pupils as adverse criticism upon the teacher, ought never to occur. On the other hand, limited time prevents the supervisor's having a conference with each teacher after his visit. Therefore, in the beginning of the year, the supervisor can explain to his teachers that some time by a mere question during the recitation he can give a suggestion. If, however, the teachers prefer otherwise, their wishes will be respected. Some superintendents adopt the plan of writing out criticisms or suggestions and leaving them on the teacher's desk. Their writing in the presence of the children, however, disconcerts a self-conscious teacher. It has been my experience that it often strengthens the pupil's confidence in the teacher to commend at the close of a recitation. The teacher surely understands that the compliment is for her, while the pupils are pleased since they take part of the "well done!" to themselves. This generally produces a very happy result.

In the answers the teachers repeatedly express the desire that the supervisors take their classes for them. This is most helpful to them since the supervisor or superintendent teaches those children with whom the teacher is accustomed to work. To quote from two replies: "I cannot think of anything more helpful to me than my supervisor's conducting a lesson for me."

"It seems to me that it would be a great help to teachers if the supervisors would conduct a lesson as they would like to have it done by the teachers."

No doubt this method of giving help has one advantage, viz., the teacher observes a person of wide experience meeting the conditions which he is trying to manage; yet the teacher must recognize certain disadvantages:

In the first place, it is almost impossible for a supervisor of a thousand or more children to know the individual names. This immediately puts a gulf between him and the class.

Second, he cannot know the individual minds as well as the regular teacher.

Third, the children are not accustomed to the supervisor's manner of questioning.

And fourth, the supervisor has not seen the successive lessons leading up to the lesson he is to give. Consequently, in the preparatory step he is apt to call for knowledge which the children do not have. He deems it necessary to teach what he supposed already taught, and does not reach the step the teacher expected. As a result some teachers are apt to pronounce the recitation a failure.

In the report thus far, I have tried to present what many teachers think of the individual help received from supervisors. Of the means employed to help teachers collectively, "visiting other schools" and "teachers' meetings" are most frequently mentioned.

3. I judge from the answers that teachers regard visiting as the best of all the methods for inspiration, especially if they see

a "successful teacher under every-day conditions." I quote from several replies:

"My visits to other schools have been most helpful when the teachers had regular work. I want to see errors made by the pupil, and see the teacher deal with them. Perfection is uninteresting and valueless, unless one can see how it was attained."

"Actual teaching that I have seen has helped me more than all talks. If some means could be devised by which teachers could see excellent work, I think they would be helped much more than by lectures."

"Visiting other schools, whether good or bad, has helped me to see the need of my own, to correct faults, and to strive for better results. Theory is good, but nothing can quite equal the seeing and doing."

"I have received my greatest and most inspiring help from visiting good schools. I mean by the really good school, one in which the teacher's love for her profession and love for the children are manifest in her work—where children's minds are developing in a fine, harmonious atmosphere. There isn't anything that anybody can tell us that is half so great a thing as this—actually seeing it done, naturally and beautifully, under the charm of someone who knows just how to do it, and who loves to do it."

"Visits are always helpful. I believe the observation of specially prepared lessons quite good. It sets a standard toward which to work. But even though the work observed be ordinary, it furnishes food for thought. Our very errors may be forcibly brought to us when observed in another."

Some answers lead me to think that there is a great deal of haphazard visiting done, from which the teachers get little help. Many express a desire for "directions for visiting;" others, a wish that they might visit their own grade in company with other teachers, and that the observation might be followed by a discussion.

Beside the general idea of observing the work of someone else, the definite purpose of the visit should be made clear to the teacher before he is sent. A superintendent has one of two objects in mind when he sends teachers to visit, either to give inspiration to a number of teachers by having them observe unusually good work, or to give help to an individual teacher in a particular line.

In the first case, the teachers derive the greatest value when they visit an unusually strong teacher who accomplishes his results artistically. They should know what things to note—the teacher's manner, voice, questioning; the amount accomplished in a recitation, etc. At about a quarter, or half-past eleven, the pupils should be dismissed and a conference held with the teacher visited. This discussion, opened by the superintendent or his representative, followed by the teachers' expressing the definite help received, and questioning the how and why of method, throws a searchlight on the work observed.

When an individual teacher is sent to visit, his particular need should be especially considered. If his weakness lies in organization, the school chosen for his observation should be particularly strong in organization; if he lacks ingenuity, he should visit a teacher of inventive genius. Before the visit he ought to be told wherein he fails. The visit is most valuable, if he is accompanied by the superintendent or supervisor. Some teachers mention that they get more if the supervisor goes with them, and afterward talks of the work observed. If it is possible to accompany a teacher, a conference should follow the visit, to ascertain if he actually has seen what he was sent to see.

In every case teachers should know where they are to go. If left to chance they often return irritated to their own work, feeling that the hours were wasted. Furthermore, some of them need instruction in how to gain the most from visiting.

One teacher remarks that, "The right kind of visitor is an encouragement to the teacher." This leads me to ask, what is the right kind of visitor? It seems to me that it is neither he who comes to see only the good (which seems to be one teacher's idea of visiting), nor he who comes to find fault; but rather he who comes with a scientific interest to study the moral and spiritual atmosphere of the schoolroom, and the teacher's method of instruction. Therefore visiting is professional not personal.

The visitor comes to examine and to learn. In the attitude of the learner, he welcomes and rejoices in all that is good and weighs method in the spirit of the student, not that of the fault-finder. If at the close of the visit the guest expresses gratitude for his privilege, points out what he liked and states in what way he has been helped, he may without fear of being misunderstood ask a question as to why this or that was done. Thus both teachers begin to weigh the merits of their respective methods. The exchange of experience is mutually helpful. This spirit of sympathetic interest is like the gift that blesses him who gives and him who receives.

4. From the answers received, I conclude that teachers' meetings, as a means of inspiration, rank next to visiting. Here again, superintendents may find encouragement in the assurance that every kind of teachers' meeting has been an inspiration to some individual. Though "a large meeting to hear some splendid address" has helped some more, others wish that there might be smaller circles where everyone would feel free to express himself.

There is a general agreement that the grade meetings are most helpful, especially when they consist of lessons given by teachers, followed by discussions something like "experience meetings," in which they compare notes and discuss individual problems. Again the teachers voice the desire to see "practical schoolroom work with average children," for many of them answer the question, "What kind of teachers' meetings have helped you most?" thus:

"The teachers' meeting where the manner of doing the work is demonstrated in regular class recitation, and not a 'show,' or 'cut-and-dried,' 'polished-till-it-shines' lesson; and then an open discussion of its merits and its faults."

"Those in which I have seen the regular class work done, and in which children make mistakes, so that I may see how others overcome them."

Hence some suggest that advanced work be presented in these lessons. One teacher offers a programme:

a) Outline of points to be made in the hands of the teachers.

b) Class demonstration by one of the regular teachers.

c) Discussion of large points in light of demonstration.

d) General discussion and concrete application to regular work cited by teachers.

The statement, "We have too much theory and not enough demonstration," made by a teacher summarizes fairly well the teacher's feeling about many of the meetings.

From the study of the answers received, I conclude that in larger places there should be a grading of teachers' meetings, i. e., there must be separate meetings for inexperienced and experienced teachers. Many of the latter comment upon teachers' meetings thus: "They are helpful to young teachers." If we combine some of the suggestions sent in, we may find a partial solution for the difficulty. Might the experienced teachers choose such subjects for these meetings as have for their fundamental principle self-activity in educational research?

A word needs to be said about the number of meetings and the time of holding them. A teacher's strength is greatly taxed when more than one meeting a week is held, or when a meeting continues several hours after the close of school. One teacher remarks that she receives little help from teachers' meetings because they are always held Friday nights after school, and that then she is "too tired to take in anything."

Since the purpose of these meetings is to help the teachers, their physical ability to receive that help must be considered in the arrangement of the schedule of meetings:

First, the teacher's mind is full of so many things in the beginning weeks of school, that many points of a meeting are absolutely lost.

Second, after April, he is so worn out with the year's work that meetings are overburdensome. Consequently, he brings little or no inspiration from them into the schoolroom.

Hence, the best time for meetings is from about the middle of October to the middle of April, with a cessation during the time the children are being tested. Then the teacher has all that he can do to mark papers and prepare lessons to clear up hazy points in the children's minds.

5. Of the many other helps, such as the teacher's associations, lectures, books, etc., many teachers have expressed their appreciation. They resent the narrowness in the choice of subject, however. One says, "In order that our interests and knowledge may be broad, the lectures we attend should not all bear directly upon our profession;" and several say they do not enjoy the study of books that are "thrust upon them." They desire a voice in the matter of selection.

Nearly all the suggestions offered in answer to question 3 are embodied in the above report. Higher salaries, fewer pupils, shorter hours receive mention. These are recognized everywhere as helpful, and will in the course of time be in effect. Therefore, I omit a discussion of them here. One suggestion expressed by several I do wish to call attention to, i. e., a co-operative planning of the curriculum. "It would increase interest through participation. All teachers criticize the course of study more or less, but for the most part unconsciously. I think it (the co-operative planning) is *the* way to get the best work for the children, and a needed means of inspiring teachers."

It was difficult to summarize the replies received, since the teachers' manner of expression is so different. However, by taking some liberties I have been able to classify them. All answers relating to the children: as for example, "watching the development of the children," "love for children," "a sense of the power to do good," etc., have been grouped under the "inspiration received from children." Allowing for this freedom in arrangement the following gives a survey of the answers received:

Seventy-nine teachers say their greatest inspiration comes to them from the children.

Of the means employed, eighty-four acknowledge that visiting other schools has been of help; while some say that visiting has been most inspiring, others say that it has always been of help. Only one says she receives little help from visiting.

In speaking of teachers' meetings: seventy-eight regard the grade meetings as most helpful and more than half of these say that the meetings are most helpful because of the model lessons given; seventeen speak of the help received from general meetings; and nine, from building meetings.

Every answer contains something about supervision. Ninety-six speak favorably of personal interviews; two, against them. Forty consider the supervisor's conducting a lesson of most help. Twenty-eight express their gratitude for words of encouragement or appreciation. Six speak especially of inspiration from enthusiastic leaders. Twelve criticize an overbearing attitude in a supervisor, and two complain against too much urging.

Forty-six write of inspiration received from strong personalities, either of supervisors, lecturers, or former teachers.

Thirty-three speak of help and inspiration received from literature, pedagogical books, and current magazines.

Five suggest that teachers need more reference books.

Thirty-two teachers speak of inspiration received at lectures; twenty-four, of the gain through coming in contact with earnest workers at county, state, and national associations. Three of these speak especially of the National Educational Association; ten, of the help received at institutes. Two who speak against institutes do so because of the length of the meetings. If the lectures were given at different times through the year, they feel that the value would be greater. Three other answers suggest closer confederations or organizations among teachers.

Sixteen teachers assert the necessity for a broader outlook; seven of these, that a teacher needs more opportunity for study and travel.

Eighteen tell of help received from normal schools; and five, from work in colleges.

Fourteen express appreciation of help received through intercourse with other teachers.

Nine tell of co-operation of parents as helpful; three of whom recommend parents' meetings as an inspiration.

Five speak of the effort which the intense desire to become a "good teacher" has stimulated; one of these says it was aroused through exhibitions.

Six tell of the great help a well-organized course of study

has been; though nine others wish that there might be a better planning, through the co-operative work of teachers with superintendents and supervisors.

Of the other suggestions received, six recommend that greater freedom be given the teacher; eight, higher salaries; five, fewer pupils; three, special schools for defective or incorrigible children; three, fewer examinations; two, that textbooks for children be made more simple; one, shorter hours; one, a larger social life.[1]

[1] I wish to express my appreciation and gratitude to the superintendents and teachers who answered the questions sent them.

THE SCHOOL PRINT SHOP AND ITS POSSIBILITIES

A. F. PROBST
Chicago

In this day of so-called new education when the aim is, or should be, to enrich the mind through the motor channels rather than by precept alone—through the hand rather than through the ear—and where the pupil is surrounded with that healthy atmosphere from which he is ever ready and eager to construct his own problems, there is no greater field and certainly none more interesting to both teacher and pupil than that of manual training. Much has been done in the last few years in the way of providing the public schools with the necessary equipment for athletics and industrial training, and now in the various departments of wood, metal, clay, textiles, domestic science, painting, and drawing, the pupil finds something to *do,* something to his taste, and toward which he has a natural bent. To quote from Professor James:

> The most colossal improvement which recent years have seen in secondary education lies in the introduction of the manual-training schools; not that they will give us a people more handy and practical for domestic life and better skilled in trades, but because they will give us citizens with an entirely different intellectual fibre.

In the midst of all these activities, and while knowing that some of my friends will say that we are already attempting to do too much, I plead for the print shop for our public schools; not that we would make printers or editors of our pupils, but that there is no department in all the school curriculum which offers greater possibilities, or better training and culture, than the well-equipped and well-managed print shop.

While there has never been, so far as I am aware, the slightest objection to our printing department, and while there has been the most loyal support on the part of both school and parents, I am fully aware that in every community there are those who, while they have been able to keep pace with the rapid progress and advancement in their own particular calling, find it very difficult and often impossible to run, at the same time, the rapid race of educational progress, and thus they oppose not only the more recent methods of instruction but also the newer and more modern equipments of which many of our public schools stand so much in need. So in the introduction of the print shop into the public schools, we meet at the very outset with two principal and common objections: first, on the ground of utility, and second, that of expense. It is from these two points of view that I wish to discuss the subject. In the first place, the printing department should have a large, well-lighted, and well-ventilated room—say 14 by 26 feet—with an adjoining room if such can be had, although one large room can be so arranged as to furnish every convenience necessary to the beginning of what can be made a leading feature of the school.

We have equipped our print shop with a fine Gordon jobber, a large Advance paper cutter, imposing stone, paper cabinet and type cabinet, type racks and cases with forty cases of type, metal and wood furniture, chases, galleys, sticks, rules, spaces, quads, quoines, and other minor accessories for about $500, and while this is not all that we desire, it is serving our purpose admirably and has furnished the nucleus around which we are gathering additional supplies from time to time from the proceeds of the press itself.

Perhaps some of the smaller village and town schools can afford neither the room nor the equipment such as I have mentioned, yet I believe that there are few schools that could not afford a print shop large enough for very efficient work and whose school boards would not be ready and willing to meet the expense if they could be made to feel that the outlay would yield adequate returns. Here, I wish to show that the material of the print shop will yield far greater returns than other apparatus of the school, much of which lies deeply and respectably buried in garret and basement dust. Realizing that material or apparatus of any kind is practically valueless except when in the hands of one who has been trained to use it, I do not hesitate to say that the person who has charge of the school print shop should nôt only be a practical printer but a teacher as well. Rarely do we find these two qualities combined in one individual, and if such a person cannot be had, it would be advisable to place the department in charge of one of the corps of teachers who perhaps has had some experience in a print shop and then furnish him with a practical printer from the local press who could give as much of his time to the work as is needed. The success of the printing department, as of all other departments, is most largely due to its management. Without proper supervision and instruction the most elaborate and expensive apparatus is of no avail and it too will soon be doomed to its final resting-place in the garret. The school print shop thus properly equipped yields its greatest returns in an educational way for the school as a whole.

Other departments of the school, and more particularly the English, French, German, history, and mathematics, have found the press very helpful and have been free to take advantage of the opportunities which it affords. For the reading-lessons, especially in the lower grades, the teacher not only selects the best, from any available source, but she composes and arranges pedagogically and psychologically much of her subject-matter, correlating it with other subjects in which the children are interested at different seasons of the year. To print these lessons, then, is the first work of the little printers in the shop. They set the type and print the leaflets in large type—18-point Caslon—and in short lines. The large type is not only less difficult for the beginner to set, but the large type and the short line are easier for young children to read. A number of proof sheets are then sent to the teacher who, together with her pupils, makes all necessary corrections. Here is offered a splendid training in spelling, paragraphing, punctuating, capitalizing, style, and arrangement. The form is then corrected and the lesson leaflets printed. Each child is provided with two leaflets, one for his immediate use, the other to be bound by the children of the bookbinding group into a reading-book, and thus the reader is enlarged by new leaflets as the work of the grade progresses. The teacher of reading in the higher grades also has the advantage of making her own selections, when it is possible to provide each individual of the class with a printed copy. Some of the finest poetry and best prose, the most beautiful sentiments and quotations can now be furnished the school at the proper time and in the right way.

What these young printers are doing for the English department they are also doing for the French and German departments. The mathematical department also comes in for its share of attention. In the lower grades, lesson leaflets are printed correlating number with domestic science, woodwork, and, as far as possible, with the work of other departments in which the pupil is engaged. In the upper grammar grades and in the high school, textbooks are supplemented by practical problems growing out of the student's own experience in nature, shop, and laboratory.

While the print shop can do all this for the public school, what can it do for the community? That the home and the school should be closely associated and mutually helpful we do not question, and it is the bringing of these into a closer and more normal relationship that the school press performs its second greatest function. In the first place, parents are always interested in the creative and constructive side of education; they not only take great pride and satisfaction in the real *doing* of the thing but, with the children, they manifest an especial interest in the finished product as the child's own accomplishment. While this much might be accorded the other manual-training departments of the school, the press goes still farther. The University of Chicago Elementary School publishes its own school paper—*The University Elementary School Reporter*—which serves as a medium for the exchange of thoughts and ideas between the children of the various rooms, and thus serves as one more point of contact between children of widely varying ages. The school paper, with its staff of young reporters, editors, and business managers, not only furnishes a splendid ethical culture but a real practical business training and in a most fruitful way.

Not long since, a distinguished English teacher visited our print shop and among the many questions which he asked concerning the work was this: "Why do you teach pupils to set type by hand, now that we have the type-setting machine?" This teacher evidently thought that to teach a boy or a girl to set type was the chief aim and purpose of the print shop. Not so, any more than the chief business of the wood department is to produce carpenters. If these young people ever become carpenters or printers, they surely will be none the worse off for having had this early training in the shop, and if they become teachers, preachers, farmers, or what not, this actual *doing things* is the making of a greater man or a greater woman. Again to quote from Professor James:

> Laboratory work and shop work engender a habit of observation, a knowledge of the difference between accuracy and vagueness, and an insight into nature's complexity and into the inadequacy of all abstract verbal accounts of real phenomena, which once wrought into the mind, remains there as lifelong possessions. They confer precision; because if you are *doing* a thing, you must do it definitely right or definitely wrong. They give honesty; for, when you express yourself by making things, and not by using words, it becomes impossible to dissimulate your vagueness or ignorance by ambiguity. They beget a habit of self-reliance; they keep the interest and attention always cheerfully engaged.

Thus, while the community, the teacher, and all the children in the school derive from the print shop a peculiar advantage, differing in kind from that of any other department, the little printer, in his *doing* the thing with a consciousness of its immediate need and value, is beginning to feel that he is more than a mere pupil of the school, that every day he is a real contributor to the welfare of the school and of the community, and thus, unconsciously, perhaps, receives the most valuable training and culture that is possible for the school to give.

In conclusion, I wish to answer the question which is sometimes asked: "Does the print shop pay financially?" To my mind, there is no other manual-training department in the school which can be made to yield larger financial returns in connection with its educational training than the print shop. The school paper has much more than paid its way, and while we have done no printing except for the school, we have realized nearly $300 from the print shop since its introduction into the school a year ago. This amount represents the proceeds from the school calendar in which the whole school had some part in its making and will ultimately share in its benefits.

Can the public school then afford a print shop? I answer, certainly it can when it can be made to yield such large educational and financial returns. Introduce the printing-press into the school, place its management in good hands, and its success is assured for certainly its possibilities are great.

ELECTRICITY AS A SUBJECT FOR STUDY IN ELEMENTARY SCHOOLS

PART I

L. DOW McNEFF
Seventh-Grade Teacher, The University Elementary School

For intense and dramatic interest, there is nothing in the realm of forces which equals that inspired by electricity. To the boy in particular, it opens a fairyland into which he needs only an introduction to be charmed and made a willing captive.

In this age of Titanic achievement in the mechanical world, when space and time are being annihilated, when there is such wonderful progress in the manipulation of raw materials, when almost in a flash nature's stores are transformed into articles of service to man, when the realms that have hitherto been unexplored are suddenly transformed into regions of light for man's searching eye to probe, when the infinite oceans of air are pierced and made to vibrate in harmony with man's intelligence, one turns breathless and bewildered with awe to that mysteriously silent and mighty force, electricity, more wonderful in reality than the Genii of the Arabian Nights in story. Were Aladdin brought to life in the twentieth century he would find that man had found an easier way to realize one's wishes than by the process of rubbing a lamp. Now he merely presses a button, or turns a lever and presto! the Genius of Electricity, flashing, silent, and mighty, is at his command, ready to leap through space in defiance of time, or to unite with the might of Thor's hammer. But, wonderful as this is, the first few letters of the alphabet only have been deciphered in the story of this mighty force.

Electricity appeals to the imagination. All of the race experience with fire, that gift of the gods which has done so much to establish man highest in the animal kingdom, is suggested by it, and all the mysticism of the flame which subconsciously we feel when near the glow of a campfire, or by the grate, exerts a subtle influence when one is near the sparkling and crackling flame of electricity.

Space and time, the two great obstacles to free communication, have been comparatively conquered by this rival of fire, and little by little it is bringing the world together into one vast social consciousness. Interest is always intense concerning things of promise, the potential, with which the imagination ever busies itself. So it is not only because of man's past conquests in the field of electricity but also the promise of still greater achievements that accounts for interest in this subject.

Almost everyone has noticed the natural interest which many boys, city boys especially, have in electricity. It is often a dominant spontaneous interest at some time between the ages of ten and fourteen.' Contact on all sides with the electrical world undoubtedly induces this interest.

As an evidence of this witness this paper which was written last year by a seventh-grade boy in the University Elementary School:

MY SHOP

I began working with electricity and mechanics when I was about eight years old. The way I got interested in this was through a boy friend of mine whose father was an electrician. I used to go to his home and watch him, and soon I got a little shop myself. I had a few batteries, a bell, and some wire, and I made push-buttons and switches out of tin. I got some sal ammoniac and made little batteries of carbon and zinc in jelly glasses. Soon my father had our barn made into a garage, and when he did this he had a room fitted up for me on the second floor, and I moved my shop from the basement of our house to this room. I got some tools and a lot of old iron and wheels and a lot of other things and put some of these things in the shape of telegraphs, little bells, and motors, but I couldn't get a motor that would run for quite a while. Soon I got a small lathe and emery wheel, and drill-press attachment? Soon after this I got interested in chemistry and put a chemical outfit in my shop and I am there now most all the time.

A little while ago I made an electric furnace which gives a lot of heat. I use this in chemistry for making metals.

A little after this I got a motor to run my lathe and I am making a pump to run by it to get air to run a blast-lamp with.

Edward Andrews

If for no other reasons than these, (1) the part which electricity plays in our civilization, a part which it is destined to play to a still greater degree; (2) the interest which children feel for it in itself; (3) the interest which the child ought to feel in one of the greatest of nature's controllable forces, these are good and sufficient reasons for giving electricity an important place in the elementary school. Certainly if one of the chief aims of education is to fit one to utilize nature and nature's forces, this cannot be done unless the school gives the child the largest possible contact with natural forces.

HISTORICAL SKETCH

Before proceeding to a consideration of the subject-matter of electricity, suitable for the elementary schools, let us first make a survey of the field in the light of historical development.

Frictional electricity has been known at least for a period of twenty-five hundred years. The Greeks knew of it through rubbing amber. Aside from this nothing further was learned until about 1600 A. D., when Dr. Gilbert, Queen Elizabeth's court physician, after much experimenting, found a considerable list of substances which like amber and jet, when electrified by friction, caused attraction. The Greek name for amber is electron and the phenomenon produced in these substances being the same as in the case of amber, he named it electrification; so it is to Gilbert electricity owes its name. He is called the father of electricity and magnetism.

The first electrical machine was a ball of brimstone mounted on an axis. When turned rapidly, if silk were held firmly against the revolving brimstone, frictional electricity was produced—barely enough to cause a spark. We owe this invention to Otto von Guericke, the burgomaster of Magdeburg, who lived about the middle of the sixteenth century. Experiments with this machine led up to an accidental discovery resulting in the invention of the Leyden jar in its original form in 1745 by Dean von Kleist. With the numerous experiments made possible by the Leyden jar and the friction machine, interest in electricity advanced by leaps and bounds. For the first time in history man could produce and control electricity of a high power. However, he was still dealing with frictional electricity. Then followed a period of play. The learned physicists and scientists of Europe entertained the courts with their wonderful toy and for a half-century it was the plaything of royalty.

A century later America entered the lists for scientific honors with Franklin as her champion. His interesting experiments soon awakened wonderful enthusiasm. In 1752, when he proved by his celebrated kite experiment that electricity and magnetism are identical, he found by his invention of the lightning rod the first means by which a knowledge of electricity could be made of actual service to man. His theories as to electricity were at first given scant recognition by the English experimenters. The French immediately accepted his theories and proved them by experiment which in large part explains Franklin's wonderful popularity with the French during Revolutionary times.

So far scientists were handicapped as the frictional electricity of the static machine stored up in the Leyden jars gave only an instantaneous spark to be experimented with. As yet no one could produce a steady flow or current of electricity.

In 1800 the invention by Volta, of the voltaic pile and later the voltaic cell, made possible a steady flow of electricity by chemical means and scientists were in a position now to study the electric current. Since then events have followed so rapidly that it is difficult for the layman merely to keep pace with them. The science and art of electricity now demands an army of experts, no one of whom can cover the whole field successfully. In 1802 Humphrey Davy produced the electric flame or arc caused by the flow of the current through the juncture of two carbon tips; in 1820 Oersted found that a magnetic needle was deflected if placed near a current. This suggested investigation of the relation between electricity and magnetism or electro-magnetism; in 1822 Faraday produced the first electric motor; in 1825 Sturgeon invented the soft iron electro-magnet, an instrument for using the temporary magnetization produced by the flow of a current of electricity.

This invention marked an epoch. The possibilities were seen to be tremendous. Since then millions of electro-magnets have been made. The electro-magnet is the essential part of the telegraph, the telephone, the sub-marine cable, the relay, the recorder, the motor, the electric signal, the electric bell, and numerous simple electrical machines.

Since the flow of electricity produced a magnetic field, Faraday in 1831 began a series of experiments with magnetism to see if it could be made to produce electricity. His researches resulted in success. His magnet led up to the dynamo which produces electricity by mechanical means. However, until about 1878, electricity had very little commercial or industrial value, aside from its use in the arc light, and in the telegraph which came into use about 1840. The telegraph has been a great aid in the development of rapid railroad transportation. The invention of the dynamo, however, made it possible to transform the energy of water power and heat into the energy of electricity at a much cheaper price than ever before and at enormous pressures. The transformer invented in 1831 made it possible to reduce the pressure at any point along the line, thus putting the powerful current under perfect control, so that it could be used for all purposes requiring currents of different control.

The more recent discovery of the X-ray and its application to medicine and surgery, and of the Hertzian waves with the development of wireless telegraphy, of the street motor-car, and of the automobile, are too recent to need an account here. While it is true that steam is still our greatest motive-power, electricity is gradually but surely supplanting it. Business men almost invariably prefer it to steam, gas, or water power, owing to its numerous advantages. Its greater cost is in many localities its only drawback. Since 1878 the development of electricity in a commercial way has been marvelous. The inventions of Edison, Westinghouse, and a host of others would fill volumes if one attempted to give an account of the innumerable ways in which they have learned how to apply the principles of electricity to solve the problem of sound, heating, lighting, transportation, surgery, communication, and almost every line of human endeavor.

For many years facts about electricity have been taught in secondary schools, in technical schools, and in universities. In engineering schools it holds of course a position of prime importance. The subject was brought during the past decade or two into some few elementary schools with the movement to enrich the school life, hoping thereby to put life into the "three R's." However, most of the subject-matter as generally taught has been chiefly concerned with experiments in frictional electricity. But frictional electricity plays a very insignificant part in the present use and applications of electricity. Historically it has played a great part in the development of the subject, as it was the point of approach. The pith ball, the friction machine, the Leyden jar, the electrophorus, etc., have held sway often almost to the entire exclusion of the larger field of current electricity. Progress in the electrical field has been so kaleidoscopic that while the pedagogue may have kept pace with a knowledge of this progress he has not kept pace in his educational practice in teaching the subject. Too often he is still manipulating his pith balls, silk and glass, Leyden jars, tinfoil apparatus, etc., evidently oblivious of the fact that the electrical world has long since left them to get dusty on an upper shelf, only taking them down to show the one-time plaything, or as evidence of the progress which they have been instrumental in bringing about. The essential applications of electricity are concerned with current electricity. Probably the fact that most textbooks begin with a treatise on frictional electricity accounts for the method of the teacher who has not yet emancipated himself from slavishness to the dog-eared textbook, which too often is written from a logical standpoint, or in the chronological order of the development of the subject.

Until books intended for use in educational work are psychologized, the teacher to do intelligent work must lay aside poor texts and present his subject so as to make the present experiences and interests of the child the starting-point. It has been well said that "the subject-matter, just as it stands for the scientist, has no direct relationship to the child's present experience."

It is my purpose, in the next article, to sum up some work in electricity done from the above point of view, illustrated by work from the seventh grade.

READING FOR LITTLE CHILDREN—Part IV

ELSIE AMY WYGANT
Second Grade, The University Elementary School

EVENING IN THE CAVE

These were happy times in the cave.

In the long evenings Old Mok and Ab sat in the firelight together.

Then the old man began to teach Ab to make wonderful things of stone.

At first Ab sat near by and watched Mok as he worked.

Then the old man gave him a flint scraper to smooth the long spear handles.

Next he taught him to chip stone.

At first Mok gave Ab only the waste flint.

And Ab spoiled many a piece.

But in time he grew skilful.

He could make a flake with as sharp a point and fine an edge as old Mok himself.

Then the old man was proud of the boy.

He taught him to make scrapers and knives, chisels and spearheads of flint.

Ab was strong too.

He could make heavy axes and mallets of redstone and granite.

He learned to chip from a piece of flint a pointed tool called a drill.

Now he could make needles of bone for his mother and bore the hole for the eye with his drill.

He found pretty shells and animals' teeth and fishes' scales.

He bored a hole in each and strung them on reindeer sinew.

These made fine necklaces to wear.

But there was one thing Ab never could learn to do.

Old Mok could carve wonderful pictures of tigers and reindeer and rhinoceras and bears.

This Ab could not learn to do.

But he would go into the forest and get the horns of the reindeer or elk.

When the men came home from a hunt he would beg the tusks and the shoulder blades.

All these he brought to Old Mok to carve.

As the old man carved pictures on the drinking-cups or knife handles, the boy would sit watching in the firelight by his side.

THE GREAT STONE KETTLE

Red-Spot was very proud of her kitchen.

There was no other in the valley so good.

She had the wood fire where she broiled meat on long sticks.

Then there were the hot coals and ashes where she roasted clams and oysters.

She covered fish with clay and baked it here.

But best of all was the place where things could be boiled.

Outside of the cave there was a great sandstone rock.

The top of this rock was nearly flat.

This was what Red-Spot wanted for a kettle.

So Ab tried to roll it into the cave.

But it was so heavy he could not move it.

Then One-Ear and Red-Spot and even old Mok helped him.

Together they rolled it into the cave.

And now the work began.

First Mok marked out a circle with his stone axe—a circle as big as a tub.

The stone had to be hollowed out within this circle to make the great kettle.

And Ab was to dig out the hollow.

He pecked and pecked with his flint chisel.

At the end of two days it had only begun to be hollow.

He tried to find a way to work faster.

He knew that he needed more weight on his chisel.

At last he brought a forked stick into the cave.

He bound the chisel into the fork.

He bound a heavy stone to the handle of the forked stick.

Now the chisel could not be driven upward when it struck the great rock.

He held the handle with both hands.

He lifted it and drove it into the hollow.

The stone weight made the chisel cut deep.

Great pieces came off at each blow.

In a few days the great stone kettle was finished.

Then Red-Spot was happy.

She was proud of Ab and his skill.

THE FEAST ABOUT THE STONE KETTLE

It was just at sunset that Ab finished the great stone kettle.

Now it happened that One-Ear had been hunting that day.

He had brought home the hindquarter of a reindeer

So they made ready for a feast.

First Bark filled the kettle with water.

Red-Spot dropped pieces of meat into the water.

Then she heated stones in the fire.

When the stones were hot she lifted them from the fire with tongs made of green twigs.

She dropped the hot stones into the water.

Soon it was bubbling and boiling.

Then a fine rich odor filled the cave.

The stew was ready to eat.

Each one rushed for a clam shell or gourd or deer horn.

With these they dipped out the stew to drink.

With sharp sticks they got the boiled meat.

Now and then little Beachleaf cried out for she wanted more stew and she was so little she could not reach into the great kettle.

They talked and laughed as they ate.

They praised Ab for his work.

When the feast was over they sat about the fire.

Old Mok told stories till Bark and Beechleaf fell asleep.

So ended the first feast about the great stone kettle.

EDITORIAL NOTES

The Loss of Professor Jackman

The loss to this journal of Professor Wilbur S. Jackman has brought with it the problem of responsibility for the further conduct of the *Elementary School Teacher* and its policy. Professor Jackman's editorials represented very vividly not only his own reactions to the problems of elementary education, but also that liberating movement in pedagogy for which Mr. Jackman and Colonel Parker before him have stood. The numbers which have appeared since Mr. Jackman's death have sought to continue the spirit and form with which he had invested the publication. It was however characteristic of its former editor's direction that the *Elementary School Teacher* reflected not only an educational movement but also an embodiment of this movement in a personality.

The Present Editorial Board

Such a direction cannot be long successfully continued when the personality has gone. While, therefore, the journal continues to represent the liberalizing movement in education with which Mr. Jackman identified himself, the responsibility for its presentation has been divided among those who we hope will be competent to represent its many sides. The editing of the *Elementary School Teacher* has passed, then, into the hands of a committee, made up from the department of Philosophy and Education in the University of Chicago, and from the staffs of the University's College of Education and the Elementary School. We have sought safety in numbers, recognizing the bewilderingly numerous phases of elementary-school teaching, and the importance of the specialist in representing these to the public whom we seek to reach. The editorial committee is a part of a larger one including that which conducts the *School Review*. The conduct of the

Elementary School Teacher will therefore have the benefit of association with an organ representing secondary education. There should result from this association broader views of problems which are common to both the elementary and high schools, and an increased confidence in presenting to those interested in elementary teaching the course which modern pedagogy should steer among its perplexing problems.

The Programme

There is little difficulty in formulating the programme of the modern pedagogy. It calls for a school so organized socially that the child may live there his own life. The experiences of school life are to be justified by their immediate value to the children as well as by their import for the activities of adults. This sort of education takes place at home—it is the only education among more primitive peoples. Its results justify the method. The character-building, the unfolding of balanced intelligence which a well-ordered home achieves, present an educational ideal which perhaps no elementary schools have ever reached. What is more natural than to demand that family life be domesticated in the schoolhouse? But in the average schoolhouse we find a régime organized with an eye single to the acquirements demanded by the after life of the man and the woman. The pupil is looked at under the perspective of the adult. It is easy to react against this unnatural attitude, by substituting for the adult interests, which are over-represented in typical curriculums, the interests, of the child; to find in the spontaneous activities of childhood the subject-matter for the child's curriculum.

The Loss of Family Morale

This reaction, however, overlooks the morale of family life. It is the dominant activity of the parents that constitutes the control, that determines times and seasons, and gives the proper perspective to the child's interest. When the child helps in the labors of the home, or bears his part in the industries that used to center there, an educational ideal arises, which could only be realized in the school, if its activities had the same compelling power. To make the school life entirely out of the child's spontaneous processes is to quite upset the natural order of the family or community life which we are seeking to copy. Education in these its natural habitats consists in relating the child's spontaneous activities to the dominant, controlling activities of the community. It is the presence of this relation in trade and professional schools that gives a morale to their pupils which is indeed purchased at the price of a certain unfortunate narrowness.

Educational Reform, Its Development, and the Reaction against It

The doors by which educational reform entered the school were those of history, the sciences, and nature-study. Today we see both a development of this reform and a reaction against it. The industrial arts have come to take the strategic position which history and nature-study earlier occupied. The reason for this is evident. The arts give a powerful motive to the child for acquiring technique, by means of which it is hoped that the desired control over language and number may be gained. The reaction is represented by the demand for drill as the pivotal element of the school teaching. It appears in the guise of modern psychology, in the demand for habits which will operate without conscious attention, or for the education of the spinal column with its reflexes and automatisms. On the one hand this reaction demands the old methods of instruction in language and number, and has no confidence in the motives that spring from the child's desire to gain skill, and to acquire techniques. On the other hand the movement has behind it the feeling that a school which follows simply the creative and outgoing impulses of the children lacks the compulsion which the child's activities at home, on the farm, and in the shop, meet in adjusting themselves to the adult processes to which they contribute.

Isolation in the School Life Where Advanced Methods Obtain

The school which merely drills is hopelessly isolated from the real life of the child. And we must make the same criticism upon a school life which is organized entirely about outgoing and creative impulses. A child who criticizes the results of his work with the severity of the artist and skilled mechanic is no longer a child. The child, because he is a child, is more interested in the process than in the result.

Here lies the crux of the problem in elementary education: How to use the child's own impulses, his native interests, material which is worthy because it has meaning for him, and the motive for getting technique which springs from interest in what he does, and yet to make felt the authoritative discipline and criticism of adult human achievement, which is as real a part of the child's normal life as it is of the adult's, though the incidence is not the same.

The Real Educational Problem

While this journal has no fixed programme to proclaim, it will continue to stand for modern educational reform in both the phases above stated, regarding with especial interest the movement toward social organization of the school as a means to the attainment of the disciplinary element in the child's development.

G. H. M.

NOTES AND NEWS

Early in November there was cabled to America news of the death of Herr Otto Salomon, director of the Slöydläraresemi-narium at Nääs, Sweden. Herr Salomon organized the school at Nääs in 1872 on a great estate contributed to the cause by his uncle, August Abrahamson, who made Otto Salomon his director. After the death of Herr Abrahamson in 1898 the foundation, by his will, became the property of the state, and is now known as the August Abrahamson Stiftelse. The fundamental purpose of the school is the training of teachers along pedagogical and technical lines. Woodwork has been the special handicraft, but in 1902 courses in gardening, cooking, and sewing were added. All courses, however, must include pedagogy, gymnastics, and games. Since the school opened its doors to foreigners, five thousand students have taken courses in sloyd, and fifteen governments have sent delegates to study the system with the idea of introducing it into their own country.

Some of Herr Salomon's more important lectures at Nääs have been published in book form: *The Theory of Educational Sloyd* and *The Teachers' Handbook of Sloyd.* These books have been translated into five different languages. An aristocrat by birth and breeding, Herr Salomon was theoretically and pedagogically a democrat. He was at once master, father, and friend to the people on his estate. As a man and as an instructor Herr Salomon made a deep impression upon all his students. They came away from Nääs with a vital consciousness of his simplicity, integrity, mental alertness, wide learning, and cosmopolitan aims and sympathies. It may be too early accurately to estimate the service of Herr Salomon to the cause of manual training, but when the history of that movement shall be finally written the name of Otto Salomon will almost certainly stand first, not only in time but in importance.

BOOK REVIEWS

A First Latin Book. By WILLIAM GARDNER HALE. Chicago: Atkinson, Mentzer & Grover, 1907. Pp. xvi+354. $1.00.

The beginning Latin book is designed to present efficiently the six essentials stated by Dr. Johnston of Indiana University in a paper on "Sanity in First Year Latin," published in the *Classical Journal* for February, 1906. These essentials are inflections, order of words, translation, syntax, pronunciation, word-lists. The method of presentation and points emphasized the more, vary in different books.

One weakness in our educational products is that some pupils go through school without learning to think. This is sometimes said to be due to the fact that the amount of work to be done is so great, that the teacher has not time to develop lessons so that the pupil will learn to think.

The beginning Latin work is great in quantity. The greatest merit in Dr. Hale's *First Latin Book* is that it covers all the essentials adequately without sacrificing correct method. The book is simple, thorough, lively, logical, and pedagogical. The steps in an individual lesson, related lessons on a case or mood, the whole book, all show a plan clearly, logically, and pedagogically worked out. Not too much is taken for granted as to the child's knowledge of English nor of his mental ability at the age of fourteen. The author makes sure of a proper preparation in the pupil's mind by a sort of printed talk on grammatical principles on which the new concept is based. Then with the aid of concrete examples the new concept is developed. The ease with which the first few lessons are mastered gains the sympathy and interest of the pupil. He is pleased to find that he can translate a Latin exercise at sight, and that Latin is not so foreign and antiquated as tradition would have it.

The teacher is surprised that Dr. Hale, who stands for advanced thought and progress in Latin, for highest modern scholarship, and for the new terminology, should be able to write a book incorporating so well that for which he stands, in such an exceedingly simple style and so well adapted to the youthful mind of the first-year Latin pupil. Inflections are arranged in a labor-saving order. After the first and second declension nouns and adjectives, the other adjectives and the pronouns appear, as they vary least from the last preceding declension. The arrangement also secures reviews from a new standpoint. Comparisons of old with new forms are repeatedly made. The active forms of the verbs in the present system are repeated on the page where the passives are found for the first time.

The Latin order is used and emphasized from the very first lesson. This stress on order from day to day forestalls and avoids the too common complaint, "I know the meaning of the words but I can't put them together."

The treatment of pronunciation is Dr. Hale's own. In division of words into syllables, the rule for disposition of consonants is changed. There is no special rule for the accent of words with enclitics attached. The length of some of the vowels is changed from the old tradition. The nominatives *hic* and *hoc* have the vowels short.

The vocabulary is abundantly large, more than nine hundred words in all, with 91½ per cent. Caesarian according to the publishers' statement. They also state that each new word is used immediately in at least two lessons. The first word-lists have a large percentage of words that easily suggest English derivatives. This aids much in the new art of learning word-meanings in a foreign language.

The exercises are modern in spirit. The sentences soon become connected discourse, and this connected discourse is continued through the book. A mimic war affords preparation for Caesar. The discourse is lively. As in most beginning books there are exercises for translation into Latin. These are the sure and severe test of knowledge with ability to think and to apply.

The treatment of syntax especially shows the pedagogical method of treatment. Every step is clearly developed and stated. Never is the pupil launched upon an unknown sea, never does he work blindly, or have to learn that for which he can see no reason. Preparatory knowledge, explanations, illustrations, precede conclusions. All the case usages are developed so as to spur thought and make understanding clear. The fundamental case idea is given and other usages are built upon that. The historical touches in dealing with the ablative and the subjunctive add interest and clearness. The presentation of the subjunctive is a happy combination of the new terminology, basic principles, and clear, simple exposition. The unity of the whole work, the harmony of the parts, the correct method of thinking given the pupil, are strong healthful features of the book.

The summary of constructions in the back of the book may profitably be used with the second year's work.

LILLIAN CARTER

PRINCETON, IND.

Geographical Stories Retold from St. Nicholas. New York: The Century Co., 1907.

Nothing, however small, that will help to bridge the chasm in the youthful mind between "reading for fun" and "literature," that will in any degree convince that good writers, as truly as poor ones, have written for the purpose of giving pleasure, and really have given more pleasure than poor ones, can be considered unimportant. Therefore every book that by its appearance or character will make boys or girls wish to read it or others like it, and will at the same time lead toward the greater and better books, has genuine educational value—perhaps greater than we at first suppose. The series of books issued by The Century Co. comprises six volumes of something under two hundred pages each: *Stories of Strange Sights; Stories of the Great Lakes; Western Frontier Stories; Sea Stories; Island Stories,* and *Southern Stories.* The stories have been read in *St. Nicholas* by such armies of children that they require no comment. They are here presented in a form as attractive as anyone could well wish, in excellent print with interesting illustration. A good deal of valuable instruction is conveyed in the six volumes, sometimes with a very thin coating of narrative. But the greatest value in such books is the lesson they give in reading as a source of pleasure.

J. A. C.

BOOKS RECEIVED

THE UNIVERSITY OF CHICAGO PRESS

Literature in the Elementary School. By PORTER LANDER MACCLINTOCK, A.M. Cloth. Pp. 305.

First-Year Mathematics for Secondary Schools. By GEORGE WILLIAM MYERS. Cloth, 12mo. Illustrated. Pp. 198. Net $1.00; postpaid $1.09.

Geometric Exercises for Algebraic Solution. By GEORGE WILLIAM MYERS. Cloth, 12mo. Illustrated. Pp. 86.

AMERICAN BOOK COMPANY, NEW YORK

The Trail to the Woods. By CLARENCE HAWKES. Cloth, 12mo. Illustrated. Pp. 176. $0.40.

Text-Book in General Zoölogy. By GLENN W. HERRICK, B.S.A. Cloth, 12mo. Pp. 386. $1.20.

Text-Book in Physics. By WILLIAM N. MUMPER, Ph.D. Cloth, 8vo. Illustrated. Pp. 411. $1.20.

Book of Plays for Little Actors. By EMMA L. JOHNSTON AND MADELENE D. BARNUM. Cloth, 16 mo. Illustrated. Pp. 171. $0.30.

Second Fairy Reader. By JAMES BALDWIN. Cloth, 12mo. Illustrated. Pp. 192. $0.35.

Explorers and Founders of America. By ANNA ELIZABETH FOOTE AND AVERY WARNER SKINNER. Cloth, 12mo. Illustrated. Pp. 310. $0.60.

The Adventures of Deerslayer. Adapted from J. FENIMORE COOPER'S *Deerslayer*, by MARGARET M. HAIGHT. Cloth, 12mo. Illustrated. Pp. 131. $0.35.

The Story of Two Boys. Retold by CLIFTON JOHNSON. Cloth, 12mo. Illustrated. Pp. 192. $0.35.

Famous Pictures of Children. By JULIA AUGUSTA SCHWARTZ. Cloth, 12mo. Illustrated. Pp. 144. $0.40.

Practical Zoölogy. By ALVIN DAVISON, A.M., PH.D. Cloth, 12mo. Illustrated. Pp. 368. $1.00.

High School Algebra. By J. H. TANNER, PH.D. Half-leather, 8vo. Pp. 352. $1.00.

GINN AND COMPANY, CHICAGO

With Pencil and Pen. By SARAH LOUISE ARNOLD. Cloth, 12mo. Illustrated. Pp. 130.

Rhymes and Stories. By MARION FLORENCE LANSING, M.A. Cloth, 16mo. Illustrated. Pp. vi+184.

Introductory Sight-Singing Melodies. By E. W. NEWTON. Cloth, 8vo. Pp. v+42. Net $0.22; postpaid $0.30.

Laboratory Exercises in Elementary Physics. By H. NEWMAN, B.S., P.D.M. Paper. Illustrated.

Examining and Grading Grains. By THOMAS LYTTLETON LYON, PH.D., AND EDWARD GERRARD MONTGOMERY, B.S.C. Cloth, 12mo. Illustrated. Pp. 101. Net $0.60.

VOLUME VIII NUMBER 6

THE ELEMENTARY SCHOOL TEACHER

FEBRUARY, 1908

SOME FEATURES OF THE GERMAN WORK AT THE FRANCIS W. PARKER SCHOOL

ARTHUR G. MERRILL
Francis W. Parker School

In this paper I shall try to outline certain features of the German work of the intermediate and grammar grades of the Francis W. Parker School.

The course begins in the first year of the elementary school and extends through the high school. Few schools begin the language so early, yet we believe that by the conclusions of many leading psychologists our experiment is justified. Certainly experience has proved that the best time for beginning a foreign language is within the language period, from four to nine years. The children at this period acquire the difficult foreign sounds easily and accurately. The work, it seems to us, possesses for them not only a very great interest, but also a real educational and social value. Again, very simple work, which is necessary to everyone beginning a foreign language, is in the primary grades the natural form of expression, and there is much available material, such as songs, nursery rhymes, and games, which will give repetition and fluency in a most pleasing and economical way, while for older children beginning a language it is much more difficult to find simple material possessing both value and interest.

The acquirement of the German language, however, is not the only purpose of the work at the Francis W. Parker School. This, indeed, is a very important purpose, but we believe the work can be of greatest social and intellectual value by making it a means of introducing the children to a new world of thought, to a world full of noble and inspiring literature, abounding in song, ballad, and legend; and particularly to a nation foremost in history and politics, in scientific research, and in education.

In the work of the Elementary School we have four definite aims in view: First, to give the children an insight into life in Germany, the manners and customs of the people, their homes and social life, for as Colonel Parker has so well said:

> A real picture of how a nation lives, the family and social relations, the education and customs, is of more philosophic value than the lives of individual men, such as Alexander, Caesar, or Napoleon; for the first furnishes the conditions through which great men become great.

A second aim is to give the pupils definite knowledge of the country, "the stage upon which the nation's history moves." A third aim is to introduce the children to the literature and music of the Fatherland. A fourth aim deals with the technique of the language, with special emphasis upon the acquirement of a good pronunciation and an adequate power of expression in the simple vocabulary of the home and school. Incidentally, a body of grammatical knowledge will be acquired, the principle of Herder being followed, that "grammar should be learned through language, not language through grammar."

In the selection of subject-matter we believe that ideal work should possess these characteristics: (1) It must be of real interest to the children or associated with some interesting experience; (2) it must have real educational value; (3) it must call forth their best efforts; (4) it must develop power; (5) it must have a social purpose, direct or indirect.

It is difficult to select the kinds of work that fulfil all the above requirements. We will present as illustrations of our material types of work which are associated with other subjects, music, art, geography, and history, hoping to show how the language work becomes a means of appreciating the German spirit from these various points of view.

The singing of beautiful songs is of great value in developing *Sprachgefühl.* Through the legitimate appeal to the child's emotional nature it tends to enlist his heart as well as his intellect. As a well-known advocate of the reform method of modern-language instruction in Germany says: "Es wirkt belebend auf den fremdsprachlichen Unterricht." This work necessarily makes a strong demand for accurate articulation of the foreign sounds.

The observance of Christmas and other holidays at the school very often includes the singing of some of the best German songs suited to the occasion such as "Stille Nacht," "Tannenbaum," "O, heiliges Kind, wir grüssen dich!" etc. This is one of the many ways in which the language becomes the means of rendering a real service in the school community. The coming of spring makes appropriate Heine's "Frühlingsgruss" and Geibel's "Der Mai ist gekommen." The study of famous places in Germany gives opportunity for the singing of such songs as "Die Lorelei," "Der alte Barbarossa," "O Strassburg," and "Alt Heidelberg," the last three only in the grammar grades. The natural interest of children in outdoor life suggests such songs as "Im Wald und auf der Heide." To understand the national spirit of Germany there is surely no more effective way than to sing their rousing patriotic songs.

As an example of the correlation of German with art and handwork I will simply mention the composition, printing, illustrating, and binding of a little German book, entitled *das gestohlene Kind.* This story of mediaeval life, a favorite with children in Germany under the name of *Heinrich von Eichenfels,* was read by a class in the seventh and eighth grades, our text being that of Guerber in *Märchen und Erzählungen,* Vol. I. After considerable study the class made a dramatization of the story. Then followed the printing of the play, the work for the most part being done outside of school hours by the boys of the class under the direction of the teacher. One edition of the play was illustrated by the pupils with water-color sketches and by illuminated letters in the spirit of the Middle Ages. To study mediaeval books, and particularly the illuminated manuscripts, several excursions were made to the Newberry Library. There also sketches were made of mediaeval coats of arms, weapons, etc., to be used in illustrating the story. The book was finally bound in leather. The art work and bookbinding were done under the supervision of the art teacher.

ERSTER AUFTRITT

(In der Kinderstube im Schlosse des Grafen von Eichenfels. Die Gräfin sitzt am Tische. Heinrich spielt in der Ecke. Margarete, das Kindermädchen, bringt die Wiege in Ordnung.)

Gräfin.

Ach, ich bin so ängstlich. Mein lieber Mann ist schon so lange fort. Wenn dieser unglückliche Krieg nur zu Ende wäre! Ich hab' schon so lange keine Nachrichten von ihm gehabt.

Margarete.

Bedenken Sie doch, gnadige Frau, es ist so schwer in Kriegszeiten Nachrichten hierher zuschicken. Ich denke, Sie werden aber doch bald von ihm horen.

Children who become intensely interested in a given topic in a foreign language are thereby acquiring a greater proficiency in the language itself. Obviously in looking for topics for our work it is important to consider the child's interests and the relation of the language to the other work of the grade. It has been stated by a well-known writer on pedagogy that from the eleventh to the fourteenth year among the strongest interests are hero-worship, imaginary journeys, voyages, knowledge of different peoples, and the grouping of facts by natural relations. All these interests may be united in the making of a beautiful book recording an imaginary journey in the country studied, with interesting accounts of great men associated with places visited, due attention being paid to the part played by local heroes in the country's development. With such a real motive for careful work children accomplish surprising results. The making of a book brings home to the children the necessity for accuracy, and neatness, and at the same time unifies their work by directing all efforts toward one end.

To gives details regarding the various parts of the Teutonic world which have been studied in this way by different grades would exceed the limits allowed for this article. The following books are illustrations of this type of work:

Sixth and seventh grades, 1906, *Das Hessenland.*

Seventh grade, 1904 and 1905, *Holland.*

Seventh and eighth grades, 1907, *Südwestdeutschland* (Heidelberg; the Black Forest; Roman sites in South Germany; Influence of Roman Civilization on Germany; Strassburg; Village life in Alsace).

Eighth grade, 1905, *Die deutsche Schweiz.*

Eighth grade, 1906, *Der Rhein.*

In the making of such books we plan an itinerary involving the study of places of special interest. Immediately we are confronted by a multitude of fascinating topics: the home life; the peculiarities of the region; the places to visit, etc. After much research we endeavor to select from an increasing number of local associations those best adapted to the particular group of children. Special reading-lessons are then prepared, consisting of material bearing on the subject in hand. The work naturally requires careful study of the best maps obtainable. In addition, it is most desirable to have illustrative material in the form of pictures, charts, steamship circulars, guide books, etc.[1] Since each child is to make a book for himself, inexpensive pictures, such as postcards, can be used to good advantage.

The plan outlined provides a natural setting for choice extracts from German literature, particularly for short poems, which the pupils learn with greater interest because of the direct association with their new experiences.

It is assumed that incidentally due attention will be given to the grammatical side of the language, as well as to formal drill to acquire accuracy in expression, but the technical work

[1] See list of illustrative material given at the close of this article.

must not be allowed to obscure the purpose of the course. It is held that even in the middle grades the gaining of experience in the use of the language is of the utmost importance, and that the greatest emphasis should not be placed on technical grammar before the ninth grade.

Whatever section of the Teutonic world may be chosen for intensive study, an effort is made to relate it definitely to the work of the grade, particularly in history, geography, and, to a certain extent, with technical English.

Following are some details regarding the making of the book on *Das Hessenland* in the seventh grade, 1905. Naturally the first problem in presenting such a subject is to establish points of connection with the child's experience. The starting-point might have been stories of Charlemagne or Barbarossa, suggested by the grade work in history. As it actually happened, we began in this way: It was found that many stories, first told to children in the Hessian lands have come to be favorites with children in America, in fact with pupils in this very grade; for example, the stories of Mother Holle and some of the Grimm tales. (The author of the latter lived for years in the heart of the Hessenland and there wrote some of his best-known stories.) The work actually began with the narration by one of the members of the class of a story of Frau Holle. On investigation different versions were found, as well as additional material on the subject. We also located places like Frau Hollenteich, the Meissner Mountain Waldmannshäuschen, etc., associated with the Frau Holle legends.

Von der Frau Holle erzählt das Volk vielerlei, Gutes und Böses. Frauen, die zu ihr in den Brunnen steigen, macht sie gesund. Blumen, Obst, Kuchen, das sie unten im Teiche hat und was in ihrem Garten wächst, teilt sie denen aus, die ihr begegnen und zu gefallen wissen. Sie ist sehr ordentlich und hält auf guten Haushalt. Wenn es bei den Menschen schneit, klopft sie ihre Betten aus, davon die Flocken in der Luft fliegen. Faule Spinnerinen straft sie, indem sie ihnen den Rock besudelt, das Garn wirrt, oder den Flachs anzündet; Jungfrauen hingegen, die fleissig abspinnen, schenkt sie Spindeln und spinnt selber für sie über Nacht, dass die Spulen des Morgens voll sind.

Some attention was also given to the stories of Thor and Woden as given in *Glück auf*. Places in the Hessenland connected with the worship of the ancient gods were also located.

Wodans Sohn war Donar (Thor), der Gewittergott. Ihm brachte man Opfer unter einer grossen Eiche bei dem Dorfe Geismar in der Nähe von Fritzlar dar.

The study of pictures illustrating conditions of life in this part of the Fatherland was of very great assistance in introducing the subject.

The children now began to ask many questions about the Hessians and their picturesque country; the homes; how the people dress; how they are governed; how they make a living; what they have done in the past.

The answers to these questions required the use of much material which is either not easily accessible or which does not exist in English. Here then is a real reason for the study of the language, aside from the desire to acquire another means of expression.

The making of the book served to give unity to the work for two terms. The most valuable material on the subject was gathered from many sources: legends and historical stories of places; important facts regarding the country from a geographical point of view; composite descriptions of pictures; suitable extracts from literature, especially very easy poems. (When in the form of songs these were sometimes sung.)

The literary and historical material is simple and is in all cases associated with the topic in hand. A visit to the Goethe House in Frankfurt a/M. suggested Goethe's boyhood in the city, with mention of places that interested him most as a boy, the walls, the Römer, and the market place. One of the reading-slips gives Goethe's own words:

Am liebsten spazierte ich auf der grossen Mainbrücke. Gewöhnlich ward dann durch Sachenhausen spaziert und die Ueberfahrt gar behaglich genossen.

Die Buden auf dem Marktplatz bei der Bartholomäuskirche waren uns Kindern sehr bedeutend. Ich erinnere mich auch, dass ich immer mit Entsetzen vor den Fleischbänken geflohen bin.[2]

A visit to the "Römer," the election place of the ancient German emperors, takes us back to the legendary founding of the city by Charlemagne, the following poem being learned:

Die besten seiner Helden, sie lagen in Sachsen tot:
Da floh Karolus Magnus, der Kaiser, in grosser Not.

[2] Goethe, *Dichtung und Wahrheit.*

"Lasst eine Furt uns suchen längshin am schönen Main!
O weh, da liegt ein Nebel, der Feind ist hintendrein!"

Nun betet Kaiser Karol auf Knieen an seinem Speer,
Da teilte sich der Nebel, eine Hirschin ging daher.

Die führte ihre Jungen hinüber zum andern Strand;
So machte Gott den Franken die rechte Furt bekannt.

Hinüber zogen alle, wie Israel durch's Meer;
Die Sachsen aber fanden im Nebel die Furt nicht mehr.

Da schlug der Kaiser Karol mit seinem Schwert den Sand:
"Die Stätte sei hinfüro der Franken Furt genannt."

Several stories of Barbarossa, whose life is also at times associated with the city of Frankfurt a/M., were read, for example, "Der Schelm von Bergen;" legendary account of Barbarossa's death; Rückert's poem, "Der alte Barbarossa" (sung by class).

A ramble about the city leads to the telling of legends concerning the places we visit. As there is a wealth of interesting material on this topic the subject grows and becomes suggestive of many lines of research. Among the Frankfurt stories read were "Die Sachsenhäuser Brücke;" " Der Erfinder vom Apfelwein;" " Die '9' in der Wetterfahne."

In a similar way visits to other places in the Hessian lands help to establish points of connection with the grade work in history and geography, at the same time preparing the way for a more detailed study of these topics in the higher grades, for example, the Luther stories associated with Worms; stories of Philip the Generous and of St. Elizabeth, in connection with Marburg.

The following letter, written by a German boy of fourteen from one of the most delightful towns in the Hessenland, gives a little glimpse into the life of a boy in Germany:

EIN NEUJAHRSBRIEF AUS DEM HESSENLAND

MARBURG AN DER LAHN, d. 1. Jan. 1906

LIEBER HERR N.! Es ist sehr lange Zeit her, dass ich Ihnen geschrieben habe und ich muss doch mal sehen, wie es Ihnen geht. Hoffentlich haben Sie das Weihnachtsfest froh verlebt und das neue Jahr recht glücklich angefangen. Möge Ihnen das neue Jahr von recht grossem Vorteile sein und viel Glück und Segen bringen.

Hier ist es sehr kalt und wir laufen Schlittschuh. Leider hat es noch keinen Schnee gegeben, doch ohne Schnee geht es auch.

Wir hatten vor einigen Wochen fünf Schaumburger bei zum Kaffee und Abendbrot; da gab es viele Witze und Geschichten zu erzählen. Der Spass dauerte bis 12. Sie haben ja eine Karte erhalten, wo sich die ganze Tafelrunde unterschrieben hat. Ihre deutschen Freunde haben Sie und werden Sie niemals vergessen.

Nochmals mit vielen, vielen Grüssen,

Ihr junger Freund

HANS

Tausend Grüsse von Eltern und Geschwistern.

One of the best short poems on the subject is the

HESSENLIED

Hessenland, liebes Land,
Sei mir gegrüsst!
Du liegst mir stets im Sinn,
Ueberall, wo ich bin.
Hessenland, liebes Land,
Sei mir gegrüsst!

Mag es auch anderswo
Schöner noch sein,
Herzen so gut, so froh,
Find' ich doch nirgendwo.
Hessenland, traulich Land,
Sei mir gegrüsst!

The following quaint night watchman's songs from the Hessenland were memorized by the class:

LIED DER NACHTWACHE

Hört ihr Herr'n und lasst euch sagen:
Die Glocke, die hat zehne geschlagen;
Bewahret das Feuer und auch das Licht;
Dass dieser Gemeinde kein Schaden geschicht.
Und lobet Gott den Herrn.

WÄCHTERRUF UM ZEHN UHR ABENDS

Hört ihr Herr'n in dieser Nacht,
Was die Glocke geschlagen hat!
Zehne ist es an der Zeit,
Lobet Gott in Ewigkeit!
Wenn andre Leute schlafen geh'n,
Dann muss ich auf der Strasse steh'n!

Wünsch' euch all'n eine gute Nacht!
Nehmt das Feuer und Licht in Acht!
Lobet Gott den Herrn!

Examples of original descriptions of pictures are the following:

Das schöne Nationaldenkmal steht auf einem Berge, Bingen gegenüber. Die grosse Figur oben ist die Germania. Die Figur ist aus Bronze. Vorn auf dem Denkmal ist der deutsche Adler.

The picture of a quaintly dressed little Hessian girl trying to open a big door suggests the following description:

"Mach' auf, Mutter! Lass mich herein. Dort kommt ein Fremder." So spricht die kleine Greta.

"Sei nicht bange, kleines Mädchen. Ich tue dir nichts zu Leide. Wie heisst du, kleines Kind?"

"Gretchen."

"Wohnst du hier?"

"Ja."

"Ist deine Mama zu Hause?"

"Ja, sie kommt gleich."

A picture card showing peasant women and girls in picturesque costumes just leaving church, is briefly described as follows:

Diese Frauen und Mädchen kommen eben aus der Kirche. Sie tragen alle blaue Röcke, weisse Strümpfe und kleine Kopfbedeckungen. Jede Frau hat auf dem Mieder eine Anzahl Knöpfe aus Metall. Die Kirche ist aus Stein. Ueber dem Eingang sehen wir ein Kreuz.

Places of historic interest described are the following: Das Lutherdenkmal, der Lutherbaum, Worms; Schloss Wilhelmshöhe bei Kassel (Napoleon III was a prisoner here, 1870); Das Goethehaus, der Römer, Frankfurt a/M.: Die Elisabeth Kirche, Elisabethbrunnen, Marburg; Wilhelmslinde, Dillenburg.

Legendary stories given are as follows: (1) Charlemagne; (2) Barbarossa; (3) St. Elisabeth (Marburg); (4) Frau Holle; (5) Der nächtliche Reiter (Dillenburg); (6) St. Boniface (Fulda); (7) Der Mäuseturm (Bingen); (8) Der Wassergeist in der Kinzig (Hanan).

The poems are as follows: Hessenlied; "Heidenröslein" (Goethe); Hessische Nachtwächterlieder; "Der alte Barbarossa;" "Gefunden" (Goethe).

Der Kirchgang in der Schwalm

Diese Frauen und Mädchen kommen eben aus der Kirche.

Sie tragen alle blaue Röcke, weisse Strümpfe, weisse Ärmel, Schnallenschuhe und kleine Kopfbedeckungen.

Jede Frau hat auf dem Mieder eine Anzahl Knöpfe aus Metall.

Die Kirche ist aus Stein. Über dem Eingang sehen wir ein Kreuz. Die meisten Hessen sind Protestanten.

Gruss aus Hes-

Miscellaneous: "Ein Neujahrsbrief aus dem Hessenland."

In conclusion, it has been proved to our satisfaction that the intensive study of a given section of the German speaking world, with careful recording of interesting material, has for several years in our school enlisted the best efforts of pupils in acquiring the German language, at the same time stimulating interest in all that concerns the life of the great German nation.

ILLUSTRATIVE MATERIAL

1. Lehmann Wandbilder (wall charts) (34½×26′), Verlag von F. E. Wachsmuth, Leipzig, are excellent. They may be imported through McClurg & Co., Chicago, or E. Steiger, New York City. The following subjects are especially good: (1) "Turnier" (Tournament); (2) "Lagerleben des 30-jährigen Krieges" (Camp Life in the 30-Years' War); (3) "Im Rittersaal" (In a Knight's Hall); (4) "Inneres einer Stadt, 15. Jahrhundert (Interior of a City, Fifteenth Century); (5) "Bürgerliches Wohnzimmer, 16. Jahrhundert" (Living-room of a Burgher, Sixteenth Century); (6) "Tiroler Dorf mit Volkstypen" (Tyrolese Village with Types); (7) "Der Dom zu Köln" (Cathedral at Cologne); (8) "Das Nationaldenkmal auf dem Niederwald" (National Monument); (9) "Die Berner Alpen" (Bernese Alps); (10) "Der Rhein bei Bingen" (Rhine at Bingen); (11) "Das Siebengebirge" (The Seven Mountains); (12) "Das Kyffhäuserdenkmal" (Kyffhäuser Monument).

2. Post cards can be used for illustrations in book-making or as general illustrative material. The writer has on hand duplicates of a large variety of artistic cards, such as are used in making of the books described. Address A. G. Merrill, 550 Webster Ave., Chicago, Ill.

BIBLIOGRAPHY

Carl Hessler. *Hessische Landes- und Volkskunde.* Band II, Volkskunde. Marburg a/L.: N. G. Elwert'sche Verlagsbuchhandlung, 1904.

Emil Schneider. *Hessisches Sagenbüchlein.* Marburg a/L.: N. G. Elwert'sche Verlagsbuchhandlung, 1905.

Stern. *Geschichten vom Rhein, und Geschichten von deutschen Städten.* New York: American Book Co.

Victor, Carl. *Sagenkranz aus Hessen—Nassau und der Wartburg Gegend.* Cassel, 1894.

Kahnmeyer und Schulze. *Realienbuch (Vollständige Ausgabe).* Leipzig: Wellhagen und Klasing, 1904.

Claudius, Martin. *Rheinsagen.* Leipzig: Ferdinand Hirt & Sohn.

Krüger, Carl A. *Geschichtsbilder für Schulen.* Berlin. J. Reutet, 1899.

Bädeker. Der Rhein.

Schoof, W. *Marburg, die Perle des Hessenlandes.* Marburg a/L.: N. G. Elwert.

THE DEEPER AND THE RICHER MEANINGS OF MATHEMATICAL TEACHING IN ELEMENTARY SCHOOLS

GEORGE W. MYERS
College of Education

MODERN THOUGHT AND TENDENCIES FAVORABLE TO MATHEMATICAL EDUCATION

This is an age of industrial and economic standards. To bewail the spirit of the time as commercialism is as futile as it is unprogressive. Earnest and prudent men do not deny facts; but accept them and deal with them. Hence, educationists are attempting to put their theories into efficient relation with economic and industrial facts. Attempts to harmonize the grounds of education with the basal facts of modern industrial conditions are being integrated into the doctrine of pragmatism. Speaking roughly and roundly, this doctrine seems to mean that truth is that which works well, frees activity, liberates thinking. Utility, broadly conceived as workability, is at the bottom of it. When educational theory veers into this course, mathematics in school work readily finds for itself both fulcrum and purchase.

The watchword of industrial enterprise is the utilization of waste products. The extent to which waste products are being converted into by-products marks the present epoch. The observance or non-observance of this law of conversion makes most of the difference between industrial successes and failures. Thus industrial survival is spelled out in terms of the closeness with which raw material balances output, with which means balance ends. Wherever accuracy of adjustment of means to ends, economic balance of effort and result, are called for, there is the place and function of mathematics. In this domain mathematics comes to its birthright, and enters pre-eminently into its own.

Consequently, whether viewed from the vantage-point of the educational theorist, or of the man of affairs, the mathematical element in education is peculiarly opportune and efficacious in the work of modern society and of social progress. But that mathematics may perform its proper office richly and liberally in educational polity, its deeper meanings must be seized and pressed into practical service. The principle of action, referred to above, that has been so well wrought out in the economic world, is freighted with significance and suggestion for the thoughtful teacher of elementary-school mathematics. This very wholesome practical doctrine has not yet been worked into the teaching of elementary-school mathematics with much thoroughness. Too large a percentage of pedagogic effort in arithmetic is devoted to mere mechanical training; and too small a proportion to educating. There are too many waste products in current processes of teaching arithmetic. No school subject, old or new, offers to well-qualified professional ability wider scope, richer opportunity, or brighter promise for improvement of output, by a completer observance of this economic law of conversion, than does school arithmetic. Lest the power of the combined evidence from educational philosophy and from practical economics fail of convincing some on this point, evidence from classroom experience may also be admitted.

MATHEMATIZED ARITHMETIC

My reason for preferring the term, elementary-school mathematics, to the customary term, arithmetic, is that the scope of the mathematical work of the modern elementary school is much broader than arithmetic, in a definitive sense. It includes form-study from the first grade through the eighth grade. It also includes the first notions of algebra under the form of general arithmetic. The form-work ripens gradually into the rudiments of geometry, before mensuration is completed. This work is all unified around an arithmetical center, and taken up at such times and places as to illuminate, to rationalize, and to reinforce the arithmetic—not primarily to prepare for high-school mathematics. In a phrase, the proper subject-matter for elementary-school mathematics may be fittingly termed *mathematized arithmetic.* It is this type of mathematical work that I have in mind, whether I use the phrase elementary-school mathematics or simply arithmetic.

DEEPER AND RICHER VALUES OF ELEMENTARY-SCHOOL MATHEMATICS

The deeper and richer meanings of elementary-school mathematics, whose importance in teaching I wish to emphasize, are:

1. Clear imaging and clear thinking.
2. Connected thinking and inference-making.
3. Concentrated thinking.
4. Independent thinking and judging.
5. Exercising the power to choose and strengthening the will.

These several virtues of mathematical work are enumerated in the order in which they should be emphasized in teaching.

In the first and second grades of many elementary schools, the arithmetical work that is done is made incidental and contributory to other school activities and subjects. No special attention is given to the number- and form-interests of children. Still the other school arts of reading and writing are begun explicitly at once. Neither the *laissez-faire* nor the occasional type of treatment is held to be good for the school arts of reading and writing in the first and second grades. For them it is conceded that a good beginning is half the battle. To me it seems a grievous error to withhold expert aid from the beginner in arithmetic as long as is customary. This is the very subject in which a poor start, or a wrong start, after working great havoc to interest and profit in school work, turns more boys and girls away from the schools, than is the case with any other school subject. The distaste that children manifest toward arithmetic is due, not to the subject-matter, but to a wrong start, or to no start at all, aggravated by poor subsequent teaching of the subject. It is the teaching, or rather the lack of it, that is the rock of offense. Boys and girls should no more be denied the opportunity of a fair start in arithmetic on the ground that they cannot do the work well, than they are denied the opportunity of getting started right in reading and writing, because at first they cannot read or write well.

THE TEACHER'S MOTIVE SHOULD BE CLEAR

But whether the programme provide help for the children at the outset or not, it is important that the teacher have clear ideas and convictions as to the phases of number- and form-work that should receive attention during the first and second school years. Even under the plan of incidental number-teaching, the teacher may render efficient service as occasion permits, by stopping now and then to stress, or to solidify a little, a number- or form-notion met in the other work. It is even more important that this be done frequently under the incidental plan, than under the plan of explicit teaching. For children of this period are greedy for sensations about everything. Many of these sensations must pertain to number, form, and magnitude. Soon this greed for sensations results in a large mass of nuclei, or cores of concepts and images. If no aid is at hand in ordering and systematizing a little this mass of material as it accumulates, it remains an unassimilable mass of detail of little use to him who has it. Indeed it often becomes a source of general confusion of mind to him. Soon this confusion becomes more confounded by the rapidly accumulating materials of sensation, and the pupil grows perplexed and annoyed. If help be withheld at these critical moments pleasure in future arithmetical progress is doomed. All this I have so often seen, both in the classroom and outside of it, that I cannot be either mistaken or exaggerating.

PURPOSE OF SECOND-GRADE WORK TO DEFINE AND CLARIFY IDEAS OF QUANTITY

In the second school year the supply of more or less poorly defined ideas becomes unwieldy. It is imperative that some defining and clarifying of these ideas be done. The notions, started through the seeing, handling, playing, and working with things in the first grade, must be given some fulness and definiteness of outline. This is done through the "how much?" and "how many?" of number and magnitude. The distinctive purpose of the second-grade number-work should be delimiting and clarifying quantitative imagery. Simple estimates, indefinite comparison of magnitudes, and the beginnings of definite comparisons and measurements should be salient features of this year's work.

The activities and materials through which the image cores of number and magnitude should be set up are: rhythmic movements, skipping plays, singing, number, rhymes, playing store, dramatic plays, committee work, making, cooking, cutting, gardening, sewing, drawing, estimating, comparing, measuring, counting rhythmically (by 2's, 5's, 10's, etc.), intuitive geometry, the number names, the digits, quick work, reading foot-rule, thermometer, and recording facts found in number dictionaries.

FORMAL WORK FOR SECOND-GRADE ARITHMETIC

The formal work of the second grade should include, at frequent intervals, such oral exercises as: "Give some numbers that, together, make 12, 14, 15," etc. Call for volunteers rapidly; write down the numbers as given, and have the class, sometimes as a whole and sometimes one at a time, add up the suggested numbers, to convince all that the numbers, taken together, do make the required number. This helps the pupil to feel the essential nature of adding, and moreover it has the psychological warrant of keeping the pupil working within a more or less vague whole to define it more fully.

Addition is thus used as a way of making vague wholes definite, as a kind of measurement. There is purpose in it for the pupil. It helps him to know some things better. Some pupil will say, directly, that 14 is a 10 and a 4. Then stop, with some such casual remark as: "Why certainly. One might see that by looking at it." Continue with enough such work to make clear the place-value of digits in two-figure numbers.

The learner thus comes first to an unknown number, as 18, *as a whole,* that he knows little about, but feels he ought to know more about. He breaks it into parts, learns it through these parts, which never get so far from the whole that the learner loses connection of whole and part. He always and continually looks at 18 in the light of its parts. This is just the opposite of the customary procedure of constructing numbers by heaping unity upon unity with the learner blindfolded as to the goal of the heaping, until the very end, when the number the teacher had in mind is reached. Under the suggested plan the constructive steps are taken in the full light of their bearing on the number, as 18, that is being learned. Then, as soon as the pupil sees that 18 is

10 and 8, ask: How many is 18 less 10? 18 less 8? thus bringing out and impressing, at once, the related character of addition and subtraction. It is wasteful in the extreme, not to teach addition and subtraction together, for ideas then have to be acquired by bits and by piecemeal. The *fragment* of an idea is difficult to acquire and next to impossible to retain.

Next, "Give some numbers that, combined, make 21, 23, 24," etc. Call for volunteers, as before. When someone says for 21, 10, and 11, stop, remarking casually: "That's what I wanted, 1 ten and 11 ones." Then treat 22, 23, etc., similarly, emphasizing as the thing you wanted, the 1, 10, and 12 ones, 1, 10, and 13 ones, etc. The bright boy will catch the point quickly; but allow the slower ones to do most of the answering, until many can at once see a two-figure number as so many tens and 11, 12, 13, 14, etc. Do not hurry the work. Give more than one day to it. This not only teaches addition at its best, but also gets ready for subtraction without the carrying and borrowing vernacular. Such work should be a feature of second-grade arithmetic. Pupils enjoy it, and so will teachers, particularly when the fruits of clear thinking and imaging begin to show. If you are skeptical about it, try it until you acquire a modicum of skill at it, and you will never return to the interest-killing unity-heaping to build numbers.

After such exercises as the foregoing, the pupil will lay hold at once of such work as: "Take 17 from 43;" thus, 7 cannot be taken from 3; but 43 is 3 tens and 13 ones; 7 from 13 leaves 6, and 1 ten from 3 tens leaves 2 tens; 2 tens and 6 ones, 26 ones. But he soon does it all more quickly than we can say it.

As 12, 14, 16, etc., are being broken into parts, ask: "Who can give 2 *equal* numbers that make 12, 14, etc.?" Then: "What number is ½ of 12, 14, 16, etc.?" Directly ask: "Who can give 3 *equal* numbers that make 12, 15, 18, etc.?" Follow at once with: "What is ⅓ of 12, 15, 18, etc.? ⅔ of 12, 15, 18, etc.?" This work suffices to show that there is an abundance of easy formal number-work adapted to second-grade immaturity, that would very materially assist in clear imaging, and would lay the foundation safe, sure, and speedy, for pleasurable and profitable progress later. For fuller work of second-grade difficulty, see also Myers-Brooks, *Elementary Arithmetic,* Part I.

THE TIMES-IDEA AND THE TABLES

The next difficulty on the road to learning arithmetic is multiplication with its inverse operation, division. Both the times-idea and the multiplication tables should be very thoroughly and rationally taught. I am opposed to drilling, or attempting to drill these matters into children. I do not agree that learning the multiplication tables is a grim struggle of pure memory, the rigors of which can in no wise be mitigated. I am confident that the teachers of this state who give the Myers-Brooks *Elementary Arithmetic* a fair trial will agree with me before two years, if they do not now agree, that learning the tables is one of the most interesting as well as one of the most illuminating parts of arithmetic. This book first teaches, and teaches thoroughly, the tables. Then it drills amply upon them.

The most helpful pedagogic means of teaching the tables is measurement. This is not because measurement is numbering; but rather because the physical acts that must be gone through in measuring run so closely parallel to the mental steps that must be taken in numbering, that all the motor imagery of the former serves to reinforce and to guarantee the correct mental imagery of the latter. The cyclic acts of putting down, taking up, noting the end-point; again putting down, taking up, and noting the end-point, doing it again, etc., until the magnitude in question is measured, are so rhythmical, so repetitive, as to suggest inescapably the rhythmical balancing of the parts in a whole, which is the essence of the times-idea. The multiplicand is so clearly the standard of measurement, the multiplier, so clearly the number of times the standard is to be used, to be put down and taken up to give the product, that multiplication must, perforce, be sensed by the learner as a kind of actual, or imagined, measurement.

TEACHING THE MULTIPLICATION TABLE

Teaching the tables rationally includes (1) a reconnoiter of each part of the table; (2) constructing the table diagrammatically, as with squares, or on squared-paper; (3) building the tables additively; (4) a first attempt at committing the tables, during which most, not all, of the committing will be done; (5) drill upon the tables, not once for all, but pretty copiously, at this stage, and then systematically for a brief time every day or two; and (6) applying the tables in problems.

In reconnoitering the part of the table being taught, the common denominate number standards that are related to the particular table in question should be used in easy problems that can be solved and understood, *by common-sense methods without the table.* This impresses the pupil with the true reason for learning the tables; viz., because they are constantly needed in common measurement. Only purposive teaching *educates;* mechanical teaching, at best, only *trains.* For example, in the 3's, 3 ft.=1 yd.; in the 4's, 4 qt.=1 gal., and 4 pk.=1 bu., and the like can be made to do valuable service, while, incidentally, most of the basal denominate number facts are taught, and much better taught, than in the old-time isolated, topical fashion. The knowledge of these facts, thus acquired, becomes a more thoroughly organic possession of pupils than the compartmental treatment makes them.

In building the tables, such facts as the following should be closely associated: $5\times6=30$; $6\times5=30$; 1/5 of 30=6; 1/6 of 30=5; $30\div6=5$; $30\div5=6$; what are the factors of 30? and such variations as: 6 5's=how many 6's? 4 7's=how many 4's? etc.; and 7 15's=how many 7's? 8 25's=how many 8's? etc.; 2 3's are 6; how many 3's in 2 6's? in 3 6's? in 5 6's? etc.; 3 6's are 18; how many 6's are 2 18's? 3 18's? 4 18's? and so on through the 6-series of products; then the 8-series; 10-series; 12-series; etc.; ¼ of 40 is 10: how many fourths of 40 is 20? 30?

Obviously, the possibilities of such work as this are unlimited. Five to ten minutes a day ought to be given to it from the third grade through the eighth. Time forbids further specifications of detail on this point; but perhaps enough has been said to make my point, that clear thinking and clear perceiving will be the sure outcome of good arithmetic teaching. It may be added that the great value of this type of formal work as training in concentrated and ready thinking, in mental springiness, and mechanical freedom, are among its virtues. The work must be brisk, and snap, and there must be movement and purpose to secure concentration of attention and thought. It is better to step aside from the main line of work for three to five minutes when a number difficulty is met that drill will relieve, and give the necessary drill, then pass on, than to take a whole class period for drill. No one will admit this more readily than the real teacher.

Factoring, cancellation, and checking work by casting out the nines and by other familiar processes are of great assistance in readiness and concentration of thought if these processes are not taught as separate topics for their own sake, but as matters to be used on every proper opportunity, to shorten, to facilitate, and to guarantee work.

To complete the view of the scope of the grade work as a whole we must continue a little farther.

PURPOSE OF THIRD- AND FOURTH-GRADE ARITHMETIC

The specific arithmetic duty of the third and fourth grades is to get the bulk of the tabular machinery of arithmetic under easy working control *through teaching and using* this machinery on easy problems drawn partly from the natural situations of life and partly from set lists designed to impress the particular lesson in hand.

The broader educational purpose of this period of the curriculum is to get started well the study of number and magnitude relations and connection. The beginnings and some progress in connected thinking must here be a part of the teacher's set purpose. The rational mastery of the multiplication table has this specific educational meaning and office.

FIFTH- AND SIXTH-GRADE ARITHMETIC

The fifth and sixth grades must seek especially to extend the learner's control of the four laws of addition, subtraction, multiplication, and division to fractional number, both common and decimal. The broader educational aim here is to give some measure of control of connected thinking, inference-making, and practice in choice of means that are best suited to meet clearly defined ends. Pedagogical effort should here be directed particularly to work calculated to strengthen judgment, to encourage independence, and to confer the feeling of power actually possessed. The feeling of joy in achievement here rises to a veritable craving.

Problems must now require for their solution more than one process, and oftentimes all four of the processes, that the pupil may learn to select the appropriate process for the work, i. e., that he may be trained specifically in *when* to add, when to subtract, to multiply, or to divide, and to prove independently whether his decisions are correct. If his decision be found incorrect, he should be required himself to correct it. In my opinion, no set answers should be allowed in the classroom here. Answer books, made necessary by the demands of teachers and school officials—even correct answers—are serious obstacles in the way of independent thinking. May the time speedily come when the current tendency to cut out the obsolete and the useless and the bad may be applied to the answer pages.

THE SEVENTH- AND EIGHTH-GRADE GROUND

The new ground remaining for the seventh and eighth grades to cover is percentage and interest, and their modern applications, and mensuration. In the first of these topics the only duty of the pupil is to learn a few technical business terms and to recognize when to add, subtract, multiply, and divide, and perhaps, if the teaching is good, to learn a little of the business settings of these topics. Obsolete business topics should be excluded. As the best arithmetics are presenting the subject today, by the time the pupil reaches the seventh grade he has learned nearly all of mensuration in the study of preceding topics. It only remains in the eighth grade to systematize what has already been learned. But the most important office of these two grades is to summarize and to digest into a sort of applied science the whole of arithmetic, hitherto covered. This should be done through the agency of rationalized mensuration, on the one hand, and of generalized number on the other. The rudiments of algebra and geometry should be associated with cognate phases of arithmetic all along. Such informal questions as

$2\ x$'s$=6$, or 8, or 12, etc.; what is one x?
$\frac{1}{2}x=2$, or 3, or 5, etc.; what is x?
$8+x=10$; what is x?
$7-x=4$; what is x?
$\frac{x}{4}=3$; what is x?
$ab=12$; $a=3$; what is b?
A rectangle is 3 in. high and x inches long; what is the area?
$\frac{1}{2}\pm\frac{1}{3}=\frac{3\pm 2}{2\times 3}$ etc., leading to $\frac{1}{a}\pm\frac{1}{b}=\frac{b\pm a}{a\times b}$, etc.

are all easy and enjoyable to children, and make them neighborly with the laws of numbers.

GOOD ARITHMETIC TEACHING TRAINS TO INDEPENDENCE

Well-taught elementary-school mathematics is peculiarly well adapted to strengthening the judgment. No other school subject, old or new, can surpass it in this regard. This strengthening and steadying of judgment is accomplished in three distinct ways: (1) in setting before pupils definite standards of judging, that are unequivocal, unbiased, and highly trustworthy, without being too difficult for the child's powers of comprehension; (2) by continually calling for and insisting upon the independent proving of work and the exercise of self-reliance in the class work; and (3) by developing a conscious feeling of growing power and independence.

To secure the virtues of independent judgment in arithmetic there must be no reasoning from authority, from precedent, and least of all must there be any of the so-called substantiating of conclusions on the basis of memorized rules. No school subject so completely repudiates all semblance of authority, of precedent, and custom, as does mathematics. It is *the* school subject which, in a pre-eminent degree, demands clear reasons and cogent proof for conclusions. The learner must not, at the peril of the best that arithmetic contains for him, be allowed to rely for assurance of the correctness of his work either upon the teacher or upon the answers of a text. No mere working for answers, no arithmetical target-shooting, no hit-and-miss figuring and spotted thinking, and no guessing at the answer, can ever allow arithmetic teaching to come to its own kingdom in education. Steadiness and certainty of mental movement, confidence and dependability of verified results, are the very spirit and essence of arithmetic work. To miss these things in teaching it is to impoverish the subject immeasurably.

Consequently, the pupil must be taught methods of checking work, must be given different ways of arriving at the same result, must be required *habitually* to use these means of backing up results. It is not sufficient, either in school or out of school, to argue: "This is the way to solve this sort of problem: I did it this way, and did it carefully; my result must be correct." To err is human—not simply childish. It is human nature also to make the same error a second time, once it has been made, if the steps are gone over in the same way. Doing the work over again in exactly the same way, merely repeating the work, may ingrain bad habits and propensities and is so poor a guarantee of correctness as to amount practically to no guarantee at all. It is essential that the order of thought be changed, by obtaining the result in another way, or by checking by some wholly independent procedure. Only thus can we hope to develop that type of arithmetical knowledge "that knows that it knows"—the knowledge that predisposes its possessor to defend conclusions, when their reliability is challenged. And this disposition to defend one's findings must be encouraged as incipient tenacity of purpose, which is an index of the seriousness with which the pupil regards his arithmetic, rather than frowned upon as incipient pugnacity. It is the groundwork of that dogged persistence in the face of difficulties which counts at par in the world of affairs. Good arithmetic can do much to foster it.

But a *little* testing and checking will not suffice. The practice must become habitual with the pupil. When school work seeks to influence conduct, it must recognize the difference to be wide between intellectual recognition and assent and that power of automatic control, which is a function of the spinal cord rather than the brain.

To illustrate: the arithmetic pupil must be taught the way, then trained into the habit, of proving sums correct by adding first upward; then downward; or by adding the columns in parts; then as a whole; then comparing the results by the different processes, or by checking the results of addition by casting out the nines. Comparing sums obtained in the usual way with those obtained by adding first the 10's, then the units, is also recommended when there are only two-figure numbers to be added. Much practice in obtaining sums orally is also urged; thus, for 47 and 35, say 47 and 30, 77; and 5, are 82. Analogous considerations hold good for the other three fundamental operations.

Factoring, than which there is no more illuminating subject in all arithmetic, seems rapidly becoming a lost art in the elementary school. This is unfortunate. It is a reflection upon the teaching, coming perilously near a disgrace, to see pupils who have found the lowest common multiple by the prime-factor process, actually dividing each number into the lowest common multiple to find how many times the lowest common multiple contains it; yet this is a common phenomenon even with eighth-grade pupils. Such work is wooden, and the teaching that is responsible for it is open to severe censure.

Another practicable and effective plan of fostering independence in the pupil, that deserves systematic employment, is that of giving time—even a full recitation now and then—for explicit training in "looking ahead before leaping." When a page of problems that call for several processes is reached, individual pupils should be called upon to read a problem through, orally or silently; to take reasonable time to see what the problem means—there should be business-like dispatch, but no hurrying here—and then to state, each in his own words, how he would solve it. The rest of the class should be attending to the explanation to correct any errors in its substance. The line should not be drawn too closely on the elegance of the pupil's English, though gross errors should be quickly corrected, but not dwelt upon. The first problem disposed of, without stopping to solve it pass to the next, and so on in sufficiently rapid succession to prevent the work from dragging. Let it be rapid-fire work; keep the class a little at a loss to know "where the lightning may strike next." When a particular problem has been solved in thought, if it is not too difficult, have the solver tell also *about what the result must be.* The list of problems may then be assigned for home work, the actual solutions to be brought to class next day, or the problems may well be solved in class next day. This plan is commended as a practicable way to teach pupils *how to study.*

The following are some of the ways in which this sort of work is of explicit benefit to the learner:

1. It resolves most of the difficulty of getting the pupil to see how he may know what to do first; what next; etc. It shows him how to clear the ground for work. It reduces that biting the pencil and not knowing "whether to multiply, or to divide."

2. There is less figuring against time, or to fill the board.

3. It teaches the economy of time and effort in getting clear as to what is to be done, before setting about the doing.

4. Pupils come to sense more keenly what it is that the arithmetical processes actually do.

5. The school work helps them directly in ways of getting ideas themselves from the printed page; i. e., in how to study from books.

6. Pupils form the habit of estimating and judging closely what results must be. In decimals, there will be little of that headless not knowing where to put the point.

7. Pupils become habituated to the correct way of attacking the problems of daily life. On such problems close antecedent estimates are required, first of all.

8. Such work appeals directly first to the understanding, then to the memory.

9. Gives incidental training in the type of good English, that undertakes to say just what it means, knows when it has said it, and then stops talking.

10. Furnishes good training in knowing what you know, when you want it, i. e., in "spot-cash business." This means concentration of thought, at its best.

Every one of these phases of benefit is seen to contribute directly and materially to the learner's ability to rely on himself—to train him into the habit of self-reliance. In cases of difficulty or perplexity he calls to his help his own fund of good judgment and common-sense. He who contends that elementary mathematics is so highly perfected in purely mechanical ways as to furnish no training in judgment, but rather to replace judgment by mechanical and automatic conclusions merely, is woefully wrong as to its teaching possibilities at least.

[NOTE.—The author will continue his discussion of this subject in the March issue of this *Journal,* treating the topics: "Good Arithmetic Teaching," "A Training in Choice," "Speed and Accuracy," and "Drill Work in Arithmetic."—ED.]

FIELD-WORK AND NATURE-STUDY
PART II
THE PEDAGOGICAL ASPECT

IRA B. MEYERS
School of Education

The point which I have tried to make is that in our attempts to teach from nature the chief sources of weakness have been: (1) our failure to appreciate the true mental attitude of the child toward his nature environment; (2) Our failure to incorporate the child's normal attitude and personal interests into our teaching procedure; (3) Our belief that the act of educating is to be accomplished by some form of step-by-step procedure through a series of lessons selected and adapted with reference to communicating to the child a certain fund of knowledge which we believe essential for him to know. Our attitude of mind is that of considering nature-knowledge as something to be learned through conscious effort; something to be acquired mainly through sheer force of will, aside from any feeling of desire or need; something to be communicated to the child through a series of logically selected and arranged lessons or topics instead of considering it as something to evolve normally out of living. We present nature to the child as a mass of fragments, as consisting of innumerable facts and details, instead of a great unit of related parts. Whether the school shall appear to the child as something normal to life or something which adults have imposed upon him to prepare him for life, a preparation for which he feels no need, depends very largely upon whether his school activities include his own personal interests and impulses or whether he meets his work as something imposed upon him. Education is as much a matter of the mental attitude of the learner as it is of subject-matter; the two things are interdependent. The quality of knowledge, the mind's interpretation of the fact, depend upon the mental attitude of the individual at the time the fact enters the mind. The strongest associations are related to our spontaneous activities and mental attitudes. A falling meteor may be to us a sign from heaven or a fragment from another world, depending upon our mental attitude whereas in reality it may be neither. The child will put his own construction on the work we try to have him do in spite of us; whether we enlist the whole of the child in the work which we are trying to do in teaching or but a part of him depends upon how closely our methods of teaching are in accord with his mental attitudes. If our work is to be effective we must prepare the mind for the knowledge which it is to receive, and the individual's free response to his environment is one of the strongest factors in this preparation. The interest of the classroom must be able to match the interests of the streets and playgrounds if we expect to get the best results from the children. It is because of its richness, and its ability to cope with these other environmental influences that field-work claims a place in our school work.

One result of broad-sense experience is to retain plasticity in mental attitude; if the mental attitude of the individual evolves out of his own experiences it will remain plastic and keep in adjustment and harmony with increase in experience; if however, it is the product of accepted dogma or statement, something based on a statement of authority, teacher, or text-book, the mind becomes set and excludes all possibility for growth in that direction. In this matter of teaching we need to distinguish between static knowledge and dynamic knowledge. That six fours are twenty-four is a static fact; we cannot conceive of a time when it was anything to the mind but twenty-four, or of a time when it will be to the mind anything but twenty-four, and the sooner the child gets that fact fixed in his mind, when he is ready for it, the better. The fact as to the cause of variety in living forms is a different matter; it is the result of special creation, of evolution, of adaptation to environment, of survival of the fittest, of mutation—it is whatever the mind in the light of its experience conceives it to be.

In time the mind will conceive the explanation as it really is and it will become a fixed fact, static as the fact that six fours are twenty-four.

We can cast a prophet eye into the future and conceive of a time when the mind shall have discovered all of the final facts pertaining to this earth, when all knowledge has become a static, and the mind, having exhausted the possibilities for growth, ceases its growth and proceeds to operate in some formal routine method to retain these eternal truths. But until that time arrives let us store up our knowledge, the real and the false, in reservoirs of books, and bring our efforts to bear upon bringing the child mind into rhythmic swing with the movement essential to real growth. It is to effect this that we need to bring our school work into close harmony with the spontaneous attitudes and interests of the child and to bring the whole into close contact with the realities of things in nature. It is this "abysmal difference between learning about nature and learning from nature" which we must appreciate before nature-study becomes really effective.

The general sentiment among parents and teachers seems to be that all time is wasted for children which is not spent in taking in consciously some special idea or fixing in the mind some fact, which the adult understands or thinks he understands. Some of the most successful field-excursions which I have observed, successful because of the multitude of new and rich experiences which came to the pupils and the spontaneous interest and delight with which they received them, were dismal failures in the minds of parents because the children were more conscious of the pleasures of the day than of the number of facts learned. On the other hand these same excursions have been considered of great value by adults whose spirits were never touched or quickened, who were impressed by the facts as they were pointed out, who remembered what was said, interpreted nothing, but went home with a fair collection of artificially received facts, but with a satisfied feeling of a duty well performed. Mrs. Boole's statement: "It is curious and painful to observe how many things have been proposed by true educationalists, simply for the purpose of administering to the unconscious mind and afterwards perverted, by persons possessed with the teaching mania, to the purpose of stuffing into the children's minds some idea which is in the teacher's mind,"[1] is extremely pertinent in the matter of nature-study.

"The region of nature is for the child, as for savage and ignorant man, a domain of mystery and fancy." It should be the aim of the teacher to aid the child in establishing such relation with nature and its various manifestations that the reasonableness of things will appear. To the child the whole domain of nature is both strange and meaningless; to the city child the growing tendency is that it shall remain strange and meaningless. It should be the aim of field-work to aid the child to gain an acquaintance with the objects and phenomena of nature, to discover relationships, to know the things of nature as they actually are, to have nature appear to him in her reality; and above all the study should become a personal matter to the child. It should aim to turn strangeness into familiarity; convert meaningless things into things alive with meaning; it should replace fancy and mystery with reason and intelligence. Nature-study was introduced into the schools to aid the child to make this transition; to aid and direct him in gaining the personal experience essential to the transition; to assist him in accumulating, arranging, and interpreting these experiences so that the realities and truths of nature will appear; and out of the effort and activity involved should evolve adequate knowledge and power. If our own knowledge of nature has any purpose or value, it is to give us breadth of view that we may guide wisely in this matter of nature-teaching; it is surely not to be used for "stuffing" purposes. It seems that if there is any type of school work in which we should be able to move with directness of purpose it should be in this matter of nature-study.

The reasonableness, relationships, and truths of nature have always been present and constant. Nature was the same in the days when man believed this to be a flat stationary earth formed by special creation as she is today under the conception of a revolving earth and evolution. Much that is knowledge today,

[1] *The Preparation of the Child for Science.*

was the unknown of yesterday, and will be the false impressions and traditions of tomorrow. These changes are wholly a matter of human mind, brought about by a more extended and minute acquaintanceship with nature; of growth in mental power in the selection and arrangement of the relevant and irrelevant, until things finally appear to the human mind in exact or approximate accord with their appearance and action in nature.

Whatever we can sense we can understand in sense terms. Our first lessons should aim to give children ample opportunity for acquiring a wide range of sense impressions to teach them to rely upon the integrity of their senses, and to aid them in expressing with clearness this sense knowledge. There will be ample time and opportunity, later, for them to discover that the senses of individuals vary, that they do not all receive the same quality of a sensation, and that there is frequently a difference between a sense impression and a scientific fact; that what is color to the eye is as a scientific fact vibrations of light. After he has made adequate use of his senses, when he meets something that is too minute for the eye to sense, and the need arises, let him use the microscope and see how we have reinforced the senses with the lens. It is only by some such method that the child will come to value knowledge and appreciate human progress.

Nature-study demands that we give children ample opportunity to deal with the actual objects and phenomena of nature instead of compelling them to submit to talks and literature about nature. It asks that as teachers we try to understand the mental attitude of the child which results from his contact with nature, to understand what determines or controls mental attitude, and to acquire power to direct the activities aroused; rather than compel the child to gain our view-point by following in some routine way our directions. "Either method of study may have outwardly the true logical form but it is the former that is really educative."

Field-work claims a place in nature-study as a means for enriching the child's sense experience as opposed by the poverty of the schoolroom; as furnishing ample range of valuable subject-matter from which to satisfy natural curiosity from which to choose according to interests and needs, as opposed to no choice in the matter except to attend to the work which the teacher has chosen and assigned; as offering freedom to physical and mental activity as opposed to suppression. Nature has given us every aid in this whole matter through the sensitiveness of the child to his surroundings and his insatiable curiosity. We have thwarted her at her first step in the matter by over-confinement of the child, at his most sensitive and receptive period, to the barren schoolroom. It is but what should be expected that the plea (and practice) to keep children out of our city schools until they have reached the age of eight or ten should be growing.

THE TEACHER'S OUTLOOK INTO FIELD-WORK

Field-work should begin with a comprehensive survey of the landscape as a whole. We should seek for some underlying unity which binds the whole into a balanced organism. Something which makes the topography, rocks, plants, and animals, in spite of variety, as much a part of this landscape organism as the leaves, twigs, and roots are parts of the plant organism. Our outlook into the landscape should be with a view to comprehending the whole of it, just as our study of the plant should be with a view to comprehending it as a whole. In proceeding from the landscape as a whole to its details of contour, mineral, and life, the study of these things should not become fragmentary and isolated, something apart from the landscape organism, any more than a study of leaves, twigs, roots, flowers, and fruit should become fragmentary and appear to the mind as something apart from the tree as a whole; the one set is as much an organic part of the landscape as the other is an organic part of the tree. If the landscape has a special form of topography there is a reason for it, and it is that reason which we seek; if a tree has a special form there is a reason for it and it is that reason which we wish to understand. If the landscape has a particular mineral formation, there is a reason for it; if a tree has a peculiar leaf form or its seeds float through the air supported by a parachute of down, there is a reason for it; if vegetation is absent on an area, or we find plants without leaves there are reasons and it is these reasons for which we seek. Each set, collectively or individually, has its greatest value when seen in true relation to the whole, in its sequence of relations. In our study of our landscape environment we should seek for the dominant influence which organizes it into a great unity. This will usually be found to be some great physical event which modeled the contour of the landscape, distributed its minerals, determined its basal physical characteristic, and in so doing predetermined, directly or indirectly, all subsequent events within the area.

In our Chicago area this predetermining agent has been the lake; everywhere the region bespeaks the characteristics given it by the lake. Its ridges of sand and pebbles bespeak sandbars and spits, and on them grow the oaks; its marshes tell of barriers and inclosed lagoons, and in them have gathered a host of plants and animals adapted to a water environment. Both ridge and swamp may be traced directly to the action of the water of the lake, working under different conditions, and out of the different landscapes developed have come this difference in life. Acorns, doubtless, came to both lagoon and ridge; but only those which were dropped on the ridge grew; the seeds of the flags dropped on ridge and lagoon; but only those of the lagoon grew. The squirrels came to feed upon the acorns and live on the ridge, while the muskrats found food in the roots of flags and inhabited the swamp. To acquire the experience, and to develop power of mind in selection and arrangement, essential to having our environment appear to us as it is, to interpret the present so as to decipher the past and forecast the future—this is the fundamental purpose of field-work.

UNIT ENVIRONMENTS IN FIELD-WORK

In the evolution of the earth its surface has been modeled and molded by the forces of diastrophism, vulcanism, and gradation into great mass landscapes known as to size as continents and islands, as to elevation, as mountains, plateaus, plains. Within these mass landscapes, composing their surface are a number of minor physical regions known, according to their genesis, form, or content, as:

1. Shores and beaches of various forms with their associated features.

2. Lakelets, lagoons, marshes of various forms with their associated features.

3. Gullies, ravines, valleys of various forms with their associated features.

4. Hummocks, hills, and ridges of various forms with their associated features.

5. Levels and flats with their associated features.

Each of these type regions may be considered as a unit environment, containing its own combination of physical condition which controls the area, and unifies the various materials and phenomena within the area. The swamp is different from the ridge and both differ from the beach. Within these regions are to be found minor physical regions, such as cause zonal distribution in the marsh plants, so that we find an inner zone of water lilies, an internal zone of flags, and a border zone of sedges. A complete study of any of these type areas should lead to an acquaintance and an intelligent appreciation of the various objects and phenomena in the region, their true relation to the region as a whole, their interdependence, and the factors which control their presence, habits, and positions.

The mental content resulting from the general and detailed study of each type should, to a degree, correspond to the true facts pertaining to the region. If the action of a certain force or forces has molded the contour of the land surface of the area, and this contour has given rise to a variety in physical conditions with reference to moisture, temperature, light, air (wind), and these in turn exert control over the presence and distribution of its content of plant and animal life, then field-work should effect in us a mental attitude of recognition and appreciation of these mutual relations.

By ignoring this unity, in our treatment of subject in elementary-school work, by presenting these various phases as isolated subjects in physiography, botany, zoölogy, etc., instead of maintaining their unity through a study of the landscape itself, we have greatly reduced the effectiveness of our nature-study and science teaching and this, combined with our indoor study, has been the main reason why nature-study and elementary science have failed to exert that influence upon education which was promised by their advocates. Our problem is no longer a matter of subject-matter, it is a question of co-operation in aiding the mind to deal with the subject so abundantly at hand; of presentation and treatment in accord with the psychic stages and mental attitudes. The statement so frequently made, that teachers are not sufficiently prepared to teach nature-study and elementary science, hence their failure, is only true when we admit with it that this is not so much on account of lack of effort in the study of subject as it is that of mental attitude induced through the study.

A common type region of the Chicago area is the marsh. Something of the richness and attractiveness of this area is indicated by the number of visits which it receives annually from physiographers, botanists, zoölogists, flower-pickers, hunters, wandering children. Each comes for a special purpose; the physiographer to determine its genesis and subsequent changes; the botanist is attracted by the variety, distribution, and habits of its plants; the zoölogist by its animal life; the hunter has an eye to snipe and duck; the flower picker seeks for orchids and water lilies; to each of these the marsh is not a unit but a place where certain problems may be solved or certain things found, and they observe the things essential to their needs. The wandering children, however, approach the marsh without any prejudices, open minded, ready for any attraction the place may offer; they come with the attitude of true explorers and investigators, stirring up the ooze, splashing in the water, peering through the reeds, wading for water lilies, catching frogs, seeking for birds, alert to every sight and sound, reveling in the richness of their new experiences.

The teacher who approaches a region with her class needs to

do so in the same comprehensive way, needs to include the whole of the marsh in order to include the entire range of children's interest in the area. We may assume that from the standpoint of subject-matter an outline as follows would include this comprehensive survey.

1. Examining the area in order to gain a fairly clear impression of the general physiognomy and atmosphere of the marsh. (This impression may be expressed in a sketch or painting of the marsh or of a typical portion of it.)
2. Examining the area to determine the genesis of the marsh, and to determine the nature of the force or agent which formed it.
3. Imaging the appearance of the region at the time the marsh was born, and the changes, and the reasons for them, which the marsh has undergone since its genesis to the present time.
4. Getting acquainted with the plant life of the marsh: (*a*) variety of plants and their identification; (*b*) their zonal distribution and the factors determining this distribution; (*c*) the structures and habits of these plants which fit them to their zones; (*d*) the influence of this plant life upon the marsh.
5. (*a*) Gaining an acquaintance with the animal life of the marsh, identification, something of its habits and life history; (*b*) factors which have attracted this animal life to the region and which control its presence and distribution; (*c*) how this life reached the area; (*d*) the influence of this animal life upon the marsh.
6. Economic aspects of the region.
7. The ultimate death of the marsh and the way it may be brought about.
8. The story of the succession of changes which take place in a marsh during its birth, growth, and decline. To see the region as a place of slow action, something dynamic instead of static; to see one wave of change follow another toward the center of the area until grass land occupies the spot where water lilies grew and sparrows and field mice take the place of ducks and frogs.

It is safe to assume that the elementary student gives little attention or thought to the problems outlined. The things that appeal to him are the mud, the cat-tails, lily-pads, tadpoles, frogs, and crayfish; how the marsh got there, from whence these things came and whither they are going does not trouble him. It is sufficient that they are there and he sets to work to get all of the experience and pleasure, by observation discovery, experimentation, and collecting, which the place offers. The region as approached by the child gives him little hint of the problems outlined; these are conceptions to be evolved out of his experiences in the marsh. Our main problem is so to direct and aid him that when the time arrives he will have the sense, data, and experience out of which to construct the complete story of the region. Our success in directing will be quite largely determined by the way in which the subject is organized in our own mind and our mental attitude toward the act of teaching.

THE SUPERINTENDENTS' VIEW OF PRESENT METHODS OF INSPIRING PROFESSIONAL INTEREST IN TEACHERS

ANNA BROCHHAUSEN
Supervising Principal, Indianapolis, Ind.

In the spring of 1907, the Department of Education of Indiana University undertook an investigation to ascertain, if possible, the superintendents' and teachers' views of prevailing methods for inspiring professional interest. The report of the teachers' view has already been given. This article endeavors to present the superintendents' view.

The following questions were sent to superintendents in different parts of the United States:

I. What is being done and what can be done to inspire professional interest through salary, increase of salary, and other kinds of promotion? Please state what teachers consider promotion, and on what promotion is based. Of what value as a stimulus is the expectation of a pension?

II. Use and importance for professional interest of "school exhibitions," "visiting days," visits from school supervising officers, and recording results of children's tests?

III. Do you have any systematic way of encouraging teachers who have grown tired and dull from teaching continually in the same grade or in too limited a field in department work? What seems to be the best remedy in such cases?

IV. In the programme of work, what arrangements are made to conserve or increase the teacher's nervous force, for example, by rest periods, alternating study and recitation periods, or other means? Do teachers teach continuously? Have you observed any special effects upon the spirit of teachers from attention to the facts suggested by this question?

V. What kind of teachers' meetings are held? In what respect are they most helpful? If you have a printed programme, will you please send it?

VI. Are special efforts made to make the individual teacher achieve substantial and recognized success? If so, how important relatively is successful teaching in keeping up interest?

VII. Kindly mention any other aspect of the matter that seems to you important.

I regret that only fourteen replies have been received, but these come from the different sections of the United States, so that probably they may be considered representative.

I. (*a*) The salary question has been and is creating a vital interest. Every reply expresses a hope for an increase in the entire schedule of salaries in the near future; or, states that there has been an increase recently. The prevailing method of increasing a teachers' salary is from a minimum to a maximum, without much consideration of the quality of the work done. That there is merit in this method is shown by the fact, that the Ethical Culture School instead of the "private arrangement between the board of governors and the individual in regard to salary," which has been their method in the past, is

now considering a schedule which may be used with some freedom. The object of this is to eliminate any possible feeling that personal bias enters into the determination of salaries, to relieve the superintendent and principals from the very great care needed to discriminate in salary matters, between persons doing work in the same grade, and to hold out to the members of the staff the encouragement and stimulus of a maximum to be reached through faithfulness and progress.

Though this increase to a maximum based upon experience has been and is still the customary method of increase, there is a tendency now of special compensation for merit. Superintendent Small, of Providence, R. I., says: "If a community can focus more on quality of work as a basis of increased salary, I think growth would be stimulated." Superintendent Carroll, of Rochester, remarks:

There must of course be a fixed minimum salary for all teachers when they are first elected. Increase in salary should be regular and stated until some maximum is reached. This advance should be based upon merit to the extent that no person should be advanced or retained in service who is not successful. In addition to this, some system of merit should be adopted by means of which teachers who are clearly in a class by themselves professionally, should receive a larger salary than prescribed by the maximum.

I judge that there is something like the merit system in Boulder, Colo., for Superintendent Casey says, "In this city increase is recommended when teachers show they deserve it," though he goes on to say, "A maximum is established with increase from year to year." Also in Cleveland, O., where the teachers are grouped into three classes according to experience, the teachers are promoted to the next higher class "upon recommendation of the superintendent and the approval of the board." Superintendent Gordy, of Springfield, Mass., says, "In Springfield we have a special maximum in all the grades. For the first seven grades it is $50 above the general maximum; in the eighth grade it is $100 above; and in the ninth grade it is $200 above." These quotations show that merit is receiving financial recognition.

It is interesting in considering this question of special recognition of merit, to hear from the teachers themselves, upon the subject. By some lucky chance, a supervisor in Trenton, N. J., gave these questions to his teachers. One of these writes in reply:

> I believe that beyond a fixed maximum of salary reached by a fixed term of experience, there should be another maximum attained through successive increments by special proficiency, originality, or advanced scholarship. This will supplement the regular lines of promotion to principalships and training-school positions; first, by affording recognition to a larger number than could reasonably aspire to those limited places at the top; second, by keeping a greater number of first-class teachers in the ranks where they may serve as "the little leaven;" third, by encouraging specialization along lines of greatest interest and talent.

Another says, "There should be increases made for those teachers who are especially efficient." From another city I receive this forcible statement: "Let teachers once understand that merit, and merit alone, is the basis of promotion, and the inspiration will take care of itself."

Though merit deserves particular recognition, it is doubtful whether it alone can be made the basis of the salary schedule. Various conditions may prevent perfect justice from being done. Personal favoritism, even though unconsciously obeyed, is apt to rule a decision. Mistakes are liable simply because supervising officers are not infallible judges. Hence, a combination of the two methods, i. e., the gradual increase with experience, and the special emphasis on merit, is probably the most satisfactory scheme for salary increase. Yet there are some who hold that more pay is not always necessary for those who have special gifts, and for those who of their own free will do extra work for their contracted salary. They argue that, "Unto whomsoever much is given of him shall be much required." Money cannot—and it is well that it cannot—pay for the highest kind of service. Few working-people, however, are willing to have this principle applied to business. They hold that the natural reward of promotion to higher positions is not always feasible and that the satisfaction which comes from work well done ought not to be the only compensation.

Fifty per cent. of the cities from which I have heard reward scholarship. In Cleveland, Ohio, college graduates are eligible to the second year of the first class. In Providence, R. I., "College graduates teaching in the grades, may be transferred to the high schools with salaries ranging from $700 to $1,800, for ladies." In Springfield, Mass., where the eighth-grade teachers may receive $100 and the ninth grade $200 above the general maximum, they look for broad scholarship in teachers of these grades; in fact, try to get as many college graduates as possible. In the District of Columbia there are "examinations for promotion in salary." The following was received from Superintendent Mott, of Richmond, Ind.:

> We pay teachers holding state licenses for more than three years (five or six, or life licenses), $50 more a year than other teachers in the same work. Again we pay teachers who receive, or have received, a Master's Degree $50 more than other teachers in the same work. These different recognitions of scholarship and merit seem to inspire study on the part of teachers.

The tendency of the times toward encouraging broader scholarship, is evident from these quotations.

There still lurks in some places the plan of having the grade determine the salary. Probably first- and eighth-year teachers should receive higher salaries than those of the grades intervening; but, to me, the principle of paying a fourth-year teacher more than a third, and a fifth-year more than a fourth, seems wrong. Frequently a good primary teacher, attracted by the higher salary enters grammar-work, where she is almost a failure.

(*b*) Only six of the superintendents answered the request

to "state what teachers consider promotion," of these, five include in their answers "higher salaries." One supplements this statement with, "or, a more desirable kind of work." Another puts it thus, "Promotion to a better-paying position." Superintendent Small adds, "Some few recognize that increased responsibility, even at the same salary, is a recognition of ability, and hence, promotion." From Cleveland, I receive the answer, "Usually a change from grade to grade up the grades looking eventually to a principalship." But with such a promotion there is an increase in salary. Possibly some will be shocked at the materialistic view of the teachers' idea of promotion. Still others will recognize that in the business world the appreciation of greater worth or value is expressed by paying a higher price. This is true not alone in the trades but in the professions. An expert lawyer or physician demands a high fee. Why should teaching be an exception?

(*c*) Of the seven who have anything to say about pensions, four consider them valueless as a stimulus, one is doubtful, and two consider them helpful. One of the last says, "We encourage teachers who are becoming tired from long service by holding out to them the prospect of a pension." One reply modifies the statement, "Of no value as a stimulus," with the clause, "unless the receiving of a pension is contingent upon meritorious (or satisfactory) service." And then adds, "Certainly, a pension, however, does relieve very many teachers from anxiety, well-based as to old age. By so much it contributes to efficiency."

Again on this subject I can quote from two replies received from Trenton. One teacher says, "Teachers themselves think little of them," and another asserts that they are a stimulus "only for those who are teaching for the money."

Whether anticipation of a pension really increases professional interest, I cannot say; but I do know that the teachers of a city where the pension system was recently inaugurated, were almost without an exception, very much pleased when the law was established. One of them in speaking to me said, "It seems too good to be true."

II. (*a*) Of the twelve who speak of school exhibitions, one says emphatically, "School exhibits do not inspire teachers, because it is generally felt that such exhibits are 'doctored.' There is usually too much teacher and too little pupil to show the real work of the real school." Two writers are doubtful of their value. One of these gives his reason, "They take a great deal of time, and unless the work is watched carefully there is a good deal more of the teacher in the outward product than there is of the pupil." The other nine replies consider exhibits helpful. To quote from several:

Our school exhibits have undoubtedly played an important part in stimulating the members of our staff to excellent work. The exhibit idea, however, may easily be overdone, both in respect to the frequency of the exhibits, and to their elaborate character. If an exhaustive exhibit is held every year, it is in danger of proving extremely irksome and depressing.

F. C. Lewis
Ethical Culture School, N. Y.

Exhibits should help to raise standards, besides creating better effort in workers.

R. J. Tighe
Asheville, N. C.

We give occasional exhibitions of work of the pupils, inviting parents on such days. Simply a means of fostering a closer relationship between the home and the school.

Wm. V. Casey
Boulder, Col.

School exhibitions, if honest, are a real stimulus to the best three-fourths of the teachers; they generate healthy rivalry and stimulate new ideas.

Willard S. Small
Principal Eastern High School, Washington, D. C.

In spite of the fact that parts of an exhibit may not be the actual work of the child, I think that one who attends an exhibit in the spirit of *the learner* is stimulated. Can those of us who visited the foreign exhibits at the World's Fair say that we were not helped? Were we even questioning whether the results were children's work? If the result spoke of a better method or closer training we came away with our ideal raised and new determination. Of course, everyone will admit that there ought not to be too many of them, and each hopes that the day will come when an exhibit will consist of the children's daily work.

(*b*) Visiting is spoken of in ten of the replies. Each of these comments favorably upon this means of inspiration. One, however, contains a remark that astonishes me, viz., that it is "difficult to get more than one-third of the teachers to avail themselves of the visiting days," and that they "should be insisted upon by the administrative officers." These statements surprise me, since of the one hundred and fifty teachers who answered the questions sent out to them, only one said that she received little help from visiting, and many thought that they were not allowed to visit frequently enough. However, the above writer goes on to say, "I have never known an intelligent teacher to return from a visiting day unrefreshed."

Though some statements are unqualified in their support of visiting days as, for example, that of Superintendent Slauson, of Ann Arbor, who says, "Visiting days afford us one of the most effective means of inspiring professional interest;" others add limiting statements, such as, "valuable when directed;" "if not overdone." I will quote one reply in full:

> Visiting days, if controlled by the supervising body, so that a teacher is sent to a particular place to view particular work in which she is weak, are very stimulating. That is the course followed in this city and it is the best stimulus we find. It is varied by having a group of teachers, weak in some common line, meet the supervisor in a room where this work is very strong, and spend a session in viewing the work and discussing principles and methods involved.

Though only two speak of visiting schools in other cities, I know the custom is prevalent. I read in the Cleveland "Rules of the Board of Education," "On permission of the superintendent this privilege (visiting) shall extend to other school systems in place of our own." Superintendent Boynton, of Ithaca, N. Y., sends this word, "Once each year we close all schools and visit schools in some other city." Personally, I consider visiting schools in other cities, one of the best means of broadening the teacher's outlook.

(*c*) Only nine of the replies deal with the question of supervision, and all but one hint that the value of these visits depends upon the supervisor. Take note of these replies:

> The visits of supervising officers should be the leaven to leaven the

whole lump. Unless a teacher feels strengthened and uplifted by such visits, they had better not have been made.

Of course, visits from supervising officers depend very much upon the personality, the wisdom, and the good judgment of the officer.

Of course, the frequent visits to the classroom of those who have the responsibility for supervision are stimulating and helpful in the cultivation of professional interest, provided these visits, and the conferences that follow them, are conducted in a sympathetic and helpful manner.

I should say that the third item "Visits of supervising officers" is the most important, if the supervising officer is a true teacher, filled with the professional spirit, and has a helpful sympathizing nature.

If supervising officers say the right things at opportune times, they may be helpful to teachers.

Hence, we see that teachers and superintendents agree as to the value of supervisors' visits. They are valuable only in so far as the supervisors are gifted with a charity so broad, an experience so wide, a wisdom so discerning, and a professional spirit so vital that they are quickening in their effect.

(*d*) Of the nine statements made about children's tests, one reads, "I should not be in favor of marks or records in any grade unless it be the very last in the elementary school." Another considers them "an inspiration to about one teacher in fifteen." Two replies speak unconditionally in favor of them, viz., "Recording of tests stimulates teachers to careful and thorough work." "Unquestionably, recording results of children's tests are of considerable stimulating value to the teachers." The other five writers modify their favorable statements about tests:

Of value when not made a shibboleth.

Tests and their comparisons properly made and properly recorded should stimulate a teacher to raise the quality of her work if it is low. There is danger in some teachers becoming self-satisfied if their marks are at the head for successive periods.

Children's tests are valuable if they are made in a proper spirit, but it is very easy to make a fad of them.

Perhaps occasional tests of pupils' work stand next (to visiting) in effectiveness, provided the tests do not bear on the question of promotion, and are *fresh* and *fair*.

III. The third question, "Do you have any systematic way of encouraging teachers who have grown tired and dull?" certainly aroused interest, since every one of the fourteen who replied has had something to say upon the subject. In addition to interest, the replies show patient endeavor to give such teachers every chance for improvement. Some of the answers are concise, as e. g., "Change of work;" "Transfer to another school or to another grade or to both;" "Leave of absence with *assurance* of re-employment after a stated time of study;" "The remedy is directed to each particular case;" "We encourage them by holding out to them the prospect of a pension;" "Give them dull pupils to teach individually." The other replies are as follows:

The only remedy we have found for such cases is the inspiration of the supervisor's personally meeting such teachers, getting them to open their hearts, tell of their troubles, and by close personal contact rearouse them and lift them back to the plane from which they have slipped. Transferring them into new schools with slight changes of work but in new environment is often effective, when such transfers are represented not as punishments but as tonics.

These questions are puzzling to me. It is difficult to know what to do in the way of encouraging teachers who have fallen into routine and have reached that unfortunate stage—the stage of mental stagnation. If we could only do something to get such people out of the routine and get them interested in outside studies—but I am sure I have no suitable suggestion to offer.

Reports are required from each member of the staff. These are expected to indicate progress during the year. The constant influx of visitors, the exhibits, the supervision and the reports are intended to stimulate progress, and to prevent teachers from getting into ruts and becoming tired of their own work. With our large teaching force, it is possible for us to vary somewhat the work of individual teachers. This is not done systematically, but is attempted wherever a natural opportunity appears.

Teachers are frequently changed from one grade to another at the suggestion of the principal or supervisor. The usual means of personal interviews, grade meetings, institutes, and visitation are practically the only means at hand. In the last analysis, the principal is or ought to be the inspiration most to be relied upon. In the presence of a poor principal the condition of such a teacher as you mention is practically hopeless. Elimination is the last and necessary remedy to be applied.

The third question is a hard one. I have studied it for twenty years. A real teacher never feels in this way. In our work any good teacher who asks for a change of work is given it as soon as opportunity comes. Poorer teachers are often forced to change work that we may find where they fit best. The best remedy in such cases is for the teacher to have a "new birth."

Give them another grade, higher or lower, or department work, if fitted. I have made a good department teacher out of a poor grade teacher.

I have no regular system to apply in such cases. Simply try to show the teacher the necessity of being alive to her work; usually she is "ready to be shown."

The solution of this problem by the teachers is suggestive. They offer a variety of devices; for instance, "Get her interested in some special phase of teaching, as teaching slow, or immoral pupils; or get her to take up some special line of work as domestic science, school gardening; or help her to do something so well that the success of it will draw attention to her work and approval of it." Again, "Give them a special study to teach of which they are very fond, or change their grade." Another teacher offers three suggestions:

(1) Sufficient salary to enable them to have complete change of scene during vacation; (2) A year's leave of absence for study in some field, without loss of salary; (3) Occasional shifting from school to school, even if contrary to the temporary inclination of the teacher. Some plants require periodic transplanting to acquire new life and vigor. The influence of a new principal, new teaching associates, new classes of children, even new room, stimulates to renewal of effort.

All of these recommendations deserve thought, but few superintendents and boards of education would venture such an investment of public funds as the first two suggestions made in the last quotation. Stimulating teachers who have grown narrow, dull, or are moving in a rut has been and doubtless will continue to be a troublesome question to superintendents.

IV. Thirteen answer the question about programme; of these, six state that study alternates with recitation or that rest periods are provided. In Batavia, "Every other period she (i.e., the teacher) is assigned to the teaching of dull pupils individually. It is infinitely better than absolute rest." Superintendent Gordy writes:

We have study periods for children for two reasons: in the first place, it is better for the children to have opportunity for quiet study; in the second place, it is better for the teacher to have these rests for the nervous exhaustion. No teacher can do her best work by continuous teaching an hour or two at a time, stretching over a five-hour day. It is too much to expect if a high level of inspirational work is done during the recitation time. I have observed that the effect on the spirit of the teachers from too prolonged periods of teaching is to make them overnervous, which reacts upon the pupils and prevents good discipline, and the proper sympathetic relations between the teacher and the pupils. I regard this as a very important question.

The programme of the Ethical Culture School is so arranged that there is time when relaxation is possible; e. g., the mere presence of the teacher at chorus or assembly, and one unassigned period. Superintendent Mott says:

We, in Richmond, give most teachers two grades to teach. Generally one class recites while the other studies. However, we require that in each room programme, provision be made for one half-hour period in each half-day session for all the class or room to study, and the teachers supervise the study, or rest, or bring up odds and ends. I believe in each half-day session such a period should be provided in each programme.

In Boulder,

Study periods alternate with recitation periods, save in the primary grades and occasional double grades. We have one class in a room. An assistant teacher is provided in each building. Assistants give help where needed—to slow pupils, to pupils not up with grade work; assist with manuscript corrections, reports, etc. As to effect, have noticed no ill effects, but rather more equable temper, more enthusiastic work, and certainly profit to the pupils.

Superintendent Archer of Charleston, S. C., affirms, "We have rest periods and alternating study and recitation periods with excellent results."

In those cities where teachers teach continuously during the day, three of the superintendents think that the rest is obtained through the variety and arrangement of the subjects, and, as one adds,

This does not give the teacher opportunity for very much rest, but it does give an opportunity for rest and relaxation for the pupils themselves. This in itself is helpful and restful to the teacher. In addition there may be rest periods or study periods for the entire school.

In two of the other places where the plan of continuous teaching is followed, the superintendents doubt its wisdom. One remarks, "All of our teachers are worked too hard. . . . . I am certain our teachers are often too tired to do efficient work. Recitations drag; the work lacks force and vigor because the teacher is exhausted." And the other says, "I fear our teachers teach too continuously as they have two divisions in each class and are obliged to get through."

One writer does not consider "rest periods" for teachers a problem. He replies,

Programmes should be made to conserve the energy of the pupil, not necessarily the teacher. With a five-hour day, there is no good reason why a healthy teacher should have rest periods. Weaklings should not be in the work. It is the fret and worry, not the work, which breaks down teachers.

One might reply to this, that investigation of the health of school children would probably show that the strain is felt not only by the teachers. Sikorsky found by dictation tests that there was an increase of 33 per cent. in the average number of mistakes made by children after four or five hours of study and recitation. Experimental schools the world over aim partly to relieve the strain which their advocates claim exists in the public schools.

In this discussion of programme arrangement, one point of view has not been mentioned. Some teachers would far rather divide the school into two classes and teach continuously, than to have one recitation period with forty or more pupils, followed by a study period for the whole school. They claim they can reach more satisfactory results through this method as it gives better opportunity for individual attention.

Possibly a helpful hint for conserving teachers' energy can be gleaned from these replies received from teachers:

(1) Smaller classes; (2) special classes for delinquent and defective children; (3) proper sanitary conditions in the schoolroom; (4) restrooms; (5) sufficient salary to make ends meet.

(1) Apparatus to lessen the mechanical work of schools; (2) liberty to change programme, e. g., on damp days; (3) a definite understanding of what line of work is to be expected during the year. (A teacher should

know before her summer vacation what grade or subject she is expected to teach the next year.) (4) a larger social life; (5) a year for study.

I had not thought particularly of the salary question as belonging to the subject of "reserving or increasing the teacher's nervous force," until I had read the teachers' replies. From these I learned that some teachers do their own cooking, much of their own sewing, and sometimes even their own laundry work. Where this is true the teacher doubtless begins the day with little reserve force.

That the establishment of special disciplinary schools, schools for the instruction of mentally deficient children and assistance in teaching very slow minds, conserves the teacher's nervous energy, is now fairy generally conceded. Special schools are part of the system in nearly all large cities. The value of individual instruction is at the basis of the Batavia system, as well as the plan of having an assistant in each building. Nevertheless, these plans also serve to guard against the over-exhaustion of the teacher.

As for the change of programme suggested in the second quotation I feel quite certain that so much liberty is tacitly given all teachers. In regard to most rules, superintendents wish to be interpreted in the spirit not the letter of the law.

That teachers are a hard-working body is generally granted. The spirit that causes them to put forth this effort is admirable, but when their exertion to accomplish produces a nervous tension, a double harm is done—the children as well as the teacher suffer.

The source of this pressure is difficult to determine. Some say it is the teacher's own fault. They do far more than is asked or expected of them. I know this to be true of some teachers. Others say, it is due to too much urging on the part of the supervising officers. Yet when one hears superintendents discuss that which is best for the teachers and reads such statements as those given above, one must acknowledge that overpressure is far from their aim.

In one respect, there is danger of the cause of the strain resting with supervising officers, viz., in their unconsciously expecting all teachers to accomplish what only the strongest can do. There is a teacher of my acquaintance who had completed the work with her school fully four weeks before the close of the term. She tested her class and began the work of the next grade. It would be unwise, however, to plan a course of study to suit the ability of such a teacher. Extraordinary teachers can present an ideal, but cannot be taken as standards.

Still the source of the trouble has not been located. Can we find it in the public demand? No doubt part of the responsibility rests here also. In the present day, the public would not sanction the appointment of a teacher who had not had at least a high-school education. Teaching requires scholarship. This partly explains the pressure felt by some, viz., by those who are trying to acquire needful knowledge along with the attainment of present-day methods of education. The truth is we are in a transition period; and everyone who has ever passed through such an age has felt its constraining influence.

Nor is the strenuous spirit of Americans to be omitted from this consideration. We are an active people and tend to do with all our might whatever we undertake, hence we cannot look for a single cause for this complaint, nor will one remedy prove a panacea. More consideration from supervising officers, adjustment of programmes, relief from abnormal children will all help, but will not effect a cure. The teacher must have also a sustaining philosophy of life.

V. Teachers' meetings have become an established means of furthering the efficiency of teachers. Everyone is so familiar with the various kinds of meetings—the general meeting; the grade meeting, either with the superintendent, district supervisor, or supervisor of special branches; and the building meeting with the principal—that a discussion of them here would be out of place. Nevertheless, a study of the frequency and time of holding the meetings, particularly in relation to the teacher's strength, may be valuable.

As to the time of meeting, there seems to be one of two prevailing customs: either the meetings are called after school at night, some even so late as half-past four; or the school is dismissed for an afternoon or part of an afternoon. In addition, meetings are sometimes called on Saturdays. Generally, teachers do not favor Saturday meetings, since many of them belong to private or university extension classes that convene on that morning. On the other hand, it is sometimes impossible to get the desired speaker at any other time. In consideration of this fact, professional interest should spur those teachers who are at liberty to attend such lectures. In fact, if the meeting is called to hear some well-known lecturer, a large attendance ought always to greet that speaker.

Again, when schools are dismissed for meetings, complaint from teachers seems unjustifiable, unless there are so many meetings that they vitally hinder the work of the schoolroom. Certainly, superintendents take care that this does not happen. If they did not, the public would, by complaining of the many dismissals.

Unless it is unavoidable a meeting ought not to be called so late as half-past four. There is evidence that vitality is at its lowest at about four o'clock. If the subject of the teacher's vitality were investigated, I dare say, it would be found far below normal at that hour. Even if it were not so, many teachers would be exhausted by having their day stretched out until six o'clock.

In the previous report, I spoke of the best time of the year for holding meetings. One further caution needs to be observed, viz., the prevention, in so far as it is possible, of more than one meeting a week. If the superintendent has called a meeting, then the supervisors and principals should postpone theirs. I know this is not always practicable.

Perhaps some will say that a weekly meeting is too much. Nevertheless, if teaching is to be placed on an equal footing with the other professions, we ought willingly to give one evening a week for its study. Its science is growing so rapidly, its practice is so complicated, that the teacher must be a student to achieve success.

VI. The sixth question, "Are special efforts made to make the individual teacher achieve substantial and recognized success?" called forth an excellent response. A fine spirit breathes through the twelve answers received, but a few quotations will suffice to show this:

Constant efforts are made by all in direction of the schools to make each teacher achieve the fullest measure of success; successful effort is accorded merited recognition with the result of sustained interest on the part of the teachers.

The individual teacher who is a success is encouraged to continue a success; her example is held up to the others. It is dealing with the teacher as an individual not as a *mass* that produces results. Our system with 750 teachers is not so large but that the individual can still be kept in view.

Naturally there is more effort to make teachers individually successful than for anything else. "Nothing succeeds like success," therefore, successful teaching is, relatively, the most important of all means for keeping up interest.

VII. Only four of the superintendents have answered the seventh question. Two of these answers agree in believing that advanced study is the most stimulating means of inspiring teachers. Superintendent Small writes:

The school department of the city and the officers of Brown University have developed a series of extension courses at the University this year, at hours convenient for the teachers. Over four hundred have elected these courses, one-half of whom are seriously studying for examinations and credits which shall count toward a future degree. . . . . I am hoping that some means may be devised whereby such teachers may receive a certain extra salary credit after a certain number of scholarship credits have been received.

Superintendent Mott states that the most important work they have been able to do along this line is the university extension work. Superintendent Tighe says,

In making salary increase we have two reports from each principal a year to supplement the superintendent's judgment of each teacher. We also have a quarterly report on the work of each teacher from the supervisors, as an aid in determining the efficiency of teachers.

This certainly shows a close understanding between the superintendent and his assistants, which is, no doubt, a great help in promoting professional interest.

Superintendent Sanders finds that, "For a teacher to have in mind some *live question* (preferably pedagogical) is one of the very best means of inspiring professional interest."

I am aware that this report consists chiefly of quotations. However, I feel that the superintendents' replies either fully present a subject, or show clearly the two sides of a question. Further comment is unnecessary. Time, study, and earnest effort to reach the truth will decide which view is correct.

EDITORIAL NOTES

In connection with the meetings of the American Association for the Advancement of Science, held at Chicago recently, a new organization, known as the American Nature-Study Society, was completed. Previous to the time of meeting there had been appointed a committee on organization which committee had met and agreed upon the plan of organization and constitution to be recommended to the general meeting. The general meeting quickly and favorably disposed of the plans and constitution as recommended, elected officers, and proceeded at once to the discussion for which they had met. This discussion is the feature of the meeting in which, in this connection, we are particularly interested.

The topic announced was "The Relation of Nature-Study to Science-Teaching." Four widely known educational men had been invited to open the discussion, and the addresses from these men were followed by some twenty-five shorter discussions. These shorter discussions were contributed by university, college, normal-school, high-school and elementary-school people proportionately in the order in which these groups are mentioned. The nature of the general association with which this society met was such as to make the representation of elementary-school teachers in this discussion less than was desired. The following partial summarization gives those points which give promise of a more tangible organization and consequently more valuable result from work in nature-study.

If "science is organized knowledge," nature-study, high-school science so-called, and some so-called college science cannot make serious claim to inclusion in the subject. But if in education science is a process of organizing knowledge, that is of solving problems and of relating results to one another, all the above must be included. Science is kinetic, not static; and any definition which fails to recognize the method of science leaves out the moving force which educationally is the greater part of the subject. The child who sets himself to find out about any particular natural phenomena has set himself a problem in science of the same nature as the problem which is attacked by the student doing research work on his doctor's thesis. Of course the problem is very, very much more simple but to the child it has the same features of unexplained phenomena. To explain these he must observe more phenomena, and infer and test his inferences. The research student finds his work differing from this only in degree. Indeed, sometimes the research student has furnished for him a much larger part proportionate to the amount of data needed than does the child. If we consider carefully some of the so-called pieces of research work, we shall see in them little beside an attempt to identify in a new or partially new combination of data, principles which have been clearly demonstrated in other quite similar combinations of data. Few research men are really great enough to enable them to work with combinations of data largely unstudied previously. This is not to be interpreted as meaning that verification work is not valuable and necessary, nor that a piece of such work does not become a problem to the doer, but it does assist in showing that in higher work as well as in grade work the problems may vary in quality. So far as this quality is concerned its extremes are found in the nature-study work of the elementary schools, in the research work of the university, an din all intervening science. So far as the essence of educational science is concerned there is no line drawn between nature-study and science. If, as some maintain, nature-study is wholly unlike science in its method and result, it must fail to present nature's problems, must fail to stimulate and extend inquiry into the natural features of our environment with which our lives are inextricably related. The "exposure" and "observation" methods of teaching nature-study could be no other than disappointing since they omitted the problem aspect which really gives life and meaning to the work. Merely seeing, is wholly unlike seeing with an interpreting eye and mind, and is inhibitory to interpretive seeing.

One of the prominent educational purposes of nature-study, therefore, is to establish and develop economic and trustworthy methods of problem solving. This involves that the problems attacked must be real to the pupils and must be worth while. They must be the pupils' own problems, or must be so presented to them that the pupils feel interest in them. The best problems are those that come out of the daily life and associations of the pupils, the solutions of which bring a fuller significance to phenomena constantly observed.

In addition to this method purpose stated above, the materials acquired in nature-study furnish the concrete basis for further work of all kinds. Much advanced work loses a large part of its meaning because there is not sufficient concrete foundation to give it significance. No doubt this work would do much to make the immediate environment more attractive and to give a better interpretation of social life, and these are highly desirable. These are incidents to the larger function of supplying pictures, organization, knowledge, and processes, by means of which future thought processes may find material upon which to develop and which may enrich and organize this new material.

It must follow that if the above criteria are correct the teacher must select her material more definitely than "at random" or with the idea of preparing "busy work." One ignorant of nature or out of sympathy with it needs to begin to learn nature and thus develop sympathy, before beginning to teach it. One does not need to know all mathematics in order to teach elementary arithmetic, but one needs to have studied arithmetic at least and should have studied considerably beyond it. It is so in nature-study. Nature-study cannot be taught by those who have not studied it and who care nothing about it. It can, however, be very successfully taught by some teachers who have never had any formal courses in any natural sciences, but who of their own initiative (the best way of all) have developed insight into nature's problems and spirit.

O. W. C.

BOOK REVIEWS

Literature in the Elementary School. By Mrs. Porter Lander MacClintock, A.M. Chicago: The University of Chicago Press, 1907. Pp. ix+305.

So many books about teaching are written, and so many of them arouse in a reviewer nothing but the will to yawn, that the impulse to unreserved praise seems, even when it comes, a stranger to the heart. Yet in the case of Mrs. MacClintock's book this impulse comes to the present reviewer, and he feels timidly inclined to be wholly enthusiastic. The book is unquestionably authoritative. It is so important, so well balanced, so scientific, so artistic, so human, so exquisitely adequate to the task proposed, that it ought to become a gospel. Teachers ought to buy it as they buy dictionaries—and read it better.

It creates an ideal, but not a remote and inimitable ideal. It is not a series of bald commands to be impossibly wise and skilful. It shows by what means any teacher of respectable intelligence and taste may vastly improve herself as a teacher of literature. Take for example the ideal set up for the teaching of structure in the story. "It is a hard thing to insist upon as a matter of general theory, because written down in cold black and white, it seems to convey the impression that emphasis is placed upon mere colorless organization; as if one obliged his children to make an analytical syllabus of their pleasant tale before he regarded it as taught. But it is no such dull thing. Beauty and economy of structure lie upon the very surface of the best bits of literature, and need but the most unobtrusive reinforcement from the teacher to work their effect of pleasure and discipline. This pleasure is an artistic product which should expand and develop with the child's reading, until, when he is a mature student, the formal structure of a poem or story gives him the same aesthetic and moral satisfaction that he gets from a picture well composed, a monument well balanced. It is not a fancy or a mere pretty theory that a good story, taught as a structure, becomes a norm, a model, a clue to the child in the preservation of his own material, and in the arrangement of it economically and effectively. His attention is trained, his patience is rewarded, his judgment exercised and steadied, his imagination guided and channeled by his contact with a complete, beautiful, and logical creation, whose elements he can see and handle as he can those of the story." These words set up for the teacher an ideal sufficiently complex, but the point is that they stand at the beginning of the chapter on "Story," and that they are followed by a full discussion of the practical means by which the ideal may be realized. Not that the chapter presents a short cut of any sort, but the discussion eddies around the subject luminously, touching definite stories and their structure in a definite way.

Similar praise must be given to each of the eighteen chapters. Together they form the only complete treatment of the subject now before the public; and it is not likely that another person will soon arise who can bring to such a task so exceptional an equipment as Mrs. MacClintock's. The discussion proceeds systematically through the following topics: "The Services We May

Expect Literature to Render in the Education of Children;" "The Kinds of Literature and the Elements of Literature Serviceable in the Elementary School;" "Story;" "The Choice of Stories;" "Folk-Tale and Fairy-Story;" "Myth as Literature;" "Hero-Tales and Romances;" "Realistic Stories;" "Nature and Animal Stories;" "Symbolistic Stories, Fables, and Other Apologues;" "Poetry;" "Drama;" "The Presentation of the Literature;" "The Return from the Children;" "The Correlations of Literature;" "Literature out of School, and Reading Other Than Literature;" "A Course in Literature for the Elementary School."

To attempt to summarize these chapters is like attempting to judge the organic unity of a course of instruction by a half-hour's visit to a single recitation. All teachers who themselves resent being judged by such methods should appreciate the reviewer's restraint at this point, and should manifest the same by possessing themselves of the book. They should not rest until, in various parts of the volume, they have read what is said of "Enoch Arden," Hawthorne's *Pandora*, the Henty books, *Emmy Lou, The Midsummer Night's Dream, Robinson Crusoe, Story of the Dandelion, The Little White Hen, Peter Pan,* and *The Child's Garden,* and have pondered the reasons—often far-reaching and profound—for what is said. The sanity with which these things and a hundred others are treated may fairly be considered a touchstone to which any teacher may profitably bring any piece of literature concerning which she is in doubt. And as for the last four chapters of the book, let us hope that teachers inspired to new hope and effort by them may have some influence with boards of education.

E. H. LEWIS

LEWIS INSTITUTE
Chicago, Ill.

VOLUME VIII NUMBER 7

THE ELEMENTARY SCHOOL TEACHER

MARCH, 1908

THE SCHOOL'S RESPONSIBILITY FOR DEVELOPING THE CONTROLS OF CONDUCT[1]

W. C. BAGLEY
State Normal and Training School, Oswego, N. Y.

Not long ago I read a newspaper anecdote that will, I think, make clear the character of the problem that I wish to discuss with you. I do not know whether this anecdote is a record of an actual occurrence or merely a bit of imaginative space-filling. In either case, however, it will serve my purpose. It had reference to the long list of railroad accidents that was just then horrifying the country, and it told the story of a young telegraph operator who had been brought to trial on the charge of criminal negligence. It appeared from the evidence that a serious disaster had occurred as a direct result of this young man's failure to perform the duty that had been assigned him, and it further appeared that his failure was due to no other factor than that which, for want of a more definite term, we call "carelessness." The attorney for the defense sought to establish the young man's good character by the testimony of a number of men and women who had been the defendant's teachers when he was a boy at school. He called one of these teachers to the witness stand and asked him this question: "What kind of a boy was the defendant?" And the witness replied that he had been a very good boy—diligent in his studies, never mischievous, and always companionable with his fellow-pupils and popular

[1] A lecture delivered before the College of Education, The University of Chicago, November 21, 1907.

with his instructors. As the witness gave his testimony, the face of the defendant brightened and his attorney smiled hopefully. But when the defense had completed the direct examination and the prosecuting attorney began the cross-questioning, the bright looks vanished and the smile was changed to a frown. For, after repeating the question of his colleague and receiving the same answer, the prosecuting attorney suddenly turned upon the witness and asked: "Was this young man a careless boy at school? Was he what you would call a careless pupil?" And the witness, after an awkward hesitation, finally admitted that the boy had been a little careless, but was, withal, a good boy and an exemplary pupil. "But," persisted the attorney, "what did you do to change him in this respect? Having recognized his carelessness, what did you do to break up his bad habits and replace them with better habits?" And the witness, reluctantly and with not a little confusion, was finally compelled to answer, "Nothing!"

Now, as I have intimated, this little anecdote may be purely imaginative, but it certainly raises a possible question with regard to the functions and responsibilities of education that cannot be brushed to one side as irrelevant and impractical. After all, what is education for? We have advanced far beyond the point where we thought of education as chiefly concerned with the acquisition of knowledge—with the cramming of the mind with facts and theories and laws and principles. We have got beyond the primitive conception of education as the process by means of which youth is endowed with certain "earmarks" of culture. We have left these inadequate conceptions behind, and have gradually come to the much broader view that education must fit the child for life and work and service and production in a complex social environment to the demands of which nature has very imperfectly adapted him. Social efficiency, formulated though it may be in diverse ways, is becoming the conscious aim of all educational effort.

As a result of this development, education is coming to its own as a human institution. As one writer has intimated, it has attained to its majority and is coming into its kingdom.

And as in individuals, so in institutions, the first sign of approaching maturity is a hypertrophied self-consciousness. Like the adolescent youth, education is filled with a deep sense of its power, a yearning to know and test its function, an analytic impulse which leads it to unravel its mysteries, and to organize its efforts with foresight and intelligence toward the goal that it seeks to attain. And with these longings and strivings and yearnings, if I may continue the metaphor, is mingled now and then an undertone of foreboding, as if the task that lay before it were too stupendous for its powers; as if the problem that had been set it for solution—by far the most intricate and complicated that any human institution has yet attempted—were much too intricate and complicated for any human institution to solve. And so we find, now and then, an expression of pessimism, just as we find a marked tendency toward pessimism in individual adolescence—a tendency to distrust the power that education possesses, a temptation to repudiate nurture and hark back to nature, to discount the forces of the environment and magnify those of heredity, to take but a half-hearted hope in the school while we await, as patiently as we can, the arrival of the superman.

There can be no doubt that just such reflections upon the worth and efficiency of school training as that expressed by the prosecuting attorney of my anecdote contribute no small share to whatever pessimism one may feel. In what measure must the school hold itself responsible for the failure of its products to meet the demands imposed by social and industrial conditions? It would seem perfectly obvious that the effort of the teacher is quite without value unless, in some way or another, it modifies the conduct of his pupils. If those who come to me for instruction and training act in no way more effectively after they leave me than they would have acted had they never come under my influence, my work as a teacher must be adjudged a failure. Certainly if they act less effectively, my work is more than a failure —it is a catastrophe. And furthermore the fact that I could not foresee the results, the fact that I did my duty as I saw it, might mitigate the blame, but it could in no way mitigate the catastrophe. The pathetic lament of one of the greatest of our university presidents over the fact that so many of the men who figured prominently in the recent scandals of the business world were graduates of his own institution is a sad commentary on the failure of what we believe to be the most efficient training effectively to dominate or control conduct in really critical situations. And the terse criticism of my prosecuting attorney, whether the anecdote be fact or fiction, could find an easy sanction in the minds of thousands of business men who are looking to the schools for the raw material of efficient service.

Now it is clear that the responsibility of the school for the development of the controls of conduct must depend upon the degree in which the factors of control can be developed by the educative forces of the school. It is easy to make an offhand judgment in either direction. We can assume that the telegrapher's carelessness was due to a bad heredity, or to an inadequate home training, or to forces that operated after he left school. It would be hard to prove that all or even one of these factors could not be accounted sufficiently strong to counteract the results of school training. On the other hand, one might reasonably assert that the telegrapher's inefficiency was manifestly due to the lack of a certain set of habits which school work can and must develop, and that the admission of his teachers that these habits had been neglected is a sufficient evidence of their culpability.

It is a platitude to say that nine-tenths of human conduct is determined by the factor of habit. Educational theory has always recognized this basic truth, and, in a certain sense, it has always recognized the duty of the school to develop efficient habits. But even now educational theory is far from a due appreciation either of the wide scope or of the tremendous difficulty of the task. Indeed, until recently, educational methods, while assuming that habits were to be developed, seemed to have but a vague conception of what the development of a habit really means. One may cite the habits of speech as a convenient and definite illustration. It is only within a few years that futility of mere grammatical instruction in improving the efficiency of expression has been fully recognized. True, the study of formal grammar taught the pupil certain rules and principles that should have operated in the formation of efficient habits of expression—and doubtless did so operate in rare instances. But the kernel of habit—the purely automatic and unconscious character of its reaction—was very far from an effective recognition. When the futility of grammatical instruction was generally agreed upon, a reform movement took, as is usually the case, quite the opposite direction. It was grammar that was at fault, consequently there must be no grammar. Its place must be taken by language lessons, and since the essence of grammar is its logical coherence and organization, so the more incoherent and illogical the language lessons could be made, the greater would be the chance that they would correct the old defects. But this, quite naturally, was found to make matters worse instead of better. After all, the trouble did not lie in the mere matter of logical organization. That, in itself, was found to have rather a beneficial influence. The real difficulty lay in the comparative ease of mastering general principles and the extreme difficulty of applying these principles over and over again until the appropriate forms became thoroughly automatic. And so the next reform brought in a new factor: It attempted to provide a motive for application and repetition. The teacher of language turned to the content subjects for more interesting material, and attempted in various ways to inspire the pupil with a desire for correct expression. But this has been a long and tedious road to travel, and the results are still far from satisfactory.

I instance this specific habit of expression simply to press my point, and my point is this: If education finds it so difficult to build efficient habits in a comparatively simple field, dealing with very tangible and definite reactions, how much more difficult will be its task in the broader fields, such, for example, as that represented by the telegrapher's inadequacy in "habits of carefulness?"

And if the problem which seemed on its surface so simple has already proved so difficult what shall we say when we find that it is still further complicated by a much more important factor? Until recently it has been assumed that a habit, once established, would continue to operate in all situations of life wherever it might be needed. That this assumption failed to work out in practice did not seem to invalidate it in the least. Entire curricula were constructed under the guidance of the dogma that specific habits could be generalized indefinitely. The child might be disciplined into the most effective habits of promptness in the school, and yet fail to meet his first business engagement upon the stroke of the clock; the youth might be trained to reason with unerring certainty in his geometry, and yet fail to evince the slightest evidence of that ability in his later adjustments in business; the college student might win high honors in the study of the observational sciences, and yet find his trained observation incompetent to detect corruption in politics and chicanery in finance. These practical tests of the doctrine of formal discipline in its naïve formulation have failed upon every hand, and yet the doctrine has died a hard death—in fact, it is still far from inanimate even in contemporary educational theory and practice. But experimental investigation has clearly revealed its inadequacy. We can hammer away at tardiness until our record is perfect, and yet we cannot be sure that our pupils will be any more prompt in meeting their out-of-school engagements than will the pupils of our neighbor, whose class record is the disgrace of the school. We may drill upon correct expression until not an erroneous form creeps into our recitations, and still not know whether the first words that our pupils utter when they go out upon the playground—much less into the walks of adult life—may not represent enough samples of false syntax to satisfy the demands of even the old grammarians. And even though the telegrapher's teachers might have drilled him into the most efficient habits of carefulness and attention in his school work, we could not assume that these would *necessarily* function, even the slightest degree, in his later work. In other words, the mere formation of a specific habit or of a set of specific habits is not in itself a conclusive proof that these habits will function in situations other than those in which they have been formed, or in closely parallel situations.

On the surface, all of this seems to justify nothing but the most hopeless sort of an outlook. Truly, if formal discipline is an impossible task—if habits are adequate only to the situations in which they have been formed—what we call general education must be in a very bad way. The school must restrict its function to matters of instruction, and even in these it must assume no value other than that which accrues intrinsically to the facts and principles learned. In this case, it is safe to predict that all training must become technical and vocational, and I think that I am safe in saying that there is at present a well-marked tendency toward this very end. The college and university reveal this tendency most clearly, but the high schools are coming to feel its influence. The traditional courses which were supposed to provide general culture and discipline are being replaced by courses that are more or less vocational in character.

Even in the elementary school, the rejection of the dogma of formal discipline is exerting a modifying influence. The methods that were formerly assumed to develop the stern virtues of accuracy and industry and duty and obedience have, in many cases, been discarded or greatly modified. Indeed, why subject the pupil to the hardships of a discipline not needed for immediate ends when the chances are so few that this discipline can be applied to remote ends? Why insist upon obedience, if the habits of obedience gained in the school cannot be generalized into the attitude of respect for law and authority, upon which every civilized government must depend for survival? True, hoodlumism is increasing at an alarming rate. True, the American child is becoming more and more a law unto himself and not infrequently a source of trial and tribulation to the adult members of society. The old-fashioned parent would have settled the difficulty in a trice, but should one inflict pain upon another merely to subserve the interests of one's own comfort, when science asserts that no remote end would be gained thereby and that irremediable injury might be caused? We could formerly justify heroic measures of discipline on the ground that our personal comfort was only an incident and that it was the remote end of civilizing the little savage that impelled us to take harsh measures. But now selfishness is the only excuse.

What is the responsibility of the school (or even of the home) for developing the controls of conduct? In the light of contemporary educational theory, one is forced to answer, Nil. Responsibility goes only with power, and power is plainly denied us—at least if the contemporary theory is valid.

But is it valid? and if not, what is its fallacy? After all, have we generalized too hastily? Have we discarded the dogma of formal discipline and repudiated the value of general training with insufficient consideration? Have we really accounted for every possible factor that might influence our judgment?

Personally, while I believe that those who still cling to the dogma in its original form cannot justify their position, I also believe that those who have entirely cast aside the idea of formal training have done so too hastily. In fact, there is now some basis for a reactionary movement in the experiments which seem to indicate that memory, for example, can be markedly improved by exercises of a very formal nature. But aside from this there is still another factor that has been neglected.

In order to make clear my own position upon this matter, let me refer to a type of conduct rather different from those just discussed. Why are you and I decent and peaceful and law-abiding —assuming, of course, that we are. Why do you and I refrain from doing unseemly things? If we were brought face to face with that question, I believe that most of us would answer that we do not do unseemly things because reason tells us not to. But this is probably far from the real truth. You and I and the rest of the men and women who live ordinarily decent lives do so very largely through the force of habit. Let us suppose that you are in a jewelry store and that you see a tray of beautiful and costly diamond rings lying upon the top of the showcase. The clerks are busy in another part of the store, and you examine these rings casually and yet admiringly. Let us suppose that you have long wished to possess a diamond ring the very counterpart of one that is right there within your reach. Why do you not slip the ring into your pocket? Let us assume that you would run absolutely no danger of detection in the theft. You tell me that your judgment tells you that this would be stealing; but judgment in your case and in mine, I hope, very seldom operates in a situation like this. As a matter of fact, you do not feel the slightest temptation to take the ring. Why? Simply because habits of honesty have been drilled into you from the earliest infancy. There is little judgment involved in the control of conduct in such a situation, because the demand for judgment is not present. In reality, there is no situation there. A situation might arise under the proper conditions. Nature tells you to appropriate the thing that pleases you. But civilized society tells you to respect the rights of others, and civilized society has been having the better of it for so long that the primitive, natural craving has been quite hushed. In short, if you and I had constantly to reason ourselves into being good, we should not be good very long. We are either good by habit or we go to the bad very quickly.

Now this, it will be agreed, approaches very close to what may be termed a general habit—to the very thing that formal discipline was supposed to engender. How has this habit been formed? Obviously not from specific experiences in that identical situation. You do not need to have suffered painful consequences for the theft of diamond rings in order to build up the habit of not appropriating diamond rings when you want them.

In order to envisage a possible solution of this problem, let us vary the conditions of the illustration. Let us assume that, instead of feeling no temptation to take the ring, one does feel the very slightest impulse. In other words, let us assume that habit is inadequate to the solution of the situation. Inherited impulse, left to itself, would solve the situation disastrously. What is it that checks and controls this impulse? Is it an intellectual judgment—this act is stealing; stealing is a sin; consequently I will inhibit the impulse? I venture to say that, if the judgment were of this bare intellectual type, it would exert not the slightest inhibiting force upon the impulse. What really determines conduct in such a situation is undoubtedly an *emotional wave*—an undefined and intangible, but thoroughly conscious, *feeling of repugnance* for the act itself. Let me ask if this is not a fair description of the controlling force in your own moments of temptation—if you ever have such moments. Impulse and emotion are so closely related as genetically not to be distinguishable; and unless one can oppose an inherited impulse with an idea that is just as powerfully colored with emotion, the impulse is bound to conquer. The idea alone, as a product of intellection, has not the weight of a feather in determining conduct in critical situations. It is the emotionalized idea—it is the *ideal*—that must hold the reins of conduct when instinct is battling for the control.

And this, it seems to me, is the explanation of the barrenness of our attempts to teach morality from the didactic standpoint. We see it coming out most clearly perhaps in that horrible example of pedagogical inefficiency that we call temperance physiology. In eight years of didactic instruction in temperance, the teacher usually accomplishes less in developing real controls of conduct, even in children whose plasticity and adaptability are the hope of the race, than an unlettered temperance reformer, with the fire of enthusiasm coursing through his veins, can accomplish in a single hour with adults who might reasonably be supposed to have every factor of control irrevocably fixed. This is the reason, also, that didactic ethics has so little influence in modifying the conduct of its students. This is why every attempt to read emotion out of religion has weakened the power of the church in controlling the conduct of its communicants. The power of an efficient incentive to action is always a direct function of the emotion that is back of it.

What term will most adequately describe the prime controls of conduct—the factors that govern adjustment in really critical situations? The term that I propose is this, "emotionalized prejudice." The adjective may be redundant, but I insert it in order that there may be no doubt as to the prime factor.

A man of science was once trying to persuade me that the

trend of mental progress was toward the elimination of the emotions. As an illustration, he adduced his own clear-thinking logic engine of a mind, the workings of which, he assured me, had not the slightest emotional tinge. I could easily find it in my heart to pardon his egotism, for, with his next breath, he exclaimed passionately, "I am a priest of truth, and I worship the naked fact!" Not having with me the instruments of exact measurements with which emotions may be identified, I could not convince him that his mind was, at that moment, surcharged with a powerful affective process—but I convinced myself. And surely if the training that we give to students in science amounts to anything more than a mastery of technique and the assimilation of a few technical facts and principles, it must amount to this: the development of a prejudice, highly colored with positive emotional force, toward truth and veracity and impersonal observation and dispassionate judgment—*an emotional attitude against emotion, a prejudice against prejudice.* And similarly I should maintain that the student of mathematics should come from his study of algebra and geometry and calculus with a highly emotionalized prejudice toward that method of close, logical thinking that mathematics, above all other disciplines, represents.

It is true that not all students derive these prejudices from the pursuit of mathematics and science. Mastery of subject-matter does not involve this as a necessary consequence. But to some students, a long acquaintance with, and contemplation of, the methods by which some of man's greatest conquests over nature have been made possible give a profound sense of the worth and value of these methods—a feeling of respect and perhaps of reverence which supplies the emotional coloring essential to the modification of conduct in later adjustments. And I am certain that the efficiency of such a prejudice is a function, in part at least, of the time and effort that have been given to the mastery of the subject. After all, the things that appeal to us most strongly from the emotional aspect are the things that we have gained at the cost of effort and struggle; and the belief that the "tough" subjects of the curriculum have the greatest disciplinary value has a psychological basis in this fact.

I am here speaking of no vague, indefinite "mental power" or "mental faculty" that may be developed by the studies. The factor to which I refer may be intangible and elusive, but I maintain that it is thoroughly consistent with the accepted principles of modern psychology. The consciousness of power is often as important in gaining a victory as the possession of power. Indeed, it is the emotional force of a belief that renders the power itself dynamic rather than potential. The graduate of Cambridge may never use his mathematics in solving the situations of his later life, but it is possible that he has gained something from his mastery of mathematics that will help him more in solving a situation than he could be helped by any amount of instruction regarding the technique of that situation. The "something" that he has perhaps gained is a consciousness of conquest, or, if I may use a street phrase, the knowledge that he has been "up against" the "toughest" problems that the mind of mind can devise and has come out a victor. Certainly his mastery of mathematics does not necessarily involve this feeling of confidence; but it *may* involve it, and, in case it does, there can be no doubt of its value in making his future adjustments more efficient.

This does not mean, of course, that one would decry the virtue of that technical and vocational education which aims to furnish specific facts and principles for the solution of specific situations. I assert simply this: that far more fundamental than the technical facts are the prejudices in favor of dogged persistence, unflinching application, relentless industry, and a determination to conquer, whatever the cost. These combined with technical knowledge and skill can spell nothing less than efficiency. Without technical knowledge, they might ultimately win, but the price of victory would be unnecessarily high and the chances of failure much greater. But technical knowledge alone without these other factors must spell disaster in every critical situation.

And I should not say that these prejudices which are so

important cannot be engendered through the processes of education that give one technical knowledge and skill. I believe, however, that, as a rule, applied science is frequently less efficient, in this respect, than pure science, and applied mathematics than pure mathematics. Pure science and pure mathematics constantly emphasize the system and unity of the subject-matter. In a certain sense, the contemplation of a large system of knowledge has much in common with the contemplation of a great work of art. It is a unity in which every part is definitely related to every other part, in which there are no gaps, or lacunae, or jagged edges. And the emotional factor, I believe, is a function, in part, of this aesthetic quality—but I should not press this point.

But there still remains unanswered a question that was raised a little way back. Granting that emotionalized prejudices of a very effective sort may be engendered in the study of science and mathematics, what shall we say with regard to the generalization of specific habits such as those formed in the earlier stages of education? What is the value of disciplining the child into specific habits of promptness, or neatness, or accuracy? Will specific training give rise to emotionalized prejudices in favor of the virtues that the discipline represents? If it does, there can be no doubt that the effects of training may be generalized or carried over to situations other than those in which the training has been given.

Personally, I believe that we get most of our effective prejudices from just this source of early training, but it is, of course, true that the specific habits might be very adequately formed without at the same time engendering the corresponding prejudices. The indeterminate factor is the emotional factor. The discipline of the early home life is the great breeding ground of prejudices *because of the positive and profound emotional factors that operate.* (I mean by "positive" factors those that operate in favor of the virtues in question.) The most powerful prejudices upon which civilized society rests are engendered in the home—honesty, cleanliness, decency, self-denial. Except as these are taught by precept and example, and fortified by specific habits, and thoroughly imbued with positive emotional force, the social fabric must surely fall to pieces.

It is for these prejudices in particular that the home must be responsible. The school can do little to develop them unless the school takes over all of the educative functions of the home, and even then the weakness of the most important factor of all —the emotional factor—is apt to make the attempt abortive. But the school in turn must stand sponsor for certain prejudices that the home cannot always be depended upon to engender, and among these one must certainly include accuracy, promptness, industry, application, efficiency, order, respect for the rights and feelings of others, respect for authority, for truth, and for justice.

The important point is this: The specific habits which have reference to these various virtues are insufficient; *it is the prejudice in their favor that is the significant thing.* And this explains in part the failure of our older methods of teaching to develop efficient controls. We thought that the habit was the prime essential. We neglected the prejudice. And so we took the shortest road to the habit, forgetting that we might thereby be inducing a prejudice of quite the opposite kind—forgetting that *prejudices not only generalize habits, but sometimes negate them.* And so the net result has been very frequently to promote the very end that we sought to avoid. A prejudice against work and application and concentrated attention has often been engendered by the heart-rending, back-breaking grind of toil imposed upon the child of the farm. A prejudice against morality has been developed more than once, I believe, by the namby-pamby methods of the Sunday school. And I am more than tolerably certain that a prejudice against temperance has been promoted, in many cases, by the methods that we have taken to build temperate habits.

Again it is the emotional factor that must be considered, and this sometimes works in the most unexpected ways. Do we believe that imposing difficult tasks upon the pupil will develop in him that prejudice in favor of persistence and application and close, sustained attention, which is so necessary in meeting the situations of later life? How do we know that, instead of this, we are not developing its antithesis, and that he will not acquire a repugnance for these virtues? Do we believe that we can avoid the difficulty by catering to his interests? How do we know that we shall not develop a prejudice against all effort that is not bribed and all tasks that are not attractive? Or, do we wish to put the pupil into an habitual attitude of respect for authority? How can we be certain that we do not overshoot the mark, and make him a subservient tool, lacking in all initiative? Do we try to obviate this difficulty by leaving his inherited impulses to work themselves out without let or hindrance? How do we know that the liberty of childhood may not engender a prejudice in favor of license in manhood? Are these merely academic questions? Ask any principal of an elementary school who is face to face with the responsibility for governing five hundred children and who is endowed with both a brain and a heart. It is precisely these problems that such a man must attempt to solve at every turn of the day's work.

One can find no better example of the difficulty of solving these problems than is presented in the one department of education in which we have consciously attempted to develop an emotionalized prejudice, namely, the teaching of literature. From present indications, it would seem that our attempt to force upon the child an appreciation of art in any of its forms has been most barren in its results. The music hall still holds forth its allurements in spite of our costly experiment in public-school music. The variety stage draws with its blandishments those who have been carefully taught how to enjoy Shakspere. All the garish distractions of our great cities prosper on the earnings, not of our unlettered immigrants, but of the products of our own public schools.

Have we not in this problem of developing prejudices both the most important and the most difficult problem of educational science? Is it not the crux of the whole question of moral education? Is it not the most significant factor in social improvement? Should it not receive adequate recognition in the present radical reconstructions to which the curricula of our high schools and colleges are being subjected?

Obviously enough, the key to the situation lies in the emotional factors; but here, unhappily, we need a key that will unlock the key. At the very outset, we confront a danger that will do much to defeat our purpose. I refer to the danger of sentimentalism. Our present conception of the emotional life is far too narrow and restricted to serve as a basis for fruitful investigation from the standpoint that I have proposed. In popular use, the word "emotion" is heavily freighted with associations that make it a veritable bugbear for scientific research. And no small source of the negative prejudices that we are now developing in education is this silly, sentimental recognition of the emotional factors so-called that is little less than disgusting to the serious and self-respecting student. If you wish to give a boy a first-class prejudice against nature, put him through the average course in nature-study that has for its object the development of a love for nature's beauty. What the true emotional nature of the boy craves is not something to love, but something to respect. Love is a word that ought always to be in our hearts, but seldom upon our lips, lest we cheapen the sentiment by constant reiteration. And the emotional factors to which we give the name "love" function in only a weakened form prior to puberty, and even after puberty, the less ado that we make about them in education, the more completely, I believe, will their ideal elements emerge from the background of instinct and become positive forces in the control of conduct. Just now we hear upon every side that the child must love his school, he must love his work, he must love his teacher, he must love literature, he must love art, he must love nature; but we never hear that he must respect anything, except (and this only by implication) his own whims and fancies. Now respect is just as thoroughly a sentiment as is love, and with the preadolescent child, it is based upon a far more powerful emotion. I might also add, although I may seem unorthodox, that the only kind of love worth having is the kind that grows out of respect.

Now this is far from saying that the teacher should not have a genuine affection for his pupils. Love of that type comes from the other side and is based upon parental instincts—paternal or maternal—that are fundamental. The person who does not feel the power of these instincts is abnormal, and certainly has no place among teachers.

And so the first step in the solution of our problem must be an investigation of the emotional forces that govern conduct—using the term emotion in the very broad sense that I have suggested. This will be no simple task, but the full investment of education with scientific dignity and worth must await its outcome. We must come to know in a fairly definite and concise form the number and sources of these great controls of conduct. Now we know them only in the vaguest fashion. We know that there are certain emotionalized ideas, like the principle of religious liberty, or the principle of equality under the law, which have dominated councils of war and stained battle fields; that there are certain emotionalized standards, like honesty and chastity and personal honor, which not infrequently determine the greatest and most critical of individual adjustments; that there are certain powerfully emotionalized abstractions, like truth, or faith, or service, which may map out the entire trend of a man's life and mark the clear path of his career; that there are certain profoundly emotionalized conceptions, like friendship, or motherhood, or divinity, which only not quite defy the words of a David or a Job to formulate, or the pigments of a Raphael to depict, but which still lie somewhere deeply imbedded in every human motive that makes for what we call the right. Of these, at present, we can say with certainty only this: that somewhere during that long period of human plasticity which we call childhood and youth, they are implanted in the heart, there to work out into action and bring forth fruit of their kind. Now perhaps the seeds are sown by precept and admonition; now by objective example and conscious imitation; now by long years of growth and training and discipline; now by a sudden flash of inspiration. Many, and these doubtless the most potent, come from the home, others from the social environment, others from religion, others from the *Zeitgeist,* others from literature and art and history and biography. But some must surely come from the school, and in all of them the influence of the school must be felt. Whether we will or no, we cannot escape the responsibility.

And even if the more accurate investigations are still to be made, the very recognition of the importance of these factors should have its effect upon the actual work of teaching. When the teacher asks himself not only what he wishes to impart in the way of knowledge and train in the way of habits, but also what sort of prejudices and what sort of standards and what sort of ideals he wishes to give his pupils, the very attitude of questioning will, I believe, modify his work in the direction of greater efficiency. We cannot all be teachers like Pestalozzi or Froebel or Arnold or Sheldon or Parker, but we can all appreciate the characteristic that made these men masters of their craft. We can know that they were great and influential, not merely because of the knowledge that they possessed, but far more fundamentally because of the ideals with which they were inspired, and that their influence was due to the facility and skill with which they could pass on this inspiration to their pupils. And, knowing this, we, too, may be encouraged to strive for idealism to the end that our pupils may feel, however feebly, the uplift, and catch a glimpse, however fleeting of the sunlit peaks.

THE DEEPER AND THE RICHER MEANINGS OF MATHEMATICAL TEACHING IN ELEMENTARY SCHOOLS. II

GEORGE W. MYERS
College of Education

GOOD ARITHMETIC TEACHING IS A TRAINING IN CHOICE

I have said that many ways of doing things in arithmetic should be taught; because there is a widespread disposition among teachers to talk and teach as though there were only *one* way to do an arithmetical problem, and that all that needs be done is to learn this one way. The old-time notion that there is one method for addition, one for subtraction, etc., was the foster-parent of the method-haggling, and device-hunting that so dominated and mechanized arithmetic work in the recent past. But this is the day of the open-door policy in the matter of method and device. They are now regarded only as means to the great end of thinking. Some teachers can render the highest service through one type of method, others become more effective through another type. As with teachers so with pupils. Some pupils will more readily grasp the underlying thought through one type of presentation, and others through another type. The good teacher must have at his finger-tips many ways of exhibiting the truth being taught, and must have great resourcefulness and tact in their use. There must be more openmindedness, more mental springiness, more flexibility in the use of method and device in the schoolroom. The essential question with all method is: *to what extent does it deepen interest and clarify, intensify, and facilitate thought?*

As just suggested, different methods will meet this crucial question with varying degrees of success with different pupils. Pupils must therefore be given latitude of choice as to their methods of attacking and of working problems.

But choosing, to be effective, must be rationalized and liberated by a knowledge of the reasons on which the choice is made, and guided and steadied by suitable standards for estimating the relative merits of choices. One all-embracing standard of judgment for choosing is the principle of ease of action. This is always available for elementary-school mathematics. It throws the choice sometimes in favor of this method, and sometimes in favor of that. If the textbook has been properly written it will not fix upon a single method for each process, then carefully manufacture problems to exemplify this method to the exclusion of all others. With good teaching, problems are selected to exhibit conditions under which this or that method is the more convenient, the more advantageous; and care will always be taken that these problems shall cover fairly well the ground of the situations that arise most frequently in common affairs. The pedagogic aim must ever be so to open up and exhibit the thinking of an arithmetical topic, that its thought-values shall spread out into other than pure arithmetical fields. This is what we call the culture-value of mathematics.

Choice must also be liberated. The pupil who knows only one way suffers constraint in choosing. He necessarily takes the only route that promises a way out. In strictness he does not choose; because he cannot. He either blindly follows, or is driven. This is the necessary outcome of one-method teaching. To prevent this driving, sometimes miscalled teaching, teachers must qualify masterfully to teach pupils to choose from among different available methods of attacking and of solving problems; to choose the order of processes used in a given problem; to choose the best way of executing the several processes, and to some extent to choose problem-material. Then will arithmetic become a powerful factor in training for rational choosing in life's emergencies, and strong willing inevitably follows right choosing. Good conduct, good morals, are simply the sum-total of correct choices. Verily, good arithmetic teaching conduces to good character and right conduct.

To specify concrete opportunities, the following enumeration of alternatives of choice will serve to suggest the scope of available materials for choice:

Sums to be obtained by adding (1) upward; (2) downward;

(3) horizontally; (4) columns by parts, then the sums of the parts; (5) footing tables vertically and horizontally; (6) horizontally and vertically; (7) by grouping into 10's, 20's, etc.

Differences to be found (1) the usual way; (2) by making-up method; (3) with subtrahend over minuend; (4) subtrahend beside minuend; (5) increasing the subtrahend digit; (6) subtracting from left to right.

Products to be found (1) the usual way; (2) left-to-right multiplication; (3) by factors of multiplier; (4) by parts of multiplier, as $25 \times 36 = 20 \times 36 + 5 \times 36 = 30 \times 25 + 6 \times 25$, etc.; (5) by aliquot parts of 100, 1,000, etc.

Quotients to be found by dividing (1) the usual way; (2) quotient over dividend; (3) by factors of divisor; (4) by aliquot parts; (5) taking common factors out of dividend and divisor.

COMMON FRACTIONS

Fractions should be added and substracted—

1. By measurement exercises with common standards.
2. By divided lines, squares, oblongs, circles, etc.
3. By brisk formal exercises such as—

a) How many fourths in 1/2? In 2/2?

b) How many fourths in 1/2 and 1/4? In 1/2+2/4? In 1/2 +3/4?

c) How many fourths in 1/2 less 1/4? In 1/2+2/4? In 1/2 +3/4?

d) How many sixths in 1/3? 2/3? 3/3?

e) How many sixths in 1/3+1/6? In 1/3+2/6? In 2/3+1/6? In 2/3+2/6?

f) How many sixths in 1/3−1/6? In 2/3−1/6? In 2/3−2/6? In 5/6−1/3?

4. By the customary formal procedure.

Fractions should be multiplied—

1. By use of common standards of distance, area, bulk, capacity, weight, time, etc.
2. By divided lines, squares, oblongs, circles, etc.
3. By the customary formal procedure, first using "of" for times symbol, and later, using "times." (Distinction of partition from division is strongly advised against.)

4. Check multiplications by reversing steps.

Fractions should be divided—

1. By measurement with common standards.

2. By aid of dividing lines, squares, oblongs, circles, etc.

3. By getting common denominators, and comparing numerators.

4. By the process of inverting divisor and multiplying, rationally presented.

5. Check division by multiplying.

NOTE.—Multiplications and divisions of fractions must be as systematically and persistently checked as are the processes with whole numbers. Cancellation is of great service in this checking.

DECIMAL FRACTIONS

The meaning of a decimal fraction should be taught by relating it—

1. To whole numbers, as with monetary values, or with metric units.

2. To common fractions, as $\frac{1}{4}$=how many hundredths? etc.

3. To the system of decimal notation for integers.

After showing that the point is only a means of "pointing out" which digit, or figure denotes ones, or units, all that is needed for decimal addition and subtraction is to proceed precisely as with whole numbers, and to point the sum or difference so that the points all stand in a vertical line.

In multiplication of decimals, the pointing is a little more difficult. Here the point should be located—

1. By writing easy decimals in common fraction form, and multiplying, then, writing the product in the decimal form.

2. By multiplying as with integers, and then, by shifting the point on the principle that $\frac{1}{10}$, $\frac{1}{100}$, etc., of multiplicand or multiplier must give $\frac{1}{10}$, $\frac{1}{100}$, etc., of the product.

3. By the customary mechanical procedure, checking by deciding roughly about what the result must be.

In division, the quotient should be pointed by dividing through as with whole numbers and then—

1. Marking off in some way as many places in the dividend as there are decimal figures in the divisor, and noting that the

quotient figures are figures of a whole number until this place is reached.

$$23.5\overline{)203.04}\quad 8.164$$

2. Shifting the point over the same number of figures in both dividend and divisor until there is but one figure to the left of the point in the divisor, and then ask, About what is ½, ⅓, ¼, etc., of the modified dividend, pointing the quotient number so as to make it as near this estimated quotient as possible, by pointing alone.

EXAMPLE

203.04 divided by 2.35 = ?

$$2.35\overline{)20.304}\quad 8.64$$

3. The customary procedure, checking the pointing by estimating roughly about what the result must be.

If time permitted I would indicate for percentage and interest and mensuration similar alternatives of procedure which should be made available to grade pupils. But a word to the wise is sufficient.

SPEED AND ACCURACY

Many teachers who glibly profess themselves seeking to secure "speed and accuracy in figuring" are unfortunately not succeeding in securing either, if we may credit recent findings of both local and foreign observers. If the animating idea of teachers of arithmetic could be ascertained, I dare say that in most cases, it would be found that the thing they are actually striving to develop, instead of accuracy, is only a sort of technical deftness, or mechanical precision as to the externals of process; and, instead of speed, the thing actually produced is nervousness, feverishness, and fidgetiness. So faded, so hackneyed has the phrase "speed and accuracy" become through canting speech and canting acts, that the terms "speed" and "accuracy" need reinforming with new life and meaning. The good old wine very much needs new bottles.

I wish to attempt a closer specification than is prevalent of the meaning of these terms for arithmetic teaching. Definitions, of course, do not necessarily help classroom practice. Only such definitions influence practice as become organic to the thought-process of the practitioner. Definitions are, therefore, merely conditions precedent—not conditions sufficient—to good practice.

WHAT IS ACCURACY?

In the first place, accuracy in arithmetic is a matter of the mind. An act of thought is its *sine qua non.* No conception of accuracy can be generated in the learner, nor can the habit of accuracy be fostered, without thinking on the learner's part. One remembers or he does not remember. "He remembers inaccurately" is a contradiction, and "He remembers accurately" is tautology. There are no gradations of remembering. This is particularly true of formal number facts. They may, perhaps, be remembered perfectly or imperfectly; but not accurately or inaccurately. Pure memorizing touches accuracy vere remotely. On the contrary, there are degrees of accuracy and of inaccuracy. But the type of accuracy that has meaning for arithmetic involves the judgment.

In the next place, judgments are based on comparisons, and comparing judgments is thinking. Arithmetical accuracy involves two elements, one external and the other internal. The internal element is an idea, mental operation, or a judgment. The external element is its expression, usually in the form of a symbol or of a mechanical process. The two factors that are always present, always an organic part of arithmetical accuracy, are an idea and its expression. If either factor be lacking, all talk of accuracy is empty and misleading. The city superintendent—not in Kansas—who said recently: "We use all diligence to make our children quick and accurate in fundamental conceptions as pure memory work," must have forgotten these facts. An examination of his school the other day showed his children to be unusually deficient in both respects. Drill-masters who are striving to teach children to be quick and accurate through pure memory work, or through the agency of pure drill on the formal side of arithmetic always have failed, are now failing, and must ever fail for the reason that they are trying to make bricks without straw, and (more's the pity!) when there is available an abundance of straw. The thought-side of the work is the indispensable, inescapable, and indisputable condition to accuracy. It is clear that I am not here speaking of mechanical precision, which is quite another matter, and has its rightful place in arithmetic.

A definition of accuracy that will both work and serve as a guide in the schoolroom may be ventured at this point. *Accuracy in school arithmetic, means adequacy of expression to idea.*

All teaching that makes the pupil's ideal merely to get set results, even a large score of them, that shifts his thought from correct answers solely as a check on correct work, at once degrades his sense of accuracy, demoralizes his habits, and confuses his ideals of accuracy. Kansas teachers are not accused of such teaching; but are herewith simply warned against it.

The true conception of accuracy for arithmetic emerges for both teacher and pupil through measuring and the use of measurements. This is indeed one of the strong reasons that arithmetic work should be based on measuring, rather than on counting, ratioing, or "on the inducing of judgments of relative magnitudes," as some would have it. In measuring, the question at once arises, and remains up continually, "With what degree of closeness should measurements be made?" This question will be answered by the teacher from two points of view, and by the pupil from only one. The teacher must ascertain the smallest unit of which the pupil has, or can readily form, a working conception, and he will not attempt to require the learner to work with a much smaller unit. This is the natural limit from the educational point of view. To find it, and to keep within it, is the business of the teacher.

But the nature of the problem must guide both teacher and pupil as to the degree of practical refinement to be sought. It is in the problem that the pupil's interest focuses, not in the way of it, nor in the educational meaning of it. If the problem be to find the number of plants for his flowerbed, it is unmeaning, even foolish, to carry results to fractions. If the problem mean the cutting of a member for a playhouse, the pupil knows, quite as well as the teacher, that an eighth or a sixteenth of an inch becomes a matter serious enough to be attended to. The problem need not call for the actual cutting, save in imagination. The pupil readily pictures to himself, from the more or less indirect suggestions of the arithmetical problem, what would be required, were he to attempt to do the actual cutting and measuring. With this measuring and cutting which he does in imagination he does not willingly take unwarranted liberties and violate metrical proprieties.

SPEED DIFFERENT WITH DIFFERENT PUPILS

A little attention to the spontaneous activities of children, when spontaneity is unchecked by adults, readily reveals that each child has a certain *norm* of speed of motor discharge. Careful observing of children at work shows an analogous norm of speed of mental activity. The child's normal mental gait is as thoroughly and characteristically a part of him as is his physical gait. At this gait he dispatches work most economically and most comfortably, and the output of his effort maintains a uniformly high quality and quantity. To this pitch the music of his soul is attuned. To this chord the rhythm of his nature most fully responds.

At this gait the child is able to maintain a steady and high potential of thought-concentration. To force him by external stimuli to work at a higher rate than his norm makes his thinking uncertain, jerky, and flighty, and soon dissipates his fund of mental energy. To permit him to work below his norm is to make his thinking wobbly, and ambling, and his attention scattering. His thought-movements resemble those of the dying top, or bicycle. Low potential activity encourages mental loafing, habituates the child to going about his tasks in a half-hearted way, and tends to satisfy him with half-achievement. It engenders and fosters effort that is below the highest levels of possibility. Thus it occurs that allowing children to work below their norm of speed and forcing them by extraneous means to go beyond it end in the same deplorable issue—dissipation, rather than concentration, of thought.

The arithmetic teacher must then study his pupils individually to ascertain as nearly as possible the norm of speed for each. He must seek to hold the effort of the pupil to the level of this norm. He should be neither dragged, coaxed, nor spurred beyond this rate for any great length of time, if at all. The pupil will raise his norm by working within it and close up to it, but not beyond it. Dullness, stupidity, and something like mental flabbiness, resulting in enfeebled powers of concentration, are the outcome of abnormally low-potential activity; while fitful and nervous activity, issuing in a sort of hysteria, standing also for enfeebled concentration, are the end of abnormally high-potential activity. Thus do overstrained and understrained effort miss the mark of educational efficiency on the same side. I suggest that it is *dispatch,* which means a reasonably high rate of turning off work of a uniformly high grade of excellence with comfort to the workman, that arithmetic teaching should strive for, rather than for mere speed.

DRILL-WORK IN ARITHMETIC

There is also much canting speech and more canting action about drill-work in elementary-school mathematics. Time can be taken here only to indicate the pedagogical place of drill in the learning process. Teachers easily habituate themselves to dealing with the problems of education only from the view-point of the teaching process. We have scores of volumes that deal with the teaching process to one that deals explicitly with the learning process. Learning, with children as with adults, means acquiring, assimilating, and getting working control over new ideas and over processes for dealing with them. For purposes of a better understanding of it, the learning process may well be thought of as made up of three stages: viz., (1) the informal-use stage; (2) the formal-study stage; and (3) the application stage. Each of these may easily be subdivided into smaller steps as is exhibited below.

The formal-study stage of the learning process is made up of the following three pretty clearly marked steps: (1) the graphic step, in which the idea or process being learned is made to stand out before the learner in some pictured way. This is the psychological place for geometrized arithmetic; (2) the memory-step, in which the learner makes an explicit effort to remember the formal aspect of the object of study. This is the point at which generalized, or algebraized, arithmetic is most helpful; (3) the reflex-action step, in which the learner seeks to acquire automatic control of the new possession, to the end that the mechanics of it may no longer retard, but may facilitate, thinking. This is the psychologic moment and place for drill and it belongs nowhere earlier than this in the learning process; (4) the last stage of the learning process is the application stage. The learner here uses the newly acquired possession; but now he has already made it fully his own. He uses it with design, of destined purpose, and that he may feel how much he has added to his efficiency by having mastered it. He uses it for a time alone, and then among other familiar ideas, that he may both know it as an idea and as it appears in the midst of its natural meanings and settings.

To summarize: the learning process consists of the following stages and steps:

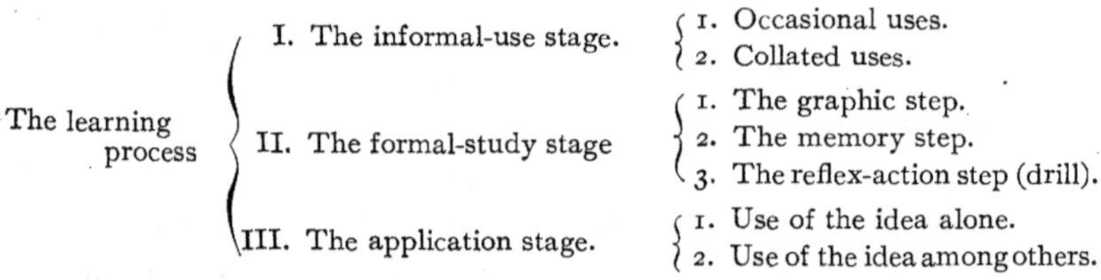

For the pupil brisk, snappy, and properly timed drill-exercises, which never should be too long sustained, perform the following important educational offices:

1. Strengthen the power of voluntary attention, or of concentration of thought.

2. Develop facility of thought and ease of action.

3. Beget and foster a sense of growth in efficiency.

4. Cultivate quickness and sprightliness of memory.

5. Give readiness, alertness, and mechanical precision.

6. Show the need and value of knowledge that is available at the instant when, and at the spot where, it is wanted; i. e., of the "spot-cash" type of knowledge.

SUMMARY

I may now summarize most of the points I have tried to make as follows:

1. The teacher may aid independence of thought in arithmetic in the following ways:

a) By accrediting the pupil's mode of thought;

b) By habitual checking of work;

c) By emphasizing the thought side of the work;

d) By impressing the thought that in arithmetic nothing is to be taken on authority;

e) By employing many semi-original problems.

2. Teachers may make arithmetic teaching a training in choice—

a) By having pupils do things in more than one way, to find the better way;

b) By showing reasons for standard conventions;

c) By allowing pupils to use their own way until the better way appeals to them as being the better way;

d) By allowing pupils to take the consequences of their own choosing of ways;

e) By using good ways themselves and by commending good ways of working when they are used by pupils.

3. Arithmetic may be made a training in judgment—

a) By teaching rational calculating;

b) By much antecedent estimating, followed immediately by measuring and calculating;

c) By having pupils to think through lists of exercises, or problems, without figuring, and to tell definitely just how they would solve them; in cases of doubt follow with the actual solutions;

d) By having pupils always on the alert to find the easy way, even where the teacher feels quite sure his way is the easy way;

e) By asking, after solutions, always in cases of doubt, whether the result seems about what it should be;

f) By independent checking.

4. Arithmetic work may be made a valuable training in concentration of thought—

a) By brisk, snappy, drill-exercises, not too long sustained;

b) By having pupils work problems with a view to seeing how soon they can solve them correctly, the demand for speed being as natural as possible;

c) By having pupils see how many exercises they can get right in 5, 10, or 20 minutes;

d) By estimating about what results must be;

e) By postponing technique and putting drill-work in its proper place in the teaching process;

f) By working always close up to, but not beyond, the pupil's norm of speed;

g) By mental calculating, counting by 2's, 3's, 5's, 10's, 4's, etc.

5. To make arithmetic work give training in clear thinking and in reasonable accuracy—

a) Give time enough, not too much, for difficult problems to be worked and checked;

b) By diagramming and sketching of figures (pictures) to advance the pupil's power to image number-relations;

c) By doing less "talky-talking" and more chalk-talking, and by the use of cross-lined paper and blackboard;

d) By recognizing in practice that attainable accuracy is different in different grades;

e) By studying habits of thinking of pupils, and insisting always on attainable neatness and system;

f) By using problem-material in which the pupil has, or may develop, an interest.

6. Arithmetic work may be made valuable training in inference-making—

a) By much preliminary estimating;

b) By careful estimating, before figuring, about what the result must be;

c) By much use of cancellation;

d) By much citation of reasons, not rules, for steps taken;

e) By rudimentary algebraic thinking, as $3x$ is 12, what is x? $3+x$ is 8, what is x? etc.

f) By the use of indirect measurements, as to get the side, or angle, of a triangle that cannot be measured directly but must be calculated from its relation to lines, or angles, that can be measured;

g) By asking why the result, as G.C.D., or L.C.M., etc., is what it claims to be;

h) By set exercises in inference-drawing.

I believe your adopted texts will, so soon as teachers get into their spirit and method, go far toward securing these very real, very useful, but too-long neglected, virtues of good arithmetic teaching. We are laying no specious claim to making the arithmetic easy; but we do claim not to be making it hard. Our problem is the improvement of arithmetical opportunities now running too largely to waste. The inclusion of the deeper and richer educational meanings of arithmetic among teaching aims necessarily adds something to the teacher's responsibility. But where is the teacher, worthy the name, who will not say at once that the slight additional burden—for it is but slight—is not eminently worth while, in view of the immense importance of the issues of educating children?

CONCLUSION

In conclusion, let me say modernizing the teaching and the substance of elementary-school mathematics is mainly a problem of enlarging the scope of pedagogic view, and of making methodology more natural and more childlike than has been the wont. This can be done by, and only by, giving teachers a larger, a truer, a less static, a more dynamic conception of their professional duties touching this particular subject. Teachers must believe in arithmetic as an educational agency, before they can succeed with it educationally. Great indeed is the need for a profounder pedagogic faith in the sentiment—

> I doubt not through the ages one increasing purpose runs,
> And the thoughts of men are broadened with the process of the suns—

even for the arithmetic. Then mellowed by that sweet docility of spirit that finds its sublimest expression in, "a little child shall lead," the teacher may go forth to meet the problems of improvement with courage, shod with sandals of wisdom and gentleness, that knows not the words failure, defeat, and discouragement. May the larger view, the more childlike view, the more hopeful spirit, and the forward look, be the inspiring watchword and portion of us all in the labor of reconstructing the good that now is into the better that is to be!

FIELD-WORK AND NATURE-STUDY
PART III

IRA B. MEYERS
School of Education

MENTAL ATTITUDE IN FIELD-WORK

Just as a sequence of related changes and events makes up the history of the genesis and development of a landscape so, also, it is through a connected series of experiences and associations that the individual mind comes to recognize and understand the content and history of the landscape in its true interrelations and completeness. True progress in nature-knowledge, in science, has been and is accomplished through the struggle of the mind with the unfamiliar materials and changes in nature to know things as they actually are, name, properties, origin, relationships, plus the application, through control and adaptation, of the facts discovered as relating to the needs and conveniences of man whereby he is gradually constructing out of these materials and forces his own social and industrial environment or kingdom. At every step progress has been through personal contact with the actual materials and forces and not through textbooks and lectures. In this growth I am not unmindful of imitation, of the influence of personality, of the power of one person to communicate the facts he discovers, the relationships which he detects, to other persons so that they may avoid going through the same blind hunt until they discover the truths already known. But I am quite sure that the person to whom a fact or discovery has been communicated will understand and assimilate the fact, not in proportion to what he has heard or read about the matter, but in proportion as he has searched for facts in the same manner, or is stimulated to search in some similar manner. Progress in nature-knowledge depends upon the way in which the individual mind meets and deals with the materials and changes in its environment; and the clearness and precision with which another mind grasps discovered facts and relationships, through any form of communication, depends upon the character of the experience it has had with its nature environment and the manner in which it has dealt with these experiences. Wherever our school work touches sympathetically upon the actual experiences of the children it gains from them a ready response, and interest and activity prevail. If we wish our work to retain this vitality we must organize our courses of study so as to give pupils a broader and richer experience than the interior of our school buildings can ever afford. We must rid ourselves of the idea that we can ever accomplish anything of worth in nature-study by telling children, or by having them read, about things with which they have had little or no personal experience. We must also appreciate the fact that children need a volume of personal-interest experiences before we begin to convert them into conscious knowledge.

Abnormal mental attitudes, induced by our artificial methods in education, are constantly cropping out in our classes and giving us glimpses of the true state of the mind. A few years ago the writer went with a class of students, all of whom were high-school graduates, to a lake shore to study the work of waves. The waves were rolling in leisurely but massively. We could see the pebbles forced shoreward by the in-rush of each wave and dragged back again by the undertow; we could hear the swish and grind of this shore-drift as it was dragged back and forth by the waves. On the beach we picked up pebbles rounded and smoothed, pieces of coal, bits of broken glass, fragments of driftwood, all with the same smoothed and rounded surface as the pebbles. The students spoke of how these various fragments must have had sharp angles and edges when first broken from their main mass, and that their rounded condition must be the result of the friction in their movement by the waves. They inferred that the pebbles must have been angular fragments of rocks worn in the same manner as the coal, glass, and wood and that the sand was to a certain extent the product of the worn-off edges. I considered that we had made the observations and interpretation essential to a clear understanding of the elementary principles of the influence of waves on shore-drift and that the facts involved had been quite thoroughly assimilated by each member of the class, when one of the students turned to me with the remark: "Now this is all perfectly clear, but how am I to know that it is really true unless I can read of it in some book?" In thinking this matter over it occurred to me that after all the connecting points were really missing; we saw no pebbles actually smoothed, no angles disappear, no sand grains formed—we inferred all. The student saw clearly the isolated facts but could not fit them together to form a chain of relationships. Only those who had pounded and rubbed stones in their childhood could really make the connection; for this our courses of study fail to provide. Fifty rods inland from the lake was a ridge, grass covered, and forested with oak. An excavation in the ridge exposed a mass of rounded pebbles and stratified sand, a duplicate of the materials found on the beach, yet the cause of the presence of that ridge was a mystery to the class. The mind which has not been furnished an adequate supply of sense experiences, nor used its experiences so as to acquire a certain independence of habit and precision in making elementary inferences as to the relations and meaning of observed facts has a poor chance of ever doing any strong work when it has to deal with materials as they exist under natural conditions. Such people will live their life and make use of socialized conditions, but they will never be positive factors in strengthening and maintaining social conditions, for they are without power to socialize the raw materials. If the memorization of knowledge, and the gaining of certain experiences through some routine, were the end, if our fund of nature-knowledge were complete, so that it was merely a thing to be learned and transmitted like the religious myths of ancient tribes, we could teach it in that way; but so long as new truths are being discovered, so long as the landscape changes, and life adapts itself to these changing conditions, so long as the mechanism of civilization is changing, we need to train the mind to deal readily with changing conditions. The mind must be kept plastic, and only a growing mind, a mind which has retained something of the plasticity of its childhood in its power and habit of going out after, choosing, selecting, arranging, and inferring from its own sense experiences under the impulse of individual interest, desire, need or sense of duty, can remain growing and plastic. It is the limitations set by our well-defined courses of study upon true self-activity which impede growth and progress. We do not attempt to raise plants by furnishing them with just what we think they need; we establish them in rich soil and open air and supplement with such aids as our knowledge and judgment dictates. So with our pupils, we must set them first to live and grow in the richest environment which we can afford; and then minister to their needs as our knowledge and judgment dictate. We are not yet wise enough to assume complete control; we must still have faith that in many places the right response to environment is surer in free nature than under the direction of the teacher; and that the tendency will be for the child to develop and adjust himself rightly if the conditions are right. Wherever there is work to be done the mind needs to be brought into an attitude of original attack on the work at hand. The character, quality, and quantity of work accomplished will be very largely determined by the attitude of the individual toward the work he is attempting and the attitude he maintains while the work is being done. We have all had the experience of seeing classes approach a piece of work with enthusiasm, only to "bog down" before the work was fairly begun. This would not be so bad if we treated the matter as we treat other natural reactions; if we considered the child a normal and natural organism, and sought a scientific explanation for this reaction, instead of assuming that laziness and perversion is a natural attitude to be overcome by some forcing process which is not in keeping with the spirit of science as a practice nor educational in result. Effort and capacity in doing work is very largely a matter of individual purpose or desire, and this depends upon how real or essential the work seems to be to the doer; upon how much of the pupil's real self we are able to enlist in the work. The boy spins his top, picks it up, tosses, catches, and balances it on his string with marvelous precision and skill, but in spite of our aid his writing remains clumsy and illegible.

The factor which determines the effectiveness of effort in any type of work is that of individual interest, purpose, or motive. Really to determine the working attitude of the mind is to find out the controlling interest or purpose which directs its activities in the main work at hand. There can be no strong action where the purpose is poorly defined and the feeling of a desire to do is absent.

The main individual purpose, in study, of the man engaged in scientific research, the child, and the teacher, differs in its character. In our teaching of nature-study and elementary science we have lost much in effectiveness through our failure to distinguish the character of each purpose and by trying to treat the whole under the purpose of the specialist.

In his study the man engaged in scientific research is ever on the alert for undiscovered forms, facts, and relationships, and his effort is to add something to the fund of human knowledge. He has chosen his special field of work, acquired a comprehensive grasp of its status in terms of present-day knowledge, and mastered the method and technique essential to the furthering of his knowledge in his chosen field. His real preparation for his work came after he had chosen his problem for study or investigation. His originality and resourcefulness as an investigator depend very largely upon the way he worked previous to the period of specialization.

The attitude of the elementary student in nature-study is in character closely allied to that of the special student in respect to dealing with new materials and phenomena and devising means for gaining a proper acquaintance and interpretation of the same, except that he is not facing the region of the unknown to science but the region of the unknown to himself. In attitude as regards their work, in conditions necessary to progress in their work, they are on a par; the main difference is in comprehensive grasp of subject, in accuracy of trained senses and mind, and in mastery of technique essential to progress in the work, and in all this the specialist has the decided advantage. That we should do honor to the one for his discoveries and deprive the other of the opportunity is to say the least not in keeping with modern reason. It is through this effort to gain individual acquaintanceship and understanding of things for himself that the child acquires that knowledge and power which makes him a valuable member to the race.

The attitude of the teacher in his approach to nature subjects with his class is a very different one. He has already in mind the forms, facts, phenomena, and their interrelations, of his subject, so far as they are known or relevant to the teaching purpose at hand; he has acquired facility in recognizing things at sight and in knowing their relationships or how to set to work to determine their relationships. He brings the materials of his subject and the pupils together, not to see how effectively they may be "crammed" with the facts and relations known to him, but to see how they lay hold of the subject at hand. His attention is not focused upon the discovery of facts in nature new to science but upon facts and relationships new to the children; and his problem is that of bringing about a contact between the materials and phenomena of nature, in the most favorable way, and then to observe the influence of this contact upon mind action and training; to note whether an acquaintance is established, whether new facts and relations are acquired, whether interest is developing, senses becoming more acute, whether these new experiences are being worked out in the mind so that the realities of things are beginning to appear; and withal whether the work is calling out the initiative of the student whereby he is going out after new experiences, observing, experimenting, interpreting, independent of detail directions; whether the pupil is really laying hold of the material at hand, and to withhold his own ready-made theories while the struggle is going on, to render aid wherever and however his judgment dictates, but to avoid, so far as possible, running ahead of the pupil's interests and needs. Situations should arise, out of the child's actual experiences, which enlist his interest and effort in solving or overcoming.

If, after we have done our best in this matter, the results

are not what we expected; if the pupils have not secured the facts and recognized their relationships as we see them and desire that they should; if they do not show the interest and enthusiasm we expected, let us retain something of a scientific attitude of mind in the matter and not place the blame wholly upon the materials with which we have been working, but let us rather look for the cause of failure in our method of treatment. Mind is surely as much a product of evolution, of natural law, as a tree. If the leaves of the tree fail in their work or the roots cease to take up moisture we do not blame the tree but seek for the cause in some abnormal or diseased condition, and having found the cause we render the aid essential to a re-establishment of normal conditions. If the child is not interested in his work, says or does stupid things, does not respond in a normal way to his school environment, no longer shows that eagerness to learn which was so prominent before his school period, let us not place the blame wholly upon the pupil but let us rather, as with the tree, seek the cause in some condition in his environment which is affecting his normal response. It is full time that we begin to believe that there is usually a physical reason for abnormal reactions in children. The entire history of civilization is one ceaseless testimony of the fact "That there is no motive that clings to man as long as the desire for wisdom." That it should be so forced an affair in the schools is to say the least a paradox. That this being, so extremely sensitive and responsive to its environment, so insatiable in its desire and capacity to learn during its first five years, should, when it enters the place organized for the economic continuance of learning, become a plodder, even resist so that we deem punishment, prizes, percentages, essential to an effectual continuance of the process, is a most unnatural condition. "It is vain that we make our children haste to rise early and late take rest and devour many carefully compiled textbooks. If their relations with the laws of nature are harmoniously established from the beginning knowledge will be given to them even while they sleep."

Theoretically no institution or system should respond so readily, or be so plastic in its adjustment to every new discovery pertaining to economic learning, as the school, but its response is extremely slow. In much of this matter there is need of considerable facing about, especially as to what constitutes real study and as to conditions and methods of stimulating genuine study; as to this matter of enforced or imposed knowledge as opposed to evolved knowledge; and in the matter of the essential mental attitude of students during their periods of study and recitation. We need to acquire ability to recognize genuine interests as contrasted with artificial interests; to know when our pupils enter into their work with the attitude of its being a personal matter, and to know when attitudes insure the accomplishment of a real purpose or work.

If our present-day fund of nature-knowledge and psychology has any one dominant value to the teacher it should be to indicate the proper method of procedure in establishing right relations between the child and his nature environment so that knowledge and power will evolve normally out of this relationship. Much valuable time has been wasted in devising courses of study designed to communicate a certain fund of knowledge, the criterion of selection being whether it was progressing in terms of subject and such as could be learned by the pupil of a given age or grade. What we really need is a course of study selected out of the child's environment, richer in content of subject-matter than any heretofore devised, the criteria of selection being its adaptation in terms of normal reaction to the psychic attitudes and tendencies of a certain age or period. So far as they relate to our nature environment these attitudes may be very generally summarized as—

1. The stage in which the child is interested in gaining a full personal acquaintance with the things around him, in finding out about this new world. In this he is impelled by a devouring curiosity the satisfaction of which is a matter of sense experience. "The cultivation of this instinctive curiosity to see, hear, handle, and secure the maximum number of sensations from any and every object is of most vital importance . . . . this inquisitiveness is naturally the vital factor in later scientific interest." The great need for out-of-door living to secure this

acquaintance and the relation of this experience to sensory training has been too fully dealt with in modern psychology to require reiteration. The truth and its proof is at hand pointing the way whenever we are ready to be guided by it. The essential thing is to spend more time out of doors, to keep in mind the unity of the landscape, to go to places where experiences, of interest to the children and essential to later and more complete interpretation, may be secured. We need to recognize the educational value of playing with pebbles and sand on the lake shore and watching the waves; of gathering flowers; of spying for birds; of wading in brooks; strolling through forests, etc.; to keep in mind that it is sympathetic contact and satisfaction of curiosity through sense experience that the child is after, rather than self-conscious knowledge; and above all to recognize that when the child has satisfied curiosity and his senses, as regards these things, there is no logical reason in his mind why he should pause to contemplate them any longer. "All these physical experiences pass up to the brain and produce some impression there. They do not constitute knowledge . . . . but they do form the unconscious material . . . . which will make his knowledge living and real and not shadowy." This failure to get a rich sense experience in childhood is father to lack of interest, originality, and initiative in youth and later manhood.

A stage slightly in advance of general sensory training is that at which children begin to take interest in connected actions or events apart from themselves, and begin to detect elementary relationships. They attach meaning to the movements of animals, can assume a certain responsibility in the care of domestic animals and pets, can appreciate the songs of birds and interpret their calls in terms of pleasure or alarm, and recognize animals by their tracks and sounds. Our course of study should scan carefully the school environment and incorporate types of experiences of this character into its course of study. Closely related are type experiences of more complex relationships. The gelatinous substance, with its black specks, found in the pond, the wriggling tadpole, and the hopping frog are to the child so many isolated objects. In the aquaria the children may see these black specks change gradually to tadpoles, and tadpoles to frogs, and these several objects become unified through the chain of observed events. Here again our course of study should scan the school and home environment to see what it offers in the way of similar observational study—the hatching of eggs, metamorphosis of insects, germination of seeds, gullying and erosion of land during heavy rainfalls, etc. The rule should be to have children interested in things doing and in doing things. Discussions, except when children are alive with wonderment and questions generated by these things which they have observed, should be reduced to a minimum. Out of these various experiences, as children grow older, will evolve questions requiring observations controlled by a conscious purpose on the part of the pupil: the cause of change of seasons; what becomes of animals and plants during the winter; factors of control in plant growth; how land surface is molded, etc. The product of this early sense knowledge furnishes the elementary basis and data for this second type of interest which may be termed intellectual interests. This second interest exhibits itself in the form of questions; it generates problems to be solved; it is the how-and-why stage of child-life, the beginning period of purposeful observation and experimentation. It is the stage of the awakening in consciousness of the power to do, to accomplish through individual initiative; and no stage, so far as relates to development of individual power and devotion to duty, needs such careful nurturing. It is the period at which our schools determine for most pupils whether they shall be dynamic powers or human automatons. Under proper guidance there will arise naturally a felt need for controlled investigations which constitutes the pupil's true preparation for the laboratory; and no pupil is really ready for laboratory work who does not carry to it a problem to be investigated. In this matter of interpretation, of detecting relationships, we enter regions where the facts and relationships are obscured by reason of their separation in time or space, or by reason of the fact that they cannot be recorded directly by the senses. It is easy to associate egg, tadpole, and frog when we have once observed the metamorphosis.

It is fairly easy to associate the rounding and smoothing of pebbles with wave action when we pick them up on the lake shore; it is more difficult to make the association when the pebbles are found in a gravel pit several miles inland, and we may fail entirely to interpret a cliff of conglomerate rock in terms of an ancient shore line. These associations depend upon the linking together of a number of elementary observations which will form a connected chain from the shore to the gravel pit and from the gravel pit to the cliff of conglomerate. Our elementary courses need to keep in mind the elementary relationships essential to these broader generalizations and follow and direct the activities of children into regions where they may be secured. The policy of failing to do this and depending on textbook statements to make these connections will always result in that lack of power to think which is at present so prominent in our school work:

> A child brought up with a sufficiently broad basis of this kind is always at home in the world. He stands within the pale. He is acquainted with nature and nature is in a certain sense acquainted with him. Whereas the child brought up . . . . with but little acquaintance with anything but the printed page is always afflicted with a certain remoteness from the actual facts of life, and a certain insecurity of consciousness which makes him a kind of an alien on the earth in which he ought to feel himself perfectly at home.[1]

Schoolwork is not suffering through lack of subject-matter but through failure to utilize to the end of educational effectiveness the common materials near at hand, through failure to recognize the value and educational content of the common things about us. We need to do more to lead pupils to appreciate the fact that the human race, since its beginning, has had nothing but these same common materials of earth, climate, life, and natural forces to study and utilize, and that during the ages these things themselves have undergone but little change. The great change has been in the attitudes of the people themselves, in the things they have found out about these various things, in the way they have used these things to aid them, and in the character and quality of their thinking.

[1] James, *Talks to Teachers.*

At some stage in the work the children should learn something of the history of the origin and growth of certain great conceptions, how great new ideas were evolved, some of the pioneers of new ideas, and how these pioneers and their ideas were received by the public. They should know something of the way in which new ideas had to struggle with old ideas to dislodge them before they could make any headway in the world. We need to develop liberal-mindedness, respect for authority, and above all how to question authority and to distinguish between prejudice and intelligent criticism.

Increase in the pupil's experience should be paralleled by information giving him corresponding increase in breadth of view of the history of the growth of knowledge and its application to progress. The efficiency of elementary field-work, of elementary education as a whole, must be judged in its totality by some standard more comprehensive than that of the successful daily recitation. Its ultimate test must be in the character of its accumulated influence on the individual, both as to right thinking and right action. If field-work had no other value it would be worth while to take pupils out of the schoolroom as a means for testing what we are doing, to develop alertness, individual initiative, and self-control. But because we are all too conscious that we are doing so little, that children are so unmanageable, and that we ourselves can explain nature better and with less fear of contradiction in the schoolroom than we can in the field and wood, or by the lake shore, we avoid the open altogether or use it but half-heartedly at its best, and then try to have it fit our books, rather than having our books fit it.

The essential factor in field-work, as in any type of schoolwork, is a comprehensive definite motive on the part of the instructor and of the school as a unit, in which the from-day-to-day lessons are steps toward this comprehensive end. Information gained through ample sense experience, impelled by strong interests, and directed by definite motives, imparts a quality to the individual quite apart from the facts learned themselves and which remains to mark the efficiency of the individual long after the several facts are forgotten.

A REPORT OF THE FIRST ANNUAL MEETING OF THE NATIONAL SOCIETY FOR THE PROMOTION OF INDUSTRIAL EDUCATION

KATHARINE E. DOPP
The University of Chicago

The National Society for the Promotion of Industrial Education was organized in New York, November 16, 17, 1906. Its great leaders (and it has great leaders) intended it to be a common meeting-ground for manufacturers, representatives of labor, social reformers, and teachers who recognize the industries as materials for education. The difficulties in the way of a society made up of such diverse elements are obvious. Each feels considerable distrust toward the other, or at least is inclined, as one party phrased it, to be "cautious." It is partly because of the conflicting and partial utterances heard from the same platform that the meeting, as a whole, was one of unusual interest. Because everybody heard so many ideas advocated that he could not accept, it was stimulating. And because the society is intended to be an organization which permits free expression, it certainly is one of great promise.

In submitting the following report, the writer is inclined to make few comments. It may not be out of place, however, to suggest to the reader the wisdom of looking for the germ of truth in the various statements, and likewise the importance of discovering the limitations of each party. For it is not the bad citizen that we have to fear so much as the good one who fails to discover the boundary line between those subjects upon which he speaks with and without authority.

The session Friday morning was presided over by Carrol D. Wright, president of Clark College, and former U. S. commissioner of labor. The subject under consideration was "The Apprenticeship System as a Means of Promoting Industrial Efficiency." The programme was so planned as to include addresses from a manufacturer, a trades-union man, and a man from a technical school. In a few introductory remarks Mr. Wright stated that the old apprenticeship system which began to decline with the introduction of labor-saving machinery has given place to a new system of apprenticeship. Referring to this new system, Mr. Wright said:

It would be too much to insist that the apprenticeship system answers the whole demand for industrial education. It is quite as needless to insist that the industrial school furnishes everything in the way of vocational equipment that can be gained through a thorough apprenticeship system. What is needed is an enlightened system that shall secure for the youth all that can be gained from an apprenticeship and all that can be gained from modern schools for trades and industrial education generally. We need a training that will secure good trade people and good citizens.

Mr. W. R. Warner, of the Warner & Swasey Co., Cleveland, Ohio, spoke as follows:

A man without an education may be likened to an automatic traveling crane worth $1.50 per day. Give the man an education and you raise his price. The old apprenticeship training is not obsolete, but it is changed. Today it is more specialized than formerly.

The motive of the manufacturer in regard to any form of industrial education is purely commercial; we need not try to disguise this fact. The motive of the schools is philanthropic. Can the two motives be combined?

Mr. Warner answered his own question in the affirmative and attempted to illustrate the good influence of the manufacturer over boys. He admitted that many boys failed, but said that there were failures in the schools. He criticized all our educational institutions as having too little of the practical, and teachers of technical schools as being inefficient. He insisted that pupils cannot think alone and that many teachers in technical schools know so little of practical operations that their instruction is of little value.

Mr. J. F. Deems, general superintendent of motive power, New York Central lines, spoke on "Trade Instruction in Large Establishments." He urged the need of industrial education at present and described the shops of the New York Central, where there are now six hundred apprentices employed learning the various trades in connection with railroad work. He believes that it is best to educate the boy in the trade, not out of it, and that the trade school can never have the atmosphere of the shop.

Night schools are failures [he continued], instruction should be given during work hours when the men are under pay. The public schools can help in this education by giving more instruction in applied arithmetic, and in the useful laws of nature. The public schools should have a curriculum that will hold the boy in school; but the United States must look mainly to the apprenticeship system for its salvation.

Mr. James O'Connell, president of he International Union of Machinists, Washington, D. C., being absent on account of business, his place was filled by Mr. W. B. Prescott, former president of the International Typographical Union, who read a paper on "The Value of a Thorough Apprenticeship to the Wage-Earner."

The apprenticeship system [said Mr. Prescott] is a survival of feudalism; its object is not to make a man, but to make money. The foreman wants results and he wants them right away. They must appear on this month's balance-sheet. The trades-unions have been blamed for the decline of the apprenticeship system. The unions feel the need of more skill than such a system gives; they feel that this system sacrifices the boy's interests for quick profits. Under specialists a trade is cut up so that a boy can neither beg, borrow, nor steal a trade. Leisure is the basis of culture and workers must share in this. When hours are long a trade education is impossible. Under long hours there is a mental stagnation and brutalization.

As an illustration of what a trade-union can do in industrial education, Mr. Prescott spoke of the work done by the National Typographical Union.

The members of this union, feeling the need of greater skill, decided to lay the basis for it in a better education. The territory to be covered was the North American continent, and hence the suggestion to establish schools was rejected on account of the expense. It was decided, however, to establish a correspondence school, charging $20 per annum for instruction and the necessary apparatus, and granting a rebate of $5 to deserving students. Believing that the field of the printer as at present recognized should be expanded so as to include a knowledge of the principles of art and their application to the work of the printer, the correspondence school offered a course treating of these subjects. In this way it is hoped to restore to the printer's art the artistic qualities which it originally possessed. The school is open to all. Correspondence instruction enables the student to receive the criticism of experts during the period of instruction and the privilege of submitting problems for help at any later time.

The tragedy of the workshops [Mr. Prescott continued] is not so much the physical accidents as the mental stagnation. The motive of the Typographical Union is to keep the mind alive. The trades-unions are not opposed to industrial education, though they may be opposed to certain schemes masquerading under the name of education. They do not object to the study of economics, but they do object to instruction which leads students to think that Adam Smith spoke the last word on economic questions, not the first. What the unions are opposed to is not education, but subterfuges. The workingmen are interested in industrial education and should have a hand in it. Where are the students of your schools to come from if the working-class is against you? It behooves the friends of industrial education not to oppose labor. The skilled man is treated as an impersonal unit. He wants to be treated less like a prisoner of necessity and more like a free man. Soft words at public functions will not suffice. We must have an industrial education that is broad enough to offer opportunity to those who desire to improve.

Mr. Leslie W. Miller, principal of the Pennsylvania School of Industrial Art, Philadelphia, next spoke, on "The Necessity for Apprenticeships."

The apprenticeship system is not dead [said Mr. Miller], but its methods are refined and readjusted. If you think you are going to ignore this truth and transfer schoolboys into the workshops without getting articulated, you are making a tremendous mistake.

Industrial education in the elementary school is a waste of public money; the schoolmaster is extinct and the schoolmistress has it all her own way. If you think women are going to teach sloyd and weaving you are mightily mistaken. Why do *all* the little boys want to be put to the carpenter's tools? It is absurd on the face of it. Industrial education should be a matter of selection; select one and leave nine hundred and ninety-nine. It is a mistake to try to make skilled workmen out of schoolboys. I am in sympathy with Mr. Warren on this matter. The educational system has failed; it is a waste of public money. The apprenticeship system is not dead; it must be controlled. I would not underestimate the trade school, but you must first catch your boy. The apprenticeship idea must dominate; it is the method that will get most money.

The subject under discussion Friday afternoon was "The Place of the Trade School in Industrial Education." Dr. Henry S. Pritchett, president of the Carnegie Foundation for the Advancement of Science and president of the society, presided. The principal speakers were Mr. Charles F. Perry, director of the Public School of Trades, Milwaukee, Wis.; Mr. Milton P. Higgins, president of the Norton Companies, Worcester, Mass.;

and Dr. Graham Taylor, director of the Chicago Institute of Social Sciences, Chicago. Mr. Perry explained the workings of the trade school in Milwaukee, which is under the supervision of the board of education. He believes that the demand for skilled workers is not supplied and that trade schools can help supply this demand, but that they should not be run by private individuals for the exploitation of the youth.

Mr. Higgins said, "Our trade schools have been largely schools with a shop attachment. What they should be is shops with a school attachment. The shop of the typical trade school must be a productive one."

Dr. Graham Taylor insisted on the need of training in occupations from the kindergarten up.

> By keeping boys and girls in the schools during the period from fourteen to sixteen years [he said] we safeguard the most dangerous period. By making use of industrial education in the schools, hereditary skill may be preserved and developed so that the trade and guild secrets may become the open secrets to all who will use them. The interests of the people must be safeguarded, however. The public must guard itself against an unlimited apprenticeship system, where the natural resources are monopolized. If by increasing the number of skilled workers we reduce the standard of living, you must not wonder that the leaders of the trades-unions are cautious in this matter. They have a right to protect their property interests in their skill. Trade schools should include in their curricula, in addition to what they now have, industrial history and psychology. One of the most serious difficulties in dealing with modern problems is that the parties have no perspective. More attention to the human elements in the problem would be of the greatest value. To discuss trade schools without reference to the co-operation of labor would be to discuss *Hamlet* with Hamlet omitted.

Among those who took part in the discussion were Miss Florence M. Marshall, director of the Trade School for Girls, Boston; Mr. Williston, of Pratt Institute, Brooklyn; and an instructor from the University of Cincinnati. Miss Marshall said that the untrained girl is a menace to our shops as well as to our homes and that where women workers are unskilled the type of civilization is low. Since so many women have charge of homes, Miss Marshall believes it wise to put the emphasis upon the duties of a director of consumption rather than upon those of the direct producer.

Mr. Williston stated that it was hardly right for manufacturers to call upon the state for that which they can provide themselves.

An instructor from the University of Cincinnati told of a most interesting experiment being carried on in that city by the co-operation of the university with the shops. Shops are used as a laboratory for the class instruction and thus far the results are gratifying.

With the exception of a stirring address by Mrs. Anna Carlin Spencer, of the Ethical Culture Society, N. Y., the education of girls was almost overlooked. This was due, no doubt, to the fact that the conception of industrial education in the minds of a majority of the speakers is that of a money-making device, limited to purely technical and trade ideas. Mrs. Spencer enumerated four fallacies underlying the belief that girls do not require an industrial education, and showed why their education presents a more complex problem than that of boys. She would have industrial training begin in the kindergarten and continue throughout successive years. She made a plea for a broad and simple foundation in the early years. "Keep your machine-shop away," she said, "until the child knows what life is."

At an after-meeting called by Miss Addams at Hull House to discuss the industrial education of women, Miss Marshall, director of the Trade School for Girls, Boston, was the principal speaker. She told of the training given in that school to girls from fourteen to sixteen years. Although Mrs. Raymond Robins and others attempted to turn the discussion into broader fields, most of the attention was given to a type of school which to many present seemed but a temporary device to tide a few destitute girls of a particular locality over a few years. Mr. Frank A. Manny, however, briefly indicated the meaning of a broader plan of industrial education and a gentleman from Helena, Mont., told of the action of that state in paying the expenses of children whose parents are not able to keep them in school.

Without attempting to outline the papers presented at the meeting held Saturday morning when the discussion centered around "The True Ideal of a Public-School System That Aims to Benefit All," it may not be amiss to state that there were as many different views expressed as there were interests represented. One would have industrial training in the hands of the public schools; another would have the public schools have nothing to do with industrial training. Some would have the schools stand for culture; others would have nothing partaking of the nature of culture in the industrial schools. In the five minutes allotted to Miss Jane Addams she gave more that was really illuminating on the whole situation than was heard at any time during the meeting. Recognizing the value of industrial training from the earliest years on, she would have it in the public schools, having its character change with the changes that come in muscular control, in interests, and in intellectual power through natural growth, Thus she would, during the seventh and eighth grades, have more attention given to skill than formerly; and, from one point of view, the handwork of this period might be termed vocational training; but she insisted that it would be a bold teacher indeed who would attempt to decide what the future work of a fourteen-year-old child should be. She also spoke of the danger at present of having the *schools captured by the manufacturers* just as several decades ago they were captured by the business men. She attempted in the few moments at her disposal to show that there is no intrinsic opposition between industrial education and culture—between work and culture—and that the child, who, in connection with his industrial occupations, has the opportunity to learn of their origin and development and the social conditions which determine and are determined by them, is getting culture in the truest sense of the term.

EDITORIAL NOTES

INDUSTRIAL EDUCATION

When the educator talks of reforms in the school system we listen with complaisance. Our emotions are mildly stirred by the pros and cons of the situation. With a sense of secure comfort in a bit of intellectual stimulus we have little real concern for the immediate future. When the leaders of industry backed by the manufacturing interests of the country take a hand in the discussion we lean forward in our seats—something is going to happen. It suddenly dawns upon us that epoch-making forces are at work and that the school system must be irresistibly drawn into their current. Such was the experience of those who attended the January meetings of the National Society for the Promotion of Industrial Education.

The Manufacturer in the Educational Situation

That industrial education was the solution of the greatest number of the defects in the school seemed to be an accepted fact. Interest was most intense on the question of what kind of industrial training would be effective. Even in its most specialized form—the trade school —it may evidently be of two kinds.

Efficiency in the Trade School

Mr. Morse, of the Massachusetts commission on industrial education mentioned that in Switzerland an apprenticeship was such that a man learned the mathematics and the physics, in fact, the whole process of making watches or music boxes. When the music-box industry was suddenly swept away by the invention of the phonograph, the entire mass of workmen, without previous training, began to manufacture motor cycles. In other words, the breadth of experience during their apprenticeship had developed the men to such an extent that they were fitted to meet new problems. What is this but culture?

There is another kind of apprenticeship which fits the man to do but one thing. In a comparatively short time, by a purely imitative process he acquires specific skill. Such a workman can turn a screw just as well as the former. The manufacturer needs only the piece-worker; therefore why produce the finer human product?

Here is the issue that concerns the future of that class of our boys and girls who at twelve and fourteen meet the stress of real life. It is to be hoped that the very conditions of supply and demand will place a premium upon the laborer who can adjust himself to the changes of the labor market.

There are analogous problems within the grammar and high schools. Is emphasis to be placed upon specific results or upon the kind of control which comes through a rich intellectual process?

Education of Americans' Initiative and Adaptability

We pride ourselves on the all-around Yankee ingenuity and adaptability of Americans. No one would consciously permit any practice to enter the school which might limit the future initiative of our people. Indeed the present movement may be taken as a wide-spread effort to develop these resources. One point in the matter seems to warrant most watchful study by the educator. Practice being somewhat controlled by habit, is much more persistent than theory. Consequently methods of organization and teaching any form of technical work do not begin to change as much as the theories which account for them. What is more probable therefore, than that the methods of the specialized forms of industrial education will find their way into the practices of the public school? The valuations of the trade school would thus be placed upon work which should aim at a broader result. Failure of industrial occupations to educate will come not from lack of right ideals but from the insidious nature of false methods.

Influence of Trade School on the School at Large

Summary

As one turns over his memories of these conferences, the immediate questions then seem to be about as follows: Is the trade school the solution of the truancy problem and does it serve the best interests of the young wage-earner? Which trade school are we to have? Is it to be the one that aims first to develop a man and then a workman, or is it to be the one that manufactures a human cog in a machine? How will the trade school affect the ideals governing industrial phases of general education? Will it prove the cultural value of technical training? Will there be an increase of industrial work in the general curriculum or will the tendency be to remove it from the demoralizing influence of the pedagogue to the supervision of the man who has come up from the bench?

Plan of the Department

It is of interest just here to note that the Department of Superintendence of the N. E. A. at its February meeting devoted a session to the consideration of the question of the place of Industries in Public Education. So largely do these questions appear in the foreground of all educational discussion that this journal will, in the future, give them special attention. We intend to note such meetings as will consider any related topics, and also the current magazine articles which deal with the situation. We are happy in the promise of contributions from those who are among the ranks of actual workers and investigators. It is our hope therefore, that we may make this department of value in keeping before our readers the live issues of the day. L. S. C.

Industrial Education and Trade Schools

It is with a real relief that those interested in the problem of our common-school education must recognize the new factor which is making itself evident in public consciousness: industrial education and trade schools. On the one hand our school systems have become so huge that educational measures can hardly command consideration upon their merits nor a field within which they can try themselves out, because the administrative problems have become too enormous and too immediately pressing to allow room for much beside themselves. And on the other hand educational reform has been prone to back up its programme by an appeal to the reality of the life outside the schoolroom, which it has never yet been able to bring inside. The mere fact that vast industrial interests demand trade schools to supply them with the skilled labor of which they are in need, indicates the presence of as real a problem in elementary and secondary education as the professional school has brought with it into the college and the university. Just as the demands of the community have increased upon its professional men, calling for skill that can only come with extended and directed training so our manufactories are calling for the skill, the competence, the ability to take responsibility which is born only of conscious technical skill and intelligently organized habits. The demand is in no small degree an admission that the specialized factory work does not train its own foremen and mechanics. Identification with specific pieces of machinery till the workman almost becomes a part of the mechanism, and the morale of the factory which is reduced to "speeding up," build up neither mind nor character. Foremen have been sought among those trained in the smaller country shops where varied occupation and responsibility for a whole product have produced the mechanic.

Demands of Industry upon the Schools Comparable to Those Made upon the Universities

There is little reason to doubt that our manufacturers, with the recognition of the need, and with the example of other countries in meeting it by trade schools, will by themselves if necessary supply their own demands for skilled men. Not a few concerns have already their own schools, and with the advantages that follow from these instances others will arise, but the educational value of this sort of schooling and the necessity of fitting it into the educational system of the country inevitably will bring it within the domain of the present common schools.

There arise at once two questions. How will these technical schools fit into the secondary system? And what is to be their relation to the elementary schools? It is not difficult to conceive of a secondary-school system which shall make these trade schools a part of itself, which will carry theoretical studies along with the practice in the shops, thus giving double value to each. Such a system in connection with the University of Cincinnati already exists in a trade school inaugurated by a manufactory in that city. The value of the shop work for study has shown itself in no uncertain way. The situation presents no

Problems Involved for Secondary and Elementary Schools

problem here that is in principle difficult of solution. The relation of this industrial training on the other hand to the elementary schools is by no means clear.

It is possible that they should have no relation, except that of preparation. In the elementary school the boy or girl might gain simply the control over language and number, the historical and scientific information which such schools are supposed to give, and await the secondary period to come into touch with industrial training. There are two reasons why this should and probably will not be the outcome. In the first place there will be an added advantage for the child who is going into trade schools, if he has had training of this industrial character, even before he is able to enter the trade schools themselves in the secondary period. Something of the nature of manual training extended all through the elementary period would fit the child for the later handling of tools, would give the education of muscles, of motor centers that is too precious to be lost, especially when the period of education is so restricted at best. The industrial school of the secondary period will inevitably extend its influence into earlier training, just as the medical and law schools have indicated premedical and prelegal courses in the university.

Value of Industrial Training for the Schools

On the other hand the school itself is in need of just the reality, which relationship with the occupations of the community gives, to give it a hold upon its pupils, and to give the pupils a hold upon what they study. The discipline of doing something and making something that is real, that is demanded by the great world into which the child longs to go, is the ideal that we look for in vain. It is inconceivable that in the end this all-important means of developing mind and character should not be taken possession of by the elementary school.

The profoundest problem arises at this point for both the secondary- and the elementary-school systems. Will trade schools develop into class schools? Will they become as narrow as the specific skill which they inculcate? Will the democratic conception which has pervaded our common schools be lost? When all the children of the community are gathered together to learn what it is essential that all should acquire, a democratic spirit is aroused that will be lost if the child is as early as possible drafted into a school which trains with an eye single to the occupation he is to follow in later years.

Interpretation of Industry by the Use of the Historical Method

The problem of meeting a narrow class attitude with a broad democratic spirit and at the same time making use of the sense of reality, which comes with constructive work as the trade school inculcates it, is the problem of interpreting the industrial activities of the community. It is the problem which in simpler forms of society has been solved by the introduction of the child into the religious and other social institutions and practices of the community. It is the problem upon which our schools have made a beginning of attack in the use of the historical presentation of social origins, of industries, and commerce. History in the common schools has suffered still more than in our colleges and universities from its exclusively political interest. It is beginning to face about toward the industrial development of the community, and in doing so comes for the first time into contact with the real problems of daily life of the majority of its citizens. The great difficulty which such a use of historical method meets is the lack of immediate contact with life which would lift the child out of story-telling into actual interpretation. How much this difficulty would be lightened if the child were actually at work in a trade, or were preparing consciously for such work within the school system is at once evident. A moment's review of the broadening effect of the sweep of industrial and commercial effort and growth into the study of our political history will make it evident that, especially for children, this point of view will enlarge rather than narrow the value of history in the curriculum. The great defect of the study of social beginnings and growth in the common schools has been that they have been presented from a literary point of view. And this has been largely necessary because only in literature could a point of departure within the child's ken be found. If this point of departure could be found in the actual instruction in trade schools, the grip gained upon subject-matter and its history would be enormous.

Learning a Trade Could Be Made the Basis of the Best Schooling

It used to be an ideal of the community that every child should learn a trade, an ideal which curiously enough finds one of its actualizations in the training of the children of the house of the Hohenzollerns. It has never been demonstrated that the best education which any child could get in the common-school period would not be gathered about the learning of a trade, in a school which could give not only the specific skill but also the interpretation thereof in the history of our industrial community, and would be able to associate the child's expression in language, and problems in number, about such a reality. These ideas are very much in the air. They are supposed to exist largely in the minds and writings of educators who are considered visionary; but any careful study of them will show that they are quite consonant with the development of the social sciences and professional schools in our universities, that the obstacles which stand in the way of their realization are either those of school administration or those of an unwitting class distinction, which has placed bookish learning above manual skill, even when intelligently informed. It is a sign of good omen for the future that in the place of the school reaching out somewhat helpless hands toward the realities of the life that lies around it, we should find industrial society knocking at the doors of the schoolhouse seeking admittance.

G. H. M.

NOTES AND NEWS

Interest in folk-dances appears to be spreading. The *Teachers Magazine* for February contains the first of a series of articles descriptive of these dances. Some of them are used in the New York schools, and in many other schools in various parts of the country.

Albert E. Roberts comments with favor in the *London Journal of Education* on the "American habit" of sometimes allowing pupils to correct each other's compositions under the teacher's general direction. He finds that it cultivates an active attitude on the part of the pupil, and a greater attention to the corrections made.

The group system of class teaching is reported as successful in Rochester. It allows the child more latitude, provides for individual promotion, and reaches the child more directly. According to Superintendent Carroll in the *Atlantic Educational Journal,* it is gaining ground in New York state, while in New England it is almost universal.

The *Educational Review* for January contains an account of legal regulation of minimum salaries for teachers, both in this country and abroad. It finds this regulation existing in those countries most advanced in education. Some of our states have laws on this subject, and in a dozen more there is a prospect of such regulation in the near future.

Mr. William Kent, of Chicago, has recently deeded to the United States 295 acres of the primeval redwood forest on the southern slope of Mount Tamalpais. This territory is about six miles from San Francisco. This most commendable gift saves to the world one more portion of one of the greatest of all displays of natural-history phenomena.

The last stronghold of child labor in New York, the tenement home, has been invaded in an investigation by the Department of Labor. "Many children of school age and even under have been found in them at work in regular employment," says *Charities.* "Some measures should be adopted to correct this weakest spot in the New York child-labor law."

The *North Carolina Journal of Education* contains an account of the systematic campaign of the last four years for the improvement of education in that state. "The school fund has been nearly doubled, the number of local tax districts has been increased from 30 to about 600 and modern schoolhouses have been erected at an average rate of one a day."

In Sweden the women teachers in primary schools, which are conducted by the state, are far better paid than those in secondary schools, which are only subsidized by the state. Such is Mr. J. S. Thornton's statement in a special report made to the English Board of Education. This situation, together with other conflicts between "public and private effort," leads to certain rather difficult problems.

The fourth annual report of the education department of New York state, transmitted to the legislature late in January, shows an expenditure of nearly fifty millions of dollars for common schools. The average cost per pupil, based on attendance, was not quite fifty dollars. This shows an increase in expense of about 2 per cent. Of the teachers in the elementary schools, about one-twelfth are men, as shown by the report.

Bulletin 195 of the office of Experiment Station of the U. S. Department of Agriculture treats of "Simple Exercises Illustrating Some Applications of Chemistry to Agriculture." Directions are given for the performance of twenty-eight simple and practical experiments. These relate to the materials and processes of making plant foods, to plant products, and to soils. The experiments are sufficiently simple for use in upper-grade natural-history classes.

Railways may be compelled by the state to carry children to and from school at half-price, is the decree of the Supreme Court, as reported by the *Outlook.* The case arose in Attleborough where the street-railway company declared that this meant a loss to them. This the higher courts denied. But their decision was based chiefly on the fact that the discrimination was not an arbitrary one, but in pursuance of the long-established policy to encourage education.

In his annual report to the New York Board of Education Superintendent Maxwell declares his dissatisfaction with the working of the present compulsory-education law. He suggests the extension of the age limit to sixteen, and would give the board power to compel parents to provide for the physical and medical needs of their children in such a way that they shall be fit to attend school. He does not seem to suggest any adequate way of bringing about such a compulsion.

Articles that appear in recent numbers of the Indiana and Illinois State Board of Health bulletins suggest that teachers in hygiene could find a source of much interesting and valuable information by securing these bulletins. The December Illinois bulletin gives a number of valuable articles on avoidance, prevention, and cure of tuberculosis, as well as descriptions of the open-air cure as it is now being administered in Illinois. A large amount of data which every teacher should know is presented.

An amusing account of an innovation in nature-study is given in the *Atlantic Educational Journal* for January. A third-grade teacher in Baltimore has inaugurated a "pets' visiting day," upon which children may bring their pet animals to the school. She contrives to endure this day once a week. Pigeons, chickens, white rats, kittens, dogs, rabbits, a parrot, and a carrier pigeon have figured among the attractions. The only exception so far made was in the case of a pet goat with a dangerous reputation.

Geology for the grades would be an appropriate subtitle for Mr. Paul's article in the January number of the *Utah Educational Review.* He gives an outline of work beginning with the first grade, and especially adapted to the children of Utah who would naturally be supposed to be interested in mines and metals. Beginning with play and work in sand, clay, and pebbles, he brings the children, by the time they have finished the grades, to chemical studies of limestone and other minerals, and to the consideration of crystallization and kindred facts.

The Bureau of Education of the United States has recently published a bulletin upon the subject of *Agricultural Education, Including Nature-Study and School Gardens,* by James Ralph Jewell. To the first section of the bulletin on nature-study fourteen pages are given, twenty-four pages are given to school gardens, and eighty-one pages to elementary agricultural education. A brief and somewhat incomplete historical statement is made of each of the three topics. A good bibliography is presented along with the discussion. The bulletin will be found highly valuable to those interested in natural-history education.

The joint report of the meeting held by the Eastern Art Teachers' Association, the Eastern Manual Training Association, and the Western Drawing and Manual Training Association in Cleveland, Ohio, May 8 to 11, 1907, has just been issued. It is especially valuable as a representative of the current thought on art and manual training.

"Manual Training at Hampton Institute and Its Relation to the Trades," a paper by John H. Jinks appearing in *Manual Training Magazine* for February, 1908, pp. 200–11; "The Manual Arts as School Subjects," by Harriet Cecil Magee in *The Educational Bi-Monthly* for February, pp. 256–61; and "Ethical and Esthetic Bearings of Handwork," by W. N. Hailman, *ibid.*, pp. 262–70, are recent contributions which are recommended to those interested in the subject.

BOOK REVIEWS

Commercial Raw Materials: Their Origin, Preparation, and Uses. By CHARLES R. TOOTHAKER. Boston: Ginn & Co. Pp. 108.

This book contains a concise description relating to the origin, preparation, and uses of over twelve hundred commercial products, accompanied by fifty maps and numerous illustrations showing the sources of raw materials and methods of preparation for the markets.

The grouping adopted is into substances of vegetable, mineral, and animal origin. Under the grouping of plants the ones first described are food-yielding, followed by those yielding both food and fiber, and then those, like the cotton plant, which supply fiber, oil, and cattle food. All materials yielded by one plant are grouped together. This same classification is used, as far as possible, with the substances of animal and mineral origin.

The book was prepared primarily as a work of reference to collections of commerical materials arranged for the schools of Pennsylvania by the Philadelphia museums but should prove a valuable aid to teachers and students interested in commercial geography and the industrial sciences.

I. B. M.

SCHOOL OF EDUCATION
Chicago

Rural School Agriculture. By CHARLES M. DAVIS. New York: Orange Judd Company. Illustrated. Pp. 270. $1.00.

This book is a manual of 143 exercises on the problems of the farm. These problems embrace such topics as the character and properties of soils, the treatment of various field crops, the testing of seeds, the effect of various chemicals and fertilizers on plants, grafting, transplanting, pruning, and spraying, as well as other more strictly botanical or entomological topics. A series of sixteen suggestive exercises is given for the field and laboratory study of corn. In each exercise the problem is definitely stated and directions are given for its solution.

The teacher who wishes to establish a closer contact between the school and the home life of a rural community will find these exercises very helpful. They show how the laboratory method may be introduced in the study of the questions arising from the pupil's experience on the farm or in the school garden. Most of the work suggested may be done in the ordinary schoolroom or in the field, with easily obtained material and very simple apparatus. The good teacher will use this book to suggest a series of exercises suited to his particular needs rather than as a manual to be placed in the hands of the pupils.

The illustrations are good and add much to the value of the volume.

GEORGE D. FULLER
UNIVERSITY HIGH SCHOOL
Chicago

BOOKS RECEIVED

HENRY ALTEMUS CO.

Poor Richard Jr.'s Almanack. Reprinted from *The Saturday Evening Post,* of Philadelphia. Illuminated. P. 128. Boards, 50 cents.

HOLBROOK BARKER CO., CHICAGO

Play—Its Value; and Fifty Games. By NINA B. LAMKIN. Cloth. Illustrated. Pp. 94.

A. S. BARNES & CO., NEW YORK

Filippo the Italian Boy. By LAURA B. STARR. Cloth. Illustrated. Pp. 112. 2 copies.

Hints and Helps from Many Schoolrooms. Arranged by CAROLINE S. GRIFFIN. Cloth. Pp. 182.

Little Talks on School Management. By RANDALL N. SAUNDERS. Cloth. Pp. 68.

WASHINGTON GOVERNMENT PRINTING OFFICE

Annual Report of the Board of Regents (of the Smithsonian Institute). Cloth. Illustrated. Pp. 546.

Agricultural Education. By JAMES RALPH JEWELL. Paper. Pp. 140. Bulletin: No. 2, 1907. Whole number 368.

THE MACMILLAN CO., NEW YORK

Linguistic Development and Education. By M. V. O'SHEA. Cloth. Pp. xviii+350.

R. B. Sheridan's Plays ("The Rivals" and the "School for Scandal"). Edited with Introduction and Notes by WILL DAVID HOWE, PH.D. Cloth. Pp. xxxiii+320. $0.25 net.

Lamb's Tales from Shakespeare. Edited, with an Introduction, by REV. ALFRED AINGER, M.A. Pp. xiii+368. Cloth. $0.25 net.

Beginner's Number Primer. One to twenty. Book I, in Eight-Book Series. Cloth. Illustrated. Pp. ix+78. $0.20 net. 2 copies.

Smith's New Intermedial Copy Books. Paper. Pp. 24. 60 cts. net per dozen. 6 numbers. 2 sets.

D. APPLETON & CO., NEW YORK

When Men Grew Tall or the Story of Andrew Jackson. By ALFRED HENRY LEWIS. Illustrated. Cloth. Pp. 331.

GINN AND COMPANY, CHICAGO

From Trail to Railway Through the Appalachians. By ALBERT PERRY BRIGHAM, A.M. Cloth, 12mo. Illustrated. Pp. 786. Net $0.50; postpaid $0.55.

Moral Training in the Public Schools. The California Prize Essays. By C. E. RUGH, T. P. STEVENSON, E. D. STARBUCK, FRANK CRAMER, G. E. MYERS. Cloth, 12mo. Pp. 208.

Commercial Raw Materials. By CHARLES R. TOOTHAKER. Cloth, 8vo. Pp. 108. Net $1.25; postpaid, $1.35.

VOLUME VIII NUMBER 8

THE ELEMENTARY SCHOOL TEACHER

APRIL, 1908

OLD SPRING CUSTOMS IN GERMANY

ANNA SCHERZ GRONOW
The University Elementary School

The spring festivals of the Germanic nations are very old. The oldest German term for spring is "Mai," which is synonymous with foliage or green, and so among the peasants on the lower Rhine a green branch is still called a "Maie." We find also that old manuscripts use the word Mayday for Springday. When, however, the spring festivals first occurred people knew only two seasons: summer and winter. June 22 was called midsummer; December 27, midwinter. The main spring festival took place in February, March, April, or May, according to locality; very often it was dependent on the arrival of such birds as the swallow or the cuckoo.

A great many customs grew out of this day; they varied greatly in different places. Here we shall try to describe only those that the German classes of the seventh and eighth grades of the University Elementary School represented at the spring festival, June 7, 1907. The old text was changed very little, only now and then passages were somewhat simplified. The music is as old as the text but required changing in regard to rhythm, etc. The present form is due to Mrs. M. R. Kern of the University Elementary School.[1]

[1] References: *Altdeutsches Liederbuch,* von Franz M. Böhme (Leipzig, 1877); Uhland's *Schriften zur Geschichte der Dichtung und Sage,* III (Stuttgart, 1866); *Die deutschen Volksfeste:* Ein Beitrag zur Sittengeschichten von Montanus (1854); *Geschichte des deutschen Tanzes,* von Franz M. Böhme.

1. In the country of the lower Rhine the *Maibrunnenfeste* are still remembered by the people. In the evening before May-day boys and girls were accustomed to go out to clean the wells so as to have pure water during the spring. They also fastened lamps to trees near the wells and watched these all night long. On the following morning it was the custom to go out and pick flowers, weave them into wreaths, and afterward lay them around the well. Eggs were often placed among the flowers, for the egg was the symbol of fertility and played a very important part in the spring festival. Our custom of decorating and giving Easter eggs is one of the survivals of ancient observances. A dance and song around the well usually ended the merry-making. (See "Der Mai ist gekommen mit Sonnenschein.")

2. In some places in Alsace a procession of children went from house to house on Mayday. The leader was a little girl, "das Maienröslein," who carried a "Maien," that is, a green branch adorned with flowers and ribbons. The other children carried baskets in which they placed the gifts they received. As they went along they sang: "Mairöslein, kehr dich dreimal um." In the songs various gifts are asked for, as eggs, bread, fruit, etc., and those that do not give, are threatened, for it was an old belief among the people that the summer would bring success only to those who were willing to sacrifice to spring.

3. The great joy and delight of the people at the arrival of spring found utterance in their spring dances, of which one was called "Siebensprung." Although this dance dates back many hundred years, it was still in use in comparatively modern times in Swabia, Bavaria, and in the Harz. It probably had a religious meaning according to Böhme, signifying a spring offering. This is indicated by the fact that this "Siebensprung" was customary on Easter Day in Westphalia. It was danced by couples; they walked up and down for eight measures, then the boy went through seven motions; he stamped the ground with his feet (first with one foot, then with the other one), he knelt, he touched the ground with his elbows, then with his forehead and so backward. During this time the girl danced around him

and both sang: "Komm, mach' mir nun den Siebensprung." After which there was a repetition of the first eight measures.

In Germanic myths the phenomena and forces of nature are thought of and presented as personal beings. The greatest contrast in nature, the strife between winter and summer, lent itself readily to personification, and so we find early reports of an allegorical play at the spring festivals called the "Strife between Winter and Summer," the actions and songs of which were full of meaning. It used to be played on the lower and middle Rhine in March; in other parts of Germany it was dependent on the arrival of the cuckoo. The villagers went out in great crowds into the meadows. Some boys, dressed in straw, represented winter; at the head marched the king with a crown of straw and a wooden sword. (Sometimes they wore furs, for the disguise had many forms.) Others represented summer. They were dressed in green and at their head was summer wearing a crown of flowers and dressed in foliage. (Summer often carried a tree bedecked with fruit, flowers, and ribbons.) Sometimes both winter and summer were accompanied by the products of each respective season, summer by grass, vine, and grain; winter by wind, snow, and fire. Many peasants followed them, all riding with summer and mocking at winter. The call of the cuckoo announced the entrance of summer who marched in singing: "Tra, ri, ra, der Sommer, der ist da." Then the hooting of an owl was heard and winter entered by the mournful tune of: "Wir Winter, wir binden Weiher und Bach." And now the strife began. It was a strife in words sung to a quaint tune. The question was who was going to be master. Summer asked winter to go, but winter refused; he threatened with the cold wind from the mountains and boasted of his white fields. Summer praised his products, grass, wine, and corn, but winter replied that in winter all this disappeared. These verses were sung alternately by the main actors, each one appealing to the spectators in the refrain: "Alle ihr Herren mein." Each also carried a big club which was meant to give weight to this speech, for it came down on his opponent's shoulders after each verse. After winter refused again to leave the country, a regular fight began with the words: " Stab aus, Stab aus," which ended in the defeat of winter. Winter was robbed of his garments which summer brought back to the music of a triumphant song: "So treiben wir den Winter aus." A dance and a song around this garment ended the play, the song containing the triumphant words of victory: "Der Sommer, hat gewonnen, der Winter hat verloren." About this play we find according to Uhland the oldest *definite* report in Sebastian Franck's *Weltbuch* (1442), which gives a good description of the custom. But earlier traces are found in a manuscript of Saint Gall of 858, where Wintar and Sumar are, however, referred to as brothers. A Latin poem, the author of which is a poet of the eighth or ninth century, speaks more distinctly. On a spring day the shepherds came down from the mountains to sing praise to the cuckoo. Spring also came with wreaths of flowers and the old winter with coarse, bristly hair. Spring wished that the cuckoo might come, a friend to everyone, but winter scolded the birds. In the fourteenth century we find a song concerning this strife that seemed to have come from the lower Rhine, and a manuscript of the fifteenth century containing songs of the Meistersinger also treats the same subject. We moreover find this theme among the works of Hans Sachs, and from there it reaches almost into present times. Such great age makes these popular festivities which have long ago lost all mythological meaning more valuable. They must have satisfied an almost national need or they would not have outlasted centuries, and it is certainly of educational value to have children get acquainted with such material.

Below follows the music of the songs as they have been made use of in the University Elementary School:

BRUNNENLIED

Der Mai ist ge-kom-men mit Son - nen-schein, Er brin-get die
Wir fe - gen die Brun-nen und machen sie rein, Und brin-gen die

2. Wir fegen die Brunnen und machen sie rein
Und bringen die Eier im lustigen Mai'n.
Er bringet die Blumen gross und klein
Drum tanzet ihr Kinder im Sonnenschein.

MAIRÖSLEINS UMZUG

2. Mairöslein, komm in grünen Wald hinein,
Wir wollen alle lustig sein.
So fahren wir aus dem Maien, etc.

3. Wollt ihr uns keine Eier geben,
So soll der Marder die Hühner nehmen.
So fahren wir, etc.

4. Wollt ihr uns keinen Wein mehr geben,
So soll der Stock keine Trauben geben.
So fahren wir, etc.

5. Wollt ihr uns kein Brot mehr geben,
So soll der Acker kein' Frucht mehr geben.
So fahren wir, etc.

DER SIEBENSPRUNG

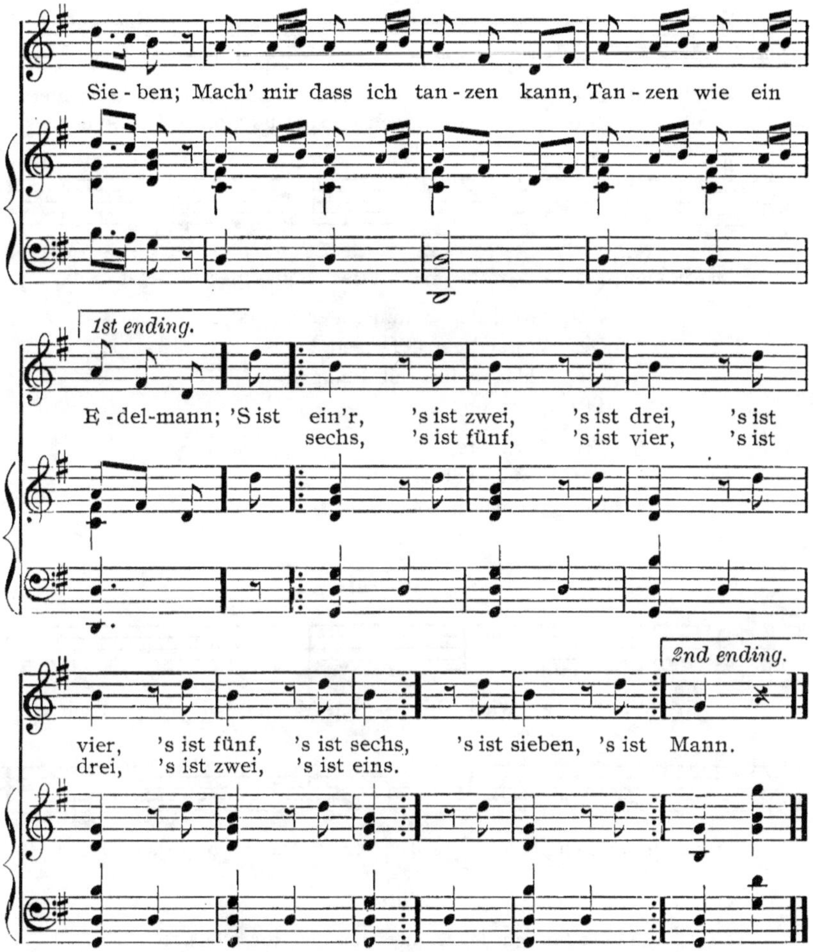

Sie - ben; Mach' mir dass ich tan - zen kann, Tan - zen wie ein
1st ending.
E - del-mann; 'S ist ein'r, 's ist zwei, 's ist drei, 's ist
sechs, 's ist fünf, 's ist vier, 's ist
2nd ending.
vier, 's ist fünf, 's ist sechs, 's ist sieben, 's ist Mann.
drei, 's ist zwei, 's ist eins.

DER STREIT ZWISCHEN SOMMER UND WINTER

Sommerleute

Tra - ri - ra, der Som - mer der ist da. Wir
Tra - ri - ra, der Som - mer der ist da. Wir

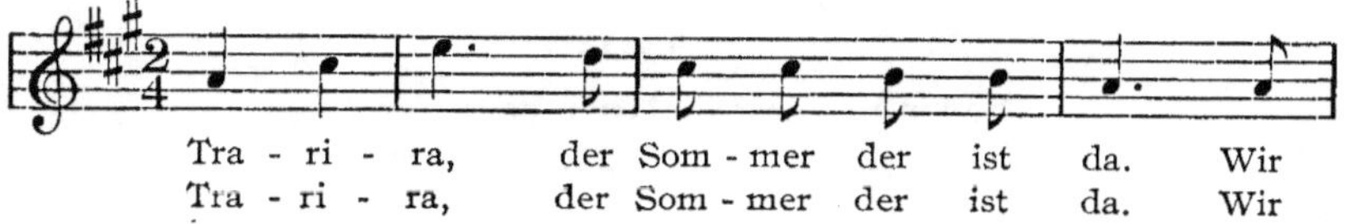

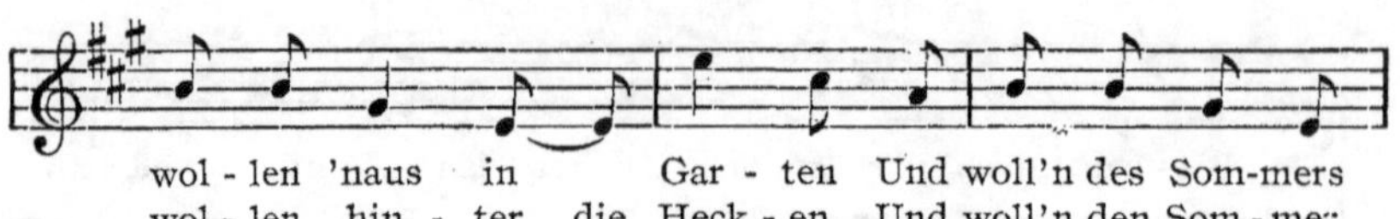

war - ten. Tra - ri - ra, der Som - mer der ist da.
weck - en. Tra - ri - ra, der Som - mer der ist da.

Tra, ri, ra, der Sommer der ist da,
Der Winter liegt gefangen,
Wir schlagen ihn mit Stangen.
Tra, ri, ra, etc.

Tra, ri, ra, etc.
Der Winter hat verloren,
Der Sommer hat gewonnen.
Tra, ri, ra, etc.

Winterleute

Winter

So bin ich der Winter ich geb' dir nicht recht,
O lieber Sommer du bist mein Knecht.
Heda, ihr Herren mein, der Winter ist fein.

Gras

So bin ich der Sommer also gross,
Zu meinen Zeiten wächst Laüb und Gras.
Heda, etc.

Schnee

So bin ich der Winter mit ganzem Fleiss,
Zu meiner Zeit werden die Felder weiss.
Heda, etc.

Wein

So bin ich der Sommer also fein,
Zu meinen Zeiten da wächst der Wein.
Heda, etc.

Wind

So komm' ich aus dem Gebirg so geschwind
Und bringe mit mir den kühlen Wind.
Heda, etc.

Korn

Mit Harken und mit Gabeln
Legt man das Korn auf den Wagen.
Heda, etc.

Feuer

Harken und Gabeln muss ich haben,
Wenn ich die Stuben warm machen will.
Heda, etc.

Korn

Es kommt ein frischer Sommer herein,
Da führt man grosse Fuder ein.
Heda, etc.

Feuer

Und was du lang einführen tust
Im Winter alles verzehren musst.
Heda, etc.

Sommer

O Winter, wir haben von dir genug;
Nun heb' dich aus dem Land mit Flug.
Heda, etc.

Winter

Wohl aus dem Land lass ich mich nit jagen,
O Sommer, du musst dich mit mir vertragen.
Heda, etc.

Sommerleute

Stab' aus, stab' aus,
Stecht dem Winter die Augen aus.

Sommerleute

Heut ist ein freu-den-rei-cher Tag, Dass man den Som-mer ge-

win-nen mag. He-da, ihr Her-ren mein, Der { Som-mer / Win-ter } ist fein!

SO TREIBEN WIR DEN WINTER AUS

So trei - ben wir den Win - ter aus Durch

un - sre Stadt zum Thor hin - aus. Wir trei - ben ihn ü - ber

Berg und Thal, Dass er nicht wie - der - kom-men soll.

WIR BRINGEN DEN LIEBEN SOMMER

Nun hab'n den Win - ter wir aus - ge - trie - ben, Und

brin - gen den lie - ben Som - mer wie - der, Den Som-mer und den

Mai - en, Der Blüm'-lein man - cher - leien.....

THE MAKING OF A PLAY

MABEL ELIZABETH DRYER
Francis W. Parker School

The children of the seventh grade who had taken part in simple plays in French and German, frequently expressed a desire to give a play in English, in which all could participate. When Scott's *Talisman* was read to them, they thought they could make a play from it, and various parts of the story were discussed with that in view. Two things seemed essential, a plot, and considerable action that could be presented in one place. The story of the stealing of the banner of England was selected as best suited to our purpose and conditions.

Individual stories of a play, based upon this part of the *Talisman,* were written by the children. Certain omissions and changes were necessary in constructing a play. For instance, Sir Kenneth's dog, Roswal, who played so important a part in Scott's story, was impracticable for our purpose.

The text was carefully read and the sequence of events outlined. Then followed the writing of the play as a class exercise. In order to have the children feel the life of the time as much as possible, it seemed desirable to use the language of Scott as far as this was consistent with our plan. Our problem was to keep the thread of the story and at the same time cut out everything superfluous.

The text of the play having been decided upon, we began our study. It required considerable drill to become familiar with the language to be used and to express the characters to be impersonated. This afforded an excellent opportunity for oral expression. In the final choice of characters, while considering to some extent the adaptability of the pupils to the characters, an effort was made to use those pupils who most needed the drill, and whose self-confidence needed developing.

In this way, several of the more gifted children were left out or were given unimportant parts.

The children were formed into committees to work out the details of costuming and scenery. As far as possible, they followed the line of their greatest interest, but throughout they showed a willingness to do anything which needed to be done.

The scenery was arranged with the assistance of the art teacher. The first act represented a moonlight scene in the camp of the Crusaders in Palestine. A canvas screen was made to fit the rear and two sides of the stage. Upon this was painted the camp, composed of a group of tents. The topography and vegetation depicted were such as the country presented at that time. A great deal of study was necessary to a knowledge of the characteristic trees and shrubs, of the style of tent used by the Crusaders, etc. Sketches were made and a composite drawing selected.

The frames for the screen were made by high-school boys, but the canvas was stretched and sized by the children of the grade. The scene was then sketched and painted, most of the children taking some part in the work. The screen formed the background for the first scene. In the foreground was built a grassy mound, from the top of which rose the banner spear, bearing King Richard's banner of red and gold.

Scene II was the interior of King Richard's tent. Two large brown screens were so placed as to represent three sides of the tent, with a rear opening overlooking the camp. Two oriental couches, a plain table, and the weapons of the king and his attendant comprised the furnishings of the tent.

The costuming was studied from an historical standpoint. In the Newberry Library the pupils had access to many rare old books depicting life in the Middle Ages. The time of the play was considered in deciding upon the costumes to be used.

Here again the children worked in groups, some sketching and designing parts of costumes, others making armor, metal belts, shoes, etc. In searching books for pictures and descriptions, they found much of interest besides the details they were after; thus their concepts of the life of the age were continually growing wider and clearer. The beautiful art and workmanship of the mediaeval period commanded their appreciation and respect, and they had a genuine desire to express, in the costuming and scenery, a true picture of the time they were representing.

A period of six months elapsed from the beginning of our study to the final presentation before the school. During this time the interest never lagged—in fact it seemed to grow stronger all the time. Throughout, there was a genuine spirit of co-operation, and a willingness to help in any way and at any time. Owing to the difficulty of getting the assembly room, because of gymnastic classes being held there, rehearsals and work on the screen had to be carried on out of school hours. Saturday morning rehearsals were cheerfully attended and there was always a group willing to work every afternoon. The spirit of unselfishness, the willingness to give up any personal desire for the good of the whole, was very marked.

Few of the pupils had taken part in such an exercise before. Some of them had suffered from their sense of limitation. In this piece of work they were drilled until they felt sure of what they were to do and say. Instead of making them seem studied, this certainty gave them self-confidence and promoted spontaneity of action. They experienced a joy in their feeling of power which grew out of their mastery of difficulties.

DRAMATIC PRESENTATION OF SCENES FROM *THE TALISMAN*

MABEL ELIZABETH DRYER AND MARGARET PERSIS BROWN
Francis W. Parker School

THE THEFT OF THE BANNER OF ENGLAND

CAST OF CHARACTERS

RICHARD CŒUR DE LION, King of England.
BERENGARIA, Queen of England.
LADY EDITH PLANTAGENET, Cousin of King Richard.
SIR KENNETH OF SCOTLAND, Knight of the Leopard.

SIR THOMAS DE VAUX, Baron of Gilsland.
CONRAD, Marquis of Monsarrat.
SIR HENRY NEVILLE, Chamberlain to the king.
ADONBEC EL HAKIM, Physician to Saladin.
NECTABANUS, A Dwarf.
EXECUTIONER.
PAGE to the queen.

SCENE I

Place: On the Mount of St. George, in the camp of the Crusaders in Palestine. The Knight of the Leopard guarding the banner of England. Time: Midnight.

(*Knight, pacing back and forth; noise from without.*)

Sir Kenneth.—Who goes there?

Dwarf.—In the name of Merlin stay thy spear or I come not at you.

Sir Kenneth.—Who art thou that would approach my post? Beware: I am here for life and death.

Dwarf.—Sheathe thy sword or I will conjure thee with a bolt from my arblast.

Sir Kenneth.—Unbend thy arblast and come into the moonlight, or by St. Andrew I will pin thee to the earth, be what or who thou wilt.

(*Dwarf comes on the stage.*)

Sir Kenneth.—Why com'st thou here?

Dwarf.—What matters it so that you presently attend me in the presence of those who have sent me hither to summon you?

Sir Kenneth.—In this I cannot gratify thee, for my orders are to abide by this banner till daybreak; so I pray thee to hold me excused in this matter.

(*Sir Kenneth resumes walk and Nectobanus interrupts him.*)

Dwarf.—Look you, either obey me, as in duty bound, or I will lay the command upon thee in the name of one whose beauty could call down the genii from their sphere, and whose grandeur could command the immortal race when they had descended.

Sir Kenneth.—Go to, Nectobanus; who is this lovely lady of whom thou speakest?

Dwarf.—Look you here, and as thou knowest or disownest

this token, so obey or refuse her commands who hath deigned to impose them on thee.

(Saying this he places a ruby ring in the knight's hand. It has a knot of carnation-colored ribbon on it.)

Sir Kenneth.—In the name of all that is sacred, from whom didst thou receive this witness?

Dwarf.—Fond and foolish knight, wouldst thou know more of this matter than that thou art honored with commands from a princess? Every minute that thou tarriest is a crime against thy allegiance.

Sir Kenneth.—Good Nectobanus bethink thyself, can my lady know upon what duty I am this night engaged? Is she aware that my honor depends on my guarding this banner till daybreak, and can it be her wish that I should leave it, even to pay homage to her?

Dwarf.—It matters little to me whether you be traitor or true man to this royal lady. Give back the ring and I will leave you.

(Dwarf turns around as if to leave the mount.)

Sir Kenneth.—Stay—stay. And may it not be postponed for even a few hours, till daybreak?

Dwarf.—She requires thy presence instantly. Harken, thou cold-blooded and suspicious knight, these are her very words: "Tell him that the hand that dropped roses can bestow laurels."

Sir Kenneth.—Hold—hold—yet a moment hold. *(To self.)* Am I either the subject or slave of King Richard, more than as a free man sworn to the service of the crusades? And whom have I come here to honor with lance and sword? Our holy cause and my transcendant lady!

Dwarf.—The ring—the ring, false knight, return the ring.

Sir Kenneth.—A moment, good Nectobanus; disturb not my thoughts. *(To self.)* What if the Saracens should attack our lines? Should I stay here to see that the king's pride suffer no humiliation, or should I speed to the breach and fight for the cross? To the breach assuredly, and next to the commands of God are the commands of my lady. *(Aloud.)* Nectobanus are you to conduct me far from hence?

Dwarf.—But to yonder pavilion of the queen.

Sir Kenneth (*to self*).—I can return instantly. I will throw myself at my lady's feet and pray her to return and conclude my watch. (*Aloud.*) Come now, good Nectobanus, let us hasten to obey the commands thou hast brought.

Dwarf.—Haste he that will, thou hast not been in haste to obey the summons, nor can I walk fast enough to follow your long strides. You do not walk like a man, but bound like an ostrich in the desert.

(*Nectobanus lags and Kenneth picks him up and carries him.*)

(*Conrad of Montserrat in disguise ascends Mt. St. George, steals the banner, breaks the staff and departs hastily. Kenneth returns to complete his watch. Finds banner gone. Searches for traces of thief. Sits down and gives way to his remorse. El Hakim the Moorish physician approaches.*)

El Hakim.—Knight of the Leopard, why art thou cast down? (*No reply.*) Cannot the physician who healed King Richard be of assistance to his noble knight?

Sir Kenneth.—Leave me, Hakim: thou hast the most wonderful science which man ever possessed, but the wounds of the spirit are beyond thy power.

El Hakim.—Not if the patient will explain his calamity and be guided by the physician.

Sir Kenneth.—Know then that last night the banner of England was displayed from this mound. I was its appointed guardian—morning is now breaking—here lies the broken banner-spear. The banner itself is lost, and here sit I a living man.

El Hakim.—(*Examining him.*) How! thy armour is whole—there is no blood on thy weapon, and report speaks thee unlikely to return thus from the fight. Thou hast been trained from thy post.

Sir Kenneth.—And if it were so, physician, what remedy?

El Hakim.—The sage flies the tempest which he cannot control. Use thy speed, therefore, and fly from the vengeance of Richard to the shadow of Saladin's victorious banner.

Sir Kenneth.—My choice were rather that my writhen features should blacken, as they are like to do, in this evening's setting sun. Leave me to recollect my sins and reconcile myself to Heaven. (*Exit.*)

(*Kenneth resumes his thoughts.*)

(*Curtain.*)

SCENE II

Interior of Richard's tent, Palestine. King Richard and De Vaux sleeping. Slow, armed tread is heard approaching tent. De Vaux wakes.

De Vaux.—Who comes? (*Knight of Leopard enters.*) Whence this bold intrusion?

Richard (*wakes*).—Hold, De Vaux, Sir Kenneth cometh like a good soldier to render account of his guard. To such the general's tent is ever accessible. Speak Sir Scot—thou com'st to tell of a vigilant, safe, and honorable watch, dost thou not? The rustling of the folds of the banner of England were enough to guard it, even without the body of such a knight as men hold thee.

Sir Kenneth.—As men will hold me no more. My watch hath neither been vigilant, safe nor honorable. The banner of England has been carried off.

King Richard.—And thou alive to tell it? Away, it cannot be. There is not even a scratch on thy face. Why dost thou stand thus mute? Speak the truth. It is ill jesting with the king. Yet I will forgive thee if thou hast lied.

Sir Kenneth.—Lied! Sir King! but this also must be endured —I have spoken the truth.

King Richard.—By God and by St. George! De Vaux, go view the spot—this fever has disturbed his brain—this cannot be—the man's courage is proof—it cannot be. Go speedily —or send if thou will not go. (*Enter Neville hastily.*)

Neville (*excitedly*).—The banner of England is gone and the knight who guarded it has been overpowered and probably murdered. (*Sees Sir Kenneth.*) But whom do I see here?

King Richard.—A traitor. (*Takes his battle-axe.*) A traitor whom thou shalt see die a traitor's death. (*Draws back weapon as if to strike, pauses a moment, then lets his weapon fall to the ground.*) But there was blood, Neville—there was blood upon the place! Hark thee! Sir Scot—brave thou wert once, for I have seen thee fight. Say thou hast slain two of the thieves, in the defense of the standard—say but one—say thou hast struck but a good blow in our behalf, and get thee out of the camp with thy life and thy infamy!

Sir Kenneth.—You have called me a liar, my Lord King, and therein, at least, you have done me wrong. Know that there was no blood shed in the defense of the standard.

King Richard.—Now by St. George! (*Heaves his arm as if to strike.*)

De Vaux (*places himself between the king and Sir Kenneth*).—My liege this must not be here, nor by thine own hand. It is enough of folly for one night and day to have intrusted thy banner to a Scot. Said I not they were ever fair and false?

King Richard.—Thou didst De Vaux, and thou wast right. I should have known him better. And yet it is strange to see the bearing of the man. Coward or traitor he must be, yet he abode the blow of Richard Plantagenet, as our arm had been raised to lay knighthood on his shoulder. Had he shown the slightest sign of fear—had but a joint trembled, or an eyelid quivered—I had shattered his head like a crystal goblet. But I cannot strike where there is neither fear nor resistance.

Sir Kenneth.—My lord—

King Richard.—Ha! hast thou found thy speech? Ask grace from heaven but none from me, for England is dishonored through thy fault; and wert thou my own brother there is no pardon for thee.

(*Noise heard from without. Guard enters and announces the queen.*)

King Richard.—Detain her—detain her, Neville, this is no sight for women. Away with him, De Vaux, through the back entrance of our tent; coop him up, and answer for his safe custody with your life. And hark ye—he is presently to die—but let him have a ghostly father—we would not kill soul and body. And stay—hark thee, we will not have him dishonored:

he shall die knightlike, in his belt and spurs; for if his treachery be as black as hell, his boldness may match that of the devil himself. And send me the executioner speedily. (*Commotion in outer pavilion.*)

Voice of Queen.—I knew it—the king will not receive us. (*Executioner enters.*)

King Richard.—Sir Kenneth of Scotland is to die shortly. And hark thee, villain, observe if his cheek loses color or his eye falters. Mark me the smallest twitch of the features, or wink of the eyelid. I love to know how brave souls meet death.

Executioner.—If he sees my blade waved aloft without shrinking, he is the first that ever did so.

Voice of Edith.—If your grace make not your own way, I make it for you; or if not for your majesty, for myself at least. Chamberlains, the queen demands to see King Richard—the wife to see her husband.

Chamberlain.—It grieves me to gainsay you; but his Majesty is busied upon matters of life and death.

Edith.—And we seek also to speak with him on matters of life and death—I will make entrance for your grace. (*Puts aside the curtain. Ladies enter.*)

King Richard (*displeased*).—What means this, Berengaria?

Queen.—Send away that man; his look kills me.

King Richard.—Begone, sirrah—what wait'st thou for? Art thou fit to look on these ladies?

Executioner.—Your highness's pleasure touching the head.

King Richard.—Out with thee, dog! A Christian burial. (*Exit executioner.*) And now, foolish wench, what wishest thou? (*Queen kneels before him.*) What seeks the lady of my heart in her knight's pavilion in this early and unwonted hour?

Queen.—Pardon, my most gracious liege—pardon.

King Richard.—Pardon! for what?

Queen.—First, for entering your royal presence too boldly and unadvisedly.

King Richard.—Thou too boldly? The sun might as well ask pardon because his rays entered the windows of some wretch's dungeon. But I was busied with work unfit for thee to witness, my gentle one, and I was unwilling besides that thou shouldst risk thy precious health where sickness has been so lately rife.

Queen.—But thou art well now.

King Richard.—Well enough to break a lance on the bold crest of that champion who refuses to acknowledge thee the fairest dame in Christendom.

Queen.—Thou wilt not then refuse me one boon—only one—only a poor life.

King Richard.—Ha! Proceed.

Queen.—This unhappy Scottish knight—

King Richard.—Speak not of him, madam, he dies—his doom is fixed.

Queen.—Nay, my royal liege, 'tis but a silken banner neglected—Berengaria will give thee another broidered with her own hand, and rich as ever dallied with the wind. Every pearl I have shall go to bedeck it, and with every pearl I will drop a tear of thankfulness to my generous knight.

King Richard.—Thou knowest not what thou sayest—pearls! can all the pearls of the East atone for a speck upon England's honor—all the tears that ever woman's eye wept wash away a stain on Richard's fame. Go to, madam, know your place, and your time, and your sphere. At present we have duties in which you cannot be our partner.

Queen (to Edith).—Thou hear'st Edith, we shall but cense him.

Edith.—Be it so. (*Steps forward.*) My lord—I your poor kinswoman crave you for justice rather than mercy. And to the cry of justice the ears of a monarch should be open at every time, place, and circumstance.

King Richard.—Ha! our cousin Edith? She speaks ever kinglike, and kinglike will I answer her, so she bring no request unworthy of herself or me.

Edith.—My lord, this good knight, whose blood you are about to spill, hath done, in his time, service to Christendom. He hath fallen from his duty, through a snare set for him in mere folly and idleness of spirit. A message sent to him in the name of one who—why should I speak it—it was my own—induced him for an instant to leave his post.

King Richard.—And you saw him then, cousin?

Edith.—I did, my liege. It is no time to explain. Wherefore I am here neither to exculpate myself nor blame others.

King Richard.—And where did you do him such a grace?

Edith.—In the tent of her Majesty the queen.

King Richard.—Of our royal consort? Now by Heaven and by St. George, this is too audacious. That you should have admitted him to an audience by night, in the very tent of our royal consort, and offer this as an excuse for his disobedience and desertion! By heaven, Edith, thou shalt rue this thy life long in a monastery.

Edith.—My honor, Lord King, is as little touched as yours, and my Lady the Queen can prove it if she thinks fit. But I have already said, I am not here to excuse myself nor inculpate others—I ask you but extend to one, whose fault was committed under strong temptation, that mercy which even you, Lord King, must one day supplicate at a higher tribunal, and for faults, perhaps, less venal.

King Richard (*bitterly*).—Can this be Edith Plantagenet, the wise and noble? Now, by King Henry's soul! Little hinders but I order thy minion's skull to be fixed as a perpetual ornament by the crucifix in thy cell.

Edith.—And if thou dost, I will say it is a relic of a good knight, cruelly and unworthily done to death by—(*checks herself*)—by one of whom I shall only say he should have known better how to reward chivalry.

Queen.—O peace—peace, for pity's sake, you do but offend him more!

Edith.—I care not, the spotless virgin fears not the raging lion. Let him work his will on this worthy knight. Edith, for whom he dies will know how to weep his memory. To me no one shall speak of politic marriage to be sanctioned by his poor hand.

King Richard (*stamping*).—Away—away, the sun has risen on the dishonor of England and it is not yet avenged. Ladies, withdraw, if ye would not hear orders which would displease you; for by St. George I swear—

El Hakim (*entering pavilion*).—Swear not!

King Richard.—Ha, my learned Hakim, come, I hope, to tax our generosity.

El Hakim.—I come to request instant speech with you—instant—and touching matters of deep interest.

King Richard.—In what can I pleasure you, my learned physician?

El Hakim.—Great king, let thy servant speak one word and yet live. I would remind thee that thou owest to the Intelligences whose benefits I dispense to mortals, a life—

King Richard.—And I warrant me thou wouldst have another in requital, ha?

El Hakim.—Such is my humble prayer to the great Melech Ric, even the life of this good knight who is doomed to die.

(*King paces up and down and speaks to himself.*)

King Richard.—Why, God-a-mercy, I knew what he desired as soon as ever he entered the pavilion. Here is one poor life justly condemned to death and I, a king, and a soldier, who have slain thousands by my command, am to have no power over it. By St. George it makes me laugh! Wife—kinswoman—Hakim—each appears in the lists as soon as the other is defeated. This is a single knight fighting against the whole mélée of the tournament—ha! ha! ha!

El Hakim.—A doom of death should not issue from laughing lips. Let thy servant hope that thou hast granted him this man's life.

King Richard.—Take the freedom of a thousand of thy captive countrymen instead. This man's life can avail thee nothing, and it is forfeited.

El Hakim.—All our lives are forfeited. But the great creditor is merciful and exacts not the pledge rigorously nor untimely.

King Richard.—Thou canst show me no special interest thou hast to become intercessor betwixt me and the execution of justice, to which I am sworn as a crowned king.

El Hakim.—Thou art sworn to the dealing forth of mercy

as well as justice. But what thou seekest, great king, is the execution of thine own will. As for the concern I have in this request, know that many a man's life depends upon thy granting this boon.

King Richard.—Explain thy words—but think not to impose upon me by false pretexts.

El Hakim.—Know then, that the medicine to which thou, Sir King, owest thy recovery, is the talisman. Severe restrictions, painful observances, are necessary on the part of the sage who uses this mode of cure, and if he fails to cure at least twelve persons within the course of each full moon, the virtue of the divine gift departs from the amulet, and both the last patient and the physician will be exposed to speedy misfortune, neither will they survive the year. I require yet one life to make up the appointed number.

King Richard.—I cannot see how delivering a criminal from the death he deserves should go to make up thy tale of miraculous cures.

El Hakim.—When thou canst show why a draught of cold water should have cured you, when the most precious drugs failed, thou may'st reason on the other mysteries attendant on this matter. Ask therefore no more questions; it is enough that by sparing this man's life you will deliver thyself, great king, and thy servant from a great danger.

King Richard.—El Hakim, when you bid Richard Plantagenet fear that a danger will fall upon him for some ill omen, you speak to no ignorant Saxon or doting old woman, who foregoes her purpose because a hare crosses her path.

El Hakim.—I cannot hinder your doubt of my words, but will you think it just to deprive the world of the benefits of this virtuous talisman rather than extend forgiveness to one poor criminal? Bethink you, Lord King, that though thou canst slay thousands, thou canst not restore one man to health. Thou canst cut off the head, but not cure the aching tooth.

King Richard.—This is over-insolent. We took thee for our leech, not for our conscience keeper.

El Hakim.—And it is thus the most renowned prince of

Frangistan repays benefit to his royal person? Know, then, that through every court of Europe and Asia—to Moslem and Nazarene—wherever honor is loved and infamy detested—to every quarter of the world will I denounce thee, Melech Ric, as thankless and ungenerous; and even the lands that never heard of thy renown shall yet be acquainted with thy shame!

King Richard.—Are these terms to me, vile infidel? (*Strides up to him.*) Art thou weary of life?

El Hakim.—Strike! Thine own deed shall then paint thee more worthless than could my words. (*Richard turns fiercely from him and traverses the tent, then hastily traces a line or two on paper.*)

King Richard (*to Neville*).—The provost will deliver this Scot to you on this warrant. Bring him hither. (*Exit Neville.*) (*King resumes pacing up and down.*) (*To El Hakim.*) Thankless and ungenerous! as well be termed coward and infidel. (*Enter Neville with Kenneth.*) Hakim, thou hast chosen thy boon, and though I had rather thou hadst asked my crown jewels yet I may not, kinglike, refuse thee. Take this Scot, therefore, to thy keeping. Use him as thy bond-slave, to be disposed of as thou wilt, only let him beware how he comes before the eyes of Richard. Is there aught else in which I may do thee pleasure?

El Hakim.—The bounty of the king hath filled my cup to the brim.

SOMETHING ABOUT THE HISTORY OF POTTERY

A MORNING EXERCISE[1]

HELEN PUTNAM
Francis W. Parker School

FIRST EXERCISE

Reading of Selections from Longfellow's "Keramos," with a Few Words of Explanation of the Poem.—H. P.

A long time ago, before people invented pottery, they used gourds for dippers and cocoanut shells for cups, and if they could not find cocoanut shells or gourds, they used wooden bowls. In countries where bamboo grows they carried water in bamboo flasks. They cut off one joint of bamboo and corked it up and put water in it. And they carried water in skin bags, and they made stone mortars to grind their corn in. And they made baskets, too. After a while they began to make pottery, and we think one way it was invented was this: Once a person went down to a pond to get some water, and it was all muddy at the edge of the water. He stepped in the sticky mud (which was really clay) and left footprints. And when he came the next day the place was dry. And he came again after a rain, and then he saw that the footprints were full of water, and he dug one out and brought it home and used it for a bowl. I made this footprint to show you how his looked. Then they thought they would make bowls with their hands. They took a solid piece of

[1] While the children of the Francis W. Parker School are working at their modeling, stories are sometimes told them of famous potters, or of the history of pottery; and they are encouraged to think out their own theories of how pottery came to be invented, and then are given opportunity to compare these theories with those of authorities on the subject. Occasionally the older children are given references to look up and report upon to the class. Out of this work grew two consecutive morning exercises based upon the material thus accumulated. The following stories are retold, as nearly as possible in the children's own words, not omitting some misstatements which were made in the telling. The illustrative drawings are taken from the *Encyclopaedia Brittanica.*

clay and dug it out in the middle, this way. That is the way we make some of our inkwells.

S. O., *4th Grade*

A long time ago, people used to have houses called *wattle and daub.* They were made of branches and twigs all woven together, with clay plastered over them. And sometimes these houses would burn, and people saw that the clay would not burn like the branches, but only got harder, so they thought it would be a good plan to make houses of the clay, and then they made bricks for their houses. And they learned to make their dishes hard by burning, too.

G. H., *4th Grade*

A long time ago, long before the white people were here, the Indians did not have pottery, but used baskets (Fig. 1, *a*) to

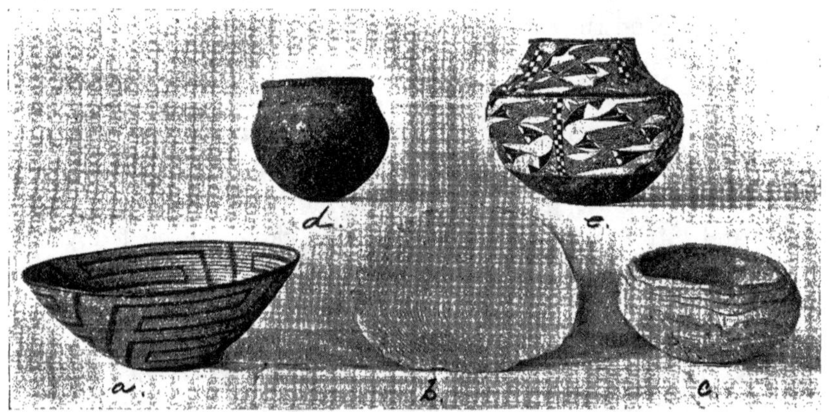

FIG. 1

cook in. And to keep their baskets from burning up they put clay on the outside. They liked that. We think that some time a woman was cooking in a basket smeared with clay, and she went off and left it over the fire and it burned up. And when she came back she found only the clay, which was still in the shape of the basket but burned hard, like this (Fig. 1, *b*). That gave her an idea, and she decided to make other bowls like that, and she told her friends about it. For a while they made bowls by sticking clay over the outside of the basket, but then they thought that if they put the clay on the inside they could build the bowl up higher by using coils, just as they used coils in making their baskets. Then it looked like this (Fig. 1, *c*). After a while they learned to scrape the bowls smooth, like this (Fig. 1, *d*) and at last to paint them (Fig. 1, *e*).

G. H., *3rd Grade*

The way that potter's wheels were first thought of was this: The ancient people used to put their vases on round stones and

FIG. 2

turn them round to shape them, and after a while they thought it would be better to keep the stand turning and shape the pots by hand. This is a drawing (Fig. 2, *a*) made from a wall painting on an Egyptian building erected about 4000 B. C. This drawing (Fig. 2, *b*) shows an Egyptian wheel, date about 2000 B. C., run by foot power like our kick-wheel downstairs. This is another (Fig. 2, *c*), a Greek one, showing the way they marked the pots. They put them on the wheel and held a stick up against the pot and it would leave lines. Maybe this way of

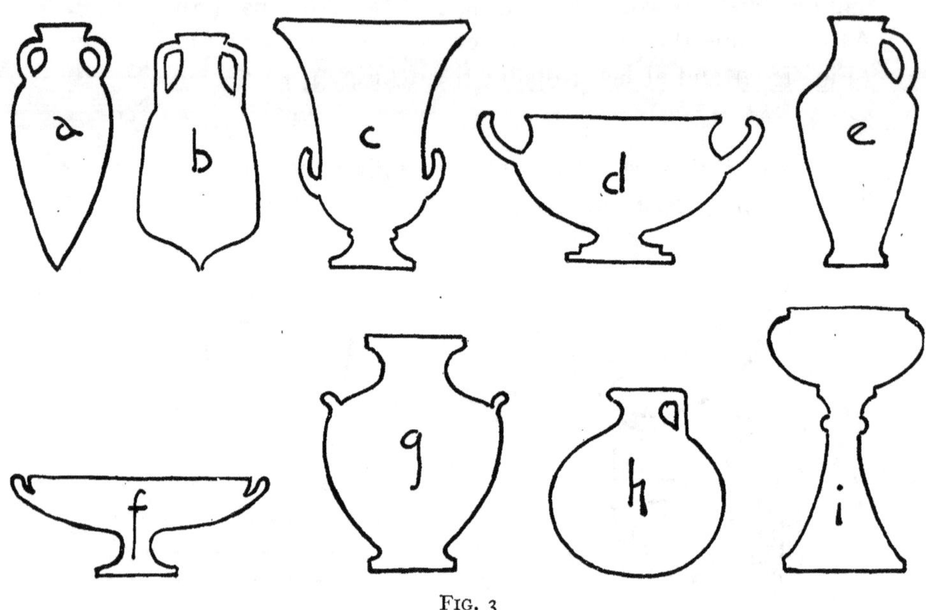

FIG. 3

marking was the result of some potter going off and leaving his work on his wheel, and some mischievous boy coming along and turning the wheel and sticking a stick up against it while it moved. In the Middle Ages, they had a potter's wheel that was driven by turning a crank, and after a while they fastened a treddle to the wheel and ran it with that. After that they used steam, and now they use electricity.

P. H. G., *8th Grade*

I want to tell you something about Greek vases. The Greeks used their vases in the beginning to hold grain and wine. Their first vases (called Amphorae) were on this order (Fig. 3, *a*), and were stretched on ropes in the room. This Amphora has two handles. This is a second kind (Fig. 3, *b*). Sometimes the points were long enough to stick into the ground. This (Fig. 3, *c*) is a Krater, which is perhaps the largest of all the Greek vases. It was used for mixing wine with the water. We get our word *crater* from this word. This (Fig. 3, *d*) is a drinking cup, called Kantharos. From the large Krater they poured the wine into a pitcher (Fig. 3, *e*) and then into the drinking cups, which were very beautiful, the most beautiful being a Kylix (Fig. 3, *f*) which was used for the wine offered to the gods. This large jar (Fig. 3, *g*), the Hydria, was used for storing grain. This round jug, called Aryballus (Fig. 3, *h*) was for carrying water for the bath, and the Lebes (Fig. 3, *i*) was a jardinière.

The decorations on Greek pottery are divided into four great classes. This (Fig. 4, *a*) shows the earliest stage—just straight

FIG. 4

lines and circles and triangles, and you can see how they correspond with our Indian designs (Fig. 1, *e*). The second (Fig. 4, *b*) shows how they used fishes and seaweed, and small plants and things of that nature, for their designs. The third (Fig. 4, *c*) is the largest class of all, the conventional design. The fourth class is perhaps the most important. That is the class decorated by figures of people. It is the most important because it is a great source of history. We learn a great deal of Grecian history from their vases. The Greeks decorated their vases with figures of heroes and kings. We can tell their dress from these vases, their customs and habits, and something about their religion and their wars and battles. Sometimes Greek artists would put a whole battle on a vase.

T. M., *11th Grade*

Perhaps you will remember reading in the *Recorder* that the fourth-grade children are furnishing a room in a Greek house. Some of the children are making pottery for it. Some of them have made Amphorae, and some vases, and some others have made lamps (Fig. 5). Besides these toy ones, three of the children are making Greek vases for the fourth-grade room. The Greek clay is red when it is baked, and our clay is white. We haven't any red clay, so we have painted the vases and pottery to make them look like the Greek. We had to find out how

FIG. 5

to make these vases so we studied pictures and went to the Art Institute and studied the lamps and vases there, and in that way found out how to make them. When we go out on our field trip to Glencoe, we are going to bring home some of the common clay. Some people say that common clay when it is baked turns red, and we are going to try and see if it does.

SECOND EXERCISE

Reading of Selections from Browning's "Rabbi Ben Ezra," and from Omar Khayam.—Mrs. B.

The pottery about which we talked to you yesterday was earthenware. We are going to talk to you today about porcelain. Porcelain is made of very fine white clay called kaolin, or else of a compound made to imitate kaolin. When broken, it shows white and glassy all the way through; earthenware does not. Porcelain requires a great deal more heat to fire it than earthenware does; for that reason earthenware was invented before porcelain. The first porcelain we know about was made in China, probably about the time of Christ. We know that the American Indians did not make any. They did not use the potter's wheel, and even the Greeks never made porcelain, although they worked with the potter's wheel and made wonderfully beautiful earthenware. Porcelain did not come into Europe at all until about the fourteenth century. Then various European countries began to make it. Can you think why it started just then? You of the older classes know that after the Crusades the people of Europe began to trade with the Orient a great deal more than before. They had found out what riches there were there, and travelers worked farther and farther to the East, looking for trade, until finally, in the fourteenth century, Marco Polo and his father went into China; and among the things that Marco Polo brought back to his people from China were pieces of porcelain, which he introduced into Europe by the name of chinaware; that is why we call it *china*. The people of Italy and Spain were the first Europeans to make porcelain. Of course you know that Marco Polo was an Italian. A great many of the travelers were Italian or Spanish, and when they made their ware they copied the Chinese porcelain, not only in material but also in coloring and decoration. We are going to tell you this morning of some of the ware they produced in trying to make these copies, and of one kind in particular—Majolica. This was made on an island by the name of Majorca, a Spanish island in the Mediterranean Sea. H. P.

Palissy, a Frenchman, was the first potter to invent a porcelain of artificial kaolin. He was a rather poor man, whose profession was painting stained glass windows for churches. He happened to see a piece of Majolica ware in a Paris museum, and from that time on he had no peace of mind until he could try to make a ware like it. So he went to a pottery near by and got some pieces of their jars, which he ground up and tried to use, but this did not work at all well because the jars were poorly made, and there were pebbles in the clay, and the only kiln he had to used was that of the glass foundry, which was too hot. But he tried other clays and kept on working, spending all his money in trying to find out what materials to use, though his wife, who had no sympathy with his aim, made his life miserable with her scolding and complaints. Finally he went to one of the larger potteries to look and see how the ware was made, but they would not let him in. So he came back, but on his trip he saw the Majolica ware again, and it was so wonderful that it was like an intoxication to him, and he *had* to work at it. So he built a kiln, but that did not work very well, and he had to build another. At last, after more and more successful experiments, a day came when he felt sure that he was going to succeed. He had a fire in his kiln, but his fuel gave out, so he went into the house and broke up the chairs and tables to burn. His wife and neighbors tried in vain to stop him. Then his fire started to go out again, and he went into the house and tore up the floor. That finished the firing, and when he opened the kiln, he had the white opaque glaze for which he had worked so long. After that he worked as a potter, and he chose some very queer decorations; he used to take not only flowers and fruits, but insects and frogs and lizards as ornamentations on his dishes. Palissy was a Huguenot, a sect at that time greatly hated by the Royalists, but the king liked his ware so well that he was taken to court to work there. Later, however, he was thrown into prison because he was a Huguenot, and died there.

C. G., *9th Grade*

The Chinese ware was clearer and better than the European ware; it was whiter and it lasted longer, so everybody in Europe was trying to find real kaolin to use in pottery instead of the artificial mixture. There was a German physician and chemist, Dr. Boettger, who was interested in pottery making. One morning his servant came in with the doctor's wig freshly powdered and feeling strangely heavy. Dr. Boettger always investigated everything, so he asked about the powder, which looked and felt, he thought, like the Chinese kaolin. The servant told him he had gotten the powder from a neighboring blacksmith, who was selling it. The smith said he had been out riding and had gotten some white clay in his horse's hoof. When he scraped it out, it powdered so finely that he thought it would make good wig powder, so he had gotten some to sell. Dr. Boettger investigated it and found that the clay was kaolin. Then he began making pottery, and became very much interested in it. The king of Saxony saw his ware and liked it, and sent Dr. Boettger and his assistants to a castle near Dresden, where they could work without having the secret found out. This was the beginning of the famous Meissen pottery, which is one of the best known porcelain wares today.

S. R. S., *9th Grade*

Besides the highly colored Chinese wares, such as Canton, which led to the bright-colored European pottery, like Majolica, there is a great deal of old Chinese porcelain that is blue and white—for example, the Nankin ware. Some of the Europeans liked the blue and white better than the brighter-colored china, so they tried to imitate it. At first they copied the Chinese designs as closely as they could, but later they began to make their own patterns. The people of Delft, in Holland, became famous for their blue and white porcelain. Their older pieces show the influence of the Chinese patterns, but their later work is decorated with pictures of objects they saw about them—boats, windmills, etc. Some of the Meissen ware, notably the well-known onion pattern, is also blue and white. There is a blue and white English china that is a very close copy of the Nankin ware. That is the famous "Willow pattern," a real Chinese pattern, with a Chinese legend attached, although the arrangement for the dishes was designed by the famous English artist, Turner. Alice is going to tell you the legend.

H. P.

Once upon a time there was a merchant, and this merchant lived in a very fine house, and he had a very beautiful daughter.

And there was a man who liked her very much. He was a poor man and lived in a small house across the river from the merchant (you can see both houses on the plate). One day this merchant went out, and the poor man came and took the merchant's daughter, and led her under the willow trees and across the bridge to his house. One of her servants went with her. When the merchant came home, he was very angry at his daughter and the young man, and he got into his boat and started across the river to catch them. They were very much afraid he was going to catch them, so they prayed to the Spirit of the Air to help them, and he turned them into birds, and they flew away and were happy ever after.

A. K., *3rd Grade*

Josiah Wedgewood was born in England in 1730. He came from a family of potters and naturally became one. He was taken from school when quite young, and went into partnership with his uncle. He was employed as thrower—that is, he made shapes for jars on the potter's wheel. After a few years he went into partnership with another potter, and they built a place known as the Bell Works. The reason they called it that is because they had a bell on the top that called all the people to work. Wedgewood took great interest in his laborers. He built them comfortable houses and made their working conditions as good as possible. In this building, the Bell Works, he made what is known as *queensware*. The reason he called it this was because the first piece of it he made, he gave to the queen, and she ordered so much of it that he got rich. About this time, the Duchess of Portland had an auction of some of her possessions. Among them was a wonderful vase which had been brought from Italy, and Wedgewood wanted it to copy. So he tried to bid it in at the auction, but a young man, a nephew of the Duchess, wanted it too, to keep it in the family, so he bid against Wedgewood. At last when the bidding had gone up very high, the young man went to Wedgewood and asked him what he wanted it for. Wedgewood told him he was a potter, and he wanted to try to make some ware like it. They finally agreed that the young man should buy it, but Wedgewood was to borrow it until he could get his copy made. The copies he made are known as jasper ware, and the modern jasper ware is what we call Wedgewood. The reason why Wedgewood went into the scientific part of pottery-making is because he lost his leg; he had to have it cut off, and could not work at the wheel any more.

M. L., *9th Grade*

Reading from Kipling's "Letters from the East," of the description of his visit to a Japanese pottery.—H. P.

EDITORIAL NOTES

THE LINE OF LEAST RESISTANCE IN EDUCATION

The meaning of the term "line of least resistance" as applied to school work seems to be somewhat confused. Many seem to interpret it as equivalent to the lazy man's doctrine of *laissez faire;* thereby reading into it the idea that Johnnie should not be compelled to do anything which his whim does not prompt him to do, but must work only as his teacher is able to catch and to hold his interest. Conversely, "line of greatest resistance" is understood to mean the course by which Johnnie's nose is held firmly to the grindstone and in which he is made to do what he does not want to do; because grandpa was brought up that way, and because in his future career he will always have to do many things that he does not want to do; and, finally, because it is good for Johnnie to get used to this sort of thing—he needs discipline; and, they assume, discipline must be imposed from without rather than from within.

Popular Misconceptions

This dispute over the question of whether, in matters educational, we shall follow the line of least resistance or not, arises from a confusion of the terms license and freedom, and from a failure to comprehend the correct meaning of the term "line of least resistance." Hence it is a mere battle of words, and will be settled as soon as the terms are properly defined.

The term "line of least resistance" is borrowed from physical sciences; and, therefore, for its definition we must turn to science. In the realm of natural phenomena, resistance is the source of useless work; and it is, therefore, the chief obstacle in the way of constructing a perfect machine—a *perpetuum mobile,* as it is often called. Were it not for resistances of various kinds, it would be

Scientific Meaning of the Phrase

possible to build a machine that would convert all the energy supplied to it into useful work. Such a machine would be a perfect machine, i. e., its efficiency would be 100 per cent.

But since resistance is inherent in all transformations of energy from one form into another—as from coal into steam power or electric light—and since economy demands that as little of the energy available for a given machine be spent in useless work, it is clear that, in order to convert the greatest possible amount of the available energy into useful work, the machine or system must be so constructed that the resistances inherent in the situation are as small as is possible—taking into account, of course, the limitations and constraints necessary to the conditions of the problem. Hence, in physics, to follow the line of least resistance means to construct machines or other physical systems which shall have the maximum efficiency that is possible under the limitations imposed by the nature of the case.

Line of least resistance is thus equivalent to line of maximum efficiency.

In the light of this definition, the scene of the controversy is shifted; for everyone of us has been trying his best to make his school or his teaching attain maximum efficiency. So we must all agree that we have been trying to follow the line of least resistance in this sense, which is the true sense. This definition does not, however, settle the problems of education by any means; for we have now to determine how we may find the line of maximum efficiency in any given case.

Application to Education

Before attempting to answer this question, let me point out that this statement of the problem of education renders wholly irrelevant the arguments of those who would run the schools on the good old lines on which they were run when Adam was an urchin. It is as far beside the mark to claim that because the classics and the doctrine of formal discipline have been tried and seem to have proved useful in educating us, they therefore furnish the sole means of attaining maximum efficiency, as for an engineer to claim that because certain devices invented by

Watt had been tried and seemed to prove useful in his engines—which burned twelve pounds of coal per horsepower per hour—they therefore furnish the sole means of attaining maximum efficiency in the modern engine, which burns but one pound of coal per horsepower per hour.

The problem of definitely finding the path of maximum efficiency in the schools is at present rather indeterminate. In the case of the engine, or any other physical system, we are generally in a position to say definitely what the path of maximum efficiency is in the light of our present knowledge; in most cases, we can, and we actually do, foretell how an engine or an electric-light plant shall be constructed and managed in order to attain this end. We are able to do this as well as we do because we have developed an accurate system of measuring both the efficiency of the finished plant, and the properties of the various factors that enter into its construction. In the case of the schools, this is not so. We possess no system of accurate measurement for determining either the educational efficiency of a school plant, or that of a single teacher; nor have we found out how to tell whether a given pupil is developing his maximum efficiency in the social system.

Educational Problems Indefinite

Hence, before we shall be in a position definitely to answer the question as to what is the path of maximum efficiency of a school system or a teacher, some system of measurement will have to be devised, and the laws that relate the properties of the parts of the system to one another—for example the laws relating the individual to society—will have to be worked out. This means much experimentation and many failures, just as has been and still is, to some extent, the case in the domain of engineering. But if the problem is attacked in a truly scientific way—and no one will deny that it is being so attacked now all along the line—there is every reason to believe that the efficiency of the schools will gradually increase, even as that of steam engines is continually doing. But without such study and experimentation, and without an eye constantly on the future, rather than on the past, such progress will be slow indeed.

How to Make the Problem Definite

It must now be clear that *license* plays no part in determining the line of maximum efficiency, while *freedom* does. In constructing an electric light plant, for instance, it is never a question of whether the copper will or will not conduct electricity. Since we know some of the laws relating copper and electricity, we are able to place the copper so that it will realize its own nature most completely in serving the plant. If we but knew the laws of the relations of the individual to society, and those of the development of the mind, and a few others of like nature, we would be able to treat Johnnie as we treat the copper; i. e., we could place him in the system so that he would always be in freedom to realize himself in the service of society—for true freedom consists in coming into harmony with law.

The Possible Solution

C. R. M.

In making the rounds as an art teacher of a public-school system, it once fell to the lot of the writer to spend a weekly half-hour at a small country school. On one occasion an illustrative drawing was in progress. A small boy with more initiative than the rest put a fence in his picture, whereupon the good country schoolmarm pounced upon it with the reproof, "Why Johnny, Miss C. did not tell you to draw a fence! Never do anything that the teacher doesn't tell you to do!" One sometimes feels a suspicion that we as a teaching profession are waiting to be "told" before we really do anything in the matter of industrial education. Looking over the files of educational journals and reports of educational meetings we find that during the last ten years they have been filled with discussions of the subject. One reaches the stage of fairly loathing its mention, and so far to what has it all amounted? In meetings—a long confession of faith—in schools—joints and Morris chairs. And now the public has taken it up and is beginning to demand as President Roosevelt expressed it, "The schools train toward and not away from the farm and the shop." When one reads the opinions expressed at the recent meeting of the Department of Superintendence of the N. E. A., he becomes hope-

Results versus Discussion of Industrial Education

ful that something will be done. When he stops to think what it means to alter or introduce one simple exercise in a school machinery as large as that of Chicago or New York he knows that the school man will hesitate before he multiplies any possible mistake by the child population of a metropolis. Consequently the chances are that the manufacturer will act while the educator still hesitates, and so the movement will lack that breadth which would result from their combined efforts.

Utilization of Social By-Products in the School

In our school system great social by-products go to waste. In the cities we realize the value of the country life affording natural stimuli. We long to build a school house in the middle of a farm, feeling that the whole problem would be solved if the curriculum were built around such ideally real conditions. But do the rural schools make use of this material? In towns and cities schools are next-door neighbors, perhaps, of great manufacturing industries or it may be they overlook the comings and goings of a world's commerce. What could be more desirable than that the school system should connect with these natural centers of community life, making use thereby of a fund of experience which under other methods is altogether wasted. Is this done? The trouble is that we spend our time making out uniform courses of study. We see its absurdity when we find that we have taught the Philippinos to make Swedish models—flour sacks, and bread boards. It is just as bad, if not so evident, when we fit the school in Ruralville with the same garment that we cut for the community at Fall River.

The Duty of the Government to Organize Educational Laboratories

But we are quite right in proceeding with caution. The manufacturer never turns his entire plant into an experimental laboratory. Every progressive one does, however, maintain a small shop in which he tries new ideas and when they prove fit and ready for the market he adopts them in his business. Why should not the government treat education in the same businesslike and scientific way? It maintains experimental stations in connection with its fisheries. It spends money in developing agriculture. It considers it worth while to send out free seeds to farmers all over the country in order that it may study the needs and possibilities of various soils. Are educational interests of less account? Why should not the Department of Education at Washington equip and carry on a school in some typical rural community, making there a scientific investigation of the best methods of developing the resources and of making up deficiences? Such a school should be small and should have for its purpose the working out of the proper rural school curriculum. A similar experiment should be maintained in industrial and commercial centers. An educational laboratory is the only economical and scientific way to study the present situation. Let us hope that this national interest in the question will find an outlet in some such sane and immediate results.

L. S. C.

NOTES AND NEWS

INDUSTRIAL EDUCATION FROM THE POINT OF VIEW OF THE DEPARTMENT OF SUPERINTENDENCE OF THE N. E. A.

The recent meeting of the Department of Superintendence of the N. E. A. at Washington was of peculiar interest because of its emphasis on industrial education. This subject held the center of attention and was discussed from every side. The standpoint of the manufacturer, the teacher, the psychologist, and the child received equal attention. In its many-sidedness this convention differed somewhat from the meeting of the National Society for the Promotion of Industrial Education which met in Chicago last January.

The papers read at the Washington meeting were necessarily brief, being limited to ten minutes. They are to be published in the report of the meeting. It will be sufficient if we give here merely the outlines from which each person spoke. It will be noted that the topics were assigned in such a way as to make of the combined separate papers an ordered and cumulative presentation of a single topic.

SYMPOSIUM: *THE PLACE OF INDUSTRIES IN PUBLIC EDUCATION*

OUTLINE OF DISCUSSION OF FIRST PROPOSITION—JAMES E. RUSSELL

I. *Our Government the Resultant of Contending Forces.*

1) Forces making for aristocracy or oligarchy.

a) In new country leaders always necessary.

b) Earliest educational institutions were for training of leaders.

2) Forces making for democracy.

a) Desire for "liberty, equality, fraternity."

b) Equality of opportunity basic principle of national life.

II. *Inefficiency of Present Educational System.*

1) Schools planned for those going on to colleges.

2) "Average" man unprovided for.

3) Vocational training omitted.

III. *Changes Necessary in Educational System.*

1) Real equality of opportunity given to all.

2) Early years of school curriculum enriched.

3) Technical training between ages of 14 and 20 at public expense.

IV. *Results.*

1) Greater efficiency of workman contributes to wealth of nation.

2) Greater pride in his work makes workman better citizen and more conservative member of society.

3) Industrial rank of nation raised.

SYMPOSIUM: *THE PLACE OF INDUSTRIES IN PUBLIC EDUCATION*

OUTLINE OF DISCUSSION OF SECOND PROPOSITION—EDWARD C. ELLIOTT

I. *The Essential Elements of Educational Opportunity.*

1. The American public school and its relation to political opportunity.
2. The translation of political opportunity into economic opportunity.
3. The *fiction* of equality of educational opportunity.
4. The maintenance of an "educational equilibrium."

II. *Forces Contributing to Vocational Selection.*

1. Social; economic; personal; educational. Each acting from:
   a) Conscious motives, or
   b) Unconscious motives.
2. Selective function of the public school.
   a) Horizontal social selection versus vertical *vocational* selection.

III. *Vocational Selection through Industrial Education.*

1. Effective operation of dependent upon
   a) Determination of the extent of industrial *demand* and *supply* of individuals.
   b) Determination of the *quality* of the demand of specific industrial capacities and interest.
   c) Determination of supply of actual and potential individual possession of specific industrial capacities and interests.
2. Character of the industrial capacities and interests.
3. The public school as an instrument for "industrial determination;" the extent of necessary reorganization so as to *prevent* positive mis-selection.

IV. *The Significance of Vocational Selection for the Maintenance of the Educational Equilibrium.*

Outline of Paper by James F. McElroy, Albany, N. Y., on the Subject of "The Most Urgent Need of Our Educational System is an Adequate Provision for the Vocational Needs of Children Destined for Industrial and Domestic Pursuits."

GENERAL PROPOSITION

1 Our public schools do not furnish to the boys and girls, destined to perform their life work in our industries, the education they require.

2. The course of study in our schools is based upon the theory that the student will continue throughout the entire course and graduate at the high school, and this course is designed to prepare the student for admission to colleges.

3. This plan is unjust, unfair, and unreasonable, so far as it relates to over 60 per cent. of the students who enter our grammar schools.

4. After inquiry concerning one hundred mechanics, I have not found one that is a graduate from the high school or even from the grammar school. These men all left school before completing their grammar school course to take up the work of learning a trade.

5. The object of education is to give students the best preparation for their life work and to give them such an education as will be conducive to their happiness and well-being.

6. The crying need of our schools is that they shall give to the laboring class an entirely different kind of instruction and something better suited to their needs.

7. The manual-training high schools do not meet this requirement, because, (1) students must enter upon their life work in the industries before such a course in the high school can be completed; (2) as a rule, young men are not financially able to complete the manual-training high-school course; (3) the work of the manual-training high school fits young men better for foreman than for positions as mechanics.

8. The technical schools do not supply the demand, because graduates of technical schools will not work in factories at $3.00 to $3.50 per day, nor will their technical efficiency in shop work compare with those who have been trained outside of the technical schools. As a rule, the technical graduate seeks work that is less arduous and that demands bigger pay.

9. Trade schools do not exactly meet the requirements, because, (1) a boy enters a trade school before he has sufficient knowledge of mechanics and sufficient experience in the world to know what trade he ought to enter, or what kind of work he is best able to perform; (2) a trade school is narrowing, limiting the student to the work of a particular trade. This is especially objectionable because of the division of labor made necessary by modern industrial methods which still further limits his experience to particular operations in manufacturing.

10. Our great educational need is to provide for the 60 per cent. of our grammar-school enrolment that now drops out before the grammar-school course is completed. This can best be done by the establishment of industrial schools *where a student can get a working knowledge of several trades,* because, (1) a knowledge of several trades broadens the knowledge and experience of men and makes them more efficient; (2) No knowledge of a machinist is complete without knowledge of the trade of the blacksmith who forges the material upon which the machinist works, or the patternmaker and the foundryman who prepares the castings upon which the machinist works; (3) A knowledge of several trades gives men a wider experience and fits them for positions of leaders and foremen to look after men performing several kinds of work; (4) With a knowledge of several trades, he can then enter any one of the several trades which offers him the opportunity he seeks for employment; (5) Such knowledge also enables him to adapt himself to the line of work for which he finds he is best qualified by natural ability and by education; (6) It enables him to take up work in a trade where labor is scarce when labor may be too abundant in the line in which he was educated in case his education was confined to a trade school; (7) The best and most efficient mechanic is the all 'round mechanic who understands all of the processes entering into the line of manufacturing and studies his own trade in connection with the processes which precede and which follow the line of work in which he is engaged; (8) A working knowledge of a number of trades is important, because the modern tendency is to classification of labor, to systematizing and to confining men to one class of work. This comes as a

result of modern methods of manufacturing. If he is to acquire a broad knowledge of mechanics, he cannot get that broad knowledge in our large industries, but he there becomes only a part of a large working machine whose work is to turn out a certain product. In our modern industries a man never works at all parts of a trade, but works on the shaper or the lathe, or the milling machine, or some other machine, performing a small part of the total work on any piece of material; (9) A working knowledge of several trades makes a man broad-minded, makes him more intelligent, and makes him able to estimate the value of the work performed by others. It also helps the employer because he is enabled to shift his men to bring up a certain part of the work of a factory when that part falls behind.

11. It is impracticable and unreasonable to expect the manufacturer with a more or less changing list of employees to carry on a system of instruction of apprentices. A young man cannot be bound to a manufacturer for a certain number of years of service as in the old apprentice system. He leaves the employ of the maufacturer at will and if he has gained a good knowledge of mechanics and has become a good machinist, he readily gets employment elsewhere at good wages. Furthermore, the manufacturer cannot afford to establish schools for educating workmen.

12. This work should be done in connection with our grammar schools and the industrial schools should receive the boys that now leave the grammar schools in order to learn something "practical." These schools should have the air of the shop. They should be places where things are done. Work on machines should be accompanied by work in making mechanical drawings. They should also have instruction in the sciences which pertain to the particular trades which are taught.

SYMPOSIUM: *THE PLACE OF INDUSTRIES IN PUBLIC EDUCATION*

PROPOSITION 4*b*. INTERMEDIATE INDUSTRIAL SCHOOLS

(*Extract from letter of Chas. F. Morse.*)

. . . . In regard to the remarks which I shall make at Washington, I will say that it is my opinion that this country cannot adopt a system which is in vogue in other countries of having industrial schools for certain classes of people and culture schools for other classes; that industrial education, as I understand the term, should not be undertaken with pupils under 14 years of age, and then should be a question of election with parents and pupils, with assistance in choice rendered by teachers who have given serious consideration to the question.

I believe heartily in manual training from the kindergarten through the grammar and high-school courses.

In my opinion, to attempt industrial education in cultural schools can only result in an injury to the cause of industrial education; that for the smaller communities a school for several towns, with a vocational motive, would be desirable. In the larger towns we should continue to have the cultural school, the manual-training school, and parallel with these an industrial school. . . . . The principals of the high schools of the state . . . . are almost unanimous in the opinion that trades cannot be taught successfully in existing high schools and that the work should be done in independent schools.

SYMPOSIUM: *THE PLACE OF INDUSTRIES IN PUBLIC EDUCATION*

PROPOSITION 4*c*. TECHNICAL HIGH SCHOOLS FOR THE EDUCATION OF INDUSTRIAL LEADERS—GEORGE H. MARTIN

1. Avowedly vocational purpose will exclude general courses; industrial character will exclude college preparatory courses.

2. May be commercial, agricultural, mechanical, or polytechnic.

3. The age of pupils, length of courses, and entrance requirements should correspond with high schools of other sorts.

4. Threefold work: (1) to furnish technical knowledge and skill; (2) to promote intelligence and culture; (3) to develop a sense of civic obligation.

5. For first purpose there should be appropriate drawing, mathematics, and science; also shop practice under shop-trained instructors producing salable commercial product.

6. For the other purposes the course should include history, economics, civics, physical training, English, vocal and instrumental music.

7. No attempt has been made to indicate the sequence of studies, time distribution, or mode of administration, financing, and governmental relations of the school.

8. There has been no thought of throwing away the existing high school nor of substituting a technical high school for it.

The only definite conclusions reached were that the public school with its present organization is inadequate, and that industrial education has a legitimate place in the course of study, somewhere; just where, however, was not decided. Some thought in the elementary school, others, at the close of the elementary school, and still others, in a separate continuation school. With a view toward making a definite recommendation the subject was carried over to the July meeting of the N. E. A., there to be brought up for further discussion.

One of the most valuable contributions to the general discussion was the address of welcome given by President Roosevelt in the East room of the White House. The *Washington Post* gave the speech in full as it is here reproduced:

SPEECH OF THE PRESIDENT

Gentlemen and ladies: Of all the bodies of citizens that I have received here at the White House, there is none which occupies a more important relation than yours. I am tempted to say none has come that has occupied as important a relation to the nation, because you men and women who deal with education, who represent the great American policy of education for all children, provided by the public as the prime duty of the public, bear a relation to the family, a relation to the future of our whole people, such as no other like number of individuals can bear. I own six of the children that you educate, and I am prepared to extend cordial sympathy to some of you.

Seriously, friends, it is idle for any man to talk of despairing of the future of this country, or feeling unduly alarmed about it, if he will come in contact with you here, and with the forces that you represent. Fundamentally this country is sound morally, no less than physically. Fundamentally, in its family life, and in the outside activities of its individuals, the country is better, and not worse, than it formerly was. This does not mean that we are to be excused if we fail to war against rottenness and corruption; if we fail to contend effectively with the forces of evil; and they waste their time who ask me to withhold my hand from dealing therewith. But it is worth while to smite the wrong for the very reason that we are confident that the right will ultimately prevail. You who are training the next generation, are training this country as it is to be a decade or two hence; and, while your work in training the intellect is great, it is not as great as your work in training character. More than anything else, I want to see the public school turn out the boy and the girl who, when man and woman, will add to the sum of good citizenship of the nation. It is not my province, nor would it be within my capacity, to speak about your pedagogic problems. You yourselves are far better able to discuss them. But, as a layman, let me say one or two things about your work.

In the first place, I trust that, more and more, our people will see to it that the schools train toward and not away from the farm and the workshop. We have spoken a great deal about the dignity of labor in this country, but we have not acted up to our spoken words, for in our education we have tended to proceed upon the assumption that the educated man was to be educated away from and not toward labor. The great nations of mediaeval times who left such marvelous works of architecture and art behind them were able to do so because they educated alike the brain and the hand of the craftsman. We, too, in our turn, must show that we understand the law which decrees that a people which loses physical address invariably deteriorates, so that our people shall understand that the good carpenter, the good blacksmith, the good mechanic, the good farmer, really do fill the most important positions in our land, and that it is an evil thing for them and for the nation to have their sons and daughters forsake the work which, if well and efficiently performed, means more than any other work for our people as a whole One thing that I would like to have you teach your pupils is that, whether you call the money gained salary or wages does not make any real difference, and that if, by working hard with your hands, you get more than if you work with your head only, it does not atone for it to call the smaller amount salary.

The term, "dignity of labor" implies that manual labor is as dignified as mental labor; as of course it is. Indeed the highest kind of labor is that which makes demands upon the qualities of both head and hand, of heart, brain, and body. Physical prowess, physical address, are necessities; they stand on a level with intellect, and only below character. Let us show that we regard the position of the man who works with his hands as being ordinarily and in good faith as important and dignified and as worthy of consideration as that of business men or professional men. We need to have a certain readjustment of values in this country, which must primarily come through the efforts of just you men and women here, and the men and women like you throughout this land.

I would not have you preach an impossible ideal; for if you preach an ideal that is impossible you tend to make your pupils believe that no ideals are possible, and therefore, you tend to do them that worst of wrongs—to teach them to divorce preaching from practice, to divorce the ideal that they in the abstract admire from the practical good after which they strive. Teach the boy and girl that their business is to earn their own livelihood; teach the boy that he is be the homemaker; the girl that she must ultimately be the homekeeper; that the work of the father is to be the bread winner, and that of the mother the housekeeper; that their work is the most important work by far in all the land; that the work of the statesman, the writer, the captain of industry, and all the rest, is conditioned; first, upon the work that finds its expression in the family, that supports the family. So teach the boy that he is to be expected to earn his own livelihood; that it is a shame and scandal for him not to be self-dependent, not to be able to hold his own in the rough work of actual life. Teach the girl that so far from its being her duty to try to avoid all labor, all effort, that it should be a matter of pride to her to be as good a housewife as her mother was before her.

The effort should be made to teach everyone that the first requisite of good citizenship is doing the duties that are near at hand. But, of course, this does not excuse a man from doing the other duties, too. It is no excuse if a man neglects his political duties to say that he is a good husband and father, still less is it an excuse if he is guilty of corruption in politics or business to say that his home life is all right. He ought to add to decency in home life, decency in politics, decency in public life.

So my plea is not that the homely duties are all sufficient, but that they are a necessary base upon which to build the superstructure of the higher life. Our children should be trained to do the homely duties in the first place, and then, in addition, to have it in them so to carry themselves that collectively we may well and fitly perform the great and responsible tasks of American citizenship.

Superintendent Lucy Whipple of Pierce County, N. D., has consolidated the ninety-nine schools of that county into one, with a large new building. The pupils are carried by team, and in case of heavy storms can remain for a day or two in the building, living on canned goods and crackers.

Teachers in Vienna are following the American example in demanding more pay. Under the present system, says the New England *Journal of Education*, they may receive, after six years' service, the munificent salary of $360 a year. After six years more they are promoted to $520, and after thirty-five years may hope, if everything goes well, for $840 a year.

According to the New York State official report, 82 per cent. of the juvenile offenders have been in the last year appreciably benefited by the probation system. The old practice of sending the boys of the tenements to prison for offenses which country boys and even college men commit as a joke and consider the expression of animal spirits, is bound to pass sooner or later.

For five years, according to the *Journal of Education,* there has been but one case in Franklin, Ind., in which a contagious disease made the closing of a classroom necessary. On this occasion the school was closed because of the one case, and there was no further spread of the disease. These results have been accomplished by the heroic measure of a weekly fumigation of school buildings.

A plea for humor in the schoolroom is made by Superintendent Bevins in the North Carolina *Journal of Education*. Humor there will always be, he contends, and unless the teacher shares it and directs it, it will be directed against him in the form of practical jokes and ridicule. By humor he means to cover rather broadly everything that makes for a spirit of naturalness and relaxation in the schoolroom.

The Salem Normal School, Salem, Mass., has obtained good results with one year of school gardening, in spite of very adverse conditions in the way of soil and situation. The second grade had a flower garden; the three highest grades, a vegetable garden. Closer touch with nature, acquaintance with outdoor work and with many facts of food-production and a pleasanter social relation between pupils and teachers are among the results recorded in Miss Learoyd's article in the *Journal of Education.*

Hannibal, Mo., has been combining geography, history, and several other less well-defined subjects in a concrete study of textiles. The incentive seems to have come from an article in the Chicago *Rcord-Herald,* of last August, describing some mills of Fall River, Mass. Managers of many mills were written to, and were found quite willing to furnish samples of their particular goods at the various stages of its manufacture. With this as a beginning, the subject naturally carried the children into the consideration of markets, transportation, and geographical relations in general.

Since 1842, there have been few marked changes in the public-school system of Pennsylvania, says T. B. Noss in an article in the *Journal of Education.* Improvements in practical working have been made, but the organic features of the system have been but slightly altered. The beginning of a forward movement was made by the appointment last year of an educational commission to collate all the school laws and to prepare new bills. It is hoped that the results of this commission will mark a distinct advance in American public-school education.

Amusing examples of foreign influence on the spelling of school children in New York City is given in the *Educational Review* for February, by Julia Richman. The words were selected at random from classes of immigrants. "Kitchen" was spelled in seventeen different ways in a class of twenty-four, the ways ranging from "cichan" to "citjhen." Miss Richman makes a classification of difficulties and urges that many of them are due, not only to the characteristics of the students' native tongue, but to inherent inconsistencies of the English language. She makes a strong appeal for spelling reform.

Rising interest in school-music was shown by the creation last January in Chelsea, Mass., of a municipal music commission. Concerts are to be given frequently in the school halls in all sections of the city. In the primary schools, says the *Journal of Education,* a plan is being started for the study of the lives of great composers with musical illustrations adapted to the appreciation of the youngest children. In the grammar schools a system of glee clubs is begun, directed by one of the teachers. Members of these clubs progress gradually through the High School Glee Club to the choral club of the city.

Midland Schools contains a symposium of over forty superintendents and presidents of schools giving suggestions for the new School Law Commission in Iowa. Apparently the commission will not lack material for consideration. Compulsory closing of schools where the enrolment is excessively small is one of the measures frequently recommended; and connected with it is the demand for larger and more efficient consolidated schools in the rural districts. The lawful election of school superintendents for a longer period than one year is another reform asked by many. Questions of salary also receive the usual amount of attention.

The *New England Magazine* contains an article by Professor Warren on the advancement of the appreciation of art by means of the schools. He deplores the tendency in education to force a merely practical and utilitarian training into the schools. "Most children are naturally sensitive to the simpler kind of beauty. But criticism and analysis are repellant and so harmful." "The child's immediate surroundings in the schoolroom should be beautiful." The love of flowers and gardens should be cultivated, also the sense of order. Drawing lessons should aim at concreteness—and should develop accuracy of observation. But Professor Warren thinks that art museums are not especially valuable for the younger children.

BOOK REVIEWS

Moral Training in the Public Schools. Five Essays by CHARLES RUGH, T. P. STEVENSON, EDWIN D. STARBUCK, FRANK CRAMER, GEORGE E. MEYERS. Boston: Ginn & Co., 1907. 12mo, cloth, pp. 208.

Educational science is confronted with no more difficult or more important problem than that of moral training in the public schools. The reason why so much that is irrelevant and impractical has been said upon the subject is, that science has not settled in any definite and authoritative way what the determining forces of conduct are nor to what extent and by what means these forces can be generated or controlled by the conscious processes of education. The results of experience and experiment are no less vague and unsatisfactory than the pronouncements of science. The educational practitioner may therefore be excused if he is more or less at sea.

"If to do were as easy as to know what were good to do," our course would be plain. It is easy to teach creeds and catechisms; it is easy to teach the ten commandments and all the prohibitions and injunctions of the sternest moral code. But though "the brain may devise laws for the blood, yet a hot temper leaps o'er a cold decree." We may envy the simple faith of those who believe that he who knows what is right and *our* reasons for thinking it right will practice the right, but when we interrogate science and human experience for a justification of that faith we are disappointed. Since there is no exact method of determining the moral efficiency of the public schools, that efficiency is naturally underrated by those who are appalled by what they conceive to be the increasing if not unparalleled immorality of their day and generation. On the other hand, those who have faith in the character forming power of dogmatic instruction on morals are quick to devise a system of instruction which they think will be a panacea for all our social, political, and industrial ailments. Since there have long been schools in which formal instruction in religion and morals has had a regular place on the daily programme, and since in every city of the United States there are today schools in which the same formal teaching occurs, it seems that an examination of the results of such schools might be made in accordance with scientific methods. If the pupils of these schools are found to be more manly and womanly than the pupils of the public schools, more chaste in speech and thought, more respectful to their parents, more fervent in business, stronger to resist temptation, more faithful to their employers, more strictly law abiding, the case for dogmatic instruction in religion and morals would be at least half won. In the absence of such results established by thorough investigation, skepticism in regard to the efficacy of following the young about with "a movable pulpit" has grown apace. And yet we may be nearer salvation than when we believed. This skepticism forces the students of educational science to a profounder study of these questions: Whence cometh character? What are the limitations of the school's responsibilities? By what means can they perform their whole duty in the training of "exemplary citizens?"

The conditions under which the public schools work may well allay the ecstacy of our enthusiasm in regard to the magnitude and speed of results to be achieved by any system of moral training. That the public schools reach no children until the home and the street have wrought upon their inherited instincts for five years, that it loses one-half of them by the time they are twelve years old, and three-fourths of them by the time they are fourteen years old, that it has them not to exceed five hours out of the twenty-four, and only for five days in the week, and that they bring into the school the spirit of their outside environment, should temper our enthusiasm with sober caution.

Such are the reflections evoked by the little book under discussion. The controversial spirit is encouragingly absent from it: "Two things," says the author of the fourth essay, "have been permanently settled by the American people; the children of the nation shall be educated in the public schools, and religious instruction shall not be given in those schools." For the most part the authors of these essays accept as a postulate, that "adjustment to persons is the heart of morality," and as far as they seek sanctions for the moral code they find them in the inexorable necessity of our social organization.

The reading of these essays seems to force upon us these conclusions: (1) That the personality of the teacher is the controlling factor in any solution of the problem they discuss; (2) That antecedent to any considerable improvement in results we must have a greater proportion of more mature and professionally trained teachers; (3) That in this professional training must be included a broad discussion of the subject of moral training in the public schools; (4) That textbooks for teachers, not for pupils, must be provided in order that there may be available, suitable and systematically arranged material; (5) That our work must be as systematic in this subject as in others, though at any cost it must be divested of that formal, spiritless, wooden character, which in the opinion of competent judges has often rendered moral instruction futile if not harmful; (6) That when all is said success depends in this, as in other subjects, upon the intelligence, tact, earnestness, and personal character of the teacher.

The essays, especially the first, abound in definite practical suggestions. Among the most valuable of these suggestions are those on pp. 39 to 49, which treat of "Punishment, and the Reformation of the Wrongdoer." On the whole, sound, sane, suggestive, instructive, inspiring, seem to the reviewer the adjectives that most fitly describe this little book. It is worthy the attention of teachers.

CHESTER T. LANE

FORT WAYNE HIGH SCHOOL

The Later Cave-Men. By KATHARINE E. DOPP. Chicago: Rand, McNally & Co.

This book is the third in a series whose full significance it is hard to estimate. *The Tree-Dwellers* and *The Early Cave-Men* were pioneer works—new educational tools in fact, and in our devotion to books made in the form of those we have been long accustomed to, it is not strange that every teacher does not know how to use this new resource at once. On the other hand to many who realize that schooling is primarily a matter of doing and thinking rather than of mechanical adjustment, this organization of material has proved to be of real service.

The transition to more connected discourse in the present volume has been well made. One misses the more dramatic effect of *The Tree-Dwellers*, but the new story holds the attention and both children and adults are found to be unwilling to lay it down until they get through the "next chapter." It will take time for the point of view here represented to lead in schools, and other types of material will need to be employed in the same way that has been used here. In the meantime it is interesting to notice the appeal that the books are making to children on their own merits, quite apart from school use. They seem also to have a function for older pupils; for instance, in one of the leading settlements they were found to be well adapted for club work and in a technical school after the first show of resentment against "baby books," the girls came through them to an appreciative study of industrial problems. A very capable modern-language teacher in Europe is planning to use them as English reading material for German and French children—the combination of simple vocabulary and construction with interesting, instructive, and substantial thought material would seem to promise success in this undertaking as well. In our search for means of moral instruction the natural development shown through invention and general increase of control would seem of much greater value than the direct application methods or such lessons as Mr. Thompson-Seton's *Natural History of the Ten Commandments.*

FRANK A. MANNY

Examining and Grading Grains. By THOMAS LYTTLETON LYON, PH.D., and EDWARD GERRARD MONTGOMERY, B.S.C. Chicago: Ginn & Co., 1907. Illustrated. Pp. 101. $0.60.

This book is a laboratory manual, including a series of exercises in field crops, to be used by students in agricultural colleges. Careful studies are made of wheat, corn, oats, barley, hay plants, with a chapter on seed-testing. A classification of the species of each crop is given with a detailed study of the characters used in testing, grading, and judging the crop commercially. Some attention is also given to variations in treatment for common diseases.

No attempt has been made to discuss the methods of teaching, but the authors have prepared a separate pamphlet containing many practical suggestions on collecting materials and teaching which can be had from the publishers.

SCHOOL OF EDUCATION
Chicago

BERTHA CHAPMAN

The Ifs of History.. By JOSEPH EDGAR CHAMBERLAIN. Philadelphia: Henry Altemus Company, 1907. Pp. 203.

This attractive volume will doubtless prove particularly welcome to those educators who believe in "training along the lines of least resistance." It is much easier for the pupil to guess at what might have happened than to attempt seriously to find out what actually did happen. The work is written in an entertaining style. That he may arrive at the proper dramatic climax the author does not confine himself to simple facts in his statement of historical conditions. It would be wearisome, and would spoil the romantic flavor of the book, to point out all the technical inaccuracies in the different chapters. The author writes with a charming disregard of all probabilities, and limits his speculations by possibilities only.

S. E. THOMAS

CHARLESTON, ILL.

Introductory Sight-Singing Melodies. By E. W. NEWTON. Boston: Ginn & Co.

This little book of forty-two pages contains exercises and short songs for use in the earlier grades. The exercises are graded much as usual and present no striking feature. The novelty and worth of the book lie in the exercise songs which form a welcome contribution to the musical literature for primary work.

Since the value of the school song is primarily cultural, its choice should not be restricted by the technical problems its presents, and to tear apart a lovely and beloved rote-song to find a phrase suitable for notation and reading, is often to rob it of its charm. Few of the primary songs given as sight-reading material possess enough musical worth to render them worthy of laborious study,, while drill on barren exercises degenerates into drudgery. Wide-awake teachers, therefore, have been searching for suitable material apart from the fine rote song, and have been using devices of alteration and composition—both usually dangerous—to meet the need. In this little volume appears a generous supply of the very material desired. The songs show an experienced touch and are set to sensible and charming texts. They are four or eight measures in length, are carefully phrased, and run through the nine common keys. A few are so written that two melodies with the same text may be sung together, forming a two-part song suitable for use in third-grade work. Problems of $\frac{2}{4}$, $\frac{4}{4}$, $\frac{3}{4}$, and $\frac{3}{8}$ measure are taken up and consecutive or frequent intervals used. Further enhanced by a good piano accompaniment, these tiny songs should delight the children.

M. R. K.

Larger Types of American Geography. By CHARLES A. MCMURRY, PH.D. The Macmillan Company, 1907. Pp. vii+271. $0.75 net.

This is the third of a series of geographical readers, and is intended for children of the seventh and eighth grades. Eight important geographical types are presented: the Appalachian Mountains, the Rocky Mountains, the Pennsylvania Railroad, the first Pacific railroad, the Mississippi River, the iron and steel business, cotton mills and cotton manufacture, and New York City.

The purpose is to show, in a simple way, the causal relation between physical and industrial and social conditions. The treatment of each topic is careful and scientific; the chapters are interesting and suggestive; and as a supplementary reader, the book ought to be of the greatest help in giving to children something of the spirit and meaning of geography. H. G.

From Trail to Railway Through the Appalachians. By ALBERT PERRY BRIGHAM, A.M. Boston: Ginn & Co., 1907. Pp. 188. $0.50.

To understand and appreciate the changes that have taken place since the buffalo traces and Indian trails were the only paths by which to travel toward the west, is to understand the best part of American history. *From Trail to Railway* makes their appreciation possible for boys of the seventh and eighth grades.

The maps are excellent, showing the topography clearly. The pictures are well chosen. Of special interest are the chapters on "The Erie Canal," "The National Road," "The Great Valley," and "To Kentucky by Cumberland Gap."

M. L.

BOOKS RECEIVED

AMERICAN BOOK COMPANY, NEW YORK

Plane and Solid Geometry. By EDWARD RUTLEDGE ROBBINS. Cloth. Pp. 412. $1.25.

Outline for Review in English History. By CHARLES BERTRAM NEWTON AND EDWIN BRYANT TREAT. Cloth. Pp. 76. $0.25.

Selections from Irving's Sketch-Book. (Gateway Series.) Edited by MARTIN W. SAMPSON. Cloth. Pp. 315. $0.45.

The Autobiography of Benjamin Franklin. (Gateway Series.) Edited by ALBERT HENRY SMITH. Cloth. Pp. 287. $0.40.

Spanish Prose Composition. By G. W. UMPHREY. Cloth. Pp. 174.

Elementary Algebra. By FREDERICK H. SOMERVILLE. Half leather, 12mo. Pp. 407. $1.00.

A Reader of French Pronunciation. By JULIUS TUCKERMAN. Cloth, 12mo. Pp. 128. $0.50.

Laboratory Lessons in Physical Geography. By L. L. EVERLY, R. E. BLOUNT, and C. L. WALTON. Manila, 4to. With maps and illustrations. Pp. 246. $0.56.

GINN AND COMPANY, CHICAGO

Fairy Tales—Vol. I. (The Open Road Library of Juvenile Literature.) Compiled and edited by MARION FLORENCE LANSING. Cloth. Illustrated. Pp. 179.

THE MACMILLAN COMPANY, NEW YORK

Selected Poems of Robert Burns. Edited by PHILO MELVYN BUCK. Cloth. Pp. 323. $0.25.

Spenser's Faerie Queene—Book I. Edited by GEORGE A. WAUCHOPE. Cloth. Pp. 294. $0.25.

Shakespeare's The Tempest. Edited by SIDNEY C. NEWSOM. Cloth. Pp. 152. $0.25.

Methods in Teaching. (Being the Stockton Methods in Elementary Schools.) By ROSA V. WINTERBURN. Including a chapter on "Nature-Study" by EDWARD HUGHES. Cloth. Pp. 355. $1.25.

Graphic Algebra. By ARTHUR SCHULTZE. Cloth. Pp. 93. $0.80.

HOUGHTON, MIFFLIN & COMPANY, BOSTON

The Beginner's Primer. Cloth. Illustrated. Pp. 126. $0.25.

The Bailey-Manly Spelling Book. By ELIZA R. BAILEY AND JOHN M. MANLY. Cloth. Pp. 154. $0.30.

LITTLE, BROWN, AND COMPANY, BOSTON

The Wide Awake Second Reader. By CLARA MURRAY. Cloth. Illustrated. Pp. 191.

HENRY ALTEMUS COMPANY, PHILADELPHIA

The Ifs of History. By JOSEPH EDGAR CHAMBERLIN. Cloth. Pp. 203.
The Boy Geologist. By E. J. HOUSTON. Cloth. Illustrated. Pp. 320. $1.00.

GOVERNMENT PRINTING OFFICE, WASHINGTON

Bureau of Education Bulletin No. 3, 1907, Whole No. 376: The Auxiliary Schools of Germany. Six Lectures by B. MAENNEL, translated into English by FLETCHER BASCOM DRESSLAR. Pp. 137.

THE KINDERGARTEN MAGAZINE COMPANY

A Baker's Dozen for City Children. (Kindergarten Songs.) Music by ISABEL VALENTINE; words by LILEON CLAXTON. Linen cover. Pp. 16. $0.50.

THE UNIVERSITY OF CHICAGO PRESS

The Seventh Yearbook of the National Society for the Scientific Study of Education, Part I: The Relation of Superintendents and Principals to the Training and Professional Improvement of Their Teachers. By CHARLES D. LOWRY. Paper. Pp. 78. $0.78.

EDUCATIONAL PUBLISHING COMPANY, BOSTON

Studies and Observations in the School-Room. By HENRY ELTON KRATZ. Cloth. Pp. 224. $0.80.

GOVERNMENT PRINTING OFFICE, WASHINGTON

Report of the Commissioner of Education for the Year Ending June 30, 1906; Vol. II. Cloth. Pp. 664.

CARNEGIE LIBRARY, PITTSBURGH

Catalogue of Books Annotated and Arranged and Provided by the Carnegie Library of Pittsburgh for the Use of the First Eight Grades in the Pittsburgh Schools. Paper. Pp. 331.

A CLASS IN METAL–WORKING

VOLUME VIII NUMBER 9

THE ELEMENTARY SCHOOL TEACHER

MAY, 1908

THE COURSE OF STUDY OF THE UNIVERSITY ELEMENTARY SCHOOL

The University Elementary School for several years has been making an experiment toward the solution of those problems of the school which are the outgrowth of the new conceptions of the nature of mental growth and of the changed conditions of modern social life. It presents its course of study for next year in a form which it is hoped will suggest the conclusions so far reached in its efforts.

The subject-matter is arranged by departments instead of by grades, to show as clearly as possible the development of the industrial arts and of the older subjects of study, and the relation that should exist between these two kinds of work in a unified curriculum. Just at present the interest taken in industrial education by business men and manufacturers is forcing upon the schools of the country in general the consideration of the ends to be attained by such training. There is a demand for education that gives pupils assistance toward the greatest efficiency in the industrial and social life upon which they will enter after leaving school. A feeling exists that much of our school work is not directed consciously toward such efficiency. There are suggestions which tend to change our grade schools into trade schools, where the child may learn directly something of the work in which he will become engaged later. While specific training looking toward particular occupations would be to throw upon the child before he is able to bear it the burden of the economic struggle and would be undesirable, still the impulse that comes from vital contact with the things which concern the outside life is necessary to putting forth the best efforts in study.

In the course of study here given the attempt is made to show that social efficiency is the aim of all the work.

Children live among surroundings which are so limited and one-sided that they afford but few experiences which tend to relate them consciously to the larger social organism. This is true of the favored minority as well as of the large percentage who must enter some highly specialized bread-winning occupation at the earliest age limit. Here is a constant tendency to build up class distinctions and to disintegrate a social organism, the very existence of which depends upon a consciousness of mutual contribution and therefore mutual dependence.

It seems not to be overstating it, to say that the Elementary School has the grave responsibility of redeeming its youth from class isolation. This means that it must develop in the individual the greatest possible power to control environment. From the beginning to the end of these eight years the materials of knowledge must be arranged with reference first, to the child's ability to make the problems his own, and second, to his opportunity constantly to grow in power to order for himself the means by which he accomplishes a projected end.

The child's consciousness is vague and the interests through which he approaches the outside world are as unorganized as those of a primitive group. He reaches out from a few centers of experience—largely play—to a great unknown. The chasm between himself and the highly developed processes of modern life he cannot bridge by a flying leap.

The period is short. It necessitates economy. In the light of child-study there can be but little time for abstractions. Actual living, actual doing, must create conditions by which the dead tools of learning are made over into the live realities of experience. Economy places a premium upon the selection of processes which contain universal and typical values. This has never been ideally accomplished. Perhaps it never can be, owing to the difficulty in creating artificially problems that contain the element of reality which enlists the best efforts of students.

At the present time industrial education seems to come the nearest to reaching this end. On the side of government the organization of children in groups for the purpose of co-operative work and the development of necessary protective restrictions establishes in their minds the logical basis for all government. On the side of subject-matter and technique an industry such as pottery, textiles, metal, wood, or agriculture is so universal that it furnishes a point of contact with all phases of organized knowledge. Pottery and textiles, for example, represent the earliest efforts of man to utilize the materials of environment. In the weaving of a rush mat or the building of a "coiled" bowl the process of modification is but slight and depends upon no tool but the hand.

The discoveries and inventions that occur in the development of these crafts from the beginnings to the modern machine are milestones marking the progress of the race in control of environment. In their earliest stages they cannot be separated from the central activities which contribute to physical maintenance, yet mathematics, history, science, art, are bound up in this primitive industrial life. Proportionate to racial progress these various sides of control become more and more clearly defined to the point of the highly organized specialization of modern life. Consequently no one of these crafts can be followed without becoming in turn a problem in science, mathematics, history, or art.

Experience with these typical hand-processes must result (*a*) in an intelligent valuation of labor which is a basis of economic standards; (*b*) in the understanding of the qualities and limitations of materials, knowledge of which is fundamental to aesthetic and industrial ideals.

The social fabric is woven together by an intricate network of reactions between consumers and producers—a network in which not only utilitarian and aesthetic problems are involved. They become moral issues as well.

If we ever bring about a real social democracy, we must free the elementary schools of the demands of specialization, whether these come from the professions working back through the college and high school, whether they come from the commercial interests dictating certain expedients, or whether they come from the manufacturer who asks us to fit the prospective wage-earners more snugly into their future grooves.

What we want in the Elementary School is not a training which has in it the class or vocational idea, but a set of large social experiences which are equally valuable to the boy destined for the professions and to the one who will work at the bench.

In our school we try to select those activities which have universally contributed to the sum of human experience and which consequently may be used as a point of departure leading to the more abstract statements of knowledge which appear as mathematics, history, geography, nature-study, etc.

While these problems have their beginnings in concrete experiences, it is highly essential that they should emerge from this first unity and develop each in its own line. Just as physiologically the hand and eye attain most perfect co-ordinations only when each functions most distinctly, so the ultimate end of our curriculum must be the differentiation of the various subjects. Correlation will then be the act of the individual by which he relates the common elements in the ever-growing complexities of his experience. When he gains the power to do this, no matter how narrow his sphere of action, the youth will reach out from it and seek to relate himself to a larger whole.

ART WORK IN THE ELEMENTARY SCHOOL

The following is a general statement to show what subjects may advantageously be selected from the regular content of each grade from the standpoint of art; and what points of art content they bring to the child's experience.

Below the fifth grade power is developed almost unconsciously on the child's part. After the age of ten, however, his interest is very consciously active on the scientific side, and instead of merely accepting the instructions offered he discovers the things he does not know and is eager for help along these very definite lines.

While the subject-matter and technique are here stated separately, they do not so occur in the course of study. They represent but two phases of the same operation.

Subject-matter is analogous to the problem or individual end. Technique is the means of solution. Throughout the course fine examples of color and composition are used for reference as a guide and source of help to the children.

First Grade

Subjects for drawing, painting, and clay-modeling are chosen from the interests developed during the nature-study excursions; work in the cooking class; study of various forms of shelter and modes of living among peoples of primitive conditions; study of Eskimo and Indian collections at the Field Museum; observation of pet animals.

In this work the emphasis in technical control is, in Form, the recognition and representation of forms, such as sphere, ovoid, and cylinder, with modifications made so as to conform with natural objects differing but slightly from such general types; in Color, study of the spectrum, two intensities, three values; in Perspective, observation of the sky and ground and meaning of the horizon; in Composition, selection of dimensions for pictorial panel and its margin, and placing of important objects in the panel; in Design, unconscious exercising of the instinct for rhythm and order in simple arrangments of pattern.

Second Grade

Subjects for drawing, painting, and clay-modeling are chosen from interests developed during the nature-study excursions; the industrial excursions; the study of the "Story of Ab," the study of collections at the Field Museum; study of shepherd peoples; study of pet animals and flowers. The technique of the year includes, in Form, the recognition of types in more complex forms; in Color, further experience in the work begun in the first grade; in Perspective, the comparison of near and distant objects of the same size; in Composition, introduction of more subject elements, with their arrangement in the panel; in Design, rhythm in areas, in tone, and in color.

Third Grade

Subjects are chosen from work in history and literature of the Greeks and Vikings; from the geographic study of their typical environments; from the study of plant development, and the life-history of the butterfly; from the study of the landscape in winter, and spring flowers.

The technique includes in Form, closer visual analysis; in Color, three values and two intensities; in Perspective, exercises in memory and imaginative drawings; in Compositon, simple emphasis by means of areas differing in color values; in Design, development of the consciousness of rhythm and balance.

Fourth Grade (One Semester)

Subjects:

History

Landscape composition showing Chicago scene.

Geography—

Study of southern plant forms—sugar, rice, cotton, tobacco.

Nature-study—

Study of animal and bird forms.

Work with bulbs—in various stages of growth.

Literature—

Picture-study (fine example) in relation to fairy tales.

Illustration of story.

Metal-work—

Designs for bowls and other articles.

Technique—

Use of natural forms in pattern, and their adaptation to the limitations of certain materials.

Increased accuracy in visualizing.

Ability to see outlines.

More advanced knowledge of perspective.

Addition of two more values in dark and light.

Fifth Grade

Subjects:

History and Geography—

Illustration of "Landing of Pilgrims," supplemented by study of Howard Pyle's *Landing of Pilgrims.*

Study of colonial quilt, and blue and white china. Design for same.

Study of tobacco plant. Design for book-cover.

Landscape illustrating *Legends of Sleepy Hollow.*

Nature-study—

Out-door sketches of swamp in color. Seasonal changes.

Technique—

Complementary colors taught. Special emphasis on harmony of color.

Principles of composition as developed in textile designs.

Use of three values and two intensities in textile materials.

Perspective. Receding lateral and vertical planes bounded by parallel lines. Common examples in walls, streets, and rows of trees.

Sixth Grade (One Semester)

Subjects:

Nature-study—

Flowers in color.

Out-door sketches in color.

Paintings of fall fruits and vegetables.

Compositions of same for book-covers.

Thanksgiving subject—Landscape of sheaves of wheat.

History—

Study of Greek figures.

Illustration of portion of the *Iliad.*

Design for Greek pottery.

Excursions to Field Museum.

Technique—

Beginning art history—Greek.

Principles of design traced in historic Greek art.

Proportion and action of human figures to be used in composition.

Continuation of color-study.

Continuation of principles of perspective as given in preceding grades.

Seventh Grade

Subjects:

History and Geography—

Landscape illustrative of early western emigration.

Excursions to Field Museum. Sketches of South American animals.

Coloring of maps in unified tones.

Metal—

Designs for brass and copper articles.

Technique—

The technique of this grade holds little that is new. The effort is one to fix the points already made in the preceding grades; and establish firmly the child's hold on real art values.

Eighth Grade

The drawing and painting is the continuation of the decoration of the schoolroom. The subjects of the frieze decoration are characteristic conditions of life in the Middle Ages, this selection of subjects having been made owing to the history interests in the grade.

The work includes the study of photographs and lantern slides of early Italian mural decorations in the school picture collection and excursions to the Art Institute. The chief problem is the balancing of areas through distribution of harmonious color and tones.

In addition to the subjects mentioned in the various grades all the children of the school work on the Annual School Calendar which is designed, printed, and sold by them.

TEXTILES

The subject of Textiles in the Elementary School covers the study of clothing and household fabrics, and deals with them from the standpoints of economics, hygiene, history, geography, and design.

The object of the study is to give children experience in the textile arts of spinning, dyeing, weaving, basketry, and sewing, and so to relate that experience to lessons in history, geography, biography, and design as to give the subject its fullest educational value.

All work done is social in its character, that is, it is to fill genuine social need which is recognized and felt by the worker; it also is planned in such a way as to call for the exercise of the children's individual taste and initiative.

Regarding clothing and home-making as subjects of fundamental race importance, it is hoped through the years of continuously related training to give to the children skill and taste in the crafts; logical sense of textile arts as race activities; an appreciation of the work done in them, and an intelligent understanding of the workers who have wrought results in these arts.

Mats, rugs, carpets, and curtains are woven or stenciled by children of the first grade for their playhouse. Designing of these introduces problems of color, light and dark, proportion, and line. Cotton, wool, linen, and silk are studied as materials of clothing. Specimens of each are mounted with pictures of sources and processes, and labeled in written words and sentences learned for the purpose. As a means of awakening the minds of the children to the general subject of clothing, a series of lessons is given upon the clothing of animals, the function of coverings, and their adaptation to environment.

In the second and third grades mats and baskets for picnics and luncheons are made from primitive materials gathered in the home locality. In the making of these the greatest encouragement is given to originality and invention. The simplest form of loom is designed, and experiments in weaving are made. Wool and linen fibers are twisted into thread by means of primitive spindles, and the children are given lessons upon the clothing processes of such primitive peoples as the North American Indians, the Lake-dwellers of ancient Switzerland, and the Eskimos; also of the shepherds of Arabia, and later of the Norsemen and Ancient Greeks. Numbers, weights, measures, and arithmetical processes are taught in the use of dyeing and weaving materials.

The children of the fifth grade design a small pocket or belt, and weave it on a hand-frame invented and made by them with the knowledge gained from their second- and third-year's experiences. Weaving progresses to the point of making a rag rug. The materials used are dyed by the children with vegetable dyes. A special study is made of cotton and wool fibers. The history of the early American colonists and of the textile arts of their homes accompanies this work; also a study of the spinning-wheel and of the colonial loom.

The sixth grade is occupied in designing, making, and using stencils as textile decoration. They make pillows, scarfs, curtains, according to the choice of the individual child. Appliqué or simple embroidery is also used to carry out these designs. In connection with this work stories of mediaeval tapestries and ancient embroidery form part of the history of the Middle Ages.

In the seventh grade both boys and girls do some weaving on the Swedish loom, making scarfs or rag rugs, and learning to do both plain and pattern weaving. They design and carve wooden blocks for block-printing, and study clothing and the clothing industries by means of industrial excursions. They study the fabrics in common use, and learn something of manufacturing and trade conditions and of the development of the textile industries in the United States.

CLAY-MODELING

As a medium for art expression, clay seems ideal for children of the lower grades. It is easily manipulated and gives opportunity for free expression without involving the problem of perspective. It is, therefore, used in the first four grades as a medium for recording observations made in the field excursions and impressions of incidents in history and literature which especially appeal to the imagination. The aim is freedom of expression and the development of appreciation of form.

The clay-modeling of the upper grades is illustrative of the history and literature.

The making of pottery involves the study of applied design, the problems of shaping an object which shall serve the purpose for which it is made, of planning an ornament appropriate to the shape of the object decorated, and of arranging a harmonious color scheme for the object as a whole.

The serious study of pottery is not begun before the fourth grade. In this grade useful articles are made and decorated with the simplest ornament and glaze. Much of the material used in design is found in the field.

By the time the child has reached the sixth grade, a considerable amount of skill has been acquired and more difficult problems are attempted. The work of this grade centers about the study of Greek pottery. A red burning-clay is therefore used and a painted decoration.

In the seventh grade the children illustrate pioneer history. In pottery, they are restricted to such forms as are suitable for slip-decoration and to simple glazes.

The eighth-grade modeling is illustrative of the life of the Middle Ages. A part of the year is devoted to a study of pottery, involving a résumé of the processes studied in the lower grades and an outline of the history of ceramics.

DOMESTIC SCIENCE

Domestic Science in the Elementary School deals with problems of food and shelter which in the past and present have been chiefly related to life in the home. The social, technical, and scientific aspects of these industries are studied with an endeavor so to place the emphasis as to meet the psychological development of the child.

The subject aims to furnish means for expressing ideas, opportunities for self-direction and control, application for common scientific truth, training in co-ordination of mind and hand, and content and meaning in the common things of life. It seeks to foster such ability as will enable a child to perform home duties and tasks to better individual satisfaction, and enable him to take a place in the family life through being able to contribute to it.

In the lower grades the conection is most closely made with garden, number, and history; in the upper grades with science and hygiene. In the first grades one hour of cooking, a half-hour for written work, a half-hour for number or reading, are allowed per week; in the upper grades one and one-half hour for cooking and one hour for science.

First Grade

(One semester.) The work here furnishes largely an opportunity for "free play." It deals with simple home duties suggested by the season, special occasion, or the grade outline of work; washing and ironing of school aprons and dusters; cooking and serving of cereals, cocoa, sandwiches, toast, cranberry sauce, popcorn, cookies, candy; and the care and preparation of any garden product.

Second Grade

(One semester.) The cooking directly aids the history of that year through the use of primitive utensils in carrying out early cooking. Natural foods are gathered on excursions, primitive methods of fire-building are attempted—baking on heated stones; parching in baskets; broiling over the fire; and boiling by means of hot stones. All this is contrasted with present methods of preparation and a luncheon is given the mothers.

Primitive cooking: rice cakes, acorn bread; parched corn, boiled wild artichokes, broiled bacon and beef, roasted nuts.

Modern cooking: pickling beets from garden, jelly making, boiled potatoes, potato salad, cookies, sandwiches, and Christmas candy.

Third Grade

Cooking: drying of grapes; grape juice and jelly, preserved pumpkin; study of starch in vegetables, cooking of starchy vegetables; cream sauce, cream soups; strong and sweet-juiced vegetables; study of milk with cheese and butter making.

Science: experiments in evaporation to determine conditions influencing quantitative work in evaporation; effect of fruit skins on rate of evaporation; iodine test for starch, litmus for acid; classification of vegetables according to rough composition and part of plant used; rough determination of starch and water in a few vegetables; change of starch to sugar; density, from study of milk and cream; determination of amount of fat in milk.

Fifth Grade

Colonial cookery. Study of home industries. This period contrasted with present time.

Cooking: hominy, corn-pone, bake beans, brown bread, apple-butter, samp, doughnuts, pumpkin pies, baking powder and soda biscuits, and gingerbread.

THE SIXTH GRADE CHRISTMAS CANDY SALE

Science: Study of corn as colonial grain; early methods of preparation; samp making; use of germ, hull and starch in corn; wheat: graham and white flour; visit to mill; composition: use of starch, gluten, and bran. Experiments to show how flour holds a gas; soda and baking-powder as sources of gas; acid and alkali. Soap and candle making (see History outline).

Sixth Grade

Study of yeast, mould, and bacteria in relation to food; its preparation, preservation, and manufacture.

Canning, preserving, pickling of fruits; making butter, cheese; manufacture of cider and vinegar; making bread and biscuit and simple doughs and batters when CO_2 is obtained from some source other than fermentation; study of yeast, mould, and bacteria; conditions of growth, food, temperature, and moisture; observation under microscope; products of fermentation; acid and alkali (continued from fifth grade); gases in expansion; visit to bakery.

Seventh Grade

Study of different foods leading to a simple classification as, (1) carbohydrates, (2) fats, (3) proteids; temperature effects on each food; principle and work in cooking based on the composition of the food.

Cereals, cream sauce, croquettes, cream soups, corn starch desserts; egg cookery, custards, salad dressings, ice cream, divinity creams; fish and meat.

Study of heat: thermometer, Centigrade and Fahrenheit; cause of change in boiling-point; comparison of materials as conductors of heat; transmission of heat in solids and liquids; study of freezing temperature.

Food tests; iodine for starch, ether for fat, Millons for proteid, Fehling for sugar.

Eighth Grade

Study of the home, in its broad and varied aspects. Historical development of the house; selection of "site" for building, construction of basement, first and second floors, with special emphasis on kitchen, pantry, and dining-room arrangements; study of heating, lighting, plumbing, and ventilation; cleaning of surfaces; study of dirt and its relation to disease. Pure food supply and cooking where occasion lends itself. Much laboratory work is done and frequent excursions are made.

THE SCHOOL GARDEN

The work of the school garden is a part of the natural history work of the school. It presents opportunity for several important activities on the part of the children. It provides place for out-of-door, open-air work with the soil, with plants and animals. Part of the garden space is given to trees, shrubbery, roses, gooseberries, etc., these areas being, in a general way, the property of all the children, since all may take part in the care and enjoyment of them. Another part of the garden is reserved for plots in each of which an individual pupil may have ownership, opportunity, and responsibility relative to the things with which he works.

In the individual plot, the pupil plants such things as he may select from the list of possibilities offered him by his teacher. These things are planted according to a plan previously designed by the pupil. The pupils are encouraged to look upon the individual plot, and not the entire area, as the unit, and to make their plans accordingly. Some children arrange designs for flowering plants only, some for vegetables and other economic plants, and some for both. A wide variety of results is produced.

After the earth is spaded, the work is done by the pupils until the beginning of the vacation time, during which a caretaker must be employed. Some work is done in the garden by the children who are in school during the summer, and in the autumn all who had plots in the spring take up the work again. The opportunities, rights, and obligations of the owner of a plot are always kept prominent in the minds both of those who have and those who do not have individual gardens. Each pupil is entitled to enjoy, and to profit by the result of his own labor. He may have produced an attractive garden which may be visited and enjoyed by others. More diligent attention may result in his garden being prominent because of its excellence, or negligence may make it necessary to cite it as an illustration of failure to appreciate opportunity. The growth of some slightly known economic or decorative plant may make one garden the center of general interest. The flowers produced in one plot may justify all the work expended in growing them through the pleasure of giving them to a friend, or to some other worthy cause. The vegetables produced may serve to give an idea as to real values in agriculture.

The work of the garden offers an incomplete substitute to city children for the light work done by the children of the country. City children have less opportunity for developing through everyday experience the faithfulness to regularly recurring duties as found on the farm. If the garden is properly used it may help to meet this increasing need on the part of city children.

The garden is a center of many divergent lines of natural history interest. The winter in-door work with soil, climate, bulbplants, etc., is directly related to garden work. Much of the work in cooking is related to materials produced within the garden. Almost all animal life studies in one way or another are made fully significant by means of contact with animal life in the garden. It is hoped that the animal life aspects of the garden may be greatly extended. Many other activities of the school find their basis in illustration in the agricultural, climatic, industrial, and aesthetic experiences of the garden.

WOODWORKING

The work does not follow any of the well-known "systems" of manual training, but depends, rather, upon the plan of the grade. For instance, the work of the first grade centers about home life. Playhouses are made in the manual-training room. Each child furnishes his own playhouse, or helps in furnishing a group playhouse. The work in textiles lends itself to the making of rugs for the floors, and the lessons in drawing and painting are devoted to the designing of wall paper. Thus the different departments of the handicrafts co-operate with one another, and in so doing discover the kinship of their special subjects and develop the correlated plan.

It is through correlation as a medium that the handicrafts, instead of being presented formally as so many isolated subjects, really become to the child methods of easy and natural self-expression.

Another use of woodworking is the making of Christmas presents. The children are alert for this chance, and each autumn in all the grades the pupils select, design, and make with great care and great secrecy the presents to be given at Christmas.

Still another use of woodworking is the making of things

for the grade room, the school, the school grounds, or the children themselves. The work represents group or co-operative planning, and individual work.

If, however, the immediate needs of the school have been supplied, the children follow, under guidance, their own wishes in the choice of things to make.

In these years there are (*a*) freehand drawing for proportion and design; (*b*) reduction of these drawings to working-drawings; (*c*) blueprints of these mechanical drawings—gradually introduced according to the skill of the pupils.

All, in proportion to their development, study (*a*) the history of the growing tree; (*b*) the process of lumbering; (*c*) something of lumber physics; and (*d*) myths of trees.

Throughout the work there is growing emphasis on technique, with instruction concerning the care of wood, finishing, the mixing of stains, and polishing.

Second Grade

The children make industrial trips and in previous years have built toy reproductions of some of the places visited. They work in groups, making a grocery, bakery, milk depot, grain elevator, freight depot, dock, boats, trains, and bridges. The grocery is approximately three feet square by two and a half feet high, and the others are built in proportion. This year, there is to be no woodwork in this grade, cooking and textiles taking its place.

Third Grade

Making boats and freight cars (see history for third grade). Construction of portfolios—an exercise valuable not only for the concrete result, but also for the careful measurements involved. As a natural sequence may follow library fittings, such as penholders, trays, paper-knives, desk-boxes, blotting-pads, and paper-files. These are the personal property of the children who make them, and may be taken home or donated to the school for use. The tools involved in the construction of these articles are the plane, ruler, try-square, saw, hammer, gauge and mallet, bit and brace, spoke-shave, and file. The children are expected to have acquired a fair degree of skill in the use of tools previous to this year, and the articles are designed with reference to the increasing power of technique on the part of the child.

Fourth Grade

(1) Desk-boxes, fern-stands, doll furniture, etc., for Christmas presents, made in hardwood, in which the child meets the same problems as in previous years; (2) various articles needed by the school. Study of lumbering.

Fifth Grade

Study of the characteristics of the Dutch house and furniture. Excursions to furniture shops for the purpose of identifying such furniture. Illustrative articles made in the manual training room. Simple mechanical drawings made by the class. The children also work out individual problems.

Sixth Grade

The study of colonial history suggests the opportunity of making a brief study of colonial furniture. Its chief features are taken up: (*a*) the principal articles of furniture in a colonial house; (*b*) the kinds of wood used; (*c*) the characteristics of the "colonial style." An excursion is made to a leading furniture store for the purpose of further illustration and identification of colonial furniture. It is hoped that in some of the articles which the children make for the school room, or the school or for their own use, it will be possible to carry out simple outlines and designs suggested by this study.

Freehand sketches for outline and proportion precede the making of all articles in wood. These are followed by a working or mechanical drawing. A few blueprints are made by the children of those designs which the class, as a whole, considers the best.

Seventh Grade

Method: working-drawing for each construction; a careful study of plans and principles involved. Articles made for use in home or school, the pupil given a choice when practicable.

The class designs electrical machines and apparatus (see "Natural History"), demanding part of the construction in wood. Some pupils will make motor boats, others, articles of interest growing out of the science work.

A study of the history and distribution of some important cabinet woods; characteristics of bark, branching, and leaves, by which trees may be recognized; grain and finish of wood; lumbering.

Eighth Grade

The making of articles for use in the school; the making of articles for individual use, with emphasis upon staining, polishing, and care of wood. In drawing there are: (*a*) freehand drawing for proportion and design; (*b*) reduction of these drawings to working-drawings; (*c*) blueprints.

METAL-WORKING

Metal-working as an industrial art is begun in the fourth grade; but as a part of the study of invention is used in the third grade where the children cast in the simplest manner in lead and pewter. As an art it offers a material which appeals to the children from both the artistic and utilitarian standpoint. Working with it develops a control unlike that found in the other handicrafts. As a medium of expression it may seem at first unsympathetic and stubborn, but on the contrary it is most responsive to those who understand its nature.

Metal has a very intimate place in daily life, and the use of it suggests questions in science and history which, if answered, show the development of civilization from the earliest times. Metal-work has many possibilities, among them the following: (1) Simple articles for social use, on which decoration may be etched, pierced, chased, or engraved. (2) It may be used as decoration on woodwork or in connection with pottery. (3) It is the material best adapted for jewelry, as brooches, belt buckles, hatpins, etc., including all the processes necessary to the jeweler's craft.

Fourth Grade

The children begin metal-work in the fourth grade. It consists (1) of hammering from copper and brass articles for which they have immediate use, either at home or in school, such as bowls, spoons, pin-trays, pencil-trays, letter-files, picture-frames, calendar-frames, etc.; (2) of the application of simple designs in etching. The majority of the children not only get some idea of the possibilities of the metal in beaten copper, etc., but learn to rivet, to use the brush carefully and accurately in painting the design, and to bring out the beauty of the metal by simple processes.

Seventh Grade

The metal-work in the seventh grade consists not only of hammering articles from flat sheets but also of applied design. The work is so arranged that the individuals are allowed great freedom in their choice at first. Then the work of each child is so carefully and systematically followed up that he gets a wide range of experiences and he gains in technique in each piece. The seventh-grade work consists of (1) hammering; (2) application of design in etching, piercing, appliqué, and repoussé; (3) riveting and soldering.

Eighth Grade

In addition to the work in the seventh grade, some of the children get experience in chasing which is the foundation of jewelry. They apply the knowledge already gained in previous grades in making large pieces, such as serving-trays, nut-sets, lamp-shades, lanterns, smoking-sets, desk-sets, etc. They may, if they wish, make simple jewelry toward the end of the course.

BOOKBINDING

Eighth Grade

The work in this department is extremely simple, but effort is made to acquaint the pupil with a general knowledge of book-construction in forms suitable to his hand training. Various blank and printed books are bound in pamphlet, case, and library bindings, using materials best adapted. Various deviations from a prescribed outline are made, as the individual needs of the children in the school arise. Lessons have been put into simple but substantial form by some members of the bookbinding class, and a few copies of the curriculum have been bound for the library.

Excursions are made from time to time to some large printing and binding establishment to see and compare machine methods, and to smaller hand binderies to view the work from the more artistic side. In the history of bookbinding as an art, the work correlates with the study of the mediaeval arts. A visit to the Newberry Library is then made.

THE MUSEUM AND COLLECTIONS

The school grows through study and criticism of its own work. To afford better opportunity for this, the pupils place in the museum, for the purpose of study, the various articles of handwork which they have completed in any semester, and these remain there in the custody of the school during the next ensuing semester. A photographic record of such work is kept for future reference.

The museum is also made the center of appropriate working collections, gathered on field-trips and otherwise, just as the library is the center of interest in books. The work in history, geography, and the arts is supplemented by exhibits which show something of the industrial and artistic development of the race.

It is not the chief aim to fill the museum with the unusual, the rare, or the curious, but rather to make it an illustrative adjunct to the common things that are studied. It contains a large number of mounted specimens, which illustrate the chief topics in nature-study, physiology, zoölogy, botany, geology, and mineralogy.

In the museum continuous records are kept of the weather conditions, such as temperature, barometric pressure, wind velocity and direction, rainfall, and sunshine. In connection with this the Weather Bureau's daily, monthly, and annual records, and publications describing apparatus, are posted or conveniently filed. In addition, an excellent clock of the world, hydrographs, apparatus for taking soil temperature, and a skiameter in the garden, are available.

A large camera obscura is placed upon the central tower. This throws a six-foot picture of the surrounding landscape for a radius of several miles with all its moving objects upon a stage in a dark room underneath. It is used in the study of physics, nature-study, and art.

During the past year a number of groups representing the life-history of the bald-faced hornet, yellowjacket, moth, ant lion, and salamander has been added to the collection.

THE VOLUNTEER FIELD TRIPS

A field trip open to the students, parents, and teachers, is conducted each Saturday throughout a greater part of the year. Trips are made to the following places among others: East Chicago—slow-running stream and small-timbered woods; Clark Junction—swamp life; Calumet River and State Street—small area of virgin river forest; Palos Park—typical stream, springs, hills, and beautiful woods; Willow Springs—oak woods, hills, Drainage Canal, Desplaines River; Millers—combination of forest, sand dunes, river, lake, ponds, swamps, and fisheries. Bulletins of these trips are posted each week, on the Elementary School bulletin board and in the Museum.

The variety of natural phenomena to be observed at these places is very great. In the autumn the students see the declining year with the attending beauty of color and the preparations which plants and animals make for the coming winter, and the decay and failure to survive of so many forms. On these trips much material is collected and kept in the vivarium corner of the Museum, in as natural conditions as possible throughout the winter.

On the trips in the spring the students see these phenomena reversed in the revival of the forms which survive the winter. They see also the failures which many forms have made to adapt themselves to the conditions which surround them during the winter. In some instances the students have seen forms in the act of hibernating in the fall and in the spring have seen the same forms in their awakening and further development.

Collections are made during the spring as well as in the autumn. The material is brought to school in glass jars, pails, lunch boxes, etc., and placed in the aquaria and cages. It consists of many forms, both aquatic and terrestrial; bats, lizards, snakes, turtles, fish, frogs (their eggs and tadpoles), salamanders, crawfish, fairy shrimp, mussels, snails, and many forms of land and aquatic insects, and their larvae, and many kinds of plant life. The children see on these trips also several of the larger mammals and birds of the region, in their natural habitats; woodchucks and their holes, chipmunks, squirrels, muskrats and their villages covering acres of the marshes, and nearly all the birds common to this area, and several of their nests, eggs, young, and care of the young. Considerable attention is given to the physiographic features of the places visited, such as dunes, beaches, ravines, streams, lakes, lagoons, the work of waves, running water, and ice, and attention is also given to the weathering.

In connection with this volunteer work, and hand in hand with it, the students have prepared a good many exhibits showing the life histories of the ant lion (with its trapping and feeding habits), cabbage butterfly, cecropia-moth (with one of its parasites), crane-fly, dragon-fly, wasp, snail, salamander, and frog. These exhibits are used for illustrative purposes throughout the school; and in the art work, for designs in drawing, modeling and textiles. The students make photographs of the activities of these trips and the resulting exhibits.

Rabbits, squirrels, two pairs of doves, and a few other pets are kept and cared for in the vivarium corner and in the classrooms. Among these vivaria the students observe the full life cycles of many forms—mammalian, avian, batrachian, and protozoan.

NATURAL HISTORY

In presenting the following statement of the work in natural history it is to be especially emphasized that this course is not regarded as a final solution of the natural-history problem. The results secured from the teaching of this course, however, are such as to justify the belief that the course is at least a partial solution of the problem, and to warrant further use of these and similar lines of work.

In organizing this course its teachers have attempted to recognize the spirit, the purpose, and the content of such natural-history work as is possible within the limits of conditions in which this school is located. An excellent statement of the spirit was made by Professor W. S. Jackman when he said:

> The spirit of nature-study requires that the pupils be intelligently directed to the study of their immediate environment in its relation to themselves; that there shall be under the natural stimulus of a desire to know, a constant effort at a rational interpretation of the common things of life.

The educational purposes of work in natural history may be stated as twofold: (1) so to use the phenomena of nature that there may be a constantly increasing and constantly better organized body of concrete data which later shall furnish the basis for abstract thought, such data necessarily including material which relates to the industrial and social environment; (2) so to use these phenomena that proper attitude, methods, and efficiency in solving problems may be developed.

If these educational purposes are to be met in the best way the phenomena selected for study must include those which contain some real significance to the pupils—interest in what things are, what they are doing, how it is being done, how this affects other nature phenomena and man's interests. Furthermore, the difficulty of the problems presented must be graded and adjusted to the interests and abilities of pupils of different degrees of advancement.

In the lower grades problems presented are somewhat isolated, very little attempt being made to develop conclusions reaching beyond the phenomena under immediate observation. In the intermediate grades, where the work centers more largely around the school garden, more is done toward forming general conclusions, while in the upper grades special types are given more extended consideration and general conclusions derived therefrom.

Kindergarten

Autumn and Winter: The areas around which the year's work centers are: (1) garden, (2) lake shore, (3) the Midway and playground, (4) the parks. Observations: seasonal changes—effect of frost on plant life, animals, and people; habits of late birds; gathering seeds and noting how they are distributed; study of nuts, fruits, and vegetables, according to the way they may be preserved and stored for the winter. Care of animals.

Spring: Effect of warm winds and sun upon the earth; effect of moisture, heat, and light upon growth of seeds, incidentally noted; return of birds and insects; watching the bees at work. Observing plants in the garden and vacant lots. Learning to know some of the common plants.

First Grade

The children are taken on such trips and excursions as bring them into relation with various forms of nature. In the fall they go to a good farm, the lake shore at Jackson Park, Beverly Hills, and Lincoln Park. In the spring they again visit these places, possibly substituting Thornton for Beverly Hills at the time of spring blossoms.

Especial attention is paid to animals. In the country are seen horses, cows, sheep, pigs, and fowls, and some of the provisions for their care and use. In the school they study pets: rabbits, squirrels, chickens, cat and kittens, a lamb, doves, turtles.

Some wild animals, polar bears, and seals, in connection with Eskimo life, and deer, buffalo, and foxes, with Indian life, may be noted, especially at Lincoln Park and at museums.

In the fall the children set out bulbs in flower-pots for winter forcing.

When for any reason in connection with the study of harvesting, planting, Arctic conditions, or everyday experience, the question of "weather" enters, simple observations are made. In noting directions of wind, children learn the points of the compass and where they are in relation to school, home, and lake.

With the study of the Eskimo, the children gain some notion

of the barren, treeless snow fields and ice-bound country of the North. With the study of Indians, they picture the grassy prairies and forested hills. They connect these closely with their own experiences as a beginning of geographical imaging.

Second Grade

The following trips are selected as furnishing experiences full of interest, typical, and essential to later interpretation of land forms, and of plant and animal life:

Thornton, to see fruit trees in bloom and to gather wild flowers; Ravinia, to see autumn coloring and clay bluffs; Clark Junction, in autumn and spring, to observe and collect swamp material. Sand dunes at Miller's Station, to get idea of desert region; Flossmoor, where there are, a swift flowing stream, many trees, and wild flowers; Sixty-third St. and City Limits, to gather golden rod and asters and to see typical prairie area; Cheltenham Beach and Jackson Park, to gather beach material and make frequent records of seasonal changes.

Upon all these trips the material gathered is brought to the school for further use, to be arranged on the sand table in miniature imitation of the region visited, or to be kept alive in aquaria, the insect cage, or earth box.

In this grade attention is given to a few common animals. A pair of rabbits and a pet lamb have been selected as the particular care and property of the second grade, and homes will be made for these in the inclosure outside the grade room.

We find that the Indians who lived in the vicinity of Chicago depended upon the following wild plants for their vegetable food: acorns, roots of arrow leaf, roots of water lily, tips of cat-tails, stems of reeds, roots of wild hyacinth, wild rice, cranberries, chokeberries, wild grape, nuts, and sunflower seeds. We take trips for the purpose of gathering these foods, and prepare them for eating as the Indians did.

In a similar way we go out to gather those vegetable materials which the Indians and early settlers used for dyes. Grasses, sedges, bulrushes, and reeds are gathered for experiments in weaving.

In the spring the children of this grade have a small group garden where they may plant what they choose from the following list of vegetables or flowers: lettuce, radishes, pumpkin, gourd, nasturtium, calliopsis, morning glory or scarlet-runner, poppies, verbena, salvia, aster.

In the autumn the children plant crocuses and snow-drops in the lawn. Chinese lily bulbs are planted in the room, and the children have the daily care of these together with the ferns and blooming plants.

Third Grade

1. Excursions: To Jackson Park, Wooded Island, South Shore, Beverly Hills. The special interests of the children are noted and followed. Birds, bird-notes, building of nests, some ways of food-getting; the woodpeckers, kingfishers, swallows, robins are observed. Materials gathered on these excursions are cared for, insects and cocoons are placed in an insect case, noted and followed up as far as demanded by them. Birds, bird-notes, building of nests, some ways of food-getting; the frog's eggs, tadpoles, salamander's eggs, snails, larvae of mosquito, dragon-flies, etc., are kept in an aquarium in the room; turtles, snakes, and toads are cared for in the school museum. The habits of the animals with which the children have become acquainted during the summer are talked of and compared with the animal pets kept in the school, as a squirrel, rabbit, canary, etc. The life-history of the silkworm is observed in this grade.

2. Garden: This class has a group bed for a few easily grown vegetables and flowers, as radishes and lettuce, giving quick results, and candytuft, oxalis, forget-me-nots, marigolds, phlox, snap-dragons, mignonette, etc. Preparation is made for this out-door work by planting seeds in the schoolroom with simple experiments to discover favorable conditions of plant growth. Slips are made of a few plants, as coleus and geraniums, in order that the children may see various ways plants have of reproducing themselves. Bulbs are also planted by the children in the window box. Willow branches are kept in water to develop roots and are then planted. Seeds

are collected to bring out various types of distribution, by wind and water, by twisting and shooting, by burs and animals and to see how they are protected.

3. Seasonal changes are noted throughout the year.

Fourth Grade

I. Animal Life: (1) The study of the squirrel—study of the habits of a tamed squirrel in the room: (*a*) Prehension of food, comparison of prehensile organs, nature of food, ways of obtaining it, etc.; (*b*) Comparison with kindred and different animals; (2) Birds—continuous bird calendar for the year, noting name of bird, general coloring, food, location of nest and materials used, time with us, economic value, and the laws of the state for bird protection. General habits of birds with study of adaptation to their environment.

II. Garden: (1) These children have individual garden beds where they will grow chiefly plants of economic value, common garden vegetables, grains, flax, hemp, sugar beets, tobacco, cotton, household herbs, peanuts, etc. (2) Soil, various types; gravel, sand, clay loam and its relation to plant growth and water supply. (3) Conditions favoring plant development, as light, moisture, heat, air, and the work of the roots, leaves, stems of the plant. (4) Bulbs are planted for winter and spring blooming. Seeds are planted and slips prepared by the children in the schoolroom, and plants therefrom used in the garden.

III. Seasonal changes noted in migration of birds: winter and spring buds of a few common trees of our streets and parks. Keeping of simple weather records, including temperature, direction of mind, clouds, frost, snow, and varying length of night and day.

IV. Excursions: Excursions are made to (*a*) the Wooded Island, (*b*) South Shore, (*c*) Glencoe, (*d*) neighboring swamps, (*e*) Beverly Hills.

Fifth Grade

Garden: The work of this grade centers about the garden where each child has his own plot of ground.

1) The greatest emphasis is put on the plant and its work. A study of the uses of the various parts of the plant, as the flower. Pollen and its distribution by various insects and wind.

2) Bees: the children observe their work and study the life of the hive.

3) Butterflies observed, collected, and life-history of common forms studied. Note taken of destructive work of caterpillars on plants of garden.

4) Other plant and animal visitors, both friends and foes, noted as various weeds, ground-squirrels, snails, earth-worms, grasshoppers, beetles, plant lice, and scales.

5) The wild flowers of the region studied and given familiar common names.

6) Gathering of seeds and fruits of the garden for use next year and studying a few common foods to give the children an idea of how the world supplies our simplest meals; salt, pepper, spices, chocolate, tea, coffee, sugar.

Excursions: Beverly Hills; Stony Island; North Shore; Parks.

Sixth Grade

The nature-study of this year is based on excursions to a given area. The sand dune and swamp area is suggested as affording several types of study: (1) The genesis of the areas; (2) Plants and animals of both sand and swamp area; (3) Factors governing distribution of plants and animals. A definite record of the reappearance of animal and plant life in these areas will be kept by the class.

During the winter the class makes a study of common rock and mineral forms found in the city and home, with the detailed study of local industries, as coal and iron. This work should widen into a study of larger land forms, including the region selected for special study.

Weather Chart: This chart consists of a graphic representation of daily conditions and shows the interrelation of the following topics: (1) Length of day and night; (2) Cloud, sunshine, precipitation; (3) Temperature; (4) Wind; (5) Barometer.

1. Physics of air with reference to weight, pressure, winds, heating and ventilation.

2. Making of both thermometer and barometer.

3. Composition of air. Tests for oxygen. Also composition of water. Separate by electrolysis and test the gases.

Seventh Grade

An increasing appreciation of things having economic value as well as intellectual interest is the special basis of this year's work. The biological subjects that are chosen are studied from both the biological and the historical standpoints, and the processes employed in using these things receive some attention.

Autumn: (1) Cultivated plants; corn, wheat, oats; sugar cane, sugar beet, sugar maple, millet, apple, potato, coffee, cocoanut, flax, rubber tree, cotton; (2) Domesticated animals; horse, cow, sheep, hog, dog, goat, and chickens; (3) by-products of each, methods of manufacture, etc.

A class study is made of a few of the above and then each child is assigned a topic to work out alone. His reports are presented to the class as he gathers information from specimens in the school museum, the Field Museum, various industrial institutions, and the library. The print-material furnished by the Department of Agriculture at Washington and by the departments of the various states has been appreciated by the children and used as much as possible. The children are aided in preparing a bibliography and collection of illustrative materials.

Carpenter's *How the World is Fed,* Adams *Commercial Geography*, and Redway's *Commercial Geography* are used for supplementary reading and reference.

Excursions are made to a wholesale coffee, tea, and spice house, the International Live Stock Show, and the Corn Show at the Coliseum.

Winter: Electricity. An experimental study of current electricity is made because of its intense interest to children of this age and because of its wide application along industrial and commercial lines. Static electricity is given little attention except from a historical standpoint. The children construct illustrative and experimental apparatus at home and in the school shop, and this serves as a basis for much of the classroom work. The following are constructed: wet cells, dry cells, storage cells, electro-magnets, a compass, a simple telegraph instrument, electric switches, buttons, motors, signals, a

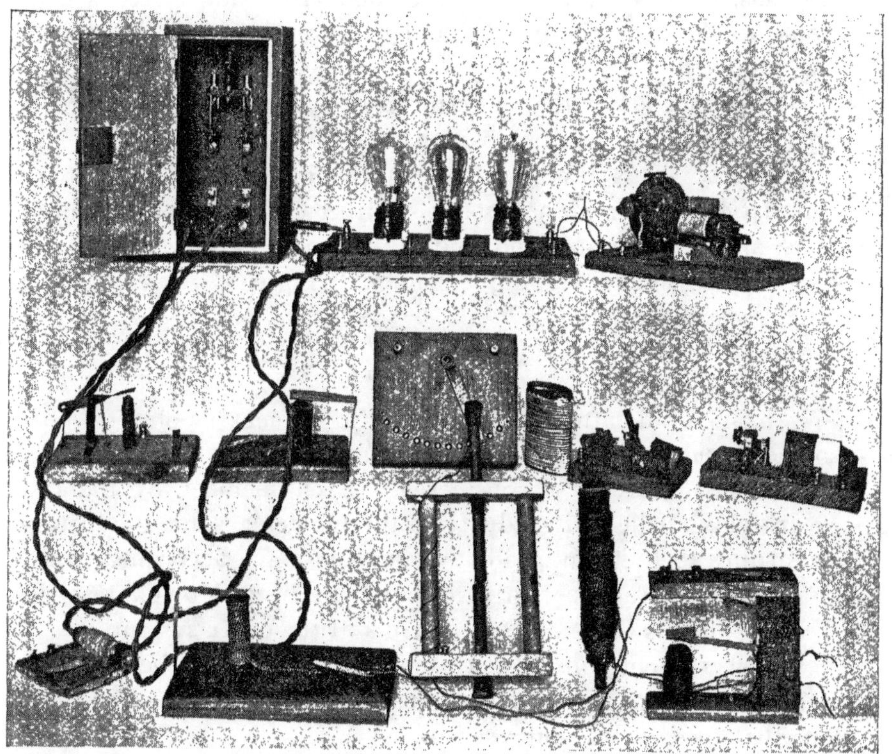

APPARATUS MADE AT HOME AND AT SCHOOL BY SEVENTH GRADE PUPILS WHILE STUDYING ELECTRICITY

small trolley car, or an arc light. The telephone, the telegraph, wireless telegraphy, the submarine cables, the *X*-ray, the phonograph, and other electrical achievements, and the part each plays in our complicated social and industrial life receive as much attention as the children appreciate.

Harper's *Electricity Book for Boys* is used as supplementary to the experimental work.

Excursions are made to the University electric plant, and the Annual Electric Show at the Coliseum.

Spring: Hygienic physiology: A study of the respiratory, circulatory, and digestive systems with special reference to the application of the experience gained in the work outlined under "Home Economics;" a study of the effect of gymnastic exercise, games, out-of-door life, and pure, wholesome foods, upon the growth and functions of the heart, lungs, and stomach.

In connection with the respiratory system we study experimentally the air: its composition; carbon dioxide; oxygen; and impurities. This leads up to (1) the problem of the proper ventilation of our homes, schools, street cars, and public buildings, and (2) the dust and smoke problems in cities.

Supplementary reading: Gulick "Hygienic Series," Book II, *Town and City*.

Eighth Grade

In this grade attention is directed to elementary physical phenomena and the industrial applications of physics. Heat and heat measurement are first considered. Each member of the last year's class made and graduated a thermometer, some graduating according to the Centigrade system, and some according to the Fahrenheit. Each performs calculations needed to express the readings of his thermometer in terms of the other system.

Each student constructed a miniature hot-water heating system, using glass tubing, corks, flasks, and sealing-wax for making the pipes, joints, and reservoir.

Water distilling apparatus was constructed by means of which each pupil could demonstrate distillation, and could estimate the amount of time required to produce a given quantity of distilled water. To some of the better stills a gas meter was attached and the amount and cost of gas required to produce a gallon of distilled water was determined. An explanation of wide differences in results was sought in differences in the construction of apparatus. Comparisons were made between the cost of distilled water from this source and from commercial supply houses.

The principles of simple pumps, then those of more complex ones are studied, and used in the construction of small pumps.

Throughout this work there is constant discussion of the principles involved. The work has led to home construction of physical apparatus by several of the pupils.

In connection with the home economics work this class considers the following natural-history topic: Plants associated with the household and health—bacteria, yeasts, and moulds. Insect pests of the home. In connection with the work in geography and history this class makes the following excursions: to the North Shore to study the beginnings of ravines, to Thornton to study the development of stream valleys, to Dune Park to study the phenomena of sand dunes, down the Desplaines valley to Lockport to study the drainage canal and the wide river valley in its relation to the geological history of Chicago.

GEOGRAPHY

The aim of the work in geography is to aid the student in gaining power to interpret his physical and social environment. The ability to understand his surroundings is obtained through a study of the physical forces which have shaped and are shaping the earth's surface and are determining its life; and through an appreciation of man's response to his physical and social surroundings. Opportunity is given even to the young children to observe the results of the work of the great forces of nature, and, when possible, to see these forces in action. This is done through field-trips to the country within a radius of thirty miles of the school. The work of waves, winds, rivers, and glaciers is well illustrated within the above limits.

Through gardening and visits to farms a touch of the fundamental industry of agriculture is gained; and through visits to the manufacturing centers an appreciation of man's control and use of natural materials and physical forces is obtained. The knowledge gained in the study of the building of this city becomes the basis for the understanding of all urban populations; the imported materials, both natural and manufactured, and the foreign peoples, if traced to their origin, lead to all the countries of the world.

The proper study of foreign peoples in relation to their physical and social environment develops a sympathetic appreciation of their relative position in the world's families of nations. It also affords an opportunity to see our own people from the view-point of the foreigner, thus broadening our horizon, placing our virtues in a rational perspective, and giving a consciousness of our faults, which is the first step toward correction and improvement.

The germ of interest in processes is nurtured from the beginning by simple experiments and explanations. This interest grows until in the fourth and fifth grades its satisfaction leads to the study of many of the simple phases of physiographic processes that are more fully developed by the older children.

During the elementary-school period the children are alive to all knowledge, regardless of utilitarian values which for the most part dominate the adult. This is the time to bring them into contact, as far as possible, with the various phases of the earth and the heavens.

In the early grades, from the first to the fourth, when interest in causal relations does not carry the pupils far from simple picturing of conditions, the children gain fundamental geographic imagery of type regions through a study of primitive peoples living in regions of extreme geographic control, as the Eskimo or Chukches of the Arctic regions, a Brazilian Indian tribe in the tropics, the Arabs in the desert, the Norwegians in the mountains, and the Indians of the plains. Through stories of travel the earth is circumnavigated, resulting in the discovery of the continents and seas.

The ideas gained in the earlier grades are organized and expanded above the fourth grade by the study of continental land-masses, islands, and seas. North America is studied as a type, in its aspect of human control and simple physiographic expressions; South America, as a tropical continent; Eurasia, as the home of civilization; Africa, as the continent of present colonization; Australia and New Zealand, as seats of important civic experiments.

The fundamental geographic principles and to a great extent the type-imagery are repeated in the study of each continent, thus giving the desired review of important ideas related to new situations.

Current events are always a source of vital interest and lead to a survey of various parts of the earth. They also furnish a needed review of the world, for memory retains in strong definition little that is not in constant use.

When the nature of the unknown can be realized by such experience, all problems arising in the study of geography are solved by experimentation. To this end a laboratory has been constructed where running water, rain, and waves may be controlled in action upon sand. The garden and the physical and chemical laboratories are also called into requisition in the solution of geographic problems.

Second Grade

The experience in typical areas and with natural materials gained in the field-trips forms the basis for geography.

After the trips the children make plans in sand or on paper of the routes followed and areas visited. No attempt is made at conventional map-making, the teachers' problem being to discover when and how children make the transition from purely picture records to the conventional representation.

Trips to the lake shore furnish collections of the common pebbles, and limestone, sandstone, quartz, chert, greenstone, granite, and iron pyrites become familiar. The children make crystals from various substances and this work culminates in our rock-candy for the Christmas tree.

As a background for the stories told in the history period the following regions must be pictured: a temperate forest area with caves and swift-flowing river; the desert, and portions of Persia, Greece, and Switzerland. Stories, reading-matter, visits to the stuffed-animal section of the Field Museum and to the "zoo" at Lincoln Park, feed that absorbing child-interest in wild animals.

Third Grade

(1) The neighborhood. On all excursions the natural features are observed. The lake shore—shore line, bluffs, different kinds of beaches. Beverly Hills—the ravines, brook-basins. Swamps—ridges with trees. (2) Typical environments. Mountain landscapes: Norway and Greece as types; narrow valleys, rapid rivers, falls, lakes; forest-covered, barren, and snow-covered mountains. Coasts: bays, headlands, fjords, islands, harbors. Animal life of the northern forests; animals of the northern seas. Study of such typical environments with relation to their social occupations, fishing, lumbering, hunting, trade (see "History").

Given typical physiographical features, the children plan routes of travel by sea and land; construct maps in sand and on the blackboard. These maps are made to record first imaginary trips and later the journey of the Norsemen to America, the caravan travel through the deserts, Columbus' discovery of America.

The children picture Arctic scenery with Nansen's journey, and tropical scenes with Livingstone and Stanley. The earth as a ball is introduced with the study of Columbus, and the different oceans and land masses noticed with relation to one another. The children construct simple compasses, and learn to use them on their excursions.

Fourth Grade

First semester: first six weeks only. Special point, ravines and river valleys, flood plains, divides, work of running water; excursions to (*a*) Thorton, (*b*) Beverly Hills, (*c*) Glencoe.

In connection with the history: (1) The St. Lawrence and the Mississippi basins; (2) geography and topography of Illinois; (*a*) old river routes; (*b*) appearance of the country; (*c*) routes to the East.

Lumbering (see "Woodworking").

Second semester: (1) Study of mining (see "Metal-working"); (2) Study of clay (see "Modeling"); (3) Special study of Mississippi basin industrially considered: (*a*) cotton belt, (*b*) grain belt, (*c*) sugar-cane belt, (*d*) rice belt, (*e*) grazing belt, etc. (4) Excursions: The last six weeks are again devoted to excursions: South Shore: (*a*) formation of sand bars, lagoons, swamps, and ridges; (*b*) reason for piers. Swamps: conditions for formation and change. Dune Park: (*a*) formation of dunes and swamps; (*b*) cause of succession of dunes. Beverly Hills: special features—forests, wide ravines, swamps, and prairies.

Fifth Grade

The general work in geography is a study of North America. During the first semester the geography is closely allied to history, which is a study of the colonies (see "History"). A general study of glaciation is made with special application to New England. From a knowledge of the rocky soil, and also through the use of pictures and descriptions, the class studies the rivers, forests, hills, boulders, water power, and climate of the region, in relation to the principal industries—manufacturing, agriculture, and fishing. Excursions are made to Stony Island, where the influence of the glacier on bed-rock and glacial drift can be seen, and to Purington for larger deposits. The location of many towns and cities, as determined by topographic causes, is noted. Other sections of the country are studied by different groups of children, who work out characteristic occupations of the areas and present to the class the results of their work.

During the second semester the study of the entire continent, including the polar and tropical regions, is continued. Visits are made to industrial plants in or near the city, which supplement the work of the classroom. A part of the work in home-economics is the cooking of cereals, and the work is supplemented by a study of the location of the areas devoted to the raising of the grains which the children cook. In the work on New York history, constant reference is made to Holland, and, in order to make this work more vivid, the general geography of Holland, including the subjects of erosion, formation of islands, and transportation of soil, is studied.

During the entire year current geography has an important place in the curriculum, and a period each week is devoted to current events.

Sixth Grade

The children are coming into contact with foreign people at school, at home, and in the great city outside; they are seeing products of foreign countries in the stores as they go shopping alone or with their parents; they or their parents have traveled abroad, or are anticipating such travel. The scope of their interests is great enough now to include the many people and countries contributing to the life around them. They are ready to see the interdependence of peoples; to appreciate the contributions of nations to progress, material and otherwise—are really very open-minded and sympathetic in this direction. At this time much can be accomplished by a somewhat thorough study of foreign people here in our city, and in their own countries abroad. If this study is deferred a year or two, the children's questions are answered haphazard outside; the children make abstractions and come to wrong conclusions, which the truth, learned later, does not always eradicate. So, to satisfy the demands of the children at this time, Eurasia is studied.

Eurasia: Physical features: great mountain systems, plateaus, plains, and rivers. Climatic features: tundras, forest belt, steppes, desert belt; characteristic products of each; effect of each upon human life. Regions of wheat, flax, etc.; grazing, mining, etc. A general picture of the great continent.

We see the three great civilizations: the European, pressing on and on over the great western peninsula, and even across the sea to the New World; the Chinese (Japanese, Corean), clinging in the past to its own soil and looking backward, with its wonderful background of written history; the Hindu in the southern peninsula, looking to the spiritual, living in the future life, as it were, leaving only buildings to tell its past.

A study of France, England, and Greece, somewhat in detail, is made in connection with the history. The European is studied as a traveler, a discoverer, an explorer. Our commercial relations with the leading countries of the continent are emphasized, and a study is made of special food products.

Seventh Grade

1. North America: The study of North America begun in the Fifth Grade is reviewed here from the standpoint of the relation of the geography of the country to the history of the development of the people. Points considered: topography of the continent as a whole; the topographic divisions; the climate of each in connection with the daily weather maps of the United States Weather Bureau (see "Natural History"); the agricultural, mineral, and commercial advantages of each; state of development; the effect of these geographic factors upon the life of the people; the relation of the geography to the history. Blackboard chalk-modeling of topography; field trips and the geographic laboratory are used as aids in the study of physiographic processes. Maps, pictures and lantern slides are also used.

2. South America: A continent similar to North America in structure, but differing in its climatic conditions, hence differing in its agricultural, commercial, and social relations. The same general plan is followed as in the study of North America. The museum collection is used to illustrate the trade relations between Chicago and South America.

3. Africa: "The continent of contrasts" (Keane); a continent differing in structure from those already studied; a continent greatly retarded in its development because of its desert conditions, plateau formation, and slightly eroded river valleys. Points to be considered and purpose to be attained are the same as in the previous study.

4. Australia: A continent similar to South America in location, but differing from it in climatic, industrial, and commercial features.

A study of current events continued during the year serves to unite all continents with our own. References for pupils: Carpenter, *North America, South America, Africa, Australia;* Shaler, *The Story of Our Continent;* books of travel; magazine articles.

Eighth Grade

In this year the class sums up the geography of the preceding years, including the physiography and political geography, but from a new point of view. The geographical conditions under which man is living on the earth, and the effect of these conditions upon his life, form the background of the work.

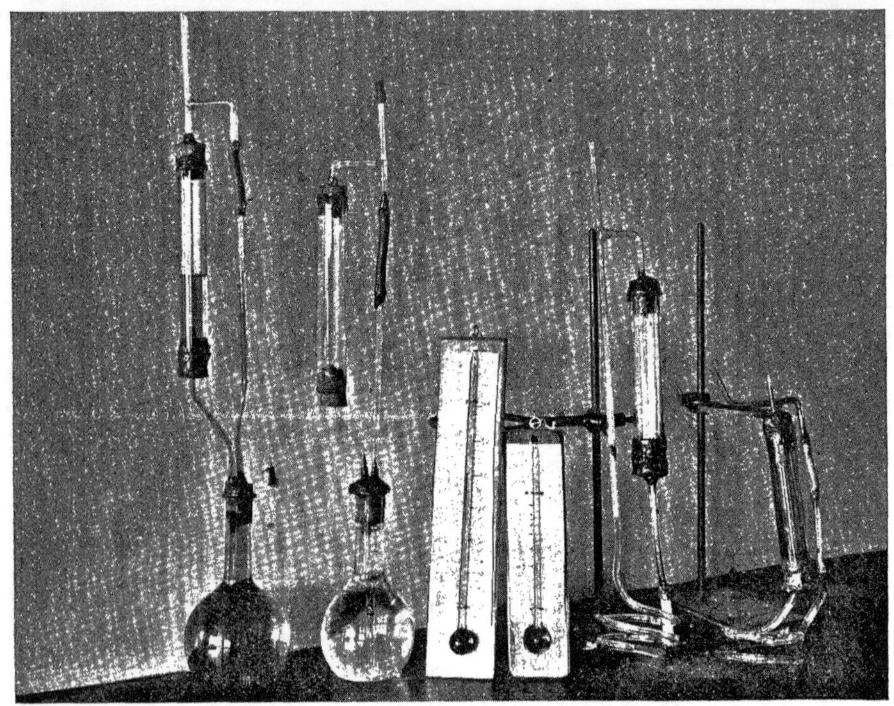

Physics Apparatus Made in Class by Eighth Grade Pupils

Starting with the world as a whole, attention is directed to the distribution of land and water on the earth, the mountain masses, the great plains, river basins, deltas, flood-plains, and coastal plains, the glaciated areas, tundras, and forests. This involves the study of the distribution of sunshine and heat on the earth, and the terrestrial winds. The children review their work of former years on weather and climate, and learn by experiment more definitely the principles governing atmospheric pressure and winds and rainfall.

The class visits several of the large commercial stores and manufacturing plants, to learn what the different countries are sending us, and what we are sending them in return. This involves a thorough review of the commercial and political geography of the preceding years.

In the study of climate the class uses the meteorological instruments and records in the school museum, and makes a visit to the United States Weather Bureau Station in the Federal Building.

In studying the relation between the nature of a country and the lives of a people, constant reference is made to the books in the school library, to magazine articles, and especially to Herbertson's geographies, which are a series of extracts from the best books of travel.

The excursions are to the following regions: (1) Glencoe; (2) Fraction Run, near Lockport, and the Drainage Canal; (3) Dune Park; (4) Thornton (see "Natural History"). On these excursions the class uses the contour maps of the United States Geological Survey.

HISTORY

The modern school has revised its course of study, giving a prominent place to the industrial arts. Although this addition to the number of studies which are now considered essential subtracts something from the time which might otherwise be devoted to history, it gives an opportunity for a far better treatment of the subject than was possible in earlier curricula.

The use of the constructive activities is the best possible introduction to the study of history, for, by the children's attempts to deal with the materials and forces of nature, they come to know the causes upon which the facts of history depend. The impulse of the things which they feel are vital to the outside life, is carried over into their study, and, instead of trying to remember mere statements of effects, they comprehend their underlying conditions. By this means, history becomes to the child the story of how other people have done work similar to that which he is doing and what social results have followed from changes in industrial methods. When there is no such relation of history and experience, the children are often driven to learn things which have no meaning to them and consequently no value for them.

In history, we bring into the child's consciousness the larger meaning of his own experience. We hold up to him a standard by which to judge of his own achievement. Thus history gives the background and interpretation of the activities which are carried on in the school and the environment.

The aims of this course are primarily the cultivation of an appreciation of social life and the ability to meet social responsibilities.

Kindergarten

Autumn: Subject—homes. (1) Our own homes—inside and out. (2) Homes of animals: (*a*) domestic animals for which homes are provided, such as dogs, pigeons, chickens, horses, cows, sheep, pigs; (*b*) animals which find their own homes, such as rabbits, squirrels, bees, birds. (3) Relation of farm to the home.

Winter: Subject—baker (kitchen and shop), grocer, milkman, postman.

Spring: Subject—market gardener—close relation to grocer and to our life. Our own garden—in relation to that of the market gardener. Plans in sandpans of yards, gardens, playgrounds, and setting for stories.

First Grade

Children of the sixth or seventh year of their experience have a large fund of unorganized facts at their command gained from their own observation and from stories and pictures. The idea in the study of history or social industry of the first school years is to bring together these loosely connected notions so as to explain and give meaning to the activities nearest the child-life. It is always necessary, however, to keep in mind the fact that six-year-olds are still very much concerned with play—play as a business, as a recreation, and altogether desirable. Hence they should be allowed and helped at every turn to dramatize, in their own way, bits of the life they are studying; to bring from home toys or treasures for illustration; and to make at school, and *then to play with,* such crude models as they are able to fashion.

The principal divisions or subjects for work are: (*a*) the farm, as a base of our supplies, with careful attention to the shelters and care of farm animals; (*b*) the playhouse as a simplification of the children's own homes; (*c*) the general activities of the Eskimo people, with a special study of their summer and winter shelters; (*d*) the same with the North American Indian.

From the summer's experience some children are sure to bring memories of the farm. These are worked out in miniature on the sand-table, the building being constructed of boxes, cardboard and paper, and the fields planted with wheat, corn, oats, and grass. They make butter and cheese, and grind corn and wheat into meal and flour. In the spring they lay out a larger farm in the garden, planting grain and such vegetables as will mature early in the season. Especial attention is paid to the germination of seeds and some experiments are carried on with different conditions of light and water.

The old large playhouse will be entirely renovated with new paint, curtains, wall-paper, rugs, and revarnished furniture and sent to some other children for Christmas. In the latter part of the year the children will make small individual playhouses, of three or four rooms, from fruit or soap boxes, furnish them throughout and take them home when finished. In past years it has been found that some of these playhouses afford considerable pleasure at home for a long time.

The study of the Eskimos and Indians more nearly approaches "history," the picturing of what other peoples do under circumstances different from our own. From our extremely cold days the children build up some idea of Arctic conditions. From pictures and stories of Eskimo life and a visit to the excellent exhibit at the Field Museum, they construct winter and summer scenes and "play" Eskimo.

In much the same way they study the Indians. They visit the exhibit at the Field Museum, become saturated with Indian myth and story, make wigwams, cradles, canoes, and bows and arrows, grind corn in stone mortars, and dance Indian dances.

Possibly, the consideration of these simple and primitive people will by its vivid and striking contrast give more meaning to the complex lives of the children.

Second Grade

The industrial history of the second grade serves to give background to the activity which predominates during a given season, cooking in the autumn, textiles in the winter, and gardening in the spring.

During the autumn the preparation and distribution of food in Chicago is seen through trips to a farm, South Water Street, the docks, an express depot, a bakery, a wholesale fish market, and a cold-storage plant.

To contrast and give meaning to this complex process with its great division of labor and interrelation of workers, stories are told of the simple ways of primitive people. Stories of the Indians of the plains, and of the Cave Man, with Waterloo's "Story of Ab" as a basis, serve as illustrations of the hunter stage of civilization where the food problem is reduced to its lowest terms.

The children experiment in fire-making without matches, out-door cooking, pottery making, and the gathering and preparing of those wild vegetable foods which were the staples of the Indians about Chicago (for further details see "Cooking" and "Natural History" for second grade).

In connection with the textile work the children experiment in shearing, carding, spinning, dyeing, and weaving. The industrial history gives background to this by means of stories of shepherd people, using as types the Arabs of the desert, the shepherds of Palestine, the people of Persia, and the Navajo Indians.

To compare their crude attempts with the great products of industry trips are made to rug stores in the city, a carpet weaver's establishment and the Field Museum (see "Textiles" and "Natural History" for second grade).

The spring is spent in the making and care of individual gardens. The children are told of the beginnings of agriculture, emphasis being laid upon the change from the nomadic life to settled homes. They do some experimenting with primitive plowing, reaping, threshing, and milling. The people of New Guinea, the Lake Dwellers of Switzerland, and the Pueblo Indians are used as types of this civilization (see "Natural History Outline" for second grade).

Third Grade

The work in history in the primary grades is a study of types of society in various environments. Some of these types are: the farmer, the hunter, the shepherd. The principal topics in this study have been: shelter, means of getting food and clothing, which includes occupations and industries, means for defense, social customs, games, etc. Side by side with the consideration of these topics, which constitute the historic aspect of the subject, the environments in which these types of society were found has been given some attention; this is the geographic aspect of the subject. Forms of shelter, industries, and modes of living in a primitive society are very largely the result of certain external conditions: climate, topographic forms, and soil. In order, therefore, to understand the peculiarities and stage of development of a certain type of society, a study of these external conditions is necessary. The factors which make Eskimo society different from Indian society, and the farmer's life different from that of the shepherd, are largely geographical. In one case we have an arctic climate, with absence of soil and vegetation; in the other case, a temperate climate, with extensive prairies; in one case, valley and river, with fertile soil; in the other, forests, with an abundance of game. To sum it up: History in these grades deals with types of primitive society; geography, with an analysis of various environments, which have surrounded man at different stages of his development.

The reasons why such types of society as the shepherd, farmer, and hunter are taken up in the first and second grades are obvious. The forms of community life on which they are based are extremely simple in all their phases, socially, industrially, and politically. The farmer's or shepherd's life has many analogies in the child's own life; it is therefore easily comprehended, and arouses his interest and sympathy. What the hunter does in a primitive society is closely akin to the things that the child himself would like to do, and very often can do. The problems and ideas which claim the attention of the hunter seem familiar and worth considering to the child in the first and second grades.

As before stated, the social, industrial, and political organization of these types of society are extremely simple. Their energies are spent mainly in obtaining the necessaries of life directly from nature. As there is no trade, there are no luxuries. They form self-sustaining communities, with no intercourse with the outside. Means of transportation and communication are undeveloped, and travel and exploration find no encouragement. It is easy to understand that the study of such a society appeals to the children in these grades. Their problems and occupations are similar to those of the society which they are studying.

In the history work of the third grade we advance one step. From the simple, self-sustaining communities of the hunter, farmer, and shepherd, the child is led to consider a type of society where man no longer is entirely dependent upon nature through his own efforts, but where he obtains the necessaries of life, and some of its luxuries through the intercourse and interchange with other people.

Such a study involves, of course, such topics as: beginning of trade, of exploration, and of travel; development of means of transportation and of a diversity of arts; expansion of industrial, social, and political life. As concrete illustrations of such a society, some phases of Greek and Norse history have been selected for study in the third grade.

In this connection the children are brought face to face with geographical conditions, more definite than and different from those that they have studied before. In both Greece and Scandinavia the country is mountainous, with a scarcity of soil. The coast is cut by deep inlets and is skirted by innumerable islands. The relation of these geographical facts to the life of the people is easily understood by the children. The study of this typical environment, with its results in industries and modes of life, furnishes material for the work in geography for the third grade.

No attempt is made to have the children reason out in a logical order the various steps and stages which led from one type of society to another, from a farming to a trading community. Such a philosophical study would be far beyond the powers of comprehension and the interest of the children. The material is not selected because it marks the beginning of proper historical study, nor because it emphasizes historical sequence. The aim is rather to furnish the children with historical material that is simple, but not too simple; material which will bring into relief their own problems and ideals; material which will delight the child and at the same time stimulate to right action. It makes no difference to the child in the third grade whether the stories of heroism, of adventure, and of simple life are taken from the beginning of history or from the present, from this country or from foreign countries; only this is necessary: they must satisfy the child's cravings for life in the forms that he can recognize and act upon. For this purpose other chapters of history might have furnished suitable material. One reason, however, for selecting Greek and Norse life is, that the material is easily accessible and embodied in great literary master-pieces. In the sagas of the Norse and in Homer, we find a literature which adequately describes the age and which charms the children by the grandeur and simplicity of its style.

DETAILS OF OUTLINE

Geography of Scandinavia and of Greece. The aim is to bring the children into close, personal contact with mountain and coast scenery by the aid of pictures, stereopticon views, descriptions, sand-modeling, and reading. Such features as mountains, valleys, islands, fjords, bays, and harbors should become living realities to the children, as much so as features of their own home environment. These features in their climatic setting will be studied in relation to the life of the old Greeks and the Norse, in determining industries and modes of living. The study of the formation of such topographic forms as mountains and valleys—that is, physiographic processes—will not be touched upon in this grade.

Geographic conditions which encouraged early navigation and commerce: islands, harbors, scarcity of soil, etc.

Resulting industries and occupations.

Development of Trade. How trade was carried on; means of transportation by land and by water. Colonization by the Greeks; discoveries and expansion of geographical knowledge.

The Vikings; where living; their houses, weapons, etc. Discovery of Iceland, Greenland, and America (Vinland) by the Norse. For comparison, stories will be told of modern explorers, as Nansen, Livingstone, Stanley; their equipment and aims as compared with those of the ancient explorers. The story of Columbus embodying the spirit and aims of exploration.

Study of Greek and Norse boats; comparison. Models of boats and vessels from the most primitive craft up to our modern vessel: the ancient vessel, the Norse boat, the galley, the boats of Columbus.

Pictures mounted on charts to show the evolution of the boat. Discussion of the slowness and inconvenience of these various crafts. How to find the location of a place on the ocean, by the stars, by the sun.

Social conditions of the people; home life, classes of people, games and sports, warfare and warlike conditions.

Standards of measurement, currency, use of metals. Ideals of the time and religious beliefs.

ILLUSTRATION OF METHOD

For the study of the Norsemen, the sagas of King Harold and Björn Farmand are told and read to the children. For the study of the Greek, the *Odyssey* in Palmer's translation, is read and told. From the reading and discussion of these pieces of literature and of related stories, the children work out the points enumerated above (see "Details of Outlines").

The play element is emphasized strongly in this work. The children imagine themselves Norsemen and Greeks; dramatize the stories; play trader, viking, captain, skald, and king.

When one group studying the Norsemen discussed how they best could tell their story to the Greek group, they planned the following scheme: to represent on a large sand-table the country surrounding a viking's home; to make trees with which to cover the mountain sides, and also animals, which live in the forest; to construct houses, ships, and men, and place these in the country made on the sand-pan. The children divided themselves into groups in order to work out this plan, each group having its chairman to direct the work and thereby give it unity. After this construction work was finished, the children embodied their knowledge of the life of a trader, in a story which they themselves composed. This story was absolutely original and composed by the group as a whole.

From the child's standpoint, a need arises for metal arrow-points, spear-points, battle-axes, money, weights, etc. This is the teacher's opportunity to have the children realize the difficulties which primitive man experienced in dealing with a new material, metal. In this as in all his constructive work, the child is confronted with his own particular problem and is left to use his own initiative in experimentation. After having discussed present uses of metals and where found, the children experiment in order to find out what metals they can use for their purposes. After trying to smelt different metals, they decide upon lead and tin. They plan and build small furnaces in which to smelt their metals, make molds, and carry on the whole process of molding in lead and tin.

A system of currency has been invented by the children, the value of a man (slave), an ox, and a sheep being represented by coins bearing the stamp of a man, or the head of an ox or a sheep.

When the children dramatize Greek or Norse life, they use,

of course, the money, weights, scales, and armor which they themselves have made.

In studying how to furnish their Greek or Norse houses, or how to make their pottery, armor, and utensils, the children have tried to express Greek and Norse ideas and ideals in the designs, On the pottery, for instance, pictures from mythology appear—fierce heads of dragons on the Norse cups, while suns and waves adorn the Greek cups.

It is believed that the many-sidedness of the work here presented will call forth the varied powers in each child; that it will give wide scope for his imagination and for expression in simple but beautiful language as well as in the arts; that the child will find numberless opportunities to develop initiative through invention and constructive work; and that the social aspects of the subject-matter itself, and of the methods used in carrying it out, will train the child in social service.

Fourth Grade

The child in the fourth grade takes a very keen interest in his surroundings. He finds himself in a community with which he feels no intimate connection excepting through family relationships. The lower grades' work has put him in sympathy with the industries about him but has not made him feel the close co-operation of many people necessary for the advancement of a city, nor has it shown him his own relation to this larger community. It is the object of the fourth grade to make him feel pride in his own city and to feel a personal responsibility and deep interest in its welfare.

First semester: A study of Chicago as it is now—its location, population, principal industries and relation to the United States and Illinois. The functions of the government of the city and county which come closest to the child: (1) The mail service; (2) water supply; (3) sanitation; (4) fire department; (5) improvement societies; (6) streets and bridges; (7) life-saving service. The civics ought to be used all through the year to show the child his responsibilities and give him a chance to put his ideas into practice in connection with the school work.

Second semester: The story of Chicago is carried back to its beginnings at the time of the exploration of the French in the Mississippi Valley. (1) Early French explorers and the motives which led to founding of Chicago: (*a*) religion; (*b*) adventure; (*c*) acquisition of territory. (2) Industries developed by French along St. Lawrence and Mississippi: (*a*) fishing; (*b*) trapping; (*c*) fur trading. (3) Story of Marquette and Joliet. (4) Story of LaSalle—his insight into the commercial possibilities of the Great Lakes and Mississippi River—the chains of forts for the fur trade which lead up to (5) Fort Dearborn: (*a*) trading post; (*b*) building of fort; (*c*) coming of pioneers. (6) Village of Chicago: (*a*) the beginnings of mail service; (*b*) streets and bridges; (*c*) water supply; (*d*) sanitation, by contrast with Chicago as it is now.

Fifth Grade

Typical colonies are studied in this grade—New England, Virginia, and New York. The geographical environment of each colony is carefully noted to show the influence of geography upon occupations. With this basis the children trace the effect of occupations upon social life and of social life upon government. These colonial types represent comparatively primitive and simple conditions, conditions easily grasped by the children. With interest in biographies which are used as a foundation for the study, it is easy to connect the story of the growth of the colonies and the evolution of various institutions. There are vivid and striking contrasts between the life of New England with its varied industries and that of Virginia dependent upon its staple product, while New York presents another type, the result of its great opportunities for commerce.

The story of the Pilgrims proceeds with Governor Bradford's *Journal* as a basis, and the children read Nina Moore's *Pilgrims and Puritans.* With the study of each colony much time is spent in constructive work. The settlement of Plymouth is set up on the sand-table and the pupils construct a miniature plantation with its great fields of tobacco, mansion house, many laborers, river, wharf, and the ship from England with its manufactured articles. A miniature New Amsterdam is also made and drawings of scenes of old New York illustrate the conditions of the early colony. Hans Brinker furnishes a vivid picture of life in Holland, and the story of the siege of Leyden illustrates the character of the people. The legends of Sleepy Hollow and Rip Van Winkle are read and parts of them dramatized.

The primitive industries of weaving, cooking, candle and soap making are repeated and contrasted with our own modern methods of manufacture. By expending this effort, the child realizes in a measure the difficulties which all pioneers must have overcome, and this is a great factor in enlarging his social interest. (See outline for cooking.)

With the history there is also some study of the functions of our own city government as contrasted with similar functions of colonial government. The methods of the firemen of today are traced from the time of the "bucket brigade," and the work of the policeman is contrasted with that of the tithing-man and other officers of colonial times. The development of modes of illumination from the use of the pine knot to electricity is traced. This continues the civic study of the previous year.

Sixth Grade

The first half of the year is devoted to Grecian history. The starting-point of this work is the *Iliad,* since from this source may be gained the background for the study of the early Greek life—the Homeric period of Grecian history. In the first few weeks no effort is made to differentiate the literature from the history, the *Iliad* being the best embodiment of the Greek spirit and ideals, from which the children may proceed to a study of Grecian history with the sense of contact with the people. Following this study of the Homeric period, the *Iliad* is continued as part of the study of literature, while the history continues separately to show the development of the Greeks from the Homeric Age through the Age of Pericles.

The Olympic games, the life in Sparta and Athens, the contrasting ideals of education, government, homes and home life in the two Greek states, the Persian wars, the subsequent development of Grecian art and architecture, and of Greek drama, form the main types around which the work centers.

The children delight in the renewal of their acquaintance with the Greek myths begun in the third grade. Especial emphasis is placed upon the story of Hercules, in connection with the study of the Temple of Zeus at Olympia, and many of the other Greek myths are retold as they are suggested by passages in the *Iliad* or by the study of Grecian sculpture.

The Greek ideal of citizenship and how it resulted in a beautiful city is emphasized with the purpose of arousing questions and discussion of our own opportunities for making a "city beautiful" with a study of how people are organized in Chicago to secure that end. An excursion to the Art Institute furnishes a rich experience in the study of Greek architecture and sculpture, including also a study of the Greek vases—a direct contribution to the work in clay-modeling (see "Art").

The second semester continues the American history of the fifth grade.

The French in America: conditions, geographical, social, political and industrial that led to their coming. The fishing industry is studied in detail since it so largely controlled the first movements of the French in America. The development of the fur-trading industry, its organization, its far-reaching consequences in the later history of the French colonies, the coming of the missionaries, the establishment of fur-trading stations and missions, the progress of exploration, until all the Great Lakes, the Ohio, and Mississippi valleys were added to the French domain, are the central topics of this study. Cartier, Champlain, Marquette, and LaSalle are the central figures in the story.

Comparison of French and English colonial life, the contrast, geographically, between the two regions, resulting in different industrial and political conditions. The French and Indian War —and how its outcome affected the development of the English colonies.

The industrial development of the English colonies, showing

the growth of manufacturing and trade. The relation of the navigation acts and internal taxation to the Revolution.

Study of the Revolution; the geographic control of the different campaigns. The slow but certain growth of national independence. How was our struggle for independence like that of the Greeks in the Persian wars?

Seventh Grade

The work for the year in the seventh grade follows the movement of the people across the continent from the Atlantic coast plain to the Pacific Ocean. The history of the crossing of the Appalachian barrier and the settlement and conquest of the land between it and the Mississippi River centers about Daniel Boone, the maker of the Wilderness Road; George Rogers Clark, who won the Northwest Territory for the United States; Robertson, the founder of Nashville; and Rufus Putnam, who led the sturdy New Englanders to Marietta. This requires a careful study of the life on the frontier to make the children appreciate the problem these men solved. Their study is reinforced by the drawing or painting of homes and forts. The various occupations are used as subjects of work in clay. The children are allowed to choose what life experiences they wish to represent, and then are guided in the modeling of statuettes illustrating their experiences. (See outline of work in clay-modeling.)

The settlements of Boone and Robertson furnish the opportunity for a study of the simple forms of government which were found necessary when people were separated from the old established government of the coast region. In this presidential year there will be a special study of the national government under the constitution, to show how a president is elected.

The problem of government survey arises as the settlement of government lands in the Northwest Territory begins.

This suggests a study of the method employed which easily connects that time with the present, making clear how titles to land in this region are good today, while those held in Kentucky have been an unending cause of trouble. By this means the idea of the meaning and value of a national government grows stronger. In this connection comes the beginning of the public-school system in the Northwest, in the setting aside of Section 16 in every township as a source of school funds. (That a portion of this section is today held by the Chicago Board of Education for this purpose is always a source of surprise).

The problem of trade in the West leads to a study of trade routes and methods and of the political difficulties which grow out of the commercial separation between East and West. The invention of the steamboat, as set forth in Knox's *Fulton,* the Cumberland Road, in Brigham's *From Trail to Railway,* the Erie Canal and railroad, in Spark's *Expansion of the American People,* and Hart's *Contemporaries,* furnish a most interesting study and result in a certain new appreciation of the present conditions from seeing what efforts they have cost and through what slow stages they have evolved. Questions of internal improvement and the tariff grow naturally out of these industrial topics.

Well-developed trade routes and transportation resulted in a unified North. The same result was brought about in the South by the development of the cotton industry. The history of the cotton industry is amplified in the work in textiles which forms the handwork for the first half-year. By experience the children learn to appreciate the effect of machinery in time-saving. (See outline of textile work.)

The crossing of the Rocky Mountain barrier is treated in a similar way, noting the occupations which led the pioneers on, and the social and political problems which grew out of these occupations. The history of our country has been thus far largely a frontier history, and the story of the pioneers with the strength of character which they developed in their advance seems particularly adapted to the needs of children of this grade. The problems of social life and government are so simple that they can to a large extent make them their own problems. The ideals set before them are those of earnest effort, simple living, and true democracy.

Eighth Grade

The European history immediately preceding the discovery of America. Following the American history of the seventh grade, the eighth grade takes up that period of European history which immediately precedes the discovery of America. The work which centers about the Renaissance is selected because it is the background of American history; because it may be used in solving some of the social and governmental problems which appeal to these pupils; because the spirit of chivalry, service, and heroism finds a ready response in the adolescent years; because knowledge of the conditions which surround modern labor shows the value of the freedom in work which resulted in the art and architecture of the thirteenth, fourteenth, and fifteenth centuries. The subject is presented according to the following outlines:

1. The period of discovery and the growth of geography: (*a*) Geographical knowledge previous to the fifteenth-century voyages; ideas of the Greeks and Romans. (*b*) The Crusades; their effect upon the routes of travel. (*c*) The journeys of the Polos; increase of geographical knowledge and the breaking-up of routes of trade. (*d*) The invention of printing; books of the Middle Ages; mural paintings; effect of printing upon knowledge.

2. Feudalism and chivalry; the growth of feudalism; the life of the people; the growth of the church.

3. The guild system of labor contrasted with our modern factory system. Art: (*a*) The towns of the Middle Ages; their position on lines of trade; trade guilds. (*b*) Florence and Nuremberg—typical expressions of the thirteenth century; the cathedrals of Europe, illustrations of Gothic architecture. (*c*) Results of the guild system of labor—compared with modern factory system.

LANGUAGES

I. ENGLISH

The work of the school in English includes training in expression through language, and cultivation of an appreciation of literature. Since language implies thought to be expressed, it is impossible to consider it without taking into account all the other interests of the children. Language in the school is therefore used as an aid to accurate thought in all the subjects of study and as a means of organizing knowledge. Here, as in the arts and occupations, there is an opportunity for a co-ordinate development of thought and expression.

The earlier work is chiefly oral, and, as the children gain in ability to write, the amount of written work increases. Wherever there is a genuine need for writing, that is, a necessity for conveying thought to others, the children put forth their best efforts, and in such work they gain rapidly in skill. Writing done merely as an exercise fails to secure good results, either in spirit or in form.

In the eighth grade formal grammar is studied, and the study of the literary drama is begun.

The pupils of the school are publishing monthly a magazine, *The School Reporter*. They themselves do all the work and meet the financial obligations. The special value to the school of this interest lies in its effect upon the work in English.

Speech, oral reading, and dramatic art.—It is the aim of this work, first, to bring about freedom and expressiveness of voice and body; clearness, distinctness, and beauty of speech—good spoken English—by training the ear to hear, and the speech organs to form, well-shaped vowels and distinct, clear-cut consonants; second, to train the children to read intelligently and with a purpose; and to read aloud simply and naturally, with a clear perception of meaning, emotional content, and form. This will be done through the interpretation of literature, by means of extemporaneous speaking, and by the writing and acting of original dramas. Whenever possible, the literature being studied in English, French, and German is utilized for these purposes. The aim throughout is so to organize both the study and expression that the children shall acquire, not only independence in the use of reference books and literature, and freedom and spontaneity in expression, but also ability to think and do—that persistence and continuity of thinking which enables them to handle new material—new literature—with intelligence, purpose, and increased power.

With the majority of children real, living interest in reading seems to develop rapidly about the fourth year of school life. If up to this time the background has been well filled in by the constant functioning of words when the child felt the greatest pressure for their use, he has a key to the situation. Technical difficulties are mastered under the new impulse with marvelous ease and skill. By the time he reaches the eighth grade he not only can read for his own pleasure and entertainment, but also has developed gradually a definite motive for reading, and is able to use books intelligently in the study of subject-matter.

The organized social life of the school, the daily morning meetings, the special-day exercises, and the festivals of the year give motive and opportunity for practice in oral and dramatic expression.

With the purpose of laying the foundation of an abiding love for what is noble and beautiful in our literature, the teacher interprets a limited number of suitable selections to the children which they can understand and enjoy, but cannot read for themselves.

It is the aim to note every speech-defect, to watch the child, and, at the proper time, to give him the necessary help toward overcoming his defect.

Kindergarten

Literature.—Rhymes and Poetry: From Lear, *Nonsense Rhymes* and *Mother Goose:* "Hickory Dickory Dock," "Sing a Song of Six-pence," "Little Jack Horner," "Mary, Mary, Quite Contrary," "Hey, Diddle, Diddle," and others; Christina Rossetti: "Mix a Pancake," "What Does the Donkey Bray About?", "What Does the Bee Do?" (from *Sing Song*); Robert Louis Stevenson: "The Rain Is Raining," "Birdie with the Yellow Bill," "When I Was Down beside the Sea," "The Swing," "My Shadow."

Stories: From *Six Nursery Classics,* edited by O'Shea: "The Old Woman and the Six-pence," "Chicken Little," "The

Three Bears," "The Little Red Hen;" from Aesop, "The Lion and the Mouse;" from Dasent, *Stories of the Field:* "The Pancake," "The Pig and the Sheep," "The Lad Who Went to the North Wind;" from Dasent, *Popular Tales from the North:* "Billy Goats Gruff," "The Gingerbread Man;" from Thaxter, "Peggy's Garden and What Grew Therein;" Helen Hunt Jackson, "St. Christopher;" adapted from Cary, "Peter at the Dike."

First Grade

English.—(1) Literature: (*a*) Rhymes and poetry: Lear's *Nonsense Rhymes* and *Mother Goose;* repetition of those given in kindergarten; Christina Rossetti: "What is Pink?" "Brown and Furry," "If a Pig Wore a Wig;" Robert Louis Stevenson: "Bed in Summer," "The Wind," "Foreign Children," "The Whole Duty of Children," "The Cow," "Singing;" "Little Gustava," Celia Thaxter; "I'll Tell You How the Leaves Came Down," Susan Coolidge.

(*b*) Stories: From Dasent's *Popular Tales from the Norse:* "Boots and His Brothers," "Gudbrand on the Hillside," "The Sheep and the Pig who set up House," "Why the Bear Is Stumpy Tailed;" adapted from Grimm: "The Wolf and the Seven Young Kids," "Cinderella;" from Grimm's *Fairy Tales:* "The Shoemaker and the Elves," "One Eye, Two Eyes, and Three Eyes," "The Town Musicians;" from Howell's *Christmas Every Day in the Year and Other Stories:* "The Pony Engine," "Christmas Every Day in the Year;" "The Sleeping Beauty," Perrault; Whittier's *Child Life in Verse;* "The Bell of Atri," from Baldwin's *Fifty Famous Stories Retold*; "German Legend of the First Christmas," *St. Nicholas;* "The Birth of Christ," read from Luke; *Fables of Aesop:* "The Wind and the Sun," "The Lion and the Mouse."

(2) Reading: (*a*) The work in phonics begins immediately and continues throughout the year. The children learn the sounds of all the consonants and combinations of consonants, the simple vowel sounds, and also some of the more unusual combinations as *oy, aw, ight,* etc. At first the work is largely in the form of games, but gradually the attempt is made to bring the knowledge thus gained into working use in reading.

(*b*) On the blackboard the children see constantly words and sentences in connection with their work. Through much repetition they learn to recognize words and are able to follow simple written directions. Recipes are written and sometimes printed, for them. They also have printed short reading lessons or records of what they have done in connection with their history or science. (*c*) Books used in reading are *Heart of Oak*, No. 1, *Aesop's Fables, Hiawatha Primer,* and *Eskimo Stories* by Mary E. Smith, *Lights to Literature,* Book I, and various other simple readers.

Second Grade

English.—(1) Literature: (*a*) Rhymes and poetry: Repetition of Robert Louis Stevenson's verses given before; the following ones added: "The Lamplighter," "Young Night Thoughts," "The Sun Travels," and "Nest Eggs." "Hunting Song," Coleridge; "The Lamb" (first stanza) and "The Shepherd," William Blake; "Fairy Folk," and "Wishing," Allingham; "Seven Times One," Jean Ingelow; "March," Wordsworth; "The Wonderful World" (three stanzas), William Rand; "The Birds in Spring," Thomas Nashe; "Seal Lullaby," Kipling; "The Swallow's Nest," Edwin Arnold; "The Sun with His Great Eye" (a fragment), John Keats. Most of the poems mentioned above may be found in *The Posy Ring,* edited by Kate Douglas Wiggin.

(*b*) Stories: Adapted from Grimm: "Snow White and the Seven Little Dwarfs," "The Enchanted Stag;" from Hawthorne's *Wonder Book:* "The Golden Touch," "The Miraculous Pitcher," and "The Chimera;" "Little Thumbling," Perrault; "Old Pipes and the Dryad," Stockton; "Muleykeh," adapted from Robert Browning; "Mowgli's Brothers" and "Toomai and the Elephants," Kipling; from Dasent's *Tales from the Field,* "Japer Tom," "Boots and the Beast;" from Dasent's *Popular Tales from the Norse,* "Boots and His Brothers."

(2) Oral reading and dramatic art: The poems given above under "Literature," and the selections to be printed for the children's reading, listed above, offer opportunities for gaining skill in reading aloud. Certain of these are memorized for morning

exercises and festivals, and are used as a means of entertainment at our social periods.

(3) Reading: The children's own reading is from books, printed slips, and script. Each child has at the beginning of the year covers for printed slips. These include the following subjects: Sketches and stories of shepherd life and descriptions of the desert, by Jennie Hall; stories of hunter life and adaptations from Waterloo's *Story of Ab;* descriptions of Arabia, Palestine, and Switzerland; "Threshing in Greece," by Jennie Hall; selections from children's poetry, some rhymes of Christina Rossetti, and the words of the children's songs. We use "Little Black Sambo" and "Peter Rabbit," and selected articles from the following readers: *Lights to Literature; Heart of Oak,* Vols. I and II, Lane, *Stories for Children; The Blodgett Reader; The Culture Reader;* Dopp's *The Tree-Dwellers, The Early Cave-Man,* and *The Later Cave-Man.*

Third Grade

Literature: Poems, by Robert Louis Stevenson, "The Land of Story Books," "The Little Land," "North-West Passage," "Travel," "Where Go the Boats," "Escape at Bedtime," "Windy Nights," "Foreign Lands," "Fairy Bread," "Farewell to the Farm," " Looking Forward;" "The Fairy Folk," Robert Bird (Posy Ring); "Is the Moon Tired?," C. Rossetti; "The Wind and the Moon," George MacDonald; "Robert of Lincoln," Bryant.

Stories: the saga of King Harold the Fair-Haired, the Volsunga saga, and the sagas of Eric the Red and Lief Ericson told and read to the children; the *Odyssey,* parts read by children from Palmer's translation, parts read or told by the teacher; Norse myths: "Thor's Journey to Jotunheim," "The Death of Balder," "The Gifts of the Dwarfs," and others (Mabie's *Norse Stories* are recommended); Greek myths and hero-stories: "Apollo and the Python," "Hermes and the Cave of Winds," Perseus, Theseus, and Hercules (Hawthorne's *Wonder Book* and Kingsley's *Greek Heroes* are used.) Fairy-tales to be told: "The Land East o' the Sun and West o' the Moon," "The Twelve Wild Ducks."

Dasent's *Popular Tales from the Norse.* Fables: "The Country Mouse and the City Mouse," "The Man, the Boy, and the Donkey," "The Fox and the Grapes," "The Shepherd and the Wolves," and others from Aesop.

Poems and stories with which the children are familiar from previous years will be used constantly in the story-telling time.

(2) Oral reading: Poems and stories, of the greatest literary value, which at the same time are easy enough for the children to read, are selected for oral reading; they are studied especially with a view to rendering them in a beautiful way to others. All of the selections from *A Child's Garden of Verse,* some of the fables, the selections from the *Odyssey,* and the sagas are included in the oral reading.

(3) Reading: For some of the children considerable phonic drills and reading of very simple stories are necessary. Others use silent reading mainly for study in science, history, and geography, oral reading being used only for social purposes. At the end of the third grade the children should have acquired ease in reading whatever thought-matter is adapted to them, and in giving an intelligent oral rendering of the same.

Fourth Grade

English.—(1) Literature: Story of Siegfried. This is read and told by the teacher from William Morris, *Sigurd the Volsung.* The children also read "Aladdin, or the Wonderful Lamp," "Ali Baba, or the Forty Thieves," "Sinbad, the Sailor," from Mabie, *Stories Every Child Should Know;* Kingsley, "Greek Heroes;" and Kipling's *Jungle Book;* dramatization of Sigurd Stories and of Fairy Tales; poems from *Golden Numbers* and *Poems Every Child Should Know,* as: "The Mountain and the Squirrel," "How the Leaves Came Down," Autumn poems, Christmas poems.

(2) Oral reading and dramatic art: (1) dramatization of a part in the celebration of the yearly festivals. (2) Study of a group of celebrated horse-back rides in literature: (*a*) "John Gilpin's Ride;" (*b*) "How the Good News Was Carried from Ghent to Aix;" (*c*) "Sheridan's Ride;" (*d*) "Paul Revere's

Ride." (3) Other poems and dramatic stories which develop the power to express intelligently the reader's interpretation of the author's meaning.

Fifth Grade

English.—(1) Literature: The literature of this grade is Pyle's *Robin Hood,* Irving's *Rip Van Winkle* and *Legends of Sleepy Hollow,* and seasonal poems.

Reading: Nina Moore's *Pilgrim and Puritans,* Carpenter's *North America,* Tarr and McMurray's *Geography.*

Oral reading and dramatic art.—The interpretation of *Miles Standish* by the teacher; study and dramatization of parts of Robin Hood or of Rip Van Winkle; dramatic training in the staging of the French and German plays. Poems of the seasons are interpreted to the children and some of them are committed and recited at morning exercises. This class takes an active part in the Thanksgiving festival.

Sixth Grade

English.—(1) Literature: The *Iliad* is the principal selection of literature for the year. We use Bryant's translation. The children read and tell stories from the *Iliad,* from books they may have, or find in the library. Some books of the poem are left untouched, and others read only in part. "King Robert of Sicily," Longfellow; "King of the Golden River," Ruskin.

Prose and poetry of the seasons are read. Burroughs' "Signs and Seasons," "Wake Robin," "The Apple;" parts of Thoreau's *Excursions;* extracts from Bradford Torrey; Riley's "Dream of Autumn;" Whittier's "Fisherman;" and Longfellow's "Paul Revere's Ride."

Home-reading: Andrews' *Ten Boys on the Road from Long Ago to Now;* Guerber's *Story of the Greeks* and Hall's *Men of Old Greece;* Kipling's *Captains Courageous;* Martineau's *Peasant and Prince.*

Oral reading and dramatic art.—Parts of the *Iliad,* interpreted by the teacher to the class. Construction of a drama founded upon some of the incidents of the *Iliad;* the selection is determined by the feeling of the class. Dramatic training in French and German plays. Oral readings of *Paul Revere's Ride* (review), *King Olaf's Christmas* and other Norse sagas, and Browning's "Herve Riel." Interpretation by the teacher of season poems. Some of these are committed and recited by the children. Interpretation by the teacher of Browning's "Pheidippides" and other poems; also of "The Ship That Found Herself."

Seventh Grade

English.—(1) Literature: King Arthur Legends: the children read Lanier's *The Boy's King Arthur* and selections from Mallory's *Morte D'Arthur* and Tennyson's *Idylls of the King;* Poe, *The Gold Bug;* Hawthorne, *Tales of the White Hills.*

Reading: Extracts from original sources; three of the following as home reading: Hulbert, *Pilots of the Republic* (selections); Lighton, *Lewis and Clark;* Kinzie, *Wau Bun;* Brady, *The Conquest of the Southwest;* Parkman, *Oregon Trail;* Irving, *Astoria;* Hale, *The Man without a Country;* Taylor, *Eldorado;* a biography of Lincoln; Thwaites, *Daniel Boone;* and Churchill, *The Crossing* (first part).

Oral reading, and dramatic art.—Old English and Scotch ballads, autumn lyrics, Browning's "Herve Riel;" Kipling, "The Ballad of East and West." Interpreted to the children: Kipling, "The Explorer;" Longfellow, "The Building of the Ship;" Lowell, selections from *Biglow Papers.*

The reading and recitation of poems, orations, and other selections for the school festivals. The dramatic training required for the presentation of the children's English, French, and German plays.

Eighth Grade

Literature.—Shakespeare, *Julius Caesar;* Aldrich, *Friar Jerome and His Beautiful Book;* Henry Van Dyke, *The First Christmas Tree;* Lowell, *The Vision of Sir Launfal;* Scott, *Marmion and Douglas,* and selections from *Ivanhoe;* Arnold, "*Sohrab and Rustum;*" Longfellow, "Keramos."

Home reading: As throwing light upon the history the

following poems and books are recommended for home reading. Some of the poems may be read with the class. Longfellow, "Venice," "The Belfry of Bruges," "Nuremberg," "Giotto's Tower," "The Sermon of Saint Francis," "Walter von der Volgeweide;" Scott, *Ivanhoe, The Talisman;* C. M. Yonge, *The Little Duke;* Gunsaulus, *Monk and Knight;* Pitman, *Stories of Old France;* Harding, *The Story of the Seven Hills;* Bulwer Lytton, *Last of the Barons.*

Pupils are expected, before completing the work of this grade, to have acquired the habit of spelling correctly, skill to write legibly, and power to express their thoughts clearly in both oral and written language. Systematic instruction in grammar to this end is a part of the work in English. There is a study of the sentence (subject and predicate, modifiers, phrases, clauses, kinds of sentence, forms—simple, complex, and compound). The parts of speech are learned, and some work is done in inflection. Scott and Buck's *Brief English Grammar* is used as a textbook.

Oral reading, and dramatic art.—Subjects for oral reading are chosen from the general work in nature-study, history, and geography, from the subjects listed under "Literature," from Julius Caesar, and selections from Scott, and from other orations and dramatic selections to be used in the morning exercise. The oral reading of subject-matter bearing on these general topics is used to give the class information not otherwise to be obtained. The study of oratory has for its object the training of the pupils to speak with purpose and power to an audience.

II. FRENCH

Fourth grade, second semester.—Instruction wholly oral. The vocabulary in this grade is obtained from songs, games, rondes, and activities which the children can perform themselves.

Fifth grade.—Instruction largely oral, with special emphasis on ear-training and pronunciation. The vocabulary is based on songs, games, objects in the room, and the simple phrases of common use in the classroom. Each child keeps a notebook containing the songs and exercises. The reader used in this grade is Hotchkiss' *Premier livre de français.*

Formal work: Attention is called to the definite and indefinite articles, the pronouns, and the verb-endings in the present tense. There is some dictation.

Sixth grade.—Vocabulary of the Fifth Grade reviewed and enlarged through the learning of more difficult songs and games. Sight-reading of stories in Guerber's *Contes et légendes,* Part I. Retelling and dramatization of stories; more dictation; writing of answers to questions and some work in the writing of original sentences. Stories read or told by the teacher, and retold by the class. The activities of the day, the seasons, etc.

Formal work: Verb-forms in the present and past indefinite of the first conjugation. The demonstrative and possessive adjectives.

Seventh grade.—A study of the geography of France. Special study of Brittany. Songs, legends, and tales connected with certain places are learned by the class. Reading of Hervé Riel. This class will probably read Guerber's *Contes et légendes,* II. Written exercises based on reading matter.

Formal work: Review of grammar of previous years. The imperfect, imperative, and future of first conjugation verbs, the present of some irregular verbs. Drill in phonetic reading.

Eighth grade.—A study of some events in French history. Poems and songs in connection with this work. Class will probably read Malot's *Sans Famille.*

Formal work: Grammar of previous years summed up. Conjugation of verbs of first, second, and third conjugations. Impersonal verbs. Irregular verbs of most frequent use. Singular and plural of nouns and adjectives with exceptions.

III. GERMAN

Fourth grade.—This class will commence German at the beginning of the second semester. Instruction will be largely oral. Basis of vocabulary: nursery-rhymes, songs, riddles, games and actions which can be executed in classroom.

Fifth grade.—This is a beginning class; a great part of the work therefore will be oral. Special attention will be paid to the acquisition of a good pronunciation, and to the training of the ear. Free oral expression will be encouraged. Basis of vocabulary: rhymes, songs, riddles, games, actions, and little stories. Everyday expressions, especially those of the schoolroom, will be memorized.

The class may begin to read: Foster's *Geschichten und Märchen.*

Formal work: Definite and indefinite article, different pronouns, a few verb endings, singular and plural of nouns which occur.

Sixth grade.—The vocabulary of the fifth grade reviewed and enlarged. Basis of vocabulary: activities of the day, meals, the house, its furnishings and rooms, stores, animals, etc. More colloquial terms and songs. Sight-reading from Foster's *Geschichten und Märchen.* Verbs in present and past tenses, singular and plural of nouns, possessive pronouns. Some dictation.

Seventh grade.—Vocabulary: Activities during different seasons, festivals, as Christmas, etc. The class begins to study the geography of Germany. Sight reading from Guerber's *Märchen und Erzählungen,* Vol. I.

Formal work: Review of the work in previous grades; future of verbs; reflexive verbs. More dictation work (phonetic spelling).

Eighth grade.—Vocabulary: Geography of Germany, historical legends, poems, and songs. Sight-reading from Seligmann's *Altes und Neues.*

Formal work: Conjugation of verbs, declension of nouns and adjectives.

MATHEMATICS

Kindergarten

In the kindergarten number is used constantly in choosing children for games in groups of 2, 3, 4, 5, and 6; in building, in designing; in allotting space indoors and in the garden; in selecting material.

First Grade

Measuring is continued in the first grade in constructing cardboard buildings for a farm, and furniture for a playhouse, also in papering walls of playhouse, and in making book-covers. In cooking, the cup is used as a unit of measure, and ½, ⅓, ¼, ¾, and ⅔ of a cup become familiar. Most of the work in number is incidental to cooking and making. As the number interests multiply, they arrange themselves around various centers of number concept which are systematized somewhat now, so that the mass of material will not be confusing, and as opportunity seems fitting, certain facts are emphasized by special drill.

Second Grade

The work of systematization begun in the first grade is emphasized in the following year. The number images are clarified and made definite. Estimates and indefinite comparisons followed by the beginnings of definite measurements and comparisons are the important features of this year's work. These are brought about through the various activities; keeping accounts of school supplies, addition of two columns of figures, and subtraction of numbers under 100 are used, and pieces of money become familiar. In cooking, gardening, construction of candy boxes, valentines, etc., and in scientific experiments, fractions—halves, fourths, thirds, eighths, twelfths, and sixteenths—are used; simple mixed numbers are added; plans are made to a scale; the following units of measure are used: gram, ounce, pound, gill, pint, quart; linear, square, and cubic inch; and the following figures are constructed: square, rectangle, right-triangle, equilateral triangle, circle, and hexagon.

The children count by 2's, 5's, 10's, 4's, and 3's; they build up numbers and take numbers apart, as, 10+8=18; what numbers added make 18, 15, 21? What two equal numbers make 12, 16, 18? What is ½ of 12, 16, 18? What three equal numbers make 12, 15, 18? What is ⅓ of 12, 15, 18? What is ⅔ of 12, 15, 18?

Third Grade

The work of the third grade in keeping accounts, in gardening, in construction, in cooking, and in scientific work, involves problems of many kinds, and the result is more mathematical concepts, new centers, and more facts. This necessitates a greater emphasis upon classification and tabulation, and the specific work of this year is to get the tabular machinery of number fairly under way.

The children keep accounts for materials used and do simple bookkeeping in this connection. In cooking, weights and measures are used, proportions are worked out in cooking recipes. In scientific experiments the amount of water contained in fruits, the amount evaporated in drying, etc., is found; weight of water transpired by bulbs and evaporated from bulb-jars is computed. Plans for woodwork are worked out to scale, and demand use of fractions.

Fourth Grade

The fourth grade completes the work of learning the tables begun in the third grade, and the work of the year is to get the tabular machinery under working control through using it in problems arising in the environment, and in problems, formal and concrete, added to these to give emphasis to the principle involved. The tables are built up through measurement, compound numbers, areas, etc., as, 1 bu.=4 pk.; 2 bu.=2×4 pk.=8 pk.; or 1 row=9 sq. ft.; 2 rows=2×9 sq. ft.=18 sq. ft. Cross-section paper is used in making the tables and in factoring. At the time $7\times 8=56$ is learned, $8\times 7=56$, and $\frac{1}{7}$ of $56=8$, and $\frac{1}{8}$ of $56=7$ are learned, as well as $56\div 7=8$ and $56\div 8=7$, and 7 and 8 are factors of 56.

Tables through the twelves are learned as well as tables of linear and square measure, dry and liquid measure, as far as the facts are used in the work.

Averages are found in three ways: $\frac{a+b}{2}$, $a-\frac{a-b}{2}$, and $b+\frac{a-b}{2}$.

Linear and square and cubic measure is used in study of gardening and ventilation. United States money is used in accounts, simple bills are made out and receipted.

Fifth Grade

The work of the fifth grade gives the child an independent hold upon the fundamental processes so that he feels he has control of them. He proves his problem, depending upon himself to know whether his answer is correct. He also transfers the fundamental processes to fractions, common and decimal. With this feeling of control comes free use of the processes, and choice of ways to reach the desired end. The cooking and textile work give rise to various problems in fractions, while the garden and material for looms and Christmas gifts call for linear and square measure, right-angle and parallel lines. Cross-section paper is used in study of areas, factoring, and fractions.

Sixth Grade

The work of fractions, common and decimal, goes on in the sixth grade, and the aim is for independence in technique as well as in mathematical thinking. And as the fifth grade gives independence in dealing with the four processes with integers, the sixth grade works toward control of these processes with fractions. There is proving of answers, rapid work, and choice of method, as, $6\frac{1}{2}\times 7\frac{1}{4}$: (*a*) multiply as it reads; (*b*) change to improper fractions and multiply; (*c*) change fractions to decimals and multiply.

Mathematical language and form are emphasized, the equation is used, the letter used for the word, as, What is the width of a rectangle whose area is 78.4 and whose length is 7, appears in this form:

$$w\times 7=78.4$$

$$w=\frac{78.4}{7}=11.2.$$

Work in geography demands knowledge of ellipse, foci, horizontal, vertical, perpendicular, angle, degree, use of compass and protractor, measure of latitude and longitude. How to bisect a line, draw parallel lines, and find center of a circle are problems that find a place here. Rectangle, triangle, trapezoid, polygon, circle, their perimeters and areas are studied. Commercial and scientific problems arise. Cross-section paper is used constantly.

Seventh Grade

Through a study of the organization and operation of modern business institutions the pupils of the seventh grade become familiar with the commercial transactions, as met in the everyday common life, of banking, handling loans, promisory notes, interest, stocks and bonds, taxes, discount, insurance, commission, and profit and loss, thus making the various operations in percentage their own. Mensuration comes to them in working drawings for manual training; designing for simple electrical and mechanical appliances; drawing to scale tracts of land, farms, maps, field measurements, area of circle, volume of cylinder, as in gas and oil tanks. Surveying is taken up in connection with *Pioneer Life* in history.

Mathematical form and language are emphasized: (*a*) the use of the equation; (*b*) the letter standing for the number; (*c*) the equation read, using letter, and also read in full. The problem: What is the length of a rectangle whose area is 14 feet and whose width is 7, is written

$$7 \times l = 14$$
$$l = \tfrac{14}{7} = 2.$$

Later it appears thus,

$$7\,l = 14$$
$$l = \tfrac{14}{7} = 2$$

to solve for *x*, and finally,

$$7\,l = 14$$
$$l = \tfrac{14}{7} = 2.$$

This comes *gradually*, following much work of this kind in the sixth grade: $n=3$, give value of 4 *n's*, 7 *n*'s, etc.; 7 *n*'s$=21$, give value of *n;* 9 *n*'s$=27$, find value of *n*. Finally the *s* is dropped and they have $9n=27$, etc. The equation is read $7l=14$ and also interpreted as the particular problem and read: "What is the length if the area is 14 and the width 7?" The problem:

For what insurance at 3 per cent. will the premium be \$75, is stated in this way:

$$\text{Prem.} = \text{Ins.} \times r$$
$$\$75 = \text{Ins.} \times .03$$
$$\text{Ins.} = \frac{75.00}{.03} = \$2{,}500$$

and later it appears thus:

$$\$75 = .03\ \text{I.}$$
$$\text{I.} = \frac{\$75.00}{.03} = \$2{,}500.$$

The independence secured in the sixth grade is strengthened by concise mathematical form, for example, the familiar law of product and its relation to the other terms of the problem is here stated thus:

$$16 \times n = 64$$
$$n = \frac{64}{16} = 4,$$

and later abbreviated to

$$16\,n = 64$$
$$n = \frac{64}{16} = 4.$$

In this way the field of arithmetic that has been covered is *reviewed* with a new interest; a simple, concise, accurate means of expression helps to clarify as it generalizes, and gives a feeling of control not possible to a student while hampered by clumsy language.

Eighth Grade

The work of the eighth grade is largely to summarize and systematize the knowledge of arithmetic already gained. The work of generalized number begun in the seventh grade is a potent agency in this review.

The rudiments of algebra and geometry are associated with cognate phases of arithmetic through the year to clarify the arithmetic rather than to anticipate the study of algebra and geometry in the high school. For example, the problem of addition and subtraction of fractions is generalized in this way:

$$\frac{1}{3} \pm \frac{1}{4} = \frac{4 \pm 3}{2+4},$$

and later

$$\frac{1}{a}+\frac{1}{b}=\frac{b\pm a}{ab}.$$

The various laws of mensuration are stated in the same concise way. The area of a triangle is found by multiplying the base by ½ the altitude, is stated:

$$\text{Area of triangle}=\text{base}\times\frac{\text{altitude}}{2},$$

and later

$$\text{Area of triangle}=\frac{ba}{2}.$$

Laws of simple machines, problems in force and weight, and laws of mensuration give free use of equations, and the laws of equations are worked out.

Relation of angles of polygons is shown experimentally and by measurement. Lines are drawn making given angles with lines. Proofs of principles are made by actual superposition of representative figures. Laws of similar triangles grow out of field-work.

Mechanical drawing: scale plans and elevations of accessible objects. Scale drawing in manual training; representative drawings of accessible and remote tracts of land, etc.

MUSIC

Each child in the school has three half-hour periods of music-instruction and two periods of chorus-singing a week in morning assembly. As the school is divided into two sections for the morning assembly, the lower five grades alternating with the upper ones, songs are chosen with reference to this division. The first five grades are given one set of songs suitable for assembly singing, while the upper grades have another repertoire.

In the year 1907–1908 the following songs have been used and found effective:

"Gipsy John" (upper grades) .... *Frederic Clay*
"Hark the Lark" (eighth-grade girls) .... *Schubert*
"The Wanderer's Song" (upper grades) .... *Schumann*
"Aurora Borealis" (two-part) .... *Rheinberger*

From the Fourth Book of "Model Music Series," by Eleanor Smith (Silver, Burdett & Co.)

"Nutting Song" (upper grades) .... *Eleanor Smith*
"The Earth Is the Lord's" (upper grades) .... *Eleanor Smith*
"Early Spring" (three-part) .... *Mendelssohn*
"The Volga" (eighth-grade boys) .... *Russian*
"Finland's Forest" .... *Finnish*
"The Wild Rose Tree" .... *Eleanor Smith*
"The Wood Minstrels" (four-part) .... *Mendelssohn*
"Come All Ye Shepherds" (four-part) .... *Bohemian*
"John Peel" .... *Folksong*
"Maypole Dance" .... *Folksong*

From the Third Book of the same series:

"A Snowy Day" (lower grades) .... *Altenhofer*
"Welcome Wild Northeaster" (upper grades) .... *Jaspersen*
"We Merry Minstrels" (lower grades) .... *Purcell*
"Santa Lucia" (two-part) .... *Venetian*
"In the Tempest" (two-part) .... *Tyson Wolff*

From the Second Book of the same series:

"Harvest Home" (lower grades) .... *E. Richter*
"Old Christmas" (lower grades) .... *Lorraine*
Two-part Round .... *French*
"Frosty Days" (upper grades) .... *Jaspersen*

From the First Book of the same series:

"Oriole's Nest Song" .... *Eleanor Smith*
"The Squirrel's Thanksgiving" .... *Eleanor Smith*
"Winter Song" .... *Chadwick*
"The Laughing Rill" .... *Adams*

From Ed. Grieg's *Children's Songs:*

"Goodnight Song to Dobbin" (lower grades)
"Sea-song" (upper grades)
"Fatherland Psalm"
"Courage" .... *Franz Abt*

From Schumann's *Children's Songs:*

"The Snowdrop" .... *Robert Schumann*

From *Songs in Season* (Flanagan pub.):

"As Joseph Was A-walking" .... *Coonley Ward*

From operetta *Robin Hood:*

"The Armourer" (upper grades) .... *de Koven*
"The Skye Boatsong" .... *Jacobite*

From Reinecke's *Children's Songs:*

"Ye Shepherds Arise"
"O Violet, Darling Violet"
"Shake the Apple-Tree" (in German)
"Kling, Glöcklein, Kling"
"Der Besen"

Technical work in music begins with the first grade, although in the kindergarten ear-training is given through imitation of whistles, bells, etc. The first technical subject taken up is rhythm. The children are led to clap and swing two, three, and four-pulse rhythm, to recognize these rhythms in simple melodies, and to picture by means of circles drawn on the board the time of familiar songs.

The scale syllables sung up or down the scale are thoroughly mastered, the children notating the scale on the board. Song-singing forms the chief part of each lesson, short melodies of simple intervals being taught as well as the larger songs for assembly use.

In the second grade song-singing is again emphasized. Technical work occupies less than half of the music-period. Rhythm is reviewed and six-pulse measure is added. Time-symbols, whole, half, quarter, and eighth notes are introduced; also the bar. Starting with melodies formed on scale-progression, the children are led to notate songs of four or eight measures.

Sight-reading is introduced in the third grade by means of short and simple exercises. A musical value is given these by the addition of a piano accompaniment after the reading is accomplished. Phrases chosen from familiar songs are notated. Rests, whole, half, quarter, and eighth, are used. Rote songs are taught for assembly singing.

In the fourth grade the children are encouraged to read independently suitable songs for their chorus work. They take pleasure in feeling their control of technique and enjoy having it tested. This is an important period in their musical development. Arbitrary rules for finding the key-note with any signature are given as preparation for later scale-analysis. Two-part singing by means of rounds and scale exercises is begun. Parts of familiar songs are notated.

Although sight-reading for practice is a part of the work throughout the upper grades, rote-singing is also continued. Two-part work is carried on into duets of increasing difficulty.

In the fifth grade, scale-structure is studied and rules are developed for building through the sharp keys. The children notate their original songs.

A thorough drill in signatures and keys is continued in the sixth and seventh grades. Chromatic scales and exercises are studied. Songs with strong, musical inspiration are chosen for assembly singing. Pupils are encouraged to play or sing for one another in class, an opportunity for this exercise being given once each week.

Emphasis is laid throughout the course upon the importance of writing as well as reading music. The vizualization of simple forms is tested by the children's ability to write simple phrases. Rhythmic and melodic analysis of tunes is followed by notation of portions, and later, of the complete melody.

Realizing that the foundation for good vocal development as well as good technical development must be laid in the elementary schools, voices are carefully watched and made as normal and tuneful as possible. Care is taken to secure good tone quality; correct attack and intonation are insisted upon. The attention of parent and physician is called to physical impediments to normal use of the voice in the children, and influence is exerted for their removal or amelioration. Unmusical and imperfect speech is corrected.

Original texts rewritten and set to music in all grades, different children contributing to the whole. The melodies are then written out by the pupils. Interesting and characteristic composites are often produced.

HYGIENE AND PHYSICAL EDUCATION

The physical well-being of the children and the conditions under which they pass their time while at school are of fundamental importance. The recognition of this fact has led the

School of Education to establish a medical supervision which extends over the school activities of the child, directs his physical exercise and outlines his work in hygiene.

Physical work.—The earliest plans of the school included a generous provision of time and equipment for physical exercise. Physical work ranks both in dignity and importance in the curriculum with the other work of the school, and the same regularity and system are required in this as in other subjects.

Equipment.—Two gymnasia, a spacious playground already equipped with volley and basket-ball courts and a running-track, and the expanse of the Midway furnish ample space for the outdoor class work, for organized plays and games, and for unrestricted play.

Costume.—Leather gymnasium shoes are required for all. Boys of the three upper grades wear gymnasium suits which should not be purchased until directions are given by the teacher. The school costume for the girls of the same grades should be loose and simple (Peter Thompson, sailor, jumper) without tight belts, in three pieces, waist, bloomers, and skirt, and so arranged that the skirt can be easily and quickly removed at class time. The most sensible costumes for girls of the lower grades includes bloomers like the dress.

Gymnastics.—All children are required to take the class work. This is arranged to counteract the more common physical defects and is of such a character that any child who is in physical condition to take part in other school activities can participate. The extent of the participation in this, as in his mental training, may be modified by the results of the physical examination. Every class receives three lessons each week, including dancing, in the gymnasium or on the playground, and exercises in the schoolroom between recitations when considered advantageous.

The class lessons aim to accomplish three objects: training in posture and correction of defects, education to quick and definite reactions, and recreation. The methods used in presenting the work are designed to develop pleasing bearing, carriage, and address, and such mental and moral qualities as responsibility, consideration, courage, initiative, order, and obedience to authority, qualities fundamental in developing useful and desirable members of society.

In this as in other subjects the teachers can only lead and direct; the child's cheerfulness of mind and manner and volitional interest are necessary if results are to be accomplished.

Plays and games.—These are presented in such a way that they eventually go to the playground as material for the morning and noon recreation periods and are of such a nature that they may be played without supervision.

Dancing is of high value in the physical programme. Properly taught it trains a sense of rhythm and gives a control of body which emphasizes grace and distinction. It invigorates both mind and body, and like plays and games promotes sociability. The folk-dances as well as national music introduce the children to the life of other peoples.

Class lessons are arranged progressively with the following outlines as guides:

First Grade

Gymnastics and games.—Marching, running, body movements and breathing, jumping and games; work arranged to require little form or application; largely imitative; proportion of formal work to jumping and games one-third. Music accompanies all parts of the lesson. Games of sense, inexact imitation, of no purpose, of variety of motion, and games involving all the players. One lesson each week in rhythm. Relation of directions and the different parts of the body discovered; their relation to various musical rhythms.

Second Grade

Gymnastics and games.—Beginnings of formal work in marching and running; add fancy steps; postural work and breathing still imitative; beginning of exercises on apparatus (hanging); games. Proportion of formal work to apparatus and games one-half. Music accompanies all but apparatus and games. Begin games of exactness of motion.

Dancing.—First five positions for the feet; bows; grand

right and left; beginning exercises leading to the waltz and two-step; galop square; marking the rhythm by hand; clapping in the waltz, two-step, and galop.

Third Grade

Gymnastics and games.—Marching, running, fancy steps, postural work and breathing, and jumping and games. Work still imitative, but increasing importance attached to proper respect for, and response to, command. In increasing the emphasis upon the advantages of method and system, begin methods of formally placing the class on the floor for postural work. Hand apparatus introduced in postural work. All formal work still accompanied by music. Begin games of low organization, and simple games of competition and co-operation.

Dancing.—First ten positions with the feet; bow; grand right and left; waltz and two-step in couples; galop in couples; galop square, polka square.

Fourth Grade

Gymnastics and games.—Lesson plan same as for third grade. Proportion of lesson given to formal exercise increases. Shorten reactions by the addition of commands while running. Combination of movements demanding finer discrimination and co-ordination. Begin games of a higher type of co-ordination.

Dancing.—Waltz; two-step; polka; galop; folk-dances; clap dance; sailor's hornpipe.

Fifth Grade

Gymnastics and games.—Further development of volitional control through problems in new co-ordination in postural and apparatus work and jumping is sought. This age of children demands the addition of antagonistic and competitive work which requires special adaptation of running, vaulting, and jumping exercises. Games involve increased endurance and skill.

Dancing.—Waltz; two-step; galop; polka; three folk-dances; London dance; sailor's hornpipe; clap dance.

Sixth Grade

Gymnastics and games.—Lesson plan the same as that of the fifth grade. Girls and boys in separate classes. Additional control of distance and direction in running and marching; increased mental and physical values through tactics executed without music at command. Training for increased dexterity and alertness through introducing insistence upon

A Gymnasium Class of Girls

form, as well as uniformity in the details of changing the direction of facing or position of the class upon the floor. Games still involve all players, but emphasize the additional element of choice.

Dancing.—Waltz; two-step; galop; polka; square dance ("Prairie Queen"); Highland fling; lilt; gymnastic dancing for girls: (1) Highland fling; (2) cachucha; (3) Greek dance; (4) nursery rhymes.

Seventh grade

Gymnastics and games.—Lesson plan the same as in previous grades. Girls and boys in separate classes. Marching and running as well as postural exercises and apparatus demanding increased volition and concentration of attention. This is a period of rapid growth—new functions develop, as well as large amounts of new tissue. Hence all exercises tend to special development of heart and lung actions, care being taken to avoid strain. Special attention to breathing exercises. Games of higher organization are added which prepare for team play and require endurance and develop judgment.

Dancing.—Waltz; two-step; square dance ("Prairie Queen"); Irish washerwoman; rejane; gymnastic dancing for girls: (1) Swedish weaving; (2) Spanish dance; (3) Greek dance; (4) Irish lilt.

Eighth Grade

Gymnastics and games.—Results more than ever depend upon the attitude and interest of the pupil. The training should begin to show dexterity and co-ordinate action in both girls and boys, and power of endurance in members of the boys' classes. Proportion of formal exercises to games now becomes two-thirds. Exercises chosen for direct bearing upon the growth and development of the period. Exercises of skill and precision with hand apparatus. Fundamental exercises on hanging and resting apparatus. The best games of the previous years are used for the free play at the close of the lesson, and, in addition, preparatory work for the highly organized competitive games.

Dancing.—Waltz; two-step; square dance ("Prairie Queen" or "Samson clog"); buck and wing; lilt.

INSTRUCTION IN HYGIENE

Through the co-operation of the grade and science teachers the children should be taught even in the lowest grades why certain methods have been adopted in maintaining the general health, in the care of the eyes, ears, nose, mouth, teeth, and skin—why we eat, sleep, wear clothes, need exercise and air; and the advantage of an erect posture. This work has already been established in some of the upper grades and will be extended as rapidly as possible.

Progressively new points are introduced and discussed in an informal way until in the upper grades growth and structure of the body and civic hygiene are dealt with more or less technically.

The instruction is placed as far as possible on an experimental rather than a didactic basis.

MEDICAL SUPERVISION

Medical supervision includes three groups of activities: The regulation of the hygiene of the institution, the control of contagious diseases, and the personal examination of each child, to determine his fitness to carry on the regular work of the school and to serve as a basis for the modification of his curriculum, mental and physical, if necessary.

School hygiene.—In regulating the hygiene of the institution such problems are dealt with as lighting, heating, cleaning, ventilation, sanitation, water supply, school furniture, the proper apportionment of mental and physical effort and of work and play.

In 1907 a filtering plant was installed in the University, and all the drinking-water in the building passes through this plant; the lunch-room is the only exception, and there hydrox is used.

The grade rooms are equipped with adjustable desks and chairs, which are fitted to the child at the opening of school and are changed on later inspection whenever indicated by the growth of the child.

Contagious diseases.—The danger of spreading contagious diseases in the school is reduced to a minimum by the system of investigating the cause of every absence before the child is allowed to return to his classes, by the prompt exclusion from school of all children who have contagious disease, and the enforcement of proper regulations in regard to other children in the same family.

Any child who has been absent from school for even one day, unless it is known that the absence is not due to sickness of himself or some other member of the family, is required to report to the office of the school physician before returning to his classroom. In case a child remains away from school for two days the cause of the absence is investigated by telephone or letter. Any pupil taken ill during school hours is sent at once to the school physician for examination and advice.

In regard to exclusion for contagious disease the following rules are in general observed, but the department reserves the privilege of shortening or lengthening the period of exclusion if it is satisfied that such procedure would be safe and desirable under the circumstances.

Chicken pox: Child is excluded during contagious period, about three weeks or until the skin is free from desquamation.

Diphtheria: Period of contagion lasts until bacteriological examination shows the throat free from diphtheria bacilli.

Measles: Period of contagion about three weeks, or as long as catarrhal symptoms are present.

Mumps: Period of contagion about three weeks, or ten days after the glandular swelling has disappeared.

Scarlet fever: Period of contagion about six weeks, or as long as any signs of desquamation persist. Notification is required from the Board of Health that the premises have been properly fumigated.

Whooping-cough: Period of contagion about six weeks, or until the spasmodic cough has disappeared.

Pupils may be excluded from school because of exposure to contagions other than those noted above.

Every pupil is required to present on entrance a certificate of vaccination. Revaccination may be required by the school physician in case the previous operation did not have a typical result, or if seven years or more have passed since the last successful operation.

Physical examination.—The physical examination of the child aims primarily to determine his working efficiency, his capacity for putting forth effort. Any physical defects which interfere with the proper exercise of his powers are particularly noted. Special stress is laid on the observation of circulation and respiration, of posture and bone relations, and on the detection of abnormalities of eyes, ears, nose, and throat.

Every child is examined at least once a year and further examinations are given to those whose condition calls for it. Children who are in school for the first time and those who are below the average physically or mentally are given the preference in the order of receiving examination.

Parents and teachers will be notified of such indications for special treatment, mental or physical, as may be brought out by the examination.

Programme

ARRANGEMENT OF ARTS AND INDUSTRIAL WORK

Grade	First Semester	Second Semester
First..........	Clay-Modeling Drawing and Painting	Clay-Modeling Drawing and Painting Home Economics
Second........	Clay-Modeling Drawing and Painting Home Economics	Clay-Modeling Drawing and Painting Textiles
Third.........	Home Economics Wood Drawing, Painting, Clay-Modeling	Textiles Drawing, Painting, Clay-Modeling
Fourth........	Clay-Modeling Wood	Drawing and Painting Metal
Fifth..........	Textiles Home Economics	Textiles Wood
Sixth..........	Home Economics Drawing and Painting	Clay-Modeling Wood
Seventh........	Metal (or Wood) Textiles	Wood (or Metal) Home Economics
Eighth.........	Home Economics, and choice of Wood, Metal, Clay-Modeling, Bookbinding, Printing	Drawing and Painting and choice of Wood, Metal, Clay-Modeling Bookbinding, Painting

The normal amount of time given weekly to each subject is as follows:

History	4 periods ½ hour each
Geography	4 " ½ " "
Mathematics	4 " ½ " "

Nature-Study	4	periods	½	hour	each	
English	2	"	½	"	"	
Literature	2	"	½	"	"	
Music	3	"	½	"	"	
Gymnastics	2	"	½	"	"	(lower grades)
	2	"	¾	"	"	(upper grades)
Dancing	1	"	¾	"	"	
Arts and Industrial Courses	2	"	1	"	"	(shorter periods in lower grades)
French, German, or Latin	4	"	½	"	"	

THE UNIVERSITY ELEMENTARY SCHOOL CURRICULUM

FRANK A. MANNY
New York City

Historically no other elementary-school curriculum has interest for workers in education equal to the one presented by the University Elementary School. There is a convergence here of important streams of influence and one is tempted to look for the results of one and another of the forces that have been at work. Present function and form are however of much more importance than origins, although these latter would necessarily be considered in any thorough study of the former.

The new statement takes advantage of the present concern in industrial education and brings to a focus in this field the various efforts that have been making to socialize the subjects of study and to organize the course from the standpoint of the activities of children and young people who also have relations to the larger social organization. Unity, integration, correlation, inclusiveness,. scope are regarded, but one may question whether the principle of differentiation is sufficiently in evidence. In the introduction it is stated that this is the "ultimate end of our curriculum," but there seems to be a division of the field between these two factors, rather than a recognition of their joint activity. This dualism may be as serious in its results as the more common one, which counts habit and drill as the lot of the elementary years, while attention and thinking are reserved for adolescents.

One may wish to defer the trade school until the age of sixteen and appreciate the need of more wisdom than has yet appeared in the use of the elective system in higher schools, without at the same time regarding vocational training as something beyond the elementary period or holding rigidly to one course for all during these years.

It would be a real service if this problem were more definitely stated. The differentiation of function on the part of children in school as evidenced by a wider range of subjects; specialists as teachers; smaller classes; participation in producing, criticizing, teaching, and governing is certainly an important stage of vocational training and differs from that of later periods more in its experimental character and its lack of fixity than in other features. Again, the relationship of the industrial to the moral deserves clearer definition than is given to it. One feels that the high school, college, commercial interests, and other factors in the larger social situation are regarded too much as outsiders and even as ogres. We have all suffered from the results of their domination, but they are resources which are indispensable in working out the freedom desired.

There is a marked freedom from external domination seen throughout the course. This is refreshing for one turning from the grind of many elementary schools, but on the other hand does this outline consider sufficiently wider relationships? The pupils probably are ready to do good work in the next stage, but one sees little evidence that this problem is taken into account. There are so few institutions in which there is an opportunity for the educational situation to be seen in such wide ranges as at Chicago and Columbia universities that we naturally turn to these for help in understanding the meaning of the large sections with reference to one another—in this case the significance of the elementary school in relation to secondary and higher education.

In the statement, on the whole, the emphasis is upon ideas rather upon execution and administration. The method in a large sense does not appear as a problem—details of subject-matter and in several cases the work of single grades and especially of departments are projected with considerable clearness but the course as a whole does not build itself up with sufficient coherence out of the excellent studies of social demands and psychological needs that are presented.

It seems ungracious to write thus of a curriculum which marks the latest development of forces which have worked so successfully in freeing us from the old schemes in which real needs were choked and smothered by an orderliness so complete that it left little room for activity and life. In one sense statement always lags behind practice and that the course may be of most help to the schools of this country (and those in Europe which I found using the *Elementary School Teacher* as a valued adviser) there is need that the logical orderly, executive aspect of the school's life, so important in the good work it is accomplishing, should be formulated and communicated rather than be taken for granted. The material is there, and also movement and direction, but organization is lacking. I repeat that it is not domination or fixity that is needed but a projection of an ideal of the whole and an expression of the methods of operation brought to light by this larger forecasting.

It is a pleasure to see how much evidence there is of the results of the work of the children in the making of the curriculum. A school must have an excellent spirit whose course shows so many signs of listening to the pupils and of observing what makes for their growth. There is a minimum of "awakening the minds of the children," of "letting," "restricting," "permitting," etc. In the same way "solving" and "solutions" give way to natural progress. The sentence, "the school grows through study and criticism of its own work," is suggestive, and one of the best expressions of execution is found in connection with the positive function of the museum. But there is limitation in that the "study and criticism" made by pupils, teachers, and departments is not supplemented by that of the secondary school, the college, the outside examiner, and others who must necessarily consider the problem as a whole.

It would be interesting to be told what is the basis upon which omissions of subjects in particular grades are made, also the sequence of subjects in some doubtful cases. There are times when prospective or retrospective reference is assumed beyond the power of the ordinary student to determine it. There is an evident intention to see the past in the light of present needs, but it would be interesting to have a study made of this past material with reference to its justification in each instance as to simplicity, etc., and a comparison of the claims of less remote substitutes.

The modern-language announcements are somewhat disappointing. The work seems advanced for beginners and questions come to mind which a little fuller statement would have cleared up. One feels that some of the sections were written rather for teachers who could fill in details of relationship from direct acquaintance with the work than for those of us who are too far away to have this opportunity. The modern-language work in most elementary schools is in an unsatisfactory condition and institutions which have favorable opportunities have also serious responsibilities. The music department of this school has had a wide influence, but the published course does not seem to do this section justice in several important fields.

Each of the departments invites questions and comment. There is in some of them almost an overwhelming amount of material. One wonders whether this does not signify at times a sacrifice of control to appreciation and whether the attack in many cases could not be more direct and effective and more attention be paid throughout to that factor which in the secondary school we do not hesitate to recognize as scientific.

Despite the apparent tendency of the present critic to emphasize negative features the announcement marks an advance in curriculum-making and gives evidence that the corps behind it is almost ready to give us a whole equal in quality to the best of the parts.

EDITORIAL NOTES

This journal is fortunate in being able to send out with the programme of the University Elementary School Mr. Manny's comments upon it. Mr. Manny has been identified from the first with the educational movement for which the University Elementary School stands. Indeed he had an active part in the beginnings of the University School. He is just completing a two-year study of schools in Europe and America. With this rich and sympathetic background his criticisms should be especially noteworthy. We may wince at some of them, and not the least at some we accept. Others we may feel disposed to debate and rebut. But in any case we shall agree that it is through such sympathetic, yet frank, criticism that the "cause" is advanced. To quote from the programme: "The school grows through the study and criticism of its own work."

Mr. Manny's Criticism on the Elementary School Programme

However, one or two comforting things may be kept in mind in reading the curriculum and Mr. Manny's comments. The statement of a curriculum may work injustice, and in two ways. The logical balance and syllogistic sequence of the curriculum of a school of the old formal type creates the impression of a continuity in method and material, for which one looks in vain in the actual operation of the school. On the other hand, in a school whose curriculum is just the on-moving life of the community, any attempt to abstract the material from the currents and eddies of the movement itself is sure to work injustice in the opposite direction. The curriculum of such a school when abstracted from the connecting motives which cannot be put on paper is sure to indicate less continuity, less method, than really exists. It is a case of attempting to separate the "what" from the "how." And this always vitiates both. Method is nothing but the material in operation. The "how" is the "what" specified by "when" and "how much." It may be, therefore, that Mr.

The Problem of Programme-Making

Manny's suggestion of a lack of attention to method in the statement of the curriculum expresses an inherent difficulty in putting on paper the curriculum of such a school, short of a complete account of the working of the school. Any published curriculum of such a school must be taken as only an illustration, as a sample, of what the real curriculum is. This should be kept in mind in reading Mr. Manny's remarks on the departments of Music and Modern Languages. Also it should be remembered that such a school does not hope to work out a finally complete curriculum. It is not attempting to "make" *a* curriculum. It recognizes that the curriculum cannot be made, that it cannot be prescribed; that it grows from day to day as does the social life from which it springs, or rather of which it is a part.

The Problem of the Elementary School

Yet these general considerations cannot obscure the fact that although the curriculum "grows," it does not grow as Topsy or the lilies of the field. It is a growth beset with problems on every side. To quote again from the programme: "It seems not overstating it to say that the Elementary School has the grave responsibility of redeeming our youth from class isolation." This is especially timely in view of the current assumption of class struggle as a solution of our social and economic problems.

And this suggests that when we say that the curriculum must be taken from the community life we are not to understand by this that the curriculum is constituted by taking over certain occupations that happen to be now going on in the community. It must consider the problematic side of these occupations, their drift, the new occupations, and the questions that spring from them. Thus, as Mr. Manny says, we are now confronted with the trade-school problem. Whatever our views about the trade-school movement, it is an issue we must face. We cannot ignore it. It is indeed a part of the larger problem of maintaining the sense of reality and vitality. We all know that this demands something more than a mere contact with "real things." We are aware that the sense of reality depends as much on the method and motivation of the "contact" as upon the thing. So long as the contact at school was backed up by contact with similar material at home and in the shop there was no problem of reality. We have taken over the industrial material abandoned by the home. But who is bold enough to say that we have yet succeeded in reaching the kind of reality, the degree of inevitableness in the motivation that the old industrial home supplied?

Continuity and Correlation

Then there is ever with us the problem of a genuine continuity and correlation. For example, we cannot simply pick up the contents developed in the studies of nature and society and use them without more ado as material for art and literature. We cannot assume that the material of any scientific or social "interest" will be equally interesting in art. We must distinguish those scientific and social experiences that *call* for artistic and literary expression from those that do not.

Freedom from the Schoolmaster's Dogmatism

Of the connection between the elementary school and the high school, of the problem of the relation of appreciation and abstraction, raised both in the introduction and in Mr. Manny's comments, there is not space here to speak. Suffice it to say that both programme-makers and their critic are sufficiently alive to all these problems and to the transitional character of the present stage of industrial education to keep the programme and criticisms upon it free from the schoolmaster's dogmatism which used to characterize much educational discussion. A. W. M.

NOTES AND NEWS

Compulsory education in Italy applies only to children from six to nine years. Most juvenile arrests take place there between the ages of nine and twelve. Crimes against property cause almost one-half the commitments.

While Pennsylvania and Illinois have been appointing commissions to codify and improve school laws, West Virginia has adopted an entirely new set of such laws, greatly improved in every point. State Superintendent Miller is to be congratulated on his speedy success.

"No wonder the Japanese prints are the most wonderful works in line-drawing and composition the world possesses," says D. C. Watson in a discussion of art-training in *Home Education*. "No Japanese boy is considered educated unless he can draw at least five thousand delicate forms to indicate as many letters, words, or expressions." Mr. Watson continues with an enthusiastic defense of drawing as a training in motor control and discriminating appreciation of form.

Popular Educator for March contains an instructive article on "Written Expression." In Italy, says M. V. O'Shea, the pupils spend a long time in simply "making lines" before they are allowed to write a single letter. Very great formal beauty of written characters is obtained, but efficiency in the content expressed suffers from minute and constant attention to the technical skill of beautiful letter-making. The article is interesting as a comment on a prevailing trait of the Latin nations.

Not only the universities have summer schools. The *Journal of Education* contains an account of the Norantum Summer School of about 400 boys and girls, where the children learn sewing, cooking, basketry, reseating chairs, and several other interesting and profitable occupations. Part of the time is devoted to training in out-of-door sports. This school, like so many of the valuable experiments in modern education, was begun by a social science club and later taken over by the municipality.

The Boston department of school hygiene, is, according to the *New England Journal of Education*, the first in the country. Besides the inspector and director and assistant directors, it includes a corps of school nurses, with an appropriation of $25,000 for the nursing work alone. These nurses are said to be especially valuable in forming a link between home and school and in giving good advice to mothers. In the case of the children at least our customs are becoming most rapidly socialized.

The Massachusetts legislature has under consideration a bill requiring a playground in every municipality of above ten thousand inhabitants, with at least one additional playground for each increase of twenty thousand inhabitants. These grounds are to be put in charge of committees the members of which receive no salary. If this bill is passed it will prove a great step in advance in the matter of school hygiene and morals.

Much better progress is being made in Chinese elementary and middle schools than in the higher educational institutions, says an article in *Indian Education*. This is due to the fact that the local authorities have a freer hand and many public-spirited men have established schools at their own expense. "The boys have a uniform and go through a course of drill, while mathematics, general history, and geography help to broaden their minds." The magnitude of the educational upheaval through which China is passing is hardly to be appreciated by the western mind.

Few things have developed faster within the last ten or fifteen years than the medical inspection of schools. In Boston such inspection was first introduced in 1894, and was applied especially to the isolation of germ diseases. Today it includes examination of sight and hearing, and a general physical examination for the purpose of determining the pupil's fitness for work. This examination is required annually. Thirty per cent. of all public-school children in the elementary grades are over the normal age of their grade, and this backwardness is often found to be due to curable physical defects.

So the rod is not to be restored to New York City, in spite of the agitation in favor of it. The subject has caused a great deal of discussion, nearly all the civic associations of the city having passed resolutions against corporal punishment. The decision of the board could hardly be called unanimous, 21 to 17, yet it seems likely to be a final decision, as the matter has been so thoroughly gone over. If New York, with its school problems increased by the numbers of foreign-born children, accustomed to severe methods of treatment, decides in favor of "moral suasion," it seems hardly likely that the rod will win out in any city of the country.

Of thirty or more "school cities" organized in the public schools of Philadelphia, all but one or two have been discontinued. O. P. Corman points out in the *Journal of Education* some of the defects of the school city. He thinks they arise from the fact that any system of self-government which attempts total control has to be under the surveillance of the authorities to such an extent that it becomes a thinly veiled paternalism. A questionnaire answered anonymously by the pupils in a school city showed "unwillingness to hold office, because the duties of that office conflicted with their ideals of honor and friendship." "The answers of many of the younger pupils showed that they had entirely missed the significance of the plan."

BOOKS RECEIVED

LITTLE, BROWN AND CO., BOSTON

In the Golden East. An Illustrated Journey in Eastern Wonderlands. (A Geographical Reader.) By CHARLOTTE CHAFFEE GIBSON. Cloth. Pp. 197.

The Louisa Alcott Reader. A Supplementary Reader for the Fourth Year of School. Cloth. Illustrated. Pp. 222.

SILVER, BURDETTE AND CO.

The Little Helper. A Supplementary Primer to Accompany the Rational Method in Reading. By MILLICENT BAUM. Cloth. Illustrated. Pp. 96. $0.28.

A First Practice Reader. By LIBBIE J. EGINTON. Cloth. Illustrated. Pp. 128. $0.30.

THE UNIVERSITY OF CHICAGO PRESS

The Logical Basis of Educational Theory from the Standpoint of "Instrumental" Logic. (A Ph.D. Dissertation.) By DANIEL AMBROSE TEAR. Paper. Pp. 58. $0.53 postpaid.

THE MACMILLAN CO., NEW YORK

School Reports and School Efficiency. By DAVID S. SNEDDEN AND WILLIAM H. ALLEN, for the New York Committee on Physical Welfare of School Children. Cloth. Pp. 183. $1.50 net.

Educational Woodworking for Home and School. By JOSEPH C. PARK. Cloth. Illustrated. Pp. 310. $1.00 net.

The Management of a City School. By ARTHUR C. PERRY, JR. Cloth. Pp. 350. $1.25.

VOLUME VIII NUMBER 10

THE ELEMENTARY SCHOOL TEACHER

JUNE, 1908

A UNIQUE SCHOOL SYSTEM

NATHANIEL BUTLER
School of Education, The University of Chicago

"On the Art of Living with Others" is the title of a charming essay by Sir Arthur Helps. The phrase may be accepted as one more, and perhaps one of the best, of the expressions of the present-day conception of the end of educational effort. It is a colloquial way of saying that the school is an agency which society organizes for "socializing" its members—for developing or setting up in the individual such impulses, prejudices, habitual reactions, that when an occasion presses the button, the response will be what is, then and there, the fitting and adequate response. This obviously demands more of the school than that it be a purveyor of information, a teacher of "lessons." It must rather be a gymnasium, or better a laboratory, wherein the pupil may practice all sorts of intelligent self-direction, in which, having become expert, he has, so far, mastered the "art of living with others."

This familiar commonplace is to be borne in mind in judging of the value of a system of schools. And when it is said that a system of schools is "unique," it is first of all to be understood that the system in discussion has solved with peculiar success for its own community the problems which that peculiar community presents. But it may also be fairly assumed that a system whose success is unique has worked out the solution of certain problems of importance to every community.

When anyone familiar with education in American cities

enumerates the systems that have impressed the country as having done these things with eminent success, he names among the first the city of Cleveland. In the succeeding article Superintendent Elson gives a modest account of the educational features of that city. But another hand than his may perhaps more freely point out certain directions in which these schools have advanced along paths of their own, or advanced farther than most along familiar paths.

In organization the school administration is entirely separate and distinct from municipal administration, "the board of education having entire responsibility and power with reference to its tax levies, and having power to issue bonds and being in no sense subject to review by any part of the municipal administration." The "topical" method of supervision is found in few if any other cities. Probably in no other city is the high-school work organized into so complete a unit of effort.

Cleveland is, if not the leader, certainly among the few cities that are leading in the experimental solution of the problem of industrial education, in distinction from what is understood by "manual training." In the new technical high school, to be opened in September, technical work will be emphasized, receiving equal attention with academic work. The latter will, indeed, be arranged chiefly with reference to the former and because of the bearing of the selected academic studies upon "the intelligent control of the problems involved on the technical side." "The school has a four-years' course, and is open to both boys and girls (in segregated classes) who have completed an eighth grade of the elementary schools." The school is frankly to be dedicated to technical training. For example the girls will be trained in (I quote from a statement by the superintendent) "hand and machine sewing; dress, garment, and costume making; fall, winter, and spring millinery; plain, fancy, and invalid cookery; first aid to the injured; hygiene, sanitation, house planning and decoration; home management and household accounts." Here is a high school devoted chiefly to training in the techniques which the pupils will be called upon to use. And specializing is not excluded, for while the first two years will follow a prescribed course, pupils will, during the last two years, be allowed to specialize along lines to which they are particularly adapted.

Cleveland probably leads American cities in its development of the school garden. This feature will be watched with especial interest because of its possibilities for both school and community. And perhaps most of all, in Cleveland, the school has reached out into the community in its provision for "special classes"—the mentally deficient, the deaf, epileptics, and those who are "backward" for any cause. Here a systematic and determined effort is made to modify the law of the survival of the fittest, by rendering the unfit fit to survive.

Superintendent Elson regards it as one of the special features of the Cleveland schools that "the three R's are well taught, particularly spelling and reading." He obviously believes that it is necessary not only to "prove all things," but also to "hold fast that which is good." His schools rest solidly upon the old foundations, and in this respect may possibly put forth a chief claim to be regarded as unique in days when so few are adhering, not merely because of tradition, but intelligently and of deliberate purpose, to the faith once delivered to the saints.

CLEVELAND PUBLIC SCHOOLS

WM. H. ELSON
Superintendent of Schools

The public schools of Cleveland operate under the State School Code which vests their control in a Board of Education. This board consists of seven members elected at the regular municipal elections upon a separate or school ticket, nominations for which are made by political parties or by petition. The period of service is four years and there is no compensation to members, except that by recent enactment they are allowed their actual expenses. The board appoints a director of schools, for a period of two years, who has charge of the executive or business department, and a superintendent of schools, for a period of five years, who has charge of the educational affairs of the schools. The Code empowers the superintendent to appoint all teachers, subject to the approval and confirmation of the board.

SUPERVISION

The system of supervision is centralized, the superintendent's staff consisting of two assistant superintendents whose duties are both supervisory and administrative, a number of supervisors of subjects, and principals who are supervising principals in their respective buildings. The method of supervision is essentially topical, i. e., a given person supervising one or more studies through several or all grades, in some cases with the help of assistants. There are supervisors in charge of each of the following: English, German, arithmetic, geography, and history, substitute teachers, kindergartens, penmanship, music, drawing, manual training, physical training.

HIGH SCHOOLS

Cleveland has six academic high schools and is about to open a technical high school. These seven schools accommodate something over 5,000 students. The academic high schools offer the following courses: classical, scientific, commercial. A two-years' course in shop-work for boys and a two-years' course in applied art for girls are offered in the academic high schools. Similar courses are offered in the technical high school and in addition a third and fourth year of practical work along lines of the mechanic arts for boys and the domestic and applied arts for girls. The principals of the high schools and the superintendent of schools constitute a Board of High-School Principals which meets once a month for comparison of ideas and experiences and for establishing common policies of instruction and administration. At these meetings every phase of educational and executive activities is considered. High-school teachers in all the leading subjects have organized themselves into groups which meet regularly for the consideration of matters relating to their respective departments. The course of study, educational values, and methods of instruction furnish topics for discussion at the monthly meetings. Through these organizations teachers make helpful contribution to a unified system of high-school instruction which is a composite of the best experience and judgment of the entire teaching force. In athletics the high schools operate under a code adopted by the Board of Education. This code provides faculty coaches and places all schools upon a common basis, insuring the smaller school in the least favored district as efficient coaching as that given the larger school in the more favored locality. The tendency of this code is to sink athletics into its proper place in the list of high-school activities.

NORMAL SCHOOL

The normal school covers a two-years' course for graduates of a four-year high school. It has about two hundred students and graduates, each year about one hundred. This school is open to a limited number of high-school graduates who are admitted upon competitive examination. Twelve weeks of practice work in the training schools are afforded—the student-teacher assuming responsibility for the conduct of regular lessons under the supervision of critic teachers.

MERIT SYSTEM OF PROMOTION

In both elementary and high schools a merit system of promotion prevails which recognizes both experience and efficiency as factors in salary advancement. Instead of the usual promotional examination, a record of efficiency is made the sole test. This includes also evidences of growth and progress. The rating is based upon written data submitted by all in official relation to the teacher.

TEACHERS' PENSION FUND

The Teachers' Pension Fund is created by joint effort of the Board of Education, which contributes annually 1 per cent. of the total income for school purposes, and the teachers who pay at the rate of $20 per year—$2 being deducted from the salary each school month. The maximum annuity is $300. There are about eight hundred members who contribute to the fund and about twenty beneficiaries.

SPECIAL SCHOOLS

Schools for defectives are established, each school having a maximum of fifteen pupils. These are in charge of teachers especially trained for this work. One of these schools is for epileptics. In some cases age and advancement is made the basis of classification, older and larger pupils being segregated and the work especially adapted to their needs. Special classes for backward pupils have also been established, the assignment to these schools being limited to twenty-five pupils. These include children who learn from books slowly and with difficulty, those who for any reason are seriously behind their grade, nervous children, or those unfavorably affected by class requirements. An oral School for the Deaf enrols about sixty-five children and has eight teachers. In these special schools transportation is paid for the children who live beyond reasonable distances from the school. Handwork and work in the school gardens is emphasized with these children.

SCHOOL GARDENS

The organization of this work under the direct charge of the curator of school gardens now includes, besides school gardens, the planting and care of trees, shrubs, and flowers with the purpose of beautifying school grounds, a propagating center, botanical garden, and exchange garden, and lectures on gardening at various schools. A number of large school gardens have been established and several small grounds developed in connection with special schools noted above. It is proposed to establish gardens in connection with cooking schools where conditions are favorable. During the past year the Home Gardening Association gave the schools more than 8,000 bulbs as prizes for flower shows, and these were used for both indoor and outdoor planting. The association also contributed $600, which was expended by a committee in the purchase of shrubs and plants, for a tool-house, and for soil and labor for the botanical garden.

MANUAL TRAINING

In the first four grades in the elementary schools drawing and manual training are united and placed under one supervision. In the grammar grades the drawing and manual training are closely related but under separate supervision. In the fifth and sixth grades boys are given work in soft wood while the girls have a course in sewing, including the making of simple garments. In the seventh and eighth grades the manual training is given in "centers" to which children in these grades from a number of nearby buildings receive their instruction—the cooking is offered for girls and the bench work for boys. Individual equipment in cooking is provided, each girl cooking every article under consideration. These lessons are given once a week—one hundred minutes in length.

In the high schools a two-years' course is offered to boys including mechanical drawing, wood turning, and cabinet work—five double periods per week with a credit allowance equivalent to one academic study. Boys of high-school age are entitled to more than the acquisition of technical skill such as is required from the making of small exercises or miniature useful articles—hence large projects of a distinctly utilitarian end are given. In the Technical High School specialized work of pattern making, forge and machine shop-work is offered. Throughout an attempt is made to relate closely the mechanical drawing to the shop activities. Designs for use in the shops form a fundamental part of the work of the students in mechanical drawing. In the two-years' course offered in the academic high schools, familiarity with working drawings and the ability to read them, together with sufficient skill in preparation of simple shop drawings, is sought while the more technical side of mechanical drawing is developed only in the Technical High School.

APPLIED ARTS

An art course is offered extending from the kindergarten throughout the elementary and high-school grades. This work includes freehand drawing, composition and design, constructive and applied design. In the primary grades the work includes also construction and in the grammar grades co-operates with the department of manual training. Decorative borders and surface coverings are used in connection with articles constructed of cardboard, wood, and in the domestic art department. In the high school a credit course in applied arts is offered as an elective and parallels the courses in manual training. Five double periods a week are given with a credit allowance equivalent to one academic study. This work is taken chiefly by girls and has recently been inaugurated. Girls may in this way secure, as a part of their regular high-school course, a training which looks to art-industry activities. The craft work includes cardboard, pottery, and textiles the first year, for the second year leather, lettering, and illuminating. In the Technical High School third- and fourth-year work is offered including pictorial and decorative composition and design, also block printing, bookbinding, and art-metal work as crafts.

PHYSICAL TRAINING

The system of physical training includes medical inspection for the prevention of communicable diseases, discovery and treatment of abnormal and subnormal children, sanitary provisions and constructive measures of physical training and athletics. The Board of Health employs twenty-six district physicians who act as school inspectors. Each is assigned a group of public schools which he is required to visit. He sees such children as principals and teachers may bring to his attention. His service is essentially designed to prevent the spread of communicable diseases and in this effort it is successful. Attempt is made to ascertain the defects of school children. A close correlation is found between these defects and the retardation of the progress of pupils through the grades. Doubtless many children leave school because of unsatisfactory progress due to physical defects. Much waste is doubtless caused by conditions which are avoidable, hence the value of medical inspection which includes the care and treatment of children that are abnormal and subnormal. Much attention is given to the securing of sanitary environment including ventilation, comfortable hygienic furniture, sanitary toilet facilities, and ample light well distributed. The buildings erected during recent years in Cleveland have excellent provisions as to light and ventilation. The desks and seats used are of an improved type designed by the physical-training department, having seats and backs which are automatically correct and with a range of adjustment adapted from measurements of several thousand children in the local schools. Sanitary drinking-fountains, having a constant flow, do away with the use of cups. Toilet rooms are thoroughly and independently ventilated by the exhaust system through fixtures which are automatically flushed. Only unilateral lighting is now employed, with a minimum window surface equivalent to 20 per cent. of the floor space, rising in most cases to 25 per cent. The use of adjustable shades aids in solving the problems of windows exposed to the sun.

In the arrangement of the daily programmes, subjects which are most expensive of nervous energy are assigned to the morning period while those that are predominantly motor alternate with more exclusively mental subjects. Attention is given to the length of the recitation period, restrictions in the amount of home work, the use of three or more daily "two-minute drills," consisting of deep breathing and stretching and bending the body to stimulate respiration and circulation and to relieve congestion. All children are required to leave the building during the recess period except in stormy weather. Not only are gymnastic exercises given, but interest is stimulated in games and sports. There is some equipment of school yards with play apparatus. The outdoor games offer opportunity for social development and for cultivating the spirit of "fair play."

CONTINUATION SCHOOLS

The continuation schools include evening schools, summer schools, and free lectures and social center development. These represent an attempt to secure to the community the largest possible return on the investment in school buildings.

EVENING SCHOOLS

Fifty evening schools for elementary instruction in English are opened. They enrol about five thousand students. There are also four evening high schools which enrol about nine hundred students. In the high schools students are almost wholly American born, while in the elementary schools they are predominantly foreign born. An evening trade school for machinists and a similar school for instruction in brick laying were opened during the past winter. In these the classes were limited. There is increasing demand in the evening school for vocational training accompanied with instruction in other studies which bear a direct and vital relation to industrial subjects.

SUMMER SCHOOLS

Regular provision is made for these schools and during the past year sixty-five instructors were organized under one supervisor and an assistant supervisor. These schools continue eight weeks, the sessions extending from 8:30 to 11:30 A. M. (high schools from 8 A. M. to 12:30 P. M.) five days each week. The total registration last year was 3,642 distributed as follows:

High schools	303
Grammar schools	856
Primary schools	588
Boys' school	168
Kindergartens	437
Manual training	200
Playgrounds	1,090

Of these, 171 high-school students and 453 grammar-school

students passed all of their examinations at the close of the summer term and many others made up a part of their work.

FREE LECTURES AND SOCIAL CENTER DEVELOPMENT

The importance of this work is indicated by the fact that a regular committee of the Board of Education has charge of the details of the work. Forty-four school auditoriums have been utilized by residents of the districts under the guidance of this committee, giving entertainments, lectures, and concerts that have been pleasing and instructive. As a result of this work the co-operative spirit is growing in the community. The courses offered are varied and extensive, appealing both to the instruction and the entertainment of the people. The building of auditoriums as a feature of school equipment is growing in the appreciation of school patrons. They afford a common place of meeting and bring the home life and school life into harmonious relation.

SCHOOL GARDENS

LOUISE KLEIN MILLER
Curator of School Gardens, Cleveland Public Schools

The late Colonel Francis W. Parker repeated again and again to the students of the Cook County Normal School: "The only way to help yourself, is to help others."

This admonition has come to me many times with renewed significance. In connection with the assistance we have given in establishing school gardens in different parts of the country, I have realized that the work in the Cleveland schools is influencing for good or ill the introduction and progress of school gardens elsewhere. We have endeavored to pursue a sane policy and make our work an integral part of the regular school work.

The school-garden work is managed by the director of schools and any co-operation with the educational departments must be effected through the superintendent of instruction and heads of departments. The nature-study, geography, arithmetic, manual-training, drawing, music, and domestic science supervisors have been most cordial in their efforts to correlate their work with that of the school gardens, and good results have been reached.

The activities listed under "School Gardens" are various in scope and far-reaching in influence. Limitation of space in school grounds has forced us into intensive gardening, which doubtless is the most effective and educative method, because it impresses upon the children an appreciation of the yielding capacity of a small plot of ground. We have found that when it is possible to have a garden in a school yard, it serves as an object-lesson to all the children, and although they are not able to engage actively in cultivation, they have had the experience of seeing other children in their work. As a result of the stimulating influence of such observation, we have today in Cleveland thousands of well-planned, well-planted, and well-cared-for home gardens in as many back yards, which until recently were the dumping-ground for an accumulation of rubbish, threatening the community with disease, and constituting a civic blemish.

The regular work is divided into that for normal, defective, and delinquent classes of children. Warren School garden may be considered a type for normal children. It is in the school yard, contains forty beds each six by twelve feet, surrounded by a six-foot flower garden, which produces a succession of blooming flowers from April to November, and inclosed by a hedge of *Ligustrum oralifolium.* The officers of the garden are elected by the children from the list of gardeners, and the selection is generally a wise one, efficiency being the qualification. The superintendent keeps all records of attendance and products, the head gardener has charge of tools and all practical work, and the assistant gardeners are responsible for work done in their sections. The gardeners are responsible to the section leaders; section leaders to the head gardeners; head gardeners to the superintendent; and the superintendent to the curator.

The Doan School garden in a vacant lot back of the schoolhouse has been improved by a summer-house and pergolas.

The Rosedale School garden is possible, because, in order to secure the property for the school, the Board of Education was obliged to purchase a "blind lot," which affords space for a rock garden, formal flower garden, vegetable garden, and herbaceous botanical garden. Thousands of persons visited this garden last year; some came week after week to see the succession of blooming flowers, each bearing away a higher appreciation of an orderly well-kept garden, of harmonious color effects, of the beauty and wonder of growing things, and an impetus to go and do likewise. We hope that the botanical garden started this spring will not only be interesting, but instructive. Space and conditions forced us to limit our planting to sixty-six orders. The planting was done according to the classification of Britton and Brown.

Children can readily learn to which great groups of plants we are indebted for our food, clothing, and shelter. The *gramineae* or grass family, containing ornamental grasses, bamboo, wheat, rye, oats, barley, and rice, bears a vital relation to men and animals. This garden will be of educative value to students of nature-study, physical and commercial geography, and botany.

A kitchen garden has been established at Oakland School, a manual-training and domestic science center. The plan calls for an arrangement of vegetables and herbs, which shall produce an attractive effect of foliage and fruit. A bed is devoted to perennial flowers and another to supplies of material useful in the household—flax, cotton, broom corn, hemp, buckwheat, castor beans, etc. The supervisor of domestic science is anxious that the girls shall be familiar with the habits of growth of plants they are learning to cook.

Last year as an experiment we established a garden for mentally and physically defective children, which proved so successful, that we shall have one for each of these schools. One which promises to be of especial interest is at the Outhwaite School, where there are two classes, one a mixed class of boys and girls, and another composed entirely of boys, between the ages of twelve and sixteen years. The children take active interest in their work and are stimulated and benefited by the exercise in the air and sunshine. There are so few avenues open to these unfortunate children, that we hope this work will demonstrate to them the possibilities of the soil.

Between the time when boys are arrested for petty, and more serious offenses and their trial, instead of being sent to jail, they are taken to the Detention Home for Boys. From 8:30 A. M. to 1:30 P. M. they go to school in a small cottage fitted up by the Board of Education for the purpose.

Mr. Charles Orr, director of schools, who is greatly interested in all phases of this work, has made it possible for us to have a garden for these boys, in the space surrounding the cottage, where the boys can raise vegetables for the home, learn to care for flowers, and keep a lawn in order. Anyone at all sympathetic with boys, and especially with those who are full of energy, but on the wrong track, must enter upon this work with intense and hopeful interest, realizing that if we can afford a legitimate outlet for this misdirected energy, it may be possible to give them a different point of view, a different attitude of mind, and that the opportunities afforded by practical gardening may lead them to appreciate the sanity of an upright way of living. When the subject of a garden was proposed to the boys, it was greeted with satisfaction and appreciation, by all except one boy. He told me he was not able to work. Charlie is an Italian. His lower limbs are crippled and withered, and he walks on two crutches. He has been refused admission to every institution in the state, and sent from the public schools on account of his violent fits of temper. He was made superintendent of the garden. All directions are given to him and he sees that they are executed. He is intelligent and efficient and will secure good results. The whole expression of his face has changed. Another boy who has done good work is a lad who ran away from home and had slept in a box for a week. A boy who ran away from the Institute for Feeble-minded at Columbus was our most efficient worker. He could be a valuable assistant on a farm.

Mr. Orr has opened an employment bureau at school headquarters, where those who want assistants for farm, truck, or home gardening can leave their names, and the boys who have had experience in school-garden work can make applications for positions. Many of the boys have gone out into the country during the summer and have not only had a pleasant, wholesome experience, but earned enough money to secure books and clothing for the following winter.

The work is delightful, but it fulfils its mission only if it stimulates to industry and effort.

Another phase of the work is the improvement of the school grounds. We seek to make the school grounds centers for civic improvement. As each school has its problem to solve the work is diversified. The Home Gardening Association has been an efficient aid in all our efforts. The children bought more than 250,000 penny packages of seeds last year, which were used in the home gardens. The autumn flower shows give evidence of the interest and efforts of the children.

The most promising feature of our work is that it is strongly progressive. Children do better work each succeeding year, and the home grounds and gardens give evidence of increasing knowledge and more artistic taste in arrangement. Illustrated lectures have been given in schools, libraries, churches, and before women's clubs. Boys and girls, men and women, listen to the discussion of preparation of soils, fertilizers, nitrifying bacteria, trees, shrubs, birds, insects, vegetable and flower gardens, with an intelligence quite gratifying. Interest in gardening is cumulative. There is a vital touch about it which nothing else seems to supply. Fresh air, sunshine, exercise, contact with the soil, the wonderful mysteries of nature, afford a strength and poise which may be helpful in physical, moral, intellectual, and spiritual development.

DO WE EDUCATE?

IDA AHLBORN WEEKS

This question, in the face of the large sums of money that we spend for education, may sound like an impertinence. But, as people may spend largely for food and dress and be neither well fed nor well clad, so they may spend largely for education and still fail of being rightly educated. We may even have pure food laws and yet be ill nourished; and we may have excellent school legislation and yet many a child go forth into life without the training that the school ought to have given him.

General statements like the above weigh little; but, if we throw into the scale with them a single specific instance, the weight becomes significant.

In a state that has an excellent compulsory school law, that has a common-school course so extended that it must often prove a weariness of flesh to teachers, in such an enlightened state a child grew up to the age of sixteen years. Her home was in a beautiful and healthful town of about two thousand inhabitants. The family was poor, the father addicted to drink and subject to epileptic attacks. Moreover, love for strong drink was a family heritage. As one might expect, the mother took in washing to help in the support of the household. In such a home the child lived, and grew familiar with a destitution that frequently sent her begging from door to door. But the worst thing befell the family when the mother was placed in the insane asylum. After a short time she returned, but soon went back as a permanent inmate of the institution, though her insanity is said not to be hereditary. For a few years—until his death—the father kept the children together in a fashion.

It would not be strange to hear the inquiry, What good thing can come out of such a domestic Nazareth? Five children came out of that wretched home, children of apparently average endowments as to mind and body. One of them was a comely girl of sixteen. What has the great state of her nativity done to educate her?

The state failed at two points: first, it failed to give her such an education as is provided for by the common-school course of study and by the compulsory school law; secondly, it failed to take her needs and gifts into consideration and thus to train her along lines where she could have been trained to advantage.

In extenuation of the state, it may be said on the first point, that the education of such a child constitutes a very hard problem. Let her put the case. "I always had to stay at home and take care of the younger children while mother was washing. I went about one day in the week. I hadn't clothes like other children." Her irregular attendance along with her dulness as to books kept her far behind most girls of her age. When she was fourteen she was in the third grade, and beyond this grade she never advanced. "I was good in numbers," she said with some pride. But she can neither read nor write. "The teacher never made me read on account of my eyes," is her explanation. (Her defective sight might have been remedied by glasses, as has since been done.) Her teacher, being visited, corroborated the statements; and added, with some disgust, a tribute to the stupidity of her former pupil, revoking it, however, in almost the same breath by saying, "If it was doing anything about the room, such as cleaning the desk or shelves, Susie was eager to do it, and she did it quite well."

The teacher indicated a line of training that might have been given to this girl to advantage, the line of manual training. Her ignorance at this point is dense and destructive. She cannot sew. This does not mean that she cannot make a gown; it means that she cannot hem a coarse dish-towel in a fitting manner. Her stitches can easily be surpassed by many a little maker of doll's garments. She cannot bake bread; her attempts resulting in ill-shaped, heavy loaves unfit for food. She cannot cook; she had never heard of baking a potato. She does not know how to make a bed, or sweep a room, or iron a napkin. A little coarse scouring and cleaning she can do. For such work she has both the muscle and the energy. Another point in her favor is a disposition that stands the severe test of constant criticism and correction of her work. She improves under instruction. Undoubtedly the state could have done much for her if it had trained her mind largely through her hands.

Of right ideas of living, which the school, in a measure, might have imparted to her, she is almost destitute. Thus, while she lacks a tooth-brush and other indispensable toilet articles, she does not lack perfumery or face powder or chewing-gum. Comfort and becoming simplicity in dress she was taught neither at home nor at school; and hence she shivers in her insufficient clothing and offends good taste by her tawdry finery. Appearances are everything with her: an embroidered shirt-waist to wear to a big dance, the third outside skirt for Sunday wear, bought on the instalment plan, and—the less said about under-garments the better. Her lack of warm clothing she explains by saying, "I spent my money going to the the*a*ter." Pleasure, a good time, is her aim in life; and that her pleasures are cheap and shallow is partly the result of her faulty training.

It may seem that a girl of sixteen is still quite young enough to make good, in some degree, her educational loss. Granting that, who is to compel her to do it? No one has any legal authority over her. She would never consent to pay for private instruction out of her small wages; nor would she consent to re-enter the public school and suffer the humiliation of ranking with little children. Not even a free night-school where she could receive individual instruction would appeal to her. She would not sacrifice finery or pleasure or pride to learn to read and write. The desultory manner of her school attendance, so far from awaking in her a thirst for knowledge, seems rather to have turned her away from books and all they stand for. Unskilled labor must remain her field, and that she will translate either into domestic service, to the trial of any mistress, or into factory work along some line as limited as pasting labels on bottles. Out of some such position she is likely to pass early to the grave responsibilities of a home of her own, modeled, in all probability, on the home in which she was reared. If society gets off as easily as this, it may well congratulate itself upon escape from severer penalty.

One swallow does not make a summer; and we may add, with equal truth, that one snowbird does not make a winter. Neither does one instance of the kind described wholly condemn the educational policy of a state; yet, regarding this young girl with pity in her want and ignorance—for which she is but slightly responsible—and knowing how dire and far-reaching are the consequences of these, and conjecturing that the one case implies the existence of similar cases, I repeat the question, "Do we educate?"

THE SCHOOL OF EDUCATION

BERTHA PAYNE
The School of Education

It seems fitting, in this closing number of the seventh year of this *Journal,* to record something of the present organization, scope, and aim of the school of which it is an organ. The School of Education is soon to enter on its eighth year of activity as a professional school of the University of Chicago. Its function, the training of teachers for all grades and departments of work, has necessitated a complex organization in which many problems have confronted its organizers, some of them unique in the history of the training of teachers. That they will not long remain unique is to be presumed, as other "schools of education" are springing up in other universities. To those who are as yet unfamiliar with this kind of situation some description of this organization, and of these questions, may be of interest.

Some of these problems are: First, the relation of the School of Education to the University of Chicago as a whole; second, the relation of the College of Education to the Elementary and High Schools; third, the organization of a curriculum for the Elementary and High Schools that shall be without gaps and breaks from the Kindergarten through the High School; fourth, the organization of a socialized course of study for these schools in which practical and formal control, individual purpose and social relation, initiative, and habituation, shall be kept in true proportions; fifth, the keeping of a true relation between the fine arts and the handicrafts, the humanities and the sciences.

To make the first question more clear, it may be explained that the School of Education is made up of three integral divisions, the College of Education, the University High School, and the University Elementary School.

While distinct in organization, the College of Education is

parallel in most respects to the Colleges of Arts, Literature, and Science. Its courses are to a certain extent interchangeable with these, on the system of credited electives. It differs greatly in this respect, that its Junior and Senior years are distinctly professional in character. It therefore is in one sense an undergraduate college, and in another a professional school, as are the schools of law and medicine. The graduate work in education is given or controlled by the Department of Philosophy and Education. With this brief statement it may easily be surmised that the problems of adjustment are not simple and that the possibilities have been realized far enough to make the future one of great interest and promise.

Of all the problems catalogued above, those relating to the organization and course of study of the Elementary and High Schools contain the kernel of the present educational situation at large. These are the laboratories for the students of the College of Education, and here then lies also the vital and essential heart of our whole institution.

When the School of Education was first instituted on the University campus in a temporary building, it consisted only of the College of Education and an elementary practice school, all under Colonel Parker. When it moved into its permanent building five years ago, under the directorship of Dr. John Dewey, there was added the University Elementary School which had been for some years widely known as the laboratory school for the Department of Education, developed under Dr. Dewey's management. At the same time two secondary schools were merged under the same organization and were moved under the same roof, the Chicago High and Manual-Training School, with its organizer and head, Dr. H. H. Belfield, and the South Side Academy, under Mr. William B. Owen. While this gave to the School of Education the advantage of large and well-established secondary schools as practice and experiment ground for prospective teachers in high schools, it complicated vastly the questions of organization and course of study.

The opportunity is here presented of shaping an elastic and

continuous plan that shall express and answer the social needs of children throughout the nine school years.

The continuity of the educational process is a perfectly valid theory, but it has never been realized. We therefore say advisedly, the opportunity "*is* presented," for although these divisions of the school are and have been operating on a very carefully thought out course of study, and one that has been tested in experience, yet we believe that the course of study will always be in the process of shaping itself. The school no longer stands alone. Nor does it lag so far behind its age as formerly. It rests on a society which is itself not fixed but evolving. The school, one great expression of society's needs, is not to be fixed. If the school utilizes social experience, assimilating its knowledges, its forms of control, its processes, and its ideals, then it must necessarily be progressive in its *mode* of utilizing this experience and in turning it back to the social whole that has thus surrounded, fed, and inspired it. The ideal of the relative functions of school and society may not change, but the mode and materials of utilization must alter as society moves. As science discovers, religion changes its emphasis, industry alters its methods of production, and the forms of social organization are modified, the school will change its focus and particulars of content. Moreover, as the light of research in psychology and child-study are turned upon the course of study, it must be that we shall test the validity of our procedure by increasingly definite standards of the normal and best in content and control throughout the successive stages of school life. It is this unfolding perspective that gives to teaching the allurements of the unattained and the enticements of the undiscovered country.

This then is the great opportunity of a school which has as its "advisory council" those who are working in psychological and philosophical research, and as its laboratory a school in which experiment is not forbidden, but whose faculty are, on the contrary committed to the policy of carrying out and testing modern educational theory.

This does not mean that this school stands apart and isolated from the public-school problems, but rather that it exists for the sake of public education, being under conditions that permit freedom in experiment. Whatever is of worth in ideal or procedure is being sought, not for one small set of children in Chicago, but for its worth to the school at large. Unless results of value can be turned over to the public schools this particular school will have failed utterly to realize the aim of its founders. It is for this reason that the *Elementary School Teacher* exists, first, as a bulletin, or "report of progress," for all who may be interested in such reports, and, second, as a medium through which news of any similarly experimental or independent work may be circulated.

The question of the relation of school work to the industrial life of home and of society has not merely brought another element into the course of study; it has been the determining factor in shaping it. The two conceptions that have been effective in this reconstruction are the genetic ideal, and the belief in the relation of school and society. We might add a third factor, which has been in the past the *raison d'être* of school, its ruling principle for generations; namely, the idea that the school's function is to put the child in possession of the formal tools of thought and communication, the instruments of knowledge.

The genetic ideal is a guide to obtaining continuity, the social ideal gives grip, vitality, motive power, and casts the form of much of the work, while the need of control makes the demand for a smooth working process—a demand which ideally comes from the child's own appreciation of the advantage of more ready adjustments. Thus drill follows the perception of meaning, drill comes after not before the seeing, grasp, and solution of the problem, drill arises as a felt need on the child's part, not wholly as an enforced discipline. The studio, the garden, the shops for metal and woodworking, modeling, pottery, and textile work, all are significant as outward and visible signs of this belief in the meaning of productive work.

What is the relation of this productive effort to the ends of knowledge and discipline? It is a relation so close as to be scarcely analyzable into "subject" and "demonstration." Just as the shuttle flies back and forth from side to side of the web, so knowledge, the aim, passes over into effort, achievement, or adjustment, and returns bringing control; knowledge made definite, workable, the aim renewed, cleared, strengthened, passes back into further effort, and again the reaction. Purpose, motive, persistence, criticism, and reflection are all parts of the total activity. The pageantry of life moves on. The school does not shut its doors upon it, nor does it open them to let the children plunge into the bewildering throng. Yet this pageant of life, the moving, changing, producing life of humanity and the life that we call "nature" is the absorbing process to which we all respond in what we are pleased to term impulse, interest, or curiosity, what you will. The response is, in the little child, overt, concrete activity in the shape of imitation and play. He becomes participant of human activity through play. Experience becomes *his* experience in play modes. His knowledge and understanding grow through this kind of response. The shops therefore scarcely exist for him as places of real production. He needs not so much great technical knowledge and skill in his teacher, as readiness and resourcefulness in helping him to clear his vague ideas and hold his fleeting images in expressive acts of drawing, building, modeling and dramatizing.

The child who, a little older, is laying out his little farm, is probably playing still, but with more persistent purpose and detailed imagery. The children of a still older grade are interested both in realizing work that will stand the test of real use, and in working out the steps or processes by which a people or race has achieved a result of common and universal meaning, such as the steps involved in preparing a textile fabric.

The older children bring greater critical power. More co-operative ability to the work. The trips and excursions reveal to them the conditions under which people work, the complicated modern tools of production, and something of the stupendous scale on which production and exchange are carried on. The larger social significances are beginning to come into consciousness.

In the intermediate and older grades technical control is a necessity in the teacher. In the groups just beyond the kindergarten skill and knowledge are as essential, and yet experience has taught us that the danger of disintegrating the child's mental control is great where his school time is distributed between many teachers though each be a specialist in her own line. A plan of simplifying the variety of arts and reducing the number of teachers has been set in operation here as an experiment for the past year.

In the secondary school more thorough differentiation begins. This seems to be the place where special interests are stronger and individual preferences are assertive, and the place where, if ever, choice may be made between one handicraft or another. Somewhere in these years the test of *actual* participation in commercially valued industry might begin. The break has been pointed out between the production of work in which children are satisfied to meet the tests of value found in their own appreciation or criticism, or in that of companions, of family, or of those in their immediate social group, and that production which must meet the test of a larger public, in other words, the commercial test. Is the high school the field for bringing the learner into a positive working relation with the life in which he has previously been spectator, playful participant, and *semi* real participant?

So far, no statement has been made of the theoretic or practical relationships maintained between science and the industrial arts, nor can any but the briefest statement be made in the limits of this article. In a word, science illuminates the process, and shows the nature and treatment of the materials of production. Science gives also the method of experiment used not only in the field of nature-study, but in that of invention. Reciprocally the arts give focus and definiteness to scientific inquiry—or, to put it more simply, to investigation.

The practical, artistic, and industrial aspects of the school afford a genuine ground of social intercourse. Further than this the games and sports, clubs, general assemblies and festivals stand for the social side of school life.

The heads of departments are in charge of their subjects in the Elementary and High Schools. This is theoretically true and practically carried out in the Elementary School, and is being worked out in the High School. The curriculum of the Elementary School is shaped and revised for each ensuing year through a series of conferences between the departmental teachers, the grade teachers, and the principal. The teacher of the grade is the one who is finally responsible for the work of her group, and she, with the departmental teachers who are working with her children for any given quarter, try to hold the work in an organic relation by planning together wherever such relation seems essential.

No briefest sketch of the school would be complete without at least a mention of the Parents' Association, which, keeping watch and ward over it has been in a collective and personal sense the guide, mentor, and friend of all its activities.

LITERARY EXPRESSION IN THE THIRD GRADE

JESSIE E. BLACK
The University of Chicago Elementary School

Teacher and pupils, in the course of studying a subject, frequently reach a point where the essential and the only adequate means of expression is through words, in some form. The pupils are interested, primarily, in getting the idea expressed, but this process of expression, once started, is found to be, not alone the expression of a thought, but the analysis and organization of it, as well. How is the idea to be appropriately stated? Is it essentially forthright and peripatetic, so that it may be expressed best, in *narrative* form? Is it dramatic, so that it should be thrown into a *play?* Or does it appeal to the emotions in such a way that the *lyric,* only, sets it forth adequately?

That is to say, we are confronted by the practical problems connected with the artistic purpose and the means which should be used to carry out that purpose. This relation is at once as ancient as the sagas and as modern as the high-school pupil's theme. It is, moreover, real. Far from being mere fanciful dresses in which to trick out writings, the historic literary forms, *narration, drama, lyric, exposition,* and the like, are an outcome of these varied relations of the teller or writer to his material.

Now these relations exist for the young child endeavoring to express himself, quite as truly as for the older pupil wrestling with his "theme." Indeed, it is possible that there would be no wrestling with a "theme," in later years, if there were a perfect understanding of these relations, in what corresponds with the "theme" in the earlier years of school life.

We remember when the "pathetic fallacy" swept over the elementary grades, and plant, post-box, or pony were alike forced to yield, in terms curiously similar, the story of their lives; it was the day when "dear Mother Nature" babbled inane, pointless tales, often untrue! That we have made a great advance in setting forth the thought in form appropriate to the substance, is seen where the bulb yields a record of growth, beautiful in its simple scientific exactness; the post-box calls forth an exposition; the pony suggests a narrative, and even Mother Nature herself may be relied upon for a spring lyric!

The following illustrations are limited to expression in English arising from *The Odyssey,* in history, studied during the latter part of the autumn quarter, in the third grade.

The teacher told the story, read aloud from Palmer's translation of *The Odyssey,* or the pupils read from easier sources. Certain of the adventures of Odysseus took strong hold on the interest and the imagination of the children; they were all eager to tell them to a group of younger children. But only one may tell a story, although many may suggest what shall be told, and how. So the tales were mulled over, "my" thought becoming "our" thought as the material, organized under healthy stimulating social conditions, one suggesting, another adding or altering, took various forms. The incident entitled "The Joke" naturally fell into narrative form. In the oral composition of it, the point persisting in appearing before due preparation had been made, the children were impressed with this principle in narrative: "success in it consists in having a point, and in not passing it or omitting any essential thing by the way."

Nor was this all. The distinction between direct and indirect quotations, the greater effectiveness of the former, training in sentence recognition, the omission of the connective "and," capitalization, punctuation, and the like were all a necessary part of the work. Small as the unit is, and simple, yet the qualities of the modern short story are there—vividness, compression, unity.

THE JOKE

"What is your name?" asked Polyphemus.

"My name is 'Nobody,'" answered Odysseus.

The giant, Polyphemus, killed Odysseus' men, so Odysseus blinded the wicked giant in his cave. He howled with pain. The giants outside asked who was hurting him.

"Nobody is hurting me!" cried Polyphemus.

The other giants answered, "If nobody is hurting you, then you surely are not hurt." Then they all went away and left Polyphemus.

The children found that they needed definite directions for playing the Greek games. After consulting their Greek stories, and photographs of Greek statues, they composed orally the following exposition of discus throwing. Then they wrote the directions and followed them. The problem was to state only the points actually needed to throw the discus successfully, and to state them as needed—just the problem of any exposition, whether in the third year of the elementary or in the third year of the high school, and involving exactly the same principles.

"The discus is held in the right hand. 'It' is thrown backward," as first suggested, was shown to leave uncertainty as to whether the hand or the discus was thrown backward. The relative "which" was selected after a brief search as the best word to use—a natural advance from the simple to the complex form of sentence.

THROWING THE DISCUS

In throwing the discus the upper part of the body is bent downward, toward the right. The right leg is bent. Upon it the left hand rests, for balance. The weight of the body is thrown on the right foot. The left foot barely touches the ground. The discus is held in the right hand, which is thrown backward. The head is turned toward the discus. Then the discus is thrown with great force.

"The Palace of Odysseus" is the beginning of a number of short descriptive pieces written for a higher grade which was also interested in the Greeks.

THE PALACE OF ODYSSEUS

A stone wall surrounds the palace. It protects the people. The main hall of the palace is very large. In the center is a fireplace, and around it are oaken couches. The women's rooms are back of this hall, etc.

The siren incident cried aloud to be played, so the dramatic form was chosen. As the play was fashioned, the teacher wrote it on the blackboard so that all might see it and add or change at will. When the siren's song was needed, a lyric was composed, of which one pupil suggested the rhythm, another a line, another an improvement, and so on. The teacher's aid took the form of reading aloud several lyrics, such as "Sweet and Low," and "Ye Mariners of England," while the pupils marked the rhythm in various ways. The style of the play, throughout, caught as it was from the great *Odyssey* itself, is direct, and even rapid, simple, yet high in thought and expression. The formal training side of the work can readily be seen, as in the punctuation of possessive plural, contraction, and the like. The great opportunities for development of the imagination, the judgment, the grasping of the situation and the choice of appropriate expression for it, must also be apparent.

ODYSSEUS AND THE SIRENS

(A Play Made by the Third Grade)

CHARACTERS: *Odysseus* and his companions, *The Sirens.*

SCENE: On the sea in a Greek boat.

Odysseus: Ho, my men! Now that the wind is fair, let us be off.

(ACTION: *Men loosen the cables, rush to their oars, and the wind fills the sails. The men row.*)

Odysseus: Listen, comrades. I have sad news to tell you. Circe told me that we should come to the island of the Sirens. She warned me to fill your ears with soft wax to escape the voices of the Sirens. She bade me, only, to hear their voices. Bind me upright to the mast. If I motion to you to free me, you must only tie more ropes around me.

(ACTION: *Men furl the sail. They whiten the waves with their oars. Odysseus cuts a cake of wax with his sword. Then he kneads it in his hands.*)

A Sailor: How shall we tie you, great leader?

Odysseus: So, comrade, with many strong cords.

(ACTION: *Odysseus stops the sailors' ears with wax. The sailors bind Odysseus hand and foot to the mast. The boat glides toward the Sirens' islands.*)

Sirens (sing "Sirens' Song"):

Bring your ship ashore, Odysseus, listen to our song!
No one's ever passed us in a black hulled ship,
'Til from our lips they've heard our song, then gone upon their way,
For we know all that's happened on the boundless earth!

CHORUS

O come, Odysseus come!
Listen to our song!

(ACTION: *Odysseus motions to his men to set him free. Two men tie more ropes around him.*)

First Sailor: No! No! We will not set you free. You commanded us not to.

Second Sailor: Great Odysseus, remember your wife and son.

(ACTION: *The Boat passes the Sirens' island. The song becomes clearer and sweeter.*)

Sirens (Repeat their song.)

Odysseus (wildly): Untie me! Let me free!

(ACTION: *Men row their hardest. The boat glides swiftly past the island. The song becomes fainter, until it cannot be heard.*)

Odysseus (motioning): Take the wax from your ears. The danger is past.

(ACTION: *Sailors unbind Odysseus.*)

All: Sing "Odysseus' Boat Song"

I

Pull deep on your oars for the wind is high,
The waves are strong and sea-gulls fly,
The white-caps rise on the deep blue sea,
While Penelope's waiting at home for me.

II

We pass the rocks on the islands drear,
While fearful foes are hiding near,
But swiftly over the waves go we,
For Penelope's waiting at home for me.

GEOMETRY IN ELEMENTARY SCHOOLS

H. J. CHASE
Newport, R. I.

"It has never been done," was the driver's explanation of the fact that English locomotives were not provided with cabs. The same explanation comes near enough to fitting a good many other situations.

Of all the branches studied in our schools, geometry is the one to which the inductive or experimental method is the most easily and completely applicable. The apparatus and material are simple, inexpensive, everywhere procurable, and always ready for use. The experiments can be performed anywhere, at any time and under any conditions; they can be suspended at any point and resumed at that point whenever it is desired. The results are as certain and as determinable as in any other field. In other words, being equipped with a ruler, a pair of compasses, a pair of scissors, and a supply of unruled paper—light-brown wrapping-paper will answer very well—any boy or girl capable of reading ordinary English and performing the ordinary operations in common fractions can take up the study of geometry and pursue it with unusual mental profit. With this simple outfit and these modest attainments, a pupil can discover for himself all the facts of elementary geometry and obtain a better grasp of those facts than nine out of ten pupils succeed in doing who study the subject in the usual way.

But if this is true, why is not geometry taught in our grammar schools? Why has it not been made a common branch, like arithmetic or geography? "It never has been done," because it never has occurred to our educators that it could be done. Nevertheless, the fact that it can be done is just as obvious as the fact that English locomotives can be provided with cabs.

In a school edition of Euclid, largely in use in many parts of the British Empire, there occurs the recommendation that the pupils verify all the propositions with ruler and compasses. If the facts can be verified with these instruments, why can they not be discovered with them? They can be. All that is needed is plain directions, and there is no trouble whatever in making these so plain that anyone not absolutely an imbecile can carry them out without difficulty.

Let us take an illustration which will be as clear to the readers who have not studied geometry as to those who have. In the ordinary textbook it is stated that the three angles of a triangle are together equal to two right angles, and a formal demonstration follows. Now, see how easy it is for the pupil to discover this fact for himself, which of course is better for him than to get it as a piece of information.

He draws a triangle. He adjusts his compasses so that the distance between the points will be somewhat less than the length of the shortest side of the triangle. Setting the steel point upon one of the corners of the triangle he describes a curve between the sides that form that corner. He repeats with each of the other corners. On another part of the sheet he describes a circle, and from any point on its circumference lays or spaces off the three curves one after the other. He finds that they extend half way around the circle. He has already learned (by experiment) that half a circumference measures two right angles. He repeats the foregoing operations with the different kinds of triangles, equilateral, isosceles, etc., and the result is always the same —the curves described between the sides always extend half way around the circle, no more and no less. If occasionally there is a small variation, he at once suspects it is due to his not having taken sufficient care in making his measurements. By the time he has concluded his experiments, it is not necessary to tell him that the three angles of any triangle are together equal to two right angles. He has found out the fact, and therefore he *knows* it.

"But," it may be objected, "he doesn't know *why* the three angles are equal to two right angles." No, he does not, and in this life he never will. We don't know the "why" of a single one of the facts of geometry. Admirers of the deductive method of reasoning (which far be it from my intention to disparage) seem to think that it is the only method by which we can become convinced of what they sometimes style, "the eternal verities." They seem to think that no one can be sure that the three angles of a triangle are together equal to two right angles until he has learned to demonstrate the proposition in the usual way. They seem to think that, however many triangles he may test with the compasses, he never can be certain that there cannot be constructed a triangle to which the test will not apply. Very well, then, let him set his doubts at rest by learning the deductive demonstration. The point I wish to make is this: It is far better for a boy to discover a fact by experiment first and to reason it out afterward, than to be furnished with the fact and a formal demonstration thereof, with seldom or never the suggestion that he verify by experiment. That is the way boys and girls are taught geometry today; that is the way they have been taught it ever since Euclid's time, and it is exactly the reverse of the right way.

Let us consider some of the results of this Chinese way of teaching. At least five-sixths of our school children never get the opportunity to study geometry, or, at best, any more than the meager amount in the ordinary arithmetic. The study has to be postponed until the high-school course is begun, and the vast majority of our children do not attend the high school. It is true that in the grammar schools of some cities a smattering of geometry is given, but scarcely enough to be of any consequence. Practically at least five out of six of our school children are debarred from studying the subject.

But don't they have enough to do at present in the lower grades, without trying to crowd in geometry? They may have enough to do, but a great deal of it is of far less educational value than geometry, and some of it of no value at all. Instead of promoting, some of it actually retards, intellectual development.

It is impossible, of course, to go into details with regard to what is taught in our schools. It suffices to assert, without fear of disproof, that nothing taught therein is of greater educational value than the rational study of geometry would be. The facts of geometry are as important as any to which the pupil's attention can be directed, and the mental discipline obtained by getting hold of those facts in the right way is exactly the kind that will enable him to deal with the problems that will confront him after he leaves school. A little less "analyzing and parsing," a little less memorizing of descriptive geography and the battles and sieges in history, a little less oral speling, etc., would give time enough for geometry in the grammar school.

Another result of the Chinese method is, that the comparatively few who get the opportunity to study geometry fail to get a good knowledge of the subject. To appreciate deductive reasoning, the mind must have attained a degree of maturity that is rare in the case of even high-school pupils. The average student of geometry, in both recitations and examinations, relies upon memory more than upon his power to reason. No instructor will dispute this contention. In pursuing the inductive method, the faculty of memory cannot enable the pupil to appear to have a knowledge that he does not possess. He is put to precisely the same kind of test that a man pretending to know how to set type would be put to in a printing office. He either can or cannot do the thing required. If he cannot, the possession of the most prodigious memory would not enable him to make the slightest concealment of his inability.

In probably every high school and college in the country, instructors in mathematics accept every day recitations that they very well know are unsound; that is, they know that the pupil doesn't fully understand what he is talking about, and that a little close questioning would make the fact too obvious to be overlooked. But what can they do? There are pupils who may be good in everything else, and perhaps brilliant in some particular subject, but who cannot get hold of mathematics. It seems hard that they should not be allowed to graduate with the others. So far as geometry is concerned, there is no reason why anyone cannot learn it, or enough of it to pass any fair examination.

Excluding idiots and imbeciles, was there ever a boy so stupid that he could not learn how to do farm work, or a girl so stupid that she could not learn to do housework? How is such work learned? Simply by doing it. We don't give a boy a book containing disquisitions upon farming tools. We give him a hoe and set him to hoeing. However awkward he may be at first, sooner or later he becomes able to accomplish something.

In all my experience, I never have found a boy or girl so stupid as not to be able to learn how to use a ruler and compasses and to make discoveries by using them. More than this, I never have found a boy or girl who did not immediately become interested in this kind of work and inclined to keep on with it. I have had one opportunity to try this method in the schoolroom, that is, to give it a full and fair test. That was in a mixed school in a southern state. The pupils, with a single exception, were very backward. All of them who could do fractions, and some who could not, were formed into a geometry class. In four months' time this class had covered all of plane geometry and had made a beginning in solid geometry. The close of the school year prevented the test being carried any further and the opportunity to repeat it has not occurred. Several pupils who had been left out of the class because I supposed them to be too young to derive any benefit from the exercises, after watching the others for a few days, teased to be allowed to join. They remained until the end of the term, and one of them became unusually proficient in the work.

The recitations took place the last thing in the afternoon—that is, at a time when children are likely to be thinking more about getting away than anything else. It was a common occurrence however, for the recitation to be prolonged beyond the hour of closing. Anyone who wished was at liberty to leave at this time, but no one ever availed himself of the privilege. On several occasions I had to insist that the investigation under way be postponed until next day.

I do not allege that all these children mastered the elements of plane geometry, but many of them acquired a fair knowledge of the subject, and every one of them obtained much more than a smattering.

Unfortunately, no one in the place was capable of appreciating the significance of the result of this test—a result that far surpassed my expectations. It convinced me that there is no good reason why all our school children should not learn elementary geometry. It is simply a case of "it never has been done."

GOVERNMENTAL CO-OPERATION IN INDUSTRIAL EDUCATION

In an earlier number of this *Journal* the suggestion was advanced that experimental schools be made possible by grants from the federal government. These experimental schools would attack the very difficult problem of the relation of industrial training to elementary schools. The suggestion called for schools which should find the center of their interest in agriculture and in the mechanical and domestic arts.

It is evident that secondary schools can with comparative ease be adapted to industrial training. There is in Europe and this country sufficient experience in this direction to indicate the success of such institutions and the possibility of combining with the technical training considerable general education.

But little or no effort has been made to relate elementary education to industrial training. And yet it is abundantly evident that practically all the education which the bulk of people receive must be gained in the elementary schools. It is equally evident that an elementary education which should be planned with reference to later industrial training and occupation must materially assist in that training and might so interpret the process as greatly to increase the intelligence and morale of the workman.

It is true that the introduction of school gardening and manual training and some phases of domestic science into the grades is a step in this direction, but in our huge city school systems or in the poorly equipped country schools thoroughgoing experiments in these directions cannot be made. We have agricultural and manual-training high schools. Up to this time no state has attempted to organize elementary schools about agriculture or the mechanical and domestic arts; and until this is done we are likely to have no satisfactory data to guide our educational policy. It is for this reason that we have suggested that the government aid those states which will make this experiment by subsidies which would be analogous to those given to agricultural colleges. This policy was inaugurated by the first Morrill in 1862 and has been enforced by later and more generous enactments. There is at present an amendment to this legislation before congress "to provide for the advancement of instruction in agriculture, manual training, and home economics in state normal schools of the United States." We quote below the substance of a communication from the acting secretary of the interior, Hon. Frank Pierce, with reference to this bill. The secretary recommends finally that the most practical immediate step would be to authorize the commissioner of education to make a thorough investigation of the whole field within which government aid may wisely be granted to state education.

This bill is one of several which have been introduced at this session of Congress, providing for national aid to education in the several States and particularly for national aid as regards education in agriculture, home economics, and other industrial subjects. The fact that several bills, touching in different ways upon this same subject, have been brought before Congress, is a clear indication of public interest in this matter. The principle involved in the granting of such aid to the states by the general government has already found definite lodgement in the policy of the national government, as is shown by the appropriations made under the second Morrill act of 1890, and the Nelson amendment of 1907, providing for more complete endowment and support of agricultural and mechanical colleges.

It is generally agreed that the working of this principle, in its bearing on the support of the land-grant colleges, has been extremely beneficial. One indication of the value of such appropriations is seen in the fact that they have encouraged rather than retarded the support of these state institutions by the several state governments. The information at hand in the Bureau of Education shows that in the year 1896 these land-grant colleges received in the aggregate 29 per cent. of their support from the national government. Ten years later, in 1906, owing to the increase of state appropriations, this proportion of their support from federal funds was reduced to 15.4 per cent. In this ten-year period the congressional grant was increased by 19 per cent. In the same time the amount which these institutions received from their several states was increased by about 240 per cent. Whereas in 1896 twenty-five of these institutions received more than one-half of their support from the national government, in 1906 only fifteen received more than one-half of their support from the national government. These figures show a wholesome tendency. They would seem to indicate that the granting of national aid for the promotion of education might safely be extended to other classes of institutions; provided it can be shown that there is a national need that these institutions be advanced more rapidly in their educational efficiency than they can be advanced without such national aid.

The land-grant colleges were intended to meet what was clearly a national need, that of institutions in all of the states which should promote agricultural improvements by providing the higher grades of agricultural instruction. This has been found to be an extremely difficult undertaking. Even with the encouragement provided by the first Morrill act of 1862, the development of these institutions was painfully slow. Since the granting of an annual appropriation for their better support under the second Morrill act of 1890, their usefulness has been very rapidly extended and increased. During this period, however, industrial changes have gone forward with great rapidity, the tendency of our rural population to gravitate toward the cities has continued, and the need of a better industrial education for our city populations has been emphasized by the increasing severity of world competition. For all of these reasons the problem of a better education of an industrial type, in both country and city, has steadily become more acute. It is extremely doubtful whether these growing needs can be met in the near future in a majority of the states unless the encouragement of federal appropriations be added to the efforts of the states and of local communities. There is, however, good reason to hope that any appropriations which may be made to this end by the national government will encourage and promote such provision by states and communities as will in good measure meet the need.

Senate Bill 3,392 is concerned with the training of teachers of agricultural, domestic, and other industrial subjects, in the regularly established state normal schools. The Nelson amendment of March 4, 1907, contained a provision permitting the use of a portion of the new funds for the training of teachers in land-grant colleges. Presumably the teachers trained under this provision would for the most part become teachers in high schools and in state normal schools. There would still be need, if such instruction is to be widely extended among schools of elementary grade, that additional provision be made on a large scale for the training of teachers of elementary schools in these special subjects.

It will appear from what has been said above, that Senate Bill 3,392 seems to call for warm approval in principle. It seems proper also that the administration of any fund devoted to such purposes as those contemplated in this measure should devolve upon the Department of the Interior and be carried on through the Bureau of Education in that Department. There are, however, numerous questions to be considered in connection with this bill, and with other proposed bills closely related thereto. It is clearly important that any forward step which the national government may take in the encouragement of public education should be carefully weighed, and be given its proper place in a well digested general policy. Furthermore, the conditions in the several states are widely different, and any bill should be framed with full knowledge of these differing conditions in order that it may be made sufficiently flexible to accomplish the best results in all parts of the country. It is conceivable that in some portions of the country money for the training of teachers on agriculture at the normal schools is more urgently needed at this time than money for the support of instruction in agriculture in schools of other kinds, while in other states this condition may be reversed. And still further, a wise economy in any one of the states might call for the concentration of such funds upon the training of teachers in the earlier years of the movement until a corps of competent teachers has been secured, while thereafter a larger proportion of the same funds might profitably be devoted to high schools of agriculture and the mechanic arts, a relatively smaller proportion being needed for the training of teachers. These considerations suggest the need of a thorough inquiry into the state and needs of industrial education in different parts of the country as a basis for a wise and economical appropriation of federal funds for the encouragement of such education. I respectfully recommend therefore that no appropriation be made at this time along the lines indicated by Senate Bill 3,392; but ask you carefully to consider an amendment of the Bill by striking out all after the enacting clause and substituting the following:

"That $100,000, or so much thereof as may be found necessary, is hereby appropriated out of any funds in the Treasury not otherwise appropriated, and made available immediaely and until expended, to be used by the commissioner of education, under the direction of the secretary of the interior, in an investigation and the preparation of a report to Congress concerning the needs and best methods of distribution and administration of federal appropriations in aid of industrial, agricultural and related forms of education, such report to be made to Congress on or before January 1, 1910."

Such an investigation will make it possible for Congress to act upon bills like S. 3,392 with full knowledge of the situation and the needs of the country.

It is very much to be hoped that this amendment above suggested be passed. The federal government will then be in a position to take a deliberate and constructive attitude toward the most serious problems which industrial education is forcing upon us. The problem is so really national that national appropriations are quite as legitimate and as desirable as in the cases of agricultural colleges or experimental stations.

The commissioner of education should be able at this critical period in our educational evolution to indicate the largest and most important phases of the problem and to direct the assistance of the government toward those educational experiments which can aid us in solving these problems. It will be the policy of this *Journal* to urge during the coming year the advisability of establishing such experimental schools and of the use of the grants of the federal government to forward such important experiments.

L. S. C.

EDITORIAL NOTES

CHARACTER AND EDUCATION

In modern discussions of the ends of education there seems to be an increasing disposition to recognize character as the most comprehensive expression of the ultimate aim. In a general sense there can be no question that the term *character* embodies a large amount of what is commonly recognized as most significant in the outcome of the educational process. But it is to be feared that serious misapprehension will arise through an unduly naïve interpretation of the basis and meaning of character.

Character the Aim of Education

If one listens to the average speaker before an audience interested in educational problems, it will generally be found that in assigning the formation of character as the fundamentally important end to be held before teachers, there is in mind primarily the instilling by precept and example of the ordinary maxims of conventional morality. If the schools turn out young people who neither lie nor steal nor are unchaste in thought or deed, they have accomplished their fundamental purpose.

Character Building by Precept

Now no one will question that such results in the lives of our young people are essentially indispensable, if civic integrity and high ideals of personal worth are to prevail among us. But this statement of the case and the view which underlies it is far too simple-minded to do justice either to the complexities of the actual growing human mind on the one hand, or to the unprecedented and wholly novel complications of the existing social order on the other.

This Method at Variance both with Psychological Method and Moral Practice

If we examine from the side of psychology the growth and significance of character, we find that it is synonymous throughout with the growth of control. This control we find is directed in the first instance to the ordering of certain great impulses or instincts which crop out as natural possessions in every human being, and which require

Psychologically Character Means Control

mutual organization in terms of the proper functions of each. These instincts and impulses represent the great dynamic factors in human life. They supply the energy which keeps the machine going. As essential parts of the mechanism by which control is established we find the great processes of knowledge with their foundations in the activities of sense perception and their superstructure high up in the regions of abstraction and inference. The knowledge process from its simplest to its most complex expressions finds its final significance precisely in the fact of the intelligent control over conduct which it permits. By means of knowledge we are enabled to recall the results of our past impulsive acts, and by means of such recall to plan for and anticipate the future. Experiences which in the past have been chiefly disagreeable and unprofitable are in this process likely to be discouraged. Those of a different character are cultivated and increasingly embodied in our established habits. Clearly, then, from the psychological side alone, to say nothing of the social aspect of the problem, a training of character instead of furnishing us a short cut to the formation of proper educational aims which can be readily applied even by the inexpert, brings us face to face with the problem of disciplining to the fullest degree all the great fundamental aspects of the mind.

In Practice Character Means Ability to Form New Moral Judgments

A well-trained character is not simply one which can be trusted neither to lie, nor to steal; it is one which in these perplexing days of changing standards and ideals can justly discern wherein stealing and lying consist. The established industrial order under which we are living countenances and encourages through the process of competition forms of human suffering which not a few leaders of social reform stigmatize as essentially theft and murder. Without assenting to the extremer interpretations of these conditions, it should be perfectly clear that one of the results which modern education should achieve for those who receive it is the ability freshly to face such problems as these and pass intelligent judgment as to the exact lines of distinction between the right and the wrong. Such capacity means fineness of intellect and fineness of feeling and indomitable energy of will. It means, in short, rich and fully developed character.

Character the Achievement of the Whole Educational Process

We assent, therefore, enthusiastically to the proposition that character is the most fundamental of the ends of education, but we protest against any interpretation of this dictum which would find in the formula a cheap and easy road to educational expediency instead of recognizing, what is the fact, that such a definition points to the hard but lofty pathway of the most difficult educational idealism.

J. R. A.

NOTES AND NEWS

Reading, Penn., is the only city in the country with a larger board of education than New York. What does Reading do with it all?

So women are acually to get the same pay as men in the New York city public schools. The senate passed the bill by a vote of 35 to 10.

The New York city board of education does more toward educating the public through evening lectures than all the other boards of education in the United States.

Boyes estimates that 8,000,000 American children under fifteen are constantly schoolless. He bases his conclusions on the latest report available, that from 1904–5.—*Midland Schools.*

France has no truant schools and no effective attendance law, nor can imprisonment be inflicted on the parents. The industrial and reformatory institutions of that country are for criminals only.

Chicago is not up to the standard in the matter of children's playgrounds, according to an address by G. S. Hall. It devotes seventy-three acres to them, while Philadelphia gives one hundred and ten, and Boston two hundred.

The average pay for men teachers in this country is $55 per month, and for women $42, the latter constituting 96 per cent. of all. Of our nearly half-million teachers, between one-third and one-fourth leave the profession every year.

In many small towns where bird-study has become a part of the regular school course, the milliners refuse to carry hats adorned with birds, saying that the demand is so small that nothing is to be made of such stock.—A. D. CROMWELL, in *Midland Schools.*

The Illinois Farmer's Institute, in a convention at Peoria, petitioned the educational commission for a bill making elementary agriculture a necessary part of a teacher's equipment. Would the farmers want this requirement made for every town and city in Illinois?

The school children of Cincinnati have been making a heroic attack on insect pests this spring, under the leadership of the superintendent of the parks. It is to be hoped that the average citizen finds its effects more noticeable than the results of the "street-cleaning day" in Chicago.

The New York public library is trying to get into closer connection with the public schools. Twice a month 393 educational institutions are visited by library assistants, who give addresses on the use of the public library, and post notices concerning educational affairs connected with it.

The Louisville *Courier Journal* says that Kentucky has for years been burdened with 5,000 school trustees who can neither read nor write, and 10,000 more who are absolutely devoid of any idea of the duties of a school trustee. Of course we must allow for the round numbers of newspaper exaggeration.

West Virginia has passed a revised school law. Two of its most progressive clauses provide for the increase of the compulsory attendance age limit to fifteen years, and the consolidation of schools and transportation of pupils in the rural districts when asked for by 75 per cent. of the voters in the sub-districts affected.

The opponents of prohibition are at last aroused to the necessity of carrying the fight into the enemy's country. Signs of their interference in educational matters have already begun. The German-American Alliance, of Davenport, Iowa, has sent a letter to the school board protesting against "a one-sided course in temperance physiology." Hitherto the prohibitionists have had things their own way in physiology at least.

Boston has appropriated $58,000 for the beginning of a play-ground scheme. The work of the vacation schools has been absorbed into a new department, "the Department of School Hygiene," which is to develop these playgrounds. To the department also will be turned over six playgrounds now under the park commission, each of them to be in charge of instructors in athletics. Playgrounds now attached to schools are to be thrown open at other than school hours.

The Home Gardening Association of Cleveland is a flourishing organization. The children of the parochial as well as of the public schools are receiving seeds this year, and prizes are awarded each autumn for the best gardens of various kinds. A training-garden has been in operation for two years for seventy-five boys recommended by their teachers. They receive practical instruction with a view to directing them to gardening, farming, forestry, and kindred pursuits.

The *Chicago Teachers' Federation Bulletin* contains an interesting list of social machines that have sprung into activity during the past quarter-century, all of them touching the public schools at some point. The following are a few: day nurseries, school children's aid society, free kindergarten associations, Religious Education Association, Social Education Association, Juvenile Court, parental schools, Vacation School and Playground Committee, Public School Art Society, parents' and teachers' clubs.

The sixth and seventh grades of Webster, Mass., have a novel method of studying civil government. They looked up the number and character of the local public offices, formed two parties, nominated candidates and held an election. By the courtesy of the town clerk the loan of a "sure-enough ballot-box" was procured. All the detailed formalities of election were followed. Then the successful candidates were required to familiarize themselves with the duties of their offices. It must have been both amusing and instructive.

English has at last been almost universally adopted as the language in the Porto Rican schools. It has come about quite naturally, no direct attempt having been made to change the language of instruction for fear of antagonizing the people. But the new custom seems to have come about, according to Commissioner Faulkner's report, through a certain prestige of aristocracy which immediately attached itself to the so-called "American-schools," and led to the overcrowding of all English-taught classes. Ponce and San Juan were the first towns to adopt English regularly.

The Chicago public library board has located two of its sub-stations in public school buildings—one in the Burr School and the other in the Washington School—the board of education furnishing the rooms, fixtures, heat, light and janitor service. The advantages of this plan should be numerous. The children will learn the uses of the public library, while the reading public that patronized the substations will be led to visit and take an interest in the schools and is it too much to hope that with the substations in the schools the children will derive benefit in the selection of their books from the influence and advice of teachers?

Boston's present board of education has done a good thing in establishing a special class for delinquent and wayward boys, says the *Journal of Education.* Hitherto the courts have been the only means of dealing with such boys. The present class is an attempt to correct delinquency without branding the boys by a court sentence, and a term in a reform school, and in it only those boys are put who under the old practice would be brought before the judge. Especial work in gymnasium and manual training is given them. The class has justified tself, for only one out of twenty-five boys was finally sent to court for continued misbehaviour.

Each country seems to have a different way for solving the problem of education in morality. Germany has enforced religious instruction in the public schools. The parents of each child may choose for it the Catholic, Lutheran, or Jewish instruction, which is then given by teachers approved both by those churches and by the state examining board. In France, the public schools were secularized twenty years ago and religious teaching forbidden in them. But fearing an increase in juvenile immorality, on account of the void thus created in the curriculum, the French made strenuous efforts to supply the defect by a new kind of moral instruction for every grade. Love of country and the instincts of the gentleman are made into a kind of secular religion. America has as yet reached nothing but the most desultory kind of training in all such matters. This, thinks G. S. Hall, in an address reported in *Midland Schools,* is the great failure of our education, and one which needs immediate attention.

BOOK REVIEWS

The Bailey–Manly Spelling Book. By ELIZA R. BAILEY AND JOHN M. MANLY. Boston: Houghton, Mifflin & Co. Pp. 154.

As the years go by with their new and their renovated educational theories, they seem to establish conclusively the fact that decent spelling will always be considered a matter of considerable importance. The teacher who can complacently overlook a mass of deaf, dumb, and blind orthography is fortunately rare, and is evidently not going to control the situation. Yet to many others, doubtless no problem is more baffling than that of the mispelled word, and the whole question of textbook and of method has seemed dark.

To them, as to others, this new book should be far more than interesting. It is given out as the result of several years of successful experiment in more than one school. In scope, it is more than a mere list of words; it includes a thorough course in punctuation and the use of capitals. The most important addition, however, is pointed out in the prefatory "Suggestions to Teachers": "The teacher should aim to have pupils gain the ability to use correctly all the words that they learn to spell."

As to the problem of spelling itself, it would be hard to find a discussion of the same length more practical than that in the "Suggestions," while there are interesting suggestions in the Preface. One thing worth noting is the emphasis wisely put on syllabification and distinct enunciation. Another is explained in the Preface: "The old method of bringing together in a list words spelled and pronounced alike was a mistake. The pupil who could learn such a spelling lesson perfectly was often at a loss how to spell the words correctly under the conditions of actual use. But the method now gaining currency in some quarters of entirely dissociating words containing similar elements, and treating each word as if it and its derivatives stood alone, is equally wrong, psychologically and practically. . . . . The authors have tried to avoid both these errors." Another interesting feature is the use of selections of prose and poetry as exercises, in addition to correspondingly short lists of detached words. One may not be able to go far with the authors in their hope that these little scraps of quotation will create a desire for good reading, but at least they are sound and good; and they do of course attain the object of teaching the word as it is used. Finally, one great excellence is the effective gradation of the work for the different years.

Altogether the book is an application of clear intelligence and uncommon sense to a difficult and important problem, and deserves at the least careful examination.

JOHN M. CROWE

THE UNIVERSITY HIGH SCHOOL

How to Invest Your Savings. By ISAAC F. MARCOSSON. Philadelphia: Henry Altemus Co. Pp. 120.

Under the present conditions it may be held that the last thing to put into the minds of children should be the desire to make money. But since they are growing up into a world not only of money-making, but of reckless speculation and financial extravagance, a book which inculcates prudence and modesty may have its usefulness for them. Therefore this little volume of papers first printed in the *Saturday Evening Post,* under the title "Your Savings," is worth noting. It is not only conservative, but practically instructive, giving useful information about the various forms of investment, as well as illustrations of the value of economy.

J. M. C.

Nature-Study Made Easy. By EDWARD B. SHALLOW AND WINIFRED T. CULLEN. New York: Macmillan. Pp. 136. 40 cents.

The title of this book and the introductory paragraph in the preface may suggest to some teachers that the long-looked-for has been found. That paragraph is: "The position of nature-work in the school curriculum is established. It has passed the experimental stage. Its value as an educational factor is recognized." Other prefatory statements are: "The lessons are given in a simple, pleasing manner; a second lesson, in different form, sometimes following the first to impress or fix it." "The lessons, though grouped according to the subjects to which they relate, may be given in any order." The opening statement of the first chapter serves further to present the author's point of view of nature-study.

"'Oh, Mary, what a beautiful flower!' cried little Nellie Brown, as Mary Hooper came into the room, holding aloft a delicate pink rose. 'Where did you get it?'

"'My Aunt Susan gave it to me,' said Mary. 'She had just brought it from her garden. She gave one just as pretty to Lucy.' . . . .

"'How sweet!' said Nellie. 'What will you do with it?'

"'Oh, I am going to put it at once in water. You know cut flowers cannot live without food, and water is their food.'

"So saying, she filled a vase with clear water, and placed her pretty flower in it."

Then follows some discussion as to why the flower stems are cut as they are, this result in an upbuilding and ennobling conclusion on the part of Nellie which leads her to say, "I am glad you told me that. I shall always cut flowers, hereafter, instead of breaking them." Later, in a discussion at dinner table of the fact that plants in the absence of sunlight do not become green, we have Lucy coming upon the scene again with, "Then is that why celery is always white? Please pass me some. I will try to see if I can taste any sunlight on it."

The authors believe in impersonation of the plants and ascribe to them memory, emotions, and ambitions worthy of the children by whom the lessons are to be studied. Quite often at the close of the chapters the writers are reminded of a poem; in fact it sometimes becomes evident before the close of the chapter that the authors are preparing to be reminded.

There is a great deal of good and usable material in the book, but it is so badly confused with make-believe conversation, impersonation, emotionalism, and faulty science, that instead of *making nature-study easy,* it would seem to the reviewer that the book must join that mass of pseudo-nature literature which is really making it very hard for a real nature-study to take a place in the school curriculum.

Nature-study will take care of its enemies if only its friends will cease committing blunders under cover of its name.

O. W. CALDWELL

COLLEGE OF EDUCATION

Catalogue of Books Annotated and Arranged and Provided by the Carnegie Library of Pittsburgh for the Use of the Grades in the Pittsburgh Schools. Pittsburgh: Carnegie Library, 1907. Pp. 331.

The Carnegie Library at Pittsburgh boasts the only training-school in the country devoted to the training of children's librarians. Possibly this serves as an incentive for the very careful and systematic work which has been done there in developing the co-operation between the schools and libraries, and in working out the best reading for children.

In the preface of this catalogue of books for schools, which is a revision of an earlier publication, a short but comprehensive account of the history of the work and its present scope is given. The list of books for high schools and the reference books for teachers have been omitted and will be issued in separate form. The arrangement of the catalogue is admirable and can best be described in the words of the preface:

"The title and annotation for each book is repeated in every grade to which the index assigns it. . . . . It enables the teachers to use each grade as a complete list without referring elsewhere for the annotations. There has been no attempt to furnish anything in the nature of supplementary textbook reading as a part of the routine school work. The aim, has been, rather, to provide collateral reading in history, biography, travel, adventure, simple science, and good fiction to be used in the schoolroom and sent into the homes of the children. It is hoped that the annotations, which are made chiefly for the teachers and from their standpoint, may help them in guiding the children in their choice of books, and in fitting the right book to the right child."

IRENE WARREN

SCHOOL OF EDUCATION

BOOKS RECEIVED

C. W. BARDEEN, SYRACUSE, N. Y.

The Condition and Tendencies of Technical Education in Germany. By ARTHUR HENRY CHAMBERLAIN. Cloth. Pp. 108.

Our Children, our Schools, and our Industries. By ANDREW SLOAN DRAPER. Cloth. Pp. 136.

THOMAS Y. CROWELL CO., NEW YORK

Montaigne and Education of the Judgment. (Pioneers in Education Series.) By GABRIEL COMPAYRÉ. Translated by J. E. MANSION. Cloth, 12mo. Pp. 139. $0.90.

HENRY ALTEMUS COMPANY, PHILADELPHIA

Get-Rich-Quick Wallingford. A Cheerful Account of the Rise and Fall of an American Business Buccaneer. By GEORGE RANDOLPH CHESTER. Cloth, 12mo; illustrated. Pp. 448. $1.50.

HOUGHTON, MIFFLIN & CO., BOSTON

The Life of Alice Freeman Palmer. By GEORGE HERBERT PALMER. Cloth. Illustrated. Pp. 349. $1.50.

THE MACMILLAN CO., NEW YORK

Departmental Teaching in Elementary Schools. By VANEVRIE KILPATRICK. Cloth. Pp. 130. $1.60.

Nature-Study Made Easy. By EDWARD B. SHALLOW AND WINIFRED T. CULLEN. Cloth. Pp. 136. Illustrated. $0.40.

Principles of Secondary Education. (Processes of Instruction, Vol. II.) By CHARLES DEGARMO. Cloth. Pp. 200. $1.00.

The High-School Song Book. Compiled and arranged by EDWARD J. A. ZEINER. Cloth. Pp. 244. $0.85.

Government by the People. By ROBERT H. FULLER. Cloth. Pp. 261.

CHARLES SCRIBNER'S SONS, NEW YORK

Mind in the Making. A Study in Mental Development. By EDGAR JAMES SWIFT. Cloth. Pp. 329.

The Elementary School Teacher

June, 1908

Vol. VIII, No. 10

THE UNIVERSITY OF CHICAGO PRESS
CHICAGO AND NEW YORK
OTTO HARRASSOWITZ, LEIPZIG

Outdoor sports best reflect glow and vigor when the skin is healthy

Avoid the cause of red, rough skin; insure a matchless complexion, soft, white hands and wholesome comfort by using the purest soap—

PEARS' SOAP

OF ALL SCENTED SOAPS PEARS' OTTO OF ROSE IS THE BEST.

The Elementary School Teacher

PUBLISHED MONTHLY EXCEPT IN JULY AND AUGUST

CONTENTS FOR JUNE, 1908

The Elementary School Teacher is published monthly from September to June. ¶ The subscription price is $1.50 per year; the price of single copies is 20 cents. ¶ Postage is prepaid by the publishers on all orders from the United States, Mexico, Cuba, Porto Rico, Panama Canal Zone, Republic of Panama, Hawaiian Islands, Philippine Islands, Guam, Tutuila (Samoa), Shanghai. ¶ Postage is charged extra as follows: For Canada, 30 cents on annual subscriptions (total $1.80), on single copies, 3 cents (total 23 cents); for all other countries in the Postal Union, 46 cents on annual subscriptions (total $1.96), on single copies, 6 cents (total 26 cents). ¶ Remittances should be made payable to The University of Chicago Press, and should be in Chicago or New York exchange, postal or express money order. If local check is used, 10 cents must be added for collection.

Otto Harassowitz, Querstrasse 14, Leipzig, Germany, has been appointed agent for the European continent and is authorized to quote the following prices: Yearly subscriptions, including postage, M.8.25 each; single copies, including postage, M.1.10 each.

Claims for missing numbers should be made within the month following the regular month of publication. The publishers expect to supply missing numbers free only when they have been lost in transit.

Business correspondence should be addressed to The University of Chicago Press, Chicago, Ill.

Communications for the editors should be addressed to them at The University of Chicago, Chicago, Ill.

Entered October 12, 1903, at the Post-Office at Chicago, Ill., as second-class matter, under Act of Congress March 3, 1879.

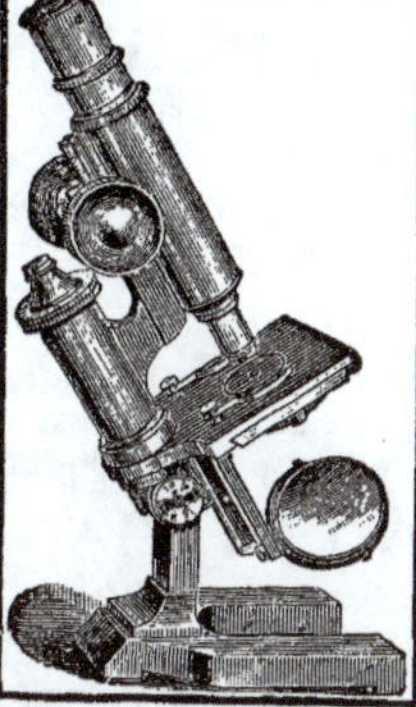

POND'S EXTRACT quickly relieves the pain of burns with a cooling, soothing effect most grateful to the sufferer.

For Sixty Years the Standard.

Nothing takes the place of POND'S EXTRACT in the home for healing helpfulness.

Sold only in sealed bottles—never in bulk.

LAMONT, CORLISS & CO., Sole Agents, 78 Hudson St., New York.

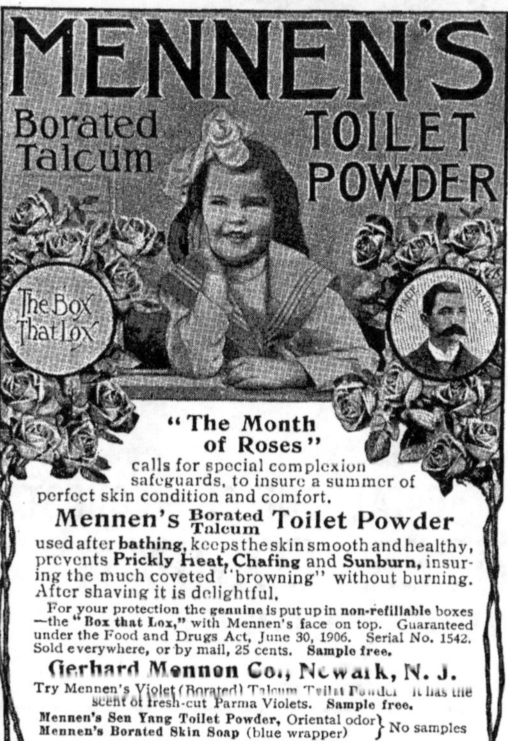

Intending purchasers of a *strictly first-class* Piano should not fail to examine the merits of

THE WORLD RENOWNED

SOHMER

It is the special favorite of the refined and cultured musical public on account of its unsurpassed tone-quality, unequaled durability, elegance of design and finish. Catalogue mailed on application.

THE SOHMER-CECILIAN INSIDE PLAYER SURPASSES ALL OTHERS

Favorable Terms to Responsible Parties

SOHMER & COMPANY

Warerooms Cor. 5th Ave., 22d St. NEW YORK. 7

PABST EXTRACT
The Best Tonic
MALT HOPS
PABST BREWING
PABST EXTRACT
The Best Tonic
MALT HOPS
PABST BREWING

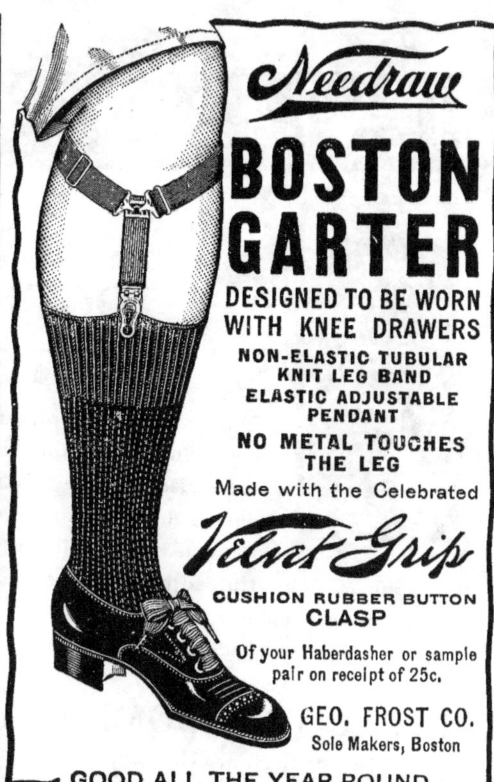

People Tell Each Other About Good Things

Twelve years ago few people knew of such a preparation as a Powder for the Feet. Today after the genuine merit of Allen's Foot-Ease has been told year after year by one gratified person to another, there are millions who would as soon go without a dentifrice as without Allen's Foot-Ease. It is a cleanly, wholesome, healing, antiseptic powder to be shaken into the shoes, which has given rest and comfort to tired and aching feet in all parts of the world. It cures while you walk. Over 30,000 testimonials of cures of smarting, swollen, perspiring feet. It prevents friction and wear of the stockings and will save in your stocking bill ten times its cost each year. Imitations pay the dealer a larger profit, otherwise, you would never be offered a substitute when you ask for Allen's Foot-Ease, the original powder for the feet. Imitations are not advertised because they are not permanent. For every genuine article there are many imitations. The imitator has no reputation to sustain—the advertiser has. When you ask for an article advertised see that you get it. Refuse imitations.

LANTERN SLIDES

OF SUPERIOR QUALITY.

BLACK SEPIA, NATURAL COLORS.

SCIENTIFIC AND LECTURE WORK SOLICITED

A. G. ELDRIDGE & CO.

3 W. 29th St., New York.

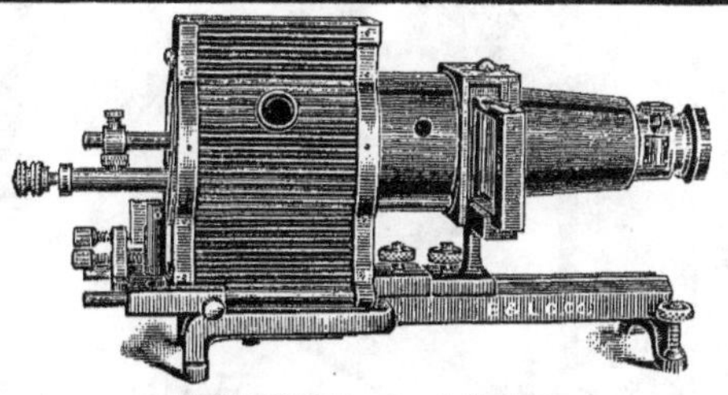

BAUSCH & LOMB
NEW SCHOOL PROJECTION LANTERN C

Every teacher today recognizes the advantages to teacher as well as pupil of the wider use of the Projection Lantern in the classroom.

Our Lantern C has been especially designed for school work. It is a thoroughly high-grade apparatus, and while equipped with our latest improvements we can offer it at a price which brings it within the reach of even the elementary school. The construction of this lantern is such as to permit the instant change from ordinary projection to microscope projection, and thereby adds greatly to its scope of usefulness.

The advantages of a lantern in the social affairs of a school will also readily suggest themselves.

This device is simple, efficient, portable—may be easily removed from one room to the other—and practically covers the whole range of school projection work. Price, complete, **$50.00**; with Acetylene Burner, **$45.00**.

Send for descriptive circular.

Bausch & Lomb Optical Co.

Carl Zeiss, Jena — B·L Z S — George N. Saegmuller

Offices: New York, Boston, Chicago, San Francisco, Washington, London, Frankfort

ROCHESTER, N. Y.

BUFFALO LITHIA WATER

Strong Testimony from the University of Virginia.

IN URIC ACID, DIATHESIS, GOUT, RHEUMATISM, LITHAEMIA and the Like, ITS ACTION IS PROMPT AND LASTING.

Geo. Ben. Johnston, M.D., LL.D., *Prof. Gynecology and Abdominal Surgery, University of Virginia, Ex-Pres. Southern Surgical and Gynecological Assn., Ex-Pres. Virginia Medical Society and Surgeon Memorial Hospital, Richmond, Va.:* "If I were asked what mineral water has the widest range of usefulness, I would unhesitatingly answer, **BUFFALO LITHIA WATER** **In Uric Acid Diathesis, Gout, Rheumatism, Lithaemia, and** the like, its beneficial effects are **prompt and lasting.** . . . . **Almost any case of Pyelitis and Cystitis will be alleviated by it, and many cured.** I have had evidence of the undoubted **Disintegrating Solvent and Eliminating** powers of this water in **Renal Calculus,** and have known its long continued use to permanently break up the gravel-forming habit."

"IT SHOULD BE RECOGNIZED AS AN ARTICLE OF MATERIA MEDICA."

James L. Cabell, M.D., A.M., LL.D., *former Prof. Physiology and Surgery in the Medical Department in the University of Virginia, and Pres. of the National Board of Health:* "**BUFFALO LITHIA WATER** in Uric Acid Diathesis is a well-known therapeutic resource. It should be recognized by the profession as an article of Materia Medica."

"NOTHING TO COMPARE WITH IT IN PREVENTING URIC ACID DEPOSITS IN THE BODY."

Dr. P. B. Barringer, *Chairman of Faculty and Professor of Physiology, University of Virginia, Charlottsville, Va.:* "After twenty years' practice I have no hesitancy in stating that for prompt results I have found nothing to compare with **BUFFALO LITHIA WATER** in preventing Uric Acid Deposits in the body.

"I KNOW OF NO REMEDY COMPARABLE TO IT."

Wm. B. Towles, M.D., *late Prof. of Anatomy and Materia Medica, University of Virgina:* "**In Uric Acid Diathesis, Gout, Rheumatism, Rheumatic Gout, Renal Calculi and Stone in the Bladder,** I know of no remedy comparable to **BUFFALO LITHIA WATER** Spring No. 2.

Voluminious medical testimony sent on request. For sale by the general drug and mineral water trade.

PROPRIETOR BUFFALO LITHIA SPRINGS, VIRGINIA.

www.ingramcontent.com/pod-product-compliance
Lightning Source LLC
LaVergne TN
LVHW010516100826
845148LV00001B/18

* 9 7 8 1 4 2 5 5 7 3 9 7 3 *